Social Mobility and Class Structure in Modern Britain

JOHN H. GOLDTHORPE

(IN COLLABORATION WITH
CATRIONA LLEWELLYN
AND CLIVE PAYNE)

CLARENDON PRESS · OXFORD

Oxford University Press, Walton Street, Oxford OX2 6DP

Oxford New York Toronto
Delhi Bombay Calcutta Madras Karachi
Petaling Jaya Singapore Hong Kong Tokyo
Nairobi Dar es Salaam Cape Town
Melbourne Auckland

and associated companies in
Beirut Berlin Ibadan Nicosia

Oxford is a trade mark of Oxford University Press

Published in the United States
by Oxford University Press, New York

First edition 1980
This edition first published 1987

British Library Cataloguing in Publication Data
Goldthorpe, John H.
Social mobility and class structure in
modern Britain — 2nd ed.
1. Social classes — Great Britain
2. Social mobility — Great Britain
I. Title   II. Llewellyn, Catriona
III. Payne, Clive
305.5'0941   HN400.S6
ISBN 0-19-827286-3
ISBN 0-19-827285-5 Pbk.

Library of Congress Cataloging in Publication Data
Goldthorpe, John H.
Social mobility and class structure in modern Britain.
Bibliography: p.
Includes index.
I. Social classes — Great Britain.   2. Social mobility —
Great Britain.   I. Llewellyn, Catriona.   II. Payne, Clive.
III. Title.
HN400.S6G64   1987   305.5'0941   87-7916
ISBN 0-19-827286-3
ISBN 0-19-827285-5 (pbk.)

Set by Grestun Graphics, Abingdon, Oxon
Printed and bound in
Great Britain by Biddles Ltd,
Guildford and King's Lynn

Preface to the First Edition

This book is in more than one way the outcome of collaborative effort. First of all, several of its chapters result from work undertaken jointly with Catriona Llewellyn or Clive Payne (and in one instance with both). These chapters, it should be said, were originally written as working papers, and some were then published as journal articles. In their present form they are revisions of these papers and articles, and I alone carry responsibility for the changes that have been made. For the most part, however, my revision has not touched on matters of substantive importance but has rather been aimed at clarifying the place of the chapters in the book as a whole, at imposing terminological consistency, and at correcting the occasional error.

Secondly, this book is one of the by now rather numerous publications to have emerged from the work of the Social Mobility Group at Nuffield College, Oxford. One of the two research projects on which the book is based was a collective undertaking by the Group as a whole; and the second was conducted under my direction by a research team within the Group. I would therefore wish to acknowledge my indebtedness to all those who were at any time members of the Group from 1969 onwards, and to give my special thanks to the following for their repeated assistance and encouragement: A.H. Halsey, Anthony Heath, Catriona Llewellyn, Kenneth Macdonald, John Ridge, Joe Schwartz, and Phyllis Thorburn. It would also be appropriate to add here my thanks to members of the Research Services Unit at Nuffield (latterly metamorphosed into the Computing and Research Support Unit of the Faculty of Social Studies) who for long periods became effectively members of the Social Mobility Group and contributed very substantially to its work. I am especially indebted to Clive Payne, Director of the Unit, and to Brian Lienhard and Tim Thomas.

Thirdly, I wish to record the enormous benefit that I have derived from 1972 onwards from my membership of the Research Committee on Social Stratification and Mobility of the International Sociological Association. The meetings of the Committee that I have been able to attend—in Rome in 1972, in Warsaw in 1974, in Geneva in 1975, in Dublin in 1977, and in Uppsala in 1978—were major sources of intellectual stimulus. Furthermore, they were occasions on which I was fortunate enough to be able to form highly rewarding working relationships, and indeed often close personal friendships, with sociologists drawn from a wide range of countries and academic traditions. In particular, I have gained great advantage and pleasure from my association with Rudolf Andorka, Daniel Bertaux, Robert Erikson, Roger Girod, Bob Hauser, Frank Lancaster Jones, Uli Mayer, Walter Müller, Lucienne Portocarero, Kaare Svalastoga, and Wlodek Wesołowski. All of the latter have contributed, and perhaps in more ways than they are aware of, to the present work.

In addition to the foregoing acknowledgements, there are several others of a more usual kind that are also called for.

Valuable comments and criticisms in regard to specific chapters were received from a number of colleagues and friends apart from those already mentioned: namely, R.M. Blackburn, Philip Brown, Frank Critchley, Ralf Dahrendorf, Elizabeth Gittus, David Glass, T.H. Marshall, Clyde Mitchell, Colm O'Muircheartaigh, and Sir Henry Phelps Brown.

Both the research projects earlier referred to received financial support from the Social Science Research Council, and I am duly grateful. At the same time it must be said that it would certainly not have been possible to undertake these projects, and to report on them, on the basis of this support alone. A comparable contribution of resources was made by Nuffield College in the form of salaries, accommodation, and technical, library, and secretarial services. In the latter respect, I should add, my personal thanks are due to Jenny Barton, Margaret Bett, and Audrey Skeats for help over and above the call of duty.

Finally, since neither collective research nor solitary writing are always conducive to sweetness of temper, I must acknowledge the remarkable—if not entirely unfailing—forbearance shown to me by my family over the long period in which this book has been in the making. They are, I am sure, still more relieved than I that it has been eventually completed.

J.H.G.

Oxford, November 1978

Preface to the Second Edition

The reception given to *Social Mobility and Class Structure in Modern Britain* when first published in 1980 was in various ways encouraging. The book attracted the attention of the press, television, and radio to a degree that was quite unanticipated; its findings were widely discussed in the political weeklies; and when reviews later appeared in professional journals, they were, for the most part, generous. A number of critical issues were of course raised, and in some instances these led to debates which I, at least, found enjoyable. The only reactions of an entirely hostile character came in equal measure from the dogmatists of the Marxist Left and of the 'new' Conservative Right—which was exactly as it should have been, and especially gratifying. But most rewarding of all has been the longer-term response in the form of new research projects which are currently pursuing various lines of inquiry that were initiated in the book, or which are replicating in other national societies the investigations and analyses that it reported.

I would like to think that in stimulating studies of this latter kind the book has helped me to repay some of the debt which I owe to the international community of sociologists working in the fields of social stratification and mobility, and which I acknowledged in my Preface to the first edition. That debt, however, still accumulates; and I must here record the invaluable intellectual and moral support that I have continued to receive from colleagues in three centres in particular: Stockholm, Mannheim, and Warsaw. It is in their company that I feel most strongly a sense of common purpose in trying to develop further the kind of sociology that *Social Mobility and Class Structure in Modern Britain* was intended to represent: that is, a sociology which addresses issues of theoretical importance—and political relevance—through systematic research and the use of the best available techniques of quantitative analysis.

The decision to produce a second, extended and updated, edition of the book was certainly made easier by the reception accorded to the first, but was more directly prompted by an awareness of the major—in some respects, epochal—changes that have occurred in British society since the time (1972-4) when the original research was carried out. A further consideration was the desirability of keeping the book available and attractive for use in the teaching of sociology. Its continued presence will, I hope, make it increasingly difficult for students—and their teachers—to avoid the conclusion that a modest statistical competence is now essential to the serious discussion of issues that are central to any curriculum.

In its new form, the book is divided into two main parts. Chapter 1 of the first edition, 'Social Mobility and Social Interests', now serves, virtually unaltered, as a general introduction, which is followed by Part One, 'Class Mobility in Britain: Trends, Patterns, and Concomitants in the Post-War Period'. This is made up of chapters 2 to 8 from the first edition in only a slightly revised form. Some minor errors have been corrected, a few obscurities removed, and new references have been added to the Notes; but no attempt has been made to rewrite these chapters from the standpoint of the present, even by changing tenses. Part Two, 'Class Mobility in Britain: Issues of the Present Day', then comprises a further three chapters, 9 to 11, each of which is entirely new. The first of these chapters extends the analysis of trends in intergenerational mobility from the post-war years through to the early 1980s; the second treats the highly topical question of the class mobility of women—though not, I fear, with results that will mollify the feminists who were outraged at its previous neglect; and the third attempts to view class mobility in modern Britain in a cross-national perspective, taking advantage of the major advances in comparative mobility research that have recently been achieved. Finally, chapter 12 is an extensively revised, indeed almost entirely rewritten, version of the original chapter 9, 'Conclusions and Prospects'.

Revisions apart, the only matter omitted from the first edition is the Appendix in which technical details were given of the 1972 and 1974 inquiries. The Annexes to chapters 3 and 4 might also have been omitted, since to *cognoscenti* they could now appear somewhat quaint—as also perhaps will the way in which the results of multiplicative modelling are presented throughout. However, the costs of making changes in these respects would have been far greater than could be warranted simply to create an appearance of modernity, and some readers will still no doubt find the Annexes of value.

In addition to my general indebtedness to colleagues in the field, to which I have already referred, I must acknowledge various other forms of more specific assistance received in the course of producing this new edition. The preparation of the data utilized in chapters 9 and 10, which were written together with Clive Payne, was financed in part by a grant to the authors from the Economic and Social Research Council, and was also aided indirectly by a grant made to our colleague, Anthony Heath, by Jesus College, Oxford. Steve Elder and his staff at Social and Community Planning Research were efficient collaborators, and research assistance in Oxford was provided by Sheila Hedger. The data drawn on in chapter 10 derive from a large-scale study of comparative social mobility in which I am presently engaged in collaboration with Robert Erikson of the Swedish Institute for Social Research at the University of Stockholm. This project is financed by the Stiftung Volkswagenwerk, and is being undertaken from the Institut für Sozialwissenschaften of the University of Mannheim.

Financial and institutional support of this kind is indispensable to modern sociological research; but no less so is the readiness of colleagues and friends to share their specialist knowledge and expertise. In this respect also I have been extremely fortunate. The names of some of those who have helped most generously have already been mentioned in other connections: Robert Erikson, Anthony Heath, and Clive Payne; and to these should be added the following (at least): A. H. Halsey, Johann Handl, Wolfgang König, Susan McRae, Gordon Marshall, Clyde Mitchell, Walter Müller, Joan Payne, Lucienne Portocarero, Martin Range, and Henrik Tham.

Finally, I should record my good fortune in being able to work as an Official Fellow of Nuffield College, Oxford. This is a position which affords me many privileges—not least of which are the services of Audrey Skeats, my secretary, and of Christine Kennedy and her ever-willing staff in the College Library.

J.H.G.

Oxford, November 1986

Acknowledgements

Earlier versions of chapters 2, 3, 9 and 10 of the present volume appeared as articles in *Sociology* (vol. 11, 1977; vol. 12, 1978; and vol. 20, 1986, nos. 1 and 4); and an earlier version of chapter 5 appeared as an article in the *British Journal of Sociology* (vol. xxviii, 1977). I am grateful to the Editors of these journals and to Routledge and Kegan Paul, the publishers of the *British Journal of Sociology*, for permission to reprint the substance of these articles.

To
KAARE SVALASTOGA,
President, and to my fellow members
of the Research Committee on Social
Stratification and Mobility of the
International Sociological Association
1972–1978

———◆•••◆———

Lovers of small numbers go benignly potty,
Believe all tales are thirteen chapters long,
Have animal doubles, carry pentagrams,
Are Millerites, Baconians, Flat-Earth-Men.

Lovers of big numbers go horridly mad,
Would have the Swiss abolished, all of us
Well purged, somatotyped, baptised, taught baseball:
They empty bars, spoil parties, run for Congress.

W.H. AUDEN
from 'Numbers and Faces'

Reprinted from W.H. Auden's *Collected Poems*, by
permission of Faber & Faber Ltd. and Random House Inc.

Contents

CHAPTER 1

Introduction
Social Mobility and Social Interests

In the quarter of a century since the end of the second world war, social mobility has become established as a major area of sociological inquiry. Indeed, in terms of certain criteria—for example, the scale of individual research projects, the extent of international communication and collaboration among research workers, and the degree of sophistication of techniques of data collection and analysis—it could well claim a position of pre-eminence. Nor can one discern any slackening of research effort: on the contrary, new investigations, and often ones breaking new ground, whether in their location, scope, or methods, are apparently being launched in a steady succession.

At the same time, however, one must recognize that in the midst of all this activity doubts have not infrequently been expressed, and by those engaged in mobility research as well as by members of the wider sociological community, concerning the ultimate purpose and significance of much of the work that is being undertaken.[1] Misgivings would appear to be particularly widespread in two respects. First, it is felt that students of mobility have of late become too much caught up with technical, and specifically statistical, problems associated with the determination of the extent and pattern of mobility and of its causes and consequences; and thus that the development of techniques is often pursued with too little concern either for their appropriateness to data of the kind that the sociologist has usually to work with or for their relevance to the major substantive issues which he must face. Secondly, the charge has been made, from a variety of Marxist and other left-wing positions, that mobility research is ideologically biased in that it gives to mobility a central place within the study of stratification and thus serves to devalue other more basic problems, notably those of class division and class conflict. More extremely, it has been held that the emphasis placed on mobility by western, and especially American, sociologists represents a more or less conscious attempt to divert attention away from the facts of domination and exploitation under modern capitalism and to celebrate the latter as being the true realization of the 'open society'.[2]

It could be thought that these two lines of criticism tend to be somewhat inconsistent: a preoccupation with excessively esoteric techniques would not seem likely to go along with a commitment to spreading an ideological message. But in fact critics have also contended that the more advanced techniques favoured in mobility research are founded upon assumptions which show a marked ideological—that is, an individualistic and liberal—coloration; and further that the tendency to define problems for investigation largely in terms of what these techniques can accomplish is an effective way of closing off other, less congenial, avenues of inquiry. In other words, a close link has been claimed not only between the choice of a particular focus for sociological inquiry and an ideological attachment, but further between that attachment and a particular *style* of inquiry.

The issues which arise here are clearly ones of some complexity, and it cannot be our present aim to argue through them in detail to the position that we would ourselves adopt.[3] To do so, with the attention to specific examples of research that would be required, would be to write another book. What, for our present purposes, seems to us important is that we should acknowledge that these issues exist, and that we should then *state* the stance, and the strategy, that we intend to adopt in regard to them.

Our basic position may be represented thus. On the one hand, we would maintain that whatever has actually been the case in mobility studies in the recent past, there is no *necessary* connection between a research interest in mobility and any specific ideological attachment, liberal or otherwise; and further, that the techniques that are commonly used in mobility research have, at all events, a much wider range of ideological neutrality than most critics have allowed. On the other hand, though, we would recognize, and insist upon the need to recognize, that mobility research is an ideologically loaded area—in the sense that underlying a research interest in it, one must expect there to be also an 'interest' of a different kind, which in some way derives from the researcher's own socio-political experience, values, and commitments.

We do not, we must make clear, equate the existence of such an interest with simple partisanship, nor do we see it as at all incompatible with a due respect for rules of evidence and argument. In fact, there is, in our view, no reason to regard it as in any way regrettable, or as detracting from the scientific standing of sociology, that interests in the sense in question should very generally lie behind the formulation of problems and the conduct of research. On the contrary, we would believe that if sociology is to fulfil its potential, and not only as a social science but as itself a mode of social consciousness, its practitioners must recognize that their problems—however much they may subsequently wish to redefine them—are to be taken far more 'exogeneously', from the development of their society and their own response to this, than 'endogeneously', from the development of their subject. To be sure, the connection between interests and inquiry may be more or less direct, more or less sophisticated. But where it becomes quite hidden from view, then we would not, at least in an area such as mobility research, regard this as a matter for satisfaction so much as for suspicion. We would be inclined to see it as an indication either that the investigator had interests that he wished to conceal—as, say, beneath the guise of social-scientific purity; or that, as a result perhaps of pursuing the logic of techniques too much for its own sake, he had lost his way in the sense of having become detached from the interests and the related substantive problems from which he had begun. In sum, we believe that it is through the awareness and the expression of the interests that prompt and guide his work that the sociologist may best keep clear, both to himself and others, what in fact he is about.

The concerns of this introductory chapter are directly related to the position that we have taken up. The major aim of the chapter is to review, even if only sketchily, the variety of interests out of which, over the last century or so, the study of social mobility has sprung. Such a review is intended to serve two purposes. First, by showing that this variety is indeed considerable, it should reinforce the claim we have made that mobility is by no means a topic that can attract attention only within a limited ideological range. Secondly, our review will enable us to situate, and to define rather precisely, our own interests in the topic; and this in turn, we hope, should help to make clear to the reader why we have concentrated our attention on those particular substantive problems that are treated at length in the chapters that follow, and why we have adopted certain methods of investigation and analysis rather than others. Thus, anyone who may share in doubts about current mobility research of the kind that were previously noted should at least have no great difficulty in deciding whether or not they are warranted in the present case.

In one of the few previous attempts to consider historically the question of the 'social motives' underlying mobility research, van Heek has advanced the argument that an ideological context conducive to the study of social mobility came into existence only after the end of the last century. 'Nineteenth century liberalism' he writes, 'was blind to the problem [of mobility] : Marxism attached little importance to it. It was especially the revisionist socialist movement and the radical current within liberalism which laid the foundation for mobility research.'[4] This assessment is, we believe, an essentially correct one, but one which, inevitably in view of its sweeping nature, allows for a good deal of elaboration and refinement. In what follows, therefore, we shall take van Heek's observation as our text, but seek to develop his argument and, further, to extend the analysis through from the early days of mobility research to the present.

In the case of van Heek's discussion of nineteenth-century liberalism, there is relatively little to add. As he notes, its 'blindness' to the problem of mobility stemmed from the belief that ample opportunity existed under liberal democracy for every individual to occupy a place in society suited to his capacities. This belief, van Heek contends, had its basis in a social Darwinism 'which pretended to notice in human society the same evolution resulting from the struggle for life that biologists had observed in nature'. Thus, attention was diverted away from socio-cultural influences bearing on individual achievement and, at the same time, whatever distribution of individuals to positions of greater or lesser privilege and power might emerge could be legitimated as reflecting 'the survival of the fittest'.[5]

The one point which it would seem important to append here is that, in the British case at least, the belief in the essential 'openness' of liberal democratic society had also a moral grounding, which in fact antedated its scientific, or rather pseudo-scientific, grounding in evolutionism. The most striking illustration of this is of course provided by the Smilesian doctrine of 'self-help', in which differences in social origins and upbringing *and* in natural endowments are alike played down as determinants of worldly success—as indeed are any aspects of the individual's 'fate' lying outside his own control. Instead, the emphasis is placed on such personal attributes as determination, perseverance, diligence, and integrity—in other words, on the moral character of the individual. As one commentator has insightfully remarked, Smiles's aim was 'to reconcile men to the station to which it had pleased God to call them, by insisting upon their duty of discovering for themselves what that station was'.[6] The greater part of *Self Help* and of other of Smiles's books is in fact made up of accounts of the spectacular mobility achieved by men of humble origin through their own unremitting efforts within their calling.[7] But what is striking is that the extent of opportunity for such advancement or the nature of the limits upon it are at no point taken as problematic. For Smiles, opportunity is boundless: the question is simply how far men are capable—that is, possess the moral calibre—of rising to the challenge that it poses.

The only potentially serious modification to the liberal position came in the work of certain economists who recognized a source of imperfection in the labour market in that between 'different grades of labourers', to quote John Stuart Mill, there existed so strong a demarcation 'as to be almost equivalent to an hereditary distinction of caste; each employment being chiefly recruited from the children of those already employed in it, or in employments of the same rank with it in social estimation . . .' However, Mill himself saw this state of affairs as one that was in fact being rapidly transformed by the development of capitalist industrialism, so that 'the habits or disabilities which chained people to their hereditary condition are fast wearing away, and every class is exposed to increased and increasing competition from at least the class immediately below it.'[8] It was not until much later in the century, notably in the work of J.E. Cairnes and of Alfred Marshall, that the phenomenon of 'non-competing groups' within the labour market became accepted as a more durable problem and led to a concern with, in Cairnes's words, 'the limitations imposed by social circumstances on the free competition of labour'[9] —or, within the radical current in liberalism to which van Heek alludes, to a concern with inequality of opportunity.

Turning now to the case of Marxism, van Heek's claim that in its classical, 'unrevised' form, Marxism attached little importance to social mobility is again one which may be accepted as generally valid. As van Heek notes, mobility is given a prominent part in the analysis of capitalism only as an aspect of the *Verelendungstheorie*, in which it is envisaged that with the growth of the capitalist economy, peasants, small entrepreneurs, artisans, and the like will be increasingly forced downwards into the ranks of the proletariat. As a form of socialist doctrine, Marxism dismissed the possibility of upward movement from the working class as merely a liberal myth: in fact, the chances of such ascent were negligible and irrelevant—the only form of advancement to which members of the working class could realistically aspire was that of collective advancement to be gained through the labour movement, class struggle and, ultimately, revolution.

However, while Marxism no less than liberalism thus foreclosed on the question of mobility, the further point that we would wish to bring out here is that, *so far as Marx's own writings are concerned*, the significance of mobility is in fact a good deal greater than has usually been supposed. It is true that Marx discusses mobility directly only, as it were, in the context of other problems, and then at no great length. But what he has to say on these occasions would appear none the less to have been often theoretically seminal; and further, it can be shown that in at least one version of Marx's interpretation of the long-term development of capitalist society, the phenomenon of mobility is in effect quite extensively assumed or implied, even where not expressly treated. To appreciate both the overt and the covert significance of mobility in Marx's analyses is, we believe, important in understanding why in the case of revisionism, and also of some varieties both of liberalism and of more recent Marxist writing, a powerful interest in mobility is created.

To begin with, it is evident from a number of passages in Marx that he *explicitly* recognized social mobility, apart from that involved in 'proletarianization', as inimical to the process of class formation. Most notably, in his observations on American society Marx more than once draws a contrast between this and older European societies in that while the latter possess 'a developed formation of classes', in America, although classes can be said to exist, 'they have not yet become fixed but continually change and interchange their elements in constant flux.'[10] In particular, rather than proletarianization, there is a 'continuous conversion of wage labourers into independent self-sustaining peasants. The position of wages labourer is for a very large part of the American people but a probational state, which they are sure to leave within a longer or a shorter term.'[11] In relating this situation to the immature character of the American working-class movement,[12] Marx may then be said to have initiated what has since become a dominant concern within the study of class structure: namely, that of the relationship between class formation and action, on the one hand, and the extent of mobility between class positions, on the other. Thus, two authors writing over a hundred years after Marx can state: 'The cardinal variables of class theory are two. They refer to the two fundamental processes of class dynamics: *class consciousness* and *social mobility*. It is no exaggeration to say that the history of any class structure is to a large extent the history of the interplay of these two great social forces.'[13]

Moreover, it is clear that Marx also saw how, even within a 'developed' class society, mobility might still serve as a stabilizing, anti-revolutionary process: that is, in the form of 'recruitment from below'. In a discussion of the evolution and functions of the modern banking system, he notes that with the increasing availability of credit 'a man without fortune, but possessing energy, solidity, ability and business acumen may become a capitalist . . .', and he continues as follows:

Although this circumstance continually brings an unwelcome number of new soldiers of fortune into the field and into competition with the already existing individual capitalists, it also reinforces the supremacy of capital itself, expands its base, and enables it to recruit ever new forces for itself out of the substratum of society. In a similar way, the circumstance that the Catholic Church in the Middle Ages formed its hierarchy out of the best brains in the land, regardless of their estate, birth or fortune, was one of the principal means of consolidating ecclesiastical rule and suppressing the laity. The more a ruling class is able to assimilate the foremost minds of a ruled-class, the more stable and dangerous becomes its rule.[14]

Once more thus Marx broaches a theme which has subsequently become one of major concern: that of how the process of what might be termed 'meritocratic incorporation' into dominant classes or élites, while perhaps injecting greater dynamism and efficiency into the working of economic and political institutions, is essentially conservative in its implications for the class structure as a whole.

From the foregoing, then, it can be seen that mobility was by no means a topic into which Marx lacked insight. At the same time, though, grounds do exist for supposing that it was not one which he found especially congenial, for reasons that are, perhaps, not too difficult to appreciate. Not only were the insights that we have illustrated left more or less undeveloped, but further there is one major respect in which Marx rather conspicuously treats the question of mobility only obliquely—or skirts round it altogether—even though the logic of his analysis would seem to require that he confront is as a quite central issue. This is in the case of his discussion of 'intermediate strata' within capitalist society—that is, of strata made up of occupational groupings whose class situation is neither that of the bourgeoisie nor of the proletariat but, in some sense, lies between the two.[15]

For Marx, the 'third parties'—*dritte Personen*—which existed along with the two great classes of capitalist society could be said to be of two clearly different kinds. On the one hand, there were those groupings which, as already noted, were destined, according to the *Verelendungstheorie*, to social and numerical decline: that is, those of small 'independents', whether in agriculture, trade, or manufacture, who were unable to survive under the economic and technological conditions of advanced capitalism.[16] On the other hand, however, there were third-party groupings which were clearly in expansion: either new groupings, largely created by the development of capitalism itself, or groupings which, while of earlier origin, had found it possible to survive, and to flourish, within capitalist society.

For example, most evident among the new groupings were those of industrial managers and supervisors and of business administrators and their staffs. These were brought into existence by the rise of the joint stock companies and by the increasing scale of industrial plant and commercial enterprise. Capitalist production, Marx argues, because of its antagonistic character, calls for greater control from above than that which would be necessary simply to ensure functional co-ordination: 'the exploitation of labour costs labour.'[17] Thus, in the capitalist factory an extensive managerial superstructure to carry out the 'labour of superintendence' becomes essential. And similarly, Marx seeks to show, the logic of the advancing capitalist system, in particular the need to ensure an effective 'circulation of capital', also makes for an expansion of 'office' functions and employees.[18]

In the case of groupings which, although antedating capitalism, were, so to speak, given new life by it, the most important were those of 'public' servants— that is, officials of the State—and those whose members provided the bourgeoisie with various private services, whether professional or more menial. Marx notes that while the bourgeoisie was in its *parvenu* period and had 'not yet subjected to itself the whole of society, the State, etc.', its spokesmen took a critical view of the State apparatus in particular and of 'unproductive' workers in general. However:

When on the other hand the bourgeoisie has won the battle, and has partly itself taken over the State, partly made a compromise with its former possessors; and has likewise given recognition to the ideological professions as flesh of its flesh and everywhere transformed them into its functionaries, of like nature to itself; when it itself no longer confronts these as the representative of productive labour, but when the real productive labourers rise against it and moreover tell it that it lives on other people's industry; when it is enlightened enough not to be entirely absorbed in production, but to want also to consume 'in an enlightened way', when the spiritual labours themselves are more and more performed in its *service* and enter into the service of capitalist production—then things take a new turn, and the bourgeoisie tries to justify 'economically', from its own standpoint, what at an earlier stage it had criticised and fought against.[19]

Furthermore, as well as engaging in more 'enlightened' consumption, the bourgeoisie was also, in Marx's view, pushed willy-nilly into increased consumption of a grosser kind: 'When a certain stage of development [of capitalist production] has been reached, a conventional degree of prodigality, which is also an exhibition of wealth and consequently a source of credit, becomes a business necessity to the 'unfortunate' capitalist. Luxury enters into capital's expenses of representation.'[20] Hence, the bourgeoisie becomes surrounded by a growing body of retainers, akin to those of the feudal lords, who minister to its needs for forms of enjoyment of a conspicuous and prestigeful kind.

It is then evident enough that Marx's more complete analysis of capitalism, as both evolving mode of production and social formation, led him to a quite different position from that suggested by the *Verelendungstheorie* alone. The progressive disappearance of the small independents would not in fact result in the polarization of capitalist society into the two great classes of bourgeoisie and proletariat because of the counter-tendency for intermediate groupings of a different kind to increase in number. This outcome is indeed several times explicitly recognized by Marx; and, moreover, so too are its effects in consolidating the capitalist order. For example, in a critical comment on Ricardo's understanding of the consequences of rising productivity, Marx writes:

What he forgets to emphasise is the constantly growing number of the middle classes, those who stand between the workman on the one hand and the capitalist and landlord on the other. The middle classes maintain themselves to an ever increasing extent directly out of revenue, they are a burden weighing heavily on the working base and increase the social security and power of the upper ten thousand.[21]

And again in discussing Malthus, Marx refers to the latter's 'supreme hope' that in order to reduce the number of those condemned to severe toil and to improve their chances of escaping from it, 'the mass of the middle class should grow and that the proletariat (those who work) should constitute a constantly declining proportion (even though it increases absolutely) of the total population.' Marx notes that Malthus himself regarded this hope as being a more or less utopian one; but Marx then states baldly that 'This in fact is the *course* taken by bourgeois society.'[22]

If therefore it is the case that in the more advanced stages of capitalism the intermediate strata do, taken as a whole, proportionately increase, and that the middle class thus succeeds the proletariat as the expanding class of society, the question must arise, as it did with the proletariat, of the sources from which its rising numbers are drawn. And to the extent that this recruitment is from the ranks of the proletariat, then, following Marx's own argument earlier noted, the further question may be posed of the implications of the 'flux' and 'conversion of wage labourers' that is involved for working-class solidarity and consciousness. Nowhere, it must be said, does Marx bring himself to address directly even the first of these questions—although it is difficult to believe that he could totally overlook their existence. But, we may note, as a by-product of his concern with a more or less separate issue, Marx does in fact at one point go beyond his analysis of the necessity for the growth of new elements within the intermediate strata, as part of the logic of the development of capitalist production, and offers an account, albeit indirect and to some degree implicit, of their actual formation: that is, an account of the mode of mobility through which these growing occupations are supplied with personnel, largely from out of a (proportionately) contracting industrial work-force.

As is well known, Marx contended that with the mechanization of production, and hence the increasing productivity of industrial labour, there will, under capitalism, be brought into existence an 'industrial reserve army' of the unemployed: this view he advanced against the apologetics of such writers as Ricardo, who maintained that as employment opportunities of one kind were eliminated or reduced by technological progress, others would automatically be generated. However, it would appear important to recognize here that the disagreement between Marx and those whom he criticized was far from being total. Marx is in fact prepared to acknowledge that the arguments of Ricardo and others are in part correct, and specifically to accept that '*in the long run* the labour that has been released [by rising productivity] together with the portion of revenue or capital that has been released, will find an opening in a new sphere of production or in the expansion of an old one . . .'[23] It is, however, a further part of Marx's case that because of the demands of capitalist development earlier noted, the reallocation of labour that occurs will be primarily to 'non-productive', middle-class occupations of a managerial, administrative, or service kind: that is, to occupations whose members are remunerated directly out of revenue, and whose increase thus means that, even with a constantly rising revenue, no proportionately larger part of the total product need be available for industrial wages. The point of his criticism of Ricardo for overlooking the expansion of the middle class is precisely that in this way Ricardo is led to overestimate the employment possibilities for the body of industrial labour that at any one time exists. This criticism then relates closely to the charge that Marx was chiefly concerned to make against the bourgeois economists: namely, that in representing the redistribution of labour consequent upon technological advance as a more or less automatic process, they fail to show the short-run costs that it occasions—economic, social, and human—and how these fall overwhelmingly on the proletariat. It is the industrial wage-workers, Marx stresses, who bear what he ironically refers to as the 'temporary inconveniences' of being thrown out of work, while the subsequent benefits go rather 'to *those who succeed the displaced men* [i.e. often non-productive workers] than to the displaced men themselves'.[24] This is so, Marx argues, basically because 'the shifting of labour and capital which increased productivity in a particular branch of industry brings about by means of machinery etc., *is always only prospective*'; the new employment opportunities created, that is to say, are not immediately available to those made redundant, but rather are taken up only later, and possibly much later, by others—'perhaps the children of those who have been thrown out, but not these themselves'. The victims of progress merely 'vegetate' in their old occupations, or drop down into a 'lower grade of labour', or become paupers.[25]

Thus, in seeking to bring out the exploitation and injustice suffered by industrial labour as it increases its own productivity, Marx in effect adumbrates a rather modern-sounding theory of the 'social metabolism' that accompanies the development of the capitalist economy. What he suggests in effect is that the process of the reallocation of manpower within an occupational division of labour that is continually changing, and most notably through the growth of occupational groupings within the intermediate strata, is accomplished less through *intra*generational mobility—that is, through men moving into the new occupations in the course of their working lives—than through *inter*generational mobility. The new occupations as they emerge tend to pull in men of a different generation—or more precisely, one might say, of a different birth cohort—from those whose employment has been downgraded or destroyed.[26]

How in the end Marx would have wished to relate his understanding of the causes and processes of the growth of the middle class to his analyses of the evolution of capitalism which pointed to its eventual collapse must remain a matter of some doubt. But there would, at all events, seem much in the foregoing to support an interpretation of his work in which emphasis is placed on his strong awareness of the existence of counter-tendencies in capitalism to those making for economic crisis, class polarization, and revolution.[27] For our present purposes, however, this question need not be pursued: what is more directly of relevance is the way in which in 'revisionist' Marxism, and in democratic socialist thought more generally, precisely those issues of the wider socio-political implications of the expansion of the intermediate strata, which in Marx are clearly raised but then left largely aside, become ones of quite central concern.

In the initial statement of the revisionist position made by Eduard Bernstein to the German Social Democratic Party in 1898, a comprehensive critique of the *Verelendungstheorie* was a prominent feature.[28] On the basis of statistical materials, Bernstein attacked the theses both of working-class immiseration and of the progressive elimination of *dritte Personen* within the class structure. While rejecting the labour theory of value as a means of assessing the degree of exploitation of the proletariat, he none the less took from Marx the idea that with technological advance a steady increase in the productivity of labour—in the 'social surplus' as he termed it—led to an increase in nonproductive, chiefly service, occupations, many of which were of 'intermediate' status. Moreover, Bernstein also challenged on empirical grounds the claim that in the course of capitalist development the numbers of small entrepreneurs and self-employed workers was destined to decline: on the contrary, he argued, the evidence for the more economically advanced European countries testified to the ability of the 'little men' to coexist along with large-scale capitalist enterprise, even if under its domination. In sum, what Bernstein insisted on was that 'far from society being simplified as to its divisions compared with earlier times, it has been graduated and differentiated both in respect of incomes *and* business activities.'[29]

On the matter of mobility specifically, Bernstein himself had relatively little to say, apart from noting the steady growth of opportunity. For him it was the actual existence of a burgeoning middle class which was of major importance—pointing, as he believed, to the weakness of any 'catastrophe theory' of capitalism, to a decline in class antagonisms and to the need, consequently, for the labour movement to change its strategy: that is, to pursue socialism not through revolution but rather through reform, in collaboration with more radical middle-class elements. However, there were others, both within German revisionist circles and elsewhere, who were ready enough to push further into questions of the effects and significance of the mobility permitted by the changing 'shape' of the class structure—and moreover to do so out of socio-political interests which were by no means always the same as those of Bernstein himself.

In this connection, one may consider first of all, within the group of academics sympathetic in some degree to the German Social Democratic Party, the case of social scientists such as Sombart and Michels, whom van Heek rightly numbers among the pioneers of the sociological study of mobility. The concern of these writers with mobility—as they were at no pains to conceal—is indeed grounded in their socio-political preoccupations. But what would also seem clear is that this concern chiefly developed as for them, in the course of the first two decades of the twentieth century, the promise of socialism became clouded and, in particular, as they came increasingly to feel doubt in the proletariat as the historically appointed agent of either revolution or moral regeneration.

For example, Sombart, who was initially a powerful advocate of the 'evolutionary' socialism favoured by Bernstein and regarded organized labour as its main engine, grew increasingly sceptical of the capacity of the proletariat to continue the struggle for a socialist society under the conditions of economic expansion which capitalism could, evidently, provide. As early as 1906 in a justly celebrated essay, *Warum gibt es in den Vereinigten Staaten keinen Sozialismus?*, Sombart was driven to the despairing aphorism: 'All socialist utopias have come to grief on roast beef and apple pie',[30] and as regards the American case specifically, he followed Marx in seeing a further obstacle to class formation and the development of the labour movement in the high rates of mobility that prevailed from the ranks of the industrial proletariat into farming and minor entrepreneurship.[31] However, while for Marx this situation of high mobility was clearly a temporary one, Sombart shows a good deal of uncertainty and ambivalence in his estimation of the future. Although he recognizes that a 'hardening' of class divisions and class relations could well occur and thus aid the emergence of a strong socialist party, he also emphasizes the pervasiveness in the United States of an individualistic and achievement-oriented ideology which could effectively inhibit a 'class' interpretation of the social structure and of the fate of individuals within it. Moreover, in his later work, and consistently with his move towards a more voluntaristic conception of social action, Sombart appears to generalize this latter possibility. Given a decent standard of living and reasonable opportunities for individual mobility, there is no compelling reason why members of the working class *anywhere* should follow the historic path that socialism requires of them: they may choose to pursue goals of a quite different and, to socialists, uncongenial kind.[32]

In the case of Michels, the link between an intellectual concern with mobility and political disenchantment, although somewhat different in its nature, is no less apparent. Michels took the view—consistently with Marx's position on the development of class relations—that 'the certainty of being condemned to hired labour throughout natural life is one of the most important causes that lead to the rise of anti-capitalist movements in the modern masses.'[33] He also accepted that under the conditions of modern capitalism the chances of a wage-worker becoming a substantial property owner and employer, which had never been great, were being further reduced. At the same time, though, Michels became increasingly impressed by the extent and persistence among the working class of aspirations for mobility, even if of a more modest kind. In his later writing the point is made recurrently: 'As the superior stratum of the middle class aspires to enter into the nobility in an aristocratic country, so the proletariat aims to form a part of the middle class . . . Anyone may see that the impulse towards social capillarity in the proletariat is very strong and clearly evident.'[34] Thus, for Michels the significance of the greater mobility opportunities that were created by the expansion of intermediate occupations—and also, he noted, by the increasingly controlled fertility of the middle class—was not simply that working-class aspirations for social ascent could be more often realized: it was also that their prevalence was made quite manifest. A constant pressure for individual advancement in the social scale became undeniable. The implications were therefore sombre for all those who looked to the proletariat as the 'class of the future', whether as destined to achieve the revolutionary overthrow of capitalism *or* as the bearer of new anti-competitive and collectivist values which could inspire and guide a reformist movement. In this context, a particular irony for Michels, and yet what seemed a particularly apt illustration of his argument, was the way in which for many more able and ambitious members of the working class the labour movement itself served as an instrument of mobility (*eine Klassenerhöh-ungsmaschine*) and thus, he claimed, of bourgeois incorporation.[35]

In Michels's work, in other words, the phenomenon of mobility becomes seen in the end as something more than simply an empirical counter-tendency to class formation and the growth of class-consciousness to which socialist strategy will need to adjust. It is taken also as reflecting a basic self-regarding predisposition—or, in Paretian terms, a 'residue'[36] —which is found within the proletariat no less than within other classes, and which represents an abiding problem for socialist theory. Michels's ultimate interest in mobility, one could say, stems from his concern to lay bare the inexorable social processes and associated psychological drives, the existence of which had forced upon him a radical reconsideration of his faith in socialism and in its supposed vehicle, and hence which gave rational grounds for the pursuit of some alternative means of socio-political advance.[37] A direct parallel is in fact apparent with the motivations of Michels's better-known concern with the problems of party and union bureaucracy.[38] Alongside the 'iron law of oligarchy' as a barrier to the attainment of the ideals of the democratic-socialist movement, there can also be placed what might be termed the 'iron law of mobility' or, at least, of mobility aspirations.

One further notable instance, also cited by van Heek, of the study of mobility having its provenance to some extent in democratic-socialist concerns, and also in the socio-political upheavals of the period of the first world war, is of course provided by the work of Sorokin.[39] Here, though, there can be still less doubt than in the case of Sombart or Michels that the underlying interest of the work is not in fact that of socialism, and that the author wishes to be understood as writing from the standpoint of one who, in the light of experience and reflection, has moved beyond the possibility of a socialist commitment. Indeed, it would seem that one of Sorokin's leading concerns was to take social mobility as a strategic area of study from which to criticize, both empirically and theoretically, the social-scientific basis claimed by Marxist and other socialist doctrines of his day.

Empirically, Sorokin aims first of all to confirm the failure of the *Verelen-dungstheorie* in all its aspects, and to stress in particular the extent and rapidity of the growth in capitalist societies of the new middle class of salaried employees—without, apparently, any awareness of Marx's own observations on the matter.[40] Secondly, he seeks to show that the results of the available statistical studies of mobility in such societies all point to the same general conclusion: namely, that a considerable volume of both intergenerational *and* intragenerational mobility occurs, at least in occupational terms, and that in the recent past the trend appears, if anything, to have been towards an increase in mobility, notably in the movement of men from manual work into the expanding forms of nonmanual employment.[41] Theoretically, Sorokin then concentrates on the implications of these findings for notions of class and class struggle. In the light of the evidence, he argues, the membership of most occupational groupings in modern societies should be seen as having two different elements: 'one relatively stable and permanent; another permanently changing, entering an occupation for a time and then going out of it'—and the latter element is, apparently, becoming the more numerous. This being the case with occupational groupings, Sorokin maintains, it must be true also 'in regard to large social classes';[42] and this in turn means 'that there is a fallacy in the statement of many theorizers of class struggle who continue to talk about the present social classes as though they were still a kind of caste. They forget completely about the fluid composition of present occupational groups.'[43] Sorokin acknowledges that there is some measure of support for class theory in that children appear more likely to enter their father's occupational grouping than any other, and in that mobility is more likely to occur between occupational groupings within the same class than between groupings in different classes. None the less, the extent of mobility is still sufficient to invalidate any characterization of the upper class as simply an aristocracy of birth or of the working class as made up entirely of 'hereditary proletarians'.[44]

It follows then, for Sorokin, that to look to the working class as an agency of social transformation, within a mobile society, is doubly misguided. On the one hand, increasing mobility undermines its revolutionary commitment: 'the narrow-proletarian psychology and ideology—in the form of social democratic and communist affiliations' is likely to prevail only among the declining 'permanent' element within the working class; and will be rejected by the expanding fluid element.[45] On the other hand, the revolutionary capacity of the working class is also destroyed: since it becomes increasingly made up of those incapable of social ascent plus the 'failures' of higher strata, the calibre of the leaders it throws up diminishes, and hence, even if the dictatorship of the proletariat were to come about, it would be likely to achieve nothing but complete social collapse with 'an aggravation of the situation of the proletariat itself' as the first result.[46]

Finally, one may note, Sorokin uses the phenomenon of mobility, viewed in a wide-ranging comparative and historical perspective, as a basis for arguing against all 'directional' interpretations of social evolution. Mobility rates and patterns, he contends, are themselves unpatterned over time, showing merely a 'trendless fluctuation'. Theories such as that of class polarization are not only mistaken empirically but also in principle. There is no reason to suppose an immanent logic in history which requires a certain development of classes and class relations as the route towards a new socialist phase of society.[47] Western societies of the present show in fact relatively high and apparently rising levels of mobility, and there are no forces working *inexorably* against the continuance of this situation. Thus, while Sorokin also discusses at some length the possible destabilizing consequences of mobility for both individuals and societies, he concludes that there is no need for those who, like himself, on balance favour a mobile society to concern themselves with prophecies of its demise. Their task is rather to do all within their power to preserve and enhance its institutions:

. . . . if our aristocracy would try to be a real aristocracy, strong in its rights and duties, creative in its achievements, less sensual in its proclivities and free from parasitism; if it would raise its fecundity; if the channels of climbing are open to every talent among the lower strata; if the machinery of social testing and selection is properly reorganised; if the lower strata are raised to levels as high as possible; and if we are not permeated by the ideologies of false sentimentality and 'humanitarian impotence', then the chances for a long and *brilliant* existence of present mobile societies are great and high.[48]

With Sorokin, thus, the shift is complete from what might be termed a 'negative' socialist interest in mobility—that is, an interest in mobility as a phenomenon which complicates, impedes, or blocks the achievement of socialism via the labour movement—to a 'positive' liberal interest: an interest in mobility as a value to be preserved and maximized. Moreover, from Sorokin on, and notably in the years following the second world war, it was this latter concern which undoubtedly grew in importance among social scientists attracted to the study of mobility. In this period, it could be said, it was the problems of liberal democracy, rather than those of the achievement of socialism, which provided the major socio-political context of mobility research. And in turn, then, it was this reorientation which eventually—by the 1960s—provided the basis for left-wing criticism of mobility research as being ideologically slanted and as essentially directed towards the legitimation of the liberal-democratic order. However, in what follows it will be our aim to show that while such criticism may be valid in some instances, it is important to display more discrimination than commentators on the Left have been wont to do, and to recognize at least two complications: that a commitment to liberal democracy need not be associated with a quite unequivocal approval of mobility as a value to be pursued; and, conversely, that a positive interest in mobility can in fact stem from other ideological positions than that of liberalism alone, and including that of socialism.

The first point is best illustrated by reference to the American case, the second by reference to the British.

As earlier noted, Marx, and then Sombart, regarded American society as being distinctive in the amount of mobility than it displayed, and especially in the apparent ease with which men could escape from wage-labour into smallholding or other forms of self-employment. For Marx, writing in the middle of the nineteenth century, this situation could be seen as one in which the normal development of class relations under capitalism had been retarded by special circumstances, for example, the existence of the open frontier. For Sombart, however, the same situation viewed half a century later was evidently a good deal more problematic. For him—as for a number of native observers—a complex of forces existed, some making for sharper class formation and class-consciousness, but others for continuing high rates of mobility. In other words, by the beginning of the twentieth century, the question of American 'exceptionalism' had become a moot one, and moreover the actual course of development of American society over the early decades of the century was not such as manifestly to resolve the issue one way or another. Rather, a protracted controversy was carried on, in political as much as social-scientific terms, in which upholders of the official liberal ideology of America as the 'land of opportunity' faced not only unwavering Marxists but also dissident liberals or conservatives of the kind Peterson has described as 'nostalgic Americans'.[49] Although out of opposing concerns, both of these latter groups sought to promote the idea that, as a result of urban-industrial development and more specifically of the growth of big business and the labour unions, American society was becoming progressively divided into relatively stable and homogeneous classes on what was taken to be the pattern of the older capitalist societies of Europe. While for Marxists the objective was that of fostering revolutionary hope, for the 'nostalgic Americans' it was that of drawing attention to the dangers which they saw threatening the republic unless a return was made to the individualistic ethos of the past.

It is, then, against the background of this debate, which was still actively pursued into the 1940s and 1950s,[50] that the two major American contributions to the study of mobility in the post-war period must be appraised: that is, those of Lipset and his various collaborators and of Blau and Duncan.[51] While both contributions are clearly made from a liberal position, and indeed share in a quite explicit concern with the conditions favourable to the stability of a liberal-democratic order, the nature of the interest that is found in mobility can be shown to differ in important respects from one case to the other.

On the questions of 'exceptionalism' and the trend of mobility rates in recent American history, Lipset and Blau and Duncan accept factual conclusions which are broadly similar. 'Mass' mobility rates in the United States, they agree, are not substantially different from those recorded in other economically advanced societies, but what these societies have in common is a level of mobility which is on any reckoning *high*. There is, moreover, no indication in the United States, or for that matter elsewhere in the western world, of mobility rates moving into a secular decline: if anything, a generally rising trend is to be observed. Part, at least, of the explanation of this is to be found in the steady expansion of the nonmanual occupational sector. In other words, contrary to the anticipations of Marxists and the fears of traditionalists alike, capitalism does not produce an increasing rigidity of social stratification: rather, it could be said, high mobility appears as an invariable concomitant of *industrialism.* Given, then, the nature and extent of this factual consensus, one could well expect a further similarity in these authors' evaluations of the mobile society from the standpoint of their chosen socio-political commitment: in fact, however, a quite marked divergence occurs.

For Blau and Duncan, the prevalence of high mobility in industrial societies stems from a 'fundamental trend' in such societies towards *universalism* :[52] that is, towards the application in all aspects of social life of standards of judgement or decision-making which derive from considerations of rationality and efficiency and which are detached from the particular values or interests of different membership groups. To begin with, the underlying structural causes of the high mobility of industrial society have, Blau and Duncan suggest, a common source in the dominance of universalism: for example, it is universalism which generates the drive to technological and economic advance, which then constantly reshapes and upgrades the occupational division of labour; while, on the other hand, the weakening of the particularistic ties of kinship and neighbourhood encourages the geographical movement of individuals from low- to high-opportunity areas. Further, of course, universalism implies 'objective' criteria of occupational and of social selection generally: that is, criteria based on achievement rather than ascription—on what the individual has himself accomplished rather on 'who he is in the sense of what family he comes from'.[53] Thus, even apart from the effects of structural change, greater variation tends to be produced between the social positions of parents and their children.

In turn, then, Blau and Duncan see the emphasis on universalism, as expressed through high mobility, as in several ways helping to resolve or accommodate what might be regarded as the basic problem of order within liberal democracy: namely, that of inducing the less-advantaged groups and strata to accept their situation of inferiority, rather than engaging in action of a collective and organized kind to the extent that directly or indirectly the *status quo* is threatened. First, the steady widening of opportunity for upward mobility, which results from economic growth and the expansion of higher-level occupations, contributes to preserving attitudes of individualistic acceptance:

For these conditions make it unlikely that large numbers of underprivileged men experience oppression, despair of all hope, and become so disaffected with the existing system of differential rewards as well as with political institutions that they join extremist political movements committed to violent rebellion . . . . Men who see little opportunity for improvement in their own economic status or, at least, that of their children, have greater inducements than those anticipating advancements in status to organise a union to raise wages or to vote for a party that advocates higher taxes for the wealthy . . . . Inasmuch as high chances of mobility make men less dissatisfied with the system of social differentiation in their society and less inclined to organise in opposition to it, they help to perpetuate this stratification system, and they simultaneously stabilise the political institutions that support it . . . .[54]

Secondly, the fact that it is considerations of achievement rather than ascription which are held to be paramount in social selection aids in legitimating existing differences in reward. This is possible, if not through an appeal to the fairness of giving special privileges to men with socially valued abilities, then at least through an appeal to the greater benefits likely to accrue to all if such men are supplied with the incentives to nurture their abilities and to enter those occupations in which they can best be applied. Thirdly, the greater the actual occurrence of mobility, and the more impermanent the positions that individuals hold in the stratification hierarchy at any one point in time, the less evident will be either classes or status groups as abiding socio-cultural entities, and the less therefore their influence upon individual conduct, either directly through 'in-group' pressures or indirectly through provoking 'out-group' reactions.

In sum, Blau and Duncan (and most clearly, perhaps Duncan, in his independent work)[55] go beyond the idea, already present in Marx, that mobility inhibits class formation to envisage a more extreme possibility: that is, the development, in a society in which universalism and the values of achievement prevail, of a type of stratification which has no inherent tendency to give rise to distinguishable collectivities of any kind with which individuals might identify or which could provide a basis for socio-political mobilization. If the stratification of American society at the present day is in some degree exceptional, it is not on account of its historical origins, but through it having evolved furthest towards this type—with other industrial societies following in its path. Duncan, it may be noted, plays down the importance of writers such as Marx, Weber, and Veblen in providing concepts suitable for the study of 'specifically American social stratification', and sees as more useful the work of Sorokin and, before him, that of Cooley.[56] The model of stratification most relevant to the American case is not one which postulates a structure of interrelated social groupings within which individuals can be located, but rather a continuum, or perhaps a series of continua, of positions of differential 'socio-economic' status on which individuals can be ranged.

One rather paradoxical consequence of a model of this kind is then that the idea of mobility, in the sense of the movement of individuals between collectivities, becomes itself deprived of content. As Duncan indeed suggests, it appears appropriate to restate the problem of mobility as that of the determinants of (socio-economic) 'status attainment'. Class or family origins may number among these determinants, but must be expected to be of declining importance as against achieved attributes, such as educational level, qualifications, etc.[57] Furthermore, if this approach is taken, the possibility must be recognized—and, in the light of his own findings, Duncan believes it to be a very real one—that status attainment will prove to be in some large measure undetermined by influences of a socially structured kind and to depend a good deal on what, from a sociological standpoint, must be regarded as individual 'luck'.[58] In other words, the way would seem open here to another formulation of the classic liberal position from which the problem of social mobility more or less disappears from view. In nineteenth-century versions, as we earlier noted, the part played in the social distribution of individuals by natural endowment might be modified by a Smilesian emphasis on moral calibre. In the twentieth-century version, the role of personal achievement is seen as being importantly qualified by a variety of chance events: birth and *virtù* alike are overlaid by *fortuna*.

It is, therefore, in regard to the work of Blau and Duncan that left-wing misgivings become most understandable. Not only is a concern with the question of the stability—and of the legitimation—of liberal democracy quite unconcealed, but further is associated with an attempt to characterize American social stratification as being 'open' and structureless to the point at which to think in terms of mobility becomes of much reduced value. Moreover, while this attempt is made in part overtly, through seeking to show empirically the influence of achievement—or of 'career contingencies'—as against ascription in the process of status attainment, it is also, as critics have pointed out, made in some part covertly through what has been called 'presuppositional bias': that is, by postulating the issue of achievement versus ascription as *the* sociologically crucial one for stratification research, to the neglect of others, and including that of the social-structural constraints which operate on the stratification process independently of individual characteristics. For example, the lack of attention given by Blau and Duncan to the constraints imposed by the institutions of private property or by the extent of the 'fit' between the patterns of occupational 'demand' and educational 'supply' has frequently given rise to objections, and not from the Left alone.[59]

However, what for our immediate purposes is of importance is not to pursue such criticism here but, rather, to show that Blau and Duncan's liberal commitment by no means *entails* certain of the basic—though disputed—features of their analysis: in particular, the emphasis they place, both empirically and normatively, on the prevalence of universalism and their view that a highly open form of stratification is that functionally most consistent with a liberal-democratic order. This can be done by turning to the very different perspective on America as a mobile society that is offered by Lipset.

From his liberal standpoint, Lipset is prepared to view mobility positively in a number of respects. He would, for example, agree with Blau and Duncan that a high level of mobility weakens the solidarity and oppositional potential of the working class by encouraging individual rather than collective attempts at advancement—and, in addition, by producing an influx into the working class of downwardly mobile persons who still adhere to the beliefs and values of their class of origin and seek to return there.[60] Furthermore, Lipset sees high mobility as favouring popular acceptance of a liberal-democratic regime in so far as élites are thereby made more accessible, and visibly so through the social and cultural heterogeneity of their members, and an ideology of openness and 'moral equality' is given some factual basis. At the same time, though, it must be noted that Lipset apparently regards these stabilizing functions of mobility as being of greatest importance where such a regime is seeking to establish itself in the relatively early stages of industrialization—at which point, he believes, the threat from extremist 'class' politics is most acute.[61] Within the context of a more mature liberal democracy, in which, in his view, class antagonisms will have been muted by economic growth and greater equality of condition, the implications of maximizing equality of opportunity and levels of mobility clearly become far more problematic for Lipset. Indeed, in this case it would be true to say that the major concern that is revealed in his work is with the socially disruptive and politically *de*stabilizing consequences which may ensue.

To understand this concern it must be recognized in the first place that Lipset never falls into the attitude of unreflecting approval of the ethos of achievement which is characteristic of Blau and Duncan: on the contrary, he is quite prepared to call it into question. For example, in the concluding chapter of *Social Mobility in Industrial Society*, he and Bendix explicitly raise the issue of how tenable are 'some basic value assumptions which appear to have been accepted by almost all research workers in this field during the past decade or more' and, in particular, the assumption that 'rapid and increasing social mobility is a good thing because it increases the opportunities of the under-privileged and hence enlarges their freedom, while the corresponding reduction of privilege among the few does not seriously jeopardise their position.'[62] This argument, Lipset and Bendix claim, is part of the nineteenth-century intellectual tradition and, whatever validity it might have had for that period, it would seem hazardous to take it as a basis for present and future mobility research. Moreover, to view a high rate of mobility as an unalloyed good is to ignore the mounting evidence from recent research of its psychological cost to the individuals involved: 'a cost that is probably high in terms of the combativeness, frustration, rootlessness, and other ills that are engendered . . . .'.[63] Whether or not the cost is *too* high is, Lipset and Bendix admit, a matter ultimately for moral and political judgement; none the less, they urge, the negative aspects of mobility should be recognized as an important and neglected area of research. One question, for example, which should be investigated is that of how far the lack of motivation for educational and occupational achievement among certain groups and strata should be seen as a problem to be overcome—or, rather, as a valuable built-in safeguard against the psychological burdens that mobility imposes.

It is, then, from these misgivings about the effects of mobility at the individual level that there stems Lipset's larger anxiety about the implications for social and political order. High mobility may generate not only personal satisfaction, and hence attitudes of socio-political acceptance; but also personal insecurity and *ressentiment*, and hence serve to alienate individuals from the *status quo* and increase the possibility of their recruitment by extremist social movements. Moreover, these negative effects may result not simply from the fact that mobility can be downward as well as upward, that is, can imply failure rather than success, but further from the fact that all mobility creates the likelihood of individuals being brought into inconsistent or ambiguous situations within the stratification hierarchy. Lipset clearly operates with a more elaborated model of stratification than that favoured by Blau and Duncan. While recognizing the existence of different forms or dimensions of social inequality, he also conceptualizes the stratification hierarchy as a complex structure of more or less distinguishable, even if overlapping, social groupings. Thus, for Lipset, mobility is not merely a matter of movement along socio-economic continua: it also typically involves processes of detachment from and attachment to particular collectivities, and these processes may be made more complicated, and more stressful psychologically, on account of mobility being often only partial—that is, being effected only in one dimension and not in others. For example, individuals and groups who have been upwardly mobile occupationally, in consequence, say, of economic growth, may not succeed in being similarly mobile in terms of social status or political power.[64]

In Lipset's view it is in fact individuals and groups who experience such 'status inconsistency' who are particularly likely to seek a solution to their personal and social dilemmas through politics of a kind which reject 'democratic restraint' and aim at some radical transformation of the existing order. For example, in later nineteenth-century Europe, members of various marginal groups—most notably, Jews—who had gained considerable economic success but who were still excluded from the highest status levels figured prominently in the leaderships of nascent socialist and communist parties. However, in the context of twentieth-century America, what has mainly concerned Lipset is the threat to liberal democracy which similarly marginal groups pose *from the Right*. In the American case, he argues, it is *nouveaux riches* who have tended to form a powerful source of support for extremist right-wing movements through their status insecurity being expressed in 'over-conformity' with what they suppose to be the American political tradition. Furthermore, a potential mass basis for such movements is to be found in a variety of other groups whose members have in some way or other become disadvantaged within the mobile society and who now 'have more of a stake in the past than in the present': for example, members of the old middle class, especially in the South, whose present economic fortunes belie the status eminence they once claimed; small businessmen whose position within the corporate economy is increasingly precarious; or manual workers who have failed to achieve affluence to the same extent as others of their kind.[65]

It is, thus, as one who believes that liberal democracy 'is the good society itself in operation'[66] that Lipset is concerned to show up the seamy side of mobility and to bring out the problems that must inhere in any naïve commitment to the ideal of the open society. What Lipset's analysis suggests is that in the interests of enhancing the stability of a liberal-democratic order, the thoroughgoing universalism which Blau and Duncan see as wholly beneficial may well need to be in various respects modified: that is to say, it may not be desirable to allow the value set on achievement as against ascription and on openness to be always overriding. As a specific illustration of this point, it may be noted that in one of Lipset's more recent contributions he is at pains to stress the difficulties—and danger—involved in efforts to create still greater openness in modern societies through radical reform in the field of education. The difficulties are those of overcoming intergenerationally transmitted inequalities of a subcultural kind other than by an 'imposed uniformity' in the rearing of children: the danger then lies in the possibility that uncompromising attempts to maximize equality of educational opportunity will in fact be pushed to the point of undermining the family and of devaluing 'the needs and satisfactions served by the family'.[67] In other words, the theme recurs that an unremitting emphasis on universalistic values may lead ultimately to socially disruptive rather than to socially integrative effects.

It should then be clear that if criticism at an ideological level is to be directed against Lipset from the Left, it can scarcely be on the grounds that his interest in the study of mobility is to provide a celebration of modern America, or of modern capitalism generally, in virtue of its openness. It could, rather, be more accurately claimed that, while maintaining that mobility is already at a high level in all forms of industrial society, Lipset seeks also to draw from mobility research evidence to sustain a conservative stance against the more radical social policies which might, still in the name of universalism, be attempted. As Miller has acutely observed, with Lipset clearly in mind, the great attraction of 'mobility-as-an-explainer'—of personal and social disequilibrium and political extremism—was that it provided a convenient possibility for an 'enlightened', yet anti-radical, critique of American society in the 1950s and 1960s: 'It was a way of saying: Watch out for the price to be paid in conforming to the American motif of onward and upward'—with the implication being that efforts to bring the American reality into closer accord with the American Dream might be somewhat less strenuously pursued.[68]

Lipset thus provides our example of a liberal interest in social mobility which, if it could not be described as actually negative, is at all events highly ambivalent and qualified. As an illuminating contrast, we may go on now to the British case and to an instance of an interest in mobility which is of a far more positive kind, but which stems in fact from a major tradition of socialist thought: namely, from Fabianism and British 'ethical' socialism. As several scholars have remarked, close affinities exist between this tradition and the German revisionism whose role in stimulating the study of mobility we have already considered.[69] At the same time, though, one difference must be noted which, for present purposes at least, is highly consequential. Rather than developing in any very significant way from out of a debate with Marx or Marxism, Fabianism and ethical social-ism were to a large extent formed indigenously, and notably in opposition to the tenets of classical British liberalism. This fact is then in several ways re-flected in the stance which their exponents adopt towards questions of mobility specifically and of class formation and class life-chances more generally.

To begin with, there was relatively little concern shown by British socialists of the earlier twentieth century that the growth of mobility opportunities or aspirations among the working class might seriously undermine the strength of the socialist movement. As a result of their commitment to gradualism and to legal and democratic—that is, essentially parliamentary—means of pursuing socialism, the importance that they gave to working-class solidarity and to class struggle was inevitably less than in the case of their Marxist counterparts. Class conflict was seen not so much as the necessary historical process through which the victory of socialism would be gained, but rather as an evil engendered by capitalism which the socialist movement would progressively eliminate.[70] Thus, social changes which tended to reduce the homogeneity of the working class or to blur the lines of class division could be viewed with equanimity or even with some approval. It was, for example, possible for British socialists to stress, in occasional polemics with Marxists, the growth of intermediate strata—to assert in fact that 'A society that is increasingly proletarian is a thing of the past. The society in which we live is an increasingly bourgeois society'[71]—*without* this in any way undermining their socialist faith and commitment. Rather, the lesson that was typically drawn was that the appeal of socialism should be widened, in part by changes in programme but also by force of argument and moral suasion, so as to bring new social groups into its support.[72]

Furthermore, the basic strategy of the attack which British socialists launched on classical liberalism was that of exposing the gap that existed between liberal ideology and social reality: and in this respect the liberal claim that equality of opportunity was a principle of capitalist society was an obvious target. As an outstanding example of the strategy in operation one may cite chapter III of Tawney's *Equality*. What Tawney was here concerned to establish was not only that the extent of mobility in British society fell far short of what would be required to make liberal ideology credible, but further that this ideology was inherently vitiated in seeking to use the principle of equality of opportunity to legitimate the existing degree of inequality of condition. For, as a matter of sociological necessity, the latter *de facto* situation must rule out the possibility of the principle ever being maintained, other than in some purely formal sense:

All careers may be equally open to all, and the wage-earner, like the property-owner, may be free to use such powers as he possesses, in such ways as he is able, on such occasions as are open to him, to achieve such results as he is capable of achieving. But in the absence of measures which prevent the exploitation of groups in a weak economic position by those in a strong, and make the external conditions of health and civilisation a common possession, the phrase equality of opportunity is obviously a jest, to be described as amusing or heartless according to taste. It is the impertinent courtesy of an invitation offered to unwelcome guests, in the certainty that circumstances will prevent them from accepting it.[73]

The nature of this attack was then in itself such as to lead British socialists to place a positive value on 'real' equality of opportunity and social openness, in contrast with the liberals' effective disregard. In this, as in other respects, it could become the socialists' claim that it was they who were the true custodians of liberal principles, which were far too important to be left to the liberals themselves. It was, of course, at the same time implied that to take the objective of equality of opportunity seriously meant considering it together with that of equality of condition. But rather than seeing these two goals as being to some large degree contradictory, as in the manner of both liberals and Marxists, British socialists were inclined to see them as essentially complementary. And hence, one may note, a positive interest in social mobility was for at least two further reasons encouraged.

First, while it was insisted upon that greater equality of opportunity could be achieved only through greater equality of condition, it was also believed that if some movement towards a more genuinely open society could be made, this would in turn aid in reducing status and class differences. For example, to the extent that 'artificial' restrictions on the use of available talent in society were eliminated, and talent, wherever located in the class structure, was permitted to develop, this would not only imply greater equality of educational level but, further, the greater supply or potential supply of qualified labour would serve to reduce differentials in occupational rewards. In other words, the greater the degree of equality of opportunity that could be attained, the more could market forces themselves be turned, as it were, against the *status quo* and enabled to work to an egalitarian effect.[74]

Secondly, it was characteristic of socialists in the British tradition that they were ready to discuss in more detail than were most Marxists the nature of the future society to which they aspired and, moreover, that they did not conceal their view that in this society the problem of equality would be a continuing one. Some inequalities, it was recognized, would persist because they were inescapable—as, for example, in political power and authority; and others would be created—as the result, say, of the desirability of giving exceptional rewards to those undertaking exceptional efforts or responsibilities on behalf of the community as a whole. It followed, therefore, that it would be of particular importance to establish maximum opportunity for mobility as a feature of socialist society, both to ensure that positions which were in any way privileged were truly open to talent and to guard against the danger of the formation of permanent élites.[75] It is significant in this connection that whereas the contribution that high mobility could make to social efficiency was regularly referred to, the possibly negative effects, whether psychological or social, were not seen as a cause for concern—provided that a basic equality of condition prevailed. It was rather on the personal and community costs of *im*mobility associated with extreme *in*equality of condition that the emphasis was placed.[76]

While the major exponents of British socialism did not themselves engage directly in research into questions of stratification and mobility (though most were social scientists of some kind), it is evident that in the research which was undertaken in this area in Britain, from the 1920s through to the 1950s, their influence was a dominant one. The most striking illustration of this is the extent to which the particular interest in mobility outlined above is reflected in what was undoubtedly the major study of the period, as well as a landmark in mobility research generally—that is, the work carried out by D.V. Glass and his colleagues at the London School of Economics in the years immediately after the second world war.[77]

It is, for example, very notable that Glass and his team show little concern with the issue, on which so much earlier European and American work had been focused, of the implications of mobility within a growing capitalist economy for working-class homogeneity and cohesion. Glass indeed states explicitly at one point that their research was designed primarily to investigate mobility in terms of social status or prestige and not to deal with class 'in the classical [*sc.* Marxist?] sense of the term'.[78] Moreover, it is clear that the attention of the LSE group is directed more towards the higher than the lower levels of the stratification hierarchy, and that a particularly marked concern is with the process of social selection for 'élite' professional, administrative, and managerial positions.[79]

Empirically, Glass and his colleagues were able to show that the transmission of social status in Britain tended in general to operate 'within, so to speak, a closed circuit',[80] and further that in recruitment to positions towards the peak of the stratification hierarchy, the degree of restriction was such that the ideal of equality of opportunity was quite blatantly negated. Recruitment was heavily concentrated among the sons of men who had themselves held high-status positions, whereas the chances of access for the sons of semi- and unskilled manual workers were negligible.[81] A key device used by Glass to bring out the extent of inequality of opportunity was to relate—through 'an index of association'—

the mobility flows actually observed to those that would have been expected under conditions of 'perfect mobility': that is, if the status of sons had been entirely independent of that of their parents.[82] This procedure, one may suggest, is in effect the direct statistical homologue of the critical strategy adopted by Tawney, namely, that of taking liberal ideology seriously.

Certainly for Glass, the reporting of his results took on the nature of an *exposé*, and he does not seek to hide his own value-commitment to the goal of a genuinely open society. Apart from considerations of social justice, those of economic and social rationality must also weigh in its favour 'since with a fluid social structure there is more likelihood that positions requiring high ability will in fact be held by individuals who possess high ability'; and, in turn, there should be 'less feeling of personal frustration and a greater possibility of social harmony'. But at the same time, and again characteristically from the standpoint of the socialist interest in mobility that we have depicted, Glass wishes to see equality of opportunity always in relation to equality of condition. Thus, on the one hand, he emphasizes that post-war attempts to widen opportunities, notably through educational reform, may well be limited in their effects, and especially on the recruitment of élites, if certain basic economic and status inequalities are allowed to remain—for example, those embodied in the independent-school system; while, on the other hand, he is concerned to argue that in so far as a more meritocratic method of élite recruitment *is* established, it is important that this should not be seen as legitimating prevailing inequalities of condition, but rather as itself increasing the need to diminish them. Otherwise, Glass warns, the outcome of meritocratic selection could be to produce between élite and mass a socially sharper, and psychologically more abrasive, division than any existing hitherto. Although functional exigencies may necessitate some degree of inequality of reward, there is no reason, Glass contends, why 'employment in occupations requiring high ability and long training and carrying high social status should be the only means of gaining social prestige; there are other ways of serving the community and there should, correspondingly, be other paths to social prestige.'[83]

The contrast between the position taken up by Glass and that of Lipset is thus particularly marked. The two have in common an awareness that dangers may follow from increased mobility, especially that resulting from the more general application of universalistic methods of social selection. But the ways in which they would define these dangers, and the appropriate socio-political response to them, are quite divergent. For Lipset, it would seem reasonable, in a society in which, in his view, the more glaring inequalities of condition have been removed, to reconsider the maximization of mobility opportunities as an overriding priority—on the grounds of reducing personal and social stress, such as that arising from situations of status inconsistency, and in turn thus, the possibility of political upheaval. For Glass, prevailing inequalities of both condition and opportunity are still far too great to be acceptable, and the continuing aim, from the standpoint of both individual and societal well-being, must be to diminish both together; meritocratic selection leading to greater mobility is one means to be adopted but, in order to counter its own potentially damaging and divisive effects, it must be accompanied by further efforts to create a form of stratification which is not only less extreme but also one in which 'inconsistency' is in fact increased through the recognition of more diverse entitlements to status.[84]

By now, we would hope, a sufficient basis has been provided for our point, made at the start of this chapter, that an intellectual concern with problems of social mobility may stem from a variety of ideological positions, and that there exists no simple one-to-one relationship between the research interest and the interest of the researcher in the wider, socio-political sense. However, in order to complete the review that we have undertaken—and to return thus somewhat closer to the main issues from which we began—it remains for us to comment on the treatment of mobility that is found in the work of a number of recent authors who write either explicitly as Marxists or under the evident influence of Marx and from a position which might perhaps best be described as 'post-Marxist'.

In some instances, the Marxist response to the growing volume of mobility research over recent decades has not in fact gone further than the charge of ideological bias: that is to say, there has been a refusal to respond intellectually to this research other than by trying to explain or situate it as an activity reflecting the class attachments of those engaged in it. Thus, whatever may have emerged of value to a Marxist sociology of knowledge, a contribution to mobility studies *per se* has obviously been precluded. Two further essentially defensive and unfruitful reactions are also to be noted. First, it has been argued that the Marxist concern is with class structure in the sense of a *structure of positions* constituted by the prevailing relations of production, and that from this standpoint the question of the distribution of individuals among these positions is of quite minor significance. Poulantzas, for example, writes:

. . . . il est évident que, même dans la supposition *absurde* où, du jour au lendemain, (ou d'une génération à une autre), tous les bourgeois occuperaient les places des ouvriers et vice versa, rien d'essential ne serait changé au capitalisme, car il y aurait toujours des *places* de bourgeois et de prolétariat, ce qui est l'aspect principal de reproduction des *rapports* capitaliste.[85]

Secondly, it has been contended that, whatever status may be given to mobility theoretically, it can be of little actual consequence for class relations and the class struggle: this is because mobility across the fundamental line of class division within capitalist society—that between the major owners of the means of production and the mass of employees—is held down, by the very nature of the transmission of capital, to so low a level as to be quite negligible in its effects.[86]

The inadequacies of both these arguments are best brought out by the manner in which sociologically more sophisticated analysts, working within the Marxist tradition, have moved beyond them. For example, Westergaard and Resler, in offering a Marxist account of the British class structure maintain the view that questions of mobility '. . . . concern the recruitment of people to classes; not the brute fact of the existence of class', and hold the latter to be the primary phenomenon.[87] They likewise accept, indeed insist upon, the crucial part played in the shaping of the class structure as a whole by the division between those who are involved in the ownership and control of concentrations of private capital and those who are not. But at the same time Westergaard and Resler recognize the wide differences in class situation that are to be found among the latter—that existing between manual wage-workers and salaried employees being of most obvious importance.[88] And in turn then, while themselves stressing the essentially self-reproducing character of the capitalist class, Westergaard and Resler are well aware that the extent and pattern of mobility occurring *within* the mass of those of employee status—who constitute in fact the large majority of the population—cannot be disregarded. Rather, in a way which, in the light of our earlier discussion, would seem entirely in the spirit of Marx, they argue that 'a central focus of interest must be the possible implications of social mobility and immobility for people's responses to their class situation: for class consciousness and class organisation.'[89] In other words, to avoid discussion of questions of mobility, either in the manner of Poulantzas by simply dismissing them as 'une problématique bourgeoise'[90] or by mere definitional *fiat*, results in the neglect of what should be a major consideration so far as the possibility of any transition from 'class in itself' to 'class for itself' is concerned.

Moreover, in the case of certain other writers who do not commit themselves to Marxism but who none the less take at least the work of Marx himself as an important point of departure, one may find approaches to the study of mobility which may from one point of view appear as fairly radical critiques of Marxism but, from another, as natural progressions from a position of the kind adopted by Westergaard and Resler. Giddens, for example, rejects the conceptualization of class structure in 'positional' terms, which has been accepted by most Marxist writers, and which means that mobility may be treated 'as if it were in large part separable from the determination of class structure'.[91] Giddens wishes, rather, to see classes as *aggregates of individuals* which will be more or less identifiable according to the *degree* of 'structuration' which happens empirically to exist. However, for Giddens, the most generalized process of structuration, in advanced societies at least, does in fact result from 'the distribution of mobility chances which pertain within a given society': more specifically,

 . . . . the greater the degree of 'closure' of mobility chances—both intergenerationally and within the career of the individual—the more this facilitates the formation of identifiable classes. For the effect of closure in terms of intergenerational movement is to provide for the *reproduction* of common life experience over the generations; and this homogenisation of experience is reinforced to the degree to which the individual's movement within the labour market is confined to occupations which generate a similar range of material outcomes. In general we may state that the structuration of classes is facilitated *to the degree to which mobility closure exists in relation to any specified form of market capacity.*[92]

In the end, then, the difference between Giddens on the one hand and Westergaard and Resler on the other would seem to be the following. Both see mobility as a process of central importance to class formation, but for Giddens its importance lies not only in the development of class-consciousness and organization, that is, in the emergence of classes 'for themselves': it also extends back to the formation of classes as recognizable social phenomena, that is, as classes 'in themselves'. This might be taken as a difference at a quite basic, ontological level; but one could equally well argue that the differences in market, work and community situations recognized by Giddens are conceptually equivalent to the structure of inequality of condition and power which for Westergaard and Resler represent 'the brute fact of the existence of class'. In this case, then, the main issue would seem to be the essentially definitional one of whether the idea of a 'class in itself' is to refer to a constellation of positions or, more demandingly, to a relatively stable aggregate of individuals occupying such a set of positions.

In a somewhat similar fashion to Giddens, Parkin has also made an apparently sharp break with the Marxist tradition in taking over Blau and Duncan's view that it is the occupational order that provides 'the backbone of the class structure' in modern western societies.[93] But it is in fact clear that in so doing, Parkin does not seek to minimize the significance of the distribution of property and of property relations. Rather, like Westergaard and Resler, he seeks to give adequate recognition to the fact that important class differences, albeit closely conditioned by the capitalist context, do exist among those who, as excluded from the commanding heights of ownership and control, make up the bulk of the population.[94] Moreover, while Parkin, like Giddens, has treated mobility patterns as a major determinant of class structure, in his more recent work such patterns become relevant not only for questions of class boundaries but further for those, of central concern to Marxism, of class action and class conflict.

The idea of dichotomy implicit in any analysis of such conflict, Parkin argues, is best expressed not through zero-sum categorizations, but rather in terms of opposing 'strategies of closure', which contending classes (and also contending groups within classes) may pursue.[95] Classes or groups may either aim to exploit, and thus preserve, a situation of superiority within the stratification hierarchy by practising various techniques of exclusion—from rewarding positions and opportunities—against inferior classes or groups; or, those in an inferior situation may seek to exploit their solidarity and organizational strength, for example, via their control over labour supply or their 'disruptive potential', in order to win for themselves higher levels of reward and opportunity, challenging where necessary the existing distributional system and the advantages of their superiors. Thus, the extent and modes of mobility prevalent within a given society become indicative, on the one hand, of the effectiveness of strategies of exclusion and, on the other, of the chances of success of counter-strategies of solidarism—which, as Parkin points out, are highly dependent on the participants being ready to commit themselves to collective interests and aspirations rather than individual ones.

In sum, then, in the case of Giddens and Parkin, no less than in that of Westergaard and Resler, a concern with mobility derives basically, as in the work of Marx himself, from an interest in the conditions of class formation and of the development of the struggle for advantage and power among classes. These writers may be placed together as working within a Marxist or post-Marxist perspective, as distinct from a liberal or ethical socialist one, in that, rather than viewing class conflict negatively or 'regretfully', they see it as being within capitalism the major vehicle of socio-political change. At the same time, though, in some contrast perhaps with Marx, and certainly with many would-be orthodox Marxists, they find no difficulty in accepting mobility as an abiding, indeed integral, feature of capitalist society, and seek thus to treat it in something more than a merely defensive or apologetic manner. While differences undoubtedly exist among them in their estimation of what the future form and outcome of class conflict is likely to be, and perhaps also in their preferences in these respects, an interest in class conflict for them requires, in one way or another, that questions of mobility should occupy a central place in any analysis of capitalist society and in any assessment of the possibility of its transformation.

The foregoing account of the variety of 'social motives' that have prompted mobility research in the past provides, we would hope, an appropriate context for the remaining task of this chapter: that of setting out the nature of our own interests in mobility in relation to those of our predecessors in the field, and thus of indicating the rationale for our choice of the substantive issues on which our attention is subsequently focused. The interests that we shall acknowledge may appear ones that are somewhat difficult to relate to each other but, we shall seek to show, they do in fact have their own coherence.

To begin with, we must declare an interest of a positive kind in mobility, in so far as it is associated with greater openness: that is to say, with a tendency towards greater equality of chances of access, for individuals of all social origins, to positions differently located within the social division of labour. However, we must at the same time make it clear that we shall certainly not wish to regard *all* mobility as being conducive to openness in this sense. Furthermore, we should also clarify our position here by stating that the source of the interest we have declared is not primarily a concern for the stability or legitimacy of liberal democracy—which, for us, falls some way short of being 'the good society itself in operation'. The source is, on the contrary, a concern with the extent to which characteristic features of the social structure of liberal democracy in fact prevent individuals of certain social origins from realizing their full potentialities as citizens, or indeed as human beings. In other words, we would, in agreement with Glass and in opposition to Lipset, regard greater openness as a goal still to be actively pursued rather than as one which needs now to be modified in the interests of socio-political stability; and in turn we would ally ourselves with Tawney and the ethical socialists generally in seeing the degree of openness that actually prevails as an issue on which liberal ideology is highly vulnerable—in particular, of course, in respect of the claim that a true equality of opportunity can coexist with substantial inequalities of condition. The obvious counterclaim, as we have seen, is that inequalities of opportunity and condition can only be reduced together, and that any adverse personal or social consequences of mobility will also in this way be minimized.

At the same time, we would reject the views, fashionable in various quarters on the Left, either that openness as we have defined it is an essentially 'bourgeois' notion and that equality of condition, understood primarily in economic terms, is all that matters; or that mobility is only a problem for so long as a socialist society is unrealized since under socialism the problem will simply disappear, together with those of social inequality and stratification in general. The question of how individuals become distributed among different positions and roles within the social division of labour seems to us to be one that is, analytically at least, quite independent of that of the distribution of economic resources, and one that must remain central—even though with different possibilities for its solution—in advanced industrial societies of a socialist as well as a capitalist kind.[96]

However, while our interest in mobility from the standpoint of openness will be repeatedly apparent in the course of the chapters that follow, it is not in fact that which has been of greatest influence in determining the focus of our research. Of prior importance has been an interest in mobility from the standpoint of its implications for class formation and class action. Here, then, we draw not on the tradition of ethical socialism but rather on one of a Marxian or at least a *marxisant* character. We do not, we should stress, hold to any historicist view in which the working class and class conflict appear as the destined agency and means of a revolutionary transition from capitalism to socialism. And we do not therefore see in any social process which is conceivably inimical to class formation and conflict—such as that of mobility—a basic threat to the validity of our entire world-view. At the same time, however, we do regard it as a major shortcoming of ethical socialism that it has neglected and underestimated the historical significance of class conflict. Most clearly in the British case, as a result of the commitment to parliamentarism, and also perhaps of the influence of Christian socialism and of Fabian élitism, ethical socialists have failed to appreciate sufficiently that they need the working class, not merely as the object of their solicitude, but as the social vehicle through whose action, electoral *and otherwise*, their ideals have by far the best probability of being realized. For our own part, the fact that we largely share in these ideals—among which that of a genuinely open society is central—must imply that we share also, with students in the Marxian tradition, an interest in the dynamics of class relations. And we would in turn then accept, in company with writers from Marx himself and the revisionists down to the 'post-Marxists' of the present day, the general proposition that in these dynamics social mobility plays a crucial role—although, we would wish to add, a more complex one than has been usually supposed.

In sum, it will be evident that we view social mobility under two different auspices. On the one hand, we see a particular pattern of mobility as representing a goal that is to be pursued—the pattern that would characterize greater openness as we have defined it. On the other hand, though, we recognize that whether or not this goal is likely to be attained will importantly depend on the pattern of mobility that actually prevails in our society, and indeed to some extent on how far this pattern deviates from that of openness. The logic of this position may at first sight seem somewhat odd—or to Marxists, perhaps, richly dialectical; but we believe it is in fact fairly straightforward. The achievement of a genuinely open society would imply, it may be supposed, the decomposition or at all events the serious attenuation of classes in the sense of aggregates of individuals, or families, identifiable in the extent to which they occupy similar locations in the social division of labour over time. However, class structures are ones highly resistant to change: those groupings who enjoy positions of superior advantage and power cannot be expected to yield them up without a struggle, but will rather typically seek to exploit the resources that they can command in order to preserve their superiority. Change is therefore only likely to be brought about through collective action on the part of those in inferior positions, relying on their numbers and above all on solidarity and organization. Hence, an interest in factors influencing their preparedness and capacity for such action— and likewise the strength of resistance on the part of those who are thereby threatened—must follow directly from an attachment to any ideal that is incompatible with a class society. To this extent at least we would agree with Marx: that *if* class society is to be ended—or even radically modified—this can only be through conflict between classes in one form or another.

The first consequence of the guiding interests that we have set out, so far as our treatment of social mobility in modern Britain is concerned, is then that this is carried out essentially in terms of mobility between classes or, to be rather more precise, between class positions. We would accept, with the same glosses as those supplied by Parkin, Blau and Duncan's view that in the advanced societies of the West it is now the occupational order that forms 'the backbone of the class structure'. But, unlike Blau and Duncan, we seek to follow through the logic of this argument by using occupation (understood in a more qualified way than usual) as an indicator of class position rather than of prestige or of socio-economic status. In having a 'class' rather than a 'status' basis, our analyses do indeed depart from the usual practice of post-war mobility research, which, as we have noted, was influenced chiefly by Glass's study of 1949: we return rather, and appropriately enough, to the earlier tradition of inquiry conducted within the context of 'the debate with Marx'.

Secondly, the duality of our interest in mobility—in relation both to openness and to class formation—is reflected in the fact that in our empirical work the focus of our attention shifts between two different aspects of mobility. On the one hand, we are concerned with what we would term absolute, or *de facto*, mobility rates: that is, the rates of mobility that we actually observe via the procedures and categories of our research. But, on the other hand, we are also concerned with relative mobility rates: that is, those that result when absolute rates are compared against some norm or standard, or when an absolute rate for one social grouping is in some way compared with that for another. It is mobility between class positions viewed in absolute, *de facto* terms that chiefly concerns us in regard to our basic interest in the implications of mobility for class formation, and the greater part of the analyses that we present are in fact ones of absolute rates—of their overall patterns, of trends through time, of the relation between inter- and intragenerational movement etc. We do, none the less, also give a good deal of attention to relative mobility rates—or, as we would alternatively say, relative mobility chances—expressed in various ways: in part, because it is in these terms that we believe that issues of openness can best be empirically treated; and in part too because, as we shall seek to show, the analysis of relative mobility can contribute importantly to the understanding of absolute rates and to attempts at assessing, albeit speculatively, their likely pattern in the future.

In this connection, however, we should also say that one matter which we do not pursue, or at least not in any direct way, is that of the explanation of mobility or of occupational attainment in terms of variation in individual attributes, including perhaps ones of a psychological as well as a social kind. We have doubts about the validity of the analytical approach that is usually followed in this respect[97] but, in any event, the matter is one that has only a rather limited bearing on our central concerns. It is of relevance only in so far as the question might be raised of how far a lack of openness, in the sense of a high inequality of relative mobility chances determined *ex post*, should be regarded as a situation of inequality rather than as one in which equal opportunities were unequally taken. But, for present purposes at least, we would stand on the position that if evidence of a striking inequality in such chances is presented, then the onus of proof must rest with those who seek to uphold the idea of equality of opportunity by arguing that this inequality is explicable in terms of individual differences of, say, a genetic or a moral kind, which operate *independently of* the location of individuals within the social structure.[98]

Thirdly, and finally here, we may note one other way in which our dual interest in mobility will be manifested in what is to follow: that is, in our discussion of the consequences or concomitants of mobility. From the standpoint of the debate on the desirability or otherwise of a truly open society, we shall wish to examine how far there is evidence, in the British case, that the experience of mobility is associated with discontinuities or strains in the individual's primary, and other, social relations—resulting, say, from status shifts or inconsistencies—of a kind that could be thought likely to induce psychological stress or disequilibrium. But our interest in class formation and in the potentialities for class action will require us to consider further what are the implications of the typical concomitants of mobility at the societal level; that is, for classes as collectivities. For example, we shall wish to ask to what extent observed mobility patterns appear likely to increase 'cross-class' social ties or, alternatively, to sharpen the degree of class segregation, to contribute to the internal subcultural heterogeneity of classes or to heighten their distinctiveness. In other words, we shall be concerned to examine the crucial question of whether mobility acts as primarily an integrative or a disintegrative phenomenon in both a micro- and a macro-sociological perspective.

The substantive themes that we have spelled out above are not dealt with in subsequent chapters in a highly ordered manner; they tend, rather, to be taken up at a number of different points. It may therefore be helpful to the reader if, in conclusion, we review briefly the content and objectives of each chapter in turn.

In Part One, chapter 2 begins the presentation of our basic data on the pattern of class mobility that we have observed in modern British society in the context of a critique of three leading theses on the relationship between mobility and class structure drawn from the work of contemporary British Marxist and 'post-Marxist' writers (principally, those discussed above, pp. 24–7). A recurrent point in the critique is that these writers have not sufficiently appreciated the distinction between mobility as viewed in absolute and in relative terms. In chapter 3 we then examine at length an issue already broached in chapter 2, namely, that of trends in class mobility over the period to which our main data-set relates—roughly, the last half-century. Here the distinction between absolute and relative mobility rates is shown to be of major importance, in that our conclusions regarding the existence and direction of trends differ radically depending on which aspect of mobility is considered. The particular attention that is in fact given to relative mobility chances in this chapter—in part because of the need to treat the conceptual-cum-technical problems involved with some care—is continued in chapter 4. In this case, we are specifically concerned to analyse the pattern of relative chances that underlies the observed pattern of intergenerational mobility as previously presented in chapter 2. It is, therefore, in chapters 3 and 4 that the reader will find most of our results that are directly relevant to the question of the openness of British society over the post-war period. in chapter 5 our attention shifts back decisively to patterns of observed mobility: here our chief objective is to fill out our previous analyses, especially those of chapter 2, by examining in greater detail how both stability and instability of class position, as seen in intergenerational perspective, are mediated through processes of work-life movement. In this chapter, thus, we complete our assessment of the extent to which patterns of mobility, and immobility, *per se* contribute to the formation of classes in the sense of aggregates or collectivities that maintain their identity over time. In the next two chapters, 6 and 7, we again move on to seemingly rather different concerns: that is, with the concomitants of mobility, as achieved via different work-life routes, first for kinship relations and secondly, for various other kinds of social relationships, both primary and secondary. In chapter 8 we are also in a sense concerned with the concomitants of mobility as we have defined it, but specifically in this case with the extent to which our definition is reflected in the subjective experience and awareness of those men from whom our data derive. How far, we ask, is there a correspondence between our constructs and those through which they themselves seek to make sense out of the course of their social lives? In Part Two we then turn to three issues of more current concern, each of which, however, at the same time enables us to resume themes initiated in Part One. In chapter 9 we examine trends in class mobility rates, relative and absolute, after the ending of the 'long boom' of the post-war years; in chapter 10, the class mobility of women; and in chapter 11, class mobility in Britain in a comparative, cross-national perspective. Finally, in chapter 12, we attempt to bring together the major conclusions that we have arrived at in the preceding chapters and, on this basis, to provide a general statement on social mobility and class structure in modern Britain, plus some speculation on future prospects. At the same time, we necessarily assess how satisfactorily our research has responded to those interests by which it was initially prompted.

NOTES

1. See, e.g., Karl Ulrich Mayer and Walter Müller, 'Progress in Social Mobility Research?', *Quality and Quantity*, vol. v, 1971; S.M. Miller, 'The Future of Social Mobility Studies', *American Journal of Sociology*, vol. 77, 1971; Daniel Bertaux, 'Questions de stratification et de mobilité sociale', *Sociologie du travail*, vol. 13, 1971; Reinhard Kreckel, 'Toward a theoretical re-orientation of the sociological analysis of vertical mobility' in

Walter Müller and Karl Ulrich Mayer (eds.), *Social Stratification and Career Mobility,* Paris and the Hague: Mouton, 1973.

2. This latter argument is advanced in particular by Eastern European Marxist writers of an orthodox cast. See, e.g., H. Steiner, 'Grundzüge und Entwicklungstendenzen der westdeutschen Soziologie' in H. Meissner (ed.), *Bürgerliche Ökonomie in modernen Kapitalismus,* Berlin: Dietz, 1967; and G.B. Osipov, 'The Class Character of the Theory of Social Mobility' in P. Hollander (ed.), *American and Soviet Society,* Englewood Cliffs: Prentice Hall, 1969.

3. Although the sole author of this chapter, I use the first person plural in the interests of consistency throughout the volume. It should not, however, be taken as committing the co-authors of other chapters to the views here expressed.

4. F. van Heek, 'Some Introductory Remarks on Social Mobility and Class Structure', in *Transactions of the Third World Congress of Sociology,* London: International Sociological Association, 1956, vol. iii, p. 131.

5. Ibid., pp. 130–1.

6. Royden Harrison, 'Afterword' to the 1968 Sphere edition of *Self Help*: London, 1968, p. 262 (1st edn., London: John Murray, 1859).

7. See in particular, *Lives of the Engineers*, London: John Murray, 3 vols., 1861–2.

8. John Stuart Mill, *Principles of Political Economy*, London: John W. Parker, 1848, vol. i, pp. 462–3.

9. J.E. Cairnes, *Some Leading Principles of Political Economy Newly Expounded*, London: Macmillan, 1874, pp. 70–3. Cf. Alfred Marshall, *Principles of Economics,* London: Macmillan, 1890, book IV, ch. 6 especially.

10. 'The Eighteenth Brumaire of Louis Bonaparte', in Marx-Engels, *Selected Works,* Moscow: Foreign Languages Publishing House, 1958, vol. i, p. 255.

11. 'Wages, Prices and Profits', *Selected Works*, vol. i, p. 444.

12. See, e.g., the letter to Weydemeyer, 5 Mar. 1852, reprinted in Lewis S. Feuer (ed.), *Karl Marx and Friedrich Engels: Basic Writings on Politics and Philosophy*, London: Fontana, 1969, pp. 494–5.

13. Joseph Lopreato and Lawrence Hazelrigg, *Class, Conflict and Mobility,* San Francisco: Chandler, 1972, p. 115.

14. *Capital,* Moscow: Foreign Languages Publishing House, 1959, vol. iii, p. 587.

15. The treatment of intermediate strata in Marx's work has of late aroused some considerable interest. However, the outstanding critical contribution, to which our own discussion is much indebted, remains that of Abram Lincoln Harris, 'Pure Capitalism and the Disappearance of the Middle Class', *Journal of Political Economy,* vol. xlvii, 1939.

16. 'The lower strata of the middle class—the small tradespeople, shopkeepers, and retired tradesmen generally, the handicraftsmen and peasants—all these sink gradually into the proletariat, partly because their diminutive capital does not suffice for the scale on which Modern Industry is carried on, and is swamped in the competition with the large capitalists, partly because their specialised skill is rendered worthless by new methods of production. Thus the proletariat is recruited from all classes of the population.' Marx-Engels, 'Manifesto of the Communist Party', *Selected Works*, vol. i, p. 41.

17. *Theories of Surplus Value*, London: Lawrence & Wishart, 1969, part three, p. 355. Cf. also pp. 496–7; and *Capital*, vol. i, pp. 331–2.

18. 'It is clear that as the scale of production is extended, commerical operations required constantly for the circulation of industrial capital, in order to sell the product existing as commodity-capital, to reconvert the money so received into means of production, and to keep account of the whole process, multiply accordingly. Calculation of prices, bookkeeping, managing funds, correspondence—all belong under this head. The more developed the scale of production, the greater even if not proportionately greater, the commercial operations of the industrial capital, and consequently the labour and other costs of circulation involved in realising value and surplus value.' See esp. *Capital*, vol. iii, p. 293.

19. *Theories of Surplus Value*, vol. i, p. 300–1 (emphasis in original).

20. *Capital,* vol. i, p. 594.

21. *Theories of Surplus Value*, part two, p. 573.

22. Ibid., part three, pp. 62–3 (emphasis in original). Marx, it is true, occasionally seeks to apply a version of the *Verelendungstheorie* to the new middle classes also, suggesting, for example, that with increasing public education the supply of qualified labour will grow and its wage levels thus fall. (See, e.g. *Capital*, vol. iii, pp. 294–5). But an argument on these lines is never worked out at length, and elsewhere Marx envisages a rising standard of living for nonproductive workers (see, e.g., *Theories of Surplus Value*, part two, pp. 561–2).
23. Ibid., part two, p. 560 (emphasis added).
24. Ibid., pp. 572, 560 (emphasis in original).
25. Ibid., part one, pp. 217–18 (emphasis added).
26. Cf. the discussion in O.D. Duncan, 'Occupation Trends and Patterns of Net Mobility in the United States', *Demography*, vol. 3, 1966.
27. See in particular Harris, 'Pure Capitalism and the Disappearance of the Middle Class'; also Martin Nicolaus, 'Proletariat and Middle Class in Marx; Hegelian Choreography and Capitalist Dialectic', *Studies on the Left*, January 1967, and Paul M. Sweezy, *Modern Capitalism and Other Essays*, New York: Monthly Review Press, 1972, part two.
28. The statement was developed in *Die Voraussetzungen des Sozialismus und die Aufgaben der Sozialdemokratie*, Stuttgart: Dietz, 1899.
29. Ibid., p. 49. For a definitive study of Bernstein, see P. Angel, *Eduard Bernstein et l'évolution du socialisme allemand*, Paris: Didier, 1961.
30. Tubingen: J.C.B. Mohr, p. 126.
31. Ibid., part three, 'Die Flucht des Arbeiters in die Freiheit'.
32. For an illuminating account of the political involvements and intellectual development of Sombart (and also of Michels) see Arthur Mitzman, *Sociology and Estrangement,* New York: Knopf, 1973.
33. Robert Michels, *First Lectures in Political Sociology* (trans. Alfred de Grazia), New York: Harper & Row, 1965, p. 82. The lectures were initially published in 1927.
34. Ibid., pp. 80–1. Cf. also pp. 103–4, and more generally Michels's study *Umschichtungen in den herrschenden Klassen nach dem Kriege*, Stuttgart and Berlin: Kohlhammer, 1934.
35. This theme is in fact one which dates back to Michels's writings in his syndicalist days. Cf. Mitzman, *Sociology and Estrangement*, ch. 25. Cf. also Michels's *Political Parties* (trans. Eden and Cedar Paul), New York: Dover, 1959, pp. 271–82.
36. The influence of Pareto on Michels's later work was considerable, and in particular Pareto's theory of the circulation of élites—which may in fact be taken as representing another kind of specifically anti-Marxist interest in mobility that we do not consider here. See, however, the interesting discussion of Pareto in Lopreato and Hazelrigg, *Class, Conflict and Mobility*, pp. 43–60 esp.
37. Ultimately, and unfortunately, this proved to be, as in the case of Sombart also, the fascist movement.
38. See *Political Parties,* part one.
39. Pitirim A. Sorokin, *Social Mobility,* New York: Harper, 1927, 2nd enlarged edn., *Social and Cultural Mobility*, Glencoe: Free Press, 1959. Sorokin was a member of the (non-Marxist) Social-Revolutionary Party in Czarist Russia, subsequently a member of Kerensky's cabinet, and eventually expelled from the Soviet Union by Lenin.
40. *Social and Cultural Mobility*, pp. 38–46, 118–28.
41. Ibid., ch. XVII.
42. Ibid., p. 428.
43. Ibid., p. 438.
44. Ibid., p. 478.
45. Ibid., p. 439, Cf. also p. 510.
46. Ibid., p. 457.
47. Ibid., ch. VII.
48. Ibid., p. 545. (emphasis in original). For Sorokin's views on the less-encouraging aspects of mobility, see further below, pp. 254, 265
49. William Peterson, 'Is America still the Land of Opportunity? ', *Commentary,* vol. 16, 1953.

50. Notable academic contributions include: Elbridge Sibley, 'Some Demographic Clues to Stratification', *American Sociological Review,* vol. 7, 1942; Gideon Sjoberg, 'Are Social Classes in America Becoming More Rigid', *American Sociological Review,* vol. 16, 1951; J.O. Hertzler, 'Some Tendencies Towards a Closed Class System in the United States', *Social Forces*, vol. 30, 1952; August B. Hollingshead, 'Trends in Social Stratification: A Case Study', *American Sociological Review,* vol. 17, 1952; Natalie Rogoff, *Recent Trends in Occupational Mobility*, Glencoe: Free Press, 1953; Ely Chinoy, 'Social Mobility Trends in the United States', *American Sociological Review,* vol. 20, 1955; Gerhard E. Lenski, 'Trends in Inter-Generational Occupational Mobility in the United States', *American Sociological Review,* vol. 23, 1958.

51. See in particular S.M. Lipset and H. Zetterberg, 'A Theory of Social Mobility', in *Transactions of the Third World Congress of Sociology*, vol. iii and Lipset and Reinhard Bendix, *Social Mobility in Industrial Society,* London: Heinemann, 1959; and P.M. Blau and O.D. Duncan, *The American Occupational Structure,* New York: Wiley, 1967.

52. Ibid., p. 429. The following paragraphs draw on pp. 425–42 esp.

53. Ibid., p. 430.

54. Ibid., p. 440.

55. See in particular, 'Social Stratification and Mobility' in Eleanor B. Sheldon and Wilbert E. Moore (eds.), *Indicators of Social Change*, New York: Russell Sage Foundation, 1968.

56. Ibid., p. 675. The reference is to C.M. Cooley, *Social Process,* New York: Scribners, 1918.

57. Ibid., pp. 695–6. Cf. *The American Occupational Structure*, ch. 4.

58. Ibid., pp. 174–5; also Duncan, 'Inheritance of Poverty or Inheritance of Race?' in Daniel P. Moynihan (ed.), *On Understanding Poverty*, New York: Basic Books, 1968.

59. For the most forceful attack from a Marxist standpoint, see N. David Crowder, 'A Critique of Duncan's Stratification Research', *Sociology*, vol. 8, 1974. But see also Aage Sørenson, 'Models of Social Mobility', *Social Science Research*, vol. 4, 1975; Raymond Boudon, *L'Inégalité des chances: la mobilité sociale dans les sociétés industrielles*, Paris: Colin, 1973; and Ray Pawson, 'Empiricist Explanatory Strategies: the Case of Causal Modelling', *Sociological Review*, n.s. vol. 26, 1978.

60. See, e.g., Lipset and Joan Gordon, 'Mobility and Trade Union Membership' in Lipset and Bendix (eds.), *Class, Status and Power,* London: Routledge, 1st edn., 1954; and Lipset, *Political Man*, London: Heinemann, 1960.

61. See, e.g., 'The Changing Class Structure of Contemporary European Politics', *Dædalus*, vol. 63, 1964, and *Revolution and Counter Revolution*, London: Heinemann, 1969, ch. 7 esp.

62. p. 284.

63. Ibid., p. 285.

64. Cf. Lipset and Zetterberg, 'A Theory of Social Mobility', pp. 571–3; Lipset and Bendix, *Social Mobility in Industrial Society*, ch. X.

65. See in particular in this connection Lipset's two contributions to Daniel Bell (ed.), *The New American Right*, New York: Doubleday, 2nd edn., 1963, 'The Sources of the "Radical Right"' and 'Three Decades of the Radical Right: Coughlinites, McCarthyites, and Birchers'; and also Lipset and Earl Raab, *The Politics of Unreason*, London: Heinemann, 1970. (The phrase quoted is from the latter work, p. 460.)

　　It is notable that while Lipset gives such importance to both mobility and status inconsistency effects, Duncan, consistently with his conception of the nature of American social stratification, tends to be generally sceptical about whether it is necessary to postulate such effects, in relation to political or other behaviour, as something other than the effects, in additive combination, of the variables used to define mobility or inconsistency in the first place. See 'Methodological Issues in the Analysis of Social Mobility' in Neil J. Smelser and Lipset (eds.), *Social Structure and Mobility in Economic Development*, London: Routledge, 1968.

66. *Political Man*, p. 403.

67. 'Mobility Patterns and Socialist Concerns', cyclostyled, 1972, subsequently published

in abridged form as 'Social Mobility and Equal Opportunity', *The Public Interest*, Autumn 1972; cf. also 'La mobilité sociale et les objectifs socialistes', *Sociologie et sociétés*, November 1972. For essentially similar views expressed by a European liberal, see Raymond Aron, *Progress and Disillusion: the Dialectics of Modern Society*, London: Pall Mall Press, 1968, pp. 80-1.

68. 'The Future of Mobility Studies'. For a detailed critique of the general thesis of 'status' politics and an insightful analysis of its origins in the liberal political commitments of its exponents, Lipset included, see Michael P. Rogin, *The Intellectuals and McCarthy: the Radical Specter*, Cambridge, Mass.: M.I.T. Press, 1967.

69. See, e.g., Angel, *Eduard Bernstein*, deuxième partie, ch. 1, esp.; and Peter Gay, *The Dilemma of Democratic Socialism*, New York: Columbia University Press, 1952, ch. 4.

70. See, e.g., R.H. Tawney, *Equality*, preface to 3rd edn., London: Allen & Unwin, 1938.

71. E.F.M. Durbin, *The Politics of Democratic Socialism*, London: Routledge, 1940, p.112.

72. Cf. ibid., parts IV and V; Tawney, *Equality*, ch. VI.

73. Ibid., 5th edn., 1964, p. 110.

74. Cf. Tawney, ibid., pp. 116-17, 144-5. It was at this point that the concerns of the democratic socialists converged with those of more radical liberals who were exercised by the extent to which 'social circumstances' prevented effective competition in the labour market. Cf. in this respect the remarkable collection of papers found in T.H. Marshall (ed.), *Class Conflict and Social Stratification*, London: Le Play House Press, 1938.

75. Cf. Tawney, *Equality*, pp. 112-15.

76. Interestingly enough, C.A.R. Crosland, in what may be regarded as the last comprehensive statement of the British ethical socialist case, reviews much of the same literature which led Lipset to call into doubt the wisdom of always giving mobility an overriding priority, and, while obviously intrigued by the idea of 'status politics', none the less concludes 'that the case often made against the mobile, equal-opportunity society both exaggerates the evils and underestimates the compensating gains'. *The Future of Socialism*, London: Cape, 1956, p. 231.

77. D.V. Glass (ed.), *Social Mobility in Britain*, London: Routledge, 1954.

78. Ibid., 'Introduction', p. 10. Glass's work exercised a major influence on other national studies of social mobility in the 1950s and early 1960s and not least in encouraging the adoption of a 'status' or 'prestige' frame of reference. Perhaps the most sophisticated inquiry in this line of development is that undertaken in Denmark by Kaare Svalastoga, *Prestige, Class and Mobility*, Copenhagen: Gyldendal, 1959. Another notable study of this period which is however rather exceptional in adopting primarily a 'class' frame of reference is that carried out in Sweden by Gösta Carlsson, *Social Mobility and Class Structure*, Lund: CWK Gleerup, 1958.

79. The LSE research in fact grew out of a projected study of the 'formation and structure' of the British middle classes—which was a matter of considerable public discussion in the years immediately after the second world war. For example, from more traditional quarters fears were being expressed that as the old middle class of independent businessmen and professionals became 'diluted' by growing numbers of salaried employees, the middle classes would lose their capacity to play their vital functions within the social order—those of invigorating economic life, providing community leadership, 'preserving standards' and, above all, standing out against the influence of the State. On the other hand, more progressive opinion tended to see in the new salariat the *cadres* of a more rational, efficient, and just society, poised to challenge the power and privilege of established groups whose claims to competence and public spiritedness alike were becoming increasingly doubtful. A useful impression of the debate, though from a traditionalist angle, can be gained from Roy Lewis and Angus Maude, *The English Middle Classes*, London: Phoenix House, 1949, and *Professional People*, London: Phoenix House, 1952.

The LSE group decided eventually against limiting their research to the middle classes, since they came to realize that studies of particular groups and strata could not be satisfactorily carried out without reference to the nature of the social hierarchy as a whole, and thus that such studies 'needed as background, a *general* investigation of social status and mobility in Britain', *Social Mobility in Britain,* 'Introduction', pp. 3–5.

80. Ibid., p. 21.

81. See in particular, ch. VIII, Glass and J.R. Hall, 'Social Mobility in Britain: a Study of Inter-generation Changes in Status'.

82. For further discussion of the index of association, see below n. 16, p. 65 and pp. 95–6.

83. Ibid., p. 26. Glass's warning about the potential dangers of meritocracy was developed by another (at the time) socialist intellectual, Michael Young in his *The Rise of the Meritocracy,* London: Thames & Hudson, 1958.

84. An interesting parallel may be noted here with current thinking in some Eastern European societies. Cf. W. Wesołowski and K. Słomczyński, 'Reduction of Social Inequalities and Status Inconsistency' in Polish Sociological Association, *Social Structure: Polish Sociology 1977,* Wrocław: Ossolineum, 1977.

85. Nicos Poulantzas, *Les Classes sociales dans le capitalisme aujourd'hui,* Paris: Seuil, 1974, p. 37 (emphases in original).

86. Cf. e.g., H. Frankel, *Capitalist Society and Modern Sociology,* London: Lawrence & Wishart, 1970; G. Carchedi 'Reproduction of Social Classes at the level of Production Relations', *Economy and Society*, vol. 4, 1975.

87. John Westergaard and Henrietta Resler, *Class in a Capitalist Society: A Study of Contemporary Britain,* London: Heinemann, 1975, p. 280.

88. Ibid., part two.

89. Ibid., p. 285. For a similar, but less extended, treatment of the same issue by another leading representative of British Marxist sociology, see T.B. Bottomore, 'The Class Structure in Western Europe' in Margaret Scotford Archer and Salvador Giner (eds.) *Contemporary Europe: Class, Status and Power,* London: Weidenfeld & Nicolson, 1971.

90. *Les Classes sociales dans le capitalisme aujourd'hui*, p. 37.

91. Anthony Giddens, *The Class Structure of the Advanced Societies,* London: Hutchinson, 1973, p. 107. Giddens is of course also parting company here with distinguished non-Marxists, such as Schumpeter and Dahrendorf.

92. Ibid. (emphases in original). This process of class structuration, through patterns of mobility and immobility, Giddens refers to as 'mediate': he also distinguishes processes of 'proximate' structuration, which operate in a more localized manner, and reflect features of particular market, work, and community situations.

93. Frank Parkin, *Class Inequality and Political Order,* London: MacGibbon & Kee, 1971, p. 18, Cf. Blau and Duncan, *The American Occupational Structure,* pp. 5–7.

94. *Class Inequality and Political Order,* pp. 23–8.

95. 'Strategies of Social Closure in Class Formation' in Parkin (ed.), *The Social Analysis of Class Structure,* London: Tavistock, 1974.

96. As regards the former view, Miller has aptly remarked that 'Even if income differences were very much narrowed, the kind of activities that people are engaged in, the tasks they do on their jobs, are still important . . . This is what social mobility is about–that people can change their jobs from those of their parents and throughout their lifetimes.' S.M. Miller, 'Social Mobility and Equality' in Organisation for Economic Co-operation and Development, *Education, Inequality and Life Chances,* Paris: OECD, 1975. As regards the latter view, we believe that Tawney and others among the ethical socialists were entirely correct in showing a concern for the part that mobility should play within –as well as in the process of achieving–a socialist society.

97. Cf. the items cited in n. 59 above.

98. One could, of course, readily go further here and point to the difficulties that arguments of this kind encounter. In particular, one might note that to show, in the manner of Blau and Duncan, a shift in emphasis in processes of social selection from 'ascribed' to 'achieved' criteria in no way guarantees a claim that equality of opportunity has been enhanced. Cf. Parkin, 'Strategies of Social Closure in Class Formation' n. 6, p. 16.

Part One
Class Mobility in Britain:
Trends, Patterns, and Concomitants
in the Post-War Period

CHAPTER 2

Class Mobility in Britain:
Three Theses Examined

(*with* CATRIONA LLEWELLYN)

Of late, an encouraging aspect of British writing in the field of social stratification has been the attempt to restore a concern with rates and patterns of social
mobility to a central place in the discussion of issues of class formation and class
action. In the years immediately following the second world war a tendency was
evident for the study of mobility and of class structure to diverge. For reasons
partly ideological and partly methodological, most major inquiries into mobility
undertaken in this period were conducted in terms of hierarchies of prestige or
of socio-economic status rather than of class; while analysts of class structure
showed a reluctance to avail themselves of the methods or results of survey
research and, in the case of some Marxist authors, went so far as to deny that the
study of mobility was of any relevance to their concerns. However, as we have
noted in the previous chapter, in the recent work of leaders of Marxist sociology
in Britain, such as Westergaard and Bottomore, and also in the work of other
writers whose position we have described as 'post-Marxist', notably Giddens and
Parkin, a serious effort has been made to give the idea of mobility a major role
in the renewal of class theory and, further, to incorporate the findings of mobility
research as an important element in substantive accounts of the contemporary
class structure of Great Britain and other industrial societies.

As we have remarked, two different, though clearly related, approaches have
been followed. First, mobility has been seen, to take over Giddens's terminology,
as a basic source of class 'structuration': it is the rate and pattern of mobility
that will determine the extent to which classes may be recognized as collectivities
of individuals or families occupying similar locations within the social division
of labour over time. Secondly, it has been suggested that the extent of mobility
evident within a society may be taken as a significant indicator of the prevailing
balance of advantage and power in class relations and, further, of characteristic
modes of class action. Parkin, for example, has argued that class conflict is to an
important degree expressed in the form of strategies of exclusion, chiefly adopted
by more advantaged groupings; and counter-strategies of solidarism, which are
typically the resort of those in less advantaged situations. Mobility rates and
patterns can thus serve to reveal, on the one hand, the effectiveness of the former;
and, on the other hand, at least the potential for success of the latter—which
must depend on participants being ready to opt for collective interests and
aspirations rather than individual ones.

In their analyses of modern capitalist society, the writers in question have
then, following these approaches, advanced several theses which link mobility in
a more or less explicit fashion to the form of the class structure and to the
character of class relations. Although, as we shall see, their arguments do not
always prove to be as precise as one might wish, they have the merit of being
sufficiently so—while at the same time holding considerable substantive interest

—to make it of value to submit them to fairly detailed empirical testing, and in fact to take them, in this chapter, as the framework within which we present and discuss our basic data on class mobility. Our attention will focus on three related theses, as applied to modern British society: that of a marked degree of 'closure' existing at the higher levels of the class structure; that of a 'buffer zone' restricting the extent of mobility across the division between manual and nonmanual occupations; and that of the offsetting or 'counterbalancing' of any rising trend in upward mobility *inter*generationally by a declining trend in such mobility *intra*generationally.[1]

DATA AND THE CLASS SCHEMA

Our data derive from a survey inquiry made in 1972 by the Social Mobility Group at Nuffield College, Oxford, into occupational mobility among men aged 20 to 64 and resident in England and Wales. A full account of this inquiry is given in an Appendix to the first edition of this book. Here it will be sufficient to note that a sample of a stratified two-stage design was drawn from the population in question, using the Electoral Registers as the frame for the selection of individuals; and that interviews producing usable information were conducted with 10,309 men, representing a response rate of 81.8 per cent.

For purposes of applying the data of this inquiry to questions of class mobility, we have formed, as described below, a sevenfold class schema or, more precisely, a schema of class positions, by aggregating categories from the collapsed (36-category) version of the Hope–Goldthorpe occupational scale.[2] A distinctive feature of these categories is that they provide a relatively high degree of differentiation in terms of both occupational function *and* employment status: in effect, the associated employment status is treated as part of the definition of an occupation. Thus, for example, 'self-employed plumber' is a different occupation from 'foreman plumber' as from 'rank-and-file employee plumber'. On this basis, then, we are able to bring together, within the classes we distinguish, occupations whose incumbents will typically share in broadly similar *market* and *work* situations which, following Lockwood's well-known discussion, we take as the two major components of class position.[3] That is to say, we combine occupational categories whose members would appear, in the light of the available evidence, to be typically comparable, on the one hand, in terms of their sources and levels of income and other conditions of employment, in their degree of economic security and in their chances of economic advancement; and, on the other hand, in their location within the systems of authority and control governing the processes of production in which they are engaged.

The schema, together with some explanatory and interpretive comments, is as follows.

Class I (H–G categories 1,2,3,4, and 7):[4] all higher-grade professionals, self-employed or salaried; higher-grade administrators and officials in central and local government and in public and private enterprises (including company directors); managers in large industrial establishments; and large proprietors. It might appear unfortunate, and immediately contrary to the principles of the schema, that in Class I employer, self-employed, and employee categories should be combined. However, the shortcoming is more apparent than real. In the case of many of the occupational roles in question, employment status tends in fact to be rather ambiguous—as with company directors, 'working' proprietors, or managers with sizeable ownership interests; or turns on rather artificial distinctions introduced primarily for national insurance or income tax purposes. In any event, the employer and (nominally) self-employed members of Class I amount to less than 8 per cent of the total. What Class I positions have in common is that they afford their incumbents incomes which are high, generally secure, and likely to rise steadily over their lifetimes;[5] and that they are positions which typically involve the exercise of authority and/or expertise within a range of discretion, and thus offer considerable autonomy and freedom from control by others. Class I might therefore be taken as very largely corresponding to the higher and intermediate levels of what Dahrendorf, following Karl Renner, has termed the 'service class' (*Dienstklasse*) of modern capitalist society— precisely the class of those exercising authority and expertise on behalf of corporate bodies—plus such elements of the classic bourgeoisie (independent businessmen and 'free' professionals) as are not yet assimilated into this new formation.[6]

Class II (H–G categories 5, 6, 8, 9, 10, 12, 14, and 16): lower-grade professionals and higher-grade technicians; lower-grade adminsitrators and officials; managers in small business and industrial establishments and in services; and supervisors of nonmanual employees. Typically, Class II positions guarantee income levels that rank directly below those of Class I, and also carry 'staff' status and conditions of employment. The occupational roles of Class II members tend to be located in the middle and lower ranges of bureaucratic hierarchies of one type or another, so that they exercise some degree of authority and discretion in the performance of their work-tasks while at the same time being subject to more or less systematic, if not particularly close, control from above. Class II could, in other words, be seen as complementing Class I of our schema in representing the subaltern or *cadet* levels of the service class.

Class III (H–G categories 21, 25, 28, and 34): routine nonmanual—largely clerical—employees in administration and commerce; sales personnel; and other rank-and-file employees in services. The level of incomes of men in Class III positions is clearly lower than that of men in Classes I and II, and indeed falls below that of men in various kinds of manual employment. The majority of Class III positions do, however, provide relatively high security of employment, and tend in some degree to be integrated into the base of bureaucratic structures, often thus offering at least some features of 'staff' status.[7] Men in the occupational roles covered are not usually engaged in the exercise of authority or, if so, only through the application of standardized rules and procedures in which their discretion is slight; on the other hand, they are themselves likely to be subjected to quite detailed bureaucratic regulation. Comprising thus largely subordinate positions, Class III is to be regarded as separate from the service class, and might rather be seen as representing a 'white-collar labour force' functionally associated with, but marginal to, the service class.[8] For some purposes, we shall find it useful to refer to Classes I, II, and III together as our three 'white-collar' classes. However, more usually, we shall treat Class III, along with Class IV and V, as being an 'intermediate' class—that is, as being structurally located between the service class and the working class.

Class IV (H–G categories 11, 13, 19, 24, 29, and 36): small proprietors, including farmers and smallholders; self-employed artisans; and all other 'own account' workers apart from professionals. Class IV, in other words, may be equated with that of the 'petty bourgeoisie'. The market situation of its members is distinctive in virtue of their employer or self-employed status, although income levels show considerable variability. Economic security and prospects must also be regarded as generally less predictable than in the case of at least salaried employees. Small 'independents' of the kind covered by Class IV are always exposed to the possibility of severe market constraints on their activities, operating as they do within, so to speak, the interstices of the corporate economy. At the same time, though, they have the advantage of some amount of capital; and also of a high degree of autonomy, in the sense of freedom from direct supervision, in the performance of their work-tasks.[9]

Class V (H–G categories 15, 17, and 20): lower-grade technicians whose work is to some extent of a manual character; and supervisors of manual workers. Class V positions afford relatively high income levels, comparable almost with those of Class II, and reasonable security of employment may also be supposed. On the other hand, though, it would seem probable that their incumbents have less favourable economic prospects than do staff in positions that are more completely integrated into administrative or managerial bureaucracies. In their occupational roles, men in Class V are typically involved in some degree in the exercise of authority and discretion—more so, for example, that the routine nonmanual employees of Class III—but again subject to close monitoring and control from above. Class V might thus be seen as representing a latter-day aristocracy of labour or a 'blue-collar' élite, its members being set apart from the mass of wage labour by their functions and to some extent by their conditions of employment within the enterprise, while remaining however still marginal to the management group proper.[10]

Class VI (H–G categories 18, 22, 23, 27, and 30): skilled manual wage-workers in all branches of industry, including all who have served apprenticeships and also those who have acquired a relatively high degree of skill through other forms of training.

Class VII (H–G categories 26, 31, 32, 33, and 35): all manual wage-workers in industry in semi- and unskilled grades; and agricultural workers.

We would equate Classes VI and VII together with the working class. Men in Class VI tend to have higher income levels than do those in Class VII (although there is a good deal of overlap—as also between the incomes of men in both Class VI and VII and those in our three intermediate classes). Again, skilled men tend to have greater job security than the nonskilled and also somewhat more autonomy in work, whether deriving from the inherent nature of their tasks or from greater work-group or union strength. However, what members of Classes VI and VII have in common and what chiefly distinguishes them from members of other classes is, first, the basic feature of their market situation—that they sell their labour power in more or less discrete amounts (whether measured by output or time) in return for wages; and secondly, the basic feature of their work situation—that they are, via the labour contract, placed in an entirely subordinate role, subject to the authority of their employer or his agents.

One further, general comment remains to be made about the class schema. It should be clearly recognized that the aggregation of categories of the H-G scale in order to form the classes was carried out without reference to the position of categories in the ordering of the scale—which its authors present as one indicative of the 'general desirability' of occupations in popular estimation (but which could also be taken as one of occupational prestige or even, perhaps, as proxy for one of socio-economic status).[11] Since the category numbers show their rank order in the scale, it can be seen from the foregoing that while Classes I and II overlap only slightly, if at all, with the remaining classes in terms of the 'general desirability' of their constituent occupational groupings, the latter comprise groupings which overlap to a considerable extent. Thus, when we describe Classes III, IV, and V as 'intermediate', we refer, as we earlier noted, to their structural location, and not to their position according to the H-G scale. Our class schema should not then be regarded as having—nor should it be expected to have—a consistently hierarchical form. As Giddens has aptly observed, divisions between classes do not always 'lend themselves to easy visualisation in terms of any ordinal scale of "higher" and "lower", as [statistically defined] strata do—although . . . this sort of imagery cannot be escaped altogether.'[12] One immediate implication—others will emerge later—is therefore that in discussing mobility on the basis of our schema, we must always take care to consider whether or not it is appropriate to describe its direction as being 'upward' or 'downward'. In general, we shall in fact speak of upward mobility only in the case of movement into Classes I and II, whether from the intermediate classes or from Classes VI and VII, and conversely of downward mobility only in the case of movement out of Classes I and II.

THE 'CLOSURE' THESIS

Within the current literature of mobility research, a wide measure of agreement is apparent on what is taken to be the generic form assumed by occupational mobility patterns within modern industrial societies. The essentials of this agreement may be summed up in the following three interrelated propositions:[13] (i) mobility is most likely to occur between groupings which are at a similar level within the occupational hierarchy, whether this is conceived of as one of desirability, prestige, or socio-economic status: (ii) mobility will tend thus to be greatest in the intermediate levels of the hierarchy and least towards its extremes —if only because at the intermediate levels the possibility will exist for mobility to occur within its most frequent range both upwards and downwards, whereas, as the extremes are approached, one or other of these possibilities will tend to be precluded; (iii) the least mobility of all will be found towards the peak of the hierarchy, since those who hold the superior positions may be presumed to have not only a strong motivation to retain them, for themselves and for their children, but further the command over resources to enable them to do so, at least in terms of whatever aspects of social advantage and power it is that defines their position as superior in the first place. The consensus prevailing on these points, as will emerge, has been of very general influence on the writers whose work concerns us: in regard to the closure thesis specifically, the third proposition is of course that of most direct relevance.

Assuming a broad congruence, at their higher levels at least, between the occupational hierarchy and the class structure, the writers in question have upheld the view that at these levels, in Britain and other comparable societies, a significant degree of 'closure' exists.[14] That is to say, in the composition of the constituent groupings of these levels, self- and inter-recruitment intergenerationally play the major role; and in so far as 'external' recruitment does occur, then—consistently with the first of the foregoing propositions—this involves mobility which is predominantly of a short-range kind. Elite groupings will contain no more than quite negligible proportions of men whose recruitment has entailed *long-range* upward movement as, say, from a working-class social background. Thus, the effective operation of various strategies of exclusion is suggested; and it is characteristic of groupings located towards the peak of the occupational and class structures that they possess a particularly marked homogeneity in terms of the social origins of their members. In turn, then, this serves to maintain their subcultural distinctiveness, and provides favourable conditions for a high degree of ideological and socio-political cohesion. It is important to note here that the argument advanced is clearly in terms of absolute mobility rates, and that 'closure' should not therefore be understood as the strict opposite of 'openness' in our sense: this concept, as we have stressed, we would wish to discuss in terms of relative mobility chances.

By way of relating the findings of our mobility inquiry to the closure thesis, we present in Table 2.1 an 'inflow' mobility matrix. This shows the composition of each of our seven classes according to the class origins of those of our respondents allocated to it, as indexed by the occupation of the 'head' of the respondent's household, normally his father, at respondent's age 14.[15] Since it is well known that mobility within the agricultural sector of a modern industrial society follows very distinctive patterns—and there is some reason to believe that the authors who concern us may have been concentrating their attention on the non-agricultural sector—we give our basic results in this chapter both excluding and including agricultural categories. However, as can be seen, the difference is generally slight, if not negligible, on account of the small size of the agricultural sector in Britain from early in the present century.

For our present concern, what is immediately striking in Table 2.1 is that, directly contrary to any notion of closure at the higher levels of the class structure, Class I of our schema displays, on any reckoning, a very wide basis of recruitment and a very low degree of homogeneity in its composition. Although a quarter of the men it comprises are themselves the sons of Class I fathers, it can also be seen that the remainder of the membership is drawn from the other six classes of our schema in a remarkably even manner, with each contributing at least 10 per cent. It is true that if recruitment to Class I is judged, in the manner of Glass and his colleagues, against the standard of 'perfect mobility'— which would imply that the distribution in each internal column of Table 2.1 would reproduce the row marginal distribution—then self-recruitment to Class I is over three times greater than the perfect mobility expectation and recruitment

Table 2.1

Class composition by class of father[a] at respondent's age 14

| Father's[a] class | Respondent's class (1972) | | | | | | | N | % |
| | I | II | III | IV | V | VI | VII | | |
				percentage[b] by column					
I	25·3 (24·2)	12·4 (12·0)	9·6 (9·1)	6·7 (6·0)	3·2 (3·0)	2·0 (1·9)	2·4 (2·0)	680 (688)	7·9 (7·3)
II	13·1 (12·5)	12·2 (11·8)	8·0 (7·6)	4·8 (4·4)	5·2 (4·9)	3·1 (3·0)	2·5 (2·2)	547 (554)	6·4 (5·9)
III	10·4 (10·0)	10·4 (10·0)	10·8 (10·2)	7·4 (6·1)	8·7 (8·2)	5·7 (5·4)	6·0 (5·3)	687 (694)	8·0 (7·3)
IV	10·1 (13·0)	12·2 (13·9)	9·8 (12·2)	27·2 (36·5)	8·6 (10·6)	7·1 (9·6)	7·7 (12·3)	886 (1,329)	10·3 (14·1)
V	12·5 (12·0)	14·0 (13·5)	13·2 (12·5)	12·1 (9·4)	16·6 (15·6)	12·2 (11·4)	9·6 (8·6)	1,072 (1,082)	12·5 (11·5)
VI	16·4 (15·7)	21·7 (21·0)	26·1 (24·8)	24·0 (19·2)	31·1 (29·2)	41·8 (39·4)	35·2 (30·3)	2,577 (2,594)	30·0 (27·5)
VII	12·1 (12·6)	17·1 (17·8)	22·6 (23·6)	17·8 (18·5)	26·7 (28·5)	28·0 (29·4)	36·6 (39·3)	2,126 (2,493)	24·8 (26·4)
N	1,230 (1,285)	1,050 (1,087)	827 (870)	687 (887)	1,026 (1,091)	1,883 (2,000)	1,872 (2,214)	8,575 (9,434)	
%	14·3 (13·6)	12·2 (11·5)	9·6 (9·2)	8·0 (9·4)	12·0 (11·6)	22·0 (21·2)	21·8 (23·5)		

Notes: (a) Or other 'head of household' (see text). The two basic questions in the 1972 inquiry from which the data of the table derive were: 'What is your job now?'—following on several questions on earlier occupations; and 'What was your father's (or other head of household's) job at that time (i.e. at respondent's age 14)?'—following on several other questions about respondent's family circumstances at that age. (b) Bracketed figures are those produced if farmers (H–G category 11) and smallholders (H–G category 24) are allocated to Class IV, and agricultural workers (H–G category 31) to Class VII.

from Class II more than twice as great, while the inflow from Classes VI and VII is at only about half the expected level.[16] However, *if* the focus of one's interest is on class formation—rather than on questions of equality of opportunity— assessments of mobility in such relative terms would seem not altogether to the point: it is absolute, *de facto* patterns which must surely be accorded greatest importance. In other words, what matters is not so much the degree of equality or inequality in chances of access to a class for persons of differing origin, but the *outcome* of these chances, whatever they may be, in terms of the compo- sition of the class.

Continuing, therefore, from this point of view, a further aspect of recruit- ment to Class I which calls for comment is the extent to which, in absolute terms, it is in fact made up of men of working-class origins. Here, the relative size of classes is a crucial factor. In Table 2.1, men allocated to Classes VI and VII together constitute well over 50 per cent of the fathers' distribution, while Class I accounts for less than 15 per cent of the respondents' distribution. Thus, although the sons of manual wage-workers are represented in Class I in much less than their due proportion, relative to the norm of perfect mobility, they still account for over a quarter of its membership. It may also be noted from Table 2.1 that the sons of Class V fathers, that is of lower-grade technicians and foremen, are recruited to Class I at close to the perfect mobility level. In this way, then, a further quite sizeable component of its membership—around an eighth—may also be reasonably thought of as comprising men who will at all events be more likely to have a blue-collar than a white-collar social back- ground.[17]

On the basis of these findings, therefore, the claim that access to the higher levels of the British class structure is tightly controlled, thus creating at these levels a marked homogeneity of social origins, would seem open to serious doubt. However, we must at this point consider one rather evident possibility: namely, that the Class I of our schema, covering as it does some 10–15 per cent of the active male population, is more broadly conceived than the élite groupings envisaged by those who have advanced the closure thesis, and to an extent that the relevance of our findings is much diminished. In this respect, it must be said, a major difficulty arises. The writers in question show a good deal of imprecision or uncertainty in their conceptualizations, and not least when they come to relate them to empirical material. In particular, confusion arises from a failure to make, or to make consistently, the distinction between what could be termed élite occupations, on the one hand, and, on the other, élites *within* these occu- pations.[18]

Our inquiry was designed to investigate mobility of an inter- rather than an intraoccupational kind, and consequently our data enable us to say little about recruitment to élites in the stricter of the two senses defined. If, therefore, the closure thesis is intended to apply *only* to these numerically very small (however socially powerful) entities, our findings are not ones which would allow us to call it into question. Indeed, we would recognize that in this delimited form, the thesis appears to be generally supported by a number of more specialized studies;[19] and we would add that in an analysis reported elsewhere, we have shown that if an 'élite' is distinguished within our Class I in terms of high income

—defined as £6,000 p.a. and over in 1972—then in this case evidence much more suggestive of closure in recruitment is to be found than when Class I is considered as a whole.[20] But it could scarcely be maintained that the closure thesis is always, and unequivocally, restricted to the form in question; and where it *is* given a wider application, our data do become pertinent, and must amount, we believe, to a refutation of it. For example, it is difficult, in the light of Table 2.1, to accept the argument that 'movement from the working class into the upper class is very limited in any society and notably so in Britain' *as is shown by* the pattern of recruitment to such occupational groupings as those of higher-grade civil servants or business managers; or the suggestion—at least if construed in inflow terms—that there is relatively little working-class recruitment to 'established middle-class professions'; or again, the claim that industrial managers 'are mainly drawn from the propertied and professional classes'.[21] Rather, if what is in question is the composition of what we have characterized as the upper and intermediate levels of the service class of modern British society, rather than that of élites *stricto sensu*, our findings must lend strong support to Dahrendorf's argument that 'If any class bears witness to the comparative openness of [contemporary] European societies, it is the service class', and that this class typically contains a sizeable component of men recruited from working-class families.[22]

Finally in this connection, we may note that in their preoccupation with the degree of closure at the higher levels of the class structure, the writers with whom we are concerned appear to have neglected the point—of obvious relevance to their theoretical interests—that far greater homogeneity in terms of social origins is in fact evident at the lower levels, and in particular among the body of manual workers. From Table 2.1 it can be seen that those of our respondents who were allocated to Classes VI and VII were preponderantly the sons of men also allocated to these classes, or to Class V. To put the matter most sharply, the data of the table indicate that if one were to take a manual worker at random from the present-day population, the chances would be greater than three in four that he would be 'second generation blue-collar' in the sense that his father would also have been engaged in some kind of manual work or as a foreman or lower-grade technician. In contrast, if one took similarly a representative of Class I of our schema, the chances would be no more than even that his father held *any kind* of white-collar occupation—that is, any occupation falling within our Classes I, II, or III. While, then, our data on recruitment to the service class afford little evidence of the practice of, at all events, any very successful strategies of exclusion—despite there being wide inequalities in chances of access—and would lead one to expect some considerable socio-cultural diversity within this class, it could, on the other hand, be suggested that the pattern of intergenerational inflow to the working class is one which, so far at least as common social origins are concerned, offers a very favourable basis for strategies of solidarism.[23]

THE 'BUFFER-ZONE' THESIS

The buffer-zone thesis, no less than the closure thesis (with which it has an obvious connection), reveals the influence of the generally received ideas on the form taken by occupational mobility patterns which we earlier set out. It proposes the division between manual and nonmanual occupations as a fundamental line of cleavage within both the occupational hierarchy and the class structure, and as one which is of major importance in preventing mobility of a long-range kind. It is accepted in statements of the thesis that a large amount of mobility does in fact occur across the manual–nonmanual division, both intergenerationally and in the course of individuals' working lives. But this, it is held, is largely short-range movement between groupings on, as it were, the margins of the division, and thus still relatively 'close' to each other in socio-economic terms: the wider significance of the area of high mobility around the division—the buffer zone—lies in the way in which it effectively blocks off longer-range mobility, which would lead to the introduction of markedly hetero-geneous elements into the groupings on either side of it.[24]

Expressed, then, in more specific terms, the buffer-zone thesis could be said to claim the following: (i) that while the sons of higher-level, that is to say, skilled manual workers will be significantly more likely than the sons of semi- and unskilled workers to achieve nonmanual occupations, such occupations as they do achieve will for the most part be ones at the base of the nonmanual hierarchy, and the chances of men of manual origin gaining access to nonmanual occupations of superior grade will fall off to the point of being almost negligible; and (ii) that while the sons of lower-level nonmanual workers, that is, of clerks, salesmen, supervisors, petty entrepreneurs, etc., will be significantly more likely to be found in manual work than will the sons of men higher in the nonmanual scale, such movements will be very largely into skilled manual grades rather than into semi-skilled or labouring jobs.

Given this formulation of the thesis, it would appear that the classes of our schema are so defined as to make it a very suitable basis on which to organize our mobility data for the purposes of an empirical test. To begin with, we may consider, in Table 2.2, the same data as were previously used in Table 2.1, but now presented in 'outflow' rather than 'inflow' form; that is, in the form relevant to showing what, for the period covered by our enquiry, has been the amount and pattern of mobility experienced by men of different class origins.

Referring to this table, we may examine, first, the extent of differences in outflow patterns between men whose fathers were skilled manual workers (Class VI) and those whose fathers were nonskilled (Class VII). It can in fact be readily seen from the appropriate two rows of the table that the only sizeable difference is in the proportions of those men who in 1972 were themselves to be found in skilled or nonskilled manual work. So far as mobility across the manual–non-manual division is concerned, what is striking is the similarity that the two distributions display. Thus we must conclude that, in the light of our findings, England and Wales, at all events, appear as a conspicuous exception to the argument advanced by one author in expounding the buffer-zone thesis that 'it is very generally the case . . . that the chances of intergenerational mobility out of the working class are heavily concentrated within the skilled manual category.'[25]

Secondly, we may ask to what extent is the mobility that does occur 'out of the working class', that is, from Class VI and VII origins, restricted in its range to the lower levels of the nonmanual hierarchy. Here again, as in discussing

Table 2.2

Class distribution of respondents by class of father[a] at respondent's age 14

Father's[a] class	Respondent's class (1972)							N	%
	I	II	III	IV percentage[b] by row	V	VI	VII		
I	45·7 (45·2)	19·1 (18·9)	11·6 (11·5)	6·8 (7·7)	4·9 (4·8)	5·4 (5·4)	6·5 (6·5)	680 (688)	7·9 (7·3)
II	29·4 (29·1)	23·3 (23·1)	12·1 (11·9)	6·0 (7·0)	9·7 (9·6)	10·8 (10·6)	8·6 (8·7)	547 (554)	6·4 (5·9)
III	18·6 (18·4)	15·9 (15·7)	13·0 (12·8)	7·4 (7·8)	13·0 (12·8)	15·7 (15·6)	16·4 (16·9)	687 (694)	8·0 (7·3)
IV	14·0 (12·6)	14·4 (11·4)	9·1 (8·0)	21·1 (24·4)	9·9 (8·7)	15·1 (14·4)	16·3 (20·5)	886 (1,329)	10·3 (14·1)
V	14·4 (14·2)	13·7 (13·6)	10·2 (10·1)	7·7 (7·7)	15·9 (15·7)	21·4 (21·2)	16·8 (17·6)	1,072 (1,082)	12·5 (11·5)
VI	7·8 (7·8)	8·8 (8·8)	8·4 (8·3)	6·4 (6·6)	12·4 (12·3)	30·6 (30·4)	25·6 (25·9)	2,577 (2,594)	30·0 (27·5)
VII	7·1 (6·5)	8·5 (7·8)	8·8 (8·2)	5·7 (6·6)	12·9 (12·5)	24·8 (23·5)	32·2 (34·9)	2,126 (2,493)	24·8 (24·6)
N	1,230 (1,285)	1,050 (1,087)	827 (870)	687 (887)	1,026 (1,091)	1,883 (2,000)	1,872 (2,214)	8,575 (9,434)	
%	14·3 (13·6)	12·2 (11·5)	9·6 (9·2)	8·0 (9·4)	12·0 (11·6)	22·0 (21·2)	21·8 (23·5)		

Notes: (a) See note (a), Table 2.1.
(b) See note (b), Table 2.1.

recruitment patterns, it is important to recognize that different judgements may be arrived at according to whether mobility is assessed in absolute or relative terms. Viewing the data of Table 2.2 against the standard of perfect mobility—that is, comparing row percentages with corresponding column marginal percentages—some support for the idea of a buffer zone might perhaps be claimed. For example, while the sons of manual workers, skilled and nonskilled, are represented in Class V, that of the blue-collar élite, in about their due proportions, and not far below this level in Class III, that of routine nonmanual employees, they become progressively under-represented as one moves from Class III to Class I. Thus, in Class I, as we have already noted, there are only around a half as many men of working-class origins as the assumption of perfect mobility would require. Again, as a means of comparing the chances of access to higher-level nonmanual positions of the sons of manual workers with those of men of other class origins, one may show from the data of Table 2.2 that of sons of Class VI and VII fathers in our sample, around 16 per cent were found in Classes I or II, as against 30 per cent of men originating in Classes III, IV and V, and 60 per cent of those respondents whose fathers were themselves allocated to Classes I or II. These proportions may then be expressed in the form of a 'disparity ratio' of the order of 1:2:4 for the chances of access to Class I and II positions for men of the three different origins distinguished.[26]

Both these ways of looking at the matter reveal, thus, marked inequalities in mobility chances to the disadvantage of men of working-class background. But, at the same time, it could still be thought doubtful whether the degree of limitation on longer-range mobility out of the working class that exists is *sufficiently* stringent to justify the idea of a buffer zone, which does after all, in the metaphor in which it is embodied, suggest some absolute rather than merely relative constraint. Certainly, if we consider the relevant data of Table 2.2 in absolute terms, the fact that around 7 per cent of the sons of working-class fathers in our sample appear in Class I and a further 9 per cent in Class II would seem difficult to reconcile with the view that mobility of this range is very rare; and further, as we shall shortly indicate, there are reasons for supposing that this proportion somewhat underestimates the actual chances of social ascent of the kind in question.[27]

Thirdly, we may turn to the evidence relating to mobility across the manual/nonmanual division in the reverse direction, and specifically to examine how far Table 2.2 shows differences among men originating in nonmanual classes in the likelihood of their being discovered in manual employment. Once more, one could say, the distribution of relative chances that is revealed is broadly what the buffer-zone thesis might lead one to expect. On the one hand, judging against the norm of perfect mobility, men originating in Class V are represented in Classes VI and VII at not greatly below their due level, but as one moves from Class V to Class I, the degree of under-representation steadily increases until for Class I itself outflow to Classes VI and VII is down to little more than a quarter of the perfect mobility value. On the other hand, in terms of chances relative to class origins, it proves to be the case that 15 per cent of our respondents whose fathers were in Classes I and II are in manual work, as compared with 34 per cent of the sons of Class III, IV, and V fathers, and 57 per cent of the sons of manual workers themselves. That is to say, for men of these three different levels of origin, the disparity ratio for the chances of their being found as manual employees more or less reflects that—the 1:2:4 ratio—which holds for their chances of access to positions within what we have characterized as the service class. However, once more too the argument applies that while this pattern of inequality of chances—or rather, one should perhaps say, of risk—may appear as consistent with the buffer-zone thesis, this is less evidently so with the absolute amount of long-range mobility, that is, from Classes I and II to Classes VI and VII, which is involved. Having regard to such downward movement, no less than to the corresponding upward flow, the suggestion of a 'buffer' effect would seem to be in excess of what the data of Table 2.2 could warrant.[28]

Finally from this table, we may observe that in the case of men of Class I and II origins—and likewise of those of Class III and IV origins—who were in manual wage-earning occupations in 1972, there is no tendency towards concentration in skilled, rather than nonskilled grades. Since the numbers in our sample in Classes VI and VII are almost the same, it is easy to see, by comparing their respective columns in Table 2.2 that both the extent of outflow to, and of under-representation in, these classes is very similar for each class of origin from Class I down to Class IV. In other words, the distinction between skilled and nonskilled manual work, on which exponents of the buffer-zone thesis have placed a good deal of emphasis, appears in our data to have no very important effect on the pattern of class mobility in *either* direction across the manual–nonmanual division.

On the evidence of Table 2.2, therefore, the idea of a buffer zone, in the form in which it has been advanced, appears to give rise to some specific propositions which are empirically invalid, and to be in general somewhat inapt to the nature and extent of the intergenerational movement that the table displays. However, it must be recognized that an outflow mobility matrix of the kind in question brings with it certain difficulties of interpretation which mean that it cannot be taken as an entirely unproblematical basis on which to evaluate the buffer-zone thesis in all respects alike. In particular, it must be kept in mind that since our sample is one of men aged 20–64, the 'present' occupations reported in 1972 will of course be those of men at widely differing time-periods away from their origins as we have defined them: some will be at the very start of their work careers, while others will be on the verge of retirement. Thus, in treating all respondents on, as it were, an equal footing, regardless of age or position in the life-cycle, as we do in Table 2.2, we run the very real risk of giving a distorted picture of mobility chances if, as one might reasonably suppose, there exist certain recurrent processes of intragenerational, or work-life, mobility, through which our respondents will have passed, or have had opportunity to pass, in varying degrees.

The only approach that can be taken to this problem is to seek to establish salient patterns of work-life movement actually experienced by men in our sample, and then to consider the implications of these same patterns continuing into the future. Using the further information that we have on our respondent's *first* occupations on entry into the work-force in combination with the data of Table 2.2, we have drawn up a series of 'three-point' mobility tables which show for different age-groups the outflow of men originating in each of our classes at the stage of their entry into work, and thence to their class positions in respect of their occupation in 1972. Since each of these tables has $7^3 = 343$ cells, they are difficult both to read and to reproduce. Fortunately, for present purposes the essential patterns which they reveal can be set out in the simplified graphic form of Figure 2.1, in which we have collapsed our class schema into a threefold one, and also confined our analysis to men aged 35 and over. By this age, one could maintain, men will tend to have achieved a stage of relative 'occupational maturity', in the sense that from then onwards one may expect if not a cessation,

Figure 2.1
'Three point' mobility patterns: flows representing 3 per cent or more of all in classes of origin, men aged 35 and over, 1972[a]

(A) *Class I and II origins (N=661)*

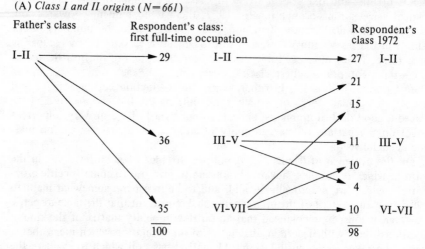

(B) *Class III–V origins (N=1605)*

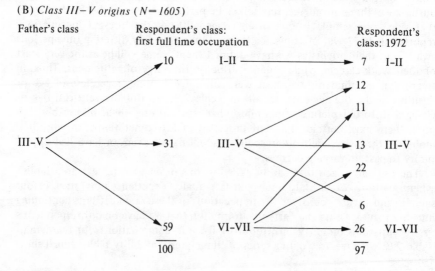

(C) *Class VI and VII origins* (*N* = 2955)

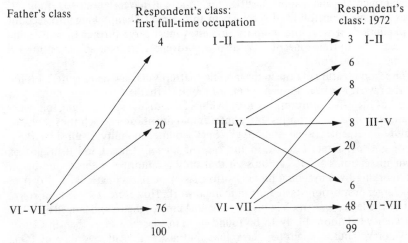

Father's class　　　　　　Respondent's class:　　　　　　　Respondent's
　　　　　　　　　　　　·first full-time occupation　　　　　class: 1972

Notes:

(a) Agricultural categories excluded.

(b) Respondents were asked: 'What was your very first full-time job after you finished your full-time education? (By full-time education, I mean a period of continuous full-time education not interrupted for more than two years except by National Service).' In other words, we sought to record the respondent's 'real' first job, excluding, for example, holiday jobs undertaken while a schoolboy or college student. Apprenticeships could count as first jobs while also, for other purposes, counting as full-time education. But jobs held for less than two years while a man was specifically waiting to take up an apprenticeship were discounted. See also n. 33 p. 66.

at all events a marked falling-off in the probability of job changes which involve major shifts of occupational level.[29] Thus, one may regard the patterns of movement displayed by these older men in our sample as giving some indication of at least the main directions in which it would be reasonable to 'allow for' work-life mobility in attempting to assess intergenerational mobility chances from data relating to the sample as a whole.[30]

With regard to the buffer-zone thesis, there are two features of the information presented in Figure 2.1 which are of particular significance. First, it can be seen from section (C) that men of Class VI and VII origins in our sample have experienced a quite considerable amount of work-life mobility taking them away from these origins. Most notably, while three out of four followed their fathers into manual jobs on entry into work, more than a third of these men were subsequently mobile to one or other of the nonmanual classes. The greater part of this mobility, it is true, was to Classes III, VI and V. But what is also apparent is that the mobility which *has* occurred from working-class origins to Classes I and II has far more often been achieved via work-life advance—that is, after initial employment as a manual worker, or in a lower-level nonmanual job—than by, so to speak, 'direct entry'. The implication is, therefore, that on the basis of Table 2.2, one will tend to form an unduly low estimate of the chances of men of Class VI and VII origins moving out of the working class, and especially of their chances of access to the higher levels of the class structure, since for the younger men in our sample insufficient time will have elapsed for 'indirect' routes to have been followed through. In this respect, then, taking into account the likelihood of work-life mobility processes must serve further to undermine the idea of a buffer zone of any great effectiveness, at least so far as upward movement is concerned.

The second feature of note in the mobility patterns displayed in Figure 2.1 is the extent of what has been termed 'counter-mobility': that is, of work-life movement which has the effect of returning an individual back to his class of origin, following some initial shift away on his entry into employment, and which thus serves to promote intergenerational stability.[31] Such counter-mobility is most marked, and of greatest interest to us, in the case of men of Class I and II origins, as shown in section (A). It can be seen that only a minority of these men began their working lives by going directly into Class I or II occupations, and that in fact a larger proportion started off in manual work. However, at some later stage, most of the latter were mobile into nonmanual employment, and indeed by 1972 were somewhat more likely to be found back in Classes I or II than in Classes III, IV, or V. Thus, it might here be argued that just as the 'all ages' data of Table 2.2, taken at their face value, are likely to suggest unduly low chances of upward mobility from working-class origins, so they are likely to give an exaggerated idea of the risks of men of relatively high-class origins being relegated to the ranks of manual labour, or at least permanently so: for some sizeable number of the individuals which the table represents as being thus downwardly mobile may be seen as 'destined' for counter-mobility at some later stage in their careers.

Accepting this argument, then, one might be tempted to conclude that if there is not a buffer effect operating against upward movement across the manual–nonmanual division, there could well be something like one in the case of downward movement. And hence, one might be inclined to take up some other, more appropriate image by which to capture this effect—such as that suggested by Blau and Duncan, on the basis of their American data, of this division acting as a 'one-way screen', permitting upward, but checking downward, mobility flows.[32] However, from Figure 2.1, it may be pointed out, we now know that as well as concealing to some degree the probable effects of counter-mobility, Table 2.2 also for certain conceals the full extent to which men of Class I and II origins have at some time been downwardly mobile into manual work, even if only temporarily. While the phenomenon of counter-mobility is obviously of relevance to any attempt to study mobility patterns in relation to class structure, so too is the fact that intergenerational stability at the higher levels of the class structure appears to depend so heavily upon mobility of this kind—rather than being achieved primarily by men of advantaged social origins proceeding directly to positions comparable to those of their fathers. Furthermore, while in some instances counter-mobility may be a more or less automatic process—as, say, where the heir to a family business works for a time as an apprentice—one cannot assume that this will generally be the case, and that the downward mobility involved is thus more apparent than real. Where, for example, counter-mobility depends, as it often must, on acquiring a professional qualification or on securing successive promotions within a bureaucratic hierarchy, it is obviously of a far more contingent nature; and even though its objective probability may be high, it could still well be that, in these circumstances, the individuals concerned see a lasting *déclassement* as being in fact only too real a prospect.[33]

Our own conclusion would thus be that attempts to comprehend currently observable mobility flows and their implications for class formation in any way which can be summed up in some simple metaphor are unlikely to be very enlightening. And this conclusion, we may add, will be reinforced when later, in chapter 5, we provide a more detailed investigation of the complex interplay between work-life movements of differing routes and timing and patterns of both mobility and continuity as seen in intergenerational perspective.

THE 'COUNTERBALANCE' THESIS

If it appears surprising that exponents of the buffer-zone thesis have themselves given so little attention to the complicating factor of work-life mobility, their concurrent adherence to the 'counterbalance' thesis could provide a very adequate explanation. As we made clear, our attempts to take processes of work-life mobility into account in assessing intergenerational mobility patterns in present-day society must rest on the assumption that such processes evident in the experience of our respondents are continuing, and will continue for some time ahead, more or less unchanged. However, central to the counterbalance thesis is the claim that there are powerful forces already operating against such continuity; and, in particular, that the occurrence of work-life advance on which we placed major emphasis, whether in the form of 'indirect' ascent on the part of men of low-level origins or of counter-mobility on the part of those of high-level origins, is becoming steadily less probable. This is the result, it is held, of growing 'professionalization, bureaucratization and technical complexity in work', which means that access to the middle and higher levels of the occupational hierarchy is made increasingly dependent upon formal educational qualifications, while the importance of experience and of 'training on the job' declines.[34]

It is on the basis of this argument, then, that the counterbalance thesis becomes differentiated from that, more widely advanced, of a 'tightening bond' between educational and occupational attainment. For while adherents of the latter view have tended to see this development as likely to promote greater mobility, on account of educational expansion and reforms aimed at reducing inequality of opportunity,[35] the counterbalance thesis maintains that any increase in upward mobility achieved in recent decades via educational channels will have been offset by the decrease in chances of advancement in the course of working life. The self-sustaining properties of the class structure— as one of differential power and advantage—will be little altered by reforms which do not touch basic inequalities of *condition*; and since these inequalities have remained little altered in recent decades, change in the dominant modes of 'social selection' will simply affect the channels of mobility without increasing its extent, and without the lines of class division being made any less definite. To the extent, thus, that the counterbalance thesis is valid, one may see class-mobility patterns as becoming in effect increasingly simplified: the complexities introduced by work-life movements of the kind that have previously concerned us would be of clearly diminishing significance.

To test the counterbalance thesis means entering into the difficult area of the assessment of mobility trends. We shall use the data of our inquiry to treat this topic in the detail which it merits in the following chapter. But, for present purposes, resort to a relatively crude procedure will suffice. In Figure 2.2 we present 'three-point' mobility data in the same form as in Figure 2.1, but distinguishing two broad birth cohorts: those of men born 1908–27 and 1928–47. Results for men in the latter cohort of age 35 and over—i.e. born 1928–37—are shown in brackets.

If the counterbalance thesis is correct, what one would most obviously expect to find in Figure 2.2 is evidence of more 'direct entry' into Classes I and II, on the part of men of all class origins, in the younger cohort than in the older one; and a compensating decline in the extent of access to these classes following entry into work via a lower nonmanual or working-class occupation. Looking first at the data for the two cohorts in section (A), a strong upward trend can indeed be seen in the proportion of men of Class I and II origins who were found in Class I and II positions after having moved directly into such positions on completion of their full-time education: that is, from 23 per cent for men born 1908–27 to 38 per cent for men born 1928–47. And at the same time, some decline is indicated in the proportion over all who have been counter-mobile from lower-level entry occupations back to Classes I and II. However, less favourably for the thesis, it must also be noted that this apparent decline disappears in the case of men born 1928–37—that is, who are aged 35 and over and may be assumed to have reached relative occupational maturity;[36] and further, that there is no change in the *probability* of being counter-mobile for those men who *do* initially move to a lower-level occupation. For both cohorts alike, this probability may be calculated at just under 50 per cent.

Secondly, turning to sections (B) and (C) of Figure 2.2, relating to men of Class III, IV, and V and Class VI and VII origins respectively, we may again see clear evidence of an increase in access to Classes I and II directly on entry into work; or, in other words, evidence of increased upward mobility achieved, presumably, via educational channels. But again, too, no 'counter-balancing' effect is shown up—there is no indication of any falling off in access to Classes I and II via work-life advance. From the older to the younger cohort, the relevant flows remain of more or less unchanged volume; and thus, if anything, the chances of men of lower nonmanual or of working-class origins being found in Class I and II positions, after having started work at some lower level, tend to improve. It may, moreover, be added here that the data presented also go contrary to a modified version of the counter-balance thesis advanced some time ago by one of the present authors. This restricted the argument of declining chances of work-life mobility to men who entered work via manual wage-earning occupations. For such men, it was suggested, manual work was 'becoming more than ever before a life-sentence'.[37] As it stands, this proposition is contradicted by the data of Figure 2.2 taken over all—the chances of a man being found in manual work after having started in such work are effectively

Figure 2.2
*'Three-point' mobility patterns by birth cohort: flows representing 3 per cent or more of
all in classes of origin*

(A) Class I and II origins

Respondents born 1908–27 (N=426)

Respondents born 1928–47 (N=588)
(results for respondents born 1928–37
(N=234) in brackets)

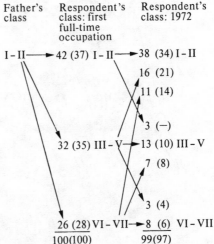

Father's class | Respondent's class: first full-time occupation | Respondent's class: 1972

```
I - II ──► 25     I - II ──► 23   I - II
                           20
                           16

        36       III - V ──► 12   III - V
                           11

                            4
        39       VI - VII ──► 12  VI - VII
       ───                  ──
       100                  98
```

Father's class | Respondent's class: first full-time occupation | Respondent's class: 1972

```
I - II ──► 42 (37)   I - II ──► 38 (34) I - II
                               16 (21)
                               11 (14)

                                3 (−)
        32 (35)   III - V ──► 13 (10) III - V
                                7 (8)

                                3 (4)
        26 (28)   VI - VII ──► 8 (6)  VI - VII
       ───────               ─────
       100(100)              99(97)
```

(B) Class III–V origins

Respondents born 1908–27 (N=1048)

Respondents born 1928–47 (N=1173)
(results for respondents born 1928–37
(N=557) in brackets)

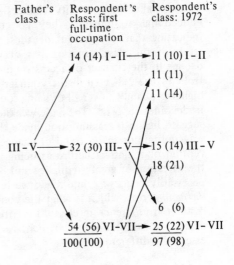

Father's class | Respondent's class: first full-time occupation | Respondent's class: 1972

```
             8    I - II ──► 6    I - II
                          13
                          10

III - V ──► 31    III - V ──► 13  III - V
                          22

                           5
             61   VI - VII ──► 29 VI - VII
            ───               ──
            100               98
```

Father's class | Respondent's class: first full-time occupation | Respondent's class: 1972

```
           14 (14)  I - II ──► 11 (10) I - II
                            11 (11)
                            11 (14)

III - V ──► 32 (30)  III - V ──► 15 (14) III - V
                            18 (21)

                             6 (6)
           54 (56)  VI - VII ──► 25 (22) VI - VII
          ───────               ─────
          100(100)              97 (98)
```

(C) *Class VI and VII origins*

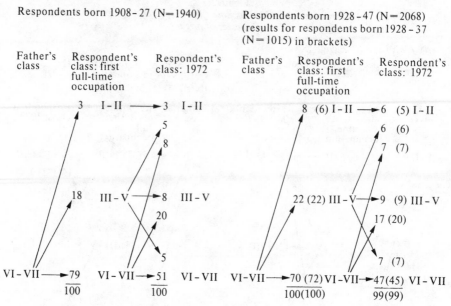

Respondents born 1908–27 (N=1940)

Respondents born 1928–47 (N=2068)
(results for respondents born 1928–37
(N=1015) in brackets)

the same for the two cohorts; and even if the proposition is taken to refer (as was the intention) to men of *manual origins* who begin work in manual jobs, the data of section (C) still do not uphold it.

In sum, then, while our findings could perhaps be taken as lending support to the claim that mobility chances are becoming increasingly influenced by educational attainments, they go contrary to the counterbalance thesis in indicating that, over recent decades, an increase in direct entry to the higher levels of the class structure has occurred without there being any apparent decline in the chances of access via indirect routes. In other words—as is evident from Figure 2.2—men in the younger of the two cohorts we distinguish have a higher probability over all of being found in Class I and II positions than do men in the older cohort.[38] The basic weakness in the counterbalance thesis, we would suggest, lies in the assumption made that the class structure itself must in some way militate against a trend of change of this kind. One may share in the conception of a class structure as being in its nature highly resistant to change in the direction of greater equality and openness without, however, taking this as necessarily being of prime relevance to shifts in mobility patterns considered in *de facto* terms—which is what the counterbalance thesis, as stated, is about—as distinct from trends in class differentials in mobility chances or in the over all degree of 'social fluidity', which, as we shall show in the next chapter, are essentially different matters.[39]

THE UNDERESTIMATION OF MOBILITY

With each of the three theses examined, we have thus found difficulty in reconciling its claims with the findings of our 1972 inquiry. Furthermore, in each case alike, this difficulty has stemmed basically from the fact that our data point to more mobility, and chiefly to more upward mobility, than the thesis considered would imply. In conclusion, therefore, it would seem important to inquire into the sources of this fairly systematic discrepancy.

First, in this connection, the possibility must be raised that in drawing on the results of previous mobility research, as part of the empirical grounding of their analyses of class structure, the writers with whom we are concerned have misconstrued the significance of these results through failing to distinguish clearly enough between mobility considered in its absolute and relative aspects. They have tended, one may suggest, to take the evidence of wide and persisting inequalities of opportunity, which has been very generally produced, as if it were at the same time evidence of relatively severe and unchanging constraints on the actual extent of mobility. To make this equation may well be seriously misleading; for, as our own data illustrate, it is perfectly possible for a high degree of inequality of opportunity, which must refer to relative mobility chances, to be observed *together with* levels and trends of absolute mobility rates which mean that the closure, buffer-zone, and counterbalance theses cannot readily be borne out. Moreover, we would wish to argue that a situation of this general kind is in fact that which has been most typically revealed by, at all events, the more recent mobility inquiries undertaken in other advanced western societies.[40] In short, the lack of fit between the arguments addressed and the data we have presented comes about, we believe, more because the former go some way beyond their purported empirical basis than because our own findings are highly deviant from those reported in other comparable studies.

Secondly, though, it would also appear that some of the more marked divergencies between the theses we have considered and the data of our inquiry do reflect the fact that their authors have not sufficiently taken into account certain features of the pattern of change in British society over recent decades, and especially of the evolution of the occupational structure, which are perhaps in some degree distinctive. It has been generally recognized that in Britain, as in other advanced industrial societies, a tendency exists for nonmanual occupations to expand while manual ones contract, and that some amount of mobility, whether achieved intra- or intergenerationally, will follow from this shift. However, what would seem not to have been fully appreciated are some of the more specific aspects of the growth of nonmanual employment as it has occurred in the British case, and their further implications for mobility patterns. In Table 2.3, we present data on the changing occupational distribution of the British work-force derived from Census statistics. Two points are evident from these data that we would wish to stress. On the one hand, it can be seen that over the period covered, a *steady* decline in the proportion engaged in manual work occurs in the case of women, but not of men: the occupational distribution of the active male population remains in fact rather remarkably stable until at least some time towards the end of the inter-war period, and the shift to nonmanual occupations then comes about relatively sharply within the three decades or so previous to our inquiry. On the other hand, it is apparent that it is, in the main, the redeployment of the female work force which has, so to speak, provided for the expansion of lower-level nonmanual occupations, while the distributional shift among men, which we take to be of greatest significance for class structure,[41] has been chiefly from manual occupations to those of a higher professional, administrative, and managerial character.

If we now revert to Tables 2.1 and 2.2, we may see these two aspects of change in the occupational division of labour fairly clearly reflected, even though the categories of Table 2.3 can be aligned with our class schema in only a very approximate fashion.[42] Most obviously, the marginal distributions of our mobility tables are rendered highly discrepant: a quarter of the men in our sample are allocated to Classes I and II, but not much more than half as many reported fathers in these classes; while conversely, a clear majority of fathers—54 per cent—are in Classes VI and VII, but only a minority—45 per cent—of our respondents. Furthermore, though, via the degree of asymmetry which is in this way introduced into our basic data, the pattern of evolution of the occupational structure also importantly conditions our findings on mobility which we have set against the three theses examined.[43]

Thus, in Table 2.1 it is apparent that Class I, and likewise Class II, are, as it were, 'forced' to take in some sizeable proportion of men from other classes of origin; and behind this arithmetical requirement, one may recognize the reality of the recent growth of the service class in British society, at a rate which could not be met other than by some considerable recruitment from below. In such a context, it is evident that even though parents in advantaged class positions may exploit their advantages in order to give their offspring a high probability of themselves securing such positions, this will still not make for a marked degree of closure. During a period in which demand for professional, administrative, and managerial personnel rises quite sharply, a large measure of intergenerational stability at the higher levels of the class structure can, of course, coexist with much upward mobility into these levels; and further, any control over access so as to favour men of not greatly dissimilar social origins will be difficult to maintain at all strictly. In other words, strategies of exclusion become at the same time less necessary and less viable.

Viewing the matter then in outflow terms, it may be observed that while increasing 'room at the top' does not in itself entail any greater amount of long-range upward movement, it does none the less tell against the likelihood of their being any very decisive barriers to it, of the kind that the buffer-zone thesis would imply. In the context in question, the possibility clearly exists of such mobility growing in actual volume to some extent, at the same time as relative class chances of access to high-level positions remain unchanged. In fact, from the data of Figure 2.2, it could be claimed that something on these lines is what in fact has happened. While, as was noted, men in the younger of the two cohorts have a higher probability over all of being found in Classes I and II than do men in the older cohort, no appreciable shift occurs from one cohort to the other if disparity ratios for chances of access to these classes are calculated in the way they were previously for the sample as a whole.[44]

Finally, it is, as we have already implied, the expansion of numbers in Classes I and II which effectively undermines the counterbalance thesis: it is made possible for an increase to occur in upward mobility achieved at the point of entry into the work force, that is, presumably on the basis of educational attainments, without any compensating decline being necessary in the importance of the indirect route to higher-level class positions. And, we may add, in view of the relatively sudden onset of this expansion, and of the fact that it preceded the major expansion of British higher education in the 1960s, our finding that the importance of indirect routes has actually remained more or less unaltered—and in promoting intergenerational stability as well as mobility— is one that can scarcely be regarded as surprising.[45]

If, then, it is the case that there is more mobility, or at least more upward mobility, in advanced societies in general, and perhaps in modern British society in particular, than has been recognized by the writers who concern us, what implications does this have for their attempts to give the findings of mobility research a central place in their analyses of class structure? It might possibly be thought that the nature of our critique of the closure, buffer-zone, and counterbalance theses is such as to raise serious doubts about the value of class analysis, in suggesting that, because of the degree of mobility that prevails, class formation is likely to remain at a low level and that shared class position must be of declining importance as a basis of socio-political action. But this is not in fact the conclusion which we ourselves would wish to draw. Rather, we would take the results of our inquiry as indicating that one should now aim to move beyond the idea that the relationship between mobility and class formation and action can be understood as being invariably a simple inverse one, in the way that seems generally to have been assumed; and that, instead, one should view this relationship as potentially complex and in need of both more careful conceptual treatment and more thorough empirical investigation than it has so far received.

In particular, in the light of the analyses of the present chapter we would stress the importance of recognizing that in a historical period in which major developments in the form of the occupational division of labour, and hence in the structure of class positions, are taking place, new parameters will be set for the entire process of 'social metabolism'. Where such structural shifts occur, it is possible for the pattern of mobility to change substantially—although without there necessarily being any change in the total amount of mobility or in the degree of openness—and in ways that would appear both favourable and unfavourable for the 'formation of identifiable classes'. Where, for example, as in the case of present-day British society, mobility flows take on a markedly asymmetrical pattern, with upward movement into an expanding service class being much in excess of downward movement from this class, such countervailing influences may readily be appreciated. It is evident that increasing chances of fairly decisive mobility out of the working class, which reduce somewhat the stability and, it might be thought, the solidarity of this class, go along with decreasing long-range mobility into the working class, which must make for a

Table 2.3

Distribution of economically active population by occupational category, Great Britain 1911-71, males (M) and females (F) shown separately

Standardized census occupational category	1911		1921		1931		1951		1961		1971	
	M	F	M	F	M	F	M	F	M	F	M	F
					percentage by column							
Self-employed and higher-grade salaried professionals	1·5[a]	1·0[a]	1·6	0·9	1·7	1·0	2·8	1·0	4·5[b]	1·1[b]	6·1	1·4
Employers and proprietors	7·7	4·3	7·7	4·7	7·6	4·4	5·7	3·2	4·8[c]	3·0[c]	5·2	2·9
Administrators and managers	3·9	2·3	4·3	2·1	4·5	1·6	6·8	2·7	7·5[c]	2·6[c]	9·9	3·3
Lower-grade salaried professionals and technicians	1·4[a]	5·8[a]	1·8	6·3	1·8	6·0	3·0	7·9	4·0[b]	9·2[b]	5·5	10·8
Inspectors, supervisors, and foremen	1·8	0·2	1·9	0·3	2·0	0·4	3·3	1·1	3·8	0·9	4·5	1·2
Clerical workers	5·1	3·3	5·1	9·8	5·1	10·3	6·0	20·3	6·5	25·5	6·1	28·0
Sales personnel and shop assistants[e]	5·0	6·4	4·1	7·5	5·9	8·2	4·0	9·6	3·9	10·0	3·9	9·4
Skilled manual workers (including self-employed artisans)	33·0	24·6	32·3	20·3	30·1	19·2	30·3	12·7	32·3	10·8	29·4	9·3
Semi-skilled manual workers[f]	29·1	47·0	24·5	40·0	23·4	41·4	24·3	33·6	22·8	30·9	21·2	27·3
Unskilled manual workers[f]	11·5	5·1	16·7	8·1	17·9	7·5	13·8	7·9	9·9	6·0	8·2	6·4
Total active population (in thousands)	12,926	5,424	13,635	5,698	14,760	6,263	15,584	6,930	15,992	7,649	15,609	8,762

Notes: (a) Divided according to 1921 ratios. (The 1911 Census did not distinguish between self-employed and salaried professionals.)

(b) Divided on the assumption of a linear trend in the ratios from 1951 to 1966 (sample Census).

i.e. $\dfrac{x61}{\text{Total }61} = \dfrac{x51}{\text{Total }51} + 2/3\left[\dfrac{x66}{\text{Total }66} - \dfrac{x51}{\text{Total }51}\right]$

(The 1961 Cenus did not distinguish between self-employed and salaried professionals.)

(c) Numbers divided according to a ratio arrived at by plotting trend lines for these groups from 1951 to 1961. i.e. $P_{61} = P_{51} + 2/3 (P_{61} - P_{51})$. (The 1961 Census did not distinguish between employers and managers.)

(d) Of manual workers.

(e) Includes supervisory personnel and also a small number of self-employed workers.

(f) Includes self-employed workers.

Sources: The basic source is the Occupational Tables of the Censuses of Population for England and Wales and Scotland. We have however, drawn to a large extent on the reworking of Census data by earlier investigators although modifying their procedures somewhat, and correcting what appear to be several minor errors. In various respects, therefore, our figures differ from those of our predecessors where they might appear comparable, but not to any very significant degree.

For 1911 to 1951 we began with the work of Guy Routh, *Occupation and Pay in Great Britain, 1906–60*, Cambridge University Press, 1965, Table 1, pp. 4–5, taken together with the further information provided in Appendix A, pp. 155–7.

For 1961 we have drawn on the work of G.S. Bain, *The Growth of White-Collar Unionism*, Oxford: Clarendon Press, 1970, Table 2A 1, p. 191; and of Bain, Robert Bacon, and John Pimlott, 'The Labour Force', in A.H. Halsey (ed.), *Trends in British Society since 1900*, London: Macmillan, 1971, Tables 4.1 and 4.3, pp. 113–114.

steadily greater homogeneity of origins among its members and thus, one could argue, for a greater potential for solidarity. And conversely, while the basis of recruitment to the higher levels of the class structure has in all probability widened, and we find at the present time considerable heterogeneity of origins among men at these levels, there is also apparent here an increasingly high degree of intergenerational stability, conducive to the growth of an 'established' upper stratum.

Moreover, it is then also important to recognize that in a situation in which such countervailing influences are at work, the potential role of a variety of other factors relevant to class formation is likely to be enhanced. For example, it would seem of obvious importance to investigate the way in which transitions from particular origins to particular destinations are actually accomplished—in terms, that is, of the routes, timing, degree of decisiveness, and permanency of the mobility involved. Again, it would appear no less important to know how far differences in these respects are associated with differences in the concomitants of mobility at the level of both interpersonal and wider social relations; and further still, how far differences in the experience of mobility as we, the investigators, would characterize it are actually reflected in the subjective experience of our respondents.

These are all topics that we shall indeed return to specifically in later chapters after we have pursued further, in chapters 3 and 4, the questions of mobility trends and of the pattern of relative mobility chances.

NOTES

1. It must be made clear that not all of the authors who will concern us have explicitly committed themselves to each of the theses in question; and that where they have, their statements of them sometimes differ in their precise conceptualization, their degree of qualification, etc. We do not therefore pretend here to do full justice to the views of each writer considered individually. What we shall concentrate on, rather, is (i) the undoubted 'family resemblance' among their views; (ii) specific claims made, within this general consensus, by particular authors.
2. See John H. Goldthorpe and Keith Hope, *The Social Grading of Occupations: a New Approach and Scale*, Oxford: Clarendon Press, 1974, pp. 131–2 and Table 6.6, pp. 134–43.
3. David Lockwood, *The Blackcoated Worker*, London: Allen & Unwin, 1958.
4. From these categories of the 36-fold version of the H–G scale, the reader may, if he so wishes, determine precisely the occupational titles, in association with a specific employment status, that are covered by each class: that is, by reference first to Tables 6.1 and 6.6 in the monograph on the scale, cited in n. 2 above; and thence to the Office of Population Census and Surveys, *Classification of Occupations 1970*, London: HMSO, 1971.
5. Here and subsequently, statements regarding income levels are based on incomes data derived from our 1972 inquiry and on the Department of Employment's *New Earnings Survey 1970*, London: HMSO, 1971; likewise statements on continuity and security of employment are based on Amelia I. Harris and Rosemary Clausen, *Labour Mobility in Great Britain, 1953–63*, London: HMSO, 1967, and W.W. Daniel, *A National Survey of the Unemployed*, London: Political and Economic Planning, 1974.
6. Cf. Ralf Dahrendorf, 'Recent Changes in the Class Structure of European Societies', *Dædalus*, Winter 1964, and Karl Renner, *Wandlungen der Modernen Gesellschaft: zwei*

Abhandlungen über die Probleme der Nachkriegszeit, Vienna: Wiener Volksbuchhandlung, 1953.

7. On the generally more favourable conditions of service, apart from pay, of routine
clerical workers as compared with manual workers, see Dorothy Wedderburn and
Christine Craig, 'Relative Deprivation in Work' in Wedderburn (ed.), *Poverty, Inequality
and Class Structure,* Cambridge University Press, 1974, and also Craig, *Men in Manufacturing Industry,* Cambridge University Department of Applied Economics (cyclostyled), 1969.

8. One must, however, guard here against facile notions of the 'proletarianization' of
lower-level nonmanual employment, and in particular against that of the emerging
'office-factory'. For useful correctives see D.E. Mercer and D.T.H. Weir, 'Attitudes
to Work and Trade Unionism among White-Collar Workers', *Industrial Relations,* vol. 3,
1972, and A. Stewart, K. Prandy and R.M. Blackburn, *Social Stratification and Occupations,* London: Macmillan, 1980, and further the discussion in ch. 9 below.

9. For useful analyses of the market and work situations of members of the numerically
most important grouping within Class IV, small retailers, see Frank Bechhofer, Brian
Elliott, and Monica Rushworth, 'The Market Situation of Small Shopkeepers', *Scottish
Journal of Political Economy,* vol. xviii, 1971, and (with Richard Bland), 'The Petits
Bourgeois in the Class Structure' in Parkin (ed.), *The Social Analysis of Class Structure*;
and also Bechhofer and Elliott, 'Persistence and Change: the Petite Bourgeoisie in
Industrial Society', *Archives européennes de sociologie*, vol. xvii, 1976.

10. The marginality in question has in fact been the subject of a good deal of research.
On technicians, see, e.g., B.C. Roberts, Ray Loveridge, and John Gennard, *The Reluc-
tant Militants,* London: Heinemann, 1972; and on foremen the useful reviews con-
tained in Keith Thurley and Hans Wirdenius, *Supervision: a Reappraisal,* London:
Heinemann, 1973 and John Child, 'The Industrial Supervisor' in Geoff Esland, Graeme
Salaman, and Mary-Anne Speakman (eds.), *People and Work,* Edinburgh: Holmes
McDougall, 1976.

11. Goldthorpe and Hope, *The Social Grading of Occupations,* pp. 10–16, 132–3.

12. *The Class Structure of the Advanced Societies,* p. 106. Cf. also Ralf Dahrendorf *Class
and Class Conflict in Industrial Society,* London: Routledge, 1959, pp. 74–7.

13. Cf., e.g., Sorokin, *Social Mobility,* ch. XVII; Glass and Hall, 'Social Mobility in Great
Britain'; Svalastoga, *Prestige, Class and Mobility,* section 5; Blau and Duncan, *The
American Occupational Structure,* ch. 2.

14. See, in particular, T.B. Bottomore, 'The Class Structure in Western Europe', and also
Elites and Society, London: Watts, 1964, ch. IV and *Classes in Modern Society,* London:
Allen & Unwin, 1965, pp. 38–41; for another Marxist view, Ralph Miliband, *The State
in Capitalist Society,* London: Weidenfeld & Nicholson, 1969, pp. 36–45, 59–67; and
Giddens, *The Class Structure of the Advanced Societies,* pp. 164–70.

15. This age was chosen as that at, or around, which most of our respondents would be
making decisions important for their own occupational futures (whether concerning
their actual entry into work or their continuation in full-time education) while still
within the sphere of influence of their families of origin. Those cases where the data
do not refer to the respondent's father amount to just under 8 per cent of the total,
and in about three-fifths of these cases the head of household was female.

16. Perfect mobility, it will be recalled (see p. 23 above) implies that the class positions
of sons and their fathers are statistically independent. The 'index of association' which
measures the degree of departure from perfect mobility (specified formally below,
n. 4, p. 117), may be conveniently calculated, though perhaps with rounding errors, for
any cell of an inflow table by dividing the cell percentage by its row marginal percentage
—or for any cell of an outflow table by dividing the cell percentage by its column marginal percentage.

17. Of *respondents* to our inquiry who were in Class V occupations in 1972, 63 per cent
had begun work as manual employees.

18. e.g. Giddens (*The Class Structure of the Advanced Societies,* pp. 169–70) in a discussion
of élite recruitment appears to be adopting a relatively restricted conception of élites,
but then seeks to substantiate one of his points by referring to Blau and Duncan's data

for the U.S. in which the 'élite' is represented by their two groupings (independent and employed) of 'Professional, technical and kindred workers', which, as well as being far more heterogeneous internally than is satisfactory, account for 11.6 per cent of Blau and Duncan's sample. Cf. also the uncertainties evident in Bottomore, *Classes in Modern Society*, pp. 38-9, 57. Among the writers who concern us, Parkin is most consistent in his treatment of élite groupings and utilizes a specifically occupational basis. See *Class Inequality and Political Order*, pp. 18-19, 51, 57.

19. See, e.g., Philip Stanworth and Anthony Giddens (eds.) *Elites and Power in British Society*, Cambridge University Press, 1974; and Ivor Crewe (ed.), *Elites in Western Democracy: British Political Sociology Year Book 1*, London: Croom Helm, 1974.

20. See Royal Commission on the Distribution of Income and Wealth, Report No. 3, *Higher Incomes from Employment*, Cmnd. 6838, London: HMSO, 1976, Appendix J.

21. Bottomore, *Classes in Modern Society*, p. 38 (see also *Elites and Society*, p. 75, in which it is explicitly argued that the recruitment patterns of middle and lower-level managers are 'scarcely different' from those of top managers—members of both groupings being predominantly drawn from propertied and professional families); Parkin, *Class Inequality and Political Order*, p. 51; Miliband, *The State in Capitalist Society*, p. 39; and cf. Giddens, *The Class Structure of the Advanced Societies*, p. 169.

22. 'Recent Changes in the Class Structure of European Societies'. pp. 250, 254. It may be added here that while no strict comparisons are possible because of differences in classification, our findings on the social origins of members of Class I, when broken down by its constituent occupational groupings, appear generally consistent with those of a number of recent recruitment studies of a more specialized kind: e.g. D. Clark, *The Industrial Manager*, London; Business Publications, 1966, Tables 4.1, p. 58, and 4.7, p. 65; J.E. Gerstl and S.P. Hutton, *Engineers: the Anatomy of a Profession*, London: Tavistock, 1966, Table I, p. 25; and A.H. Halsey and Ivor Crewe, *Social Survey of the Civil Service*, being vol. 3 (1) of evidence submitted to the Fulton Committee on the Civil Service, London: HMSO, 1969, Tables 3.18, p. 52, and 4.15, p. 125. More generally, cf. the finding reported by M. Young and P. Willmott that among men aged 40 and over in a sample from the London region in 1970, 48 per cent of the managerial and professional group distinguished were the sons of manual workers. *The Symmetrical Family*, London: Routledge, 1973, p. 242.

23. Among the writers considered, only Westergaard and Resler appear to recognize this point at all. See *Class in a Capitalist Society*, p. 310.

24. See, in particular, Parkin, *Class, Inequality and Political Order*, pp. 25, 49-60; Giddens, *The Class Structure of the Advanced Societies*, pp. 108, 181-2, 231; Bottomore, *Classes in Modern Society*, p. 38; Westergaard and Resler, *Class in a Capitalist Society*, pp. 297-302.

25. Giddens, *The Class Structure of the Advanced Societies*, p. 199, cf. also. p. 111.

26. i.e. setting the chances of men of Class VI and VII origins at 1 and expressing those of the other two groupings in relation to them. As will be seen in the following chapters, disparity ratios, together with 'odds ratios' which are closely related to them, are our preferred means of representing relative mobility chances. Disparity ratios have previously been used for this purpose by Miller and by Westergaard and Resler under the name of 'indices of inequality of opportunity' (or of 'risk'). See S.M. Miller, 'Comparative Social Mobility', *Current Sociology*, vol. ix, 1961, and Westergaard and Resler, *Class in a Capitalist Society*, part 4, ch. 3.

27. It is of course in regard to particular absolute rates of this kind that the question of the degree of reliability of our data becomes most crucial. And it is relevant to note here that in so far as unreliability takes the form of random error—in data collection, coding, etc.—it will tend to lead to an underestimation of the 'true' association existing between two variables: e.g. between son's class and father's class. It is therefore quite probable that the outflow percentages cited in the text are in this way somewhat inflated. At the same time, it is also relevant to note that our Classes VI and VII are generally more restricted in their coverage than the 'manual worker' categories of other studies, excluding as they do lower-grade technicians (in Class V), self-employed manual workers (in Class IV), and some grades of service worker of an arguably manual character (in

Class III). If these groupings were to be included, an appreciably *higher* rate of long-range upward mobility from manual origins would undoubtedly be shown.

28. It might be added that a conceptual as well as an empirical objection can here be raised against the buffer-zone thesis in regard to the assumption it embodies that a crossing of the manual–nonmanual division is always involved in mobility of a long-range kind. In terms at least of the H–G scale, mobility between Classes I and III would appear no less long range than that between, say, Classes I and VI. What conception and measure of 'social distance' exponents of the thesis themselves have in mind is not always clear; and one may suggest that they tend to conflate unduly the idea of mobility between different levels of an occupational hierarchy, reflecting in some way the distribution of valued occupational attributes, and that of mobility between different class positions, defined in terms of market and work relations. It is in regard to the former that one may most straightforwardly speak of long- and short-range movement; but in regard to the latter that the manual–nonmanual division is of main relevance.

29. Cf. Harris and Clausen, *Labour Mobility in Great Britain, 1953–63*, Table 57, p. 57.

30. The exercise is, of course, essentially one in informed speculation: we cannot *know* that these same patterns will be reproduced in the experience of younger men. We would certainly agree with the comment of Westergaard and Resler that '. . . while much debate implicitly turns on the issue of emergent trends of mobility, the information obtainable necessarily relates to past experience—in that sense, hard facts about social circulation always tend to lag behind current controversy.' *Class in a Capitalist Society*, p. 286.

31. See Roger Girod, *Mobilité sociale: faits établis et problèmes ouverts*, Geneva: Droz, 1971, ch. 2 esp.; also Daniel Bertaux, 'Mobilité sociale biographique: une critique de l'approche transversale', *Revue française de sociologie*, vol. XV, 1974, and Paul Bernard and Jean Renaud, 'Contre-mobilité et effets différés', *Sociologie et sociétés*, vol. 8, 1976.

32. *The American Occupational Structure*, p.59.

33. The question of the degree of 'assurance' of counter-mobility appears to have been generally neglected in the literature cited in n. 31 above, and the fact that counter-mobility has occurred seems to be taken as in itself sufficient indication that the initial downward movement was simply part of an established career pattern, without wider social significance. It should be noted that in our classificatory system all 'trainees', 'articled pupils', etc. are coded as belonging to the occupations which they are training for. Thus, counter-mobility, as we have recorded it, does, at least, involve a definite occupational shift.

34. See John Westergaard and Alan Little, 'Educational Opportunity and Social Selection in England and Wales: Trends and Policy Implications' in OECD, *Social Objectives in Educational Planning*, Paris: OECD, 1967; also Westergaard, 'The Myth of Classlessness' in Robin Blackburn (ed.), *Ideology in Social Science*, London: Fontana, 1972, pp. 130–3; and Westergaard and Resler, *Class in a Capitalist Society*, pp. 324–33. Cf. the importance given to education in determining occupational placement in Parkin, *Class Inequality and Political Order*, pp. 62–7.

35. See, e.g., the arguments reviewed in Dahrendorf, *Class and Class Conflict in Industrial Society*, pp. 100–9.

36. As regards men born 1938–47, we cannot of course tell whether by the time they in turn have reached 'occupational maturity' a similar proportion as in earlier cohorts will have attained Class I or II positions, or whether life-cycle effects which have previously operated are now in fact just on the point of being overridden by new secular tendencies. Cf. n. 30 above.

37. John H. Goldthorpe, 'Social Stratification in Industrial Society' in P. Halmos (ed.), *The Development of Industrial Societies*, Keele: Sociological Review Monographs, No. 8, 1964, p. 108.

38. There is here, of course, a further implication for the buffer-zone thesis: the figure of around 16 per cent of men of working-class origins in the sample as a whole who were found in Class I and II positions conceals a slowly but steadily rising trend. For

the birth cohorts 1908–17, 1918–27, 1928–37, and 1938–47, the corresponding proportions are 14.1, 16.8, 17.5, and 18.5 per cent. See further Table 3.1 below.

In some statements, it might be added, the counterbalance thesis also suggests a decline in *downward* as well as upward work-life movements—offsetting, presumably, an increase in 'permanent' downward mobility on entry into the workforce. But again the data of Figure 2.2 would not support the argument: the proportion of men being downwardly mobile from their origins and failing to achieve counter-mobility falls, while there is in fact no sign of any reduction in work-life downward mobility, as between entry and present job, whether serving as counter-mobility or not.

39. At some points, Westergaard and Resler (*Class in a Capitalist Society*, pp. 318–19, 324–7) appear to regard evidence of little change over time in 'fluidity' or 'exchange' mobility as evidence supporting the counterbalance thesis. But this could only be so if the thesis were to be reformulated in terms of relative mobility chances, which they do not attempt to do, or at least not explicitly. The meaning of their term, the 'velocity of circulation' we find unclear.

40. See, e.g., the review of the relevant literature presented by Girod, *Mobilité sociale*, ch. III, 'Mobilité intergénérationelle: faut-il rejeter la théorie des barrières? ' (which embodies a powerful critique of current French theorizing on the theme of 'reproduction sociale' associated with Pierre Bourdieu and his associates and with certain groups of French Marxists). As Girod aptly comments, mobility and inequality of opportunity are 'deux phénomènes qui n'ont rien d'incompatible logiquement et que la réalité se charge d'ailleurs de faire abondamment coexister' (p. 75). See further on this point, especially for the simple, but illuminating, numerical examples provided, Girod, 'Inégalité des chances: perspectives nouvelles', *Archives européennes de sociologie*, vol. xvi, 1975.

41. Like the authors who concern us, we would argue that, at least for the historical period in question, it is the class position of males which has been the overwhelmingly important direct determinant of the class 'fate' of the large majority of families and households: in other words, the way in which women have been located in the class structure has tended to reflect their general situation of dependency. See further, John H. Goldthorpe, 'Women and Class Analysis: in Defence of the Conventional View', *Sociology*, vol. 17, 1983, and ch. 10 below.

42. On the treatment of manual workers especially, cf. n. 27, above.

43. We recognize that since fathers are represented in our inquiry only via their sons, the fathers' distribution cannot be taken as corresponding to any previously existing state of the occupational structure (cf. Ramkrishna Mukherjee, 'A Further Note on the Analysis of Data on Social Mobility' in Glass (ed.), *Social Mobility in Britain,* and Duncan, 'Methodological Issues in the Analysis of Social Mobility'); and further that this distribution will be influenced by other factors than the trend of change in the occupational structure: for example, by differential fertility, which will to some extent have contributed to the relatively high proportion of working-class fathers. None the less, it is, we believe, clear enough that the evolution of the occupational division of labour is the *major* determinant of the dissimilarities that are evident between the marginal distributions of our mobility tables.

44. However for further discussion of the question of changing relative mobility chances, on the basis of odds ratios as well as disparity ratios, see chapter 3, pp. 74–85.

45. Cf. the conclusions of earlier critiques of the counterbalance thesis, notably D.J. Lee, 'Class Differentials in Educational Opportunity and Promotion from the Ranks', *Sociology*, vol. 2, 1968; and Trevor Noble, 'Intragenerational Mobility in Britain: a Criticism of the Counter-balance Theory', *Sociology*, vol. 8, 1974.

Trends in Class Mobility

(*with* CLIVE PAYNE *and* CATRIONA LLEWELLYN)

In this chapter our aim is to treat in some detail the question of trends in class mobility in modern Britain which we have already broached in seeking to assess the counterbalance thesis. We have shown that this thesis in fact fails when tested against the data of our 1972 inquiry—and chiefly, we have suggested, on account of the relatively rapid expansion of the service class over recent decades: this expansion has made possible an increase in the extent of upward mobility achieved directly, on completion of full-time education, without any offsetting decline in the extent of such mobility achieved via indirect routes. To begin with, then, we shall attempt to provide a fuller picture of the pattern of change in absolute mobility rates that can be discerned in our data, so that the discussion of the previous chapter may be both confirmed and placed in a larger context. Subsequently, though, we shall concentrate our attention on trends in relative mobility rates—and hence on the issue of whether, over the last half-century or so, the openness of British society has increased or diminished.

In seeking to derive evidence of trends in mobility from the data of a single inquiry, we shall, as in chapter 2, follow the usual method of birth-cohort analysis: that is, we shall divide up the respondents to our inquiry according to their date of birth—using in this case ten-year intervals—and then compare the mobility experience of the successive cohorts thus formed. As a preliminary to an extended discussion of mobility trends, we may, however, note here certain imperfections and disadvantages of this method.

First, we should recognize that we are not, of course, dealing with true birth cohorts but rather with the present-day survivors of such cohorts after the erosions of mortality and migration. Distortions may thus be introduced into the data and, in our case at least, it is not possible to determine whether or not this is so. We can only hope that what we would think *prima facie* likely is in fact the case: namely, that any such distortions will not be of a magnitude capable of affecting significantly the major results that we report.[1]

A second disadvantage of the method is that problems inevitably arise from the confounding of 'period', 'age' (or 'life-cycle'), and specifically 'cohort' effects: in other words, problems of knowing how far features of the observed mobility of men in a particular cohort are attributable to their having been born at around the same point in historical time; or to their having lived for a similar number of years; or to their cohort membership *per se*, which places them in a certain relationship with the members of other cohorts which at any one time exist within the total work-force or population. We shall try to meet these problems to some extent by considering the mobility experience of our respondents over more or less determinate sections of the life-cycle, so that we can hold constant life-cycle stage for men of differing birth dates, and thus examine how far mobility over the stage in question varies from one historical period to another. But we must accept that difficulties in the interpretation of our results may still remain. For example, if for mobility during a given life-cycle stage a trend over historical time is apparent, it will not be possible for us to determine conclusively from our data themselves how far this trend is specifically a period effect, reflecting some process of secular change—as, say, in the occupational or class structure; or how far, on the other hand, it results from changing relationships over time among the totality of cohorts in existence. In such instances, we must perforce rely more on informed judgment than on statistical demonstration.

Finally, we should add that in applying birth-cohort analysis to mobility data, a practical problem that is usually encountered is that of obtaining large enough cell values to ensure a reasonable degree of reliability. Even with the generous sample size of our 1972 inquiry, we have thought it best from this point of view to maintain relatively large cell values by working essentially on the basis of the collapsed, threefold version of our class schema. That is to say, we have collapsed Classes I and II, representing the higher and lower divisions of the service class; Classes III, IV, and V—our three intermediate classes; and Classes VI and VII, representing the two divisions of the working class.[2]

TRENDS IN ABSOLUTE MOBILITY RATES

In Table 3.1 we present data to show the experience of class mobility of men in four birth cohorts for three intergenerational transitions: from origins (as indexed by father's occupation at respondent's age 14) to (A) respondent's position on entry into work: (B) his position ten years after entry; and (C) his position in 1972.

In the case of (A) and (B), the stage in the life-cycle at which we seek to assess the extent of our respondents' dispersal from their origins is reasonably well defined. It should, however, be noted that with transition (B) a problem of a different kind arises, in that in three out of the four birth cohorts, there are relatively large numbers of men for whom we were not able to record an occupation 'ten years on' in their working lives. This is the result, in the 1908–17 and 1918–27 cohorts, chiefly of men being engaged on military service, either during or after the second world war; and in the 1938–47 cohort, of men not having completed ten years in employment by 1972. 'Missing data' for this youngest cohort can in fact be reasonably dealt with, as is done in Table 3.1, by substituting respondent's 1972 occupation; but the deficiencies in our information for transition (B) so far as the two older cohorts are concerned cannot be overcome and the results we report for them must therefore be regarded as rather unreliable.[3]

In the case of transition (C), the problem of the section of the life-cycle covered obviously arises: this will, of course, vary across our cohorts, being longer the earlier the respondent's date of birth. We must, then, interpret all our findings for this transition in a more circumspect way than where we are dealing with mobility over a more or less fixed life-cycle stage. We may however to some extent mitigate the problem we face by making use of the notion that we earlier introduced of a stage of relative 'occupational maturity', attained by men at around age 35: that is, a stage at which one may expect, if not a cessation,

Table 3.1

Class distribution of respondents by class of father[a] and birth cohort (A) on entry into work, (B) ten years after entry,[b] and (C) at time of inquiry (1972).

Father's class	Birth cohort	Respondent's class									N			percentage		
		I and II			III–V			VI and VII								
		(A)	(B)	(C)	(A)	(B)	(C)	(A)	(B)	(C)	(A)	(B)	(C)	(A)	(B)	(C)
		percentage by row														
I and II	1908–17	24·8	38·4	55·1	35·9	35·4	27·8	39·3	26·2	17·0	206	164	205	12·4	11·2	11·9
	1918–27	25·4	49·7	62·5	35·1	26·9	22·4	39·5	23·3	15·1	228	193	232	12·7	14·9	12·6
	1928–37	36·8	52·7	67·9	35·1	28·5	20·3	28·0	18·8	11·8	239	239	246	13·1	13·3	13·0
	1938–47	46·4	48·6(59·4)	62·5	29·0	28·1(25·1)	24·8	24·6	23·3(15·5)	12·7	366	210(367)	363	17·7	12·9(17·5)	17·3
III–V	1908–17	7·2	13·6	24·7	31·5	31·2	38·1	61·3	55·2	37·2	501	449	522	30·1	30·6	30·4
	1918–27	8·0	21·3	31·6	30·8	30·8	35·4	61·2	47·9	33·0	565	403	585	31·4	31·1	31·7
	1928–37	14·4	24·0	34·6	29·8	33·0	36·0	55·8	43·0	29·4	561	549	581	30·8	30·7	30·8
	1938–47	14·1	20·0(26·3)	29·8	33·8	35·2(33·6)	34·2	52·1	44·8(40·1)	36·0	631	491(639)	641	30·5	30·2(30·4)	30·6
VI and VII	1908–17	2·6	5·0	14·1	19·3	23·0	29·7	78·1	72·0	56·2	957	856	991	57·5	58·3	57·7
	1918–27	3·8	8·7	16·8	17·2	17·6	27·3	79·0	73·7	55·9	1005	700	1026	55·9	54·0	55·7
	1928–37	6·2	11·2	17·5	21·4	20·4	29·9	72·4	68·4	52·6	1022	1003	1060	56·1	56·0	56·2
	1938–47	9·4	13·3(16·2)	18·5	22·9	22·3(21·6)	23·2	67·7	64·3(62·2)	58·3	1069	925(1097)	1093	51·7	56·9(52·2)	52·1
All	1908–17	6·7	11·4	22·2	25·1	26·9	32·0	68·2	61·7	45·7	1664	1469	1718			
	1918–27	7·8	18·7	27·2	23·7	23·1	29·2	68·4	58·2	43·5	1798	1296	1843			
	1928–37	12·7	20·7	29·3	25·8	25·3	30·5	61·5	54·0	40·2	1822	1791	1887			
	1938–47	17·4	19·9(26·8)	29·6	27·3	27·0(25·9)	26·8	55·3	53·1(47·3)	43·6	2066	1626(2103)	2097			

Notes: (a) The questions in the 1972 survey from which the data of the table derive are those given in note (a) to Table 2.1 and note (b) to Figure 2.1, plus the further question: 'Ten years later [after entry into work] –that would be 19 .. / that would be when you were .. –what kind of work were you doing then?'

(b) The numbers which appear in brackets for this transition, in the case of men born 1938–47, are those obtained if respondents who had not by 1972 completed ten years in employment are included in the analysis *on the basis of their 1972 occupations.*

at all events a marked falling off in the probability of job changes involving major shifts of occupational level. Accepting this notion, we would then tend to regard our data on the 1972 position of men in our three older cohorts—who would at that time be between the ages of 35 and 64—as giving a reasonably valid indication of their ultimate work-life position, while viewing the corresponding data for the youngest cohort—of men aged 25–34 in 1972—as being those most likely to show the influence of age effects.

Considering Table 3.1 as a whole, a number of broad regularities emerge. First, one may note the tendency, as one follows through the life-cycle from transition (A) to transition (C), for a higher proportion of men of all class origins to be found in Classes I and II and a lower proportion in Classes VI and VII. Furthermore, it is also the case that the proportion found in Classes III–V declines steadily within all cohorts of men of Class I and II origins, while generally increasing within those of men of Class VI and VII origins and showing a somewhat uncertain pattern within those of men who are the sons of Class III–V fathers. In other words, Table 3.1 indicates that among men of all birth cohorts and all class origins within our sample, the tendency has been for some amount of (net) upward mobility to occur into the service class in the course of working life; and likewise some shift from manual to various forms of lower-level non-manual employment.

Secondly, turning to our major interest in trends through time in a historical sense, Table 3.1 reveals that over the first three of our cohorts there is a fairly clear tendency, in the case of each transition alike, for the proportion of men of all class origins found in Classes I and II to increase, while the proportion found in Classes VI and VII falls. Deviations from this pattern result primarily from the fact that men in our second cohort—i.e. born 1918–27—were not systematically less likely to be found in Classes VI and VII on entry into work or ten years later than were men in the first cohort. In view of our previous reservations about the reliability of our data for transition (B) for both the first and second cohorts, it is reassuring that our results for this transition do not in any respect appear discrepant with those for transitions (A) and (C).

Moreover, it may be observed that the trend evident over the first three cohorts is generally sustained into the fourth cohort in the case of transition (A)—there being only one deviant cell; and likewise in the case of transition (B), if we accept the adjusted (bracketed) figures in the table, which serve to correct for the effects of missing data. With transition (C), the trend effectively disappears in the fourth cohort, but it is here, as we have earlier suggested, that our findings are most likely to show important age effects; and, given the nature of the movement over the life-cycle which we noted above, it is clear that such effects would work *against* the trend which the older cohorts reveal. In other words, the 'shortfalls' in the proportions of men in the fourth cohort who are found in Classes I and II, relative to the trend set by the three older cohorts, and likewise the 'excess' proportions found in Classes VI and VII, may be seen as reflecting the fact that many members of this cohort have still to reach the stage of occupational maturity. And in turn, then, it would seem a reasonable expectation that, in the course of time, the experience of class mobility of these younger men in our sample will in fact 'come into line' with the pattern which emerges from the experience of the cohorts preceding them (cf. ch. 9 below).

We may thus take Table 3.1 as confirming in greater detail the conclusion reached in chapter 2 that in British society in the recent past a steady increase in the amount of upward mobility has occurred. Over successive birth cohorts and at three different life-cycle stages there is evidence of a generally rising probability of the sons both of manual wage-workers and of men in our three intermediate classes having gained access to higher-level—that is, service-class—postions. At the same time, though, we should note that an increase is also indicated in intergenerational *stability* at these higher levels of the class structure, resulting chiefly from a decrease in the likelihood of men of Class I and II origins being downwardly mobile into manual work. Men originating in the intermediate classes are also steadily less often found in manual work at subsequent stages in their lives; and so too, furthermore, are men who are themselves of Class VI and VII origins: that is to say, the long-term tendency would seem to be for the intergenerational stability of the working class to decline.

These results may be regarded as ones which are at some variance with generally received ideas on mobility trends in modern Britain. The mobility inquiry undertaken by Glass in 1949 produced findings suggestive of an essentially static situation in mobility, as between status levels represented by categories of the Hall–Jones scale. Across successive birth cohorts—the oldest of men born before 1890, the youngest of men born 1920-9—no consistent trend in the amount or pattern of mobility was observed.[4] Glass and his colleagues appreciated the problems involved in seeking to determine trends from cohort analysis, and also warned specifically against extrapolating their results forwards in time. However, despite their caution—and in the absence of any later evidence going decidedly contrary to that they had produced—their finding of 'no trend' has been quite regularly taken by sociologists, and others, as if it applied not only to the first half of the twentieth century but also to the period subsequent to the 1949 study. Indeed, a number of explanations have been advanced—and from sharply contrasting socio-political and intellectual positions—for the supposed constancy in mobility rates.[5] However, while recognizing that the concern of the 1949 inquiry was with status rather than class mobility, and without attempting to make any direct comparison between the results of that inquiry and our own (there are major technical difficulties in the way of such an attempt),[6] we would none the less see the findings we have reported as requiring a rather radical change of view: that is, as making it quite evident that the static situation indicated by Glass's research has *not* in fact been maintained through to the present time.[7]

Moreover, there are features of Table 3.1 which suggest clearly enough *why* some amount of change in mobility patterns has been produced. Looking at the marginals of the table, one may note that in the case of all three respondents' distributions, the proportion of men in Classes I and II regularly rises, and that in Classes VI and VII usually falls, as one moves through the cohorts; and further, that while a similar shift is generally evident in the respondents' origins distribution, by the stage of transition (C) the latter distribution shows, in each cohort alike, a much lower proportion of men in Classes I and II and a higher proportion in Classes VI and VII than does the respondents' 1972 distribution. Indeed, across the first three cohorts—those of men whom we would treat as having attained occupational maturity—the difference in the proportions steadily widens in percentage-point terms. This pattern in the marginals of the table is of course one highly conducive to the trends in mobility rates which are shown up in its internal cells; and behind it, one may then recognize the actual course of evolution of the occupational division of labour in British society over recent decades, which we have previously documented in Table 2.3 on the basis of Census statistics. As may be calculated from this table, this evolution has resulted, so far as the employed male population is concerned, in the proportion of those engaged in professional, technical, administrative, and managerial occupations rising from under 16 per cent in 1931 to 27 per cent in 1971, while the proportion engaged in manual work fell over the same period from 71 per cent to 59 per cent. In other words, we may regard as the structural context of the mobility experience of the men in our sample an important 'upgrading' of objective mobility opportunities.

In contrast, it may be added, if we consider the more or less analogous intercensal period in relation to the 1949 inquiry—that is, 1911 to 1951—Table 2.3 indicates that the increase in the proportion of the male work-force in professional, technical, administrative, and managerial occupations was only from 14 per cent to 18 per cent, and the decline in the proportion in manual work from 74 per cent to 68 per cent. Correspondingly, we may then note, in the intergenerational mobility tables presented by Glass, the marginal distributions do not show any well defined trends across birth cohorts, nor is there any marked asymmetry between respondents' fathers' distribution and their own distribution as of 1949.[8] It would, however, seem valid to claim that Glass's research was carried out at virtually the last moment before the effects of ongoing, and quickening, changes in the form of the British occupational structure would necessarily be manifested in any observed mobility patterns. In other words, there is—as a result, as it were, of the accident of its timing—a particular *in*appropriateness in regarding the findings of the 1949 inquiry as holding good over succeeding decades.

TRENDS IN RELATIVE MOBILITY RATES: DISPARITY RATIOS

In the foregoing section we have produced evidence of a fairly systematic pattern of change in absolute mobility rates, as determined via our class schema, and we have shown that this pattern is one which has been clearly favoured by shifts in the occupational structure of the male work-force. We are thus rather naturally led on to the question of just how important to trends in absolute mobility rates is this changing structural context; or, as it might alternatively be expressed, to the question of how mobility trends would appear if they could in some way be assessed 'allowing for' or 'independently of' this context.

In dealing with such questions, sociologists have followed two quite different approaches. One approach depends upon a distinction made between 'structural' (or 'demand' or 'forced') mobility and 'exchange' (or 'circulation' or 'pure') mobility. The former is defined as that part of total observed mobility which is directly attributable to changes in the structure of objective mobility opportunities, and the latter as that part which is unassociated with such changes. Essentially, this approach has been operationalized by determining, in the case of a conventional mobility table, what proportion of all instances of mobility that are shown—that is, what proportion of all cases appearing in cells off the main diagonal—is arithmetically required, simply by discrepancies between the two marginal distributions of the table. This proportion is equated with the amount of structural mobility displayed, and the remaining proportion with the amount of exchange mobility. On this basis, it has then been thought possible to construct indices of the degree of openness or 'social fluidity' that prevails by relating the calculated amounts of structural and exchange mobility to each other and to 'perfect mobility' expectations.[9]

This manner of proceeding is not, however, one which we find satisfactory, since it appears to embody a serious conceptual flaw, not to say contradiction. What is being attempted is to use the straightforward partitioning of recorded instances of individual mobility as a means of expressing a distinction which can have meaning only at a supra-individual, or 'macro-sociological', level. Structural and exchange mobility are in effect being treated as if they were two different kinds of mobility, between which the movements of individuals may be divided up—when the distinction between them must be understood, if it is to have sociological significance at all, as relating to two aspects of mobility which are variable properties of societies, taken as units of analysis. As is now well recognized, difficult technical and interpretive problems arise with all indices of social fluidity constructed in the way referred to;[10] and these problems, we would argue, stem directly from the basic confusion of levels of analysis that is involved.

The other approach to assessing the extent of mobility allowing for structural influences—which we shall ourselves take up—also rests upon a conceptual distinction, but one which is, we hope, unproblematic: namely, that we have already introduced and implemented between absolute and relative mobility rates.

As we have seen in chapter 2, a very simple way of expressing relative mobility rates is in the form of disparity ratios between outflow percentages. Thus in a 2 × 2 mobility table, one would calculate:

$$\frac{f_{11}}{f_{1.}} \bigg/ \frac{f_{21}}{f_{2.}} \quad \text{and} \quad \frac{f_{22}}{f_{2.}} \bigg/ \frac{f_{12}}{f_{1.}}$$

where f_{11} is the frequency in the 1-1 cell, $f_{1.}$ the corresponding row marginal, etc. In using such ratios in the study of mobility trends, one is not then seeking to determine whether some supposed structural 'component' of observed mobility is becoming more or less important; but rather, whether or not changes in the structure of objective mobility opportunities over time are being equally reflected in the mobility experience of individuals of all origins alike. Thus, in the case which specifically concerns us, the substantive issue which we will most obviously wish to address may be put as follows: in the context of the expansion of the service class and the contraction of the working class, what changes, if any, have occurred in the chances of men originating in any of the classes we distinguish being found in a service-class or a working-class position, relative to the chances of men originating in other classes. In Table 3.2 we present a set of disparity ratios, derived from the data of Table 3.1, on the basis of which we may treat this question.[11]

Table 3.2

Disparity ratios showing relative chances, by class of father and birth cohort, of being found in Classes I and II (chances of sons of Class VI and VII fathers set at 1) and Classes VI and VII (chances of sons of Class I and II fathers set at 1), (A) on entry into work, (B) ten years after entry, and (C) at time of inquiry (1972).

Father's class	Birth cohort	Relative chances of being found in Classes I and II (chances of sons of Class VI and VII fathers set at 1)			Relative chances of being found in Classes VI and VII (chances of sons of Class I and II fathers set at 1)		
		(A)	(B)	(C)	(A)	(B)	(C)
	1908–17	9·48	7·65	3·90			
	1918–27	6·73	5·71	3·73		(set at 1)	
I and II	1928–37	5·97	4·72	3·89			
	1938–47	4·97	3·66a	3·38			
	1908–17	2·75	2·70	1·75	1·56	2·11	2·18
	1918–27	2·11	2·45	1·89	1·55	2·05	2·19
III–V	1928–37	2·34	2·15	1·98	1·99	2·28	2·50
	1938–47	1·51	1·62a	1·61	2·12	2·59a	2·84
	1908–17				1·99	2·74	3·29
	1918–27		(set at 1)		2·00	3·16	3·71
VI and VII	1928–37				2·58	3·63	4·47
	1938–47				2·75	4·15a	4·60

Note: (a) Based on the *adjusted* data of Table 3.1.

As regards access to Classes I and II, the clearest pattern emerges from Table 3.2 when we consider the chances of men who are themselves of Class I and II origins relative to those of men of Class VI and VII origins. It may be noted first of all that the general disparity in chances which is revealed—to the advantage of the former—is in all cohorts greatest in transition (A), but then diminishes as mobility is assessed at later stages in the life-cycle in transitions (B) and (C). Further, though, in the case of transitions (A) and (B) a steady decline in the inequality of chances is also evident across our four cohorts: in both transitions alike, the disparity ratios are in fact roughly halved from the oldest cohort to the youngest.[12] But finally, in the case of transition (C), understood as that from origins to the stage of occupational maturity, it can be seen that no such equalizing trend is present. In each of the three cohorts whose members may be thought of as having attained occupational maturity, men who were the sons of Class I and II fathers were almost four times more likely than men who were the sons of Class VI and VII fathers to be found in Class I and II positions. A broadly similar pattern, if not so regular or strongly marked, is also apparent when one considers the chances of access to Classes I and II, again relative to those of men of Class VI and VII origins, of men originating in our intermediate classes, III–V.[13]

As regards relative chances of being found in Class VI and VII positions, the information which may be gained from Table 3.2 is rather more straightforward. Looking first at the chances of men who are themselves of Class VI and VII origins set against those of men of Class I and II origins, one may observe that in each cohort alike the disparity ratios reflecting these relative chances *increase* from transition (A) to transition (C)—that is, as one extends the section of the life-cycle over which mobility is assessed; and further, that in each transition alike, the ratios tend to increase also across our four cohorts. Thus, in the case of our youngest cohort, those men who were the sons of Class VI and VII fathers were more than four times more likely than those who were the sons of Class I and II fathers to be found in Classes VI and VII in 1972; and the pattern of our data must lead us to suppose that as this cohort moves closer to the stage of occupational maturity, the disparity will *widen*. It may also be noted that when the chances of men of Class III–V origins being found in Class VI and VII positions are compared with those of men originating in Classes I and II, there is again seen a tendency for disparities to increase both over the life-cycle and over birth cohorts, even though in a less pronounced fashion.[14]

As represented in Table 3.2, then, data on trends in relative mobility rates in modern Britain create a very different impression from data on trends in absolute, or *de facto*, mobility rates, as set out in Table 3.1. The latter revealed a rather consistent pattern of change, one important feature of which was increasing rates of upward movement from working- and intermediate-class origins into the expanding higher levels of the class structure.[15] Table 3.2, however, indicates that, to judge from the mobility experience of our respondents through to the stage of occupational maturity, the increasing 'room at the top' has in fact been shared out more or less *pro rata* among men of different class origins, including those of Class I and II origins, so as to produce no change in their relative chances of access; and, on the other hand, that the contraction of the working class has been accompanied by a decline not only in the absolute chances of men of Class I and II origins being found in manual work but in their relative chances also. Over all, therefore, the picture obtained, once the perspective of relative mobility is adopted, is no longer one of significant change in the direction of greater opportunity for social ascent but rather, of stability or indeed of increasing *in*equality in class mobility chances.

What in fact would appear to have been happening over recent decades, so as to give rise to the pattern of ratios in Table 3.2, is that while some greater equality in chances of direct access to service-class positions—that is, immediately on entry into work—has been brought about, the relative chances of men of different class origins achieving such positions indirectly, during working life, have tended, if anything, to widen; and that such chances have widened most clearly in the case of mobility from career beginnings as a manual worker.[16]

Support for this interpretation can in fact be drawn from the three-point mobility analyses which we reported in the previous chapter. From Figure 2.2 it can, for example, be shown that in the case of sons of Class I and II fathers who entered work via occupations at some lower class level, a rather higher proportion had by 1972 been counter-mobile back to Classes I and II within our third cohort than within the two older ones—55.6 per cent as against 48.0 per cent; whereas, the proportions of men of Class VI and VII origins who had followed a similar course of upward mobility during their working lives suggest little change over time—13.8 per cent in the third cohort and 13.4 per cent in the two preceding ones. Furthermore, an appreciable decline can be discerned in the proportion of men of Class I and II origins who began work in Class VI and VII occupations who were found in these same classes in 1972—from 30.8 per cent in the two older cohorts to 21.4 per cent in the third. But, on the same basis of comparison, the proportions of men themselves of Class VI and VII origins who had both started work in, and who were found in, these classes shows only a slight falling off, from 57.7 per cent to 55.5 per cent.

The three-point analyses from which the above figures are derived were carried out to test—and, in the event, served to refute—the thesis of 'counter-balance' in mobility trends in modern Britain, according to which any increase that might be in train in upward mobility achieved intergenerationally would tend to be offset by a declining trend in such mobility achieved intragenerationally. However, while this thesis is undoubtedly mistaken in the form in which its exponents have actually presented it—that is, in terms of absolute mobility rates—it is interesting to note that a revised version of it, in terms of relative mobility rates, would in fact be generally consistent with the results that we have reported in this section.

TRENDS IN RELATIVE MOBILITY: ODDS RATIOS

Disparity ratios, as we have said, are a very simple way in which relative mobility rates may be represented. Used in the analysis of class mobility trends, they provide some basis for assessing how far changes in the shape of the class structure itself may have affected the relative chances of men of different class origins arriving at some specific class location. It is however also possible, and sociologically meaningful, to think of relative mobility rates, and of changes in these rates, in a somewhat more complex way which may be expressed by means of 'odds ratios'. In this case, one would, with a 2 × 2 class mobility table, be interested in possible changes across cohorts in the ratio

$$\frac{f_{11} / f_{12}}{f_{21} / f_{22}}$$

That is to say, one would be asking whether the relative chances of the son of a Class I father being himself found in Class I rather than Class 2 are changing over time at the same rate as the relative chances of the son of a Class 2 father being found in Class I rather than Class 2.[17]

In a table distinguishing a larger number of classes, more than one such odds ratio would of course be calculable—one, in fact, for every possible pair of origin classes in relation to every possible pair of destination classes.[18] A set of odds ratios of this kind might perhaps be most usefully interpreted sociologically as showing the outcome of a series of 'competitions' between men of different class origins to achieve—or avoid—one rather than another location within the class structure. The closer the value of an odds ratio to unity, the more 'equal', or the more 'perfect', is the particular competition to which it refers: that is, the lower within this competition is the association between class of origin and class of destination. Our collapsed, three-class schema requires us to think in fact in terms of nine competitions, as is shown in the format of Tables 3.3 to 3.5. In these tables, we give the corresponding odds ratios across our four birth cohorts for each of our transitions in turn.

Table 3.3

*Relative mobility chances in terms of odds ratios, by birth cohort: transition (A),
from origins to position on entry into work*

Pairs of origin classes 'in competition'	Birth cohort	Pairs of destination classes 'competed for'		
		I and II/ III-V	I and II/ VI and VII	III-V/ VI and VII
I and II *vs.* III-V	1908–17	2·99	5·37	1·80
	1918–27	2·81	4·96	1·77
	1928–37	2·20	5·07	2·31
	1938–47	3·97	6·98	1·76
I and II *vs.* VI and VII	1908–17	5·07	18·81	3·71
	1918–27	3·32	13·47	4·05
	1928–37	3·73	15·43	4·14
	1938–47	4·08	13·68	3·35
III-V *vs.* VI and VII	1908–17	1·70	3·50	2·06
	1918–27	1·18	2·72	2·29
	1928–37	1·70	3·04	1·79
	1938–47	1·03	1·96	1·90

Table 3.4

*Relative mobility chances in terms of odds ratios, by birth cohort: transition (B),
from origins to position ten years after entry into work*

Pairs of origin classes 'in competition'	Birth cohort	Pairs of destination classes 'competed for'		
		I and II/ III-V	I and II/ VI and VII	III-V/ VI and VII
I and II *vs.* III-V	1908–17	2·49	5·96	2·39
	1918–27	2·66	4·79	1·80
	1928–37	2·54	5·01	1·97
	1938–47[a]	3·03	5·99	1·98
I and II *vs.* VI and VII	1908–17	4·98	20·99	4·22
	1918–27	3·72	18·05	4·85
	1928–37	3·39	17·15	5·06
	1938–47[a]	3·16	15·19	4·81
III-V *vs.* VI and VII	1908–17	2·00	3·52	1·77
	1918–27	1·40	3·77	2·70
	1928–37	1·33	3·43	2·57
	1938–47[a]	1·04	2·53	2·44

Note: (a) Based on the *adjusted* data of Table 3.1.

Table 3.5

Relative mobility chances in terms of odds ratios, by birth cohorts: transition
(C), from origins to present (1972) position

Pairs of origin classes 'in competition'	Birth cohort	Pairs of destination classes 'competed for'		
		I and II/ III–V	I and II/ VI and VII	III–V/ VI and VII
	1908–17	3·06	4·86	1·59
	1918–27	3·12	4·32	1·39
I and II *vs.* III–V	1928–37	3·47	4·90	1·41
	1938–47	2·89	5·97	2·06
	1908–17	4·16	12·85	3·09
	1918–27	4·54	13·83	3·05
I and II *vs.* VI and VII	1928–37	5·72	17·37	3·04
	1938–47	4·29	15·56	4·91
	1908–17	1·36	2·56	1·94
	1918–27	1·45	3·20	2·20
III–V *vs.* VI and VII	1928–37	1·65	3·55	2·15
	1938–47	1·10	2·61	2·38

By inspection of the data in question, one may gain a great deal of information about patterns of relative class chances of mobility (or immobility), including, of course, patterns over time. It must, however, be acknowledged that the very volume of information contained in the tables, and its somewhat complex nature, make it difficult, if not to see the wood for the trees, at all events to tell with any certainty whether the trees form a wood of some distinctive shape. All that it seems safe to say at a general level is that while there are in all tables some quite large differences in the magnitudes of the odds ratios between cells—on a pattern that data earlier presented would lead one to expect—differences between odds ratios within the same cell, that is, across cohorts, are relatively modest; and moreover, that in no table do the set of odds ratios show any systematic tendency to increase or decrease over time. Fortunately, though, we are not, in this case, required to rely on inspection alone. A means is in fact available to us of testing statistically whether or not the odds ratios presented in Tables 3.3 to 3.5 are consistent with certain hypotheses which might be advanced relating to the association between class of origin and class of destination, and to the absence or presence of changes in this association across birth cohorts.

In the course of the 1970s, several writers, notably Hauser and his associates[19] and Hope,[20] offered a new approach to the problem of 'allowing for' structural changes in the investigation of mobility trends. This approach draws on the work of statisticians, notably Goodman, in the application of multiplicative or 'log-linear' models to the analysis of multivariate contingency tables.[21] In using the system proposed by Goodman, the analyst attempts to account for the cell frequencies of a contingency table by moving in effect through a 'hierarchy' of models, starting from one which specifies the independence of all variables, and proceeding thence to ones specifying two-way associations among variables, three-way associations, etc.—up to, if need be, the maximum complexity permitted by the number of variables involved. At each stage, he is able to test the goodness of fit of the cell frequencies derived from a model with those actually observed, or to test whether he gains a significant improvement in fit from a higher-level model than from a lower-level one taken as a base—the aim being to determine the most parsimonious model that will adequately 'recover' the observed values. A general specification of the log-linear model is provided in an Annex to this chapter.

Given, then, a concern with the study of mobility trends in a context of structural change, a model of obvious interest in regard to a table in the form of our Table 3.1, which comprises the three variables of 'respondent's class', 'father's class', and 'birth cohort', is that which specifies two-way but no three-way association: viz. that (i) an association exists between the marginal distribution of respondents and birth cohort and between that of their fathers and birth cohort—i.e. both class distributions vary over time; (ii) an association also exists between respondent's class and father's class; *but* (iii) this latter association does *not* vary with cohort—i.e. is at a constant level over time—once the effects of the marginal changes are controlled for.

This model could then be regarded as one of 'constant social fluidity', against which any more complex model, implying a change in the degree of fluidity over time, may be assessed. Reverting to the distinction earlier discussed, the 'constant social fluidity' model might be said to refer to a state of society in which change is occurring in structural mobility but not in exchange mobility; or, alternatively, in which changes in structural mobility account for all changes in total, observed mobility.

However, adhering to our own preferred distinction between absolute and relative mobility rates,[22] we may note that with this model, as indeed with log-linear models generally, what is specified may be expressed—and, in our view, expressed most concretely—in terms of odds ratios. A log-linear model is constituted by a definition of the pattern of association between variables in a contingency table in terms of odds ratios calculated from sets of four cells— each set being formed by a pair of categories from one variable and a pair from another. Thus, any such model, and any hypothesis it embodies, entail statements about odds ratios. To take a simple example, if, for a 2×2 class mobility table, one advanced the hypothesis that respondent's class and father's class are *not* associated—i.e. the cell values are determined solely by the marginal distributions—then (as we earlier implied) what the hypothesis would in effect claim would be that the odds ratio given on p. 77 above has a value of 1. In spelling out in similar fashion the content of the more complex hypothesis represented by the 'constant social fluidity' model, this same odds ratio would also be involved. But in this case, where we are concerned with a mobility table incorporating the third variable of birth cohort, interest centres not on the value of the ratio *per se*, but rather on whether there is significant change in its value across cohorts. What the hypothesis entails is that this odds ratio will be invariant across cohorts; and moreover, that with tables based on more than two classes, *all other* odds ratios of the same form that are calculable will likewise be invariant. More formally, the hypothesis as modelled states that, where k is the birth cohort variable, the odds ratio

$$\frac{f_{11k} \, / \, f_{12k}}{f_{21k} \, / \, f_{22k}}$$

and all other odds ratios that may be derived from pairs of origin and destination classes in the mobility matrix, will be constant for all values of k, and in fact equal to the weighted mean odds ratio over all cohorts.

For each of our three transitions, we have tested against the 'constant social fluidity' model, taken as the null hypothesis, the possibility that the association between respondent's class and father's class *does* vary over time: in other words, the possibility that in our mobility data the level of this association is itself associated with birth cohort, so that our observed odds ratios, as presented in Tables 3.3 to 3.5, could not be generated other than by a model in which a term for this latter, 'three-way' association was included. In the case of each transition alike, the results we obtain clearly require us, by the conventions of goodness of fit testing, to accept the null hypothesis. Indeed, in each case the 'constant social fluidity' model appears to fit our data rather well: as can be seen from Table 3.6, in which our results are summarized, the probability that the discrepancies that occur are attributable merely to sampling error is quite high.[22] Thus, we may go beyond our earlier conclusion, based on inspection, that our observed odds ratios display no clear and systematic trends, and state further that, statistically, there are no grounds for supposing any kind of generalized shift in relative mobility chances as expressed via odds ratios: that is, to repeat, in the relative chances of men of two different classes of origin being found in one, rather than another, of two different classes of destination.[24]

Table 3.6

Results of testing for 'three-way' association against the 'constant social fluidity' model taken as the null hypothesis

Transition	χ^2	df	p
(A) Origins to position on entry into work	10·37	12	0·58
(B) Origins to position ten years after entry	11·72	12	0·47
(C) Origins to present (1972) position			
All four cohorts	11·19	12	0·51
Three oldest cohorts only (men aged 35 and over)	3·53	8	0·90

At the same time, it is important that we make clear that in accepting the 'constant social fluidity' model, we do not commit ourselves to the view that *no* shifts of any sociological interest have occurred in relative mobility chances over the years to which our data relate. To be precise, what we have done is failed to reject this model as the null hypothesis in a 'global' test for changes in odds ratios across our birth cohorts. In such a case, the possibility still remains of there having been shifts of a more specific kind, which only more detailed analysis could reveal.

For example, even though the degree of social fluidity has been more or less constant on an overall view, changes could none the less have taken place affecting only particular combinations of categories of the variables with which we are concerned—that is, particular odds ratios might have varied in some systematic way across our cohorts. And to test, then, whether or not such changes have in fact occurred is only possible through disaggregating our analysis in some way and examining patterns of association in our data in a 'partitioned' form. Moreover, in view of our central interest in mobility trends, it is important that we recognize that the test we have made of the 'constant social fluidity' model takes account only of the magnitude of discrepancies between observed and expected values, and not of the temporal ordering of these discrepancies. That is to say, the test result is unaffected by whether the observed values for a particular odds ratio across cohorts show a trend about the expected (constant) value or not. If we wish to test for trends as such, we need to model hypotheses which specifically state that over time certain odds ratios have become steadily larger or smaller. For example, to revert to the simple case of a 2×2 mobility table comprising, say, a three-category cohort variable, one would represent a hypothesis of declining fluidity over time as

$$\frac{f_{111} \ / \ f_{121}}{f_{211} \ / \ f_{221}} < \frac{f_{112} \ / \ f_{122}}{f_{212} \ / \ f_{222}} < \frac{f_{113} \ / \ f_{123}}{f_{213} \ / \ f_{223}}$$

where the third subscript refers to the cohort variable.

Given these qualifications, then, it would seem advisable for us to inspect again the observed odds ratios of Tables 3.3 to 3.5 with an eye to trends, and this time with particular regard to ones which may be apparent only within a single cell or set of cells. There would in fact seem to be two such trends that are worthy of attention: one in Table 3.4, that is, relating to transition (B); and one in Table 3.5, relating to transition (C), across the three older cohorts only. In each case, the trends show up in the central cell of the table and in the three other cells lying to the left of, or below it: in other words, in all cells in which the chances of men of working-class origins are compared with those of men not of such origins in gaining, rather than not gaining, access to the service class. The difference between the trends in the two tables is in their direction: in the case of transition (B), the odds ratios decrease—the competition becomes more equal; but in the case of transition (C), they increase—the competition becomes less equal.

It is thus clearly of interest to us to set against the data of Tables 3.4 and 3.5 disaggregated models which can embody hypotheses to the effect that while in certain odds ratios 'constant social fluidity' prevails, in others, that is, in those for the four cells referred to, trends over time have occurred. Following a method described in the Annex to this chapter, we have in fact tested for the existence of *linear* trends—in the one case decreasing, in the other, increasing —in the odds ratios of these four cells. What in effect we have sought to determine is the probability that differences between values derived from our more elaborated model and those derived from the global 'constant social fluidity' model are attributable to sampling error, on the assumption that the latter—more parsimonious—model is the 'true' one.

Table 3.7

Results of testing for linear trends in certain odds ratios

Pairs of origin classes 'in competition'	Transition	Pairs of destination classes 'competed for'					
		I and II/ III–V			I and II/ VI and VII		
		χ^2	df	p	χ^2	df	p
I and II *vs.* VI and VII	(B) decreasing trend	3·44	1	0·07	0·56	1	0·47
	(C) increasing trend[a]	1·50	1	0·22	2·43	1	0·12
III–V *vs.* VI and VII	(B) decreasing trend	6·95	1	0·01	0·50	1	0·49
	(C) increasing trend[a]	0·64	1	0·44	2·14	1	0·15

Note: (a) Over three oldest cohorts only.

In the outcome, as is shown in Table 3.7, only one of the p-values returned by our tests is below the ·05 level, so that, to judge by the conventional standard, in only this case may we accept the existence of a linear trend with confidence. However, there are three other p-values that are at the ·15 level or below, and what is of particular interest is that the odds ratios to which these four lowest values refer can be seen to fall into a substantively meaningful pattern—as in turn, do those associated with the four appreciably higher p-values. If we take this patterning, as we would be much inclined to do, as itself lending further support to the idea that certain specific trends of change have in fact occurred in processes of social fluidity over recent decades,[25] these trends would be describable as follows:

(i) over transition (B), that is, from origins to ten years on in working life, the chances of men of working-class origins being found in service-class rather than *intermediate-class* positions have *improved*, relative to the chances both of men of service-class and of intermediate-class origins being found in service-class rather than intermediate-class positions; but

(ii) over transition (C), that is, from origins to occupational maturity, the chances of men of working-class origins being found in service-class rather than *working-class* positions have *worsened*, relative to the chances both of men of service-class and of intermediate-class origins being found in service-class rather than working-class positions.

In other words, while intergenerational social fluidity could be said in certain respects to have increased where attention is concentrated on the earlier stages of our respondents' working lives, in the intergenerational transition which may be taken as ultimately of greatest importance, that to the stage of occupational maturity, the tendency has been the reverse: 'exchange between classes' has in certain respects become more restricted.

Finally, if we treat the above trends as being 'real' ones, rather than features which have appeared in our data merely by accident (and this, we would stress, must remain ultimately a matter of judgement) the question arises of how exactly these trends connect with the changes in relative mobility chances which we earlier presented in terms of disparity ratios (Table 3.2).

First of all, it is fairly clear that an important contribution to the particular trends towards greater fluidity which we have discerned within transition (B) comes from the greater rate at which men of working-class origins improved their chances of achieving service-class positions compared with men of other class origins. But further, the fact that we can accept an increasing fluidity over time in regard to the competitions we considered for access to service-class rather than intermediate-class positions but not in regard to those for service-class rather than working-class ones, may be seen as reflecting another feature of disparity ratios in transition (B): namely, that they show that the chances of men of working-class origins being themselves found in manual wage-work have declined at a *lower* rate than have the chances of men of other class origins.

Furthermore, in the case of the particular trends towards reduced fluidity that we believe can be detected within transition (C), it is the slower decline that has occurred in the chances of men of working-class origins being found in manual wage-work than in the chances of men of other origins which appears as the *major* source of the shift—relative class chances of access to service-class positions having remained little altered. Where, one may note, the competition is for service-class rather than intermediate-class positions, instead of for service-class rather than working-class ones, the results of our statistical tests give us no basis for supposing that any real decline in fluidity has taken place.

If, then, one were pressed to pick out the one most consequential change in relative mobility patterns that has occurred over recent decades, one might well suggest the tendency, in the context of a contracting manual working class, for the sons of nonmanual workers to have 'avoided' manual employment to a progressively greater extent than have those men who originated within this contracting class.

We have examined our data on trends in intergenerational class mobility in a variety of ways, beginning with the analysis, in simple percentage terms, of absolute mobility rates, as observed via our class schema, and proceeding thence to the analysis of relative mobility rates. These we have treated, first, in terms of disparity ratios; and, secondly, in terms of odds ratios, taken as the components of log-linear models specifying different patterns of association among our three basic variables of 'respondent's class', 'father's class', and 'birth cohort'. We have shown that the results produced by these different methods of analysis may create very different impressions of the extent of the change that has occurred in class mobility in modern Britain. So far as absolute rates are concerned, our analysis reveals that men of all class origins in the younger birth cohorts in our sample tend to have better chances than men of similar origins in the older cohorts of gaining access to higher-level, service-class positions; and, conversely, to run lower risks of being found in rank-and-file manual employment. But this trend is obviously associated with the evolution of the occupational division of labour and thus with the changing structure of objective mobility opportunities. And when we go on to consider relative mobility rates, and in this way abstract from the effects of this changing structural context, it is then the degree of stability rather than of change that is the more striking. Overall, in fact, a model of 'constant social fluidity' would seem to fit our data rather well. Further, though, in so far as certain specific trends in relative mobility chances may be established, evidence of increased fluidity is only revealed when the class positions of respondents and their fathers are compared at a relatively early stage in respondents' working lives. When mobility is assessed from origins to a stage in working life beyond which the likelihood of further major shifts in class position falls away, such trends as are apparent are ones in the direction of reduced social fluidity.

We have described in our introductory chapter how in the United States a debate has been in progress from the 1940s onwards on the issue of whether the high degree of openness taken to be characteristic of American society in its formative period has been preserved into the twentieth century. Lipset and likewise Blau and Duncan, we have noted, have contended, as against both traditionalist and left-wing critics, that there is in fact no good empirical basis for supposing that mobility rates in America, however assessed, have displayed any general tendency to fall during recent decades. And, we may add, Hauser and his associates, having shown that several sets of American mobility data are, like our own, rather well described by a 'constant social fluidity' model, have of late further underlined the argument that no evidence for a systematic decline in the openness of American society can be adduced.[26] However, the point of contrast that we would wish to bring out here is that, in a British context, one can scarcely maintain the same perspective as these American authors. In particular, one cannot so readily regard the absence of any proof of declining openness as being a matter for satisfaction and as undermining radical criticism of the society: rather, the fact that there is no evidence of an *increase* in openness must, in the British case, serve powerfully to reinforce such criticism.

Despite the efforts of Smiles and other publicists, nineteenth-century Britain was never accepted by her own citizens as being 'a land of opportunity' in the same way as was the United States. And indeed, as we have also described in chapter 1, there was from the end of the century an increasing recognition of, and concern over, the extent of the inequality of opportunity that prevailed. This concern was gradually translated into political programmes and then— chiefly after the second world war—into actual policies of reform, primarily in the educational field. Such reforms had the explicit aim of reducing class influences on processes of 'social selection', and thus of creating greater openness in our sense: that is, greater equality of chances of access, among individuals of all class origins, to positions differently located within the social division of labour. However, what our findings on relative mobility chances must suggest is that these reforms have in fact failed to achieve their objectives. Even in the presumably very favourable context of a period of sustained economic growth and of major change in the form of the occupational structure, the general underlying processes of intergenerational class mobility—or immobility—have apparently been little altered, and indeed have, if anything, tended in certain respects to generate still greater inequalities in class chances.[27]

We have earlier remarked that we would wish to see the class structure as one constituted by relations of differential social advantage and power, and therefore as being in its nature highly resistant to change. We would then in turn regard our finding that no greater degree of openness was achieved in British society over the post-war years confirming this interpretation; and, furthermore, as raising serious questions about the nature and extent of the measures that are likely to be required if the class structure *is* to be significantly modified via legislative and administrative action.

NOTES

1. And likewise any distortions resulting from immigration.
2. We have excluded from the analyses of this chapter all instances of mobility involving movement into or out of the agricultural sector. From supplementary analyses that we have carried out, it is clear that trends in such mobility are to a large extent *sui generis*, and should be treated as such. On the other hand, the very small proportion of the total work-force engaged in agriculture over recent decades means that the exclusion can have no substantial effect on the general pattern of our results. Cf. Tables 2.1 and 2.2 above.
3. Especially as the pattern of the relevant marginals in Table 3.1 suggests that the missing data may introduce certain biasses, leading to an under-representation of men originating in Classes I and II in the first cohort, and an over-representation in the second cohort.
4. See Glass and Hall, 'Social Mobility in Britain', pp. 201–4.
5. The counterbalance thesis and the arguments underlying it (see pp. 55–6 above) represent one such explanation. For others, see J.B. Gibson and Michael Young, 'Social Mobility and Fertility' in J.E. Meade and A.S. Parkes (eds.), *Biological Aspects of Social Problems,* Edinburgh: Oliver and Boyd, 1965; and H.J. Eysenck, *The Inequality of Man*, London: Temple Smith, 1973, ch. 4.
6. The most basic and intractable of these stem from the inadequacies of the Hall–Jones scale of occupational prestige, used in the 1949 inquiry. Since the interview schedules of this inquiry have been destroyed and its data are extant only in coded form, any comparison of its findings with those of the 1972 inquiry must be on a 'Hall–Jones' basis. However, the procedures specified for coding occupations to the categories of this scale are too lacking in clarity and detail to make for an acceptable degree of reliability in its application. Cf. Kenneth Macdonald, 'The Hall–Jones Scale: a Note on the Interpretation of the Main British Prestige Coding' in J.M. Ridge (ed.), *Mobility in Britain Reconsidered*, Oxford: Clarendon Press, 1974. Attempts we have made to code into the scale occupational data for men in those birth cohorts of our 1972 sample which were also covered in the 1949 inquiry produce results which diverge significantly from those of 1949.
7. It may be added that no obvious qualifications to any of these findings are suggested if we organize the data of Table 3.1 on the basis of the full, sevenfold version of our class schema. More minor deviations are evident from the main trends that we have noted, but we would doubt the wisdom of attempting any substantive interpretation of these in view of the relatively small numbers that are often involved.
8. See Glass and Hall, 'Social Mobility in Great Britain', Tables 2, 6, and 7.
9. See, e.g., Saburo Yasuda, 'A Methodological Inquiry into Social Mobility', *American Sociological Review,* vol. 29, 1964; and Raymond Boudon, *Mathematical Structures of Social Mobility*, Amsterdam: Elsevier, 1973.
10. See, e.g., the interesting discussion in Daniel Bertaux, 'Sur l'analyse des tables de mobilité sociale', *Revue française de sociologie,* vol. x, 1969.
11. As can be seen from Table 3.2, we take here as the base for comparison the chances of those men whose class origins give them the *lowest* level of opportunity (or of risk)

of being found in a given destination. We could, of course, have equally well taken for this purpose the chances associated with either of the two other classes of origin, or the average chances of the men in the sample as a whole. Depending on which base is chosen, comparisons appear as more or less dramatic; but no change is produced in the general pattern of trends, either over the life-cycle or across cohorts, which Table 3.2 displays.

12. It should be recognized that, as in fact occurs in these cases, a narrowing in relative class chances as shown up by disparity ratios may coexist—though not indefinitely—with an actual widening of class 'differentials' expressed in percentage-point terms.

13. We again find a pattern of this same kind if we relate the chances of men of Class III–V origins being found in Classes I and II to those of men of Class I and II origins. This is more readily seen if the former are set at 1. Over the first three of our birth cohorts, the disparity ratios for the latter then decline from 3·44 to 2·56 in transition (A) and from 2·82 to 2·20 in transition (B). But in transition (C) no trend is evident, the disparity ratio remaining close to 2 in all four cohorts.

14. If the chances of men of Class III–V origins being found in Class VI and VII positions are related to those of men of Class VI and VII origins, similar trends are to be discerned so far as the widening of disparities over the stages of the life-cycle is concerned but are less regular across birth cohorts. Setting the chances of the former at 1, disparity ratios for the latter are in fact in transition (A) fairly constant across cohorts at around 1·30, while in transitions (B) and (C) they rise over the first three cohorts from 1·30 to 1·60 and from 1·51 to 1·80 respectively.

15. In a previous report on this aspect of our research ('Trends in Class Mobility', *Sociology,* vol. 12, 1978), we spoke of the increase in rates of upward mobility as representing a trend towards greater openness—which, in one sense, it is: the incumbents of higher-level class positions become increasingly heterogeneous in their social origins. But such a shift, as our data indeed indicate, does not necessarily imply greater openness in the sense that we have defined in chapter 1, and which we shall seek to retain throughout the present work.

16. From further of our analyses (see Figs. 5.1, 5.2, 5.11, and 5.12 below) it is evident that the tendency towards greater equality in chances of direct entry into Classes I and II must largely result from changes in access to professional and technical occupations, since recruitment into administrative and managerial positions is predominantly via work-life mobility even within our youngest birth cohorts.

17. The relationship between odds ratios and disparity ratios is straightforward: an odds ratio is the product of a pair of disparity ratios. Thus:

$$\left(\frac{f_{11}}{f_{1.}} \Big/ \frac{f_{21}}{f_{2.}}\right) \cdot \left(\frac{f_{22}}{f_{2.}} \Big/ \frac{f_{12}}{f_{1.}}\right) = \left(\frac{f_{11}}{f_{21}}\right) \cdot \left(\frac{f_{22}}{f_{12}}\right) = \frac{f_{11} / f_{12}}{f_{21} / f_{22}}$$

18. For an R × C table (where R is rows and C is columns) the number of odds ratios calculable is given by

$$\frac{R\,(R-1)}{2} \, , \quad \frac{C\,(C-1)}{2} = \frac{RC\,(R-1)\,(C-1)}{4}$$

19. Robert M. Hauser, John N. Koffel, Harry P. Travis and Peter J. Dickinson, 'Temporal Change in Occupational Mobility: Evidence for Men in the United States', *American Sociological Review,* vol. 40, June, 1975.

20. Keith Hope, 'Trends in the Openness of British Society in the Present Century', *Research in Social Stratification and Mobility*, vol. 1, 1981. (An earlier version of this paper entitled 'Trends in British Occupational Mobility: a replication to test inferences from cohort analysis' is published in the proceedings of the Internationale Arbeitstagung. *Anwendung mathematischer Verfahren zur Analyse sozialer Ungleichheit und sozialer Mobilität*, Bad Homburg, March 1974).

21. For an excellent review of Goodman's work, see James Davis, 'Hierarchical Models for Significance Tests in Multivariate Contingency Tables: an exegesis of Goodman's recent papers', in Herbert L. Costner (ed.), *Sociological Methodology, 1973-1974*, San Francisco: Jossey–Bass, 1974. Cf. also Clive Payne, 'The Log-Linear Model for Contingency

Tables' in Payne and Colm O'Muircheartaigh (eds.), *The Analysis of Survey Data*, vol. 2, *Model Fitting*, New York: Wiley, 1977.

22. Operationalizing the distinction between structural and exchange mobility in the new manner marks an undoubted improvement on the methods earlier referred to in avoiding their 'misplaced concreteness'. However, the tendency then is for this distinction, unlike that between absolute and relative mobility rates, to encourage speculation on what amount and pattern of mobility *would have been* observed if structural change in the occupational division of labour *had not* occurred. This may, at first sight, appear an attractive approach; but macro-sociological analyses based on such counterfactual conditions tend to run into formidable difficulties over the *ceteris paribus* clauses that need to be spelled out. See further below, ch. 11, pp. 316–17 esp.

23. We have not made any adjustment of our results to allow for 'design effect' of our complex sample. There are in fact several reasons for believing that the design effect will be close to 1. First, the sample design provided for a large number of primary sampling units (N = 417), and one may suppose that the observations contributing to each cell of the three-way tables that concern us are fairly evenly spread across these units, thus of course reducing the design effect. Independent calculations made by Professor Graham Kalton support this supposition. Secondly, it is known that the design effect for the difference between subclass means is lower than for each component separately if both subclasses are evenly spread over the primary sampling units. The estimates of the parameters of the log-linear model are derived from differences between cell frequencies, so that, by analogy, one would expect relatively low design effects in this case also. Thirdly, it is generally believed that complex statistics, such as χ^2, are associated with relatively low design effects. It should be added that any design-effect adjustment that might have been made would of course result in a *deflation* of χ^2 values, and thus, in the present instance, would have confirmed us in our acceptance of the 'constant social fluidity' model as representing the null hypothesis.

24. If we carry out the same model-fitting exercises as are reported on in Table 6 on the basis of the full sevenfold version of our class schema, the results again point to acceptance of the 'constant social fluidity' model so far as transitions (A) and (C) are concerned, but in the case of transition (B) the deviations that occur from this model are significant (just) at the 5-per-cent level. However, given our doubts about the quality of our data for this transition, we are reluctant to attempt any substantive interpretation of this result. In this connection, it is also relevant to note that from another analysis of the 1972 Oxford data, Hope has reported findings of 'no change' in what we would term social fluidity on the basis of mobility assessed over our transitions (B) and (C), although using five-year birth cohorts, a different occupational classification (one devised to 'simulate' the Hall–Jones scale) and, in the case of transition (C), an alternative index of respondent's origins, namely, father's present or last occupation. See 'Trends in the Openness of British Society in the Present Century'. In this paper, Hope also reanalyses the intergenerational mobility data of Glass's 1949 inquiry, and again finds constancy in 'exchange mobility' across birth cohorts, even though there is, in his view, clear evidence that the 1972 and 1949 inquiries differ systematically in the actual *amount* of such mobility that they show for men in cohorts for which their data overlap.

25. For discussion from various standpoints of the importance in the social sciences of complementing tests of statistical significance with assessments of substantive meaning, see the papers collected in Denton E. Morrison and Ramon E. Henkel (eds.), *The Significance Test Controversy*, London: Butterworth, 1970.

26. Hauser, Koffel, Travis, and Dickinson, 'Temporal Change in Occupational Mobility'. But for a somewhat modified view, see David L. Featherman and Robert M. Hauser, *Opportunity and Change*, New York: Academic Press, 1978, ch. 3.

27. It is worth recalling here that Glass and his colleagues, while welcoming reforms such as those that were embodied in or followed from the 1944 Education Act, clearly warned that their effects in increasing equality of opportunity might well be disappointing if major inequalities of condition remained unchanged. See above, p. 23.

ANNEX:

FITTING LOG-LINEAR MODELS

Introduction

Hauser *et al.*, give a full description of the use of log-linear models in the analysis of mobility tables.[1] In this Annex we provide the specification of the models fitted by Hauser and then give an extended specification for the more complex partitioned models which we have used in addition. A knowledge of the use of design matrices in fitting linear models is assumed.

Using the same notation as Hauser, the multiplicative model for a three-way mobility table of origin (respondent's father's) class (P) with I categories, destination (respondent's) class (S) with J categories and birth cohort (T) with K categories, under the hypothesis of no three-way interaction—i.e. constant social fluidity—is:

$$F_{ijk} = \eta \; t_i^P \; t_j^S \; t_k^T \; t_{ij}^{PS} \; t_{ik}^{PT} \; t_{jk}^{ST} \tag{1}$$
$$i = 1, \ldots I; j = 1, \ldots J; k = 1, \ldots K$$

where F_{ijk} is the expected frequency in cell ijk and the terms on the right hand side of the equation represent the parameters to be estimated. There is one parameter for each combination of the subscripts in each term (e.g. t_i^P represents the parameters t_1^P, t_2^P ... t_I^P) and there are constraints on each term so that the product of the parameters in the term is equal to 1 (so that $t_1^P * t_2^P * \ldots * t_I^P = 1$).

Similarly, the model which includes the three-way interaction is

$$F_{ijk} = \eta \; t_i^P \; t_j^S \; t_k^T \; t_{ij}^{PS} \; t_{ik}^{PT} \; t_{jk}^{ST} \; t_{ijk}^{PST} \tag{2}$$

This is the most complicated model we can fit to a three-way table and is called the saturated model. Model (1) differs from model (2) in that the parameters in the term t_{ijk}^{PST} for the three-way interaction are all set to 1. In order to compare the two models by testing whether the addition of the term t_{ijk}^{PST} significantly improves the fit with the observed valves, the conditional likelihood ratio statistic is used. This statistic, like the more familiar Pearsonian goodness of fit statistic, follows a χ^2 distribution but, unlike the latter, has additive properties which allow it to be used to compare the fit of successive models in a hierarchical sequence.

The multiplicative model can be expressed in linear form by taking natural logarithms. Model (1) then becomes

$$\text{Log } F_{ijk} = u + \lambda_i^P + \lambda_j^S + \lambda_k^T + \lambda_{ij}^{PS} + \lambda_{ik}^{PT} + \lambda_{jk}^{ST} \tag{3}$$

where the λ's are simply the logarithms of the corresponding terms (e.g. $\lambda_i^P = \log t_i^P$) and the constraints are now that the parameters within each λ term sum to zero. The log-linear model formulated in this way is analogous to the analysis of variance for factorial arrangements and can be expressed in the matrix form of the general linear model:

$$Y = X\beta + e \tag{4}$$

where Y is a n × 1 vector of log frequencies (n = I × J × K),

X is a n × p design matrix for the p parameters to be estimated,

β is a p × 1 vector of parameters and e is a n × 1 vector of errors.

An understanding of this formulation is necessary in order to fit partitioned models. Nelder gives reasons for preferring log-linear models to the analysis of variance for the analysis of factorial arrangements of frequencies.[2]

The Design Matrix

In order to estimate the parameters of a log-linear model we must, in fact, reparameterize models involving λ's since there are constraints on these and we can only estimate independent parameters. The term λ_{ij}^{PS}, for example, contains $I \times J$ parameters of which $(I-1) \times (J-1)$ are independent. The reparameterization can be done in various ways. A convenient method is to use contrasts between the first category of each variable and the remaining categories in turn. For example, for variable P with 3 categories we can define two independent parameters $\beta_1^P = \lambda_1^P - \lambda_2^P$ and $\beta_2^P = \lambda_1^P - \lambda_3^P$. Thus for the column in the design matrix for β_1^P the entry is coded 1 for category 1, -1 for category 2, and 0 for category 3; and for the β_2^P column the entries are similarly coded 1, 0, and -1. This method is called effect coding and is described by Namboodiri *et al.*[3]. The design matrix for one way terms β_i^P, β_j^S, β_k^T for a table with each of three variables having 3 categories is given in table A.3.1. Two-way and higher order terms are constructed by multiplying the appropriate columns in this matrix.

Table A.3.1
Design Matrix for One-Way Terms in a 3 x 3 x 3 table.

Cell	Col. Contrast	1 Mean	2 P_1-P_2	3 P_1-P_3	4 S_1-S_2	5 S_1-S_3	6 T_1-T_2	7 T_1-T_2
1	Log F_{111}	1	1	1	1	1	1	1
2	" F_{211}	1	-1	0	1	1	1	1
3	" F_{311}	1	0	-1	1	1	1	1
4	" F_{121}	1	1	1	-1	0	1	1
5	" F_{221}	1	-1	0	-1	0	1	1
6	" F_{321}	1	0	-1	-1	0	1	1
7	" F_{131}	1	1	1	0	-1	1	1
8	" F_{231}	1	-1	0	0	-1	1	1
9	" F_{331}	1	0	-1	0	-1	1	1
10	" F_{112}	1	1	1	1	1	-1	0
11	" F_{212}	1	-1	0	1	1	-1	0
12	" F_{312}	1	0	-1	1	1	-1	0
13	" F_{122}	1	1	1	-1	0	-1	0
14	" F_{222}	1	-1	0	-1	0	-1	0
15	" F_{322}	1	0	-1	-1	0	-1	0
16	" F_{132}	1	1	1	0	-1	-1	0
17	" F_{232}	1	-1	0	0	-1	-1	0
18	" F_{332}	1	0	-1	0	-1	-1	0
19	" F_{113}	1	1	1	1	1	0	-1
20	" F_{213}	1	-1	0	1	1	0	-1
21	" F_{313}	1	0	-1	1	1	0	-1
22	" F_{123}	1	1	1	-1	0	0	-1
23	" F_{223}	1	-1	0	-1	0	0	-1
24	" F_{323}	1	0	-1	-1	0	0	-1
25	" F_{133}	1	1	1	0	-1	0	-1
26	" F_{233}	1	-1	0	0	-1	0	-1
27	" F_{333}	1	0	-1	0	-1	0	-1

The design matrix for the constant social fluidity model (1) for the $3 \times 3 \times 3$ mobility table has 12 additional columns (for a total of 19 independent parameters) made up as follows:

$$
\begin{array}{llll}
\text{P} \times \text{S term col. } 8 & = \text{Col } 2 \times 4 & (P_1 - P_2)(S_1 - S_2) \\
\text{''} \quad 9 & = \text{''} \quad 2 \times 5 & (P_1 - P_2)(S_1 - S_3) \\
\text{''} \quad 10 & = \text{''} \quad 3 \times 4 & (P_1 - P_3)(S_1 - S_2) \\
\text{''} \quad 11 & = \text{''} \quad 3 \times 5 & (P_1 - P_3)(S_1 - S_3) \\
\text{P} \times \text{T term ''} \quad 12 & = \text{''} \quad 2 \times 6 & (P_1 - P_2)(T_1 - T_2) \\
\text{''} \quad 13 & = \text{''} \quad 2 \times 7 & (P_1 - P_2)(T_1 - T_3) \\
\text{''} \quad 14 & = \text{''} \quad 3 \times 6 & (P_1 - P_3)(T_1 - T_2) \\
\text{''} \quad 15 & = \text{''} \quad 3 \times 7 & (P_1 - P_3)(T_1 - T_3) \\
\text{S} \times \text{T term ''} \quad 16 & = \text{''} \quad 4 \times 6 & (S_1 - S_2)(T_1 - T_2) \\
\text{''} \quad 17 & = \text{''} \quad 4 \times 7 & (S_1 - S_2)(T_1 - T_3) \\
\text{''} \quad 18 & = \text{''} \quad 5 \times 6 & (S_1 - S_3)(T_1 - T_2) \\
\text{''} \quad 19 & = \text{''} \quad 5 \times 7 & (S_1 - S_3)(T_1 - T_3) & \quad (5)
\end{array}
$$

The three-way interactions in the saturated model are constructed in a similar fashion (e.g. $(P_1 - P_2)(S_1 - S_2)(T_1 - T_2)$, $(P_1 - P_2)(S_1 - S_2)(T_1 - T_3)$ etc.).

Most computer programs for fitting log-models effectively construct this design matrix in a reparameterized form for the user, providing that the model required includes *all* the parameters that make up a term. Some programs, such as ECTA[4] (Everyman's Contingency Table Analysis) convert the reparameterized model back to the original multiplicative form (e.g. model (1) or model (3) corresponding to (5)).

Partitioning the three-way interaction

The constant social fluidity model of no three-way association implies that all nine odds ratios calculated from our mobility table are constant over cohorts (i.e. all λ_{ijk}^{PST} are zero). In this section we give some examples of disaggregation of the three-way association into components which imply a systematic variation over cohorts in some (or all) of the odds ratios. The final example given below is of the modelling of the hypothesis that a linear trend is present in one specific odds ratio. There are in fact many possibilities for this more complex type of hypothesis, since we can choose a large number of subsets of the odds ratios which can vary over cohorts in a number of different ways. Each hypothesis involves the addition of parameters to the constant social fluidity model (i.e. columns added to the design matrix for model (5) formed by the product of appropriate contrasts). The conditional likelihood ratio test statistic is used to test the significance of the set of the parameters added.

Example 1

Hypothesis: The odds ratios in cohort 1 are the same as those in cohort 2 but different from those in cohort 3.

$$
\begin{array}{l}
\text{Additional parameters } (P_1 - P_2)(S_1 - S_2)\,T \\
\qquad\qquad\qquad\quad (P_1 - P_2)(S_1 - S_3)\,T \\
\qquad\qquad\qquad\quad (P_1 - P_3)(S_1 - S_2)\,T \\
\qquad\qquad\qquad\quad (P_1 - P_3)(S_1 - S_3)\,T
\end{array}
$$

where T is the contrast coded as 1 if cohort 1 or 2, -1 if cohort 3.

Example 2

Hypothesis: All odds ratios involving movements into and out of class 1 vary with cohort.

Additional parameters $(P_1 - \bar{P}_1)(S_1 - \bar{S}_1)(T_1 - T_2)$

$$(P_1 - \bar{P}_1)(S_1 - \bar{S}_1)(T_1 - T_3)$$

where $(P_1 - \bar{P}_1)$ is a contrast coded as 1 if parent class is 1, -1 if parent class is 2 or 3 and $(S_1 - \bar{S}_1)$ is a similar contrast for respondent's class.

Example 3

Hypothesis: Only the odds ratio involving origin class 1 rather than origin class 2 for destination class 1 rather than destination class 3 varies with cohort.

Additional parameters $(P_1 - P_2)(S_1 - S_3)(T_1 - T_2)$
$(P_1 - P_2)(S_1 - S_3)(T_1 - T_3)$

Example 4

Hypothesis: There is a *linear* trend in the odds ratio involving origin class 1 rather than origin class 2 for destination class 1 rather than destination class 3.

Additional parameter $(P_1 - P_2)(S_1 - S_3)T_L$

where T_L is a contrast using orthogonal polynomials to give a linear trend for the cohort variable.

In the three category case the coding is 1, for cohort 1, 0 for cohort 2 and -1 for cohort 3. For the four category case the coding is -3, -1, $+1$, $+3$. Orthogonal polynomial codings can be used to fit trends of higher order such as quadratic or cubic.

There are several programs for fitting models of these complex types. In particular GLIM[5] (Generalised Linear Interactive Modelling) has good facilities for the construction of design matrices. It is applicable to a range of types of linear model including the log-linear.

NOTES

1. 'Temporal change in occupational mobility'.
2. J.A. Nelder, 'Log-Linear Models for Contingency Tables', *Applied Statistics,* vol. 23, 1974.
3. N.K. Namboodiri, L.F. Carter, and H.M. Blalock, *Applied Multivariate Analysis and Experimental Designs,* New York: McGraw Hill, 1975.
4. Available from L.A. Goodman, University of Chicago.
5. Available from the Numerical Algorithms Group, 256 Banbury Road, Oxford.

CHAPTER 4

Class Structure and the Pattern of Intergenerational Fluidity

(*with* CLIVE PAYNE)

Following our demonstration in the preceding chapter that relative mobility rates have remained generally stable in modern British society—or, in other words, that a situation approximating constant social fluidity has prevailed—it is a rather natural progression that we should now wish to inquire further into the actual extent and pattern of this fluidity. To put the matter more precisely, what we would wish to know is the particular pattern of relative mobility rates that prevails and that, so to speak, underlies the pattern of observed, absolute rates as earlier presented in, say, Tables 2.1 and 2.2. The problem of how, technically, such a question may best be approached is, like that of how one may best assess mobility trends net of structural effects—or distinguish between 'structural' and 'exchange' mobility—one of long standing in the field of mobility studies. However, we have shown in chapter 3, following on contributions by Hauser and Hope, that a satisfactory solution of the latter problem can be provided through the application of multiplicative or log-linear models; and here, taking our lead from a further pioneering effort by Hauser,[1] we shall seek to show that the problem of determining the pattern of fluidity may also be effectively treated in this way.

In analysing mobility trends we asked, for a historical period in which structural developments had favoured—and to some extent required—systematic changes in absolute rates, whether changes had also occurred in relative rates, as expressed in the values of odds ratios. Log-linear models were then used to give a precise form to a series of relevant hypotheses: for example, to the hypothesis that no overall change in odds ratios had occurred—that there had been constant social fluidity; or to hypotheses stating that trends were present in certain odds ratios—that is, in relative mobility chances between certain origin and destination classes—but not in others. Any such hypothesis could be evaluated by fitting the model that represented it to the observed values of the appropriate mobility tables. Correspondingly, we now wish to show how, when we pose the question of what set of relative mobility chances—what 'mobility regime' as Hauser has termed it—is reflected in the *de facto* mobility experience of a particular population sample, we may likewise treat relative mobility chances in terms of odds ratios, and thus use log-linear models to represent different possibilities in the distribution of such chances. Again, the fit of a model with mobility actually observed (allowance being made in the model for structural—that is, marginal—effects) will serve to test the hypothesis it embodies.

However, while our treatment of the two problems is to this extent on essentially similar conceptual and technical lines, there is a difference in their sociological contexts of which we should take note. In investigating mobility trends, one can readily advance a number of hypotheses that are of evident theoretical interest—such as that of constant social fluidity over time; but in seeking to determine a mobility regime it is far less apparent from a theoretical standpoint just what hypotheses it would be most rewarding to model and test. It would be possible with the techniques that we shall deploy to proceed in an entirely empirical, trial-and-error fashion, so that one would be engaging in hypothesis-testing in only a rather empty sense, while in fact carrying out an essentially exploratory 'data-dredging' exercise; but, for reasons that will emerge, to do so would probably not be sociologically very enlightening. We shall therefore pursue a somewhat more ambitious goal. After outlining, in the next section of this chapter, the method proposed by Hauser for the analysis of mobility regimes, we shall attempt to develop a model of the regime prevailing in modern British society, in respect of intergenerational class mobility, which does, at least in some degree, possess a theoretical rationale: that is, one informed by an extension of the theoretical ideas implicit in the sevenfold class schema in terms of which we have made our observations of absolute mobility rates. In testing this model, therefore, we shall at the same time be testing further at least the heuristic value of this schema. Specifically, we shall be able to ask whether the basis on which we have chosen to examine the pattern of absolute mobility is a profitable one on which to examine the pattern of relative rates also.

ANALYSING THE MOBILITY REGIME: THE HAUSER MODEL

In attempting to study patterns of social fluidity sociologists for long relied mainly on a single statistic: namely, the 'index of association' introduced by Glass and his colleagues in their 1949 inquiry.[2] This index, as we have earlier noted, is the ratio of the observed frequency in a cell of the mobility table to the frequency that would be expected in that cell under the assumption of 'perfect mobility'; that is, of statistical independence between class (or other category) of origin and of destination. We have ourselves made some rather casual use of this measure in chapter 2, and believe that it is of informative value as regards the degree of *de facto* association between origin and destination positions. However, the index of association has from the first been subjected to much critical comment, and what is by now clear is that it is, at all events, a quite inappropriate measure if one's concern is specifically with patterns of association in mobility tables *considered independently of* their marginal distributions. The reason why this is so is straightforward: as Tyree and others have shown, the values of the index are conditioned by the marginal values that enter into their calculation, so that in fact the maximum value that the index can take for any cell will be the reciprocal of the larger of the two associated row or column proportions. It is thus 'easier' for cells associated with relatively small marginal frequencies to display high indices of association than for cells associated with larger marginal frequencies.[3]

Taking Tyree's argument further, Hauser has then made the valuable observation that associated with the idea of the index of association there is in fact an implicit multiplicative model of the mobility table—but one that is of an unsatisfactory kind precisely because it is founded upon the perfect mobility assumption. What this model in effect does is to identify 'interactions' in the mobility table—that is, tendencies towards mobility or immobility in particular cells that are net of marginal effects—with the deviations from perfect mobility expectations that the index of association measures. Thus, the model says that the observed frequency in any cell of the mobility table will be the product of (i) a 'scale' effect, reflecting the total number of observations—i.e. the sample N; (ii) an effect reflecting the relative size of the origin class involved—i.e. the row marginal proportion; (iii) an effect reflecting the relative size of the destination class involved—i.e. the column marginal proportion; and (iv) an interaction effect—i.e. the index of association for that cell.[4] While attractive in its form, this model is, Hauser shows, seriously flawed in its actual content, and specifically in taking indices of association as interaction parameters. The root of the difficulty, one might say, is that the index of association is being required to perform two tasks as if they were one; that is, to index the extent to which observed cell values in the mobility table depart from perfect mobility expectations and at the same time to index mobility or immobility considered independently of marginal effects.[5] But in fact these two tasks are incompatible, and it is essentially *because* the index of association is designed to perform the former, which entails that marginal effects as well as interaction effects should be reflected, that it is disqualified from performing the latter.

Hauser's positive contribution follows directly from his critique of the index of association and of the model underlying it. It is to develop a more sophisticated multiplicative model of the mobility table which incorporates effects of the same four kinds that were indicated in (i) to (iv) above, but which is based on assumptions appropriate to mobility data and is therefore capable of displaying the structure of such data without undue distortion. The model is specified formally in the Annex to this chapter but informally it may perhaps be best understood as follows.

In the case of the model associated with the index of association, the analytical strategy implied is that one should start from the assumption of perfect mobility and seek to understand the structure of the mobility table in terms of deviations from the statistical independence of origin and destination classes. In contrast, Hauser starts from the recognition that such independence is not generally found in mobility data and that interactions of varying size (*not* to be identified with the extent of departures from perfect mobility) tend in fact to be distributed throughout most of the cells of the mobility table. Thus, the strategy that he pursues is that of accommodating this fact by providing explicitly in his model for a number of different levels of interaction or, in other words, for tendencies towards mobility or immobility (net of marginal effects) of differing strength. What the model requires is that each cell of the mobility table be allocated to a particular interaction level, so that all cells placed at the same level share a common interaction parameter; and it is then the interaction parameter for a given cell which, together with the appropriate row and column parameters (and the scale effect), determines the expected frequency in that cell.[6]

The more substantive significance of the model, and in particular of the differentiation of levels of interaction, may be brought out if we revert to thinking in terms of relative mobility chances as expressed via odds ratios. In general, one could say that the allocation of the cells of the mobility table to different interaction levels is one way of representing in a condensed form the very large amount of information which, other than in a rather simple mobility table, would be constituted by the complete set of odds ratios that could be calculated.[7] Under the Hauser model, the odds ratios for any particular combination of a pair of origin and a pair of destination classes can be calculated from the interaction levels of the four cells involved in the following way:

$$\frac{F_{ik}/F_{il}}{F_{jk}/F_{jl}} = \frac{D_{ik}/D_{il}}{D_{jk}/D_{jl}}$$

where subscripts i, j refer to origin classes, subscripts k, l to destination classes, F is the cell frequency generated by the model, and D is the parameter for the interaction level to which a cell is allocated.[8]

From this equation what is first of all apparent is that all odds ratios involving combinations of cells from the *same* interaction level will have the value of 1. As we have previously noted, an odds ratio of 1 implies that the 'competition' between members of the two origin classes to obtain, or to avoid, positions in the two destination classes is entirely equal or 'perfect'; or, in other words, that within this competition no association exists between class of origin and class of destination. Thus it can in turn be seen that in the Hauser model all cells at the same interaction level form, so to speak, an 'area' of the mobility table *within which* perfect mobility prevails, while at the same time being distinguished in their rates of relative mobility from cells at other levels. In contrast with the model underlying the index of association, which is one of *general* statistical independence of class of origin and destination, that proposed by Hauser may be described as one of statistical independence *conditional upon* the assignment of the cells of·the mobility table to the several levels of interaction that are recognized.

Secondly, the equation given above also indicates that where an odds ratio relates to frequencies from cells at different interaction levels, that is, with different interaction parameters, the value of this ratio will be given by the corresponding (second-order) ratio existing between the parameters. (Note that in this case, where cells are not all from the same level, F_{ik}/F_{il} does *not* equal D_{ik}/D_{il} nor F_{jk}/F_{jl} equal D_{jk}/D_{jl}.) From this it is evident how differences between interaction parameters can be interpreted in a quite straightforward way. An odds ratio tells one that the chances of an individual of one class of origin being found in one rather than another class of destination are *so many times greater or less* than the corresponding chances of an individual of another class of origin. Given then the relationship between odds ratios and interaction parameters that we have stated, it is evident that one can in turn think of mobility or immobility propensities being so many times greater in cells at one interaction level than in those at another. Hauser himself refers to interaction levels as 'density' levels, since the interaction parameters of his model correspond directly with the idea of variations in the density of observations in cells of the mobility table suggested by previous writers;[9] and thus he speaks of the relative densities of mobility or of immobility in cells at different levels. We shall find it useful to follow this terminology, and also the convention that is adopted by Hauser of numbering the interaction level of highest density as 1, that next highest as 2, and so on.

From the point of view of an interest in patterns of fluidity, it is then clear that Hauser's analytical approach offers one the possibility of treating a range of directly relevant questions: Which cells in the mobility table may be appropriately grouped together in respect of their interaction, or density, levels? How great are the differences in density between these levels? Is it the case that densities of immobility are generally higher than densities of mobility—i.e. that cells on the main diagonal of the mobility table are generally allocated to higher density levels that are cells off this diagonal? So far as the latter cells are concerned, do they fall into density levels according to a symmetrical pattern or are asymmetries in relative mobility rates apparent between certain pairs of origin and destination classes?

However, before we attempt to design a version of the Hauser model that will adequately represent the pattern of fluidity underlying intergenerational class mobility in modern Britain, and thus enable us to discuss questions of the above kind, we must note what is, in our view, the major difficulty in using this model to interpret mobility data in the way that is proposed. As we have seen, Hauser's model, unlike that underlying the index of association, is expressly devised to fit mobility data by providing for different levels of interaction. It is therefore not at all difficult merely to obtain a version of the model that will reproduce observed data rather closely. All that is required to achieve this is to distinguish a sufficiently large number of interaction levels and to allocate cells to them, on a trial-and-error basis, so as to maximize the degree of fit. However, after having carried out an exercise of this kind, one would almost certainly find that, interpretively, one had gained little: that is to say, one would not understand the structure of the mobility table much better than one did before. If in fact the model is to be used to some effect, then, as Hauser has himself argued, there are at least two design constraints that must be recognized: first, the number of interaction levels distinguished should be substantially less than the number of cells in the table—and indeed Hauser has noted that interpretive problems may be encountered even where the number of levels is greater than the number of *classes*; and secondly, the allocation of the cells of the table to different interaction levels must be meaningful to the analyst, and is therefore best carried out on the basis of certain theoretical expectations. In other words, the interpretive value of an application of the model will in large part depend on having a design for the interaction levels that is both relatively parsimonious and as far as possible theoretically informed.

DESIGNING A MODEL

Accepting the above requirement, we had then to recognize that the procedure we should follow—indeed that which was logically required of us—was, as we have already indicated, to attempt to base a design for a Hauser-type model on the theoretical ideas implicit in the class schema in terms of which we have presented observed, or absolute, mobility rates. We have already given some account of these ideas, and we will need to elaborate on them as we set out the rationale of our design in detail. But first it would seem desirable that we should also outline what we would regard as the general considerations chiefly relevant to an understanding of the pattern of social fluidity, in the sense of relative mobility chances, between different class positions. These considerations we would group under three heads, as follows.

(i) The *relative desirability* of different class positions. This can be indicated in a general way, so far as the classes of our schema are concerned, by the position of their constituent occupational groupings on the H–G scale. One should however recognize the possibility of there being particularistic variations related to class origins.

(ii) The *relative advantages* afforded to individuals by different class origins. These may usefully be thought of in terms of three kinds of resources: (a) economic resources–that is, capital in various forms (including ongoing business enterprises and professional practices) and flow of income, availability of credit, etc.; (b) cultural resources–that is, 'cultural capital' in Bourdieu's sense,[10] and especially as this is favourable to the creation of the *famille éducogène*; and (c) social resources–that is, involvement in social networks, and also possibilities for less structured contacts, which can serve as channels of both information and influence.[11]

(iii) The *relative barriers* that face individuals in seeking access to different class positions. These may be thought of in terms of requirements corresponding to the kinds of resources indicated under (ii): for example, the requirement for capital, for educational qualifications, for 'knowing people', etc.

In producing a design for our model of the intergenerational mobility regime, by reference to these considerations and to our class schema, the first decision that it seemed necessary to make was that concerning the number of interaction levels with which we should operate. Hauser has suggested that it is sensible to begin with a relatively large number, but in the hope of being able eventually to eliminate levels in the light of empirical results. However, as we have noted, he also reports that difficulties in interpretation may arise where the number of levels exceeds the number of classes represented in the mobility table. Hence, it appeared most appropriate for us to work, initially at least, on the basis of having the *same* number of interaction levels as of classes–i.e. seven.

Having made this decision, our task then was to allocate each of the forty-nine cells of our basic intergenerational mobility table–that is, as represented in Tables 2.1 and 2.2 above–to one or other of these levels in as theoretically grounded a way as possible. For purposes of exposition, it will be convenient if we present at the outset the 'levels matrix' that resulted. This we do in Table 4.1, in which the cell entries indicate interaction, or density, levels–the level of highest density being level 1 and that of lowest density, level 7.[12] We may now proceed to the arguments which guided this allocation of the cells–bearing in mind that the theoretical rationale that we can provide is by no means one of uniformly compelling rigour. We shall in fact be concerned to make clear as we go along where our design is rather closely informed by our theoretical ideas and where, on the other hand, the latter could yield no very precise indications. Thus, when we come to test our model against our observed mobility data, we shall have some basis on which to decide whether or not to make modifications to it on empirical grounds. To do so where theoretical considerations are indecisive might well be reasonable; but to change our design in a way that would imply an obvious contradiction of our theoretical ideas would be pointless, for in this case we would gain an improvement in the fit of the model which we would be unable to interpret except perhaps in some quite *ad hoc* fashion.

Table 4.1

Levels matrix for a Hauser-type model of the intergenerational class-mobility regime, with cells allocated to seven levels of interaction

				Son's class			
Father's class	I	II	III	IV	V	VI	VII
I	1	3	4	6	7	7	7
II	3	3	4	6	6	7	7
III	4	4	4	6	5	6	6
IV	5	5	5	2	6	6	6
V	5	5	5	6	4	5	5
VI	7	6	5	6	5	4	5
VII	7	6	5	6	5	5	4

We begin with the argument that the surest advantages and the most decisive barriers in regard to intergenerational class mobility (considered independently of supply and demand factors) are those represented by economic resources and requirements. This is so, firstly, because economic resources can be more reliably transmitted intergenerationally than can cultural or social resources; and secondly, because, unlike the latter, they predominantly take the form of 'exclusive' rather than 'inclusive' goods—that is, ones which if possessed by one party cannot be possessed by another.[13] The transmission of economic resources may be expected to be particularly important within two of the seven classes of our schema, namely, Class I and Class IV. Class I comprises a minority of large proprietors and independent professionals who will often be in a position to pass on businesses or practices to their sons; and furthermore they, and also members of the majority groupings in this class, are likely to be able to aid their sons' occupational chances substantially by the use of their relatively large incomes and accumulations of wealth—for example, by buying them a privileged education, extensive training, or indeed a business or practice of their own. In Class IV we then have all other 'independents' (including farmers and small-holders) not covered by Class I. While their capitals will certainly vary considerably in size and form, one may suppose that a majority within this class will still have the potential to transmit capital to some extent. So far as the likelihood of intergenerational transmission of class position is concerned, we would therefore wish to regard these two classes as being *sui generis* and in turn we assign the I–I and the IV–IV cells in our mobility table to the highest density levels that we distinguish. In fact, as can be seen from Table 4.1, we place the former cell alone at level 1, and the latter cell, also alone, at level 2. This differentiation is made on two grounds. First, Class I positions are generally the most desirable—to judge by the H–G values of the occupational groupings involved—so that Class I sons may be expected to wish to retain positions comparable to their fathers', while Class IV sons have the possibility of seeking more desirable positions, for example, in Class I. Secondly, Class I origins can be regarded as offering greater advantages than Class IV—or indeed than any other class origins—in terms of cultural and social resources, so that in this way also the relative chances of Class I sons themselves attaining Class I positions are enhanced.

Having thus treated the I-I and the IV-IV cells as rather special cases and made over our two highest density levels to them, it will now be possible to deal with the remaining cells by working through the mobility table row by row.

As regards those in the first row—that is, those pertaining to the distribution of men of Class I origins who were not themselves found in Class I positions—we reason as follows. After Class I positions, those found in Class II are generally the most desirable. As we have earlier suggested, Classes I and II may be regarded as representing the higher and lower echelons respectively of the service class of modern British society. Thus, Class I sons who do not manage to follow their fathers into Class I will tend to look to Class II positions as the next best possibility, and will moreover have better resources than any one else for obtaining them. On the other hand, we may regard Class VII as comprising over all the least desirable positions, and Class I sons as being, because of the resources they have available to them, the best protected against relegation to such positions. It would therefore seem logical to place the I-II cell at the highest density level after the two we have already used, that is, at level 3, while allocating the I-VII cell to the lowest level available, level 7. Since the positions comprised by Class VI appear somewhat more desirable than those of Class VII, it might in turn seem appropriate, following this same logic, to place the I-VI cell at a rather higher level than the I-VII cell, for example, at level 6. But we would note here that there is a barrier to access to many Class VI—that is, skilled manual—positions which does not exist in the case of Class VII positions: namely, the requirement for an apprenticeship or comparable training, which must moreover be usually started upon at an early age, and in fact before that at which most Class I sons will have finished full-time education, even if they are academically undistinguished.[14] Taking the existence of this barrier into account, as a factor offsetting the greater desirability of Class VI positions, the I-VI cell would then seem best placed, together with the I-VII cell, at level 7. Furthermore, an essentially similar argument may be advanced to warrant treating the I-V cell as being likewise one of minimal density. Some of the technician positions comprised by Class V also require apprenticeships but, more importantly, manual supervisory positions are ones that are typically obtained via previous experience in rank-and-file manual employment, rather than on the basis of advantages of the kind that may be conferred by social origins.

We are thus left with only two cells still to be allocated in the first row of the table—I-III and I-IV. We may suppose that for Class I sons, Class III and IV positions are less desirable than Class II positions but are at least as desirable, and generally more accessible, than Class V or VI positions. It is therefore clear that we should assign these cells to density levels in the range of 4 to 6. Beyond this point, however, we have no very specific theoretical expectations, and we choose—rather arbitrarily—level 4 for the I-III cell and level 6 for the I-IV cell.

For men of Class II origins, we assume similar ideas about the relative desirability of different occupational positions as for men originating in Class I, in particular that manual employment will be found unattractive and that in any event barriers will again exist in some degree to access to Class V and VI positions. At the same time, though, we must recognize that Class II sons will be less advantaged than Class I sons, especially perhaps in regard to economic resources, and that they will thus be somewhat less likely than the latter to accede to the more desirable white-collar positions and in turn somewhat more likely to pursue, by whatever route, positions at the peak of the blue-collar occupational hierarchy. We would aim to reflect this situation therefore by allocating the II-VII and the II-VI cells, like the I-VII and I-VI cells, to the minimal density level of 7, while placing the II-V cell at level 6. The level of resources available to Class II sons also carries implications for the allocation of the II-I cell. On the one hand, this must clearly be put at a lower level than the I-I cell but, on the other hand, higher-level service-class positions will be those most attractive to Class II sons and their chances of obtaining them will be better than those of men of any other origins except Class I. It would thus seem appropriate to place the II-I cell at level 3. There remain then three cells in the second row still to be dealt with: II-II, II-III, and II-IV. Of these, we should clearly allocate the II-II cell to a higher density level than the other two, since Class II positions will be more desirable than Class III or IV ones; and there are grounds for giving the II-IV cell the lowest level of the three: namely, that while Class IV comprises positions that are not decidedly more desirable than Class III ones, there may be barriers to access to the former through the capital requirements involved. Within these constraints, we opt to place cell II-II at level 3, cell II-III at level 4, and cell II-IV at level 6.

Again for men of Class III—or lower-level nonmanual—origins, we assume the same ideas about the relative desirability of positions as for men of Class I and II origins, but also a further drop in the level of available resources. Hence, we must put the III-I and the III-II cells at a lower density level than the II-I and II-II cells; and since movement to manual employment is likely to be less avoided, we should allocate the III-VI and III-VII cells to a somewhat higher level than the minimal one of the II-VI and II-VII cells. The obvious levels to choose here would thus seem to be level 4 for the former pair of cells and level 6 for the latter pair. We do not differentiate between the cells in each of these pairs since we have no basis for judging how the countervailing effects of relative desirability and relative barriers would be likely to work out. We would moreover use an analogous argument to justify giving the III-IV cell the same density level—i.e. 6—as the II-IV cell: in this case, the greater relative desirability of Class IV positions for Class III sons than for Class II sons is taken as being offset by the still lower relative advantages of the former than the latter for gaining access to Class IV positions—the capital requirements being again the crucial consideration. We are left thus, in this row, with the III-III and III-V cells. To judge from the entries we have so far made in the levels matrix, it would seem that the former should have a density level not lower than 4, and the latter a level higher than 6. Rather arbitrarily, within these limits, we allocate these cells to levels 4 and 5 respectively.

In the fourth row of the table, we have already allocated one cell, that on the diagonal, to density level 2. Imputing this high density of immobility to men of Class IV origins implies then rather lower densities in the other cells in the row than would otherwise be expected. To begin with, although we would regard the relative advantages of Class IV sons as being at least comparable to those of Class III sons considered over all, we would see the former as being more advantaged than the latter in terms of the economic resources that are directly relevant for access to Class IV positions but as less advantaged in terms of the cultural and social resources that are more relevant for access to Class I and II positions. Thus, we allocate the IV–I and IV–II cells to a lower density level than the III–I and III–II cells—i.e. to level 5. We also place the IV–III cell at level 5, not because we suppose Class IV sons to be much less advantaged than Class III sons as regards Class III positions but rather because we would suppose such positions to be relatively less attractive to Class IV sons, given their greater advantages to succeed to Class IV positions. This same reasoning can also be applied in the case of the IV–V cell, and so we likewise put this one level lower than the III–V cell, at level 6. We are then left with the IV–VI and IV–VII cells. There seems no reason to suppose that Class IV sons should differ from Class III sons in either their desire to avoid manual employment or in the resources they have available to enable them to do so: hence we allocate the cells in question to the same low density level as the III–VI and III–VII cells, that is level 6.

As regards Class V sons, we would see them as having a slightly lower level of resources available to them from their origins than either Class III or Class IV sons: that is, they are likely to fall short of the relative advantages of the former in terms of cultural and social advantages deriving from their families' involvement in the world of white-collar employment, while falling short of the latter in terms of economic resources, notably the availability of capital. Thus, we should place the V–I cell at all events at a lower density level than the III–I cell, and we opt for level 5. It is also possible that Class V sons, because of their parental involvement in the blue-collar world, may regard lower-level white-collar positions as being little more desirable than high-level blue-collar ones. Thus, we would also incline to give the V–II and V–III cells lower density levels than the III–II and III–III cells, and we in fact allocate these too to level 5. However, in the case of the V–IV cell we would choose the same low density level—level 6—as for the III–IV cell, and on the same grounds of lack of the required resources for access. There remain the V–V, V–VI, and V–VII cells. Here, our foregoing arguments would indicate higher density levels than have been given to the corresponding cells in preceding rows, and also that the V–V cell should be distinguished from the other two by having a higher level on the grounds of the greater desirability of Class V positions. We therefore allocate the V–V cell to level 4 and the V–VI and V–VII cells to level 5.

The two remaining rows of the mobility table—those pertaining to Class VI and Class VII sons—we may usefully treat together. This is because we would regard the resources available to men of such origins, and also their ideas on the relative desirability of positions, as being to a large extent the same. As regards resources, the sons of skilled manual workers may have some advantage in economic terms over the sons of semi- and unskilled men, but one may suppose a good deal of overlap in this respect; and while the former may also perhaps have some slight advantage in cultural resources, there is offsetting this the tendency for many Class VII occupations, notably ones located in the tertiary sector, to offer greater social resources as origin positions on account of the contacts they provide with the white-collar world. On the other hand, the sons of working-class fathers of all skill levels may be regarded as essentially alike in being disadvantaged over all, relative to men of other class origins, in the competition for the most desirable positions. For this reason, then, we give lower density levels to the VI-I and VII-I, and to the VI-II and VII-II cells than to the corresponding cells in any previous row: that is, level 7—the lowest level of all—to the first pair of cells and level 6 to the second pair. This differentiation reflects our judgment that for men of working-class origins the barriers in the way of entry to Class I positions—economic, cultural, and social—will be appreciably greater than those to Class II positions. We also allocate to level 6 the VI-IV and VII-IV cells, on the same grounds of economic barriers as in the case of the III-IV and V-IV cells.

The remaining cells in the sixth and seventh rows should then clearly be given higher density levels than those already assigned, but the only differences that we would wish to make *between* the two rows is that entailed by placing the VI-VI and VII-VII cells at a higher density level than the VI-VII and VII-VI cells respectively. We would expect Class VI sons to be relatively advantaged, especially in their cultural and social resources, in gaining access for themselves to skilled manual positions, and Class VII sons, correspondingly, to be more confined to semi- or unskilled ones. At the same time, we should bear in mind here that both Class III and Class V positions present no very formidable barriers to access by men of Class VI or Class VII origins. It would thus appear that the cells in question can be treated with the minimum of differentiation necessary to meet these considerations by allocating the VI-III, VI-V, and VI-VII cells all to level 5, and likewise the VII-III, VII-V, and VII-VI cells; and by then allocating the two diagonal cells, VI-VI and VII-VII, to level 4.

We have now completed our account of the theoretical rationale for the levels matrix of Table 4.1, and our next task is therefore that of examining how well the model based upon it fits with the pattern of observed mobility. Obviously, there is little point in entering into any extensive discussion of the pattern of social fluidity that is implied by the design until it has been empirically tested in this way. However, it is perhaps at this stage worth noting that the levels matrix would appear to be a rather irregular one, and not of the kind that one would be likely to specify if the categories in terms of which one had chosen to examine mobility were formed, unlike those provided by our class schema, simply on the basis of some single hierarchical dimension, such as that of occupational desirability, prestige or socio-economic status.[15]

FITTING THE MODEL

A Hauser-type model of our basic intergenerational mobility table, with its cells allocated to interaction levels as in Table 4.1, generates the set of 'expected' cell values that are shown in Table 4.2 alongside the actually observed values.[16] The question that we must then determine is that of how well the model fits the empirical data, in the sense of adequately reproducing or describing them. To assess goodness of fit we use, as in the previous chapter, a form of the χ^2 test.

Table 4.2

Intergenerational class mobility: cell values observed and cell values expected on the basis of the seven-level Hauser-type model

Son's (i.e. respondent's) class

Father's class	I	II	III	IV	V	VI	VII	Total
I	311	130	79	53	33	37	45	688
	311·0	129·7	67·1	38·9	29·8	52·8	58·8	
II	161	128	66	39	53	59	48	554
	161·0	128·3	66·3	38·5	49·5	52·2	58·1	
III	128	109	89	54	89	108	117	694
	138·9	110·7	82·5	47·9	83·4	109·2	121·5	
IV	167	151	106	324	116	192	273	1329
	189·9	150·5	112·2	324·0	116·5	206·7	230·1	
V	154	147	109	83	170	229	190	1082
	150·9	120·3	89·7	72·5	175·7	223·8	249·1	
VI	202	228	216	170	319	788	671	2594
	171·3	229·3	231·7	187·2	326·0	805·0	643·6	
VII	162	194	205	164	311	587	870	2493
	163·0	218·2	220·5	178·1	310·2	550·2	852·8	
	1285	1087	870	887	1091	2000	2214	9434

Table 4.3

Results of testing the Hauser-type model of the intergenerational class-mobility regime

Version	Goodness of fit			Percentage of association accounted for	Percentage of cases misclassified
	χ^2	df	p		
Initial seven-level design	76·99	30	0·00	95·6	3·0
Revised seven-level design (four cells reallocated)	45·33	30	0·03	97·4	2·2
Eight-level design (six cells reallocated —two to a new minimum density level)	31·44	29	0·35	98·2	1·9

The question that is specifically asked is whether the extent of the discrepancies that exist between the values generated by the model and those observed is significant, in that it is unlikely to have resulted merely from sampling error. If we apply the test to the results displayed in Table 4.2, we do in fact obtain a highly significant χ^2 value, as is shown in first row of Table 4.3. On this basis, therefore, we are required to conclude that our model does not fit our data satisfactorily.

However, again as in the previous chapter, we would not wish to accept tests of statistical significance as our only guide to substantive, sociological significance. In Table 4.3 thus we also report two other statistics that we would take as relevant to assessing the adequacy of our model. The first is a measure of the extent to which the model accounts for the association in the mobility table between class of origin and of destination.[17] The second shows quite simply the proportion of the total number of cases represented in the mobility table (N = 9434) that the model 'misclassifies'—that is, as compared with their observed distribution across the cells of the table. What these statistics indicate is then that while the difference between the cell values generated by our model and those observed may be greater than can be attributed to chance, it is still not all that large, and that our model would seem to have been designed on broadly the right lines. In this connection, it is also very relevant to record that under the model that we have fitted the parameters of the density levels take on values that are entirely in the order that is implied by our theoretical arguments: that is, the parameter for level 1 has the highest value, that for level 2 the next highest, and so on, by fairly regular intervals, down to the parameter for level 7 which has the lowest value. Nothing in the fitting procedures, it should be made clear, guarantees or in any way predisposes for such an outcome. In these circumstances, therefore, it would appear appropriate to consider whether it is possible for our model to be somewhat modified, so as to improve its fit, but without offending grossly against any of the theoretical expectations that guided its initial specification.

From Table 4.2 it is fairly evident that most of the larger discrepancies between observed and expected values occur in two rows of the mobility table —the first and the fifth.[18] In the first row, our model most notably underestimates the mobility of men of Class I origins to Class IV positions, while overestimating their mobility to Class VI and VII positions. As regards correcting the former discrepancy, there would seem to be no theoretical objection to raising the I-IV cell by one level—i.e. to level 5—since all that was required by the rationale of the design was that this cell should fall in the range of levels 4 to 6. Likewise, while we did not anticipate the difference, there is nothing in the theoretical expectations that we set out that would actually tell against placing the I-VI and I-VII cells at a lower density level than the others allocated to level 7. The only drawback here is that this would mean creating a new, eighth level of density and, to that extent, having a less parsimonious design.

In the fifth row of the Table, discrepancies chiefly arise in that our model underestimates the extent to which men of Class V origins are found in both Class II and Class III positions, and then greatly overestimates the extent of mobility to Class VII positions. To make the reallocation of cells to density levels that would be necessary to reduce these discrepancies *would* imply some amendment of theoretical ideas earlier expressed but, it may be said, only of ones which were rather tentatively advanced. While we felt that strong grounds existed for placing the V-I cell at a lower level than the III-I cell—a decision which the results of Table 4.2 bear out—we allocated the V-II and V-III cells also to a lower level than the corresponding cells in the third row because we envisaged that subaltern white-collar positions might have a lower desirability for Class V than for Class III sons. And, in turn, we then placed both the V-VI and V-VII cells at one density level higher than the III-VI and III-VII cells. It would now appear that our speculation here was mistaken: at all events, the relative chances of Class V sons being found in Class II and III positions, on the one hand, or in Class VII positions, on the other, seem not in fact to differ greatly from those of Class III sons. However, it is, we believe, possible to drop the argument in question without any grave consequences for our theoretical position in general, and we would therefore wish to modify the design of our model by reallocating the V-II and V-III cells from level 5 to level 4, and the V-VII cell from level 5 to level 6.

What the foregoing would suggest is, then, that we may reasonably—that is, with due regard for subsequent interpretation—move from our initial design to one or other of two possibilities: that is, either to a revised seven-level design, incorporating one reallocation in the first row of the mobility table—the I-IV cell from level 6 to level 5—and the three in the fifth row, that we have just specified; or to an eight-level design which would involve, in addition to these reallocations, the introduction of a new minimum density level, to which would be allocated the I-VI and I-VII cells. From the second and third rows of Table 4.3 it can be seen how the fit of our model would be improved by these modifications to the initial design. To judge by the conventional 5 per cent criterion, the χ^2 value for the revised seven-level design is still significant, even though it is evident from the other two measures used that the differences between observed and expected values cannot be very great. On the other hand, while the further improvement that the eight-level design can effect on these latter measures is necessarily rather slight, this version of the model does reduce the χ^2 value to a clearly non-significant magnitude, and may therefore be accepted as giving a statistically satisfactory description of our empirical data.[19]

Thus, in attempting, in the final section of this chapter, to show the relevance of our modelling exercise to the discussion of substantive questions of the extent and pattern of social fluidity, it is, it would seem, the eight-level design on which this discussion may best be based. Although the number of density levels in this case exceeds that of classes, no problems of interpretation are apparent since, substantively, the differences between the eight-level version of the model and the revised, or even the initial seven-level one are so limited.

In Table 4.4 we give the values for the parameters of the density levels in the eight-level design expressed in additive form—that is, as effects on logged cell frequencies—with the value for level 1 set at zero and the other values interpreted as differences from level 1. More importantly, we also provide a matrix of the differences in densities that these parameters imply expressed in multiplicative terms. The parameter values can in fact be computed in a variety of ways, depending upon the normalization procedure that is adopted (see the Annex to this chapter); but the set of mutiplicative differences between them is their constant property, and represents the basic quantitative information that is produced by our model.[20] The matrix of Table 4.4 can be read as showing, to take, for example, the first row, that at level 1 density is one and a third times as

Table 4.4

Values of the parameters of density levels for the eight-level model (in additive form) and matrix of differences in density between levels (in multiplicative form)[a]

	Additive parameter value	Level	(j) 1	2	3	4	5	6	7	8
	0·00	1	1	1·37	1·78	2·66	3·58	4·90	7·68	12·55
	−0·29	2	0·75	1	1·34	1·99	2·69	3·67	5·75	9·39
	−0·58	3	0·56	0·75	1	1·49	2·01	2·76	4·32	7·03
(i)	−0·98	4	0·38	0·50	0·67	1	1·35	1·84	2·89	4·71
	−1·28	5	0·28	0·37	0·50	0·74	1	1·37	2·15	3·49
	−1·59	6	0·20	0·27	0·36	0·54	0·73	1	1·57	2·56
	−2·04	7	0·13	0·17	0·23	0·35	0·47	0·64	1	1·63
	−2·53	8	0·08	0·11	0·14	0·21	0·29	0·39	0·61	1

Note: (a) Values in the upper triangle of the matrix are of $\frac{D_{(i)}}{D_{(j)}}$; where $D_{(k)} = e^{x_k}$ where x_k is the additive parameter for level (k). Values in the lower triangle are of $\frac{D_{(j)}}{D_{(i)}}$ i.e. the reciprocals of the former. As an example of the derivation of the multiplicative entries of the matrix from the parameters given in additive form (i.e. as effects on logged frequencies), consider the first off-diagonal entry in the first row:

$$\frac{D_{(i)}}{D_{(j)}} = e^{(0·00 - (-0·29))} = e^{0·29} = 1·37$$

or, for the last (off-diagonal) entry in the last row

$$\frac{D_{(j)}}{D_{(i)}} = e^{(-2·53 - (2·04))} = e^{-0·49} = 0·61$$

great as at level 2, one and three-quarter times greater than at level 3, two and two-thirds times greater than at level 4, and so on; or, alternatively, as showing, to take the first column, that density at level 2 is three-quarters that at level 1, at level 3 is just over half that at level 1, at level 4 just over a third that of level 1, and so on.

As a further aid to the application of the model to substantive issues, we also give, in Figure 4.1, a graphic representation of the revised levels matrix on which the model is based. The allocation of cells to density levels is here indicated directly by the density of their shading, so that the 'contours' of the density of mobility or immobility can be readily seen. In addition, the sizes of the cells are drawn to scale with the marginal proportions in the mobility table that are accounted for by each class.

THE PATTERN OF SOCIAL FLUIDITY

We now have a well-fitting model of our basic intergenerational mobility table which is capable of showing the extent and pattern of association between class of origin and of destination considered independently of marginal effects. What, then, are the main features of social fluidity, in this sense, that the model reveals? Since the initial design of the model was guided by certain theoretical expectations—which the reasonably good fit achieved with our empirical data serves broadly to confirm—we may suppose that most of these features are, in a general way at least, reflected in the rationale for the model that we earlier presented. However, working from the final version of our model, which incorporates various modifications to the initial design made on empirical grounds, we should be able to bring out these features more fully, and further to see them in relation to each other and to attach to them some quantitative estimates.

On the basis of most previous discussion of the pattern of social fluidity, in Britain or in other modern industrial societies, one would expect two features to be prominent. First, one would expect the highest density levels to be found in cells on the main diagonal of the mobility table—that is, to be densities of immobility—because of processes favouring the 'inheritance' of class positions; and moreover, that the strongest tendency of all towards immobility would be within the more advantaged and powerful groupings commanding the more desirable positions towards the peak of the class structure. Secondly, one would expect that, in so far as the categories of the mobility table are hierarchically ordered, the lowest densities would be those in the cells furthest from the main diagonal, thus reflecting weak tendencies for mobility of a long-range kind, either into or out of the higher class levels.[21] In the preceding chapter, in considering the question of trends in relative mobility rates, we were led to remark that the thesis of 'counterbalance' between inter- and intragenerational mobility, which in chapter 2 was disconfirmed by our absolute mobility data, might however, if recast in relative terms, be regarded as generally consistent with our findings.[22] A question, then, that obviously arises here is whether a similar reformulation might not give new life to the other, related theses that were likewise critically examined in chapter 2: namely, those of 'closure' towards the peak of the class structure and of a 'buffer zone' in the intermediate levels which, while itself characterized by high mobility rates, serves to block off longer-range movement between the class positions on either side of it. From Figure 4.1 it is rather readily apparent that our model does in fact specify a pattern of fluidity which is broadly in line with the expectations that we have noted. At the same time, though, as we will aim to bring out, various deviations and elaborations are also entailed: the pattern of fluidity, within the British class structure at least, is somewhat more complex than the standard expectations allow for.

In our model the highest density level is that for the I-I cell (level 1) and the lowest is that occurring in the I-VI and I-VII cells (level 8). The greatest difference in density, we may then say, is that between the density of immobility within the higher echelons of the service class and the density of mobility downwards from such advantaged social origins into manual wage-earning positions. From the matrix of Table 4.4 it can be seen that at level 1 density is in fact over twelve times greater than at level 8; or, in other words, that the tendency, net of the influence of structural factors, for men born into Class I to be subsequently found in that class is more than twelve times stronger than the tendency for

Figure 4.1
Graphic representation of the levels matrix for the eight-level model, with the size of cells drawn to scale with the marginal proportions in the mobility table accounted for by each class.

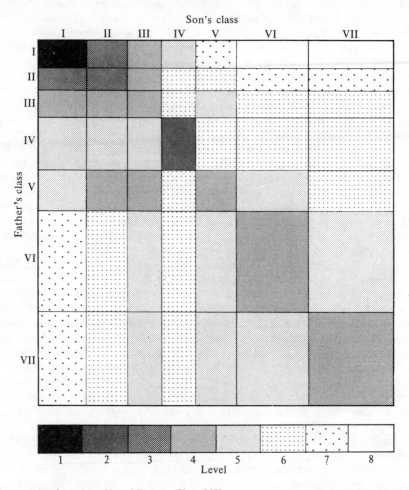

them to be found in Class VI or in Class VII.

The above difference is one that finds its expression in outflow terms; but in inflow perspective too—that is, looking along the columns rather than the rows of the levels matrix represented by Figure 4.1—the largest contrast in density levels is one that involves the same classes: that between the I-I cell and the VI-I and VII-I cells at level 7. Again by reference to Table 4.4 we may quantify this difference and say that in terms of relative mobility chances members of Class I are between seven and eight times more likely to be men who were born into that class than to be men of Class VI or of Class VII origins.

If we wish to express the extent of differences in density by means of odds ratios, this is readily done according to the equation given on p. 97 above. The highest odds ratios—that is, those indicative of the most unequal 'competition'—again relate, not surprisingly, to mobility between higher-level service-class and working-class positions. For example, we may write

$$\frac{F_{I-I}/F_{I-VII}}{F_{VII-I}/F_{VII-VII}} \quad = \quad \frac{D_1 / D_8}{D_7 / D_4}$$

or alternatively

$$\frac{F_{I-I}/F_{VII-I}}{F_{I-VII}/F_{VII-VII}} \quad = \quad \frac{D_1 / D_7}{D_8 / D_4}$$

which will, of course, take the same value. From the matrix of Table 4.4 we can then calculate that the odds ratios in question have in fact a value of approximately 36.[23] That is to say, the chances of men born into Class I being found in Class I positions rather than Class VII positions are around thirty-six times greater than the chances of men born into Class VII being found in Class I rather than Class VII positions; or, alternatively, the chances of men found in Class I being of Class I rather than Class VII origins are around thirty-six times greater than the chances of men found in Class VII being of Class I rather than of Class VII origins. And, from inspection of the levels matrix as illustrated in Figure 4.1, it is of course evident that we would obtain exactly the same result if we considered likewise relative mobility chances as between Class I and Class VI.

In Table 4.5 we give the set of all odds ratios under our model where the pair of origin classes and the pair of destination classes involved is the same. It can be seen that the competitions between men of Class I and of Class VI and VII origins are in fact the most unequal by a wide margin; and further, that the next most unequal ones are those in which men born into Class I show an approximately ten times better chance of being found in a Class I rather than a Class IV or a Class V position than do men born into Class IV or Class V. Competitions involving Class II in opposition to Classes VI and VII reveal a moderately high degree of inequality, and so too do all those that involve Class IV. But so far as the remainder are concerned, it is notable that the degree of inequality is relatively low, with odds ratios being in all cases less than 3.

From the foregoing it would then seem clear enough that the pattern of relative mobility chances associated with Class I is a distinctive one. Not only is the density of immobility within Class I the highest density of all in our model, but Class I is further set apart on the one hand, as a class of origin, in the extent to which it endows men born into it with particularly low chances of being found in any kind of blue-collar employment; and on the other hand, as a class of destination, in the extent to which it imposes particularly high barriers to entry so far at least as the sons of manual wage-workers are concerned. However, while in these respects the pattern of fluidity that we have modelled may be regarded as consistent with the standard expectations that were earlier set out, we may at this point take note also of certain other features for which these expectations would not so well prepare one.

First, while the highest density levels in our model are indeed found in cells on the main diagonal and the I–I cell has the highest density of all, it is also the

Table 4.5

Matrix of odds ratios where the pair of origin and the pair of destination classes are the same[a]

			Class			
Class	II	III	IV	V	VI	VII
I	1·78	2·66	9·68	10·38	35·86	35·86
II		1·49	7·46	2·76	8·00	8·00
III			4·97	1·35	2·49	2·49
IV				6·80	6·80	6·80
V					1·82	2·49
VI						1·82

Note: (a) The entries in the matrix show the chances of men in one class of origin relative to those of men in another of being themselves found in one rather than the other of these same two classes. Thus the entry in the I–II cell of 1·78 indicates that men originating in Class I have around one-and-three-quarters times the chance of men originating in Class II of being found in a Class I rather than a Class II position—or conversely, of course, that men originating in Class II have a similarly greater chance than men originating in Class I of being found in a Class II rather than a Class I position.

case that the model specifies a good deal of further variation in densities of immobility from class to class. The IV–IV cell is at the second highest density level, that is, level 2; the II–II cell is at level 3; and the diagonal cells for Class III and for the three blue-collar classes are all at level 4. Moreover, by reference to Table 4.4 it can be seen that the range of this variation is quite considerable. The density of immobility in Classes III, V, VI, and VII is only two-thirds that in Class II and a half of that in Class IV. What is primarily reflected here is of course our own theoretical expectation, spelled out in the rationale for our model, that a crucial factor affecting the extent of the 'inheritance' of class positions is the possibility of this being achieved via the intergenerational transmission of economic resources, and in particular via inheritance in the strict sense, that is, of property and 'going concerns'.[24]

Secondly, it should be recognized that in our model densities of immobility are not invariably greater than densities of mobility, even within the same row or column. With three of our classes, as Figure 4.1 will confirm, the tendency for intergenerational immobility is no stronger than that for movement to certain other classes. The relative chances of immobility of men of class II origins are matched by their chances of being found in Class I; those of men of Class III origins by their chances of being found in Class II or in Class I; and those of men of Class V origins by their chances of being found in Class III or in Class II. The two former instances are of particular interest since it may also be noted that, net of marginal effects, men found in Class II are as likely to be of Class I as of Class II origins, and that men found in Class III are as likely to be of Class I or of Class II origins as of Class III origins. In other words, we may discern among our three white-collar classes, despite the high density of immobility in Class I, a generally high density of mobility in what may be regarded as both an upward and a downward direction.

Thirdly, and perhaps most importantly, we should take full note of a feature of the mobility regime represented by our model which we have in fact to some extent implied in our previous observations: that is, that the model entails a rather large number of asymmetries. Pairs of corresponding cells on either side of the main diagonal of the mobility table are allocated to different density levels, thus indicating that the tendency for mobility to occur between them is stronger in one direction than in the other. Many of these asymmetries are apparent in Table 4.1 and derive directly from the rationale provided for our initial design; but the modifications subsequently made to this design on empirical grounds introduced several others.[25] In fact, our final design specifies an asymmetry in as many as twelve out of the total of twenty-one pairs of cells. In ten of these cases the difference in density is of only one level, but with the other two pairs—the I-V, V-I, and the II-V, V-II cells—there is a difference of two density levels.

These asymmetries are obviously intriguing, and further consideration of them as, for example, on the basis in Figure 4.1 will moreover reveal that they can to quite a large extent be understood as conforming to a single pattern. Under our model, we may say, mobility from any of the three white-collar classes of our schema—that is, Classes I, II, and III—into the three blue-collar classes—V, VI, and VII—tends to be less, net of marginal effects, than is mobility of the reverse kind. Thus, by reference to Table 4.4, one can see that the tendency for intergenerational mobility to occur from Class I, II, or III to Class VI or VII, or from Class III to Class V, is only from three-fifths to three-quarters as strong as the tendency for mobility in the reverse direction; while the tendency for such mobility from Class I or II to Class V is only around a half as strong as that for the counter movement. The pattern in question, which accounts for nine out of the twelve cases of asymmetry,[26] arises, we would suggest, chiefly from the way in which the mobility of men of white-collar and blue-collar origins is conditioned by different combinations of advantages, barriers, and preferences.

On the one hand, as we earlier remarked, the advantages of men of Class I, II, and III parentage—in terms of economic, cultural, and social resources—are such as to give them very favourable relative chances of retaining or, in the case of the latter two groupings, of improving their class positions, and this, we may assume, they will generally seek to do: hence the high densities of both immobility and mobility in the top-left corner of our levels matrix. At the same time, though, and again as earlier suggested, 'unsuccessful' men of Class I and II origins may face difficulties in entering occupations within Class V or Class VI because of apprenticeship and work-experience requirements, and may thus be forced into Class III as a *pis aller*. It is, moreover, possible that even where men of white-collar origins have the choice between higher-grade blue-collar work and the lower-level nonmanual employment characteristic of Class III positions, they will opt for the latter to a greater extent than would be indicated by the relatively low 'general desirability' ratings of the occupational prestige groupings that Class III comprises. Thus, the concentration of high densities in the top-left corner of our matrix is offset by the very low densities of the top-right corner.

On the other hand, so far as men of Class V, VI, and VII origins are concerned, there is generally less reason for them to seek to preserve the class positions of their fathers; and some at least of them, one may suppose, will actively pursue mobility, whether within or out of the blue-collar world. Class VI and VII sons, being particularly disadvantaged in their origins, will face major difficulties in any attempt at long-range mobility; but, as we have pointed out, the barriers to entry are less formidable in the case of Class II than of Class I, while Class III (and Class V) positions appear rather open. The net outcome is then that the relative chances of men of blue-collar origins being found in different destination classes tend, in comparison with those of men of white-collar origins, to vary less widely overall and to be rather more smoothly graded. The three bottom rows of our levels matrix, it may be observed, contain no cells of very high density of either mobility or immobility, and all cells are in fact allocated within the range of level 4 to level 7. In effect, thus, the asymmetries apparent between corresponding cells in the outlying corners of the matrix may be seen as largely the counterpart of the differences in density levels on and around the main diagonal to which we previously drew attention.[27]

In conclusion, therefore, there are two aspects of the pattern of social fluidity that we have modelled that would seem to be of chief importance. First, the pattern does in certain major respects bear out standard expectations: that is in showing a strong tendency for immobility towards the peak of the class structure, as represented by the higher professional, administrative and managerial groupings of our Class I; and very low relative chances of mobility in either direction between these groupings and those at the base, as represented by the body of manual wage-workers comprised by our Classes VI and VII. It is in fact possible for the closure and buffer-zone theses still to retain some merit if they are reformulated so as to refer to fluidity rather than to absolute mobility rates.

As we have shown in chapters 2 and 3, the chances of men of all origins, including working-class ones, to accede to higher-level class positions have steadily increased over recent decades in absolute terms; and, during this period, the heterogeneity of the social origins of those holding such positions has in consequence surely grown. None the less, these developments are not only consistent with a situation of no change in relative mobility chances, as we have also shown in chapter 3; but further, with a situation in which the inequalities in such chances that prevail are ones of a quite gross kind, at least as between the higher division of the service class and the working class. It is here, it may be said, that the reality of contemporary British society most strikingly and incontrovertibly deviates from the ideal of genuine openness. And, it should be kept in mind, we are not merely comparing the relative chances of small minority groupings in extreme class locations: Class I of our schema accounts for 10 to 15 per cent of the active male population, and Classes VI and VII together for around 45 per cent.

Secondly, however, it is evident that there are further features of the pattern of fluidity which are of obvious interest but which derive from other characteristics of the classes that we have distinguished than their hierarchical ordering alone, whether this is thought of in terms of levels (as distinct from kinds) of resources or of the general desirability of their constituent occupational groupings. From Figure 4.1, and again from the odds ratios of Table 4.5, it is clear that while the pattern of fluidity as we have represented it certainly takes on a hierarchical form to some extent, this is far from being an entirely regular one—just as, of course, is the case with our class schema itself. In fact, in both the rationale that we provided for the initial design of our model and in our discussion of its application, as empirically modified, to our data, we have sought to develop the same idea: namely, that the different classes of our schema have associated with them as both classes of origin and destination, mobility tendencies that are in some degree specific, and that reflect typical features of the range of class positions that they comprise, both in their hierarchical aspects and otherwise.

Thus, from this point of view, it is not only Class I that should be thought of as being distinctive, in consequence of the superior advantages and social power of its members and the desirability of the positions they occupy. Class IV is also quite clearly distinctive in its mobility tendencies, and by virtue of the fact, we would argue, that it is a class of proprietors and entrepreneurs, although of a small-scale kind. Again, as we have seen, Classes II and III display distinctive patterns of mobility chances in relation to each other and to Class I; and between these three classes together and Classes V, VI, and VII we have found a pattern of consistently asymmetrical mobility tendencies which, we have suggested, reflect differences in the conditions that typically attend mobility from white-collar and from blue-collar origins, including those set by entry requirements to different white-collar and blue-collar positions.

In sum, then, we feel able to claim that our class schema is of clear heuristic and analytical value in the study of the mobility regime of modern British society. As we have explained in chapter 1, we gave our study of social mobility a class basis on account of our primary sociological and extra-sociological interests in the implications of mobility for class formation and action—to which interests the pattern of absolute mobility rates is of most direct relevance. But what has emerged in the present chapter is that in regard to our further interest in openness, and hence in the determination of relative mobility chances within the social division of labour, a class perspective is also highly revealing.

So evident is this in fact that one must be led to question the predominant practice in recent mobility research of taking scales of occupational prestige or socio-economic status as the sole basis of analysis—and to question this practice not so much on ideological grounds as on the grounds, rather, that in this way significant features of mobility processes must tend to be overlooked. While analyses made in terms of such synthetic scales may be able to display certain hierarchical effects in great detail, they would seem likely to blur or obscure distinctions that we have shown to be of substantial importance: for example, those between self-employed and employee groupings, even within the same occupational area; or between groupings differentiated in their market and work situations on the lines that we have labelled white-collar and blue-collar. For occupations that are distinct in these ways will to quite a large extent be bracketed together by a synthetic scale, in the process of all occupations being ordered on the single dimension that the scale represents. The major shortcoming of such instruments, as Westergaard and Resler have observed, lies in the fact that they will often combine 'within one "status" band, groups with quite different positions in the apparatus of production'.[28]

Furthermore—as these same authors also note—this shortcoming leads to another at least potential weakness in mobility analyses based on scales of the kind in question: namely, that they will have difficulty in treating adequately 'issues connected with the transformation of the economy'.[29] Whether, for example, occupational groupings expand or contract in the course of economic development, and at what rate, has relatively little to do with their prestige or socio-economic status, as compared with the particular way in which they are situated within the social division of labour. Thus, studies of mobility conducted in terms of occupation taken as the basis of prestige or status categories may fail to capture fully the effects of structural changes as these impinge on the pattern of absolute rates; and, furthermore, to the extent that, as we have suggested, distinctive mobility tendencies are associated with occupational groupings in respect of their location within the class structure, such studies may also be insensitive to the way in which the pattern of relative rates, or in other words of social fluidity, will also be affected as the evolution of the division of labour proceeds.[30]

NOTES

1. Robert M. Hauser, 'A Structural Model of the Mobility Table', *Social Forces*, vol. 56, 1978. Hauser's model is in fact a special case of a more general statistical model proposed by Leo Goodman, 'Some Multiplicative Models for the Analysis of Cross-Classified Data' in *Proceedings of the 6th Berkeley Symposium on Mathematical Statistics and Probability*, Berkeley: University of California Press, 1972.
2. The same statistic, under the name of the 'mobility ratio' was introduced into the American literature at about the same time. See H. Goldhamer, 'The Analysis of Occupational Mobility', paper presented to the Society for Social Research, Chicago, May 1948; and Rogoff, *Recent Trends in Occupational Mobility*.
3. See Andrea Tyree, 'Mobility Ratios and Association in Mobility Tables', *Population Studies*, vol. 27, 1973. Cf. also Hauser, 'A Structural Model of the Mobility Table'. The first important critique of the index of association was W.Z. Billewicz, 'Some Remarks on the Measurement of Social Mobility', *Population Studies*, vol. 9, 1955–6. In a 'Reply' to Billewicz (ibid.), W. Scott has offered the best defence of the index, as a measure of association in a 'descriptive', or *de facto*, as opposed to an 'analytical' sense. In the former case, it is legitimate that the size of marginal proportions should influence the value of the index; in the latter, not.
4. Using standard notation, the index may be expressed as being for the ij^{th} cell

$$R_{ij} = \frac{f_{ij} N}{f_{i.} f_{.j}}$$

Alternatively, then, we may write in multiplicative form

$$f_{ij} = a b_i c_j d_{ij}$$

where $a = N$, $b_i = f_{i.}/N$, $c_j = f_{.j}/N$, and $d_{ij} = R_{ij}$.

5. 'A Structural Model of the Mobility Table', p. 924.

6. It is also possible, as Hauser has shown, to derive from his model a new mobility ratio which may be calculated for each cell of the table. See further n. 20 below.
7. Cf. n. 17, p. 88 above.
8. A proof is provided in the Annex to this chapter.
9. See in particular Harrison C. White, 'Cause and Effect in Social Mobility Tables', *Behavioural Science*, vol. 8, 1963.
10. Cf. Pierre Bourdieu and Jean-Claude Passeron, *La Reproduction: éléments pour une théorie du système d'enseignement,* Paris: Les Editions de Minuit, 1970, and Bourdieu, 'Cultural Reproduction and Social Reproduction' in Richard Brown (ed.), *Knowledge, Education and Cultural Change,* London: Tavistock, 1973.
11. Cf. Mark S. Granovetter, *Getting a Job: a Study of Contacts and Careers,* Cambridge, Mass.: Harvard University Press, 1974.
12. Hauser refers to such a levels matrix as a 'design matrix'. We would prefer to reserve the latter term to refer to the matrix which specifies the parameters to be estimated in the log-linear model. See the Annex to this chapter.
13. Cf. Bernard and Renaud, 'Contre-mobilité et effets différés'.
14. Cf. Keith Hope, 'Quantifying Constraints on Social Mobility: the Latent Hierarchies of a Contingency Table' in Hope (ed.), *The Analysis of Social Mobility: Methods and Approaches,* Oxford: Clarendon Press, 1972, pp. 180–1.
15. Cf., e.g., the design initially proposed by Hauser for modelling the pattern of fluidity underlying the 1949 mobility data for England and Wales reported by Glass and Hall on the basis of the categories of the Hall–Jones occupational scale. As Hauser observes, this design shows considerable regularity, in that 'the successively lower density zones resemble a set of concentric layers, like those of an onion'. 'A Structural Model of the Mobility Table', p. 933.
16. For purposes of testing the model, we have used the data for our complete sample (including agricultural categories), despite our previous remarks (pp. 51, 70–1) about the possibility that data for men who have yet to reach the stage of 'occupational maturity' may in certain respects create a misleading impression of the extent and pattern of mobility. We do, however, attempt to keep this possibility in mind in subsequent discussion of the model.
17. The measure is one proposed by Goodman, 'A Modified Multiple Regression Approach to the Analysis of Dichotomous Variables, *American Sociological Review*, vol. 37, 1972, based on an interpretation of the χ^2 value as the amount of variation in the frequencies that is left unexplained when a model is fitted. The measure is the percentage reduction achieved by a more complex model in the χ^2 value that is obtained when the simple independence model is fitted to each cell to the contingency table. See further Payne, 'The Log-Linear Model for Contingency Tables', pp. 131–2.
18. If residuals from the model are expressed as natural logs of the ratios of observed to expected frequencies, then, it may be noted, the cells in these rows that we consider for reallocation are all those (and only those) in the table with residuals of ± .2 or greater.
19. We should acknowledge that this value does result from modifications to our design— i.e. from a respecification of the null hypothesis—made in the light of using the χ^2 statistic itself as a fitting criterion. It is therefore reassuring that it is non-significant by quite a wide margin.
20. We could also have reported for each cell of the mobility table the new mobility ratio proposed by Hauser, which may be expressed as being for the ij[th] cell

$$R_{ij}{}^* = \frac{f_{ij}}{F_{ij}} D_{ij}$$

However, we do not in fact present these ratios since, as Hauser has himself observed, with a model that fits well, the array of mobility ratios will add little to what is known from the levels matrix and the parameters. As can be seen from the above expression, the new mobility ratio is in fact a function of the density level for a given cell and its residual under the model fitted.

21. These expectations have obviously a close affinity with those set out in chapter 2 (see pp. 43–4 above) concerning the generic form assumed by absolute mobility rates in modern industrial societies. The fact that expectations concerning absolute and relative rates have not been more clearly differentiated reflects, we would believe, in part a failure to make the conceptual distinction consistently—more common perhaps on the part of commentators than of mobility researchers themselves (cf. p. 59 above)—and in part the lack until recently of adequate techniques for applying the distinction to empirical data.

22. See above, p. 78.

23. i.e. $D_1/D_8 = 12.55$, $D_7/D_4 = 0.35$, and $12.55/0.35 \simeq 36$; or $D_1/D_7 = 7.68$, $D_8/D_4 = 0.21$, and $7.68/0.21 \simeq 36$. (Slight discrepancies in the results of such calculations may occur because of rounding errors.) We could, of course, calculate this, or any other, odds ratio from the observed cell values of Table 4.2. But having obtained a well-fitting model, we would follow the usual statistical practice of taking the values predicted by the model as being the 'true' ones, to which those resulting from our sample are an approximation.

24. It may be added here that in so far as such inheritance tends to occur at a relatively late stage in an individual's working life and to be associated with processes of counter-mobility (cf. pp. 127–9 below), the fact that our data relate to all males aged 20–64 may well mean that an unduly low impression is given of the extent of immobility within Class IV.

25. One was also removed in reallocating the I–IV cell from level 6 to level 5.

26. The other three are those occurring between the II–IV, IV–II, the III–IV, IV–III, and the V–VII, VII–V pairs of cells.

27. Again it could be argued that our all-ages data are likely to underestimate the strength of the pattern in question. Certainly, from results presented in the previous chapter (see p. 72 above), it is clear that younger men will be more likely than older ones to be found in the I–VI, I–VII, II–VI and II–VII cells, and less likely to be found in the corresponding cells in the bottom-left corner of the table—in consequence, that is, of upward mobility achieved in the course of working life.

28. *Class in a Capitalist Society*, p. 287. Examination of the Hall–Jones scale, the Duncan scale, or the H–G scale will readily confirm this claim. This is not of course to say that such scales are invalid for all purposes. For example, we would regard the H–G scale, interpreted as one indicative of the general desirability of occupations, as being very apt to serve as at least the *dependent* variable in studies of the process of occupational attainment.

29. Ibid. As Westergaard and Resler recognize, an argument on these lines against basing mobility studies simply on status or other such-like scales was advanced at a relatively early stage by Theodor Geiger. See his *Soziale Umschichtungen in einer dänischen Mittelstadt,* Aarhus University Press, 1951.

30. Interestingly, Blau and Duncan at one point appear to note precisely such a possibility in remarking that 'The fact that the very occupations that rest on proprietorship and that reveal little mobility in or out have either contracted in size or expanded less than the rest in recent decades may well be a factor that has contributed to the large amount of social mobility observable today.' *The American Occupational Structure*, p. 41. But the dominant style of their subsequent analyses is not such as to permit them to explore this possibility further. It should be added here that distinctive mobility tendencies *may* of course also be associated with occupationally defined prestige or status groupings as well as with classes. But one of the few attempts to spell out the dynamics of such prestige mobility is that by Svalastoga, and this attempt was not in fact borne out by the modelling exercise that Svalastoga based upon it. See his *Prestige, Class and Mobility*, pp. 319–27. Nor have more recent and more sophisticated 'social distance' or 'association' models proved conspicuously more successful in reproducing the data of mobility tables.

ANNEX

THE HAUSER MODEL

We have already outlined the main principles of fitting log-linear models to mobility data in the Annex to the previous chapter. Using the same notation as previously, Hauser's model for a two-way mobility table of origin (respondent's father's) class (P) with I categories, destination (respondent's) class (S) with J categories, and with each cell assigned a density (D) with K categories, is:

$$F_{ij} = \eta t_i^P t_j^S D_{ij} \tag{1}$$
$$i = 1 \dots I, j = 1 \dots J$$

where D_{ij} is chosen from the set of K density parameters t_k^D ($k = 1 \dots K$). Thus model (1) can be presented in an alternative form:

$$F_{ij} = \eta t_i^P t_j^S t_k^D \tag{2}$$
$$i = 1 \dots I, j = 1 \dots J, k = 1 \dots K$$

It can easily be shown that the (second-order) odds ratio is related to the density parameters by the equation

$$\frac{F_{ik} / F_{il}}{F_{jk} / F_{jl}} = \frac{D_{ik} / D_{il}}{D_{jk} / D_{jl}} \tag{3}$$

—where i, j now refer to a pair of origin classes and k, l to a pair of destination classes—by substitution for F_{ij} from (1) in the left-hand side of (2) as follows:

$$\frac{F_{ik} / F_{il}}{F_{jk} / F_{jl}} = \frac{\eta t_i^P t_k^S D_{ik} / \eta t_i^P t_l^S D_{il}}{\eta t_j^P t_k^S D_{jk} / \eta t_j^P t_l^S D_{jl}} = \frac{D_{ik} / D_{il}}{D_{jk} / D_{jl}}$$

since all the η and t terms cancel out.

The multiplicative model can be expressed in linear form for estimation purposes by taking natural logarithms. Model (2) then becomes

$$\log F_{ij} = u + \lambda_i^P + \lambda_j^S + \lambda_k^D \tag{4}$$

where the λs are the logarithms of the corresponding t terms. (Thus, for example, $\lambda_k^D = \log t_k^D$ and $t_k^D = e^{\lambda_k D}$). Model (4) must be reparameterized since only independent parameters can be estimated. There are I−1 independent parameters for the term λ_i^P, J−1 for the term λ_j^S, K−1 for the term λ_k^D, and 1 for the mean. The reparameterization can be done in various ways. Hauser imposes the constraint that the parameters which make up a term sum to zero, and it may be noted that his mobility ratio R_{ij}^* is based on the parameter estimates obtained with this method. We ourselves have used this method for the purposes of our analyses in chapter 3, and the construction of the design matrix for this method follows the principles outlined in the Annex to that chapter. In the present case, however, we have used a different, and more convenient, reparameterization. Here we constrain the parameter for the first category of each term to be zero by dropping the parameter from the estimation; the remaining parameters in the term are then interpreted as deviations from the category dropped. This method is the standard practice with the treatment of independent categorical variables in multiple regression.

The design matrix for this method can be illustrated by means of a 3×3 mobility table with three density levels, as shown in Table A.4.1.

Table A.4.1

A 3×3 mobility table with three density levels

Cell No.	Observed frequency	Father's Class (P) category	Respondent's Class (S) category	Density level (D) category
1	f_{11}	1	1	1
2	f_{21}	2	1	2
3	f_{31}	3	1	3
4	f_{12}	1	2	2
5	f_{22}	2	2	2
6	f_{32}	3	2	3
7	f_{13}	1	3	3
8	f_{23}	2	3	3
9	f_{33}	3	3	3

The design matrix is given in Table A.4.2. For each variable P, S, D in turn, there are N−1 columns, where N is the number of categories in each variable (N = 3 for all variables in the example). The first column for each variable has entry 1 if the cell is category 2, 0 otherwise; the second column has entry 1 if the cell is category 3, 0 otherwise and so on. There is also a column for the mean.

Table A.4.2

Design matrix for the density model for the example in Table N.4.1

Cell	Column Contrast	1 Mean	2 P_2	3 P_3	4 S_2	5 S_3	6 D_2	7 D_3
1	$\log F_{11}$	1	0	0	0	0	0	0
2	$\log F_{21}$	1	1	0	0	0	1	0
3	$\log F_{31}$	1	0	1	0	0	0	1
4	$\log F_{12}$	1	0	0	1	0	1	0
5	$\log F_{22}$	1	1	0	1	0	1	0
6	$\log F_{32}$	1	0	1	1	0	0	1
7	$\log F_{12}$	1	0	0	0	1	0	1
8	$\log F_{22}$	1	1	0	0	1	0	1
9	$\log F_{32}$	1	0	1	0	1	0	1

There are seven parameters to be estimated, and the estimates obtained for the two density parameters D_2 and D_3 are in the additive form, which is given in the case of the model we actually applied to our data in the left hand column of Table 4.4.

The GLIM program (see n. 5, p. 93 above) used for fitting this model automatically sets up the design matrix in this form for the user, who only needs to supply data in the form of Table A.4.1.

CHAPTER 5

Class Mobility: Intergenerational and Work-life Patterns

(*with* CATRIONA LLEWELLYN)

In chapter 2 we presented a critique of certain arguments advanced by contemporary Marxist and 'post-Marxist' writers on the relationship between social mobility and class structure in modern Britain. The main thrust of our critique lay in showing that these arguments largely failed because their authors had underestimated the amount of mobility, and in particular the amount of upward mobility, that has occurred in British society over recent decades. This underestimation, we suggested, resulted in part from a failure to distinguish clearly enough between the extent of restriction on absolute, *de facto* mobility and the extent of inequality in relative mobility chances; and in part from a failure to appreciate fully the nature of structural changes in the social division of labour in Britain, especially in the period from the second world war. In the course of chapters 3 and 4 we have then been able to lend some support to this suggestion by showing that the closure, buffer-zone and counterbalance theses would all have much more to commend them if reformulated so as to refer to relative, rather than to absolute mobility rates—or, in other words, to patterns and trends in social fluidity.

However, it is necessary at the same time to recognize that in this way the theses would of course become ones of most obvious relevance to the question of the degree of openness of British society, rather than to that which for their authors—as for ourselves—is in fact of chief concern: that is, the question of the implications of mobility for class formation and action. In order to address this latter question further, as we would now wish to do, we must return to the consideration of absolute mobility rates, and in fact subject these to a more detailed examination than hitherto. This task we shall seek to accomplish by way of developing more fully another theme of our critique in chapter 2, which was there left to some extent implicit.

Given the interests of the writers who concerned us, it was, we felt, somewhat surprising that they should pay relatively little attention to the way in which processes of intragenerational, or work-life, mobility could play a crucial part in mediating both class mobility and immobility as viewed in intergenerational perspective. The tendency was rather—as seen most clearly in the arguments underlying the counterbalance thesis—to regard mobility patterns within modern societies as becoming progressively simplified, as a result of the placement of individuals within the division of labour being made increasingly dependent upon their level of education and formal qualifications. Thus, it was suggested, mobility chances become effectively realized at the point of the individual's initial entry into work, on emerging from the educational system, and the likelihood of significant changes occurring in his occupational level or class position in the course of his working life is correspondingly reduced. However, contrary to this view, we were able to show that the data of our national inquiry of 1972 gave no indication of any secular decline in the extent of intragenerational movement over the last thirty to forty years—and not all that surprisingly so, it could be added, since for most of this time the evolution of the occupational structure had indeed tended to outpace that of at least 'mainstream' educational institutions.

In the present chapter, therefore, our aim is to investigate further the interplay between patterns of intra- and intergenerational mobility, with the question of the potentialities for class formation chiefly in mind. Not only is this interplay basic to the whole process of 'social metabolism', through which individuals are distributed and redistributed within the occupational and class structures over time; but further, of course, it directly conditions the nature of individual experience within this process, and would thus in turn seem likely to be a key determinant of how individuals respond subjectively to these major structural features of their society that objectively confront them.

DATA SOURCES

To some large extent we shall draw here on the same material as we have used in previous chapters: that is, the occupational mobility data of our 1972 inquiry organized in terms of our class schema. The starting point of all the analyses reported will in fact be with Table 5.1, which is a three-way mobility matrix, based on the collapsed version of the schema, and displaying in complete form the data on mobility from origins, via first occupation, to 1972 position that were earlier used in constructing Figure 2.1. However, it will be noted that in Table 5.1 the cell values are expressed as percentages of our total sample (N = 9,423) rather than, as is usual in mobility tables, of the number of respondents, or of their fathers, within a given class. Our aim here is to show the distribution of our respondents across the set of 'routes' of mobility (or immobility) that the cells of the table define.[1] For the purposes of the systematic examination of these routes that we shall undertake, it will be convenient to label subsequently the collapse of Classes I and II as S ('service'); of Classes III, IV, and V as I ('intermediate'); and of Classes VI and VII as W ('working'). Thus each of the twenty-seven routes represented in the table may be identified by a combination of these letters, relating respectively to classes of origin, of first occupation and of destination as of 1972.

Although then quite numerous, the routes displayed in Table 5.1 are still only rather crudely characterized, and we shall therefore seek to introduce greater detail into our accounts of them in two different ways. First, in examining any particular route we may revert to analysis in terms of the classes of our full sevenfold schema, and further, where it would appear appropriate, in terms of the constituent occupational categories of these classes. This we shall do especially in attempting to bring out more clearly patterns of intergenerational movement. Secondly, we shall in this chapter supplement the data of the 1972 survey with results from a follow-up inquiry carried out two years later, in which in re-interviews with men in a number of subsamples drawn from our 1972 respondents, we collected complete work-histories. In the 1974 inquiry (described in full in the Appendix to the first edition) we concentrated our attention—out of both substantive and practical considerations—on men who were aged 25 to 49 in 1974, that is, born 1925-49; and who in intergenerational

Table 5.1

Distribution of respondents by class of father at respondent's age 14, by respondent's class at time of first full-time occupation, and by respondent's class in 1972

Father's class	Respondent's class: first full-time occupation	Respondent's class: 1972			
		I and II	III–V	VI and VII	Total
		percentage of total sample			
	I and II	3·9	0·4	0·1	4·4
I and II	III–V	2·2	1·8	0·6	4·6
	VI and VII	1·7	1·2	1·4	4·3
	Total	7·8	3·4	2·1	13·3
	I and II	2·8	0·6	0·2	3·6
III–V	III–V	3·1	4·4	1·8	9·3
	VI–VII	3·1	7·1	9·7	19·9
	Total	9·0	12·1	11·7	32·8
	I and II	2·1	0·5	0·2	2·8
VI and VII	III–V	2·6	4·6	3·3	10·5
	VI–VII	3·6	9·6	27·4	40·6
	Total	8·3	14·7	30·9	53·9
Total		25·1	30·2	44·7	100·0

N = 9423

terms appeared as immobile *or* as having experienced *long-range* mobility either into or out of Class I of our schema. In Table 5.2 we show from exactly which cells of an intergenerational mobility matrix based on the schema the 652 respondents to the follow-up inquiry were drawn. As can be seen, the work-history material that we have available will relate to only sixteen out of the forty-nine intergenerational transitions possible, and its value is thus correspondingly limited, as well as by the restricted age-range of the respondents. None the less, this material can still serve to bring out in an instructive fashion some of the biographical, diachronic realities which lie behind the essentially synchronic information that the conventional mobility table provides.

We may now proceed by considering in turn the cells of Table 5.1 that are indicative of (i) intergenerational stability within the three classes distinguished; (ii) intergenerational mobility between intermediate-class and working-class positions—which, as we have earlier noted, we would not think could be usefully characterized in 'vertical' terms; (iii) intergenerational mobility which could be regarded as upward—that is, mobility into the service class from other class origins; and (iv) intergenerational mobility downward—that is, from service-class origins to other class positions.

PATTERNS OF INTERGENERATIONAL STABILITY

Of our 9,423 respondents, 730, or 8 per cent, were, as Table 5.1 shows, the sons of Class I and II fathers who were themselves found in 1972 in Class I and II occupations, this figure being equal to 59 per cent of all such sons in our sample.

Table 5.2

Distribution of respondents to the 1974 follow-up inquiry, by class of father and own class in 1972

Father's class (at respondent's age 14)	Respondent's class (1972)						
	I	II	III	IV	V	VI	VII
I	1:2 75		1:1 31	1:1a 6	1:1b 5	1:1 13	1:1 13
II							
III	1:1 51		1:1 32				
IV	1:1a 20			1:1a 31			
V	1:1b 46				1:1b 40		
VI	1:1 77					1:4 67	
VII	1:1 57						1:4 88

Key: Number of re-interviews achieved ⟶
Sampling ratio applied to 1972
respondents (age 25–49) ⟶

Notes:(a) Respondents in H–G categories 11 and 13 not included.
(b) Respondents in H–G category 15 not included.

A relatively high level of intergenerational stability of this kind found towards the peak of the class structure is consistent with what has come to be seen as the generic form taken by occupationally based mobility patterns within industrial societies: those who hold advantaged positions are presumed to have not only a strong motivation to see their children succeed them in such positions but, in addition, the command over resources, both material and cultural, to enable them to realize their ambitions in a high proportion of cases. However, what is less in line with such standard expectations is the further finding that in fact only half of the men in question, or 4 per cent of our sample, started on their working lives in a Class I or II occupation—i.e. represent the **S-S-S** pattern: the other half began work in either a lower-level nonmanual or manual occupation covered by one of the remaining classes of our schema—i.e. have followed the **S-I-S** or **S-W-S** patterns. In other words, over the period to which our data relate, intergenerational stability at the higher levels of the class structure has to a substantial degree been maintained through what we have termed countermobility: that is, work-life movement which has the effect of returning an individual back to his class of origin, following some initial shift away on his entry into employment.

Why this is the case may be made more apparent if we examine the **S-S-S** route at the level of the occupational categories which constitute Classes I and II. It emerges that this route is to a large extent confined to men entering work via one particular division or *situs* within the service class, namely, that of professional and higher-grade technical positions: men who have 'succeeded' their fathers in Classes I and II have not often gained direct access on entry into work other than via professional and technical employment. In Figure 5.1, the professional and technical groupings within Classes I and II are distinguished from the remaining, chiefly administrative and managerial groupings. It can be seen that over four-fifths of those following the **S-S-S** pattern first entered work via one or other of the former categories—and further, that these men were for the most part found in these same categories in 1972.[2]

Conversely, then, where intergenerational stability results from men of Class I and II origins achieving positions within the administrative and managerial *situs* of the service class, it is the counter-mobile, **S-I-S** and **S-W-S** routes which play the major role. Figure 5.2 shows that although access to professional and technical occupations via these routes is by no means precluded, over three-fifths of the men who had followed them were found in administrative and managerial categories. Considered in terms of our sevenfold class schema, we may add, this counter-mobility occurs through certain rather well-defined channels, the significance of which will emerge more fully later on. With the **S-I-S** route, 85 per cent of the men concerned started work in a Class III occupation, that is, in one of a rank-and-file white-collar character; and in the **S-W-S** one, 68 per cent started in a Class VI, that is, skilled manual one.

To throw further light on these patterns of intergenerational stability within the service class, we may turn to the work-history data of our 1974 inquiry relating to men (born 1925–49) who were the sons of Class I fathers and who in 1972 were themselves found in Class I occupations (N = 75). In terms of our three-point analysis, fifty-two, or 69 per cent, had followed the **S-S-S** route, and of these men, as would be expected from our more general findings, the large majority—forty-one or 79 per cent—had started work in a professional or higher technical occupation. Further, though, the work-history material brings out the point that these respondents had experienced a very high degree of work-life *continuity*;[3] only eight, or 15 per cent, had at any time moved *from* a Class I occupation to one at a lower level, and such 'absences' averaged only slightly more than two years in length[4] (in relation to an average duration of working life of eighteen years). With the remaining men, representing the **S-I-S** and **S-W-S** routes, it was also the case that, having once reached a Class I position, they had rarely moved away from it—indeed, in only three cases out of the twenty-three. But what is also revealed by our work-history data is the extent of the mobility that these men had experienced between different occupational groupings *prior to* the process of counter-mobility being achieved. If, for example, we count shifts between occupational categories which entail changes of class position within our sevenfold schema, we find that representatives of the **S-I-S** and **S-W-S** routes average 2·4 per man—as against 0·4 per man for those following the **S-S-S** pattern.[5]

What is of major interest here is the suggestion that counter-mobility to the higher levels of the class structure is by no means always a straightforward matter: rather, it seems, it may often come about only through a relatively complex series of work-life movements. The contrast is thus heightened between

Figures 5.1 to 5.6
Patterns of intergenerational stability

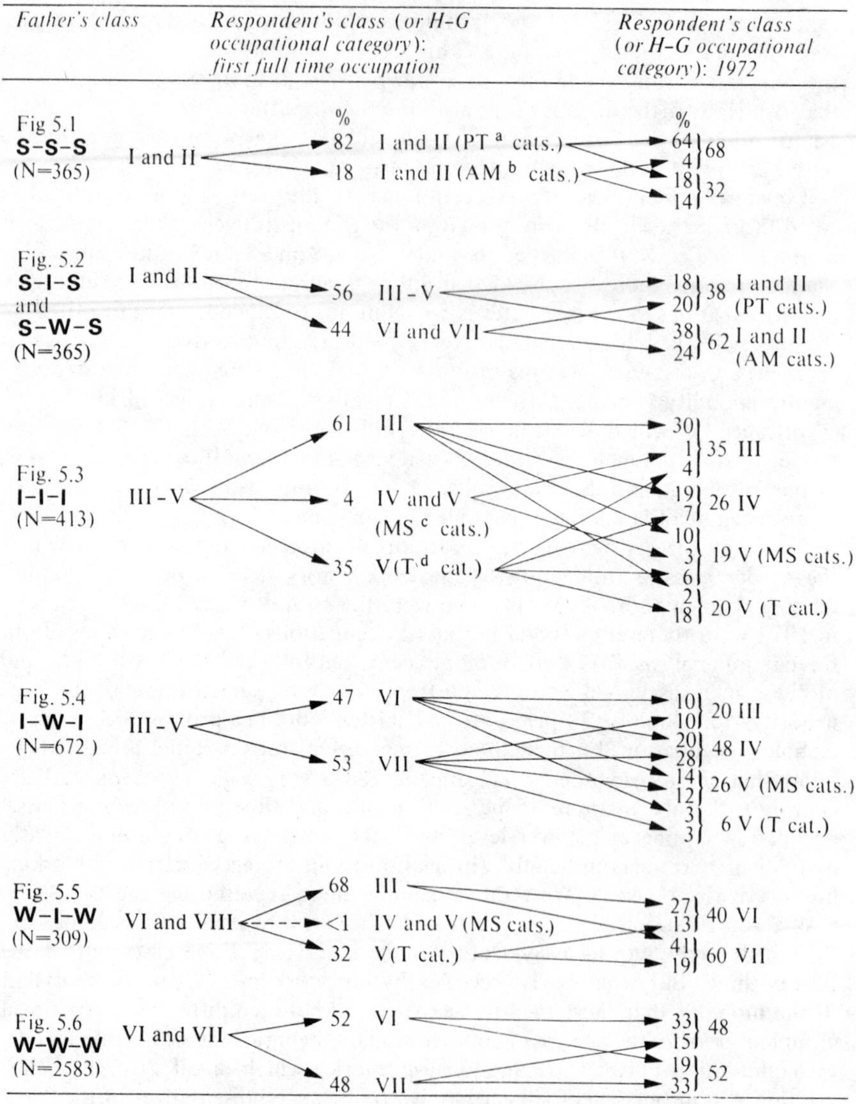

Father's class	Respondent's class (or H-G occupational category): first full time occupation	Respondent's class (or H-G occupational category): 1972

Fig 5.1
S–S–S
(N=365)

I and II

%
82   I and II (PT [a] cats.)
18   I and II (AM [b] cats.)

%
64} 68
4}
18} 32
14}

Fig. 5.2
S–I–S
and
S–W–S
(N=365)

I and II

56   III–V
44   VI and VII

18} 38   I and II (PT cats.)
20}
38} 62   I and II (AM cats.)
24}

Fig. 5.3
I–I–I
(N=413)

III–V

61   III
4   IV and V (MS [c] cats.)
35   V (T [d] cat.)

30}
1} 35 III
4}
19} 26 IV
7}
10}
3} 19 V (MS cats.)
6}
2} 20 V (T cat.)
18}

Fig. 5.4
I–W–I
(N=672)

III–V

47   VI
53   VII

10} 20 III
10}
20} 48 IV
28}
14} 26 V (MS cats.)
12}
3} 6 V (T cat.)
3}

Fig. 5.5
W–I–W
(N=309)

VI and VIII

68   III
<1   IV and V (MS cats.)
32   V (T cat.)

27} 40 VI
13}
41} 60 VII
19}

Fig. 5.6
W–W–W
(N=2583)

VI and VII

52   VI
48   VII

33} 48
15}
19} 52
33}

Notes: (a) PT cats. = Professional and higher technical categories (H–G: 1, 2, 6, 9, 10).
(b) AM cats. = Administrative and managerial categories (H–G: 3, 4, 5, 7, 8, 12, 14, 16).
(c) MS cats. = Manual supervisory categories (H–G: 17, 20).
(d) T cat. = Lower technical category (H–G: 15).

this mode of arriving at intergenerational stability and that whereby the sons of men in high-class positions proceed, on completion of their full-time education —and presumably on the basis chiefly of their educational attainments—directly into positions comparable to their fathers'. Although those following the **S-I-S** and **S-W-S** routes did first attain Class I occupations at what would seem a fairly early stage in their lives, the average age being just over 25 years, this was still almost five years more than the average for representatives of the **S-S-S** pattern. In fact, almost all of those men who were counter-mobile to Class I left school within two years of the minimum age: that is to say, they averaged almost ten years in work before counter-mobility was achieved.

Moving now to those routes which are indicative of intergenerational stability within our intermediate classes—that is, the **I-I-I, I-S-I,** and **I-W-I** patterns—we may note first that they account for 1,138 of our respondents, equal, as is shown in Table 5.1, to 12 per cent of the total sample, or to 37 per cent of all respondents whose fathers were allocated to these classes. Consistently with standard expectations in regard to occupationally based mobility flows—which imply that mobility should be greatest in the middle ranges of the social hierarchy—this latter figure represents a lower rate of intergenerational stability than that found in the case of Classes I and II. And from Table 5.1 it can also be seen that, still more than within the latter classes, such stability within the intermediate bloc is dependent upon counter-mobility. Only a third of the respondents in question, or 4 per cent of our sample, have in fact followed the **I-I-I** route. Furthermore, in the light of our earlier remarks on the heterogeneity of this bloc, it is of relevance here to note that *within* the **I-I-I** pattern, as it were, a great deal of mobility occurs among the three classes of the sevenfold schema that are involved. Indeed, we find that only a minority of the representatives of this pattern, 41 per cent, had not moved intergenerationally between these classes; and that with only 25 per cent was there stability across each of the three points of the route. In more detail, 11 per cent of these respondents originated in Class III and were found in a Class III occupation in 1972, with 10 per cent having started work in such an occupation; while the corresponding proportions for Class IV were 13 per cent and 3 per cent, and for Class V 17 per cent and 12 per cent. It must therefore be recognized that, in this case, even among men who appear as highly stable according to the typology generated by Table 5.1, some far from negligible amount of shifting between different class positions has in fact occurred.

To some extent, this amount of movement may be understood by turning again, as with Classes I and II, to examine the pattern of entry into work. Within our bloc of intermediate classes, one can, as within the service class, and indeed still more sharply, distinguish certain groupings of occupations through which entry into work is quite regularly made and others through which entry occurs only rarely. So far as the **I-I-I** pattern is concerned, Figure 5.3 shows that of the occupations taken up on initial entry into work, three-fifths were in the rank-and-file white-collar categories constituting Class III and a further third in the lower-grade technicians category of Class V (H-G category 15). Entry into work through the self-employed groupings of Class IV, or through the manual supervisory groupings within Class V (H-G categories 17 and 20) is extremely limited.[6] In other words, the sons of small independents and also of men of foreman grade have, almost entirely, had the experience of beginning work in different locations within the division of labour from those occupied by their fathers when they themselves were around school-leaving age, even if they still remained within the range of intermediate-class positions.

These restrictions on initial entry into Classes III–V are, moreover, clearly of relevance to the importance of counter-mobility. In the case of men of inter-mediate-class origins, the possibility of course exists of counter-mobility occur-ring from an initial placement in either a Class I or II or a Class VI or VII occu-pation. But in fact, as Table 5.1 indicates, the former I–S–I pattern is almost negligible, being followed by less than 1 per cent of our respondents.[7] Thus, counter-mobility back to intermediate-class positions is overwhelmingly in the form of movement from manual employment, i.e. of the I–W–I route which accounts for 7 per cent of our total sample. From Figure 5.4 it can then be seen that three-quarters of the representatives of this route were found in 1972 in those self-employed and manual supervisory occupations into which direct entry is effectively barred—as compared with less than half of those men rep-resenting the I–I–I pattern. It is also of interest here to observe that while with counter-mobility from manual first jobs back to service-class positions—i.e. the S–W–S pattern—over two-thirds of first jobs were, as we reported, in skilled categories, with the I–W–I pattern less than half were skilled.

It is thus evident from our three-point analyses alone that intergenerational stability within the intermediate classes must be recognized as very often the outcome of sequences of work-life movement. Further, though, when we turn to the relevant work-history material from our follow-up inquiry, not only is this conclusion amply confirmed, it is also shown to be one that must be devel-oped in a way that renders the idea of such stability still more problematical. For example, if we consider respondents to this inquiry who were the sons of Class III fathers and themselves in Class III occupations in 1972 (N = 32), we discover that while twenty-one, or 66 per cent, of these men had also begun work in such occupations, that is, were representatives of the I–I–I pattern, only nine had in fact, up to 1974, remained continuously in Class III or other inter-mediate-class positions. Half had on at least one occasion been in manual employ-ment, and already in the two-year period between our inquiries eight men had moved into Class I or II positions. Over all, occupational movements entailing shifts of class position, in terms of our sevenfold class schema, averaged 2.4 per man.

Again, if we examine the work-histories of respondents (N = 31) who were intergenerationally stable in self-employed, Class IV occupations (excluding those of H–G categories 11 and 13), we find, as we might anticipate from our earlier analysis, that most, twenty-five or 81 per cent, have followed the counter-mobile, I–W–I route; but further, that this information in itself gives a rather inadequate characterization of their mobility experience. This is in fact quite extensive, with the average number of work-life shifts in class position being 2.3 per man. The suggestion is thus here reinforced that counter-mobility is not to be seen as invariably a straightforward process—and not even where, as in the case in ques-tion, it might seem likely to result from the transmission of capital or of a 'going concern'. Of the thirty-one (all, it should be remembered, under the age of 50) six had in fact already moved at least once *from* self-employment *to* employee status in the course of their working lives to 1974. We have shown in the preceding chapter that there is a strong tendency towards intergenerational immobility within Class IV; but this, we can now see, should not be equated, so far at least as the lower-level groupings within this class are concerned, with a tendency towards a marked degree of either intergenerational or work-life continuity. It can safely be taken only as indicating that those men who are at any one time found in Class IV positions will have a relatively high probability of being the sons of fathers who, at one time, had also held such positions.

Finally, with men (N = 40) included in the 1974 inquiry as ones following their fathers in the supervisory categories within Class V, we find that while twenty-five, or 63 per cent, began work in manual jobs, that is, represent the I-W-I pattern, the most notable feature of their work-histories, whether constituting counter-mobility or not, is their very 'disorderly' nature:[8] in this case, shifts in class position average as high as 3.3 per man. It is of particular note that eleven men had already been in *and out* of supervisory positions—that is, back to rank-and-file manual jobs—at least once before 1972; and that nine had moved from supervisory status, to either rank-and-file or higher-level positions, between 1972 and 1974.

One is thus led to the view that within our bloc of intermediate classes intergenerational immobility, as indicated in the manner of conventional mobility tables, will often be more apparent than real. This is so because the occupational groups forming these classes would not seem to be, in comparison, say, with those of Classes I and II, ones which men have a low probability of leaving, and which may therefore be rather reliably taken as 'destinations' in their working lives. On the contrary, they are ones which, on account, as we will later suggest, of their particular structural locations, men tend relatively often to move out of, either through choice or constraint. Hence, those respondents to a mobility inquiry who are classified as intergenerationally stable on the grounds that both they and their fathers were found in such groupings at particular points in time must in fact be seen as forming a collectivity which is itself far from stable—that is, in the sense of being liable to considerable short-term fluctuations in its composition.[9]

The remaining routes leading to intergenerational stability are those pertaining to the working class—the W-W-W, W-S-W, and W-I-W patterns. From Table 5.1, the first thing to recognize is that these are numerically much more important than those we have previously considered—covering 2,915 of our respondents, or 31 per cent of the total sample. This figure represents a level of intergenerational stability within Classes VI and VII of 57 per cent, which, in line with standard expectations, is only a little below that of Classes I and II and clearly above that of the intermediate classes. However, what is also evident from Table 5.1 is that the part played in this respect by counter-mobility is far less in Classes VI and VII than in either Classes I and II or III-V. Of those men who were found, like their fathers, in manual employment, 89 per cent, or 27 per cent of our sample, had first entered work in a manual job or, in other words, were representatives of the W-W-W pattern. Of obvious relevance here is the fact that the rank-and-file manual occupations comprised by Classes VI and VII are all ones of a kind into which men may readily move on first entering work; that is, which do not show any particular tendency to recruit via work-life advancement.[10]

Where counter-mobility to Classes VI and VII does occur, then, as Table 5.1 further shows, it overwhelmingly takes the form of the **W-I-W** route, which accounts for 3 per cent of the total sample: the **W-S-W** pattern, like the **I-S-I** one, is scarcely in evidence. From the further detail of Figure 5.5, it can be seen that representatives of the **W-I-W** pattern had first jobs of a still more restricted range than did men following the **I-I-I** one. Subsequently, in 1972, 40 per cent were found in Class VI, skilled manual jobs and 60 per cent in Class VII, non-skilled jobs. Such patterns of movement, it may be argued, need to be viewed in a rather different light from counter-mobility occurring in other class contexts. They would seem to have the character, if not necessarily of failures to escape from class origins, then at all events of merely a 'detour' in the working lives of those who follow them, in the sense that they lead back only to a type of occu-pation into which many men of similar origins will have entered directly.[11]

As regards the far more important **W-W-W** pattern, further analysis indicates that although a fair amount of mobility occurs between Classes VI and VII, the extent of such shifting at the level of our seven-class schema is still appreciably less than with the **I-I-I** transition. A majority of those representing the **W-W-W** pattern—58 per cent—were found in the same class as that accorded to their father, and 42 per cent were in the same class at all three points in the route. In more detail, 28 per cent appeared as intergenerationally stable in Class VI, 21 per cent having also entered work in a skilled category; and 30 per cent appeared as intergenerationally stable in Class VII, with 21 per cent having entered work in a nonskilled category. Figure 5.6 illustrates further the patterns of work-life mobility that are involved. However, it should by now be evident that our three-point analyses vary greatly in the reliability of the impressions that they create in this respect, and once more therefore we may usefully set their results against those of our 1974 inquiry.

From this source, we have work-histories for subsamples of men who were the sons of Class VI fathers and who were themselves found in Class VI occu-pations in 1972; and likewise for the sons of Class VII fathers found in Class VII occupations. Of the former (N=67) all but five, or 93 per cent, had followed the **W-W-W** transition, the remainder representing the **W-I-W** pattern. Although only a third of these men had been consistently in skilled manual jobs up to 1974, overall the extent of occupational mobility entailing changes in class position was relatively low. The average number of such moves was 1·9 per man, and moreover 60 per cent of the total were ones made between skilled and non-skilled manual grades. In fact, forty-two men, equal to 63 per cent of all in question, and to 68 per cent of representatives of the **W-W-W** transition, had never been employed as other than manual wage-workers; and for those who had, the average length of time spent in nonmanual work was just over three years (as against an average work-life duration of twenty-one years). A particu-larly high level of consistency, it may be added, existed in the case of those representatives of the **W-W-W** transition within Class VI who had also begun work in a skilled job. These men (N=48) averaged only 1·2 shifts in class position and thirty-nine, or 81 per cent, had remained continually in manual employment.

With men intergenerationally stable in Class VII (N = 88) the degree of continuity was less, though not substantially so. The **W-W-W** pattern was again dominant, accounting for seventy-four, or 84 per cent, of the total, but only a quarter had remained in nonskilled manual jobs throughout their working lives. Shifts in class position averaged 2·3 per man, with 55 per cent being ones in and out of other—that is, skilled—manual occupations. The proportion of those whose work experience was entirely restricted to manual employment was 56 per cent, or 66 per cent of those following the **W-W-W** route; and those with experience of nonmanual occupations had spent on average just over four years per man in such work (as against an average work-life duration of twenty-four years).

From the foregoing, one may then conclude that intergenerational stability within Classes VI and VII is, at all events, associated with work-life continuity to a greater extent than within our intermediate classes: counter-mobility is of less significance, and there is in general less shifting of class positions. The comparison with Classes I and II is somewhat more complex. On the one hand, work-life movement in the form of counter-mobility is again less important to stability within Classes VI and VII; but, on the other, Class I occupations at least are, once achieved, less likely to be left than are manual ones, although the 'retentiveness' of the latter clearly varies a good deal.

PATTERNS OF INTERGENERATIONAL MOBILITY:
WORKING CLASS/INTERMEDIATE CLASSES

Among our 9,423 respondents, there were 1,385, or 15 per cent of our sample, whose fathers had been in manual employment but who were themselves found in 1972 in intermediate-class positions, this figure being equal to 27 per cent of all men of Class VI and VII origins. As Table 5.1 indicates, just under a third of these respondents, or just under 5 per cent of our sample, appear as directly mobile into an intermediate-class position on entry into work—i.e. had followed the **W-I-I** route; while the remainder, who had reached such a position indirectly, had almost entirely begun work in manual employment—i.e. represented the **W-W-I** pattern. The **W-S-I** route, like others implying downward movement from an initial occupation in Classes I or II, is of negligible importance.

As shown in Figure 5.7, men following the direct, **W-I-I** route to intermediate-class positions had first jobs which were confined to the rank-and-file white-collar categories forming Class III or to the technicians category of Class V to a similar extent to those of representatives of the **W-I-W** pattern—although with fewer having made their entry via the former groupings and more via the latter. At the same time, it may be noted that in their subsequent 1972 occupations these men were more often found in both lower technical *and* rank-and-file white-collar occupations than were those who had followed either the **I-I-I** or **I-W-I** routes. (Figures 5.3 and 5.4). With the indirect **W-W-I** route, accounting for 10 per cent of our respondents, Figure 5.8 shows that while more men began work in skilled manual categories than with followers of the **I-W-I** pattern (Figure 5.4), their 1972 distribution was similar to that of the latter in showing

Figures 5.7 to 5.10
Patterns of intergenerational mobility: working class/intermediate class

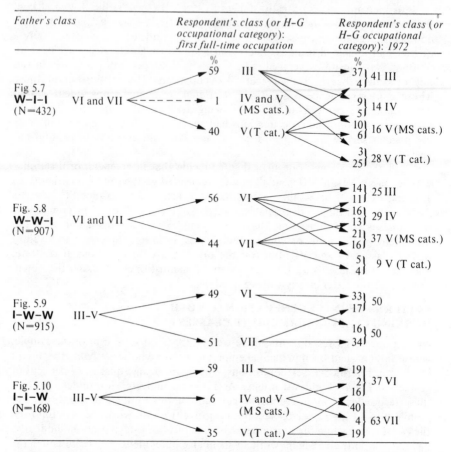

Father's class	Respondent's class (or H-G occupational category): first full-time occupation	Respondent's class (or H-G occupational category): 1972

a relatively high proportion in those intermediate-class occupations into which direct entry is more or less precluded—but with a bias towards the foremen categories within Class V rather than the self-employed ones of Class IV.

In the case of those routes shown in Table 5.1 that are indicative of inter-generational stability, we have systematically raised the question of how far they reflect work-life continuity: in the case of those routes indicative of inter-generational mobility, the question may correspondingly be posed of how far this mobility can be seen as *permanent*, in the sense, at least, of implying that the individual has made some more or less decisive departure from his class of origin. Thus, with those of our respondents who represent the **W–I–I** and **W–W–I** patterns, what we would wish to ask is whether there are grounds for supposing that the positions in which they were found in 1972 are ones of a kind in which they are likely to remain (or from which they may move on to others still further removed from their origins) or whether, on the other hand, they are ones from which they are likely to be counter-mobile back to working-class occupations like those of their fathers.

The transitions in question are not, unfortunately, ones for which our 1974 inquiry can provide work-history material of direct relevance. Nevertheless, there would seem little reason for us to depart here from the general conclusion which we reached on the basis of such material previously considered: namely, that intermediate-class positions are ones from which men move to different class positions with a greater frequency than they do from others. One implication is, then, that some of those men who have followed the **W-I-I** and **W-W-I** routes may be expected to, as it were, confirm their break with their working-class origins by moving on to service-class occupations. For example, for reasons which will emerge fully later, this may be thought especially likely among those representatives of the **W-I-I** pattern whose entry and 1972 occupations were in Class III or the Class V technical category.[12] On the other hand, for representatives of both patterns whose 1972 occupations were in Class IV or Class V supervisory categories—a far larger number of men—movement back to a working-class position must be regarded as the more probable, particularly in view of the degree of disorder which was in fact revealed in the work-histories of 1974 respondents who appeared as intergenerationally stable in occupations of this kind. Assuming that men of working-class origins would be *more* likely than the latter to move away to manual jobs,[13] the data earlier reported would indeed lead one to suppose that perhaps as many as a third of representatives of the **W-I-I** and **W-W-I** patterns found in self-employed and manual supervisory categories in 1972 would *already* have been in and out of such positions at least once before that date.

We may now turn to men who appear in Table 5.1 as having been intergenerationally mobile in the reverse fashion to those just considered—that is, who have followed the **I-W-W**, **I-I-W**, and **I-S-W** routes. Together, these men number 1,104, equal to 12 per cent of our sample and to 36 per cent of all men of intermediate-class origins. In this case it can, however, be seen that one transition, that is, the direct, **I-W-W** route, is of predominant importance, accounting for 83 per cent of all respondents involved. In so far as mobility of the kind in question has come about indirectly, it has, as Table 5.1 further shows, been effectively restricted to the **I-I-W** route.

From the more detailed analyses of Figures 5.9 and 5.10, one may note in the **I-W-W** case the close similarity of the work-life shifts between skilled and nonskilled manual categories with those occurring within the **W-W-W** route (Figure 5.6); and in the **I-I-W** case, the similarity with the **W-I-W** route (Figure 5.5), at least in the relatively high proportion of men found in 1972 in non-skilled manual grades. In other words, the patterns of collective work-life mobility of these intergenerationally mobile men would seem, at this level of analysis, fairly homogeneous with those of men who appear in our data as intergenerationally stable in working-class positions. From our work-history data we know, however, that a large minority of the latter have in fact at some time been in (lower-level) nonmanual occupations of one kind or another. Thus, while our 1974 inquiry again gives us no information of direct relevance, we may expect that among representatives of the preponderant **I-W-W** pattern, as well as among those of the I–I–W one, many men, probably in fact a majority, would already have moved at least once from a manual to a nonmanual occupation before we encountered them—the assumption here being that men themselves of inter-mediate-class origins would be more likely to make such moves than men of working-class origins.[14] Moreover, even with men of intermediate-class origins who have been continuously engaged in manual work, the recruitment patterns of Class IV and of Class V supervisory occupations in particular would make it difficult to say that counter-mobility back to intermediate-class positions was effectively ruled out for them, at least until they had reached a quite late stage in their working lives. In sum, then, it would seem safe to suppose that inter-generational mobility following the I–W–W and I–I–W routes comprises a still larger impermanent element than that occurring via the reverse, W–I–I and W–W–I routes.

PATTERNS OF INTERGENERATIONAL MOBILITY: UPWARD

We treat as upward intergenerational mobility the movement of individuals into Classes I and II from other class origins. Of our respondents, 1,639 fell into cells of Table 5.1 indicative of mobility of this kind: 855, or 9 per cent of the total sample, coming from Class III–V origins, and equal to 28 per cent of all men of such origins; and 784, or 8 per cent of the total, coming from Class VI and VII origins, and equal to 15 per cent of all such origins. As in the previous section, we may usefully distinguish between mobility occurring directly and indirectly; that is, by, on the one hand, the I–S–S and W–S–S routes, accounting for 5 per cent of our sample and, on the other, the I–I–S, W–I–S, I–W–S, and W–W–S routes, which account for 12 per cent.

As regards the former, what is of immediate interest is the relatively low proportion of our respondents who have followed them. A basic reason why this is so is that direct access to Classes I and II for men of lower-class origins is—not surprisingly—restricted to no lesser extent than for the sons of Class I and II fathers to occupations in professional and technical categories. This is illustrated in Figures 5.11 and 5.12, which may be compared with Figure 5.1.

In the case of the indirect routes—that is, ones implying work-life advance—through which mobility into Classes I and II has been chiefly gained, more detailed analysis helps in fact to simplify our presentation. It emerges that both in routes via intermediate- and via working-class entry occupations, almost exactly the same patterns of work-life movement have been collectively experienced by men of intermediate and working-class origins alike. Our data for the I–I–S and W–I–S, and for the I–W–S and W–W–S routes can therefore be conveniently combined, as is done in Figures 5.13 and 5.14.

From the former, it can be seen that men following the I–I–S and W–I–S routes entered work predominantly through the rank-and-file white-collar occupations of Class III—more so than with representatives of the I–I–I, W–I–W, W–I–I, or I–I–W patterns, and to a comparable extent to men of Class I and II origins who were counter-mobile via the S–I–S route. Like the latter also (see Figure 5.2), the respondents in question were then found in 1972 mostly in occupations in the administrative and managerial *situs* of the service class, for which the occupational categories comprised by Class III must be clearly regarded

Figures 5.11 to 5.14
Patterns of intergenerational mobility: upward

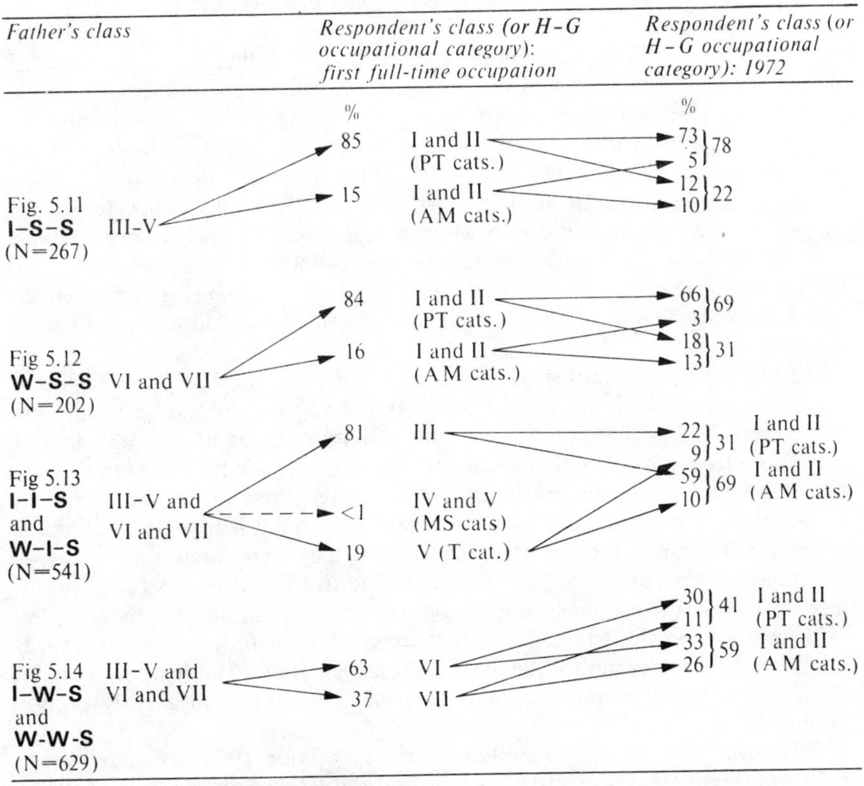

Father's class	Respondent's class (or H–G occupational category): first full-time occupation	Respondent's class (or H–G occupational category): 1972

Fig. 5.11
I–S–S III–V
(N=267)

85 — I and II (PT cats.) — 73} 78 / 5
15 — I and II (AM cats.) — 12} 22 / 10

Fig 5.12
W–S–S VI and VII
(N=202)

84 — I and II (PT cats.) — 66} 69 / 3
16 — I and II (AM cats.) — 18} 31 / 13

Fig 5.13
I–I–S III–V and
and   VI and VII
W–I–S
(N=541)

81 — III — 22} 31 / 9 — I and II (PT cats.)
<1 — IV and V (MS cats) — 59} 69 / 10 — I and II (AM cats.)
19 — V (T cat.)

Fig 5.14 III–V and
I–W–S VI and VII
and
W–W–S
(N=629)

63 — VI — 30} 41 / 11 — I and II (PT cats.)
37 — VII — 33} 59 / 26 — I and II (AM cats.)

as a crucial catchment area.[15] In turn, from Figure 5.14, it emerges that men who appear as upwardly mobile into Classes I and II after starting work in manual jobs began in a majority of cases in skilled grades—more frequently than representatives of the **I–W–I, W–W–W, W–W–I,** or **I–W–W** patterns, and again to a similar extent to men who were counter-mobile via this route to Classes I and II, that is, followers of the **S–W–S** pattern. Again, too, the similarity persists in that both those upwardly mobile and those counter-mobile from manual first jobs (Figure 5.2) divide somewhat more equally in their present occupations between the professional-technical and administrative-managerial categories than do their counterparts starting from intermediate-class occupations. Inspection of individual cases here points to the continuing importance, over the period which concerns us, of skilled manual occupations as an initial training ground both for higher-grade technicians and for professionals in engineering and related areas.[16]

Having thus elaborated the routes of intergenerational mobility leading into service-class positions, we may now move on, again as in our consideration of mobility between working-class and intermediate-class positions, to the matter of the permanency of the shifts which our data display. Already from Table 5.1, we have some indication that service-class occupations are in fact of high retentiveness, in that only a small proportion of those men who moved into them on entry into work were found in 1972 in classes other than I and II. But we can here draw further on our work-history material, there being, as Table 5.2 shows, 117 respondents to our 1974 inquiry who were intergenerationally mobile into Class I from Class III–V origins, and 134 from Class VI and VII origins. For present purposes, it will however be more relevant to divide these respondents into the 100 who have followed the direct, **I–S–S** and **W–S–S** routes – having first occupations mostly in the professional and technical categories of Classes I and II–and the remainder whose upward mobility has been of an indirect kind. Of the latter, eighty-two had followed the **I–I–S** or **W–I–S** routes, 76 per cent having started work in Class III occupations; and sixty-nine had followed the **I–W–S** or **W–W–S** routes, with 71 per cent starting in skilled manual, Class VI occupations.

As regards representatives of the direct routes, we find that, once in a Class I occupation, these men had indeed not often moved away from it to one in some other class. This had occurred with only twenty-one out of the 100–that is, little more frequently than in the case of men of Class I and II origins representing the **S–S–S** pattern. Furthermore, as with the latter, these moves were generally of rather short duration, averaging less than three and a half years; and, what is of main significance for our present concerns, they were rarely moves *back to* the respondent's class of origin. Over half were to Class II occupations, and no more than seven of the men in question had, at any point in their lives, worked in occupations in the same class as that to which their father was allocated. In other words, we may regard the bulk of these men as being authentically mobile in having, to all appearances, departed from their origins in a fairly decisive fashion.

When we turn to the mobility experience of our 1974 respondents who represent the indirect routes to Class I, we find a situation which in certain respects is similar to the foregoing but in others very different. With these men also it is the case that, having once reached Class I, they have tended to remain within it. Again, only the same smallish minority—thirty-one out of the 151, or 21 per cent—had ever subsequently moved out; again the average duration of such moves was short, in this case, less than two and a half years; and again in only very few instances—nine or 6 per cent of all—did these moves lead the respondent back to his origins, more than half being to Class II. In short, indirect work-life mobility into Class I would appear to be no less permanent, and no less authentic, in implying a departure from class origins than such mobility achieved directly on completion of full-time education.

However, while this is so, what also emerges strongly from our 1974 data is just *how* indirect the indirect routes often are. An indication of this can be given if we look, as previously, at the number of occupational changes made which entail shifts between the classes of our sevenfold schema. For men following the direct **I–S–S** and **W–S–S** routes, these average 0·9, and 65 per cent were changes between Class I and II positions. In contrast, for men following the indirect **I–I–S**, **W–I–S**, **I–W–S**, and **W–W–S** routes, class shifts per man average respectively 2·1, 2·6, 2·6, and 3·3, and in none of these cases did shifts between Classes I and II account for more than 20 per cent of the total. What, rather, is reflected here, and especially with the last three of these routes, is the considerable amount of work-life mobility experienced by the men who have followed them before they attained a position within the service class of any kind—mobility which in fact occurred chiefly, and often in an apparently disorderly fashion, between different grades of manual, lower-technical, manual supervisory, and rank-and-file white-collar occupations. That is to say, *up to the point at which they gain access to Class I or to Class II*, these respondents display work-histories which are generally comparable to those of the fairly large numbers of men who, as we have already shown, tend to oscillate between intermediate- and working-class positions.[17] Just as, then, we would see counter-mobility as being the 'hard way' for men of high-class origins to succeed their fathers, so we would see the indirect routes to high-class positions as being the 'hard way' for men of lower-class origins to be upwardly mobile. Men following these routes first attained a Class I position at an average age of just under 29 years, as compared with just under 22 years for those who were directly mobile into the service class; and also, it may be recalled, as compared with just over 25 and just over 21 years respectively for men counter-mobile to Class I and for representatives of the **S-S-S** pattern.

PATTERNS OF INTERGENERATIONAL MOBILITY: DOWNWARD

In terms of our class schema, cases of downward intergenerational mobility are those where the sons of Class I and II fathers are found in other than Class I and II positions. From Table 5.1, what is immediately striking is the generally low values that are found in cells indicative of mobility of this kind. Taken together, they account for only 512 of our respondents, or for just over 5 per cent of the total sample, although it may be remarked that this figure is equal to 41 per cent of all men in the sample who are of Class I and II origins. From Table 5.1 it is also evident that the very large majority—in fact 92 per cent—of those who appear as downwardly mobile intergenerationally become so 'directly': that is, by making their initial entry into work either via an intermediate-class occupation, as in the **S-I-I** or **S-I-W** patterns, or via a working-class one, as in the **S-W-I** or **S-W-W** patterns.

In the case of the former, a more detailed picture of the work-life mobility which those following them have experienced is given by Figures 5.15 and 5.16. With the more important **S-I-I** route, the most notable feature is the high proportion of first occupations falling into Class III—comparable in fact to that found with the upward **I-I-S** and **W-I-S** routes and, more to the point perhaps, with the counter-mobile **S-I-S** pattern. In other words, so far as the permanency of this mobility is concerned, it is difficult here to avoid the view that men whose working lives thus far correspond to the **S-I-I** pattern are themselves, and especially where still in Class III occupations, likely candidates for subsequent movement back to their class origins.[18] In some contrast, however, representatives of the **S-I-W** pattern would seem less obviously poised for counter-mobility. Figure 5.16 shows that fewer entered work in Class III occupations and more in the technical category of Class V; and further that, like others who have moved from intermediate-class first jobs to manual work (cf. the **W-I-W** and **I-I-W**

Figures 5.15 to 5.18
Patterns of intergenerational mobility: downward

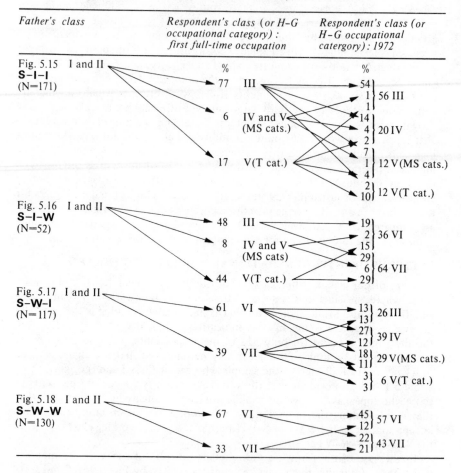

| Father's class | Respondent's class (or H-G occupational category) : first full-time occupation | Respondent's class (or H-G occupational catergory) : 1972 |

routes as shown in Figures 5.5 and 5.10), the majority of these men were found in non-skilled, Class VII categories.

Work-life mobility experienced by representatives of the **S–W–I** and **S–W–W** patterns is shown in Figures 5.17 and 5.18. In both cases, it can be seen, a relatively high proportion had entered work in skilled manual occupations, comparable to that observed with the **I–W–S** and **W–W–S** and also the **S–W–S**, patterns. Those men who were subsequently found in intermediate-class occupations were concentrated in self-employed, Class IV, and in manual supervisory, Class V categories, in a rather similar way to representatives of the **I–W–I** route (Figure 5.4); while those whose 1972 occupations were manual ones were somewhat more equally divided at that stage between skilled and nonskilled categories than they were on entry, but still with more men in skilled jobs than in any other of the routes terminating in manual work. As regards the likelihood of their future counter-mobility, one might then see respondents who appear as following the **S–W–I** and **S–W–W** routes as falling somewhere between representatives of the **S–I–I** and **S–I–W** patterns, with those who have retained Class III or Class VI occupations being seemingly the better placed for eventually attaining a Class I or II position.

To provide at least a partial check on these speculations, our 1974 data can, once more, be put to use. Table 5.2 indicates that sixty-eight of the respondents to our follow-up inquiry were sons of Class I fathers who in 1972 were found in either intermediate- or working-class occupations. Of these men, nine had entered work via a Class I or II occupation (seven representing the **S–S–I** pattern and two the **S–S–W** one). Among the remainder, on whom our interest here centres, more —twenty-three—appeared as having followed the **S–I–I** route than any other, all but one being first employed in routine white-collar occupations within Class III.

On inspection, the actual work-histories of these respondents up to 1974 reveal that, consistently with our supposition above, their departure from their class origins was indeed often of a far from decisive kind. Changes of occupation involving shifts between our seven classes averaged 2·2 per man, and while one in three had at some time been in manual employment, the more frequent moves were to (and occasionally back again from) Class I and II positions. Thus, in fact, by the time of our 1974 inquiry twelve of the twenty-three were no longer in their 1972 occupations, and all but two of these post-1972 moves were to service-class occupations—that is to say, were ones which, in terms of the typology of Table 5.1, would count as instances of counter-mobility via the **S–I–S** route.

Representatives of the other downwardly mobile patterns showed a similar frequency of class shifts in the course of their working lives but had less often moved to Class I or II positions, either before or after 1972. Again in line with what we earlier suggested, the work-histories of the eight men who had followed the **S–I–W** route would seem to point to the greatest degree of detachment from class origins: only one of these men had at any time been in a service-class occupation, and between 1972 and 1974 all had remained in manual work. In the case of representatives of the **S–W–I** and **S–W–W** transitions (N = 12 and 16 respectively) three had held a Class I or II occupation at some time before 1972 and four had become counter-mobile in the interval between our two inquiries.

In sum, then, not only is a very small proportion of our total sample to be found in those cells of Table 5.1 which are indicative of downward mobility from Class I and II origins but, further, it is evident that among these men there is at least some sizeable minority for whom this mobility can scarcely be taken as implying any lasting break with their origins.[19] In the light of our 1974 data, these men would appear to be concentrated among representatives of the **S–I–I** pattern; but in regard to the other transitions in question, we should perhaps recall our earlier finding that counter-mobility back to Classes I and II was often achieved only after a complex, and protracted, series of work-life movements.

From the foregoing analyses, we would wish to draw conclusions which are primarily of substantive significance. We may, however, first note, as a matter of major methodological interest, how adopting a diachronic or biographical perspective on mobility produces a very different picture from that derived from the synchronic, cross-sectional view of a conventional mobility table. It is in this way made abundantly clear that to interpret the main diagonal cells of such a table as indicative of a total absence of mobility or, for that matter, the off-diagonal cells as indicative of mobility of a permanent kind, may well be highly misleading; and further, that even with three-point analyses of the kind of Table 5.1, which at least enable inter- and intragenerational transitions to be distinguished and set in relation to each other, a still very inadequate idea may be obtained of the amount and pattern of work-life mobility that individuals have in fact experienced.

In addition, our work-history data, although relating to only certain sub-samples of respondents to our national inquiry, is still sufficient to show that a wide diversity exists in the actual routes and sequences of work-life movement that men have followed even between similar origins and destinations. Thus, these data must serve to undermine the idea of there being, as some writers have suggested, a 'normal career curve', by reference to which the interpretation of cross-sectional data might be aided.[20] It is true that our findings would suggest that certain relatively well-defined types of work-life 'trajectory' could be specified; but whether it would be possible to assimilate the mobility experience of the population at large to some manageable number of such types is a question which here at least, we must leave in doubt.

Given, then, that in biographical perspective the mobility experience of men in the British work-force appears as far more extensive and diverse than when represented by more conventional methods, must one conclude that the analysis of mobility patterns can, in the end, do little to illumine the nature of class structure; or further, perhaps, that the degree to which 'all is flux' is such as to render the idea of class formation itself problematic? We would not in fact regard the findings that we have reported as lending general support to arguments of this kind. While we must defer until our final chapter a full statement of the understanding of the relationship between mobility and class structure which we derive from our research as a whole, the following observations, based on the data of the present chapter, may be advanced.

First, a state of 'flux' is clearly more evident in certain areas of the occupational and class structure than in others, and, in turn, the experience of mobility within these structures is far from being evenly distributed throughout the population as a whole. In particular, it may be said, it is the occupational groupings constituting our three intermediate classes which are most closely associated with mobility of a frequent and often apparently disorderly kind. As we have seen, there are comprised here rank-and-file white-collar and lower-grade technical occupations, through which men of all class origins make their entry into work in some numbers and from which men later disperse over no less wide a range; and further, self-employed and manual supervisory occupations, to which men normally gain access only via worklife mobility but which at the same time cannot be taken as regularly representing 'final' occupational destinations.

What these intermediate-class positions have in common, and what, we would suggest, chiefly accounts for their tendency to, as it were, generate mobility, is their *marginality* in relation to the two major organizational principles or forms which underlie the occupational division of labour: namely, those of bureaucracy and the market. As the relevant monographic literature well shows—and as we have already noted in presenting our class schema in chapter 2—routine clerical and sales personnel, junior technicians, foremen, and the like are groupings characterized by an uncertain and ambiguous location between 'staff' or 'management' and the manual labour force; while small proprietors and other own-account workers could be said to operate not so much 'independently' as 'conditionally' within the interstices of the corporate economy.[21] Men in such occupations, we would then argue, have a relatively high propensity to be mobile from them, since, on the one hand, they can serve as 'stepping stones' in projects of work-life movement, whether leading away from or back to class origins; but also because, on the other hand, they are occupations which often do not afford any strong *assurance* of further advancement, or even perhaps of security, and in which therefore many projects will fail or disappoint and be reshaped or abandoned.

A detailed examination of mobility patterns is thus of value in enabling one to appreciate the full import for the analysis of British class structure of the fact that at the present time, as indeed throughout the period to which our data relate, nearly a third of the employed male population are to be found in intermediate-class positions of the kind in question (cf. Table 2.3). In the light of our data previously presented, it must be recognized that among these men the experience of class mobility, as we have defined it, will be considerable and, moreover, quite often incomplete; and there is, of course, the further implication that periods of employment in intermediate-class occupations will have figured widely in the working lives of men who are found at any one time, and who may appear as stable, in *other* class positions. Thus, in the numerically most important case of men who in 1972 were in manual, Class VI and VII occupations and whose fathers were allocated to these same classes, our work-history data would make it reasonable to assume that up to half would in fact have *some* experience of nonmanual work of one kind or another.[22]

The continuingly large number of intermediate-class positions whose marginality—in the sense we have defined—plays a major role in promoting a high frequency of work-life mobility is clearly, then, a feature of modern British society which must be reckoned with in any assessment of the potentialities for class formation. However, at the same time as we thus demarcate the main area of flux, we also of course point up those areas where the experience of mobility is less extensive. Most obviously, our attention is in this way directed to the half or more of those men who appear as intergenerationally stable in Classes VI and VII whom we may suppose to have remained entirely in manual employment—that is, who have moved, if at all, in their working lives only between skilled and nonskilled manual jobs. And further here, we may draw again on our work-history findings to suggest that even with those representatives of the **W-W-W** and the **W-I-W** patterns who *do* have some experience of nonmanual employment, this will for probably a majority have marked only a relatively short episode within their working lives as a whole. In other words, if we may identify a sizeable, though unstable and shifting, 'middle-mass'[23] made up of men moving through or between intermediate-class occupations, or between these occupations and manual ones, we may identify also a bloc of men whose mobility has been very largely restricted, in both inter- and intragenerational terms, to movement within the range of working-class positions. At a relatively slow rate, the composition of this bloc will also of course be subject to change by mobility, as some of its number move away from the ambit of the working class for the first time (and are succeeded by the sons of manual workers entering the labour force in manual jobs); but, from the data we have earlier assembled, one might estimate *grosso modo* that at any one time over recent decades those whom Sorokin would term 'hereditary' and 'lifetime' manual wage-workers will have accounted for between a fifth and a quarter of the employed male population.

Moreover, the findings we have reported would also indicate a further important restriction on mobility at the higher levels of the class structure—although not, it must be stressed, of the kind which has most usually been claimed. As we have argued previously—and the data of the present paper serve to elaborate the point—patterns of recruitment to professional, higher-technical, administrative, and managerial occupations over recent decades are inconsistent with any idea of closure : rather it must be recognized that the service class of present-day British society is in fact highly heterogeneous so far as the social origins of its members are concerned. And further, as well as comprising a high proportion of men upwardly mobile from other class origins, the service class, and especially its administrative and managerial component, has recruited to a major extent, and regardless largely of class of origin, via work-life advancement. Consequently, as can be seen from Table 5.1, there is only a small minority of the service class who have experienced the degree of continuity that is implied by the **S-S-S** pattern : the remainder have been recruited, whether inter- or intragenerationally, 'from below'. However, while our data thus reveal a widespread experience of upward mobility among members of the service class, they also point to the high degree of security with which the latter would seem to hold their present positions : in other words, to the very limited extent to which *downward* mobility is experienced, out of the service class, in the course of working life. As we have shown, from whatever origins and by whatever route service-class positions have been attained, they would seem—as ones that are, typically, 'established' within bureaucratic structures—to offer rather powerful guarantees of subsequent work-life continuity at this level.

We may, therefore, regard those men found in our Classes I and II, who amount to a quarter of the employed male population, as also forming, in terms of their mobility patterns, a rather distinctive bloc, even if in a different way from that we have identified within the manual work force. While the latter is defined retrospectively, by reference to the shared experience of mobility—or rather immobility—of its members in the past, members of the service class are to be distinguished, as it were, prospectively: by the fact that they have reached, albeit by very diverse routes, positions within the occupational and class structures from which any radical departure in the future course of their working lives may be counted as exceptional.

As well, then, as recognizing the existence of a 'middle-mass' characterized by relatively high rates of work-life mobility, we are able to point to two different ways, both of some substantive importance, in which work-life patterns evident in the population we have studied could rather be regarded as conducive to class formation: that is, by associating collectivities of individuals with the same range of class positions with some degree of permanency.

Finally, however, it is important that we make it clear that, in our view, conclusions of the foregoing kind, drawn from basic mobility data alone, can represent only *part* of any attempt to show adequately the relevance of the study of mobility for class analysis. To gain an idea of the extent and nature of variation in the experience of individuals in moving between different positions within the division of labour and class structure is in this respect a necessary and substantial first step. But one needs then to go on to examine the wider concomitants of such mobility, as these may be found in aspects of men's lives outside the sphere of work—for example, in the accompanying degree of discontinuity in their social relations with kin, friends, leisure associates etc.—and further, of course, to examine the extent to which the mobility which we would impute to individuals in fact corresponds with their own awareness of having been mobile. The schema of class positions which we have adopted as the basis of our analyses, in the light of our interests in mobility, is ultimately to be judged by its heuristic and analytical value to us in pursuing those interests. But in so far as we wish to concern ourselves with the conditions under which 'objectively' shared class positions are, or may become, a basis for socio-political action, we cannot avoid questions of how mobility, as it were, enters into the actual social relationships in which individuals are engaged and into their own definitions of their social situation. In other words, we must clearly regard as crucial the connection between, on the one hand, individuals' experience of class mobility or immobility, as we have construed it for the purposes of our inquiry; and, on the other hand, mobility in the social lives and in the 'lived' experience of those who are the subjects of our inquiry. This connection we intend to explore in the three chapters that are to follow.

NOTES

1. At the same time, it must of course be appreciated that the pattern of cell values in Table 5.1 is conditioned by the distribution of the class origins, the first occupations and the 1972 positions of our respondents. Thus, for example, in the same way as Tables 2.1 and 2.2, Table 5.1 is in fact constrained, as a matter of arithmetic, to reveal some amount of net upward mobility into Classes I and II in both inter- and intra-generational terms.

   Both 'period' and 'life-cycle' effects will influence the age-composition of respondents representing each of the mobility routes shown in the table, but in fact the average age of men in those cells comprising more than 1 per cent of the total sample is in all cases within five years of the sample average of 41.3 years. Age differences, both within and between cells, which appear of interpretive significance will be taken note of.

2. In fact, all but eight of the men in question entered work via one or other of the three

employee categories, H–G 2, 6, and 10. In the sample as a whole, men allocated to Classes I and II in 1972 were divided almost exactly equally between professional and technical and administrative and managerial categories.

It might here, as elsewhere in our analyses, appear of interest to introduce greater differentiation into 'father's class', either via our sevenfold class schema or our occupational categories. However, this would often produce greater complexity than could be satisfactorily interpreted because of smallness of numbers. We have chosen to look in greatest detail at patterns of work-life mobility, at the cost of having to retain a rather crude indicator of social origins.

3. We use 'continuity' here and elsewhere, to refer to individuals remaining in a given class *through* time, while using 'stability' to refer to their being found in the same class at two separate points in time (and regardless of their mobility or immobility in the interim).

4. It should be noted that all such statements made on the basis of our work-history material are subject to the qualification that where men had had more than three different jobs within the same year, we recorded them as belonging to what appeared to be their 'typical' occupational category for each period of rapid job changing. Such cases were infrequent, and arose mainly with men shifting between nonskilled manual employments.

5. These figures relate in fact to work-histories through to 1974; but, as will be evident from the foregoing, they will be little affected by shifts occurring after 1972, when, of course, all those in question were in Class I occupations.

6. Within our sample as a whole, Class III accounts for 30 per cent of all men whose 1972 occupations were covered by Classes III–V, and category 15 of Class V for 13 per cent; while the proportions accounted for by Class IV and categories 17 and 20 within Class V are 31 per cent and 26 per cent respectively.

7. It can in fact be seen from Table 5.1 that *all* cells implying downward movement from first occupations in Class I and II occupations have very low values—in part because of the relatively low proportion of men entering work via such occupations, but also because of the low probability of men who have done so being later found in other class positions. Since we shall subsequently say little about the several mobility routes in question here, on account of the small numbers who have followed them, the following characteristics of the totality of men involved (N = 185) may be noted: (i) their average age is 36, five years below the sample average; (ii) a relatively high proportion—39 per cent—had first jobs in administrative and managerial categories; (iii) almost half of the latter and likewise of those whose first jobs were in professional and technical categories were found in 1972 in Class III or Class V supervisory occupations. These findings would suggest to us that some sizeable proportion of the downward work-life mobility indicated may be of only a temporary character, reflecting occupations taken either for experience within a 'planned career' or in the course of 'transferring' from the professional-technical to the administrative-managerial *situs* of the service class.

8. We take this term from Wilensky to refer to work-histories in which the different occupations held by the individual cannot be seen as forming a connected sequence. See H.L. Wilensky 'Orderly Careers and Social Participation', *American Sociological Review*, vol. 26, 1961.

9. i.e. from one inquiry to another. It should be added here that it may well be in regard to intermediate-class occupations that the greatest unreliability occurs in the collection and coding of occupational information. Dividing lines are often hard to determine, and to implement consistently, between rank-and-file and higher-level white-collar occupations; proprietors of differing 'sizes'; supervisory and lower managerial positions; and lower-grade technical and skilled manual jobs.

10. Each of the occupational categories comprised by Classes VI and VII accounted for at least 2 per cent of the *total* 'first occupations' distribution of the men in our sample, and all but three (H–G 26, 27, and 33) accounted for a larger proportion of this distribution than of the 'present occupations' one.

11. The pattern we have particularly in mind here is that whereby the sons of manual

workers begin work as 'juniors' in offices or shops but then leave, or have their employ-ment terminated, before reaching adult grades and take up manual jobs themselves.

12. These men, it may be noted, were on average almost eight years younger than others following the **W-I-I** route. (But since our sample was one of men aged 20–64, it may be taken that men found in 1972 in Class III occupations were all in adult grades–that is, had succeeded in gaining a white-collar occupation beyond the very precarious 'junior' stage referred to in the previous note.)

13. As the data of Table 5.1 indicate, this assumption is valid at least so far as movement from first occupation is concerned. It may be calculated that 26 per cent of those men of working-class origins who began work in nonmanual jobs were found in 1972 in manual ones, while this was so with only 17 per cent of men of intermediate-class origins whose first occupation was nonmanual.

14. Again it is evident from Table 5.1 that the assumption is valid for movement from first occupation. In fact 51 per cent of men of intermediate-class origins whose first occu-pation was a manual one had a non-manual one in 1972, as against 32 per cent of men of working-class origins.

15. Cf. the data provided by more specialized inquiries such as Acton Society Trust, *Management Succession*, London: Acton Society Trust, 1956; Clark, *The Industrial Manager*, ch. V; and Halsey and Crewe, *Social Survey of the Civil Service*, pp. 104–6, 134–7.

16. Cf. Gerstl and Hutton, *Engineers: the Anatomy of a Profession*, chs. 4 and 6. It may be noted how here, as in several other respects previously referred to in this chapter, the distinction between skilled and nonskilled manual employment appears as an important one so far as work careers are concerned–in contrast with the relatively limited import-ance of the distinction in regard to social origins (i.e. father's occupation).

17. It should be remembered that our 1974 data relate only to men who in 1972 were in Class I occupations; but there would seem no reason why indirect mobility into Class II occupations should tend to be achieved in any less disorderly fashion.

18. The average age of these men was, at 36, five years less than that of the sample as a whole.

19. In this case, the fact that our 1974 data were limited to men of Class I origins is probably of some consequence in giving an exaggerated idea of the likelihood of counter-mobility to service class positions. Among men of Class II origins in our 1972 sample whose first jobs were in Class III–V or Class VI and VII categories, rates of 'observed' counter-mobility back to Class I or II occupations were 44 per cent and 34 per cent respectively, as compared with corresponding figures of 51 per cent and 45 per cent for men of Class I origins.

20. See, e.g., Delbert C. Miller and William H. Form, *Industrial Sociology*, New York: Harper, 1951, Part Four; and, on more sophisticated lines, Theodore Caplow, *The Sociology of Work*, University of Minnesota Press, 1954, ch. 3. We join here with other recent critics of the undue reliance on the cross-sectional approach in mobility studies, whose awareness of its deficiences has been aroused by the collection and analysis of work-history data. Cf. Jorge Balán, Harley L. Browning and Elizabeth Jelin, *Men in a Developing Society: Geographic and Social Mobility in Monterrey, Mexico*, Austin: University of Texas Press, 1973; and Bertaux, 'Mobilité sociale bio-graphique: une critique de l'approche transversale'. An earlier, but rather neglected, British study of work histories (whose findings appear broadly similar to ours to the–limited–extent to which comparisons can be made) is G. Thomas, *Labour Mobility in Great Britain 1945–49*, London: The Social Survey, n.d.

21. See the references cited in n. 9, p. 65.

22. Cf. pp. 130–1 above. Our work-history data relate, it must be recalled, only to men aged 25–49 who appeared as intergenerationally stable in Class VI or Class VII. It would seem implausible that men who were intergenerationally mobile between these classes would be significantly more or less likely to have experience of nonmanual work; but some allowance should probably be made for the fact that older men would simply have had more time in which to gain such experience.

23. We again take the term from Wilensky but give it a rather different and, we would

think, more valid meaning. Cf. H.L. Wilensky, 'Work, Careers and Social Integration', *International Social Science Journal*, vol. 12, 1960. It is also important to note that what we are suggesting here is not simply another version of the idea of a buffer-zone, in which much short-range mobility occurs between manual and nonmanual positions. The middle-mass, as we would characterize it, must be seen as including at any one time some sizeable number of individuals involved in what will eventually prove to be mobility of a long-range kind.

CHAPTER 6

Class Mobility and Kinship

(*with* CATRIONA LLEWELLYN)

So far in this volume our concern has been with analysing, in terms of both absolute and relative rates, the main patterns and trends of class mobility that have prevailed in British society over recent decades. In this and the next chapter the focus of our attention changes. We move on from the findings that we have previously presented to consider various of their implications: more specifically, to examine the consequences, or as we would prefer to say, the concomitants of the mobility that we have recorded and, in particular, of the dominant feature of the pattern of absolute mobility—namely, the relatively high and increasing rate of upward movement from working- and intermediate-class origins into the ranks of the service class. We shall be concerned with the implications of this mobility, on the one hand, for the mobile individuals themselves; and, on the other, for the larger collectivities, that is, the classes, between which we would regard these individuals as having moved. We wish to know how far mobility within the class structure, as we have conceptualized it, is associated with discontinuities in individuals' primary social relations and in their life-styles more generally, which would indicate that they have in fact been mobile between meaningful socio-cultural entities and not just between the theoretically inspired categories that we have imposed on our data. And then further, we wish to consider what is thereby entailed for the degree of internal homogeneity of the major classes that we have distinguished. Following Sorokin (cf. p. 12 above), one may envisage occupational groupings and classes in modern society as comprising two different elements: one a more or less permanent 'core', the other made up of mobile individuals of relatively recent membership and whose affiliation remains uncertain. In this view, a certain amount of heterogeneity in the social origins of the members of a class is thus presupposed; but the question remains of how far the mobility that occurs also gives rise to a more basic heterogeneity, expressed at a normative and relational level,[1] in members' characteristic patterns of social life.

We begin, appropriately, we believe, by examining some of the implications of class mobility for kinship relations. The social ties that exist between close kin, at least, are of an obviously primordial kind. Moreover, it is on account of the solidary nature of these ties that the family, rather than the individual, is usually regarded as the appropriate unit of class, or of other forms of stratification. Thus, kinship may be seen as representing for our purposes a critical or limiting case, in the sense that if intergenerational class mobility is disruptive of kinship relations and is associated with significant changes in the pattern and style of individuals' interaction with their kin, then one would be led to expect no less decisive or extensive changes in other of their primary social relations.[2]

THEORY, METHOD, AND DATA

In theoretical analyses of the nature of kinship in industrial society (mostly of American provenance) the claim that social mobility *is* inimical to the maintenance of social ties with kin has been a more or less standard feature. Parsons, for example, has argued from a functionalist standpoint that the relatively high social mobility typical of industrial societies renders inappropriate a system of extended kin relations which impose obligations wider than those deriving from roles within the nuclear 'family of orientation'.[3] Again, Schneider and Homans, influenced more perhaps by theories of social exchange, have contended that typically, in modern American society at least, mobility erodes solidarity among kin: 'upward mobile persons keep only shallow ties with members of their kindred, if they keep them at all; downward mobile persons may be neglected by their kindred.'[4] For Great Britain, Stacey has contended, in a paper much influenced by American theorizing, that 'With mobility, family connections become fewer and more tenuous' and that kinship relations 'are usually disrupted and change in quality'.[5]

Such arguments have, however, never gained extensive empirical support;[6] and as research has progressed it has rather become apparent that the connection between mobility and kinship is, to say the least, a good deal more complex than they would imply. To begin with, several studies have indicated that while, in some circumstances, mobile individuals may show a lower level of interaction with their extra-familial kin than those not mobile, this rarely means that they are entirely isolated from their kindred or that a sense of kinship obligation is dissipated;[7] and it has also been suggested that the reduced interaction is in any event more often attributable to the *geographical* mobility which is the usual accompaniment of social mobility, than to social mobility itself.[8] Further still, it has been held that even where social mobility can be shown to be associated with differences in interaction with kin independently of geographical mobility, it remains questionable whether it is the experience of mobility *per se* that is effective. An alternative possibility, it is suggested, is that the differences observed reflect the 'cross-pressuring' to which mobile individuals, unlike the non-mobile, are subject, as a result of their exposure to normative influences deriving from both their class of origin and their class of destination. Thus, from this point of view, what is required to understand the consequences of mobility for kinship relations (or indeed for any other aspect of social behaviour) is not knowledge of the mobility process itself or of any effects—say, of psychological kind—that are proper to it, but rather of the norms regulating the behaviour in question that prevail within the classes, or other groupings, between which mobility occurs. That is to say, the behaviour of the mobile may be expected to reflect, and to be accountable in terms of, some 'mix', or intermediate version, of these two sets of norms.[9]

The discussion of the impact of mobility on kinship has thus undoubtedly become more sophisticated over recent years. At the same time, though, it must be recognized that its focus has tended to shift away from issues which are of major concern if one's interests lie, as ours do, in the implications of mobility not only for the mobile individual but also, and primarily, for class formation within a given historical context. From this latter standpoint, the attempt to determine the precise structure of causal influences at work is in fact somewhat beside the point. To revert to the distinction earlier introduced, it is the actual concomitants of mobility in the given context that matter, rather than what could, in a strict sense, be regarded as its specific consequences. In other words, it is of greater importance to establish, at a descriptive level, the form and extent of the association that exists between mobility and the pattern of kinship relations than to ascertain whether it is through geographical movement, psychological factors, normative cross-pressures, or whatever, that this association is chiefly mediated.

At the same time, though, the standpoint we adopt requires that certain other methodological issues be given rather more attention than they have usually received: notably, the basis on which intergenerationally mobile and stable individuals are selected for study; and the degree of refinement required within these two broad categories in terms of the different modes or routes by which mobility, or stability, has been achieved. Virtually all studies of mobility and kinship so far undertaken have related to highly localized samples, drawn from a single town, suburb, or housing area; and, typically, their analyses have then rested on a simple fourfold division of their respondents: that is, into two 'non-mobile' groups of men found at the same 'high' or 'low' class (or status) levels as those of their origins, and two 'mobile' groups of men whose present positions are taken as indicating that, relative to their origins, they have moved in an upward or a downward direction. However, if one wishes to gain some idea of the concomitants of mobility patterns that have been observed on a society-wide basis, and which reflect, one believes, major structural changes, it is clearly desirable that one should not contract one's field of inquiry to the experiences of individuals in one—or even a number—of particular milieux. And if one is concerned with the implications of mobility for the internal homogeneity of classes, it would also seem important to recognize that comparisons made between individuals' class origins and the class positions they hold at some later point in time tell one little about the *lifetime* mobility routes which they have followed—whereas it is knowledge of the latter which would seem most relevant to determining their title to be regarded either as stable members of a class or as exemplifying mobility of a particular type.

Our 1974 follow-up inquiry, on the data of which we shall here essentially rely, was designed with the above considerations much in mind. As we have described in the previous chapter, this inquiry involved re-interviews with certain subsamples of respondents to the 1972 national mobility study who were between the ages of 25 and 49 and who, according to our basic mobility table, were either intergenerationally stable in class position or had experienced long-range upward or downward movement—that is, into or out of Class I of our schema (see Table 5.2). The 1974 interviews with these men were in large part given over to collecting a wide range of information on the pattern of their social relations and life-styles; but, in addition, we secured from our respondents the complete work-history records that we have already drawn on rather extensively in chapter 5. Thus, we have available from this source data which, although restricted in the ways we have indicated, will enable us to examine the connection between mobility and kinship relations in the case of men whose experience of mobility we can place in the context of the national patterns and trends that we have discerned *and* which we can also view in a lifetime, or biographical, perspective.[10]

We shall seek to exploit this material in the following way. Pursuing Sorokin's idea of the relatively permanent, 'core' membership of a class, we shall aim, first, to establish the patterns of kinship relations displayed by those of our respondents who would appear as representatives of such core groupings;[11] and then secondly, we shall use these patterns as, so to speak, benchmarks, against which we can assess the kinship patterns of our more mobile respondents. Among the latter, we will give greatest attention to those men who exemplify long-range upward mobility into the higher levels of the class structure which we know shows a rising trend—and especially, we may add, within the birth cohorts which our data cover.[12]

CLASS AND KINSHIP

In the 1974 inquiry we drew samples of 1972 respondents in the 25 to 49 age-range who appeared as intergenerationally stable within Class I and within the five lower classes of our schema (but with H–G categories 11 and 13 being excluded from Class IV and H–G category 15 from Class V). Reference to Table 5.2 will give the sampling ratios and numbers involved. However, from the work-history data provided by these men, it emerged, as we have seen in the previous chapter, that intergenerational stability by no means implied a high degree of *continuity* of class position. Such continuity, and hence the existence of a sizeable 'core' grouping, was most evident within Class I, on the one hand, and within Classes VI and VII, on the other. In contrast, those men who appeared as intergenerationally stable within our three intermediate classes showed relatively high rates of work-life class mobility—often of a 'disorderly' kind—and had therefore to be regarded as themselves forming a rather unstable collectivity in the sense of one liable to considerable short-term fluctuations in it composition.

We thus began our analyses of kinship relations by comparing our data for three rather conservatively defined core groupings, as follows.

(i) Men intergenerationally stable in Class I who had also entered work via a Class I or a Class II position (N = 52). Only eight of these men, as we have earlier noted, had *ever* in their working lives moved—and then, of course, only temporarily—from a Class I position to one at a lower level.

(ii) Men intergenerationally stable in Class VI who had entered work in a Class VI—i.e. skilled manual—occupation and who had never been in other than manual, Class VI or VII employment (N=39).

(iii) Men intergenerationally stable in Class VII who had entered work in a Class VII—i.e. nonskilled manual—occupation and who had never been in other than manual, Class VI or VII employment (N=45).

The outcome of these initial analyses was that men in the first of these groupings displayed a pattern of kinship relations clearly differentiated in various respects from those of the second and third groupings, while the patterns of these latter two groupings resembled each other quite closely. In other words, a contrast was suggested between, on the one hand, a higher service-class kinship pattern and, on the other, a working-class one common to skilled and nonskilled manual workers alike.

Furthermore, though, the extension of our analyses to the remainder of our respondents selected as intergenerationally stable in either Class I or Classes VI and VII revealed that their kinship relations did not diverge in any systematic fashion from the two basic patterns shown by the core groupings. That is to say, the pattern of the Class I core was also displayed by men of Class I origins who had entered work in working-class or intermediate-class occupations and had then been counter-mobile back to Class I (N = 23); and the common pattern of the Class VI and VII cores was followed by other men intergenerationally stable in one or other of these classes but who had not entered work via that class or who had some experience of nonmanual work in the course of their working lives (N = 71). Neither of these results should be thought especially surprising in view of two findings that were reported in the preceding chapter. First, men counter-mobile to Class I, although often following seemingly complex routes, had still tended to achieve Class I positions at a quite early age—on average, at just over 25 years—and were then no more likely to have been mobile from Class I than men who had entered this class directly. And, secondly, men inter-generationally stable within Classes VI and VII although with experience of nonmanual employment tended in fact to have spent only relatively short periods of their working lives in such work—on average, around three and a half years, as against an average work-life duration, to 1974, of almost twenty-three years. In Tables 6.1 to 6.5, therefore, we present data for all our inter-generationally stable Class I respondents together; and we likewise treat together all men intergenerationally stable in Class VI or Class VII.[13]

On the other hand, however, we may note that in the case of those respondents selected as intergenerationally stable within one or other of our intermediate classes—but among whom no sizeable core groupings were readily apparent—patterns of kinship relations did tend to vary with certain features of work-life mobility. Most notably, those men who had begun work in non-manual (largely intermediate-class) occupations (N = 47) displayed a pattern in most respects close to that of Class I, even though a third had at some time in their lives been manual wage-workers; while those men who had begun work in manual occupations (N = 56) showed a pattern generally close to that of Classes VI and VII, notwithstanding their intermediate-class origins and present (1972) positions. We have in fact grounds for supposing that a major difference between the two groupings is that the former contains a much larger proportion than the latter of men who have good prospects of eventual advancement into the service class and who may indeed be on well-established routes leading to service-class positions.[14] In Tables 6.1 to 6.5 we thus present results for our intermediate-class respondents divided according to the nature of their first occupation; but our commentary will in fact concentrate on the results for our two benchmark groupings, that is, for men intergenerationally stable in Class I and in Classes VI and VII.

The data of Tables 6.1 to 6.5 relate to three main aspects of kinship relations: (i) the degree of our respondents' contact with their kin; (ii) more specifically, the part played by kin in providing domestic and family help, and as associates in leisure-time activity; and (iii) the degree of acquaintance that exists between respondents' kin and other of their more frequent associates who are not kin.

The results reported in Table 6.1 on contact with kin reveal certain fairly well defined tendencies. To begin with, panel (A) indicates that quite marked differences exist between Class I and Class VI and VII respondents in the extent to which they are in regular and relatively frequent contact with 'close' kin (living outside their households). For purposes of our inquiry, 'close' kin were defined as the respondent's—and, where applicable, the respondent's wife's—parents, parents' siblings and their spouses, siblings and siblings' spouses; and, in the case of married respondents, all descendant kin and their spouses. It can be seen from panel (A) that respondents having *no* close kin whom they usually meet at least once a week amount to over half of those intergenerationally stable in Class I, but to less than a fifth of those stable in Classes VI or VII; while these proportions are then reversed in the case of respondents reporting three or more such kin who are met with this high degree of frequency.[15] However, the data of panels (B) and (C) of Table 6.1 would further suggest that as one considers the extent of contact with kin that occurs over longer time periods, that is, on a less frequent basis, the difference between the service-class and the working-class pattern diminishes. Thus, in panel (C), it can be seen that the difference in the numbers of close kin met over the course of the year preceding interview is in fact rather slight. And further, when in panel (D) we come to examine contacts over this same period with other, more distant kin, we find that these appear to have been somewhat *more* extensive among our Class I respondents than among those from Classes VI and VII.

These findings would then incline one to question whether there is in fact any *major* divergence in class norms influencing the frequency of interaction among kin: the nature of the differences shown up between our two benchmark groupings would seem more likely to be ones that reflect differences in factual circumstances and the constraints on action which they entail. In particular, one could reasonably suppose some connection between the relatively low degree of 'weekly' contact with kin on the part of men intergenerationally stable in Class I and a relatively high physical dispersion of kin, resulting from the well-established tendency for professional, administrative, and managerial careers to occasion more geographical movement than does employment in manual work.[16] While, as we have said, our main concern here is with the actual concomitants of class mobility, rather than with the processes through which they are brought about, it will be relevant to our later discussion to present the results of one simple analysis that confirm this supposition. If one considers, as in Table 3, only those of our respondents who had close kin living within easy reach of them—that is, 'within about ten minutes' walk'—it can be seen that class differences in the extent of 'weekly' contacts are greatly reduced. Although, as would be expected, having kin living near by is much less common among Class I than among Class VI and VII respondents, where such kin are present, the former appear no more likely than the latter to be uninvolved in frequent interaction with them.[17]

In Tables 6.3 and 6.4 we turn to data on the relative importance of kin as a source, first, of help in domestic or family crises, and secondly, of leisure-time associates. Table 6.3 gives the results we obtained from several questions put to respondents about whom they would look to for help in certain hypothetical situations; and also from a question about the help which they had actually

Table 6.1

Contacts with kin: respondents intergenerationally stable in class position

Class	(A) Number of close kin usually met at least once per week[a] Percentage meeting			Mean	(B) Number of close kin met in last month before interview[b] Percentage having met				Mean	(C) Number of close kin met in last year before interview[c] Percentage having met				Mean	(D) Number of other kin met in last year before interview[d] Percentage having met			Mean
	0[e]	1-2	3+		0[e]	1-4	5-9	10+		0-4	5-14	15+	DK etc.	f	0	1-4	5+	
Class I (N = 75)	55	27	18	1.5	13	43	36	8	4.9	20	55	21	4	10.2	19	31	50	6.5
Classes III-V (first occupation nonmanual) (N = 47)	45	23	32	1.7	19	40	26	15	5.1	28	38	30	4	9.9	26	36	38	4.1
Classes III-V (first occupation manual) (N = 56)	22	23	55	3.6	9	30	32	29	7.4	11	43	29	18	12.3	31	23	46	6.6
Classes VI and VII (N = 155)	19	30	51	3.6	8	32	35	25	7.0	19	37	29	15	12.3	32	38	30	5.7

Notes: (a) The question asked was: 'Which of these relatives [i.e. close kin, as defined in the text, displayed on a kinship chart] – apart from those who live in the same household as you – would you usually meet at least once a week?'

(b) The question asked was: 'Which of the people [on the kinship chart] have you met in the last month?'

(c) Directly following the question given in note (b), respondents were further asked: 'How many other people [on the kinship chart] have you met during the last year?' The data used in this panel of the table thus come from combining the answers given to these two questions.

(d) The question asked was: 'Are there any other relatives [not on the kinship chart] – e.g. cousins, grandparents, or more distant relatives – whom you have met during the last year?'

(e) Owing to an error in the coding procedure, a few instances of non-response may be included in the zero category.

(f) Mainly cases where the respondent claimed he was unable to give a precise answer because of the large numbers involved.

Table 6.2
Number of close kin usually met at least once per week; respondents inter-generationally stable in class position with kin living within 'about ten minutes walk'[a]

Class	Percentage meeting			Mean	N	Percentage of all
	0	1–2	3+			
Class I	12	41	47	3.0	17	23
Classes III–V (first occupation nonmanual)	27	27	46	2.7	22	47
Classes III–V (first occupation manual)	4	26	70	3.9	27	48
Classes VI and VII	13	30	57	3.3	96	62

Note: (a) The question asked was: 'Which of these relatives [on the chart showing close kin] live within about ten minutes' walk of you?'

received in one particular circumstance, the birth of children. Answers to the hypothetical questions show, in each instance, that kin tend more often to be envisaged as a source of help among Class VI and VII than among Class I respondents, and that the difference widens as one moves from the first, rather trivial, to the two more serious situations presented. At the same time, though, it is also the case that, as the help that would typically be required becomes more long-term and demanding, there is a *general*, and quite marked, increase in the extent to which kin would be looked to. Thus, in panel (C), in the situation of protracted illness, each grouping of respondents, regardless of their class, would be clearly more inclined to turn to their kin for help than to any other source. And, on the other hand, it may be added that with the first two situations (but not the third), class differences in the extent of reliance on kin are largely eliminated if attention is restricted to respondents with kin living near. Among such respondents, the proportions who would resort to kin, within our stable service-class and stable working-class groupings respectively, are 29 per cent and 31 per cent in the first situation and 71 per cent and 79 per cent in the second. Finally, in panel (D) of Table 4, our findings on help received at the time of the birth of children—an occasion on which support is not only needed but takes on symbolic significance for family solidarity across generations—show that the importance of kin is overwhelming; and that, in this case, class differences are in fact quite negligible.

In some contrast, the data of Table 6.4 might seem to point more decidedly to differences in class patterns. Class VI and VII respondents, it is shown, were more likely to report kin as associates in recent leisure activities than were Class I respondents. And in turn, then, kin appear as clearly more important in the associational pattern of working-class than of service-class leisure. However, these results must be recognized as quite closely reflecting those previously reported on variation in the extent of contact with kin on a 'weekly' basis—

Table 6.3

Relative importance of kin as a source of help: respondents intergenerationally stable in class position

% who would look for help to kin (K) neighbours (Ne), friends etc. (F), and other/DK[d]

Class	(A) If respondent needed to borrow tool or material[a]				(B) If respondent (and wife) ill for couple of days[b]				(C) If respondent/wife ill for several weeks[c]				(D) Percentage (of married respondents with children) having received help when children born[e] from			
	K	Ne	F	O/DK	K	Ne	F	O/DK	K	Ne	F	O/DK	Kin	Neighbours	Others/No one	N
Class I (N = 75)	15	52	21	12	46	21	21	12	51	11	13	25	80	5	15	41
Classes III–V (first occupation nonmanual) (N = 47)	15	51	25	9	66	13	6	15	53	11	13	23	86	0	14	21
Classes III–V (first occupation manual) (N = 56)	20	41	16	23	69	20	9	2	63	7	13	17	84	3	13	39
Classes VI and VII (N = 155)	26	45	17	12	72	14	6	8	77	15	7	1	83	6	11	90

Notes: (a) The question asked was: 'Supposing you were doing some emergency repairs and needed to borrow some tool or material – say, a spanner or some fuse wire – who would you go to?'

(b) the question asked, with the bracketed phrases included where applicable, was: 'If you (and your wife both) caught 'flu and had to stay in bed for a couple of days, who would you be likely to call on for help with shopping, cooking (and help with the children) etc.?'

(c) Unmarried respondents were asked: 'Suppose you had been seriously ill in hospital and then had to convalesce for several weeks. Who would most likely look after you?' Married respondents were asked: 'Suppose your wife had to go to hospital for several weeks. Who would most likely help you in the home?'

(d) 'Friends etc.' includes work colleagues. 'Other/DK' includes a few instances of non-response.

(e) The questions asked were: 'When your children were born did anyone come and help in the house?' and, if so, 'Who?'.

which, we have suggested, derive primarily from differences in the ready availability of kin rather than in normative orientations to kinship ties. If only
respondents with kin living 'within about ten minutes' walk' are considered, men
intergenerationally stable in Class I are in fact rather *more* likely to have had
recent leisure association with kin than men stable in Classes VI and VII. For
example, only 24 per cent of the former, as compared with 34 per cent of the
latter, reported having had no leisure-time contact with kin during the days
covered by our questions. Thus, while the *de facto* significance of the divergent
patterns revealed in Table 6.4 must not be lost sight of, we would none the less
doubt if the data of this table could be taken as pointing to contrasting class
conceptions of the desirability of 'kin as friends', any more than those of Table
4 could be thought to suggest widely differing conceptions of kinship obligation.

Lastly, in Table 6.5 we present data which give some indication of the extent
to which our respondents' kin were known to those individuals (or couples) who
were respondents' most frequent spare-time associates. Such associates might be
kin themselves but, as can be seen from the last column of Table 6.4, this was
the case only with rather small minorities. In Table 6.5 it is clearly the similarities
between the results for our two benchmark groupings that must be regarded as
most notable, and especially so since such differences as do appear largely reflect
the greater probability of the associates of working-class respondents themselves
being kin.[18] In the case of both benchmark groupings it would appear that a
frequent spare-time associate was about as likely as not to know (fairly) well one
or more of a respondent's kin, while one in five or six of such associates would
be well acquainted with five or more of the respondent's kin. In other words,
one might perhaps say that in both groupings alike, the degree of acquaintance
between regular spare-time associates and kin, and hence the 'connectedness' in
this respect of respondents' social networks, was at a moderately high level.[19]
The main contrast here—the possible significance of which we will suggest later—
is to be found in the results reported for our groupings of stable intermediate-
class respondents whose first occupation was nonmanual, which in Table 6.5
deviate far more than usual from the Class I pattern. It can be seen that among
these men it was far more likely than not that a frequent spare-time associate
would not know well *any* of a respondent's kin, and highly unlikely that he
would be familiar with five or more.

Taken together, then, the data of Tables 6.1 to 6.5 would imply that differences in patterns of kinship relations between our two benchmark groupings,
while they certainly exist, may easily be overinterpreted. In a number of aspects
of kinship that we have been able to consider, differences of a rather well-defined
kind have indeed been revealed: we would thus regard kinship relations as varying
with class in several significant respects. At the same time, though, it must be
recognized, first, that these differences are still not total, qualitative ones, but
rather ones essentially of degree, which we have in fact shown up through
comparing frequency distributions and means; and secondly, that in the light of
the evidence we have available, their immediate source, at least, would appear to
be more in class-linked constraints on kinship relations of a physical kind, associated chiefly with differences in the degree of dispersal of kin, rather than in
sharply divergent class norms.[20] In moving on now to examine the kinship

Table 6.4

Relative importance of kin as leisure associates: respondents intergenerationally stable in class position

Class	Percentage reporting no contacts with kin	Leisure contacts with kin and others over week-end and last week-day before interview[a]			Percentage of most frequent spare-time associates who are kin[b]
		Mean number of kin reported per respondent as associates in leisure activities	Mean number of non-kin reported per respondent as associates in leisure activities	Kin as percentage of all associates in leisure activities	
Class I (N = 75)	51	1.9	5.8	24	9
Classes III-V (first occupation nonmanual) (N = 47)	60	1.5	4.3	26	10
Classes III-V (first occupation manual) (N = 56)	45	3.1	3.2	50	20
Classes VI and VII (N = 155)	39	3.0	4.1	42	17

Notes: (a) These data are derived from leisure-time charts, covering the days in question, on which interviewers recorded details of how respondents spent their time when not actually at work. Attention was concentrated on activities, or sets of related activities, which took up at least an hour. For each such 'block' of time, respondents were asked with whom, if anyone, their activity was undertaken.
(b) Respondents were asked: 'Now thinking generally, who are the people you *most often* spend your spare time with—not counting your immediate family? For example, are there any people that you normally meet at least once a week, or a few times a month—they may be people you have mentioned already?' Interviewers recorded for each respondent details of up to three individuals or couples mentioned. In the figures reported here, couples are counted as one.

Table 6.5

Acquaintance of most frequent spare-time associates with respondents' kin.[a]
respondents intergenerationally stable in class position

Class	Percentage of respondents' first-mentioned associates knowing 'well' or 'fairly well'			Number of first-mentioned associates	Percentage of all respondents' associates knowing 'well' or 'fairly well'			Total number of associates mentioned
	No kin	1–4 kin	5+ kin		No kin	1–4 kin	5+ kin	
Class I	47	33	20	58	53	31	16	131
Classes III–V (first occupation nonmanual)	69	23	8	36	65	26	9	88
Classes III–V (first occupation manual)	42	41	17	41	38	43	19	90
Classes VI and VII	44	36	20	121	44	34	22	271

Note: (a) The data of this table are derived from the question given in note (b) to Table 6.4 and from two follow-up questions asked about each associate (or couple) mentioned: 'Does he/she/they know any of your relatives?' and, if so, 'Well or fairly well—or only slightly?'

patterns of our sub-samples of intergenerationally mobile respondents, in comparison with those of our benchmark groupings, it is important that we keep these qualifications in mind.

MOBILITY AND KINSHIP

Details of the subsamples of intergenerationally mobile men which we drew from our 1972 respondents have been provided in Table 5.2. To repeat: these men could all be regarded as having experienced long-range mobility, either upwards into Class I from working-class or lower-level intermediate-class origins or downwards from Class I origins to working-class or lower-level intermediate-class positions in 1972. However, just as it is important to raise the question of whether or not intergenerational stability, as shown up in a conventional mobility table, implies continuity of class position over time, so too, we have seen, it is important to consider whether intergenerational mobility which is thus revealed is likely to be of a *permanent* kind. In fact, as we have indicated in earlier chapters, the instances of upward and downward mobility with which we are concerned differ significantly in this respect. Analyses of both our 1972 data and of the work-history material collected from our 1974 interviews show that movement into the service class, and into its higher echelons especially, has a high probability of being permanent, and that, at least where long-range upward mobility has occurred, any subsequent return by an individual to his class of origin is rare. On the other hand, though, downward mobility from service-class origins, and especially where this is experienced in early working life, is very often impermanent. In this case, there would appear to be a quite high probability of subsequent work-life advancement—or in other words, of countermobility—through which the individual will be brought back to his class of origin. Thus, in discussing the concomitants of mobility among our respondents —whether in regard to kinship or otherwise—we shall tend to concentrate our attention on the upwardly mobile; for as well as being numerically the more important, it is only these respondents whom we can reasonably assume have experienced mobility which implies at all events a fairly decisive break with their social origins.

In addition to helping us to establish this point, our work-history data also make it possible for us to distinguish different types of (upward) mobility in terms of the route that has been followed. Previously, in dealing with mobility rates and patterns, we have made a good deal of the distinction between upward mobility into higher-level class positions which is achieved directly—that is, immediately on completion of full-time education; and such mobility which is achieved indirectly—that is, in the course of working life, after initial employment at a relatively low level. It would therefore seem desirable to retain this distinction in the present case, and especially so since one essentially similar has also figured in other recent discussion of the concomitants of mobility.[21] To do this, without numbers becoming too low, means, however, that we are constrained to work with only two broad origin categories, those of intermediate-class and working-class—in other words, we must treat together respondents of Class III, IV, and V, and of Class VI and VII origins. But, fortunately, inspection of our data suggests that we shall not in this way lose sight of any very marked or systematic variation in the kinship relations of the upwardly mobile. In Tables 6.6 to 6.10 in which our findings in this respect are presented, we have thus four groupings of upwardly mobile men; (i) men of intermediate-class origins found in Class I who had been directly mobile into service-class positions on entering full-time employment, that is, whose first occupations were in Class I or Class II of our schema (N = 52); (ii) men of intermediate-class origins who had been indirectly mobile into Class I, that is, after entering work in intermediate- or working-class occupations (N = 65); (iii) men of working-class origins found in Class I who had been directly mobile into the service class (N=48); and (iv) men of working-class origins who had been indirectly mobile into Class I (N=86).

It may be recalled here from the analyses of the preceding chapter that direct and indirect access to the service class tend to be associated with recruitment to different of its components. Men entering directly do so predominantly through, and remain largely within, professional and technical occupations; while men entering indirectly are found largely in administrative and managerial occupations. On the other hand, though, whether or not our upwardly mobile respondents had entered directly or indirectly seemed to make little difference to the degree of continuity with which they had retained service-class, or at least Class I, positions. In both cases alike only around a fifth had ever moved from a Class I position, more than half of these moves were to Class II, and their 'absences' were for the most part ones of short duration.

In Table 6.6, the contents of which derive from the same interview items as those of Table 6.1, we set data on the kinship contacts of our mobile respondents in comparison with those relating to the two benchmark groupings that we have established. The most important conclusion that may be drawn from this table is that its data are generally inconsistent with the view that mobile individuals are distinctive in their degree of isolation from kin. Most obviously, each of the groupings of mobile men shows a degree of contact with kin on a relatively frequent basis, that is, as indicated in panels (A) and (B), which tends to fall somewhere *between* the two different levels displayed by the intergenerationally stable groupings of Table 6.1. What is thus of major interest here is the fact that the numerically preponderant groupings of men upwardly mobile into Class I have in each case alike—that is, no matter which mobility route they have followed—*more* contact with their close kin than do men who have succeeded their fathers in Class I.[22]

If, on the other hand, we seek to compare our upwardly mobile respondents with stable representatives of their class of origin, rather than of destination, it is true that we do then find evidence to suggest that mobility is associated with some falling off in interaction with kin. With men of intermediate-class origins, we have the difficulty that we lack any well-defined benchmark grouping to which we can refer; but so far as men of working-class origins are concerned, our data point to a lower level of relatively frequent contact with kin among the upwardly mobile than among the stable, and especially so in contact occurring on a 'weekly' basis. For example, from a third to a half of the former report no kin who are usually seen 'weekly', as against only a fifth of the latter.[23] However, what is also suggested by the pattern of our data, and what is in fact confirmed by Table 6.7, is that differences in the physical dispersal of kin are again of major

Table 6.6

Contacts with kin: respondents intergenerationally mobile and respondents stable in Class I and Classes VI and VII

Mobility pattern	(A) Number of close kin usually met at least once per week — Percentage meeting				(B) Number of close kin met in last month before interview — Percentage meeting					(C) Number of close kin met in last year before interview — Percentage having met					(D) Number of other kin met in last year before interview — Percentage having met			
	0	1-2	3+	Mean	0	1-4	5-9	10+	Mean	0-4	5-14	15+	DK etc.	Mean	0	1-4	5+	Mean
Stable in Class I (N = 75)	55	27	18	1.5	13	43	36	8	4.9	20	55	21	4	10.2	19	31	50	6.5
Directly mobile to Class I, intermediate-class origins (N = 52)	52	25	23	1.5	6	46	31	17	5.5	25	50	19	6	10.1	13	31	56	7.5
Indirectly mobile to Class I, intermediate class origins (N = 65)	32	34	34	2.1	11	40	35	14	5.4	28	51	15	6	9.2	26	38	36	5.4
Directly mobile to Class I, working-class origins (N = 48)	46	17	37	2.4	23	33	25	19	5.7	19	50	21	10	10.3	15	54	31	4.6
Indirectly mobile to Class I, working-class origins (N = 86)	45	26	29	2.0	7	38	35	20	6.3	20	53	26	1	11.2	23	37	40	5.6
All upwardly mobile to Class I (N = 251)	43	26	31	2.0	11	39	32	18	5.8	23	51	21	5	10.3	20	40	40	5.8
Downwardly mobile from Class I (N = 68)	44	13	43	2.4	10	41	37	12	5.4	25	41	22	12	8.9	21	41	38	5.6
Stable in Classes VI and VII (N = 155)	19	30	51	3.6	8	32	35	25	7.0	19	37	29	15	12.3	32	38	30	5.7

(See notes to Table 6.1)

importance. From Table 6.7 it is evident that among our mobile respondents generally, as among our intergenerationally stable groupings, there is little variation in the extent of 'weekly' contact with kin when only those respondents with kin living in close proximity are considered. For present purposes, the most significant fact shown up by this table is then that the proportion of mobile respondents who have kin readily available—less than a third overall—is closer to that found among men stable in Class I than among those stable in Classes VI and VII. And here again, we would argue, the crucial factor is the requirement for geographical mobility that is typically imposed by service-class occupations.

Table 6.7

Number of close kin usually met at least once per week: respondents inter-generationally mobile and respondents intergenerationally stable in Class I and Classes VI and VII with kin living within 'about ten minutes walk'

Mobility pattern	Percentage meeting			Mean	N	Percentage of all
	0	1–2	3+			
Stable in Class I	12	41	47	3.0	17	23
Directly mobile to Class I, intermediate-class origins	22	33	44	2.7	9	17
Indirectly mobile to Class I, intermediate-class origins	19	33	48	3.1	21	32
Directly mobile to Class I, working-class origins	15	31	54	3.2	13	27
Indirectly mobile to Class I, working-class origins	11	37	52	3.1	27	31
All upwardly mobile to Class I	16	34	50	3.0	70	28
Downwardly mobile from from Class I	17	22	61	3.4	23	34
Stable in Classes VI and VII	13	30	57	3.3	96	62

(See note to Table 6.2)

Finally, reverting to Table 6.6, panel (C) we may observe that as regards contact with close kin on a yearly basis, where we previously found no great class differences, we in turn find no evidence of any marked or systematic deviation on the part of our mobile respondents from what would seem the generally prevalent pattern. And as regards contact with more distant kin as indicated in panel (D), what is chiefly notable is that while three of our four groupings of upwardly mobile men show lower levels of interaction than men stable in Class I (who had the higher level of our two benchmark groupings), the differences are all rather slight. If upward mobility were in fact associated with a tendency to 'drop' kin, as, for example, Homans and Schneider have suggested, one would then surely expect this tendency to be revealed sharply in the case of more distant kin, towards whom feelings of obligation would not be overriding.

In Tables 6.8 and 6.9 we turn to data on kin as a source of help and of leisure-time associates, presented in the same form as in Tables 6.3 and 6.4. So far as our mobile respondents are concerned, the findings set out in Table 6.8 would appear highly consistent in their implications with those we have just reviewed on the extent of contacts with kin. In reply to each of our three questions on potential sources of help in domestic or family crises, men in each of our mobile groupings were, with only two minor exceptions, less likely to report that they would look to their kin for help than were our intergenerationally stable working-class respondents, but more likely than men in our stable service-class grouping. In other words, in the case of respondents who had been upwardly mobile into Class I, we may say that, far from being isolated from their kin, these men appear rather more reliant upon them than do those 'born' into Class I. Moreover, the difference here in the relative importance of kin tends to widen —in the same way as between our two benchmark groupings—as the degree of help that would be typically required increases. Thus in panel (C), in the situation of lengthy illness, it can be seen that the extent to which upwardly mobile men, of both working-class and intermediate-class origins, would look to their kin for help does in fact come rather close to the stable working-class level. Further still, as another indication that for those upwardly mobile, at least, kin may be of particular importance as a source of support, we may note that among respondents who have kin living near, upwardly mobile men rather more often stated that they would resort to kin, in each of our three hypothetical situations alike, than did men stable either in Class I *or* in Classes VI and VII—the proportions being, in the first situation, 37 per cent (of men in all upwardly mobile groupings taken together) as against 29 per cent and 31 per cent in the two stable groupings; in the second, 84 per cent as against 71 per cent and 79 per cent; and in the third, 83 per cent as against 53 per cent and 80 per cent.

Lastly in this connection, the data of Table 6.8 panel (D) on help actually received at the birth of children are also of some significance. They would suggest that if our mobile respondents deviate at all from the pattern found to prevail within both our benchmark groupings, in which the importance of kin was overwhelming, it is in fact in those upwardly mobile having drawn to an even greater extent on help from this source. In the light of these findings, it can then be seen how particularly inapt it is for Stacey, in arguing that mobile couples frequently do not have their kin at hand 'when they really need them', to cite confinement as one of the occasions on which this isolation becomes apparent.[24]

The inferences we have drawn from our data so far are thus ones which would lead us, for the most part, to play down the implications of mobility for kinship relations. However, the contents of Table 6.9, on kin as leisure-time associates, show a rather different pattern from those of the preceding tables, and may serve to alert us to the danger of any oversimplified view. From the first two columns of the table and the last, it may be observed that, in this case, our mobile respondents, rather than showing a level of interaction with kin which lies somewhere between those displayed by our benchmark groupings, are clearly comparable, in their limited degree of contact with kin, to men stable in Class I. At least, then, for men who have been upwardly mobile into Class I from working-class origins, whom we can compare with our respondents stable in

Table 6.8

Relative importance of kin as a source of help: respondents intergenerationally mobile and respondents intergenerationally stable in Class I and Classes VI and VII

% who would look for help to kin (K), neighbours (Ne), friends etc. (F), other/DK

Mobility pattern	(A) If respondents needed to borrow tool or material				(B) If respondent (and wife) ill for couple of days				(C) If respondent/ wife ill for several weeks				(D) Percentage (of married respondents with children) having received help when children born from			
	K	Ne	F	O/DK	K	Ne	F	O/DK	K	Ne	F	O/DK	Kin	Neighbours	Others/ No one	N
Stable in Class I (N = 75)	15	52	21	12	46	21	21	12	51	11	13	25	80	5	15	41
Directly mobile to Class I, intermediate-class origins (N = 52)	13	52	27	8	50	21	21	8	71	6	10	13	86	0	14	28
Indirectly mobile to Class I, intermediate class origins (N = 65)	18	59	18	5	69	23	6	2	69	8	8	15	97	0	3	39
Directly mobile to Class I, working-class origins (N = 48)	27	48	19	6	60	23	13	4	65	4	13	18	85	0	15	27
Indirectly mobile to Class I, working-class origins (N = 86)	16	59	13	12	56	30	9	5	71	6	6	17	85	6	9	53
All upwardly mobile to Class I (N = 251)	18	56	18	8	59	25	12	4	69	6	9	16	88	2	10	147
Downwardly mobile from Class I (N = 68)	22	43	26	9	56	20	12	12	59	10	9	22	80	3	17	30
Stable in Classes VI and VII (N = 155)	26	45	17	12	72	14	6	8	77	15	7	1	83	6	11	90

(See notes to Table 6.3)

Classes VI and VII, we have evidence associating mobility with some reduction in the relative importance of kin (and, at the same time, corroborating that previously presented to indicate a decline in contact with kin on a 'weekly' basis). Moreover, when in this respect we 'control' for the ready availability of kin, we disclose a situation which is in direct contrast with that found when kin were considered as a source of help. Among respondents with kin living within ten minutes' walk, men in our mobile groupings have the *least* contact with kin in their leisure activities. For example, of men upwardly mobile from inter-mediate-class origins, upwardly mobile from working-class origins and down-wardly mobile respectively, 57 per cent, 40 per cent, and 52 per cent reported *no* such contact during the three days covered by our questions, as compared with 24 per cent of men stable in Class I and 34 per cent of those stable in Classes VI and VII. One is thus led to conclude that the relatively low level of interaction with kin in the context of leisure activities which our mobile respon-dents display is not adequately accounted for by their physical separation from kin alone, and reflects an element of choice as well as constraint.

From this point of view, there is one further feature of interest in the data of Table 6.9. From the third column of the table, it can be seen that upwardly mobile men of working-class origins, who have more leisure-time contact with kin than other 'mobiles', at least when kin are readily available, also report on average the largest number of other leisure associates who are not kin. One might therefore say that these men, to a greater extent than those upwardly mobile from intermediate-class origins or those in our stable groupings, 'supple-ment' their kin as leisure associates by drawing on work colleagues, neighbours and other friends, so that in this way, if not by total exclusion, the relative importance of kin in this role remains quite low—as the fourth column of Table 6.9 shows.

We complete the presentation of our findings in this section with Table 6.10, the contents of which follow the pattern of Table 6.5. From this latter table, it will be recalled, rather little difference was apparent between our two bench-mark groupings in the extent to which respondents' kin were known to those persons whom respondents reported as their most frequent spare-time associates. Our data suggested that both service-class and working-class social networks showed in this respect a moderately high degree of connectedness. From Table 6.10, however, it may readily be seen that it is in this case of class similarity that our mobile respondents are in fact more distinctive than in any other. For each mobile grouping alike, the proportions both of respondents' first-mentioned spare-time associates and of all such associates mentioned who do not know well *any* of a respondent's kin are larger than in either of our benchmark groupings, while the proportions knowing well five or more kin are smaller. In other words, we have here evidence that a concomitant of mobility, at least in any of the relatively long-range forms to which our data relate, is that mobile individuals tend to be involved in less connected or, one might better say, more segmented social networks than do those who form part of either the working-class or service-class cores. In the light of this evidence, we may add, we may now better understand the seemingly 'deviant' finding of Table 6.5, on which we earlier remarked: namely, that men intergenerationally stable in intermediate-class

Table 6.9

Relative importance of kin as leisure associates: respondents intergenerationally mobile and respondents intergenerationally stable in Class I and Classes VI and VII

Leisure contacts with kin and others over week-end and last week-day before interview

Mobility pattern	Percentage reporting no contacts with kin	Mean number of kin reported per respondent as associates in leisure activities	Mean number of non-kin reported per respondent as associates in leisure activities	Kin as percentage of all associates in leisure activities	Percentage of most frequent spare-time associates who are kin
Stable in Class I (N = 75)	51	1.9	5.8	24	8
Directly mobile to Class I, intermediate-class origins (N = 52)	52	2.5	5.0	33	6
Indirectly mobile to Class I, intermediate-class origins (N = 65)	52	1.8	3.9	31	7
Directly mobile to Class I, working-class origins (N = 48)	56	2.1	8.3	20	7
Indirectly mobile to Class I, working-class origins (N = 86)	48	2.1	6.1	26	12
All upwardly mobile to Class I (N = 251)	51	2.1	5.7	27	8
Downwardly mobile from Class I (N = 68)	57	1.6	4.9	24	9
Stable in Classes VI and VII (N = 155)	39	3.0	4.1	42	17

(See notes to Table 6.4)

Table 6.10

Acquaintance of most frequent spare-time associates with respondents' kin: respondents intergenerationally mobile and respondents intergenerationally stable in Class I and Classes VI and VII

Mobility pattern	Percentage of respondents' first-mentioned associates knowing 'well' or 'fairly well'			Number of first-mentioned associates	Percentage of *all* respondents' associates knowing 'well' or 'fairly well'			Total number of associates mentioned
	No kin	1–4 kin	5+ kin		No kin	1–4 kin	5+ kin	
Stable in Class I	47	33	20	58	53	31	16	131
Directly mobile to Class I, intermediate-class origins	59	33	8	39	67	28	5	102
Indirectly mobile to Class I, intermediate-class origins	58	33	9	45	67	27	6	112
Directly mobile to Class I, working-class origins	65	24	11	37	68	23	9	84
Indirectly mobile to Class I, working-class origins	61	24	15	70	60	28	12	164
All upwardly mobile to Class I	61	28	11	191	65	27	8	462
Downwardly mobile from Class I	50	38	12	56	57	35	8	125
Stable in Classes VI and VII	44	36	20	121	44	34	22	271

(See notes to Table 6.5)

positions whose first occupations were nonmanual report fewer ties of acquaintance between their spare-time associates and their kin than do our other stable respondents. For, as we also previously noted, a sizeable proportion of men in this grouping, as well as having perhaps experienced a fair amount of short-range mobility, may in fact be regarded as being potentially long-range mobile and indeed as actually *en route* for service-class positions.

How, then, may we best sum up the significance of the findings reported in the preceding sections—thinking first of their implications for the mobile individual and secondly for questions of class formation? To begin with, we may state in general terms what we have at several points suggested in regard to particular findings: that is, that the data we have presented go strongly against the argument that mobility is inimical to the maintenance of kinship ties. Mobile men, and, it should be remembered, men whose mobility is relatively long-range, are not isolated from their kin—unless isolation is in effect equated with physical distancing; nor do they show systematically lower levels of interaction with kin than individuals who are intergenerationally stable in class position. Moreover, in the case of our upwardly mobile respondents, we have found no evidence of a propensity to 'drop' kin but, on the other hand, several indications that for these men—whatever mobility route they may have followed—kin remain a particularly important source of social support.[25]

At the same time, though, we must not create the impression that, in the light of our findings, the implications of class mobility for kinship appear as more or less negligible. First, we have shown some grounds for supposing that upward mobility into a service-class position, from working-class origins at least, is associated with a reduction in interaction with kin occurring on a relatively frequent basis—chiefly on account of physical separation. And secondly, we have found evidence to suggest that, as a matter of choice to some extent as well as of constraint, upwardly mobile men are less likely than those intergenerationally stable to draw on their kin as a source of leisure associates; and further, that (together with those downwardly mobile) they are less likely to have leisure associates who are well acquainted with their kin.

If, therefore, we were to advance a general thesis to replace that which represents mobility as disruptive of kinship ties and the mobile individual as more or less isolated from his kin, it would, at all events, need to be one of a less simplistic kind. What is in fact suggested to us by our findings is that, rather than being isolated, the upwardly mobile man at least is typically involved in two, or possibly more, rather sharply differentiated sets of primary social relations, one of which comprises his kin and the other, or others, various categories of non-kin—neighbours, colleagues, friends, etc. We earlier maintained that no very basic differences exist between our benchmark groupings in either conceptions of kinship obligation or conceptions of the desirability of 'kin as friends'. We would now further argue that while the former are not greatly affected by the experiences of mobility between classes, the latter prove to be more mutable. In the context of leisure or 'spare' time—which is specifically associated with freedom from obligation—kin become less often the preferred associates of the upwardly mobile or are supplemented in this context by other associates who belong to a different 'social world'. Thus, one could say, the major implication of upward mobility so far as primary social relations are concerned is that, from the point of view of the mobile individual, their structure becomes more segmented and hence, perhaps, more demanding. If interpersonal problems are encountered in consequence of mobility, one might then expect them to arise not so much from the breaking of ties as from the difficulties of 'managing' a concurrent engagement in two or more social networks that are largely separate.[26] However, such management, one may suppose, is facilitated by the fact that the upwardly mobile individual does not usually remain in very close residential proximity to the majority of his kin, which means that his participation in his kinship and other networks can often be spatially, and temporally, segregated.[27]

Whether the thesis we have outlined is as applicable to the primary social relations of downwardly mobile as of upwardly mobile individuals is hard to say—because, as we earlier noted, downward mobility, at least as represented in our data, is a rather problematic phenomenon. From what we know of patterns of counter-mobility, we must assume that among our downwardly mobile respondents there will be some sizeable proportion who have not in fact made any very decisive break with their social origins and who will return to Class I positions in the course of their careers. It is then possible that where 'true' downward mobility occurs, a tendency does exist for ties with some, perhaps more distant, kin to be broken, but that this tendency is obscured in the data of Table 6.6 by the presence in our downwardly mobile grouping of men who are but momentarily displaced from Class I and whose kinship relations conform to the pattern of the Class I core. On the other hand, though, it is still the case that in Table 6.8 kin appear as being if anything of greater importance as a source of help to our downwardly mobile respondents than to those stable in Class I, which might then be taken to imply that those whose downward mobility from this class is more or less decisive, rather than merely transient, are especially reliant upon the support of their kin. And finally, following the same logic in regard to Tables 6.9 and 6.10, one would suppose that what may here be obscured is the full extent to which in the case of 'true' downward mobility from Class I, the part played by kin in leisure activity is diminished and the individual's most frequent spare-time associates are persons unfamiliar with his kin.

If we now turn to the implications of our findings for questions of class formation, it is important that we first recall the extent to which the mobility flows that concern us differ in volume, upward mobility being much more frequent than downward. Taking an inflow perspective, we may note that of all respondents to our 1972 inquiry who held Class I positions, as many as 52 per cent had been recruited intergenerationally either from Classes VI and VII or from the lower-level categories of Classes III-V[28] (as compared with only a quarter who were of Class I origins); while, on the other hand, men downwardly mobile from Class I accounted for less than 2 per cent of respondents in Classes VI and VII and for less than 6 per cent of those in *all* categories of Classes III-V.[29] Thus, even if one were to assume that such downward mobility is of a generally permanent kind (which we know it is not) it would still play only a very minor part in the composition of the working and intermediate classes, and hence can be of little consequence for the degree of their internal homogeneity. In contrast, however, the substantial recruitment to Class I that occurs via upward mobility, of a relatively long-range kind, must create the potential for quite considerable heterogeneity within this class—and the actual extent and form of this, one may then suppose, will in large part depend upon individuals' experience of mobility at the level of primary relations. Thus, the question that we may here most usefully pose is that of the significance of our findings on mobility and kinship relations so far as socio-cultural diversity within the higher levels of the service class is concerned.

Since the data presented for men in our benchmark groupings indicated that class differences in normative orientations to kinship are not marked, high mobility into the service class might not be expected to create any very great diversity in this respect; and indeed, in regard at least to conceptions of kinship obligation, the data we have subsequently presented by way of comparing the kinship relations of men upwardly mobile into Class I with those intergenerationally stable in this class would generally bear out this expectation. However, we have also argued that as a concomitant of upward mobility some decline is apparent in both the availability *and* the desirability of kin as associates in leisure-time activity; and further, that the normative shift here involved has relational consequences in that the social networks of the upwardly mobile tend to be segmented, with kinship and other primary relations being kept largely apart. Some divergence in life-style between stable and mobile members of the service class is then in this way implied, and one which would in itself suggest that the latter remain somewhat less than perfectly assimilated.

Moreover, of perhaps greater significance in this respect than differences in the structure of primary social relations are differences in participants. The fact that mobility does not lead to the disruption of kinship ties in the way that has been often supposed has consequences that go wider than the personal situation of the mobile individual. It makes it highly probable that those members of the service class who have been recruited via long-range mobility—as we have seen, a rising proportion—will be distinguished from its core members by having more relatively close social ties with persons who hold quite different class positions to their own. We may gain some idea of the basis that kinship, and in particular the family of origin, can provide for such 'cross-class' ties by turning again to the data of our national inquiry. We may note, for example, that of all men in our 1972 sample who had gained access to Class I from working-class or lower intermediate-class origins, as indexed by their father's occupation when they were aged 14, over 80 per cent had fathers who were still in this same range of class positions as indexed by their 1972 occupations, or by their last occupation if dead or not working in 1972. And further we can estimate that of these mobile men around a half had brothers who occupied such low-level positions—the proportion falling to under 40 per cent in the case of those upwardly mobile from intermediate-class origins but rising to over 60 per cent in the case of those mobile from working-class origins.[30] We do not ourselves have evidence of the actual extent of cross-class interaction with kin on the part of our mobile respondents; and the possibility of course exists of 'differential association' in that mobile men may have less contact with those kin who have remained in their class of origin than with those who have been in some degree mobile themselves. However, it may be added that data presented by Richardson indicate that while some such tendency may be at work, it is not at all a powerful one; and that mobility does serve to generate quite extensive cross-class ties via kinship relations.[31]

If, then, we accept that at least a substantial, and increasing, minority within the service class will be linked via effective kinship relations with persons who remain at the lower levels of the class structure, it becomes tempting to speculate what construction might most appropriately be put on this fact—given that good grounds exist in both theory and research for supposing that it is through the individual's primary relations that social influences bear most forcefully upon his attitudes and behaviour. Is the integrative function of mobility here underlined, in that as well as allowing able and enterprising individuals from disadvantaged backgrounds to realize their legitimate ambitions, it serves also to multiply social ties across lines of class division—thus blurring these lines, diminishing 'social distance' between the members of different classes, and reducing the likelihood of disruptive class conflict? Or is it rather the inchoate, still largely unformed nature of the expanding service class that is chiefly signified—the result of 'recruitment from below' too extensive to permit the effective assimilation of new members and now, perhaps, a potential source of socio-political instability?

However, before any such speculations can be profitably pursued we need of course to extend our examination of the concomitants of mobility to take in more than kinship relations alone. As we previously noted, kinship may be regarded as a critical case in that if the primordial ties that it entails are found to be eroded by mobility, there would seem no reason why other forms of primary relation should prove more impervious. But since we have in fact concluded that there is no clear tendency for kinship relations to be disrupted by mobility—although their social content may be modified—we must by the same logic accept that whether or not mobility is compatible with relational continuity in other respects is very much an open question. For example, it could well be the case that mobility *has* in general a 'dissociative' effect, and that kinship relations because, say, of the important element of obligation that they involve, are exceptional in being able to withstand the strain. The issue is obviously one that can be decided only through further analysis of empirical materials, and this we shall aim to provide in the chapter that follows.

NOTES

1. For an elaboration of this distinction, see John H. Goldthorpe and David Lockwood, 'Affluence and the British Class Structure', *Sociological Review*, n.s. vol. 11, 1963.
2. We define primary social relations, largely following Cooley, as ones which are recurrent, on a face-to-face basis, and which are entered into and maintained for more than specific instrumental reasons.
3. Talcott Parsons, 'The Social Structure of the Family' in Ruth N. Anshen (ed.), *The Family: Its Function and Destiny*, New York: Harper, 1949; and 'A Revised Analytical

Approach to the Theory of Social Stratification' in Bendix and Lipset (eds.), *Class, Status and Power*, 1st edn.

4. David M. Schneider and George C. Homans, 'Kinship Terminology and the American Kinship System', *American Anthropologist*, vol. 57, 1955, p. 1207. Cf. also Sorokin, *Social and Cultural Mobility*, pp. 522–5, 544.

5. Barrie Stacey, 'Some Psychological Consequences of Inter-generation Mobility', *Human Relations*, vol. 20, 1967. Stacey's position, it should be said, is a good deal more extreme than that of the writers previously referred to. It seems possible that he has in fact misunderstood Parsons's—admittedly far from unambiguous—arguments. Cf. the latter's attempt at a restatement: 'The Normal American Family' in S.M. Farber (ed.), *Man and Civilisation: The Family's Search for Survival*, New York: McGraw-Hill, 1965.

6. Studies lending some—but by no means extensive or unequivocal—support are Robert P. Stuckert, 'Occupational Mobility and Family Relationships', *Social Forces*, vol. 41, 1963; A.M. Mirande, 'The Isolated Nuclear Family Hypothesis: a Reanalysis' in J. Edwards (ed.), *The Family and Change*, New York: Knopf, 1969; and for Britain, Peter Willmott and Michael Young, *Family and Class in a London Suburb*, London: Routledge, 1960, ch. vii and Appendix 3.

7. Cf. Eugene Litwak, 'Occupational Mobility and Extended Family Cohesion', *American Sociological Review*, vol. 25, 1960.

8. Cf. B.N. Adams, *Kinship in an Urban Setting*, Chicago: Markham, 1968.

9. This approach to 'mobility effects' derives essentially from Duncan, 'Methodological Issues in the Analysis of Social Mobility'. Its main application in the study of mobility and kinship is in Michael Aiken and David Goldberg, 'Social Mobility and Kinship: A Re-examination of the Hypothesis', *American Anthropologist*, vol. 71, 1969. The approach is not, however, without its conceptual and technical problems. Cf. Keith Hope, 'Models of Status Inconsistency and Social Mobility Effects', *American Sociological Review*, vol. 40, 1975.

10. Another weakness of many studies in the field is that information on kinship was in fact obtained from interviews with the *wives* of the men sampled. As Nicholas Tavuchis has put it (in an unpublished paper, 'Mobility and Family: Problems and Prospects', p.11), 'while it is the husbands who are moving it is the wives who are talking'. In our interviews wives were in fact present in a majority of cases, and were encouraged to participate in those sections (among others) dealing with kinship relations.

11. As Sorokin pertinently observes: 'If we want to know the characteristic attitudes of a farmer, we do not go to a man who has been a farmer for a few months, but we go to one who is a farmer for life.' *Social and Cultural Mobility*, pp. 509–10. The same approach, we believe, must guide one in seeking to determine characteristic class attitudes and behavioural patterns.

12. Although this approach will essentially involve us in comparing statistical data as between our benchmark and mobile groupings, we shall not employ tests of statistical significance as a means of evaluating differences that are displayed. On this continuingly controversial issue, our position is—briefly—as follows. First, we regard the value of such tests in social research as being greatest where one is concerned with testing discrete, well-defined hypotheses for a given population, on the basis of data from a simple random sample or from a more complex sample for which, however, estimates of design effects are possible. Where such conditions largely prevailed, as in our analyses in chapters 3 and 4, we have used significance tests—although even then as providing only one among various other possible indications of how we should interpret our results. Secondly, though, where these conditions to a major degree do not apply—as, for example, in the analyses of this and the following chapter—we believe that significance tests have rather little to contribute, and that the best guide to the 'significance' of statistical data is the extent to which the total set presented reveals, or fails to reveal, particular patterns of theoretical interest, and the degree to which these patterns are, or are not, in line with those shown up by other inquiries into the same issues. In other words, informed—but at the same time, of course, corrigible—judgements must take precedence over (supposed) statistical demonstrations. For an elaboration of this position, see Morrison and Henkel (eds.), *The Significance Test Controversy*, in particular the contributions by Hogben, Lipset *et al.*, Camilleri, and the editors themselves.

13. Note that while we subsequently regard these two groupings as together forming our working-class core, they do not include men intergenerationally mobile between the skilled and nonskilled sections of the working class, who were not covered by the 1974 inquiry. However, since no systematic differences occur, in the respects that here concern us, between men intergenerationally stable in Class VI and in Class VII, we think it unlikely that they should occur between men thus stable in these classes, on the one hand, and those mobile between them on the other—and especially so since we know that *in the course of their working lives* a majority of men in the former groupings have moved between skilled and nonskilled employment. Cf. above, pp. 129–31.

14. Almost 90 per cent of those men who had begun work in a nonmanual occupation were in fact intergenerationally stable in either Class III or Class V, while almost 90 per cent of those who had started in a manual occupation were intergenerationally stable in Class IV or Class V.

15. For both Class I and Class VI and VII respondents, it may be noted, the close kin who were seen on a weekly basis were overwhelmingly (i) parents, (ii) wife's parents, (iii) siblings, or (iv) wife's siblings. The proportions of Class I respondents who reported seeing 'weekly' at least one person in these kinship categories were, respectively, 27 per cent, 21 per cent, 15 per cent, and 8 per cent; and of Class VI and VII respondents, 45 per cent, 44 per cent, 36 per cent, and 29 per cent.

16. Cf. e.g., Harris and Clausen, *Labour Mobility in Britain, 1953-63*, and F. Musgrove, *The Migratory Elite*, London: Heinemann, 1963. Note that what is being alluded to here is the dispersion of kin resulting from a high rate of geographical mobility among family members as a whole, and not just the movement of one individual or couple away from the rest of their kin. Thus it is possible for an individual or couple to become physically distanced from the majority of their kin while in fact remaining geographically *im*mobile.

17. From comparison of Tables 6.1 and 6.2 it may be inferred that among respondents who do not have kin living 'within about ten minutes' walk', the extent of 'weekly' contacts is much greater for men in our working-class than in our service-class core. In fact, only 29 per cent of the former as against 67 per cent of the latter report no such contacts. But we may suppose that kin who do not live within ten minutes' walk are still generally closer at hand in the case of our working-class than of our service-class respondents. We know, for example, that 10 per cent of the former had no close kin living within 25 miles of them and that 51 per cent had ten or more close kin within this radius, while the corresponding proportions for the latter were 36 per cent and 8 per cent.

18. If we omit from the analysis spare-time associates who were kin, we find that 53 per cent of all associates reported by stable Class I respondents knew none of their kin, and 14 per cent 5 or more, as against corresponding proportions for stable Class VI and VII respondents of 48 per cent and 16 per cent.

19. What is here termed 'connectedness' is now perhaps more usually referred to by social network theorists as 'completeness' or 'density'. Cf. J. Clyde Mitchell: 'The Concept and Use of Social Networks' in *idem* (ed.) *Social Networks in Urban Situations*, Manchester University Press, 1969.

20. These conclusions are generally in line with those arrived at in the most thorough community-based study of class and kinship to have been made in Britain, Colin Rosser and Christopher Harris, *The Family and Social Change*, London, Routledge, 1965. Rosser and Harris found that the most important class differences in contact with kin occurred in the case of the mother–daughter relation (see pp. 220–1 esp.), which is not of course covered, or at least not directly, by our data.

21. See Earl Hopper, 'Educational Systems and Selected Consequences of Patterns of Mobility and Non-Mobility in Industrial Societies: a Theoretical Discussion' in *idem* (ed.), *Readings in the Theory of Educational Systems*, London; Hutchinson, 1971; and C.J. Richardson, *Contemporary Social Mobility*, London: Francis Pinter, 1977.

22. It could be objected here that this conclusion might be different if we were to concentrate our attention on respondents' 'own'–i.e. consanguineal–kin and discount contacts with affinal kin: it is after all the respondents who have been mobile and not, necessarily, their wives. However, if we modify our analyses in the way in question,

the result remains the same: i.e. upwardly mobile men within Class I have more contact with their (own) kin on a relatively frequent basis than do men intergenerationally stable in Class I—though less contact than men stable in Classes VI and VII. The implication that there is little difference within either our benchmark or our mobile groupings in the general form of respondents' relations with consanguineal and affinal kin is in fact one consistent with the anthropological theory of bilateral kinship systems.

23. Note that such data as these can in themselves only suggest a decline in interaction with kin and not prove conclusively that this has in fact occurred. For example, it could be that through some process or other men who achieve upward mobility tend to be selected from among those in their class of origin who have relatively low levels of interaction with kin in the first place.

24. 'Some Psychological Consequences of Inter-Generation Mobility', p.6.

25. In the foregoing respects, our results may in fact be seen as generally in line, despite differences in data and methods of analysis, with those reported for the United States by Litwak, Adams, and Aiken and Goldberg in publications previously cited. They are also consistent with those reported by Richardson in his recent British study based on samples drawn from the London Metropolitan Region. See *Contemporary Social Mobility*, pp. 219–20. Of particular interest here is that our findings confirm Richardson's in indicating that, so far as kin are concerned, upward mobility achieved via an indirect, or, in his terms, 'non-sponsored', route is no more likely than mobility achieved directly to be disruptive of interpersonal relations—contrary to arguments advanced by Hopper and which seem, in part at least, to be accepted by Richardson himself. Cf. n. 21 above.

26. We did in fact ask respondents: 'Are there any relatives, whether on the chart [showing close kin] or not, you once felt very close to, but whom you no longer see so much of?' Mobile respondents were no more likely to report 'breaks' with kin of this kind than were men intergenerationally stable. For example, the proportions reporting no such instances were 59 per cent, 63 per cent, 58 per cent, and 47 per cent for respondents stable in Class I, stable in Classes VI and VII, upwardly mobile to Class I, and downwardly mobile from Class I respectively.

27. Compare with the foregoing the idea of the 'structural differentiation' of primary group relations within urban-industrial society suggested in Litwak, 'Occupational Mobility and Extended Family Cohesion' and developed in Litwak and Ivan Szelenyi, 'Primary Group Structures and their Functions: Kin, Neighbours, and Friends', *American Sociological Review*, vol. 34, 1969.

28. i.e. those covered in our 1974 inquiry: see Table 5.2.

29. These differences are of course a function both of differences in the size of the classes involved and of higher rates of upward than downward mobility, reflecting the proportionate expansion of the service class and contraction of the working class. For the birth cohorts covered in our 1974 inquiry, the discrepancy between upward and downward mobility rates is greater than for the 1972 sample as a whole. See ch. 3, pp. 73–4 above.

30. We obtained information on the 1972 occupation of one brother of each of our respondents who had a (living) brother or brothers. If the latter, the brother to whom our questions were to relate was selected randomly.

31. See *Contemporary Social Mobility*, pp.240–2.

CHAPTER 7

Class Mobility and Social Involvement

(*with* CATRIONA LLEWELLYN)

We noted in the previous chapter than arguments which claim that social mobility is disruptive of kinship relations have been advanced from different theoretical positions. On the one hand, writers such as Parsons have contended that the high rates of mobility typical of industrial societies render a system of extended kinship relations functionally inappropriate. On the other hand, writers such as Schneider and Homans have claimed that kinship ties are weakened by mobility, apparently because this tends to destroy the 'balance' of social exchange on which any stable relationship must, in their view, be founded. As we, and others, have shown there are serious objections of an empirically grounded kind that can be raised against such arguments. But it may further be remarked that in one important respect they are also analytically underdeveloped: they provide no explicit account, in terms of social action, of exactly why it should come about that kinship ties are neglected or broken off following upon the occurrence of mobility. Such an account is suggested only implicitly and—notwithstanding the theoretical differences involved—would seem in fact to derive from a largely shared set of 'taken-for-granted' assumptions concerning the nature of stratification and mobility within modern societies.

However, if in the analyses in question the content of these assumptions has for the most part to be inferred, in certain more ambitious attempts that have been made to treat the implications of mobility for primary relations in general, greater attention has in fact been given to the interpersonal processes that are supposedly involved. In these analyses—which are again of chiefly American inspiration—one finds assumptions of a very similar kind to those that seem likely to have informed discussions of mobility and kinship, but which are somewhat more fully spelled out. For the purposes of the present chapter, therefore, these more developed accounts represent a useful point of departure.

THEORETICAL PERSPECTIVES

First of all, it should be noted that in most treatments hitherto of the effects of mobility on the structure of primary relations, the form of social stratification within which mobility takes place has been conceived essentially in terms of *status*. If class inequalities have been considered at all, then they have been regarded as so closely correlated with status that, empirically at least, the distinction is of little significance. Secondly, it has been assumed that the status order is *also* a prime reality for social actors: that is to say, they are seen as having a highly developed status consciousness. They are sharply aware of the ways in which subcultural attributes serve to define status and much concerned with how their own life-styles and patterns of association will affect their status position, which they wish of course to be as elevated as possible. Thirdly, then, the crucial questions that arise for the individual who is mobile in, say, occupational or class terms have been assumed to be those of subsequent changes in his status group affiliations; or, in other words, questions of how effectively his occupational or class mobility may be translated into status mobility.

Given those assumptions, it becomes evident enough why mobility should be thought likely to place a strain on kinship relations. The mobile individual will have a different status position, potentially at least, to that of most of his kin, and this situation will tend to be damaging, or at any rate unhelpful, to the status concerns of one or the other of the parties to the kinship relation. Retaining close ties with his kin will not assist the upwardly mobile individual to establish himself at a higher status level than that of his family of origin, and to achieve this will mean giving time to the cultivation of new life-styles and acquaintances. Conversely, for the kin of a downwardly mobile individual to retain close ties with him will do little to enhance *their* status position, and could conceivably be detrimental to it.

It is also of course clear how arguments analogous to the foregoing could be developed in regard to other of the mobile individual's primary relations—with leisure and work associates, friends, neighbours, etc. Thus, one thesis which emerges from analyses of the kind in question is that mobility is likely to result in the disruption not only of the individual's kinship relations but of the entire pattern of his social life: mobility is seen as having a generally 'dissociative' effect. Moreover, the importance that is attached to considerations of status directly prompts a further thesis: that the disruption of the individual's primary relations attendant upon his mobility will not represent a merely temporary phase but is likely, rather, to bring him into a more or less enduring state of social isolation or, at least, marginality. In the case of the upwardly mobile individual, the social ties that his mobility will lead him to neglect or break— that is, ties with former associates who have not shared in his success—will not easily be replaced by others with those persons whom he would now wish to regard as his status equals. The *arriviste* will typically encounter coolness, if not actual rejection, in the social milieux that he has newly entered, since he may well appear as a threat to their exclusiveness and hence to the status of those already 'established' within them. On the other hand, the downwardly mobile individual will not wish to form new social ties in the milieux into which his decline has taken him, for this would tend to confirm his mobility which he would rather view as far as possible as being only short term. But, at the same time, he will find it difficult to maintain the primary relations in which he was previously involved before his decline became generally apparent.

Finally, then, one other thesis that has been frequently advanced is that mobility, because of the stresses that it tends to impose, is likely to be associated with some form of personal, as well as social, disequilibrium. This may find expression in feelings of insecurity and anxiety or even in more severe kinds of psychological disorder; or it may reveal itself in a pervasive *ressentiment* and in violent social prejudices and political extremism.

Among American authors, analyses on these lines have perhaps been most fully elaborated by Lipset and various collaborators, as we have described in our introductory chapter.[1] Here it may be added that basically similar views on mobility effects have in recent years been advanced by a number of commentators on British society. Stacey, for example, has claimed that those who have experienced mobility in present-day Britain 'frequently . . . suffer from being marginal people' and 'tend to live more isolated lives' than those not mobile; and it is evident that he regards the dynamics of status as chiefly determining this pattern.[2] Likewise Musgrove, writing of men who have been upwardly mobile into professional, administrative, and managerial occupations, sees them as facing serious 'problems of social isolation'. The disruptive effects of their social mobility are compounded by those of the geographical mobility in which their employment frequently involves them, thus reinforcing the situation of 'surburban loneliness' in which they are trapped. But, according to Musgrove, there is 'little doubt that social mobility, with or without geographical mobility, is associated with comparatively high rates of mental disorder'—because of the problems of interpersonal relations to which it gives rise.[3]

One other contribution of particular note is that of Hopper, who is specifically concerned with Anglo-American comparisons. Hopper addresses himself directly to the question of 'status rigidity' or, in other words, to the question of how easy or difficult it is 'for the economically mobile to acquire a legitimate position in the status hierarchy'.[4] Although he apparently regards the American status order as being inherently less rigid than the English, Hopper sees the crucial variable, so far as the experience of the individual is concerned, as being the type of mobility route that he has followed, in terms of the educational, training and selection processes that are involved. For example, upward mobility that is achieved via 'mainstream' educational channels is, in his view, less likely to be 'pathogenic'—that is, less likely to be associated with 'interpersonal isolation and loss of support'—than is such mobility achieved via other routes which imply at least an initial lack of success within the educational system. In England mobility of the former type may indeed be less pathogenic than in the United States because of the greater degree of 'sponsorship' and hence of 'status training' that is entailed. But, overall, upward mobility in England will tend to generate more social-psychological problems than in the United States, since more of this mobility occurs through 'initial rejection' routes and these routes are more likely to expose the individual to interpersonal difficulties. In contrast with the 'initial selection' routes, they provide no suitable preparation for the social hazards of the mobility they engender: 'Their career-training and status-training experiences are for the lower social classes, and are inappropriate for those who become upwardly mobile despite their having been initially rejected (and in effect incorrectly).'[5]

There is, then, no shortage of sociological argument which would treat mobility as having a generally dissociative effect, chiefly on account of the influence exerted on interpersonal relations by the status order, and specifically through patterns of social action oriented towards the enhancement or preservation of status. However, this line of argument has so far been little more successful than its particular variant relating to mobility and kinship in securing the degree of empirical confirmation required to drive alternative analyses from the field; and certain of the latter can in fact claim at least a comparable measure of empirical support.

First in this respect, one may note that even sociologists who would regard mobility as tending to disrupt primary social relations may still accept that this need not lead to the social isolation of the mobile individual. He may compensate for the difficulties he experiences at the primary level by a relatively high degree of participation in what Janowitz has referred to as 'secondary group structures'—that is, in the affairs of local communities, clubs and societies, interest-group organizations, political parties, and various other kinds of what we would generically term 'voluntary associations'. Thus, Janowitz has argued for the United States that while in the short term at least 'mobility may well contribute dysfunctionally to both individuals and to the society at large [through its effects on primary relations], there is enough evidence to indicate that social mobility creates new social relations in communities and toward large-scale organisations which are functional and integrative both for the individual and the society at large.'[6]

Further, though, the idea that mobility must always be associated with the impoverishment of primary relations has itself been called into question. For example, it has been argued by Litwak and others that upwardly mobile persons at least, and especially those working within bureaucratic contexts, tend to develop social skills in the course of their careers which enable them to form congenial and supportive social relationships relatively quickly, so that the disruptive effects of mobility, geographical as well as social, can be readily made good. Moreover, this process is facilitated where, as in modern industrial societies, even long-range mobility is a not infrequent occurrence; and still more so where employment and housing patterns tend to bring the mobile together with each other. In these circumstances, it appears somewhat inappropriate to think in terms of isolated *arrivistes* seeking acceptance within exclusive milieux and sharply defined status groups.[7]

Finally, and perhaps most radical of all, there is the position of those such as Duncan and his associates, who, as we have earlier remarked, would envisage the stratification of modern societies not as a hierarchy of status groups but rather as a virtually structureless socio-economic continuum. In turn, they would wish to see mobility as having direct and systematic implications only at a normative, and not at a relational level at all. That is to say, they would expect the effects of mobility on individuals' patterns of association to occur only via the changes brought about in norms defining and regulating acceptable forms of sociability; and further, they would expect that these changes would be towards some intermediate version of the norms generally prevalent at the levels of the socio-economic continuum between which mobility had taken place. Thus, for example, the patterns of friendship or of neighbouring of mobile individuals, or their participation in voluntary associations, would be seen as depending crucially not on the type of mobility route they had followed nor on any physical or social constraints occasioned by their mobility, but rather—in what would appear to be a highly voluntaristic fashion—on the particular normative 'compromises' that they had arrived at in these several respects.[8]

In what follows, then, we shall seek to assess the merits of these divergent views, so far at least as they apply to present-day British society. We shall proceed in essentially the same way as in the preceding chapter. That is to say, we shall try, first, to establish the patterns of social involvement that are character-istic of the intergenerationally stable respondents to our 1974 inquiry, and especially those characteristic of our two benchmark groupings, represented by men who were stable either within Class I or within Classes VI and VII of our sevenfold class schema.[9] Then we shall use these patterns as a basis for evaluating the comparable patterns that are displayed by our various groupings of inter-generationally mobile respondents, and with particular reference to the question of how far the disruption of primary relations and social isolation may be re-garded as concomitants of mobility. To the extent that there is evidence of any such connection, we shall wish further to ask how far this may be attributed to considerations of status; and to the extent that there is no such evidence, we may enquire why the dynamics of status have not operated in the way that the writers referred to above would have anticipated. Finally, however, we shall again attempt to treat the implications of our findings at the societal as well as the individual level, and with special reference to questions of class formation.

The data we have available on our respondents primary and secondary social relations are of six main kinds. At the primary level, we have rather extensive information on (i) those individuals (or couples) whom respondents reported as being their most frequent spare-time associates and on (ii) those they re-ported as being 'good friends' even though not perhaps seen very often. We shall concentrate on data on the number of such persons reported; on the way in which and time at which the respondent's relationship with them was first formed; and on their class affiliation. We also have information on (iii) the extent of acquaintance among those reported as respondents' spare-time associates and as 'good friends'; and further on the extent of acquaintance between per-sons in these two different categories. Finally at the primary level we have more limited information, chiefly data on frequency of contact, on (iv) our respon-dents' relations with their work colleagues in their out-of-work lives, and on (v) their relations with neighbours. At the secondary level, we then have a variety of information pertaining to (vi) our respondents' participation in voluntary associ-ations. We shall chiefly draw on data on the number of associations belonged to, frequency of participation, and the extent of office-holding; and further on the types of association belonged to.

CLASS AND PATTERNS OF SOCIAL INVOLVEMENT

In Tables 7.1 and 7.2 we present, for our intergenerationally stable respondents, data on their most frequent spare-time associates and on other 'good friends'. As regards the former, our two benchmark groupings of men intergenerationally stable in Class I and in Classes VI and VII show no marked differences in panel (A), in the number of spare-time associates they reported;[10] nor, in panel (C), in the length of time for which such associates had been known. Again, in panel (B), in which we show the distribution of spare-time associates by the origin of their relationships with respondents, the patterns displayed by the two groupings are broadly similar, and the only difference of note is perhaps that in the pro-portion of associates who were kin. As we previously observed, kin tend to play a greater part in the associational pattern of working-class than of service-class leisure—although in neither case are they of major importance.

It is in fact only in the remaining set of data, that of panel (D), in which we show the distribution of spare-time associates by class, that quite wide differences between our benchmark groupings are apparent in Table 7.1. What we document here, as various other inquiries have done before, is the extent to which in modern Britain segregation, or at all events highly differential association, on class lines is a dominant feature of the structure of sociability.[11] One qualification that we may however add in the light of our data is that the degree of such segregation is not uniform throughout the class structure. The distribution of the spare-time associates of men who appear intergenerationally stable in intermediate-class positions (but who, we know, have collectively experienced a great deal of work-life movement) is in fact rather even across the three broad class divisions that we distinguish in panel (D), thus throwing into sharper relief the skewness of the distributions for our two benchmark groupings.[12]

Turning then to our data on respondents' 'good friends', as presented in Table 7.2, we find here that class differences are rather more extensive. Men stable in Class I report clearly more relationships of the kind in question than do men stable in Classes VI and VII; and while there are no very great differences in the number of years over which such relationships have been maintained, interesting differences are evident in their origins. In particular, 'good friends' reported by stable service-class respondents were less likely to be relatives or old school friends than those reported by stable working-class respondents, and were more likely to be classified in the 'Other' category of panel (B)—that is to say, tended to be of more varied origin. Indeed, inspection of our interview schedules reveals that stable Class I respondents had formed friendships out of a rather remarkable diversity of initial acquaintances, although with professional and business contacts (apart from those with immediate colleagues) and introductions made at 'social' gatherings of one kind or another being especially important. Finally, from panel (D) of Table 7.2, it can be seen that differences between our benchmark groupings in the class composition of 'good friends' are yet more marked than in the case of spare-time associates. Of particular note is the degree of exclusivity that is shown in the friendships of men intergenerationally stable in Class I, four out of five of whose 'good friends' were also in service-class positions, as compared with only one in twenty who were manual wage-workers.[13]

We complete the presentation of our data on spare-time associates and friends in Table 7.3, on the basis of which we can examine the extent of acquaintance both among those persons whom respondents named in each of these categories and also between associates and friends. From panel (A) it can be seen that the spare-time associates reported by men stable in Classes VI and VII were clearly more likely to be acquainted with each other than were those reported by men stable in Class I. More technically, one could say that, at least where three associates were reported, the networks of working-class respondents were more likely than those of service-class respondents to be of a 'completely interlocking' form (as illustrated in Figure 7.1a), and less likely to be of a 'partially interlocking' or 'radial' form (Figures 7.1b–d).[14] In fact, it can be shown, if one combines data from Tables 7.2 and 7.3, that *among men reporting three associates*, these associates were involved in a completely interlocking network, anchored on the respondent, in 77 per cent of cases where the respondent was

Table 7.1

Most frequent spare-time associates: respondents intergenerationally stable in class position

Class	(A) Number reported[a]					(B) Percentage distribution of all reported by origin of relationship[b]							(C) Percentage distribution of all reported by years known[b]				(D) Percentage distribution of all reported by class[b]			
	Percentage reporting				Mean	Kin	School	Neigh-bour	Work	Vol. assoc.	Other	N	less than 5	5–10	more than 10	N	I–II	III–V	VI–VII	N
	0	1	2	3																
Class I (N = 75)	23	21	15	41	1.8	9	15	8	22	12	34	130	34	28	38	125	63	28	9	123
Classes III–V (first occupation nonmanual) (N = 47)	23	11	21	45	1.9	10	7	5	24	28	26	85	42	28	30	83	30	42	28	82
Classes III–V (first occupation manual) (N = 56)	27	16	27	30	1.6	20	10	13	16	13	28	90	13	39	48	82	25	36	39	76
Classes VI and VII (N = 155)	22	21	18	39	1.7	17	10	5	25	15	28	268	33	18	49	247	13	22	65	243

Notes: (a) Respondents were asked: 'Now, thinking generally, who are the people you *most often* spend you spare-time with—not counting your immediate family? For example, are there any people that you normally meet at least once a week, or a few times a month—they may be people you have mentioned already?' Interviewers recorded for each respondent details of up to three individuals or couples mentioned. In the figures reported here, couples are counted as one.

(b) Men who named at least one individual or couple in response to the above question were subsequently asked: 'Is he/she a relative (Are they relatives) of yours?', and, if not: 'How did you get to know one another?', 'What year did you meet?'; and then our standard series of questions designed to elicit details of an individual's precise occupation, employment status etc.

Table 7.2.
'Good friends': respondents intergenerationally stable in class position

Class	(A) Number reported[a]					(B) Percentage distribution of all reported by origin of relationship[b]							(C) Percentage distribution of all reported by years known[b]				(D) Percentage distribution of all reported by class[b]			
	Percentage reporting				Mean	Kin	School	Neigh-bour	Work assoc.	Vol.	Other	N	less than 5	5–10	more than 10	N	I–II	III–V	VI–VII	N
	0	1	2	3																
Class I (N = 75)	3	13	23	61	2.4	3	9	7	8	23	50	181	15	25	60	180	81	14	5	173
Classes III–V (first occupation nonmanual) (N = 47)	17	30	17	36	1.7	9	12	9	22	10	38	81	21	27	42	79	30	44	26	69
Classes III–V (first occupation manual) (N = 56)	30	13	27	30	1.6	9	23	10	20	5	33	88	14	20	66	85	29	45	26	73
Classes VI and VII (N = 155)	41	21	20	18	1.2	11	23	10	25	6	25	177	8	29	63	169	17	28	55	144

Notes: (a) Following the series of questions on their most frequent spare-time associates, respondents were asked: 'Are there any other people, whom perhaps you don't see very often, but whom you would still regard as close friends?' Interviewers again recorded details of up to three individuals or couples mentioned.

(b) Men who named at least one individual or couple in response to the above question were subsequently asked a further series of questions exactly the same in form as those stated in Note (b) to Table 7.1.

Table 7.3

Acquaintance among and between most frequent spare-time associates and 'good friends': respondents intergenerationally stable in class position

| | (A) Percentage distribution of sets of respondents' associates by number of links reported—i.e. associates know each other 'well' or 'fairly well.' (base: respondents reporting at least two associates)[a] | | | | (B) Percentage distribution of sets of respondents' 'good friends' by number of links reported—i.e. friends know each other 'well' or 'fairly well.' (base: respondents reporting at least two friends)[a] | | | | (C) Percentage distributions of sets of respondents' associates and 'good friends' by number of links reported between these categories—i.e. associates knowing friends 'well' or 'fairly well'[b] | | | | | | | |
| | | | | | | | | | (1) (base: respondents reporting at least one associate and one 'good friend') | | | | (2) (base: respondents reporting at least one associate) | | | |
Class	0	1-2	3	N	0	1-2	3	N	0	1-2	3-9	N	0	1-2	3-9	N
Class I	17	57	26	42	38	49	13	63	46	33	21	58	46	33	21	58
Classes III-V (first occupation nonmanual)	16	49	35	31	31	38	31	26	46	21	32	28	57	17	26	35
Classes III-V (first occupation manual)	12	47	41	32	48	43	9	32	38	28	34	29	56	20	24	41
Classes VI-VII	13	35	52	88	41	40	19	59	49	25	26	73	69	15	16	118

Notes: (a) Respondents were asked, of each possible pair of associates or friends named: 'Are they related to one another' and, if not: 'As far as you know, do they know one another? Well or fairly well? Slightly? Not at all? In the figures reported here associates or friends who were related are counted as knowing each other 'well' or 'fairly well.'
(b) Respondents were asked of each possible associate-friend pair the same questions as above.

Figure 7.1
Types of personal networks

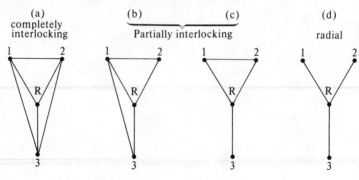

Key: R   = respondent
     1, 2, 3   = spare-time associates
     –   = acquaintance (know each other 'well' or 'fairly well').

intergenerationally stable in Class VI or VII, but in only 35 per cent of cases where the respondent was stable in Class I.

In the data of panel (B), relating to the extent of acquaintance among 'good friends', little difference is apparent between our two benchmark groupings, the number of links reported being, as one might expect, generally lower than among most frequent spare-time associates. However, if we again concentrate our attention on those respondents reporting the maximum of three, we may note that there are again more Class VI and VII than Class I respondents who are members of completely interlocking networks—39 per cent as compared with 17 per cent—while keeping in mind, of course, that the former were far less likely than the latter to name three 'good friends' in the first place.

Finally, little class difference is again shown up in panel (C1) in the extent of acquaintance between associates and friends—that is to say, where we consider only respondents who reported at least one individual (or couple) in each category. As is shown, about half of such respondents in each benchmark grouping reported one or more connecting links. However, a rather different picture is obtained if we consider, as in panel (C2), all respondents reporting at least one spare-time associate, and ask how far these frequently seen persons were linked by acquaintance to others whom respondents regarded as 'good friends' even though they might be less often seen—in other words, if we permit the fact that men stable in Class I reported more relationships of this latter kind than men stable in Classes VI and VII to enter into the analysis. In this case, our stable working-class respondents appear clearly as having the less connected—or rather the less developed—networks, so far as relations of sociability are concerned. In sum, then, we might say that while the working-class pattern of sociability is more likely than the service-class pattern to involve the individual in a highly connected set of regular spare-time associates, it is, on the other hand, less likely to involve him in wider-ranging networks which comprise, although perhaps in a more loosely connected fashion, *both* his regular spare-time associates *and* other persons with whom he maintains a tie of friendship.

The remaining data that we have on our respondents' primary social relations, namely, those of Table 7.4 on contacts with work colleagues and with neighbours, serve to confirm the view that relations of sociability within the service class are, typically, of a more extended kind than within the working class. Panel (A) of Table 7.4 shows that while a majority of men in both our benchmark groupings have no work colleagues whom they see outside work on a fairly regular basis, the average number of colleagues who *are* thus seen by men stable in Class I is still twice that for men stable in Classes VI and VII. And, rather more surprisingly, panel (B) shows an even more marked difference in the extent to which respondents were well acquainted with neighbours—broadly defined as persons living 'within about ten minutes walk of your home'. Contrary to the generally received idea (though one which has never been given strong empirical support) that intensive 'neighbouring' is an important component of working-class sociability, it can be seen that it is in fact among men stable in Class I, rather than in Classes VI and VII, that relatively close relationships with neighbours were the more frequent.[15] We may add here that inspection of our interview schedules points also to differences of a more qualitative kind in the contacts reported both with colleagues outside work and with neighbours. While in the case of service-class respondents such contacts tended more to result from arrangements made specifically for purposes of sociability—the drink together after work, the coffee or wine-and-cheese party, etc.—in the case of working-class respondents they appeared more often to be casual ones—for example, 'meeting in the pub'; or ones where sociability was still more incidental—the chance encouter 'over the garden fence', 'in the street', or 'at the match'.[16]

Lastly, then, we turn to our data on the extent of our respondents' involvement in 'secondary group structures', which pertain in fact to various aspects of their participation in voluntary associations. In Table 7.5 we present data on the extent of such participation. Class differences are once more evident, and are of a kind that the results of previous research would lead one to expect. Men intergenerationally stable in Class I belong to more voluntary associations than do men stable in Classes VI and VII; they spend more time in participation in the affairs of such associations; and they are far more likely to hold, or to have held, official positions within them.[17] Moreover, panel (D) of Table 7.5 indicates that a greater proportion of the associated memberships of service-class respondents are of relatively recent date: 53 per cent had been taken up within the five years preceding the interview, as against only 28 per cent of the memberships reported by working-class respondents. What then is suggested here is that in the typical service-class life-style voluntary associations are joined at relatively frequent intervals, so that, over the course of his life, the individual steadily accumulates memberships—even though, as a result, say, of geographical mobility, some may be dropped at the same time as new ones are entered into. In contrast, the typical working-class pattern would appear to be for associations to be joined far less frequently—and with some concentration perhaps in early adulthood—but for memberships to be continued, on average, for a longer period.[18]

Table 7.4

Contacts with work colleagues and neighbours: respondents intergenerationally stable in class position

Class	(A) Number of work colleagues seen outside work 'fairly regularly'[a]				(B) Number of neighbours known 'well' or met 'fairly often'[b]			
	Percentage reporting			Mean	Percentage reporting			Mean
	0	1–4	5+		0	1–4	5+	
Class I (N = 75)	54	27	19	2.4	37	43	20	3.2
Classes III–V (first occupation nonmanual) (N = 47)	47	40	13	2.0	60	30	10	1.8
Classes III–V (first occupation manual) (N = 56)	64	32	4	0.7	57	32	11	1.8
Classes VI and VII (N = 155)	55	37	8	1.2	60	32	8	1.4

Notes: (a) Respondents were asked: 'Of the people you work with, are there any that you see outside work fairly regularly for any reason?'
(b) The question was: 'Now I would like to ask about the people living in your neighbourhood; that is, within about ten minutes's walk of your home. Apart from the people that you see casually in the street from time to time, are there any neighbours that you know quite well or meet fairly often?'

Table 7.5

Participation in voluntary associations: respondents intergenerationally stable in class position

Class	(A) Number of associations belonged to[a]					(B) Number of associations in which respondent participates at least 2 hrs. per month[b]					(C) Percentage holding or having held office in an association[b]	(D) Percentage distribution of all associational membership by number of years' duration[b]		
	Percentage belonging to				Mean	Percentage participating in				Mean		less than 5	5–10	more than 10
	0	1–2	3–4	5+		0	1	2	3+					
Class I (N = 75)	4	31	33	32	3.6	32	36	27	5	1.1	52	53	24	23
Classes III–V (first occupation nonmanual) (N = 47)	15	62	21	2	1.7	53	28	15	4	0.6	17	50	33	17
Classes III–V (first occupation manual) (N = 56)	18	66	14	2	1.6	62	32	4	2	0.5	23	45	29	26
Classes VI and VII (N = 155)	25	53	18	4	1.5	61	25	9	5	0.6	19	28	31	41

Notes: (a) The question was: 'Now I would like to ask you about clubs, societies, associations, etc. that you may belong to, or be connected with in some way. Are you, for example, a member of, or in any way connected with, a . . . [running prompt] sports or hobby club, educational or cultural group, social club, church or church group, political party, trade union or professional association, residents' association, tenants' association, parent-teacher association, charitable association? Are there any bodies whatsoever of this kind that you have any connection with?'
In the case of positive answers, the name of the association was recorded, and a count made of all associations mentioned.
(b) For each association mentioned, respondents were also asked: 'In what year did you join?'; 'Roughly how many hours per month or year do you spend on activities connected with [the name of association]?'; 'Do you hold any official position, or serve on any committee?' and, if not: 'Have you ever done so?'

Table 7.6

Types of voluntary association belonged to: respondents intergenerationally stable in class position

Class	Percentage distribution of all associational memberships reported by type of association[a]							Total number of memberships reported
	Social	Sports (1)[b]	Sports (2)[b]	Educational Cultural Hobby	Occupational	Political Residential Religious Charitable etc.[c]	Other	
Class I (N = 75)	2	15	11	9	28	16	19	272
Classes III–V (first occupation nonmanual) (N = 47)	13	6	23	6	18	15	19	78
Classes III–V (first occupation manual) (N = 56)	12	6	23	4	26	16	13	90
Classes VI and VII (N = 155)	28	3	15	5	30	10	9	240

Notes: (a) The data of this table derive from the question given in note (a) to Table 5.
(b) Sports (1) is restricted to sports clubs of a kind which, in our judgement, have typically a relatively high degree of exclusivity, whether economically or socially based: i.e. clubs etc. concerned with golf, squash, sailing, tennis, rugby, game fishing, rowing, hockey, rally driving, flying and gliding. Sports (2) comprises all other sports clubs.
(c) i.e. including all other broadly defined 'interest groups'.

Further insight into the differences in question can be gained from Table 7.6, in which we show the distribution of the memberships reported by men in our intergenerationally stable groupings among various types of voluntary association. It can be seen that in the case of Class VI and VII respondents two types of association account for well over half of all memberships: that is, social clubs, very largely in fact working men's clubs; and occupational associations, overwhelmingly trade unions. Membership in associations of both these types is rather likely to be taken up at an early stage in working life. Among Class I respondents, on the other hand, associational involvements are clearly more diversified. Membership of occupational associations—in this case, mostly professional bodies—is of similar importance as among working-class respondents; but while participation in purely social clubs is almost negligible, membership in all other types of voluntary association that we distinguish figures more prominently.[19] The associational involvements of service-class men, one might surmise, tend to develop, along with their interests, as they move through successive stages of the life-cycle. However, what is at any rate clear is that at the secondary level as at the primary, the service-class pattern of social participation, whether or not more intensive than the working-class one, is certainly of a more extensive and varied kind.

In chapter 6 we felt the need to stress that class differences in kinship relations might easily be exaggerated, and that those differences that were observable were often the result more of class-linked constraints of a physical kind than of divergent class norms. In the present context it is evident that class differences, and ones that have an essentially normative basis, are rather well-defined. The structures of sociability and of social involvement generally within the life-styles of those respondents forming our two benchmark groupings display quite sharply contrasting features. Furthermore, we have shown that these differences go together with an often high degree of social segregation. In particular, men intergenerationally stable in Class I reveal a strong tendency to select their spare-time associates and friends from among those in a generally similar class position, and appear to be largely lacking in such ties of sociability with working-class people. In the case, then, of our mobile respondents, and especially of those who have been upwardly mobile into Class I positions, there is at all events the clear possibility of their advancement being accompanied by socio-cultural discontinuities; and in turn, therefore, any question of their assimilation into the stable 'core' of their new class will obviously require consideration in both normative *and* relational terms.

MOBILITY AND PATTERNS OF SOCIAL INVOLVEMENT

In Tables 7.7 and 7.8 we present data on the spare-time associates and 'good friends' of our groupings of mobile men alongside those for our two benchmark groupings of intergenerationally stable respondents. The first point that can be made on the basis of these tables is that they provide no support for the idea that mobility tends generally to lead to social isolation. From panel (A) of Table 7.7 it can be seen that men in our several mobile groupings show no tendency to report fewer spare-time associates than do men in our benchmark groupings, and neither do the former, taken over all, contain a larger proportion

Table 7.7

Most frequent spare-time associates: respondents intergenerationally mobile and respondents intergenerationally stable in Class I and in Classes VI and VII

Mobility pattern	(A) Number reported					(B) Percentage distribution of all reported by origin of relationship							(C) Percentage distribution of all reported by years known				(D) Percentage distribution of all reported by class			
	Percentage reporting				Mean	Kin	School	Neigh-bour	Work	Vol. assoc.	other	N	less than 5	5–10	more than 10	N	I–II	III–V	VI–VII	N
	0	1	2	3																
Stable in Class I (N = 75)	23	21	15	41	1.8	9	15	8	22	12	34	130	34	28	38	125	63	28	9	123
Directly mobile to Class I, intermediate-class origins (N = 52)	25	10	10	56	2.0	6	4	9	22	22	37	102	56	26	18	101	60	32	8	101
Indirectly mobile to Class I, intermediate-class origins (N = 65)	31	8	20	42	1.7	7	12	11	27	21	22	111	32	32	36	112	51	33	16	109
Directly mobile to Class I, working-class origins (N = 48)	23	21	15	42	1.8	7	8	8	34	21	22	84	38	28	34	79	62	28	10	80
Indirectly mobile to Class I, working-class origins (N = 86)	19	16	21	44	1.9	12	7	11	33	13	24	164	36	26	38	155	51	31	18	150
All upwardly mobile to Class I (N = 251)	24	14	17	45	1.8	8	8	10	29	18	27	461	40	28	32	447	55	31	14	440

Table 7.7 (cont.)

Mobility pattern	(A) Number reported					(B) Percentage distribution of all reported by origin of relationship							(C) Percentage distribution of all reported by years known				(D) Percentage distribution of all reported by class			
	Percentage reporting				Mean	Kin	School	Neigh-bour	Work	Vol. assoc.	other	N	less than 5	5–10	more than 10	N	I–II	III–V	VI–VII	N
	0	1	2	3																
Downwardly mobile from Class I (N = 68)	18	24	16	43	1.8	9	12	11	26	16	26	122	46	23	31	120	35	42	23	105
Stable in Classes VI and VII (N = 155)	22	21	18	39	1.7	17	10	5	25	15	28	268	33	18	49	247	13	22	65	243

(See notes to Table 7.1)

Table 7.8

'Good friends': respondents intergenerationally mobile and respondents intergenerationally stable in Class I and Classes VI and VII

Mobility pattern	(A) Number reported					(B) Percentage distribution of all reported by origin of relationship							(C) Percentage distribution of all reported by years known				(D) Percentage distribution of all reported by class			
	Percentage reporting				Mean	Kin	School	Neigh-bour	Work	Vol. assoc.	other	N	less than 5	5–10	more than 10	N	I–II	III–V	VI–VII	N
	0	1	2	3																
Stable in Class I (N = 75)	3	13	23	61	2.4	3	9	7	23	8	50	181	15	25	60	180	81	14	5	173
Directly mobile to Class I, intermediate-class origins (N = 52)	15	14	31	40	1.8	3	13	3	31	9	41	102	16	25	59	100	69	23	8	94
Indirectly mobile to Class I, intermediate-class origins (N = 65)	11	20	25	44	2.0	9	12	9	36	9	25	132	11	26	64	131	61	29	10	121
Directly mobile to working-class origins (N = 48)	19	10	19	52	2.0	9	22	2	18	20	28	98	5	29	67	93	66	29	5	90
Indirectly mobile to Class I, working-class origins (N = 86)	19	23	24	34	1.7	7	13	13	27	11	29	149	8	26	65	144	55	33	12	139
All upwardly mobile to Class I (N = 251)	16	18	25	41	1.9	7	14	8	28	12	31	481	10	27	63	468	62	29	9	444

Table 7.8 (cont.)

Mobility pattern	(A) Number reported					(B) Percentage distribution of all reported by origin of relationship							(C) Percentage distribution of all reported by years known				(D) Percentage distribution of all reported by class			
	Percentage reporting				Mean	Kin	School	Neigh-bour	Work	Vol. assoc.	other	N	less than 5	5-10	more than 10	N	I-II	III-V	VI-VII	N
	0	1	2	3																
Downwardly mobile from Class I (N = 68)	22	20	24	34	1.7	9	21	10	25	3	32	115	25	29	46	112	35	39	26	101
Stable in Classes VI and VII	41	21	20	18	1.2	11	23	10	25	6	25	117	8	29	63	169	17	28	55	144

(See Notes to Table 7.2)

of respondents who were isolated in the sense of being unable to name *any* such associates.[20] In panel (A) of Table 7.8 it is true that mobile men are shown to report on average fewer 'good friends' than stable Class I respondents; but it is also the case that they report *more* such friends than do respondents stable in Classes VI and VII. Thus, in the case at least of men upwardly mobile into Class I from working-class origins, we have evidence which, far from connecting mobility with social isolation, would rather suggest that it may lead to a more developed pattern of sociability.

Some understanding of why in these respects mobility has not had any obvious dissociative effects can perhaps be gained from the further data of Tables 7.7 and 7.8 on the origins of respondents' relationships with associates and friends. Thus, as regards associates, panel (B) of Table 7.7 shows that while upwardly mobile respondents especially were less likely than those intergenerationally stable to draw on kin or old schoolmates—in other words, on persons whom they would have known from an early stage in their lives—they compensated for this, so to speak, by drawing more heavily on work colleagues and on persons whom they had met via voluntary associations. Again, as regards 'good friends', panel (B) of Table 7.8 indicates that although the friends of mobile men come from a narrower range of sources than those of men stable in Class I—that is to say, a smaller proportion have to be allocated to the 'Other' category of the panel—the friendship relations of the mobile are, by this same criterion, still more diverse in their origins than are those of men stable in Classes VI and VII. And it can in fact be shown that just as the lower average number of friends reported by mobile individuals relative to the service-class 'norm' is attributable largely to the more restricted sources on which they draw, so can the higher number they report relative to the working-class 'norm' be in turn attributed to their greater propensity to recruit their friends from a circle of acquaintance that is wider than that provided by family, school, and neighbourhood.

Turning next to our data on the length of time over which associates and friends have been known, we find here again evidence that is on the whole hard to reconcile with the view that the effects or concomitants of mobility are of a radically dissociative kind. From panel (C) of Table 7.7, it might be concluded that there is some tendency for the spare-time associates of our mobile respondents to have been known for a shorter period than those of men intergenerationally stable in either Class I or Classes VI and VII; but in fact in only one out of the five mobile groupings is the difference at all marked. Furthermore, the corresponding data for 'good friends', as presented in panel (C) of Table 7.8, show a clearly different pattern. While the friendships of downwardly mobile men appear as being of shorter duration than those of our stable respondents, this is not the case with those of men in the upwardly mobile groupings. As can be seen, within each of these groupings alike some three-fifths or more of the 'good friends' reported had been known for longer than ten years. This is then scarcely the situation one would expect to find if mobility were regularly associated with the disruption of interpersonal relations and with the more or less permanent isolation of the mobile individual.

We can in fact produce evidence that is of more direct relevance in this last respect if we relate, on an individual basis, the dates from which associates and friends had been known to the dates from which men in our upwardly mobile groupings could be regarded as having achieved their mobility—for example, from the time of their first gaining access to a service-class position as covered by either Class I or Class II of our schema. Proceeding thus, we find that while only 19 per cent of all spare-time associates reported by upwardly mobile men were known before the respondent had attained a service-class position, this was the case with as many as 45 per cent of all 'good friends' reported. At the same time, though, we should also note that this latter figure, as might be expected, conceals a fairly wide difference between men who had been directly mobile into the service class on completing full-time education and those whose mobility had been through an indirect route: 36 per cent of the 'good friends' reported by the former were known prior to their entry into the service class, but 51 per cent of those reported by the latter.

The remaining information presented in Tables 7.7 and 7.8, in their respective panels (D), is that which pertains to the class affiliations of our respondents' associates and friends—in which respect, the tables remind us, our two bench-mark groupings were sharply, if not surprisingly, differentiated. What is indicated by the corresponding data for our mobile respondents may then in turn appear rather unremarkable if, to begin with, we express it in general terms: namely, that in the case of both spare-time associates and 'good friends', mobility would appear to be in some degree conducive to relationships that cut across class lines. This is in fact again a finding which previous research has made into a virtual commonplace.[21] However, a number of more specific points may be noted in the data that are of further interest.

First, it may be observed that the associates and friends of men directly mobile into Class I, from whatever class origins, are somewhat closer in their class composition to those of men stable in Class I than are those of men whose upward mobility was indirect. But secondly, it has also to be recognized that even in the case of men in our indirectly mobile groupings, at least a half of both the associates and friends reported were themselves in Class I or II positions—that is, a decidedly larger proportion than is found in the case of our working-class benchmark grouping or, for that matter, of our groupings of men inter-generationally stable in intermediate-class positions (see Tables 7.1 and 7.2). Thus, while our findings here would clearly lend support to the view that upward mobility reduces the extent of the individual's close personal relations with other, non-mobile members of his class of origin, they are, on the other hand, scarcely compatible with the claim that the mobile individual is likely to be cut off from such relations with other members of his class of destination.[22]

A third point of interest concerns our downwardly mobile respondents. As we have previously remarked, it is difficult to know how far the mobility of these men should be taken as representing a decisive break with their class origins, rather than a temporary shift which will in due course be offset by some process of counter-mobility. While we cannot resolve this difficulty by reference to Tables 7.7 and 7.8, it is none the less worth noting that although men down-wardly mobile from Class I would certainly appear to be less socially detached from their origins than men upwardly mobile to Class I, they do report a much lower proportion than the latter of associates and friends who are themselves in service-class positions. If then one would wish to argue—as we in fact do—that the chances of counter-mobility for such downwardly mobile men are relatively high, one must at the same time accept that the downward shift preceding counter-mobility may well have significance as more than simply a stage in the individual's occupational career which leaves his social situation otherwise unchanged.[23]

Each of the foregoing points can be usefully sharpened if we next reanalyse our data on the class composition of the associates and friends of our mobile respondents from a different angle: that is, so as to bring out the degree of homogeneity that exists *within the sets of associates and friends reported by individuals*, rather than among all those reported by a particular grouping. This is done in Table 7.9.

On the basis of this table, one could first of all claim that among men directly mobile into Class I, and especially among those thus mobile from intermediate-class origins, a clear majority (those represented in the first two columns of the table) are effectively 'assimilated' into the service class, in terms of relations of sociability; while, on the other hand, only a small minority of around one in ten (those men represented in the last column of the table) are entirely unassimilated.[24] Among respondents whose upward mobility was via indirect routes, the extent to which such assimilation has occurred is clearly less; but most still have *some* involvement with other service-class members, the entirely unassimilated minority being in this case around one in five. In this regard, it is the contrast between men indirectly mobile into Class I and those downwardly mobile from this class that is perhaps most instructive. It is the latter, it can be seen, who are clearly the more cut off, so far at least as relations of sociability are concerned, from service-class contacts. Again, then, even though we may doubt the permanence of much of the downward movement that we have recorded, mobility still appears as being more likely to militate against close relationships with members of the class from which the individual has moved than to prevent the formation of such relationships with members of the class into which he has entered.

One matter remains to be clarified. We have shown that only a minority of our upwardly mobile respondents are totally uninvolved in relations of sociability with other service-class members; and that within all upwardly mobile groupings alike, a majority of the spare-time associates and 'good friends' reported fall into our Classes I and II. But previously we noted that, in the case at least of friends, the relationships reported tended to be of quite long standing, and not infrequently dated back to before the time when respondents had first achieved a service-class position. How, then, are these two findings connected? Were relationships that antedated the achievement of mobility more likely than those formed subsequently to be ones with persons who did not hold service-class positions, and is it in this way that one may account for the lower degree of assimilation into the service class of men who had followed indirect mobility routes?

Plausible though these suggestions may appear, our data point in fact to a rather more complex situation, as can be seen from Table 7.10. It is true that in the case of spare-time associates, 28 per cent of those reported by men indirectly mobile into Class I, as against only 6 per cent of those reported by men directly

Table 7.9

Class composition of sets of spare-time associates and 'good friends' reported by mobile respondents

Mobility pattern	Class composition of sets of associates and friends reported Percentage					N [a]
	All service-class	Majority service-class, remainder intermediate-class	Other: some service-class	Other: no service-class		
Directly mobile to Class I, intermediate-class origins	25	39	28	8		49
Directly mobile to Class I, working-class origins	35	19	34	12		48
All directly mobile to Class I	30	29	31	10		97
Indirectly mobile to Class I, intermediate-class origins	25	18	36	21		63
Indirectly mobile to Class I, working-class origins	20	18	42	20		81
All indirectly mobile to Class I	22	18	40	20		144
Downwardly mobile from Class I	10	16	33	41		61

Note: (a) All reporting one or more spare-time associate or 'good friend'.

Table 7.10

Distribution of spare-time associates and 'good friends' reported by upwardly mobile respondents by class and by date of origin

Mobility pattern	Met before access to service-class Percentage			N	Percentage of all		Met after access to service-class Percentage			N	Percentage of all
	I-II	III-V	VI-VII				I-II	III-V	VI-VII		
Associates											
Directly mobile to Class I (N = 100)	36	46	18	11	6		63	29	8	170	94
Indirectly mobile to Class I (N = 151)	42	33	25	73	28		54	31	15	186	72
All mobile to Class I (N = 251)	42	34	24	84	19		58	30	12	356	81
Friends											
Directly mobile to Class I (N = 100)	73	22	5	67	36		64	28	8	117	64
Indirectly mobile to Class I (N = 151)	54	34	12	132	51		62	28	10	128	49
All mobile to Class I (N = 251)	60	30	10	199	45		63	28	9	245	55

mobile had been known prior to the respondent's access to a service-class position; and that such associates were somewhat less likely to have been in a service-class position in 1974 than were ones met only after mobility had been achieved. On the other hand, though, considering 'post-mobility' associates only, one may note that those of men who had followed direct mobility routes were still more likely to be service-class members themselves than were those of men who had followed indirect routes. Furthermore, in the case of 'good friends', it could scarcely be claimed that *any overall* tendency exists for 'pre-mobility' relationships to be less often with persons who were in service-class positions in 1974 than relationships initiated later. The greater proportion of service-class friends reported by our directly mobile than by our indirectly mobile groupings results from the fact that, while there is little difference in the class distribution of post-mobility friends, the pre-mobility friends of indirectly mobile men were less likely than their post-mobility ones to be currently in service-class positions, but those of directly mobile men were *more* likely.

In sum, our findings would indicate that in seeking to account for differences in the class composition of associates and friends among our upwardly mobile respondents, the issue of whether relationships antedated or postdated their attainment of a high-level class position is, at all events, of less straightforward relevance than much previous theorizing might lead one to suppose.[25] In particular, there is no basis here for the assumption that relationships initiated prior to upward mobility will be overwhelmingly ones with persons of a lower class position than that which the mobile individual has himself achieved. Even in the case of the spare-time associates of men indirectly mobile to Class I, where some tendency is evident for pre-mobility relations with persons in lower class positions to be 'carried-over', it still works out that a quarter of all the service-class associates whom these men report were also ones known from their pre-mobility days.

What, therefore, one is led to conclude is either that our upwardly mobile respondents, as part perhaps of some process of anticipatory socialization, had quite frequently formed relationships with 'established' service-class persons in the period before they had themselves gained access to this class; or, as we would think generally more important, that many of their current service-class associates and friends who are of long standing had also, like themselves, made their way into the service class from lower class origins and could thus be met *en route* on a basis of approximate social equality, whether in the course of their education or of their earlier working lives. The high probability of this kind of occurrence is brought out if we recall that, as previously shown (cf. Tables 2.1 and 5.1), only a minority, indeed less than a third, of all men found in Classes I and II in our 1972 national inquiry were of Class I and II origins—and that of these, only a half had also first entered employment in a Class I or II occupation; while, on the other hand, we may add, as many as 58 per cent came from the range of lower-level origins from which we selected our upwardly mobile respondents in 1974.[26]

Thus, we would believe, one major reason why in our inquiry we have found so little support for the idea that mobility leads to social marginality and isolation is that in present-day Britain the upwardly mobile at least are sufficiently numerous, as a component of the service class, to be able to provide *each other* with ample possibilities for relations of sociability, even supposing it to be the case that they encounter difficulty in forming such relations with members of the service-class core. In other words, we would endorse here the argument of Litwak and others that in an expanding industrial society, in which rates of upward mobility are relatively high, the problem of assimilation facing the mobile individual is far less severe than in societies in which such rates are low. It is not, or not necessarily, a problem of gaining acceptance, as a conspicuous outsider, into established social circles but rather, one may suppose, a problem not essentially different from that facing the stable individual—that is to say, one of forming relationships with, so to speak, his own kind, whom he can find about him in some number.

Finally in regard to our mobile respondents' associates and friends, we may examine, on the basis of Table 7.11, the extent of acquaintance that existed among and between persons thus named. We previously concluded that our two benchmark groupings differed chiefly in that the working-class pattern of sociability more frequently involved the individual in a highly connected network of acquaintance among spare-time associates, while the service-class pattern more frequently involved him in a wider-ranging, if more loosely connected network, which comprised both his regular spare-time associates and other persons whom he thought of as 'good friends'. How, then, do the corresponding social networks of men in our mobile groupings compare with these two patterns?

So far as the extent of acquaintance among spare-time associates is concerned, it can be seen from panel (A) of Table 7.11 that the position of our mobile respondents is generally an 'intermediate' one. In particular, one may note that the proportion of respondents reporting three associates all knowing each other 'well' or 'fairly well' is greater in each mobile grouping than in our Class I benchmark grouping, but less than in our Class VI and VII grouping. The respondents involved in such 'completely interlocking' networks represent 55 per cent of all cases where three associates were named among men upwardly mobile, and 44 per cent among those downwardly mobile, as against the previously reported figures of 35 per cent and 77 per cent among our stable service-class and working-class respondents respectively.

However, as regards acquaintance among 'good friends,' and also between associates and friends, a different situation is found. As is shown in panel (B) of Table 7.11, the tendency is, if anything, for acquaintance among the friends of our mobile respondents to be less extensive than among those of men in either of our benchmark groupings; and further, as shown in panel (C1), for men in our upwardly mobile groupings, taken as a whole, to report fewer links existing between their associates and their friends. In turn, when on the basis of panel (C2), we consider the question of how far men were in fact involved in networks in which links between regular spare-time associates and others regarded as 'good friends' were a feature, our upwardly mobile respondents appear as less involved than men intergenerationally stable in Class I, and indeed as very comparable in this respect to our stable working-class respondents, even though, as we observed earlier, they reported on average more friends than did the latter.

What we have here thus is some further indication—although the differences

Table 7.11

Acquaintance among and between most frequent spare-time associates and 'good friends': respondents intergenerationally mobile and respondents intergenerationally stable in Class I and Classes VI and VII

Mobility pattern	(A) Percentage distribution of sets of respondents' associates by number of links reported—i.e. associates know each other 'well' or 'fairly well' (base: respondents reporting at least two associates)				(B) Percentage distribution of sets of respondents' 'good friends' by number of links reported—i.e. friends know each other 'well' or 'fairly well' (base: respondents reporting at least two friends)				(C) Percentage distribution of sets of respondents' associates and 'good friends' by number of links reported between these categories—i.e. associates knowing friends 'well' or 'fairly well'							
									(1) (base: respondents reporting at least one associate and one 'good friend')				(2) (base: respondents reporting at least one associate)			
	0	1–2	3	N	0	1–2	3	N	0	1–2	3	N	0	1–2	3–9	N
Stable in Class I	17	57	26	42	38	49	13	63	46	33	21	58	46	33	21	58
Directly mobile to Class I, intermediate-class origins	21	41	38	34	58	28	14	36	58	21	21	33	64	18	18	39
Indirectly mobile to Class I, intermediate-class origins	10	54	36	41	50	39	11	46	69	15	15	39	74	13	13	45
Directly mobile to Class I, working-class origins	11	52	37	27	44	41	15	34	44	22	33	27	60	16	24	37
Indirectly mobile to Class I, working-class origins	7	52	41	56	40	42	18	50	53	29	17	58	62	24	14	70
All upwardly mobile to Class I	11	50	39	158	48	38	14	166	57	23	20	157	64	19	17	191
Downwardly mobile to Class I	12	58	30	40	41	49	10	39	34	34	32	44	48	27	25	56
Stable in Classes VI and VII	13	35	52	88	41	40	19	59	49	25	26	73	69	15	16	118

(See notes to Table 7.3)

in question are not strongly marked—that, so far at least as upward mobility is concerned, the disruption of primary social relations is a less probable concomitant than their segmentation. Previously we presented evidence to show that although men thus mobile were not typically isolated from their kin, they were less likely than men intergenerationally stable to draw on their kin as a source of leisure associates, and further that their kin were less likely to be known well to those persons with whom they did most frequently associate in their spare time. We now see that these regular spare-time associates of our upwardly mobile respondents, while more often well known to each other than those of men stable in Class I, tend to be somewhat less closely linked by acquaintance to other 'good friends' than are the associates of respondents in either of our benchmark groupings. And in this way, then, the impression is heightened of these mobile men being implicated in different 'social worlds' which are only rather tenuously, if at all, interconnected.[27]

The remaining comparisons that we can make between the primary relations of men in our mobile and our two benchmark groupings are in regard to their contacts with work colleagues and with neighbours. The relevant data are shown in Table 7.12. Once more, our mobile respondents are found in an 'intermediate' position, averaging fewer work colleagues and neighbours with whom relations of sociability could be regarded as well established than men stable in Class I, but more than men stable in Classes VI and VII.[28] This holds good for each mobile grouping considered separately, but with some tendency for men who had followed a direct route to Class I to report more contacts, with work colleagues at least, than men who had followed an indirect route. Again, therefore, as in the case of the number of 'good friends' reported (Table 7.8), we have evidence which would indicate that upward mobility into the service class, and in particular from working-class origins, will tend to lead not to isolation but rather to a more developed or, at all events, to a more widely based pattern of sociability, on the lines of that of the service-class core. In other words, to the extent that such mobility is associated with normative shifts influencing relations of sociability, these will be ones in a direction that will tend to offset, or to compensate for, any other concomitants of mobility which may be of a socially disruptive kind.

We argued above that one major reason why our findings have failed to confirm the idea of mobility as a generally dissociative phenomenon is that in present-day Britain the upwardly mobile form so large a component within the service class that the problem of their 'assimilation' is unlikely to be an especially severe one. We may now suggest a second, complementary reason: namely, that since movement upwards into the service class does in fact represent by far the most frequent form of relatively long-range mobility, the normative implications of such mobility will, on balance, be far more conducive to a greater range and diversity in relations of sociability than to their rupture or contraction. It is in the case of mobility downwards from the service class that the normative implications might be expected to reinforce any isolating effects: but, as we have shown, mobility of this kind is only rather rarely observed. Furthermore, it must even then be regarded as generally less decisive and permanent than movement in the reverse direction. And hence, one may add, it is not altogether surprising

Table 7.12

Contacts with work colleagues and neighbours : respondents intergenerationally mobile and respondents intergenerationally stable in Class I and Classes VI and VII

Mobility pattern	(A) Number of work colleagues seen outside work 'fairly regularly'				(B) Number of neighbours known 'well' or met 'fairly often'			
		Percentage reporting		Mean		Percentage reporting		Mean
	0	1-4	5+		0	1-4	5+	
Stable in Class I (N = 75)	54	27	19	2.4	36	41	23	3.2
Directly mobile to Class I, intermediate-class origins (N = 52)	60	27	14	2.1	52	29	19	2.5
Indirectly mobile to Class I, intermediate class origins (N = 65)	46	45	9	1.8	51	34	15	2.2
Directly mobile to Class I, working-class origins (N = 48)	48	37	15	2.2	46	31	23	3.1
Indirectly mobile to Class I, working-class origins (N = 86)	56	31	13	1.5	43	42	15	2.9
All mobile to Class I (N = 251)	53	35	12	1.8	47	35	18	2.7
Downwardly mobile from Class I (N = 68)	50	37	13	2.1	38	54	7	2.1
Stable in Classes VI and VII (N = 155)	55	37	8	1.2	60	32	8	1.8

(See notes to Table 7.4)

to find that in Table 7.11—as in panel (A) of Table 7.8—our downwardly mobile respondents are also, like those upwardly mobile, in an 'intermediate' position, although one that is somewhat further removed from the Class I pattern.

To conclude our presentation of data in this section, we may turn from our findings on primary relations to those of Tables 7.13 and 7.14 which pertain to our mobile respondents' involvement in 'secondary group structures' in the form of voluntary associations. As we noted earlier, certain writers have suggested that mobile individuals will display sharply different patterns of social participation at the primary and secondary levels—that is, in compensating for the problems they typically encounter in the former sphere by a particularly high rate of activity in the latter. However, the results that we have reported thus far have in fact given little indication that mobility *is* associated with special problems of interpersonal relations, or at all events with ones that lead to social isolation; and neither, in turn, would the data of Tables 7.13 and 7.14 support the expectation that mobile men should show a distinctively high degree of involvement at the secondary level. Rather, the main significance of these data, we would claim, lies in the corroboration and the further illustration that they provide for the main line of argument that we have developed in the immediately preceding paragraphs.

To begin with, it can be seen from Table 7.13 that on our several indicators of the extent of participation in voluntary associations, our groupings of mobile respondents once more occupy 'intermediate' positions between those of our two benchmark groupings. Their participation is generally less than that of men intergenerationally stable in Class I, while being greater than that of men stable in Classes VI and VII. Likewise the data of Table 7.14 would indicate that our mobile respondents are 'intermediate' as regards the variety of the associations in which they are involved—although memberships falling into the 'Sports (2)' and 'Educational', 'Cultural', and 'Hobby' categories figure rather more prominently in their case than in that of either of the stable groupings.[29] At the same time, however, it is also evident from Tables 7.13 and 7.14 that, in the main, the participatory pattern of the service-class core is more closely approximated by those men who have been upwardly mobile into Class I than by those who have been downwardly mobile from it; and that, among the former, this pattern is most closely approximated of all by men whose mobility into Class I was of a direct kind, that is, achieved on completion of full-time education.

Taken over all, such findings would thus appear far more in line with a theoretical argument which regards the most typical concomitant of mobility as being some rather generalized shift towards the prevailing norms of the class of destination—its extent, however, depending on the mode of mobility—rather than with one which starts from the supposition that all forms of mobility are likely to occasion more or less severe difficulties in relations at the primary level. In turn, the implication for the case of present-day Britain is clear enough: namely, that the quantitatively most important flow so far as relatively long-range mobility is concerned—that upwards into the service class—is one which will tend at the secondary level *as well as* at the primary to extend and diversify, rather than to undermine, the individual's pattern of social involvement.

We may now attempt to review the several conclusions to which the foregoing analyses have led us, with reference first of all to the conflicting arguments

Table 7.13

Participation in voluntary associations : respondents intergenerationally mobile and respondents intergenerationally stable in Class I and in Classes VI and VII

Mobility pattern	(A) Number of associations belonged to					(B) Number of associations in which respondent participates at least 2 hrs. per month					(C) Percentage holding or having held office in an association	(D) Percentage distribution of all associational memberships by number of years duration		
	Percentage belonging to				Mean	Percentage participating in				Mean		less than 5	5-10	more than 10
	0	1-2	3-4	5+		0	1	2	3+					
Stable in Class I (N = 75)	4	31	33	32	3.6	32	36	27	5	1.1	52	53	24	23
Directly mobile to Class I, intermediate-class origins (N = 52)	6	40	33	21	3.0	38	38	14	10	1.0	46	47	31	22
Indirectly mobile to Class I, intermediate-class origins (N = 65)	8	46	32	14	2.5	51	29	12	8	1.0	32	48	27	25
Directly mobile to Class I, working-class origins (N = 48)	8	44	27	21	2.8	40	37	17	6	0.9	38	45	35	20
Indirectly mobile to Class I, working-class origins (N = 86)	15	35	36	14	2.4	47	36	14	3	0.8	31	50	33	17
All mobile to Class I (N = 251)	10	40	33	17	2.6	45	35	14	6	0.9	36	48	31	21
Downwardly mobile from Class I (N = 68)	25	49	23	3	1.7	49	26	22	3	0.8	28	53	26	21
Stable in Classes VI and VII (N = 155)	25	53	18	4	1.5	61	25	9	5	0.6	19	28	31	41

(See notes to Table 7.5)

Table 7.14

Types of voluntary association belonged to : respondents intergenerationally mobile and respondents intergenerationally stable in Class I and in Classes VI and VII

Mobility pattern	Percentage distribution of all associational memberships reported by type of association							Total Number of Memberships reported
	Social	Sports (1)	Sports (2)	Educational Cultural Hobby	Occupational	Political Residential Religious Charitable etc.	Other	
Stable in Class I (N = 75)	2	15	11	9	28	16	19	272
Directly mobile to Class I, intermediate-class origins (N = 52)	4	13	17	7	32	15	12	155
Indirectly mobile to Class I, intermediate-class origins (N =65)	5	15	22	10	20	15	13	165
Directly mobile to Class I, working-class origins (N = 48)	3	13	21	10	31	12	10	136
Indirectly mobile to Class I, working-class origins (N = 86)	6	12	19	6	26	17	14	205
All mobile to Class I (N = 251)	5	13	20	8	27	15	12	661
Downwardly mobile from Class I	14	5	28	11	18	12	12	114
Stable in Classes VI and VII	28	3	15	5	30	10	9	240

(See notes to Table 7.6)

outlined at the start of this chapter, the focus of which was on the implications of mobility for the social situation of the mobile individual. Secondly, though, we shall wish to consider the significance of our findings for the issue which is our own ultimate concern, namely, that of the implications of mobility—and of its typical concomitants in the lives of individuals—at the societal level and, specifically, for the process of class formation.

A recurrent theme in our commentary on our findings has been that they do not support, and indeed go generally contrary to, any claim that mobile individuals tend to be socially isolated or marginal. We find evidence, to be sure, that upwardly mobile persons at least are likely to become detached to a greater or lesser extent from relations of sociability with non-mobile members of their class of origin; but this does not then typically result in their isolation, or certainly not in any permanent way. Many may in fact be regarded as effectively assimilated into the service class, and most are involved in some degree in relations of sociability with other service-class persons. Of crucial importance here, we have argued, is the actual volume of upward mobility into the service class that has occurred over recent decades. This has meant that the upwardly mobile individual has by no means been in a minority situation: rather, he must in most cases have been surrounded—at his place of work, in his area of residence, etc.—by many others who have followed a similar social trajectory. In such circumstances, therefore, the question that has been pre-eminent for American writers of how far occupational mobility may be translated into status mobility must seem not a little out of place, and likewise the underlying assumption of a relatively well-ordered and stable status group structure. Even if we were to accept that the service-class core, or even smaller groupings within it, may still seek to preserve their status exclusiveness and will refuse social acceptance to *arrivistes*, this would still in no way imply that the latter would be deprived of opportunities for sociability within their class of destination. And of course the very extent of the inflow into the service class must in itself have increased the difficulty of maintaining status barriers, despite perhaps at the same time sharpening the desire to do so.[30]

A further point that we have had repeatedly to make is to the effect that aspects of the sociability of our mobile respondents cannot be set in contrast with ones that are common to the sociability of our intergenerationally stable respondents as a whole, but must rather be seen as intermediate in relation to the two generally divergent patterns of social involvement that our benchmark groupings display—that is, what we would wish to regard as the distinctive patterns of the service-class and working-class cores. This is the case, for example, with the number of 'good friends' reported and with the diversity of their sources; with the frequency of relatively close social contacts with work colleagues and neighbours; and with the extent of participation in voluntary associations. In these various respects, therefore, our findings would appear highly consistent with the arguments of those who have held that, in modern societies, mobility is unlikely to have any very dramatic effects at the relational level, which could be attributed to the experience of mobility *per se*; but that its typical concomitant will be some relatively gradual process of normative change, whereby the mobile individual comes to adopt a set of norms that are an intermediate, or mixed, version of those prevailing within the social levels that he has spanned.

However, while our data can be taken as providing ample evidence of such normative change, they serve also to show that normative and relational concomitants of mobility cannot be so readily separated as may sometimes have been supposed. On the one hand, it would seem clear that the shift towards service-class norms on the part of our upwardly mobile respondents has been a further major factor, along with their relatively large numbers within the service class, in counteracting any possibility of their social isolation or marginality, since the content of these norms is generally favourable to a high degree of social involvement. On the other hand, though, we have observed that differences exist among these upwardly mobile men in the extent of their assimilation into the service class according to the type of mobility route that they have followed. Within groupings of men indirectly mobile into Class I, conformity with service-class norms of sociability would appear to be somewhat less developed than within those of men whose mobility was of a direct kind; and it is among the former groupings that we find the larger numbers of men who have few, if any, ties of sociability with other persons in service-class positions. It is, then, difficult to resist the conclusion that differing modes of upward mobility involve men, over the course of their lives, in social contexts and relations which vary in the degree to which they will promote their adoption of the norms of their eventual class of destination—periods of time spent in positions at the lower levels of the class structure affording, one may suppose, conditions less conducive to anticipatory socialization than ones spent, say, in full-time higher education.

This, it may be recalled, is in effect an argument advanced by Hopper;[31] but what we would wish to stress is not, as Hopper does, the greater likelihood of indirect rather than direct mobility leading to 'interpersonal isolation and loss of social support', for we have found no evidence that these are typical concomitants of mobility of any kind. Rather, the point we seek to bring out is that the process of normative adaptation does not go on in a relational vacuum, and that its actual outcome will be conditioned not simply by the range of the individual's mobility but also by the particular mode of its achievement.[32]

Finally here we may note that notwithstanding the relatively high level of social involvement of our mobile respondents and their tendency to move to a greater or lesser extent towards the norms of sociability of their class of destination, we have in one respect found that, among the upwardly mobile majority at least, the relational structure of their sociability does tend to be somewhat distinctive as compared with that of men in the intergenerationally stable groupings that we have taken as our benchmarks. That is to say, in comparison with the latter, men upwardly mobile into Class I would appear to have social networks of a rather more segmented kind. In particular, those persons with whom they most frequently associate in their spare-time activities are less often linked by ties of reasonably close acquaintance not only with their kin but also with other persons whom they would regard as their 'good friends'. The differences in question are not great and, in the absence of more detailed research than ours, we can only speculate on why exactly they occur—perhaps, for example, to take over Merton's distinction, because upwardly mobile men are more likely than those stable in class position to be 'cosmopolitans' rather than 'locals'.[33] None the less, such findings do serve to alert us further to the danger of moving from one extreme of regarding mobility as being, through the dynamics of status, inherently disruptive of social relations to the other of seeing it as merely a matter of moving through some structureless continuum of socio-economic positions with no specific relational implications at all.

To turn now to questions of class formation, it may usefully be recalled that in considering these in regard to our analysis of the implications of mobility for kinship, we stressed, first, the importance of taking into account the relative volume of mobility flows; and second, the importance—and the problems—of knowing not only how far the pattern of mobility may, over all, have served to reduce or blur class differentiation, but further whether, on balance, this was likely to be a factor making for a greater or lesser degree of social integration and stability.

The much greater significance of upward than of downward mobility for class composition, as this may be demonstrated in a purely arithmetical manner, need not be further rehearsed. We may however note that, in one respect, the results we have reported do enable us to confirm this point in a more specifically sociological way. We have seen that, in modern Britain, intergenerational mobility has been more likely to remove individuals from close social contact with non-mobile members of their class of origin than to prevent them forming relationships with other members of their class of destination; but we may here further observe that this tendency is clearly more marked in the data we have presented in the case of upward than of downward movement (cf. Tables 7.7 and 7.8). Thus, it is not only that the extent of recruitment into the service class of men of low-level class origins is by far more important quantitatively than is that of recruitment into the working class of men of service-class origins: in addition, the mobility involved in the latter case can be regarded as less clear cut, in the sense of less often entailing some sharp relational discontinuity. This is, of course, what we might expect since we have previously argued that such mobility tends also to be less clear cut than that into the service class in being more likely to be offset by subsequent counter-mobility. In so far, then, as we accept the less decisive character of such downward movement in these two senses together, its impact on the internal homogeneity of the working class must be still further discounted than it would be on the basis of the data of a mobility table alone; for the extent of the inflow 'from above' thus indicated would, even though quite small, still give an exaggerated idea of the importance of the fully and permanently *déclassé* element.

If in fact downward mobility of the kind in question does have significance for class formation, then this, we would suggest, is less likely to be in regard to the composition of the classes into which it leads than in regard to that of the service class itself. As we did previously emphasize, our downwardly mobile respondents *were* less involved in relations of sociability with service-class members than with persons outside this class. Thus, we can scarcely regard their mobility as being generally spurious—for example, as merely a career stage without wider social implications—even though we may make the quite justifiable assumption that it will in many cases be eventually reversed. And to the extent that it *is* followed by counter-mobility, it will therefore have the effect of bringing into the service class, and indeed into its intergenerationally stable component, men who will tend to have a different social experience and different social relationships from those whose access to a service-class position was achieved directly. From this point of view, it is then relevant to recall the considerable part that has been played by counter-mobility in maintaining intergenerational stability within the service class over the period to which our data relate; but also the fact that while over recent decades counter-mobility to Classes I and II has not diminished in its absolute volume, its contribution to the intergenerational stability of these classes *relative to that of 'direct access' routes* has slowly declined.

As regards now the dominant—that is, the upward—mobility flows with which we are concerned, we may consider first of all their implications for class formation at the normative level: in other words, their implications for normative diversity, as expressed in differences in life-style, within the expanding service class. In the case of kinship, we came to the conclusion that mobility into the service class, even if relatively long range, would be unlikely to create any very great diversity since, at least so far as conceptions of kinship obligation were concerned, no marked differences between classes were apparent. Only in the—lesser—extent to which they drew on kin as spare-time associates did men upwardly mobile into service-class positions appear to differ in their normative orientations to kin from men stable in this class. However, in the case of patterns of social involvement considered more generally, quite wide class differences are regularly displayed, in particular between the core groupings of the higher service class and the working class, and thus the implications of upward mobility for socio-cultural heterogeneity within the service class would, potentially at least, seem further reaching. In fact, the corollary of our finding that mobility typically involves the individual in some degree of normative 'compromise' is that within the service class, as a major recipient of mobility over recent decades, normative diversity will have been considerably increased. In other words, we may conclude in the present context that the service class of present-day British society is not only highly heterogeneous in the social origins of its members, as we have previously shown, but further that this heterogeneity extends into various major aspects of its members' life-styles.

Secondly, moving to the relational level, the issue that is central is that of how far upward mobility flows have blurred lines of class division by increasing the frequency of close social ties between persons in different class positions. In our discussion of mobility and kinship, we argued that since mobility was not in fact inherently disruptive of kinship relations, it is probable that increased upward movement into the service class has resulted in a growing proportion of the members of this class being involved in cross-class ties of the kind in question. At the same time, though, we were also led to ask how far kinship might in this respect be a special case, in that, through the degree of obligation that is entailed, kinship relations are more resistant than most others to the strains that mobility may impose.

In the light of the findings of the present paper, an entirely unequivocal answer to this latter question is not easy to give. It is certainly true that a majority of the regular spare-time associates and 'good friends' of our upwardly mobile respondents at the time of interview were themselves in service-class positions—that is, we may safely assume, a larger proportion than of their close or effective kin. Nevertheless, the evidence we have on the length of time for which such relationships had lasted gives us no strong basis for supposing that these upwardly mobile men had shown a greater propensity than those in our stable groupings to 'drop' associates and friends. While we cannot rule out the possibility that they may have had some bias towards keeping up relationships with persons in higher- rather than lower-level class positions, there is also, as we have noted, the—quite considerable—possibility of their having preserved long-standing ties with persons who had in fact followed the same course of upward mobility as themselves.

Moreover, what should in any event be remembered here is that the extent to which cross-class relations were reported differs a good deal among our groupings of upwardly mobile men. We have already discussed the finding, from the standpoint of their 'assimilation', that men who had gained access to the higher service class via an indirect rather than a direct route—that is, who had spent on average a larger proportion of their lives at lower class levels—had in turn a larger proportion of associates and friends in intermediate- and working-class positions. From the present standpoint, however, this finding has a further significance. What we would argue is that intergenerational *and indirectly achieved* mobility into the service class should be thought of as being particularly inimical to class formation, on account of both its ideological *and* its social implications. On the one hand, it demonstrates more strikingly than does direct mobility the extent of opportunity for social ascent, in showing that even men of disadvantaged class origins who start their own working lives in low-level positions can none the less still rise towards the peak of the class structure; and, on the other hand, as we have seen, it is also more likely than direct mobility to engender social relations —in addition to those of kinship—that imply interpersonal solidarity across class boundaries.

Finally, then, it is relevant in this context to restate the fact that over the period to which our data refer, indirect routes have been quantitatively far more important than direct ones in recruitment to the service class. For example, of all respondents to our 1972 inquiry who had been intergenerationally mobile to Classes I and II, only 29 per cent had first entered work in a Class I or II position; and 60 per cent had followed an indirect route to Classes I and II from origins in the same range of lower-level categories as those of our upwardly mobile respondents of 1974. However, we must here again enter a qualification concerning the apparent trend over time. Just as for men of Class I and II origins the importance of counter-mobility back to these classes has been declining relative to that of routes giving direct access—even though remaining little altered in its actual volume—so too, we know, there has been a decline in the relative importance of indirect upward mobility into these classes for men of lower-level origins.

We are therefore obliged to conclude, first of all, that the implications of mobility for class formation in modern Britain by no means all run in the same direction. Rates and patterns of mobility between classes have been changing in rather complex ways and, further, different modes or routes of mobility, even between similar origins and destinations, tend to have different concomitants, both personal and social. There is perhaps one respect in which we can speak with no very great qualification. Most, if not all, of what we have established about the wider implications of long-range mobility flows at least, as well as about the pattern of these flows themselves, points towards an increasingly homogeneous working class. Long-range downward movement into this class may be regarded as a very minor element in its composition, and further as being both relatively impermanent and uncertain in character. On the other hand, though, in the case of the service class, the situation that has emerged from our analyses is clearly a far more complicated one, with a number of different and often countervailing tendencies being discernible. There can be little doubt that, as a result of mobility over recent decades, the service class has become internally more heterogeneous in terms of the social origins of its members and hence also, we would argue, of their life-styles. It would further seem reasonable to suppose that men in service-class positions are at the present time more frequently involved than previously in cross-class social ties, whether ones based on kinship or on sociability alone. But at the same time we have also noted changes in the pattern of recruitment to the service class which, while they may not diminish the diversity of the social origins of its members, would appear more likely, in the longer term, to heighten rather than to reduce both their subcultural distinctiveness and their social segregation from persons located elsewhere in the class structure.

In view, then, of these conflicting tendencies bearing on the development of the service class, it would seem particularly difficult to move on to any judgement on the still larger question of the implications of mobility for social integration and stability. We will, eventually, wish to confront this question, whether or not any very clear-cut answer to it would seem possible. But, before that, we may add to the material on which it will be relevant to draw by examining the concomitants of mobility, and immobility, from one other point of view: namely, that of mobile, or immobile, individuals themselves. That groupings of men formed according to their movement between, or continuity within, the classes we have distinguished should reveal fairly systematic differences in their social relationships, as we have seen in this and the preceding chapter, is itself some guarantee that the mobility we have observed in terms of our class schema is more than simply artefactual, and reflects movement between meaningful sociocultural entities. None the less, there may still be much to learn by inquiring further into the relation between this observed mobility and the actual experience of the individuals to whom we have attributed it. This will be the concern of chapter 8.

NOTES

1. See above, pp. 17–20. A further paper that has been highly influential is P.M. Blau, 'Social Mobility and Interpersonal Relations,' *American Sociological Review*, vol. 21, 1956. This paper, written before Blau's collaboration with Duncan in *The American Occupational Structure*, employs a sociologically stronger concept of status or prestige than that found in the latter work: 'Occupational mobility, both upward and downward, poses special dilemmas for establishing interpersonal relations and becoming integrated into the community. Attributes and orientations associated with socio-economic status do not furnish unambiguous criteria of social acceptance for mobile persons. They are marginal men, in some respects out of tune with others both in their new and original strata in the occupational hierarchy . . . The upwardly mobile must choose between abandoning hope of translating his occupational success into social acceptance by a more prestigeful group and sacrificing valued social ties and customs in an effort to gain such acceptance. The downwardly mobile must choose between risking rejections for failure to meet social obligations that are beyond his financial resources and resigning himself to losing his affiliation with a more prestigeful group' (p. 290). Cf. further Bruno Bettelheim and Morris Janowitz, *The Dynamics of Prejudice*, New York: Harper, 1950, and Janowitz, 'Some Consequences of Social Mobility in the United States' in *Transactions of the Third World Congress of Sociology*, London: International Sociological Association, 1956; and Melvin M. Tumin, 'Some Unapplauded Consequences of Social Mobility in Mass Society', *Social Forces*, vol. 36, 1957.
2. 'Some Psychological Consequences of Inter-generation Mobility', pp. 5–6.
3. Musgrove, *The Migratory Elite*, p. 119.
4. 'Educational Systems and Selected Consequences of Patterns of Mobility and Non-Mobility in Industrial Societies: a Theoretical Discussion', p. 301.
5. Ibid., pp. 330–2.
6. 'Some Consequences of Social Mobility in the United States', p. 199.
7. Cf. Eugene Litwak, 'Reference Group Theory, Bureaucratic Career, and Neighborhood Primary Group Cohesion', *Sociometry*, vol. 23, 1960, and Phillip Fellin and Litwak, 'Neighborhood Cohesion under Conditions of Mobility', *American Sociological Review*, vol. 28, 1963. Cf. also Gino Germani, 'Social and Political Consequences of Mobility' in Smelser and Lipset (eds.), *Social Structure and Mobility in Economic Development*.
8. Cf. Duncan, 'Methodological Issues in the Study of Social Mobility', and also, e.g., Donald J. Treiman, 'Industrialization and Social Stratification' in Edward O. Laumann (ed.), *Social Stratification: Research and Theory for the 1970s*, Indianapolis: Bobbs-Merrill, 1970.
9. As in the case of our data on kinship, we found no indication of systematic differences within our benchmark groupings between those men forming the service-class and working-class cores, in the strict sense we initially defined (see p. 150 above), and the remainder. But again, though to a lesser extent, differences did occur among men intergenerationally stable within one or other of our three intermediate classes, according to whether their first occupation was a manual or nonmanual one. In presenting data for these men, we have therefore again divided them on the basis in question.
10. In a small number of cases men who felt unable to name any regular spare-time associates explained that this was because they had so many and could not pick out any three as being the 'most frequent'. This situation arose more often among men stable in Class I than among men stable in Classes VI or VII. However, even if the respondents in question were to be counted as having reported three associates, the mean number of associates per respondent for the former grouping would then rise only to 2.0, while remaining at 1.7 (calculated to one place of decimals) for the latter.
11. As perhaps the most systematic demonstration, see A. Stewart, K. Prandy, and R.M. Blackburn, 'Measuring the Class Structure', *Nature*, no. 245, 1973.
12. The issue may of course be raised of whether one should not take into account, in assessing the significance of such distributions, the relative number of persons of different class *available for* association. It is not in fact clear to us that this *is* a crucial consideration in regard to questions of class segregation; but we may none the less note

that if the class distribution of men in our 1972 national sample can be accepted as a reasonable basis for calculating 'expected' values, then on the assumption of statistical independence between the class of associate and respondent, the following ratios of observed to expected frequencies are obtained.

Intergenerationally stable grouping	Associates' class		
	I–II	III–V	VI–VII
Class I	2.5	0.9	0.2
Classes III–V (first occupation nonmanual)	1.2	1.4	0.6
Classes III–V (first occupation manual)	1.0	1.2	0.9
Classes VI and VII	0.5	0.7	1.5

As regards the reliability of occupational, and other, information reported by respondents for associates and friends, generally reassuring evidence is provided in Edward O. Laumann, *Bonds of Pluralism*, New York: Wiley, 1973, pp. 29–32.

13. Ratios of observed to expected frequencies, calculated on the same basis as in the previous note, are as follows.

Intergenerationally stable grouping	Friends' class		
	I–II	III–V	VI–VII
Class I	3.2	0.5	0.1
Classes III–V (first occupation nonmanual)	1.2	1.5	0.6
Classes III–V (first occupation manual)	1.2	1.5	0.6
Classes VI and VII	0.7	0.9	1.2

The greater degree of class segregation in the case of 'good friends' than of most frequent spare-time associates should not be thought surprising: the latter could include persons with whom the respondent's sociability was of a relatively specific rather than an entirely diffuse character—for example, a co-member of a 'serious' sports team or cultural body, or a colleague in some organized interest group.

14. Cf. Laumann, *Bonds of Pluralism*, p. 113 (from which Figure 7.1 is directly derived).

15. Cf. the discussion in Josephine Klein, *Samples from English Cultures*, London: Routledge, 1965, vol. i, pp. 131–42.

16. Cf. Graham Allan, 'Class Variations in Friendship Patterns', *British Journal of Sociology*, vol. xxviii, 1977, p. 391 esp. The data of Table 7.4 are generally confirmed by those we obtained from the leisure-time charts on which we recorded details of how, and with whom, respondents spent their time when not actually at work over the week-end and last week-day before their interview. For example, workmates and neighbours reported by men intergenerationally stable in Class I as having shared in some activity with them during these days averaged 1.2 per respondent, as against 0.8 in the case of men stable in Classes VI and VII.

17. Cf. C.G. Pickvance, 'Voluntary Associations' in E. Gittus (ed.), *Key Variables in Social Research* vol. 2, London: Heinemann, 1974. Our working definition of a voluntary association was adapted from Pickvance: i.e. a non-statutory, non-commercial organization which has a formal structure (e.g. a name, a constitution, a leadership and membership) and the membership of which is unpaid.

18. At the end of the section of the interview dealing with voluntary associations, respondents were asked: 'Are there any clubs, societies, etc. of the kind we have been talking

about in which you were once quite active, but which you have ceased to take part in during, say, the last five years?' The number of such associations reported by men intergenerationally stable in Class I averaged 0.9 per respondent, as compared with 0.4 in the case of men stable in Classes VI and VII.

19. Many of the latter, sports clubs especially, do of course provide ample opportunities for sociability of a diffuse kind.

20. Such respondents within our upwardly mobile groupings were, it is true, somewhat less likely than men stable in Class I to explain their inability in terms of the very large number of associates that they in fact had, but the numbers involved here are again small. If those giving the latter explanation are counted as having three associates, the average number of associates reported per respondent among our upwardly mobile groupings taken together rises to 1.9 as compared with 2.0 for our stable Class I groupings (cf. n. 10 above).

21. See, e.g., Richard F. Curtis, 'Differential Association and the Stratification of the Urban Community', *Social Forces*, vol. 42, 1963; and Edward O. Laumann, *Prestige and Association in an Urban Community*, Indianapolis: Bobbs-Merrill, 1966, pp. 130–2.

22. Ratios of observed to expected frequencies in the class distributions of the associates and friends of groupings of mobile respondents, calculated in the same way as for intergenerationally stable respondents (cf. ns. 12 and 13 above), are as follows.

Mobile grouping	Associates' class		
	I–II	III–V	VI–VII
Upward–direct	2.4	1.0	0.2
Upward–indirect	2.0	1.1	0.4
Downward	1.4	1.4	0.5
	Friends' class		
	I–II	III–V	VI–VII
Upward–direct	2.7	0.9	0.1
Upward–indirect	2.3	1.1	0.2
Downward	1.4	1.3	0.6

23. Cf. above, pp. 125–6.

24. It may be noted that in the case of respondents forming our Class I benchmark grouping, 69 per cent reported sets of associates and friends where all, or the majority, were in service-class positions and none in working-class ones, and only 1 per cent–i.e. one man–reported a set containing *no* service-class persons.

25. While it is not directly relevant to our present concerns to pursue the matter, we would think a far more important factor is that of educational experience. The origins of the pre-mobility relationships of men directly mobile into the service class with persons themselves in service-class positions in 1974 were heavily concentrated in the later years of the respondents' period of full-time education.

26. It was unfortunately not a practical possibility to obtain information specifically about the mobility of respondents' associates and friends. Pilot work revealed that respondents only rather infrequently had precise and certain knowledge about any aspect of their social origins.

27. At the same time, though, it must be noted that the segmentation of primary relations that is in question here is not displayed, as was that between kin and spare-time associates, in the case of those respondents intergenerationally stable in intermediate-class positions whose first occupation was nonmanual, and who would comprise, we argued, a sizeable number of men in the course of mobility into the service class.

28. As in the case of our intergenerationally stable respondents, the data in question here can be broadly confirmed by the further information we obtained from respondents' leisure-time charts. Workmates and neighbours reported by upwardly mobile men as having shared in some activity with them averaged 1.1 per respondent, and those by downwardly mobile men 0.9 per respondent, as against the averages of 1.2 and 0.8 previously reported for our service-class and working-class benchmark groupings

respectively (cf. n. 16 above).

29. Again, our further information on the frequency with which our mobile respondents had ceased to participate in particular associations over the last five years is generally consistent. The number of such terminations averaged 0.7 for upwardly and downwardly mobile respondents alike, as compared with the averages of 0.9 and 0.4 for our stable service-class and working-class groupings respectively (cf. n. 18 above).

30. For a general discussion of the decay of the status order in modern Britain, see John H. Goldthorpe, 'The Current Inflation: Towards a Sociological Account' in Fred Hirsch and Goldthorpe (eds.), *The Political Economy of Inflation*, London: Martin Robertson, 1978. If highly exclusive status groups can still be identified in British society, we would expect them to be associated with those élites within the service class which, we have suggested, may—unlike the service class as a whole—display closure in their recruitment patterns.

    The conclusion that mobility does not tend to lead to social isolation or marginality is also reached, on the basis of results broadly similar to ours, by Richardson in his study made in the London Metropolitan region. See *Contemporary Social Mobility*, chs. 9–11.

31. See above, p. 177.

32. This consideration appears to have been almost entirely neglected in the debate on intergenerational mobility effects, following on Duncan's proposed new approach (see n. 9, p. 172 above), which has been essentially concerned with appropriate models for specifying the relative weights to be given to the social origins and present positions of mobile individuals as influences on their attitudes and behaviour. But the theory of 'acculturation' which would seem to underlie Duncan's approach would itself clearly imply the importance in this respect of mobility routes, contexts, time-tables, etc., as well as of beginning and end points. Cf. Germani, 'Social and Political Consequences of Mobility'.

33. See R.K. Merton, *Social Theory and Social Structure*, Glencoe: Free Press, 1957.

CHAPTER 8

The Experience of Social Mobility

In designing our 1974 follow-up study, the importance of investigating in some way the subjective experience of mobility, or immobility, of those men who were respondents to our national inquiry was readily apparent to us. In critiques of mobility research, as undertaken by standard survey procedures, the question has several times been raised of how far the mobility or immobility that is observed by the investigator in terms of movement between occupational or class groupings of his own devising in fact corresponds with his respondents' actual awareness of having been mobile or immobile. And indeed evidence has been produced to suggest that the degree of this correspondence may in some instances be sufficiently low to call into question the validity of such research, at least where its central concern is with the implications of mobility for social action and social structure.[1] For, clearly, the study of any aspect of the consequences or concomitants of mobility must become more problematic than ever if some wide divergence prevails between the investigator's and actors' ideas of what should count as mobility. Moreover, even if the investigator is prepared, on theoretical grounds, to give privilege to his own categories over those of actors, the extent and nature of the discrepancy that exists between the two sets of constructs must in itself remain an obvious matter for further inquiry.

PROBLEMS OF METHOD

While recognizing, then, the need to give some place in our analyses to our respondents' own awareness and understanding of their mobility, we were, however, faced in this respect with a major problem of data collection. In basing our follow-up study on a number of relatively small subsamples, drawn from respondents to our 1972 investigation, our aim was to obtain more detailed information—complementary to that collected in 1972—from a few hundred respondents than it was feasible to collect and process from a sample of over 10,000. But one unavoidable consequence of subsampling was that the men selected for re-interview could be located in any of the 417 primary sampling units of the 1972 inquiry and were thus far more widely scattered geographically, throughout England and Wales, than would be usual in a survey inquiry on the scale that was planned. This meant therefore that it was not economically or administratively possible for us to deploy our own fieldwork team for the follow-up study, and that we had rather to draw on the services of an established social-research agency with a nationally organized field force. So far as the collection of essentially factual information was concerned, this proved to be in no way a disadvantage: the interviewers employed by the agency with whom we collaborated had a high level of skill and experience in taking respondents through structured, though often very complex and detailed, series of questions. But, on the other hand, since our interviewers did not for the most part have any specifically sociological training, limitations were clearly imposed on the extent to which we could make use of a less structured approach. In particular, what would have been our preferred method for investigating respondents' subjective mobility experience, that is, the use of open-ended questions followed up by 'informed' probing, was effectively precluded by the character of our field force, and we were therefore obliged to search for an alternative, second-best possibility

Perhaps the most obvious resort was to develop, in this respect also, the kind of structured interview items that our field force would have been capable of administering. However, on due consideration, we decided against this option because of the doubts that we felt about the degree of validity of the data that would be thus generated. From various pieces of pilot work that we had undertaken, it was clear that we could expect to find quite wide diversity in the meanings which mobility had for our respondents, and in the ways in which they conceived its various contexts and correlates. In turn, then, it seemed to us scarcely possible to devise any one conceptual schema that could serve as the basis for structured questioning *and* in terms of which the views of our respondents could be represented, without the risk of serious distortion. We could, to be sure, have formulated, from the standpoint of our own theoretical interests, a series of 'closed' questions relating to mobility awareness etc., and could have expected, in the main, to have received answers to them. But these answers would have constituted data of very dubious utility to us in our attempt to investigate, precisely, the degree to which, in regard to mobility, our categories and those of our respondents might be discrepant.

Since therefore it appeared that neither structured nor unstructured questioning could be satisfactorily taken up as a means of obtaining the kind of material we sought, the implication was that this material would have to be collected in some way other than through the interview itself. In these circumstances, the method that came most readily to mind—as indeed the classic alternative to the interview (or questionnaire) in the history of social research—was that of the 'personal document', and specifically in the form of the individual 'life-history'. Moreover, this method was one which could be regarded as being especially apt to our purpose of eliciting our respondents' own understanding of their mobility. Angell, for example, has defined a personal document as 'one which reveals a participant's view of experiences in which he has been involved', and has represented the essential aim in collecting such documents as being 'to obtain detailed evidence as to how social situations appear to the actors in them and what meanings various factors have for the participants'.[2] Likewise, Becker explicitly contrasts 'data formulated in the abstract categories of [sociologists'] own theories', which is characteristic of survey research, with the kind of material obtained from life histories which is expressed 'in the categories that seemed most relevant to the people . . . studied'. The distinctive feature of the life-history approach, Becker argues, is in 'assigning major importance to the interpretations people place on their experience', and its distinctive value is in 'giving us insight into the subjective side of much-studied institutional processes'.[3]

We decided thus to try as far as possible to link the collection of life-histories, focused on our respondents' mobility experience, to our basic survey approach, and proceeded in fact in the following manner. Each respondent to our follow-up inquiry was asked at the end of his interview if he would be willing to help us further in our research by writing for us what we referred to as a set of 'life-history notes'. The respondent was provided with a leaflet explaining in more detail what we had in mind and including a list of questions which we would particularly like him to cover. The first two paragraphs of the leaflet and the list of questions are reproduced below. Assurances were given that any material supplied would remain confidential to members of the research team and would not be used in our research reports in any way that would permit an individual to be identified. Those respondents who agreed to write notes were provided with a stamped addressed envelope in which to forward them to us, and were also told how to contact members of the research team in the case of any queries.

Extracts from the Life-History Notes Leaflet

You have already supplied us with a good deal of basic information about your education, work, family, etc. What we are now asking you to do is to tell us something about how, looking back, you view the course of your life—its patterns, its turning points, its light and shade.

Below we have a list of questions. If you would write a paragraph or so in answer to each of these, this should give us the kind of notes that we want. On the other hand, you may wish to arrange what you write in your own way, taking these questions simply as a guide to the points which chiefly interest us. (Remember in any case that you need not go over again the basic facts that you have already given us) . . .

Questions we would like you to cover in your life history notes

1. What are the biggest differences between the job and way of life of your father (or the head of your family) when you were about 14, and your job and life now? What do you think are the reasons for these differences?
2. What pattern has your working life mainly followed from the time of your first full-time job up to now? A steady advance to better and better jobs? A series of disappointments? Repeated ups and downs? A series of jobs that were just different from each other, rather than being better or worse? Or some other pattern?
3. Do you think there have been any important turning points or major crises in your working life? If so, what were they?
4. How important has luck been in your working life, compared with other things (such as family background, the way you were brought up, or your own character and abilities)? Do you feel that the same applies to most other people, or has your case been unusual? Can you give examples of how luck, or whatever it was, worked in your case?
5. How important has your work been to you in your life as a whole? Have other things had to take second place to it? Or have you taken the jobs you have because they gave you a chance to do other things? Have you ever turned down a good job because it would have meant giving up something that mattered more?
6. What have been your main goals during your working life? To work at something that interests you for its own sake? To earn more? To provide for the future? To be able to live in a particular way, or in a particular place? Or something else?

7. How far, and in what ways, do you see yourself as 'successful' in your job or in other aspects of your life? And in what ways, if any, as a 'failure'? Do you think success in your work matters more, or less, than success in other things?
8. Have you found that success in your working life has had generally good effects on your life outside work, or has success had its costs? Has any failure you may have had in your work had a bad effect on life outside work, or have other things made up for it? For example, how has success or failure affected your family, or the kinds of friends you have made?

As can be seen, the questions that we wished respondents to consider were posed in everyday language, in an entirely open-ended form and, we hoped, in such a way as to give a respondent every encouragement to 'tell his own story'. To judge at least from the sets of notes that we received, the questions were in general found meaningful and indeed stimulating. Few men answered them in a merely perfunctory fashion, and in the large majority of cases the notes that were written ran from 500 to 1,500 words in length. A number of men wrote what amounted to autobiographical sketches, several thousand words long. Moreover, from the extracts from these notes that will subsequently be cited, it will be apparent that there was often displayed a remarkable sharpness of both observation and expression, and that new perspectives on virtually all aspects of mobility were opened up.

However, the chief problem that we anticipated with the procedure we followed, and which did in fact arise, was that of persuading respondents actually to produce notes. Only a small minority refused at the outset to undertake the task; but despite two, or in some cases three, reminders, a majority even of those who had agreed in principle to write notes still failed to do so. In the end, usable notes were secured from 247 men, representing 38 per cent of the 652 respondents to our 1974 study or 27 per cent of the total number of 926 men who were selected for re-interview from our 1972 respondents.[4] Differences in the proportions supplying life history notes among our groupings of inter-generationally stable and mobile respondents are shown in Table 8.1.

What we succeeded in obtaining was thus a body of material which, while substantial in itself and apparently highly illuminating of the mobility experience of those who had supplied it, related none the less to the experience of only a minority of the men in our subsamples, and which had in consequence to be viewed with, to say the least, extreme caution so far as its representativeness was concerned. In turn, then, it was this deficiency in our data which largely conditioned the decisions that we made regarding their analysis and use. For example, there seemed little point in taking our life-history material as being, so to speak, a direct substitute for the kind of material that we might have obtained from interviews, and subjecting it to systematic quantitative treatment as, for example, through techniques of content analysis. In other words, it did not seem appropriate, given that our material derived from only a relatively small proportion of our respondents, to try to extract from it attitudes and beliefs to be taken as the attributes of specific individuals, which could then be related to other of their attributes such as, say, features of their mobility experience as expressed through the categories of our earlier analyses. It was, rather, evident to us that, from a quantitative standpoint, our life-history data would

Table 8.1
Returns of life-history notes by mobility pattern

Mobility pattern	Number returning usable notes	Percentage of all re-interviewed (1974)	Percentage of all selected for re-interview
Stable in Class I	33	44	32
Stable in Classes III–V	35	34	26
Stable in Classes VI and VII	53	34	23
Directly mobile to Class I	33	33	– a
Indirectly mobile to Class I	68	45	– a
All upwardly mobile to Class I	101	40	33
Downwardly mobile from Class I	25	37	27
All	247	38	27

Note: (a) The distinction between direct and indirect mobility did not apply in the selection of men for re-interview in 1974.

have to be used in a much cruder and more limited way. The only objective which in fact appeared feasible was to identify, for each of our groupings of stable and mobile respondents, those themes and their main variations within the life-history notes supplied by its members which could even with our very imperfect data, be reasonably regarded as salient ones; or, where the degree of diversity was such that no dominant theme could be discerned, to give as full an idea as our data would allow of the range of this diversity.

At the same time, though, it appeared to us also important to try to exploit our life-history material in a qualitative as well as a quantitative fashion; and, specifically, to use this material as a basis not only for describing our respondents' experience of mobility from their own point of view but further for making this experience 'understandable'. The personal document has been widely regarded as a means whereby individuals differently located in the social structure can communicate with each other: in Becker's words, 'it tells us what it means to be a kind of person we have never met face to face'.[5] But, for such communication to be effective, some basis of understanding—some way of 'bridging the gap' between the subjectivity of the writer of the document and that of the members of his audience—is obviously required. The key assumption that we would make in this respect is the following: that the medium through which this bridging must ultimately be achieved, in so far as it can be achieved at all, is that of rational intelligibility. In other words, we would argue that to the extent that one claims to understand the beliefs and attitudes or the actions or, more generally, the responses to events and circumstances of other persons, one is in effect claiming that, within the given situation, they are intelligible to one in rational terms: once the facts of the situation, as one may establish them, are taken into account, it is apparent to one how, at least from the observed actors' own standpoint, their beliefs, attitudes, actions, etc. are related to their situation and to each other in a rational manner.[6]

Thus in what follows we shall try as far as possible to bring out, for each of our groupings of respondents, the 'subjective logic' of the life-history notes that they presented by considering, on the one hand, the rationally intelligible (rather perhaps than the quantitatively important empirical) relationships that prevail between their dominant themes and certain factual aspects of the mobility, and also of the present social situation, of the men in question; and, on the other hand, the internal coherence that exists among these dominant themes and some at least of their variants. We shall, that is to say, attempt to interpret the collectively significant content of the life-history accounts of our several groupings of respondents in such a way that our conception of the understandability of these accounts is made explicit. At the same time, though, we hope that the amount of purely descriptive material provided, together with the data of our previous chapters, will be sufficient to give the reader some basis for forming his own view of the appropriateness of these interpretations. Finally, in this respect we may note that the implications of the incompleteness of our collection of life-history notes will be rather less serious for our interpretive efforts than in regard to quantitative analysis. If the data from which we shall work are in fact unrepresentative, the effect of this will not be in itself to invalidate the interpretations that are offered; rather, it would at most imply that some aspects of our respondents' mobility experience, because inadequately represented in our data, might be left uninterpreted.

In the two preceding chapters we have first presented data for those of our respondents who were intergenerationally stable in class position—taking those stable in Class I and in Classes VI and VII as benchmark groupings—and have then proceeded to set against these findings the comparable data that we collected from our intergenerationally mobile respondents. In the present chapter we shall follow a somewhat different pattern in that we shall treat our life history material in three sections and make comparisons between our several groupings of respondents within each one. In the first section we shall be concerned with our respondents' awareness of having been mobile or immobile, drawing mainly on material from their life-history notes which was written in response to the first three questions on our list. In the second section we shall be concerned with how men account for such mobility as they believe they have experienced, or with what we may term their mobility ideologies, again using material prompted by the first three of our questions and also by the fourth. And thirdly we shall be concerned with the significance that men attach to the mobility of which they are aware, both in the context of their working lives and more generally, using in this case their responses to the last four questions that we suggested.

THE AWARENESS OF MOBILITY

In formulating the first three of the questions on our list, we aimed to give respondents the opportunity of expressing any awareness that they might have of being socially mobile, whether by reference to their family origins or in the course of their own working lives. We may consider first here the material relating to these questions in the life history notes that were produced by those men (N = 33) who, on our categorization, were intergenerationally stable within Class I.

In the comparisons these men made between themselves and their fathers, what was chiefly notable—and, of course, from our own point of view reassuring—was that where differences were referred to, in work or in life-styles, they were very largely ones of only marginal, if any, significance for class position. For example, the differences most often noted between type of job were ones between, say, professional and administrative work or between management in the public and private sectors—in other words, ones relating not to differences in class position but rather in *situs* within the service class. Likewise, the differences recognized in life-styles were chiefly ones arising from different family situations, from different personal values, or most frequently perhaps, from differences in geographical and physical mobility.[7]

Basically, my father and myself, being professional men, both have had very similar styles of life, and a very similar outlook on life. . . My father always knew he wanted to be a surgeon and this is what he became. . . I, from a reasonable age, once I had got out of the idea of going in for medicine, knew that I wanted to become an accountant and that is where I have got to . . .

(088-2129: consultant surgeon; articled clerk—chartered accountant)

My father was a self-employed dental surgeon with one partner and two other employees. I am a salaried member of a big international company. He had much more personal freedom to arrange his working hours, but had the responsibility of running a dental practice.

(109-1302: dental surgeon; research chemist—Director of Chemical Research)

At the time I was 14 my father was a solicitor, a partner in a firm in Bournemouth. As I am a chartered accountant in Bournemouth, in many ways our jobs and ways of life are similar. The main difference is probably that my father spent most of his time in Bournemouth . . . I find that I do quite a lot of travelling . . . I have clients all over the country.

(595-1111: solicitor; articled clerk—chartered accountant)

So far then as class position is concerned, our categorization of these men as intergenerationally stable and their own subjective experience would appear to be rather closely in accord. However, the situation is a good deal less straightforward when we turn to the accounts that these same men gave of the course of their own working lives. Here the dominant theme[8] is quite clearly that of upward movement or advancement—whether 'steady' or with crucial 'turning-points', whether expressed in terms of professional achievement, organizational position or business success. Moreover, this is not only the case among those men whom we would regard as having exhibited counter-mobility, but likewise among those whose access to the service class, following on their fathers, we have treated as being direct.

My working life has been spent almost entirely with one firm of chartered accountants—first as an articled clerk, then as a qualified accountant, then as junior partner and now as a senior partner. It could be summed up as a steady advance to better and better jobs.

(595-1111: solicitor; articled clerk—chartered accountant)

My working life started off very badly. . . After working as a labourer for several months, I reluctantly agreed to become an apprentice bricklayer. . . After becoming established in the construction industry, I took a great interest in it and went all out to know both the practical and theoretical aspects of the industry. The net effect was that when I reached the end of my apprenticeship I was well equipped for advancement. . . This, coupled with a dearth of good management, allowed me to rise to a quite senior position quite quickly.

(558-2713: civil-engineering contractor's agent; apprentice bricklayer—civil-engineering contractor's agent)

Starting as a student metallurgist, educated on a Company scholarship, I then steadily progressed, every two or three years, to better (more senior) jobs within the same technical area of the steel industry.

(193-7547: building contractor; research metallurgist—Head of Research and Development Department)

The pattern of my working life has been, in common with most people with medical qualifications, one of progression from post to post, with advancement to consultant status without serious delay.

(264-2962: works manager; house-surgeon—consultant surgeon)

From the theoretical standpoint that we have adopted as investigators, it is important to distinguish movement between broadly defined occupational groupings, and in turn between class positions, from that which occurs *within* such groupings. Our research has focused specifically on mobility of the former kind, and not on what may be termed *intra*-occupational mobility. However, from the standpoint of those at least of our respondents whom we would regard as intergenerationally stable within the service class, this distinction is—not surprisingly—of far less significance. For them, it would seem, the changes both in and within occupations that they have experienced take on meaning essentially in the context of their *careers*—as representing steps, or perhaps checks or turning-points, in their progress. And even where, as in the case of those men whom we would define as counter-mobile, occupational changes have taken them across class boundaries, they have not usually been understood in class terms—for example, as actually marking their 'regaining' of the class position of their fathers. To the extent that the process of counter-mobility, as we would conceive it, is actually represented in their life-history notes, it is in 'career' terms: for example, in terms of 'finishing training', 'becoming qualified', 'being promoted to a management job', etc.

From respondents intergenerationally stable in Class I, we may move next to those supplying life history notes who were stable in Classes VI and VII (N=53). In the comparisons they made between themselves and their fathers, men in this latter grouping, like those in the former, very largely confirmed our own categorization of them as being immobile in terms of occupational level. In so far as differences in jobs were referred to, they were almost all ones between different types of manual, wage-earning employment; or respondents commented to the effect that their work was 'easier'—in the sense of being physically less demanding —than that of their fathers. At the same time, though, these stable working-class respondents, in contrast to those stable in service-class positions, could be said to show in one respect a very widespread awareness of having been mobile in an intergenerational perspective: that is, in enjoying, relative to their fathers, greatly improved pay and conditions of employment and in general a much higher standard of living.

I don't believe that there is any great difference between my job now and the job my father did when I was 14. They are different trades or types of work, but the fact that they are both manual brings them into the same category. My father's way of life and work was much harder, his pay and standard of living were nowhere near that which he and I have today.
(663-1330: auto tool-setter; electrical fitter-welder—gas fitter-welder)

My father worked 12 hours a day for 6–7 days a week, which left him with very little social life, if any, whereas I work a five-day, 40 hour week and have a great deal of free time, plus a better standard of living.
(064-2723: slag-crusher operator; steelworks labourer—roadwork labourer)

The main differences are less time at work and longer holidays; also many things my father classed as luxuries, a motor car, holidays abroad etc. I now take for granted.
(484-3435: compositor; apprentice printer—compositor)

The difference in life now is that there is more money, better working conditions and, if you wish, more leisure time. . . When I was 14, you had to work long hours for little pay—twelve-hour days most weeks.
(199-3957: office cleaner; milk roundsman—bus driver)

Such responses as these can scarcely be thought surprising; but their recurrence does none the less serve to infuse the life-history notes of our working-class respondents with the sense of their having lived through a period of major social change—with an awareness, to echo Wright Mills, of the intersection of biography and history[9]—which is largely lacking in the accounts of men stable in Class I.

When, however, we turn to the question of awareness of mobility during working life, the contrast between the two groupings, while still marked, has a quite different basis. Where our service-class respondents displayed a strong sense of (upward) movement, associated with the experience of their individual careers, the dominant theme in the accounts of working-class men is one of an essential immobility: they have either remained in much the same kind of work all their lives or, if they have shifted between different types of job, this has not amounted to any kind of progression. The only variation on this theme that is of any significance is where some advance is recognized not in level of occupation but simply in level of pay.

I have had quite a few jobs, although most of them were in one large firm. Wherever I went it was always apparent that I could never reach a higher position as the persons in higher authority were not willing to give anyone a chance to better themselves. Whatever I did, I was just a number to most people.
(385-2238: warehouseman; consignment clerk—sheetmetal worker)

My working life [has] consisted of a series of jobs that were just different . . . such as, lift attendant, window cleaner, general labourer etc., almost all boring occupations owing to their monotonous repetition.
(476-8855: dock labourer; lift attendant—bus conductor)

My jobs have been a bit different . . . When I left school I had five [years] to learn painting and decorating. When I finished this I moved to another job, paint spraying. Then I got a job as a HGV driver. All these jobs have only given me more money to try to get a good standard of living.
(498-0160: lorry driver; apprentice painter and decorator—lorry driver)

The pattern my working life has followed has been dictated by the money factor, except for the period I was employed by the GPO. Because I had few commitments, I enjoyed the outdoor life and meeting people. When I married I realised that with the added responsibility it was imperative to earn more money —from there on it was a better job but always with the money in mind.
(047-1266: wagon repairer; wagon repairer—steel-mill hand)

Finally, then, so far as those groupings we have characterized as intergenerationally stable are concerned, we may consider the subjective awareness of mobility of men who were found, like their fathers, in one of our three intermediate classes. Such respondents who supplied life-history notes (N=35) drew comparisons with their fathers that revealed a fair amount of diversity. As with men in our other stable groupings, gratifyingly few saw themselves as having moved at all decisively in terms of occupational level; but while a majority could perhaps be regarded as recognizing, more or less explicitly, a basic continuity in class life-style, this was clearly not so predominant a majority as among men stable in Class I, and the main variant was to stress, in the manner of men stable in Classes VI and VII, substantial improvements in living standards. Again in regard to work-life mobility, responses were somewhat mixed, with those we have found typical of both our core service-class and working-class groupings being well represented. In addition, though, we may here identify, as more or less specific to men in our intermediate-class groupings, a further response reflecting the experience of a notably inconsequential or 'disorderly' kind of movement, whether associated with uncertainties of choice or the force of external circumstance.

The pattern of my working life has been varied, going from types of jobs which have been completely different from each other. I did not know what I wanted to do when I left school and I still do not know seventeen years later . . . I have no goals or objectives in my working life because I do not know what I want.
(622-7144: meter reader and chart keeper; apprentice fitter—records clerk)

[Overall my working life has been an advance] but with ups and downs due to the reason that I was made redundant from all three firms that employed me. I always left the firms at the chargehand level.*
(108-2631: railway ganger; trainee car mechanic—foreman wireman)
  *In fact, two of these jobs were at assistant foreman level and
  were coded as such.

The pattern of my working life has changed quite a lot since my first job . . . I had one or two different jobs which I didn't settle into, but on reaching 18 I joined the Royal Navy and served during the war years. On leaving the Navy my brothers and I started up a haulage contract business which seemed a steady advance for the better, but after several years of working harder and harder, rising prices and heavy taxes plus work failing to come in, there was a series of ups and downs and many disappointments, so the business crumbled . . . I thought there was a turning point in my life for the better, but unfortunately . . . unforeseen happenings were against me.

(601-9814: greengrocer; greengrocery assistant—scrap-iron dealer)

As we have earlier noted, being intergenerationally stable in any intermediate-class position may well be the outcome of much work-life movement, whether among these classes or between them and the working class.[10]

In the light of the foregoing, we may thus conclude, first of all, that where we have categorized our respondents as intergenerationally stable in respect of their general location within the occupational division of labour and class structure, we have probably not, in the main, seriously contradicted the sense of their own experience. Secondly, though, we must also recognize that among the members of each of the groupings we have considered there exists a strong awareness of having been mobile in some *other* way. There is no reason for us to suppose that this awareness is in any sense spurious, or reflects social processes that are some-how less 'real' than those with which we are primarily concerned. Rather, the finding in question may serve to bring out the fact that our research has concentrated on but one of several types of mobility process, all of which may be regarded as integral to advanced industrial societies. Certainly, in present-day Britain, the centrality of the experience of career—often intra-occupational—mobility is entirely intelligible among members of the service class, whose working lives will have been largely shaped by bureaucratic, and typically *expanding* bureaucratic structures. And no less understandable is the widespread awareness of intergenerational advance in conditions of employment and consumption standards within the class of manual wage-workers, whose market situation has in the post-war decades been significantly strengthened by the effects of both economic growth and social policy. Even the rather distinctive experience of disorderly work-life mobility among men found in intermediate-class positions may be seen to reflect what we earlier suggested was the marginality of the latter, in relation to both bureaucracy and the market as the two main organizational forms that underlie the division of labour.[11] It is then important that this very general experience of social mobility of some kind among men who, from our point of view, constitute intergenerationally stable groupings, should form part of the context in which we seek to understand the mobility awareness of those of our respondents whom we would ourselves categorize as displaying intergenerational mobility, and of a relatively long-range kind.

As regards men upwardly mobile into Class I of our schema, we may say first of all that those who returned life-history notes (N=101) overwhelmingly recognized—in contrast with men stable in Class I—major social differences between themselves and their fathers. The dominant theme in their accounts emphasized not only their higher incomes and living standards but further the quite different, in fact higher-level, work in which they were engaged. And in this latter respect, we may note, their mobility awareness also of course contrasts with that of men stable in lower-class positions. Moreover, the main variation on, or addition to, this theme—most evident in the case of men of working-class origins—took the form of a fairly explicit recognition of mobility into a quite different social and cultural world to that of their fathers.

Father's job was essentially manual . . . devoid of responsibility to [his] employer and indeed [he] seemed to develop an anti-management attitude. I find myself as part manager and employer . . . Father tended to live more from week to week. His hours of work and income were very variable. . . As was the working-class pattern of the neighbourhood and era, most of the week was given to work and men's pastimes . . . I tend to spend more time in home and garden and less with other men.

(058-9704: dock labourer; laboratory assistant—Principal Scientific Officer, Ministry of Defence)

My father commenced and ended his working life in a coal mine. He was never happy with such a work situation and had lengthy spells in other jobs [manual and lower nonmanual]. The greatest difference is therefore that my father never achieved any fulfilment from work. It was merely a case of flogging himself to bring up a family . . . My own career is entirely different in that I feel much more content with my lot and obtain a great deal of satisfaction from a challenging job . . . My position carries a good salary [and] I follow a different social life in that I enjoy dining out, a drink with friends and a much more varied programme.

(512-5323: colliery datal worker; railway clerk—Administrative Officer, British Rail)

[My life and my father's] cannot be compared. My father was a semi-cripple and could only do office work, i.e. cashier work. His earnings were relatively lower than mine [and he] had to watch how the money was spent . . . I live in a different world where standards of living are higher . . . I am now able to have the luxuries which I dreamt of fifteen years ago.

(068-1050: coal merchant's clerk; apprentice fitter—civil engineer)

My father . . . has worked in the steel industry since the age of 15 and has always had to undergo shiftwork . . . My parents found it hard to subsist . . . Their life . . . was mainly one of sustaining themselves with very little money for recreation, holidays and luxuries. My job is a professional one, being in a firm of solicitors, and I am able to earn far more money than my father could ever earn and meet people from all walks of life. I am also able to enjoy luxuries such as sports car, holidays abroad, eating out and expensive clothes, stereos, tapes, etc.

(645-9408: sheet-steel worker; clerk in solicitor's office—legal executive)

Our upwardly mobile respondents were thus clearly differentiated from men stable in Class I in their experience of intergenerational ascent. Further, though, we must note that they were essentially comparable to the latter—while again placed in contrast with men stable in the same classes of origin as their own—in their awareness of work-life mobility: specifically, in their awareness of significant work-life advancement, in which the distinction between inter- and intra-occupational movement was largely obliterated within a 'career' perspective. The only difference that might perhaps be discerned here between stable and mobile members of Class I was for the latter, and especially those who had followed indirect mobility routes, to represent the course of their advance as having been erratic or somewhat abrupt rather than steady and to place more emphasis on 'turning-points' and other career contingencies.

My . . . career up to date may be described as typical . . . The only real disappointment or setback . . . was the illness that I contracted when twenty years of age, which resulted in permanent disability to my feet and a spell of over a year away from work . . . My illness curtailed my soccer career . . . and resulted in me channelling the majority of my energies to my working life . . . [The other turning-point was] the decision five years ago to leave the accountancy profession and join a commercial organisation . . . I am now Group Chief Accountant of one of the largest merchant banks in London and, therefore, my ambitions are almost realised.

(266-2584: lorry driver; articled clerk—Group Chief Accountant)

The earlier part of my working life was repetitive, dull, factory-type work. Since the age of 27 . . . I have found my niche and have made steady and fulfilling advances . . . [The turning points were] the decision to leave factory work for something better when contemplating marriage [and after] the two-year period of being in business on my own, the decision to back out and join a large selling company.

(144-6745: slitting-machine operator; warehouse boy—sales manager)

In the early stages of my railway career I was often tempted to seek other employment on the basis of thinking I was 'destined for greater things' but as promotion came rapidly compared with my contemporaries, I settled down and have since achieved a steady advance to better and more interesting jobs . . . An important turning point was . . . when I was fortunate enough to be accepted as a Management Trainee—a position normally reserved for university graduates.

(512-5323: colliery datal worker; railway clerk—Administrative Officer, British Rail)

Although, then, we have found an awareness of social mobility of some kind to be widespread among men who, in terms of our class schema, we treat as stable, we may still maintain that the mobility experience of those respondents whom we would characterize as upwardly mobile at least is of a more complete and decisive kind—and quite understandably so. Unlike the members of our stable groupings, these men show an awareness of upward movement in *both* inter-generational *and* worklife perspective; and this reflects the fact that their inter-generational shift from the lower to the higher levels of the occupational and class structure, whether or not involving mobility across class lines during their working lives, has also taken them into the range of occupations *within which* career advance, rather than being limited or precarious, tends in some degree to be institutionalized.

It remains in this section to consider whether an equally well-defined awareness of mobility is revealed by those men whom we have categorized as being downwardly mobile from Class I. In this case, we have a particularly small number of life-history notes on which to draw (N = 25), and it will therefore be still more difficult than usual to arrive at reliable conclusions. Furthermore, as regards at least the issues that concern us here, our downwardly mobile respondents showed a considerable diversity of outlook. In the comparisons they made with their fathers, none of these men claimed to hold a higher-level occupational or class position, and there was a clearly greater tendency evident than in other groupings for men to see themselves as being in some way disadvantageously placed; but at the same time the basis of these adverse comparisons varied—type of work, life-style, and standard of living being all invoked. Moreover, in other cases an intergenerational similarity in one or other, or in all, of these respects was claimed; and in others still, respondents saw themselves as being better off than their fathers in specifically material terms. Similarly, in their responses to our questions on the pattern of their working lives downwardly mobile men gave widely differing accounts. Each of the dominant themes of our other groupings that we have earlier illustrated—career advance, immobility, and disorderly movement—was in fact represented. In addition, reference was made in several instances to *voluntary* downward mobility, often of a temporary nature, which was accepted, for example, in order to gain wider work experience, to escape from over-demanding work, or to have more opportunity to pursue out-of-work interests.

In the case of men we have categorized as downwardly mobile, we cannot therefore claim a corresponding subjective experience of mobility in the way that is possible with our upwardly mobile respondents. This conclusion should not however be found surprising, since the analyses of our previous chapters have in themselves led us to recognize our downwardly mobile grouping as being a highly heterogeneous one. While it may certainly be assumed to contain some proportion of men whose *déclassement* is decisive, it is no less evident that for some further number of its members their detachment from their class of origin is a matter of degree and that real, though again variable, possibilities for counter-mobility exist. We may thus regard the diversity of the mobility awareness shown within this grouping as reflecting a comparable diversity both in the circumstances that have brought men into the situation to which our categorization relates and in their prospects of moving from it.

MOBILITY IDEOLOGIES

As well as asking respondents to comment on the major differences of which they were aware between their own and their fathers' work and way of life, we also asked them what they saw as the reasons for such differences; and, following our questions concerning the pattern of their working lives, we asked further about the part they believed luck had played in shaping this pattern as compared with other more determinate factors, such as their individual qualities or family backgrounds. On the basis of the material prompted by these questions, our aim was to form some idea of the main 'mobility ideologies' that prevailed among our respondents, in the sense of the cognitive and evaluative notions through which they themselves sought to 'make sense' of their mobility experience.

We have seen that within two of our groupings, those of men stable in Class I and of men categorized as downwardly mobile from this class, no widespread or uniform awareness of intergenerational differences in class position was present. So far then as we are concerned with the explanations for such differences that were offered by our respondents, we must concentrate on the life-history material provided by our remaining groupings. We may most usefully begin with respondents intergenerationally stable in Classes VI and VII, among whom we have observed a widespread awareness of upward mobility in terms of pay and conditions of employment and of living standards generally.

To a large extent, it would appear, these men regarded the explanation of this kind of mobility experience as being self-evident: to describe its nature—participation in a collective economic advance—was in effect to imply its cause, and the majority were content to leave their accounts in this form. There was, however, one clear variation, found chiefly in the case of men who as well as referring to higher levels of consumption also specifically cited improvements in working life, and this was to emphasize the role of trade unionism and the growing strength and expectations of the working class.

I feel the trade unions must be given a lot of the credit [for] the working man's steady progress—not that I agree with all the unions say and do. Basically the idea of unions is good, it's the officers who sometimes get misguided. I'm sure without the unions the workers of this country would be being exploited far more than they are at present by what is still a capitalist society.
(664-0780: foundry annealer; electrical assembler—crank-shaft grinder)

The power has moved from the employer to the employee, with much stronger unions who are not afraid to use their power . . . The children who now leave school are better educated and would not stand for the conditions my father lived under.
(484-3435: compositor; apprentice printer—compositor)

Whereas . . . at work [my father] was supervised for most of his working life, I rarely see a foreman or chargehand. This is solely because nowadays we have brought management to realise that workers given responsibility to manage their own job do a better and more exact job because they are not watched. There is also the different approach to work—my father was brought up to believe he was lucky to be working, while I and my generation believe we have the right to work . . .
(047-1266: wagon repairer; wagon repairer—steel-mill hand)

In this view, then, the social advancement experienced by wage-workers is represented as being in some part the result of their own efforts, rather than simply the more or less automatic outcome of a period of economic growth. None the less, it is important to note that the process is still envisaged as a collective one, involving the working class as a whole or, at all events, sizeable sections of it.

In contrast with this, we may remark first of all that in those instances where our stable intermediate-class respondents expressed an awareness of improved living standards, relative to those of their fathers, no reference to trade unionism occurred, and that long-term historical factors, such as 'increased commercial activity' or 'the growth of technology', were more often invoked. Secondly, though, as might be expected, the more important contrast is with the explanations that were provided for their mobility experience by those men whom we ourselves categorized as having been upwardly mobile in class terms. For in their case, of course, the experience that typically required explanation was, as we have seen, one of intergenerational advancement not only in living standards but also in position within the occupational hierarchy. Correspondingly, then, the accounts offered by these men tend to take on a more elaborate form. While the importance of secular trends of social change is again perceived, indeed emphasized, the changes in question are ones relevant to advancement of an individual rather than a collective kind: the dominant theme is not that of the growth of incomes or consumption, but rather that of the growth of *opportunity*. For our upwardly mobile respondents, the differences between themselves and their fathers are primarily attributable to the 'chances' which they had and which their fathers were denied. Among those men who had followed direct mobility routes, the reference was almost exclusively to the expansion of educational and training opportunities of one type or another; but among those whose mobility had been indirect, a wider view was sometimes found in which the expansion of higher-level employment opportunities was also stressed.

The main reason for the differences [between my father and myself] is, I believe, education, in the broadest sense of the word. I left school with 'O' levels and then obtained further qualifications via day-release, which enabled me to start my career further up the proverbial ladder, whereas my father had to start as an apprentice at the very bottom.
(684-6952: vehicles inspector; plastics technologist—sales manager)

Without doubt, the main reason [for my higher-level work and living standards] is that I have had the opportunity to go to a Grammar School and carry on with further education after I left school with the aid of local authority grants and courses, etc. Also . . . my father, never having had the opportunity, always was behind me to see that I did not waste [it].
(645-9408: sheet-steel worker; clerk in solicitor's office—legal executive)

My father grew up in the 'good old days' with a lack of educational facilities and a family need to get out and earn some money. The opportunities in the years 1914 (when he started work) onwards were very few and far between for anyone to progress to better things. Fortunately, when I started work, in 1953, there was opportunity for part-time day release and evening studies at the local technical college, and it was entirely up to the individual to exploit the education system.
(033-4163: garage foreman; draughtsman—development engineer)

I think the main reason for the difference [between my father's occupational level and my own] is that I started work during a period of reasonable economic activity . . . the chances for good jobs existed, and I 'stuck at it' through a poorly paid training period.
(657-4722: paper-mill labourer; engineering apprentice—contracts manager)

The main variation on this theme of widening opportunity, or more often in fact a complement to it (as the above extracts also illustrate), was some reference to individual, or perhaps family, attributes which were seen as crucial to the educational or occupational success that the respondent had actually obtained: in other words, one could say, attributes which had enabled him to *take advantage* of the opportunities that existed. However, this aspect of the mobility ideology prevalent among our upwardly mobile men is one that can be fully brought out only when we turn next to consider specifically the ways in which our respondents understood their experience of mobility in work-life perspective, and in particular the role of luck.

To begin again here with our grouping of men stable in Classes VI and VII, we may recall that their typical experience was one chiefly of immobility in working life, in the sense that they saw progress, if at all, only in their level of pay and not in the type of work they performed. One might then have expected these men to have inclined to the view that, so far at least as individual advancement was concerned, luck had been against them—that they had 'never had a chance'. However, if such a view did prevail, it was far more often implied than directly expressed. The assessments of the role of luck that were offered showed in fact a good deal of diversity, but with a majority tending to discount or to minimize its importance. In part, this resulted from luck being sometimes taken to mean simply *good* luck; but further, and more significantly for our purposes, it was evident that our working-class respondents did not, in the main, see the essentially non-progressive character of their working lives—any more than their rising living standards—as something requiring specific explanation, whether in terms of luck or otherwise. Rather, they accepted it as a more or less given, insurmountable feature of their social situation—which then in turn served to delimit their conceptions of what the role of luck in their lives *might be*, regardless of whether in the end they adjudged this important or not.

Thus, for example, where men regarded luck as being relatively unimportant, this was predominantly for one or other of two reasons. Either it was on the grounds that being working class in itself more or less precluded the possibility that (good) luck might enter into their lives, at least in any way that would transform their situation; or, more frequently, it was on the grounds that their present situation, fairly obviously, owed little or nothing to any good fortune— no one had ever done *them* any favours—and that to achieve and to maintain what they had, they were forced to rely on their own efforts and abilities.

I don't believe luck has played any part in my working life. If one is lower working-class, it's almost impossible to be anything else.
(624-1315: Electricity Board labourer; news-stand assistant—process worker)

I don't think a working-class family such as mine has any luck, they merely exist through life.
(476-8855: dock labourer; lift attendant—bus conductor)

[My working life has been] a series of jobs that were just different from each other—no major crises or important turning points. The way I see it, luck has nothing to do with it. You have to make your own way as best you can.
(147-9598: drill operator; butcher's apprentice—machine moulder)

There has been no luck in my life. All I've ever had or got, I've had to work for or do without. It's just as simple as that.
(199-3957: office cleaner; milk roundsman—bus driver)

Similarly, where these working-class respondents felt that luck *had* been important in their lives, its role was again generally seen in relation to the maintenance of their position as wage-workers—as opposed, that is, not to their advancement, but rather to their becoming unemployed, sick, or disabled. The role of good luck in working life was to help in some way to prevent their employment from being disrupted; that of bad luck was to bring this about or make it more likely.

Everything relating to my present way of life depends on my being consistently at work . . . I consider myself lucky to have been based in the South East of England . . . where there doesn't appear to be the same uncertainty about future prospects for work etc. [as in] the 'depressed areas' of Scotland, Northern Ireland or parts of Wales.
(469-4768: painter and decorator; filing clerk—painter and decorator)

I always consider that I've been lucky up to yet. I regard one of life's most important things as good health—which I've had. When one has good health, then they can work for any goal they may seek.
(602-0726: building labourer; messenger boy—diesel-engine tester)

I think luck has been important in my life as I have never been badly hurt down the pit.
(399-3967: excavator driver; colliery surface worker—colliery face worker)

[I have had] bad luck due to health reasons, causing lost working days . . . [A] major crisis [came in 1974 with the] three-day working week due to the power strike, followed by hospitalisation.
(161-1379: clicker (shoe manufacturing); milk roundsman—shoe machinist)

Moving on now to men in our upwardly mobile groupings, we may note first of all that they too, like our stable working-class respondents and indeed more strongly, favoured the view that luck had played no major part in the course of their working lives. While, as we have seen, these men were often prepared to acknowledge, implicitly at least, their good fortune in having had wider opportunities than their fathers, in accounting for the work-life advancement of which they were so overwhelmingly aware, they clearly wished to represent this as being primarily their own achievement. But there is of course no real contradiction here, and once more we can readily understand the outlook prevalent among a grouping of our respondents by relating it to those features of their situation which had greatest subjective salience for them.

So far as their working lives were concerned, the dominant reality for these upwardly mobile men, as we have previously suggested, is that of the careers that they had 'made for themselves' in their present professional, administrative, and managerial occupations and, of course, in securing access to the service class in the first place. In their lifetimes the opportunities for such mobility may have increased but these opportunities had none the less to be seized: more specifically, examinations had to be passed, qualifications gained, promotions won, new posts 'held down', and so on. The existence of opportunities in itself obviously provides no guarantee that any particular individual will succeed. Thus, viewed in this perspective, it can in no way be surprising that these men should be disinclined to accord luck any very prominent part in their advancement, and that they should rather place the emphasis on their own endeavours and on the personal qualities, plus perhaps the family support, which had enabled them to sustain their ambition over often lengthy periods. It is furthermore of interest to find that where luck did figure in the accounts they gave of the realization of their mobility, its role was, just as with our working-class respondents, defined essentially in terms of their dominant reality. That is to say, the instances of luck that were cited—good luck more often than bad—were very largely references to career contingencies, largely in fact ones illustrating in various ways the advantage of 'being in the right place at the right time'.

I can't really think luck has played a big part in my working life. I worked very hard to ensure that I had the experience and knowledge necessary to meet the requirements of each position I have held . . . I gave up all my spare time— evenings and week-ends for four years—to study for my accountancy qualifications, and have spent a lot of time since then reading and studying to keep up to date . . . I have steadily advanced, I believe, through ability.
(005-0404: Rescue Superintendent, A.R.P.; junior clerk—Divisional Administrative Manager, large brewing company)

Having chosen my intended career fairly early, luck did not enter into the picture at all. Ability to work and ability to relax have been the most important factors . . . One of our family ideas is that if you want something, you must work for it.
(638-10310: foreman fitter; army apprentice—Captain, R.E.M.E.)

I am a firm believer that you make your own 'luck' in life, by accepting, if need be, the slightest half-chance to improve your career or life-style . . . When the Sales Manager in my last employment asked me to become a Technical Representative, instead of Assistant Production Manager . . . this completely altered my career . . . At the time, I had no experience or training [in sales] and I accepted the challenge to better myself—obviously not luck.
(684-6952: vehicles inspector; plastics technologist—sales manager)

I have always believed that the major turning point in my working life was the untimely and sad death of an elderly colleague . . . I was invited to take his position but obviously as a complete novice . . . Since acceding to that position I have never looked back . . . [But] I am able to state that with [this] definite exception . . . I have achieved my present position through hard work, long hours and possibly having a personality that happens to fit this particularly erratic occupation.
(234-4705: foreman in plastics factory; order clerk—senior contracts administrator, aircraft manufacturing company)

Finally, we gain some further indication that it is the experience of career advance that basically conditions the mobility ideology of our upwardly mobile men, if we turn, by way of comparison, to the life-history notes of those groupings of respondents whom we have thus far largely neglected in this section. On the one hand, we may observe that men intergenerationally stable in Class I, who, like our upwardly mobile respondents, show a general awareness of work-life advance, also show the same strong tendency to reject the idea of luck as having been of key importance in their progress. These men, as we earlier saw, mostly recognize, implicitly if not explicitly, a continuity between their fathers' class position and life-style and their own; but they appear in fact little more likely than upwardly mobile men to attribute their work-life attainments to the good fortune of their birth or to any advantages that may have accrued to them from their family background. Rather, it is evident that the experience that is subjectively crucial for them is again that of making a career—of overcoming the successive obstacles or challenges of professional qualification or bureaucratic 'pyramid climbing'; and, in turn, the accounts that they offer of their advancement are again ones in which the emphasis is heavily on effort and ability, together perhaps with some references to how they had 'made the most' of any lucky 'breaks' that had happened to come their way.

On the other hand, we may also draw usefully, if rather selectively, on the life-history notes provided by men who were either intergenerationally stable in intermediate-class positions or downwardly mobile from Class I. Although, as we have previously described, these respondents displayed a good deal of variation in how they saw the pattern of their working lives, they followed for the most part those in other groupings in playing down the role of luck—either, that is, from the typical working-class or the typical service-class standpoint as we have represented these, depending on whether their awareness was primarily of work-life immobility or of career advance. However, within these groupings there were also to be found some few cases in which work-life experience was in fact largely accounted for in terms of luck, and what is, we believe, of some significance is that these were almost all ones where the 'course' for mobility, so to speak, had *not* taken the form of a series of career stages. Rather, the cases in question were ones of men who had either succeeded in establishing themselves, like their fathers, within our Class IV—that is, in self-employed and minor entrepreneurial positions; or who had been downwardly mobile from Class I origins chiefly as the result of entrepreneurial failure. What is implied in these respondents' accounts is the relatively insignificant role of individual striving in the face of the quite decisive influence that may be exerted by 'chance' events.

Luck was the main factor in my business becoming a success. For the first month of trying to work a round up [for a mobile shop] I was only having a moderate success. But luck came along in the form of an ex-employer. Apparently I had started my round up on the territory of a bread van driver who was employed by the same bread firm that I used to work for. On hearing of this, my old boss, the manager of the bakery, came to see me, and in a sort of compromise he offered me all his customers in the area I was working, on condition I sold their bread and cakes. It was like a dream come true and my business has never looked back.

(213-7628: grocer; shop assistant—mobile-shop proprietor)

[The crisis in my working life] was a heart attack at the age of 45. [I also had] bad luck in business due to other people's greed: i.e. manufacturers cashing in on shops and businesses by opening shops themselves in their factories and getting away with rates etc . . . Previous to my illness [my goal] was to provide for the future. Since then it has been hopeless. Success in work now is a faraway dream.

(598-4277: works manager; apprentice packer—haberdasher)

One is thus led to the suggestion that, in present-day society at least, it is not private enterprise that provides the prime social context for a mobility ideology of a distinctively 'meritocratic' kind, but rather higher-level salaried employment: in other words, not the 'free' market itself but rather bureaucracy, public and private.[12]

Perhaps the most significant conclusion to emerge from the discussion of this section is then that our respondents' attempts to account for their mobility experience tend to take on a quite different character depending on whether they view their mobility in intergenerational or in work-life perspective. Where men are seeking to explain differences of which they are aware between their own and their father's social position, they readily 'appeal to history', so to speak, and recognize the importance of secular trends of change in society at large—economic growth, the progress of the working class, the expansion of mobility opportunities—in which they have been caught up but to which, as individuals, they can have contributed only negligibly if at all. Where, in contrast, they are concerned with accounting for their present positions as the outcome of their own working lives, they are far more likely to take individual responsibility in some degree—that is to say, for the way in which they have conducted themselves *within* the actual conditions that they have encountered: for example, in the case of those who have followed their fathers as wage-workers, by responding to the 'money for effort' bargain, which, even while shifting in their favour, remains central to their work situation; or, in the case of those who achieved professional, administrative or managerial occupations, by taking advantage of the growth of educational and training facilities and of career openings.

Thus, when sociologists seek, as we have earlier done, to link the mobility rates and patterns that they have observed to the forms, and changes in the forms, of the occupational and class structures, it would seem important that they should keep in mind that the individuals who 'live through' the mobility in question may well complement a recognition of the macro-social factors involved with interpretations in which their own agency is given a central part. And, we may add, it would also appear desirable that those sociologists who have construed the mobility process in terms of occupational attainment and who have then accorded luck a substantial part in this process[13] should reflect on the distinct possibility that the majority of the individuals whom they have studied might be in serious disagreement with them.

THE SIGNIFICANCE OF MOBILITY

The life-history material on which we shall draw in this third section derives from four questions that we suggested to our respondents, each relating in some way to the place and meaning that work held in their lives, and through which which we sought to gain some idea of the wider significance for them of the types of mobility, or immobility, of which they had shown themselves aware. We shall in fact concentrate on the accounts that respondents gave of the importance that they attached to work in their lives and for what reasons—that is, in pursuit of what goals; of their degree of success in achieving these goals; and of the actual implications of their success, or lack of success, for their lives outside of work. We may best proceed, as in our first section, by considering first the accounts supplied by each of our groupings of intergenerationally stable respondents, and then those of our mobile groupings.

Among men intergenerationally stable in Class I, the dominant theme was that of work as a 'central life interest'.[14] Indeed, work was quite frequently represented by these men as *the* major commitment in their lives, to which all else had to take second place. The goals for which they strove in work could be described as essentially ones of self-fulfilment—whether to be achieved via professional reputation, promotion, or business success, or simply through the skilful performance of their work-tasks. Satisfactory monetary rewards tended to be treated as a more or less automatic concomitant of the realization of these primary goals. Where the commitment to work was in any way qualified, this was typically in regard to family responsibilities: that is to say, some limits were recognized on the extent to which the pursuit of work goals could be allowed to threaten family life. Work and family interests could be represented as compatible in so far as success in work meant a higher income and thus a raising of family living standards; but respondents often showed themselves aware of at least potentially serious conflicts between work and family in regard either to demands on their time and energy or to the requirement for geographical mobility.

Work is obviously the major factor in my life and most of my leisure activities relate to it. I regard myself as extremely fortunate in having a job that gives me enormous satisfaction, as well as subsiduary activities such as reviewing and writing that I also enjoy and give me the *entrée* to a social world in which I am appreciated . . . My main goal has been to live in a particular way, which involves privileges as well as money.

(179-9069: Gas Works Manager; management trainee—museum curator)

Where one is in private practice one's work is supremely important, and however much one may deprecate it, other things quite often have to take second place. My main goals or objects have been to carry out my professional work and duties to the best of my ability in the interests of my clients, whilst at the same time endeavouring to earn the best living and to attain the highest standard of life for myself and my family.

(551-9540: solicitor; articled clerk—solicitor)

My job is very central and most things have been subordinated to it. When you first start in the rat race, you must be ready to work hard [and to] move home to wherever the next promotion is . . . My first wife . . . couldn't stand the pace . . . The work is often intellectually boring, but this has to be accepted. There is plenty of satisfaction in setting oneself and others targets to be achieved and eventually getting there. I have always striven hard to be in a position to give orders to others.

(596–4811: Department-store manager; assistant company secretary—Chairman of group of printing companies)

[My goals in work are] to have an interesting, varied job; to contribute to the company's objectives . . . to be respected by one's colleagues as an expert and to achieve an international reputation. Obviously financial reward and status are important—but less than enjoying the job . . . I recognise that commitment to work has to be balanced with family commitments—this becomes increasingly difficult with increased seniority. Promotion may involve relocation; this would be a difficult decision—especially with three children settled at school.

(193-7547: building contractor; research metallurgist—Head of Research and Development Department)

This emphasis of our stable Class I respondents on the centrality of work in their lives, though linked sometimes with doubts and fears about the implications for their families, is then carried through into the assessments they offered of how far their life stories might be regarded as ones of success or failure. As might be expected in view of their general awareness of career advance and their tendency to attribute this to their own efforts and abilities, the large majority were ready to see themselves as being successful, to a greater or lesser degree, in career terms: for example, in having achieved professional qualifications and competence, in having reached or exceeded the level of promotion regarded as appropriate for their age, in having won the respect of their colleagues, etc. A further claim, more common as an addition than as an alternative, was to the effect that they had succeeded in that, through their achievement in work, they had provided their families with a relatively high level of material comfort and security and a rewarding style of life. However, it was at the same time on the relationship between their working and their family lives that such misgivings as these men displayed were chiefly centred: for a sizeable minority, success in the former had not been conducive to success in the latter or had indeed militated against it.

I feel I have been successful in my professional life, and have provided a good standard of living for my family. My wife would say that I have not given sufficient time to my family, and this was certainly true during the formative years of the practice. There are stresses in our family life which I hope to have time to resolve. My main regret is that there should be any sense of conflict or competition between home and work. I work hard for my family's sake, and would like to feel their support in times of stress, rather than the sense of failing them for lack of time.
(343-6056: Chartered accountant; architectural assistant—architect)

Work has steadily, over the last six to seven years, taken a more important role in my life, until now when it *is*, unfortunately, 'my life' . . . Socially, work has taken its toll, because I have not had sufficient time to spend with friends, and also perhaps I have forgotten how to enjoy myself. The biggest regret, however, is not having enough time to spend with my wife. Reading back now, this all sounds absurd. But one definitely does get further and further involved into the rat race; at first without realising it, but when you finally do, it's too late.
(542-2040: Managing Director, seed mail-order company; gardener—Executive Director, seed mail-order company)

The distinctive characteristics of the outlook of these Class I respondents can be yet more clearly brought out in contrast with the outlook typical of men stable in our Classes VI and VII. In the first place, work was clearly not for the latter a 'central life interest' in the same sense as for the former. This is not to say that work was less important to our Class VI and VII respondents, but rather that their involvement in their work was for the most part of a different, more restricted, kind. Work was not for them a sphere of life within which their ultimate goals were located; rather, these goals lay outside their work, chiefly in fact in their domestic and family lives, and the importance that then attached to work was that of being the essential *means* to their realization. The predominance of such an 'instrumental' orientation did not, it must be stressed, imply that these respondents were unaware of, or insensitive to, the possibility of deriving satisfaction directly from work; on the contrary, the desirability of having interesting, inherently rewarding work was quite frequently referred to. The fact that this was represented as an actual goal only by a minority (mainly of skilled men) has to be seen, we would argue, not as an expression of free choice but as reflecting a basic constraint of the working-class situation: that is, the lack of opportunity to obtain work in which goals of self-fulfilment *and* a relatively high income can realistically be pursued together.[15]

Work is all important. Everything takes second place to it. [My goal is] to earn as much as possible, in order to try to provide my family with the basic necessities. A decent home, food as good as can be afforded, clothing the same, and, if possible, the chance of some break from the routine of work in the form of a holiday once a year.

(469-4768: painter and decorator; filing clerk—painter and decorator)

I just take work as it comes. The only reason I think most people and myself [work] is for a better way of life . . . My main interest is to earn more so I can get the house paid for and provide a good future for my family.

(502-3899: colliery face worker: errand boy—colliery underground worker)

Education and qualifications give you opportunities for good jobs. I have neither, so I have moved to jobs to improve my pay. I go out to work because I want money to try to give my wife and children the things I never had: a decent furnished home, clothes, education, etc. . . . I like to do something that interests me, but I can't deny I sell my labour to the highest bidder.

(411-7554: textiles worker; ring doffer (wool industry)—lorry driver)

My work has been important to me for only one main reason, money—so that my family could live from week to week. My job was and still is a means to an end . . . Long ago I realised that I hadn't the educational or social qualifications needed to be able to pick my job. I had responsibilities when I was in my early twenties—a wife and baby to support; and with only a secondary school education I was destined to become just another working-class nobody like millions of others. Not that I wouldn't have liked to have been able to follow a chosen career . . .

(664-0780: foundry annealer; electrical assembler—crankshaft grinder)

The contrast between our stable service-class and stable working-class respondents is then sustained when we go on to consider the latter's judgements of the degree of their success or failure. They too in fact wish, in the large majority of cases, to see themselves as being successful. However, following from their basic orientation to work, they claim their success not in their work itself—except perhaps in being proficient at their jobs and thus able to maintain their earning power—but rather in their lives outside work and, overwhelmingly, in the achievement of their goals in regard to the well-being of their families. Consequently, we may remark, these men, unlike those stable in Class I, have no reason to be aware of, or to fear, any major tension between the demands of success in work and in family life. On the contrary, if their working lives are to be accounted as successful at all, this can ultimately be only in the extent to which benefits, material and social, have accrued to their families.[16]

Work has been important for my family life . . . I see myself as successful when I can go home to my lovely house and family. I do not think success in work would be good for me. I have other things (freedom) . . . I think by having our own house, a good car and nice friends, my family are respected.

(141-3668: french polisher; apprentice carpenter—carpenter)

I feel I have a responsibility to my family to give them the best of everything if possible, regardless of my own feelings, etc. [My goals are] to earn more . . . to be able to go anywhere and do anything, to please myself as much as I can. I feel successful in the sense that I have a place to live, a happy family, a car, all of which I have worked for myself. I have not had to ask anyone for anything.

(385-2238: warehouseman; consignment clerk—sheet metal worker)

I regard myself as fairly successful providing I only compare myself with my own class, and with people of a similar background to mine . . . I have a successful married and family life . . . Success at work from my point of view, and most working-class people that I know, is measured by the amount of money that is on your pay-slip at the end of the week.

(664-0780: foundry annealer; electrical assembler—crank-shaft grinder)

Finally, we may note that in the accounts of their orientations to work offered by our respondents stable in Classes III–V, we find basically the same themes as in those of our other stable respondents, although quite often in an interestingly mixed form. For the men in question, work has been chiefly important, thus far at least in their working lives, in much the same way as for our working-class respondents: that is, as the means of improving family living standards. However, unlike their working-class counterparts, men stable in our intermediate classes were not generally content to *restrict* their objectives in work to the achievement of a relatively high level of monetary return, and quite frequently included among their goals that of having work in which they could gain some satisfaction of an intrinsic kind. But while their aspirations were in this way more developed than those typical of manual wage-workers, they had not for the most part been realized, nor probably had the prospect of being realized, to the same extent as those of men established in service-class occupations. In turn, it is scarcely surprising that among our stable intermediate-class respondents we find, to a clearly greater degree than within our other stable groupings, assessments of success that are expressed in a relatively guarded or ambivalent manner.

My work would have to hold a certain interest for me, otherwise I would soon be looking for something else. For all that, my idea of working for a living is to earn enough, so that life is more comfortable and free of money worries, and to provide for the future. Whilst I do not consider myself a failure, I find it difficult to be able to gauge success. I suppose, in my case, success at work is knowing my job and doing it well without supervision. If I fail in anything, it is in being unable to 'push' myself into the limelight. I think that success at work is not as important as success in one's family life.

(100-3156: stocktaker's clerk; telegraph boy—wages and time clerk)

My main objects in working are to . . . work at something that doesn't bore me, to earn enough to live comfortably, and to work for a company which makes some arrangement for the future—which I do. In my job I have been 'successful' in my own eyes, as in general I am doing what I want to do, and in the way I want to do it. I believe I have been successful in having a happy family life and have never been without a week's wages since I started work. I do not consider myself to be a 'failure', probably because I am not ambitious . . . Any apparent 'failure' would be from outsiders, thinking I should have risen higher in the company than I have, but not from my own or family's viewpoint.

(017-7974: goods yard foreman; restaurant porter–goods-yard foreman)

Against this background provided by the accounts of our groupings of inter-generationally stable respondents, we may now consider the corresponding material that we have from the life-history notes of our mobile men and, in particular, from those of men upwardly mobile into Class I positions.

As regards the significance that work held in the lives of these men, one could say that their typical outlook was closely akin to that of our stable Class I respondents in that their actual work-tasks and roles were clearly a major pre-occupation and a source of much inherent satisfaction. At the same time, though, it was no less clear that the claims of family life were more widely recognized and given a rather higher priority. In other words, while the orientations to work of our upwardly mobile men could not be regarded as predominantly instrumental ones, like those of our working-class respondents, their goals in work did appear to be less sharply focused on the fulfilment of their own career ambitions than those of men who had followed their fathers into service-class occupations, and more often explicitly took in the welfare and the happiness of their families as prime considerations.

Work has been very important but not at the expense of my family. I recently turned down a promotion which meant moving to Wales . . . [My goals have been] to have a satisfying job–creative, responsible–and to provide a comfortable living standard for my family. I have never knowingly set myself any goals long-termwise.

(032-3755: lamplighter; apprentice draughtsman–Plant Engineer, large chemical plant)

Work has been very important. Most certainly other things have taken second place to it [but] my priorities, I consider, are quite clear: wife and children first, job second (as it is mainly a supporting function), hobbies and other interests last. [My] main goals in life–work orientations–have been to earn more and also to provide for the future. If it is interesting, so much the better.

(502-9324: storeman; apprentice fitter and turner–pharmaceuticals plant manager)

My work is very important, and to succeed in it and to obtain educational qualifications required that I had no time for other activities . . . [Now] my main goal is to earn enough to enable my wife and family to have as comfortable a life as possible. I require my job, however, to be both satisfying and a challenge.

(514-10044: lorry driver; architectural assistant–architect)

Until I was in my late thirties, I think it would be true to say that work came first. Since then I have turned down two very good jobs because each would have meant disrupting the family and our home life. I now realise I have achieved all I am probably going to, and want to enjoy family life and widen our social activities. I also want to be home in order to see and enjoy our daughter growing up. I obtain tremendous satisfaction from my work. I have endeavoured to be the best in order to provide a good standard of life for my family both now and in the future.

(005-0404: Rescue Superintendent, A.R.P.; junior clerk—Divisional Administrative Manager, large brewing company)

That such differences in emphasis should be found between men intergenerationally stable in Class I and those recruited into this class from below is not, we would think, very difficult to understand. From their social origins, and also in many instances from their own earlier working lives, upwardly mobile men will have had opportunity to learn the meaning of work as an activity which, even if affording little or no direct satisfaction, is crucial to the pursuit of social advancement outside work. Their mobility has removed them from those less-advantaged class situations in which powerful constraints may well lead to this being taken as the only, or the overriding meaning of work; but it remains none the less one which, in the context of their biographies, it is not easy for them to discount. In other words, they are unlikely, as compared with second-generation members of the service class, to take it for granted that work should be inherently rewarding, at the same time as providing a relatively high income more or less as a matter of course. Rather, as the above extracts illustrate, to have work that can *both* engage their interest and abilities *and* enable them steadily to improve the standard and style of living of their families might be taken as being for our upwardly mobile respondents the nub of their ambition.

In turn, then, one might suggest, having attained the kind of occupation that allows this goal to be realized, upwardly mobile men will feel less pressure than those stable within the service class to seek *continuing* career advance—perhaps to the detriment of their family relations—in order to give significance to their working lives. While the latter, as we have seen, tended to judge the degree of their success primarily by the progress they had made in *intra*-occupational terms, we find that the claims to success which were—almost invariably—made by our upwardly mobile respondents reflected more broadly, as one might expect, the *inter*-occupational, or indeed class mobility, and its concomitants, of which they were generally aware. Thus, even while perhaps being relatively modest about their achievements, or potential, *as* professionals, administrators, or managers, these men could still assess the course of their lives in a highly favourable manner by referring back to their family origins and also, in the case of those who had followed indirect mobility routes, to the low occupational levels at which they had started their careers.[17]

For ten years [I have been] pushing further and further up the ladder, as in the building trade hard work on the staff side (which I tend to revel in rather than regret) is soon noticed . . . which I find very rewarding after the dead-end jobs I originally had . . . In my early life I worked for returns at the end of the week, which we all do really, but nowadays I find I get more fulfilment from doing a good job and showing returns for it. I have only just begun to realise really how successful I have been in life compared with other people I knew in my childhood.

(265-2953: factory foreman; apprentice fitter—site engineer, construction and civil engineering company)

I suppose most people seek financial security and I am no different but . . . I do not consider work as something to be tolerated. I think of it as something interesting, challenging and mentally rewarding. It has given me a degree of importance and a status. Compared with my school friends and bearing in mind the environment from which I came, I have been tremendously successful [although] at some stage in my career, I came to terms with my ability and decided that I would find it very hard going to reach the very top and, subconsciously, I think I settled for moderate success.

(512-5323: colliery datal worker; railway clerk—Administrative Officer, British Rail)

The main goals during my working life have been: to earn more and thus live in a better way, to obtain job security, to achieve satisfaction and a challenging and interesting job . . . I see myself as successful . . . because without any formal training I have risen from the shop floor to top management—probably as far as I can go.

(219-6182: turner and fitter; apprentice printer—Works Manager, large printing company)

Finally, it is also consistent with what we have taken to be the typical goals in work of our upwardly mobile respondents that these men should not, to the same extent as those intergenerationally stable in Class I, reveal anxieties about the implications of their career success for their domestic and family lives. In this respect, the dominant theme in their accounts was in fact that the wider effects of their success in work had been quite generally beneficial: the material standards and the quality of their families' lives had been raised and, furthermore, reference was quite frequently made—in line with the analyses of the two previous chapters—to a widening (rather than a radically changing) set of friends and acquaintances and to a more varied programme of 'social' activities. While career advance might sometimes result in men 'losing touch' with former associates, in so far as any actual disruption of social relationships was mentioned, then, as with stable service-class members, this was chiefly linked with geographical movement.

I have found that being fairly successful at work, although taking up a little more of my time, does have compensations and has had good effects outside my working environment. We can entertain at home and we do have a fairly busy social life, and of course we have a very good holiday abroad each year. In retrospect, we have a wide circle of what I consider to be very close and good friends.

(473-0564: bus conductor; export clerk—Shipping Manager, wine merchants)

Success at work has meant meeting a wider type of person. I have my schoolday friends who are mainly shop-floor (shop stewards in some cases) and there are friends which I have made as I have advanced, i.e. managers, engineers. Also, with the area in which we live, the neighbours and friends are mainly professional people. I sometimes feel conscious of my background (lack of university) when I am in the company of people who have been to Public School or university [but] summing up, I feel that success in my working life has had a good effect on my life outside of work. I have many friends and my family have an active and full life.

(032-3755: lamplighter; apprentice draughtsman—Plant Engineer, large chemical plant)

My success at work has had good effects on my life outside work. It has enabled me to do some travelling in Europe and the USA . . . [and] I have also met, because of work, a greater range of people than most, ranging from uncouth, illiterate manual workers to uncouth, illiterate company directors. Success has not affected my family relationships and I still have the same friends as I had when I was at school.

(578-6434: boiler maker; laboratory assistant—Chief Development Chemist)

To succeed in my work has meant that I have had to move home. Inevitably this means that contact is lost with old friends. Nevertheless, I feel that success has proved beneficial to my family . . . in material possessions; and living in different parts of the country has given them more self-confidence.

(514-0035: sheet-metal worker; apprentice electrician—electrical engineer C.E.G.B.)

In sum, on the basis of our life history material we are clearly led to question one widely accepted stereotype of the upwardly mobile man: that is, as the excessively ambitious, continually striving 'eager beaver', whose career success is bought dearly in terms of stress in family relationships and an impoverished social life. In the preceding chapter, we have already noted certain features of the pattern of mobility in modern Britain, as we would ourselves describe it, which makes it less likely than has often been supposed that mobility should lead to social marginality or isolation. We may now suggest in addition, from the point of view of the upwardly mobile individual, that his ascent from relatively disadvantaged origins to a position in the higher levels of the occupational and class structures may well in itself be sufficient to satisfy his ambition and to give an acceptable meaning to his biography; and that, consequently, he will in fact be *less* motivated than the man for whom such a position is in effect a starting point to press for *further* advancement in his working life. In particular, he will not be inclined to pursue his career to the extent of threatening his own and his family's enjoyment of the material and social rewards of the mobility that he has already achieved, since it is likely that such benefits will, from the start, have figured prominently in what he has sought to obtain from his work.

To complete this section, we must then consider, if only briefly, a similar range of issues to those treated above in regard to our grouping of downwardly mobile respondents. These men, it will be recalled, showed in fact some considerable variation in their awareness of mobility, as we might have anticipated from our earlier analyses of the phenomenon of counter-mobility. Correspondingly, we also find a great deal of diversity in the accounts they give of their goals in work and of the extent of their success in realizing them. However, while no very well-defined themes stand out, two observations of some interest may be made.

First, only a small minority of these downwardly mobile men appear to have accepted the predominantly instrumental orientation to work that we have taken as typical of our intergenerationally stable working-class respondents. In other words, the goal of having work capable of providing intrinsic satisfaction as well as adequate monetary returns was still for the most part retained, even though, as among our respondents stable in intermediate-class positions, judgements were very mixed on whether this goal had actually been attained or was in sight.

Secondly, it was also notable that, with the exception of the one or two who had suffered the collapse of their own businesses, our downwardly mobile men were reluctant to recognize themselves as being failures in any total or decisive way. While straightforward claims to success were certainly less frequent in this grouping than in any other, a range of accounts was offered of why an unqualified judgement of failure would be inappropriate: for example, to the effect that it was as yet too early to say how one's career might work out, that the respondent was not really interested in being successful, that success in the conventional sense took second place to other goals—cultural, sporting, spiritual etc.;

I do not see myself either as a success or failure. I retain an open mind . . . I am still seeking the occupation that will give me success. At this present moment plans are afoot for me to change my job once again where the intentions are to become a self-employed haulage contractor.
(280-5057: Managing Director, dyeing company; apprentice fitter—trainee salesman)

I could not really claim to be ambitious or in all honesty, money-conscious. My main aim is to find a niche, a steady, reliable job which is not too demanding but at the same time maintains a certain amount of interest . . . My approach is one of partial commitment and . . . I am prepared for any disappointments that may transpire.
(151-0623: Contracts manager; apprentice printer—compositor)

I really judge success outside work, as I like to switch off and relax. As I play a lot of sport, I play to win, but second to enjoyment and satisfaction. I captain a successful hockey team . . . I tend not to carry my work into my outside life.
(248-2455: Army Officer; budget control clerk—travelling salesman)

Such accounts may well, of course, have to some extent the function of excusing or legitimating failure that is in fact deeply felt; but they did none the less usually appear to have some consistency with the facts of the respondent's biography and present situation. What is, at all events, confirmed is our earlier view that we cannot regard our downwardly mobile respondents as being at all a homogeneous grouping, and that this is so whether their mobility patterns and prospects are treated in terms of our categories or of their own subjective assessments.

Our principal aim in this chapter has been to investigate how far a correspondence exists between the analyses of social mobility in modern Britain that we have earlier presented, on the basis of our 1972 and 1974 inquiries, and the actual experience of mobility, or immobility, among those individuals who have been the subjects of these inquiries. Because of the problems of data collection to which we have referred, the material on which we have drawn—that is, the life-history notes written by 247 men, or 38 per cent of those re-interviewed in 1974—is not of the same degree of reliability as that previously available; and we have furthermore been engaged in the difficult task of using this material to interpret, rather than simply to describe, the ways in which our respondents have subjectively experienced mobility. Thus, the conclusions that we have arrived at in this chapter must clearly be regarded as being of a more tentative and debatable kind than most of those earlier advanced. None the less, we find it difficult to believe that those respondents who supplied life-history notes could be so unrepresentative, or our interpretations of their accounts so erroneous, that these conclusions will be wildly misleading ones. Rather, we would incline to accept them as valid, at least in broad terms, and therefore to see them as being in fact of some more general significance: that is, as largely confirming that the basic approach to the study of mobility to which we were led by our theoretical and other interests—that of viewing mobility in terms of movement between class positions—is one which is by no means alien to the understanding of our respondents themselves.

To be sure, we have found that among those men who returned life-history notes there was a very widespread awareness of having been socially mobile in one way or another, including among those men whom we would categorize as being stable in class position. In other words, we must acknowledge that there are other types of subjectively significant mobility than that on which we have chosen to focus our attention. However, in this connection, two further findings may also be underlined.

First of all, we may note that the kind of mobility experience predominant within our stable groupings is in each case readily distinguishable from that of class mobility in the sense we have adopted: that is, of the movement of individuals within the occupational division of labour such that major changes in their market and work situations are involved. Thus, for example, among men stable in Class I the awareness was of mobility essentially in the form of career advance, which was achieved to an important extent intra-occupationally, and which did not entail any sense of discontinuity in class membership (even where countermobility had occurred). Again, among respondents stable in Classes VI and VII the mobility that was widely recognized, although in this case intergenerational in character, implied collective rather than individual progress, and was in fact associated with a general improvement in, rather than an escape from, the class position of manual wage-labour. On the other hand, then, among those men whom we have treated as being class mobile, or at all events among the majority whose movement was upwards, the experience of mobility is quite evidently of a different, and indeed more comprehensive kind, involving an awareness of both intergenerational and work-life advance. Moreover, this mobility is rather clearly represented when viewed in intergenerational perspective in terms of what, on our definition, are differences in class position. Our upwardly mobile men see themselves for the most part as differing from their fathers not only in enjoying higher incomes and greater consumer power or, in other words, in having a superior market situation; but also in being engaged in higher-level occupations—ones affording greater autonomy, authority, and opportunity for direct satisfactions—or, in other words, in having a superior work situation.

Furthermore, it should be recognized that the adoption of a 'class' point of view was by no means restricted to those of our respondents who sought specifically to express the experience of class mobility. On the contrary, in seeking to account for their mobility experience of whatever kind, and to explain the goals they had pursued, our respondents quite regularly referred to components or features of their class position: that is, to factors affecting their chances in the labour market and hence to their chances of obtaining work of a particular type.

Thus, men upwardly mobile into service-class positions attributed their advancement to the expansion of educational and training facilities and of higher-level employment opportunities, and to their own success in gaining qualifications, taking advantage of career openings, etc. But intergenerationally stable service-class members also thought of themselves as having 'made' careers—rather than having followed their fathers in some quasi-automatic fashion—in that they too had equipped themselves with the necessary qualifications and work experience to be able to command a professional, administrative, or managerial post. And again our stable working-class respondents alluded to long-term changes in market conditions which had favoured labour, and to its increased organizational strength, while perhaps explaining their concentration on monetary returns from work in terms of their lack of education and qualifications and their consequent inability to obtain work in which other goals could at the same time be realistically pursued.

Similarly, we may observe, when our respondents came to discuss the wider significance of the mobility of which they were aware and of its effect on their lives, it was once more on aspects of their market and work situations, and on the more immediate implications of these, that their attention focused. Thus, the major benefits of (upward) mobility were seen as lying in higher income, improved living standards, and greater security; and in being able to obtain these greater extrinsic rewards while performing intrinsically more rewarding work-tasks and roles. References to changes in life-style also occurred, but it is notable that—in much the same way as higher living standards—these appeared to be more valued for their own sake than as being indicative of status advance. Only very rarely in fact was the experience of mobility discussed in specifically 'status' terms. In other words, we may at all events claim that our life-history material would *not* be highly congruent with the theoretical approach that sees the essential context for mobility as a generally recognized status hierarchy, and the chief significance of an individual's position in the occupational structure as being therefore the degree of prestige that attaches to it. For the men we studied, at least, other occupational attributes, in particular the economic and psychological rewards directly associated with the work carried out, would appear to be of far greater salience.

Correspondingly, we then further find that in so far as our respondents referred to the costs of mobility, these were seen as arising mainly through their work imposing excessive demands on their time and energy or requiring repeated shifts in residence, with adverse consequences for their home and family lives. Such problems were thus ones associated primarily with the exigencies of career advancement, rather than with intergenerational mobility, and they appeared in fact to be more frequently encountered among men stable in Class I than among those recruited to this class from below. The life-history notes of our upwardly mobile respondents indeed suggested that they had not for the most part experienced their mobility as socially stressful and, in particular, problems of managing status discrepancies or of translating occupational into status ascent received very little mention.

In arguing thus—that our respondents to an important extent viewed their mobility experience in 'class' terms—we do not of course wish to claim that they were 'class-conscious' in any way approaching the Marxist sense, nor even that they made regular and explicit use of concepts of class similar to those that have informed our own analyses. The point we seek to establish is of a more limited kind: namely, that the way in which these men most often discuss their mobility, and the structure of inequality within which it occurred, is one which in fact concentrates on the same basic *elements*, that is, features of market and work situations, that are also the focus of the theoretical approach that we have adopted—as distinct, for example, from one which would take as central the idea of a status hierarchy. And thus what we would maintain is that the analytical basis on which we have worked in previous chapters, expressed in practice chiefly through our class schema, can in turn be provided with more than a purely theoretical validation: it can also be seen as comprising 'second order' constructs that have an obvious affinity with—indeed represent a systematization and development of—certain of the 'first order' constructs through which the subjects of our research try themselves to make sense of the course of their social lives.

NOTES

1. See, e.g., Arnold Rose, 'Social Mobility and Social Values', *Archives européennes de sociologie*, vol. 5, 1964; and, in particular, K.U. Mayer, 'Soziale Mobilität und die Wahrnehmung gesellschaftlicher Ungleichheit', *Zeitschrift für Soziologie*, vol. 1, 1972; and *Ungleichheit and Mobilität im sozialen Bewusstsein*, Dusseldorf: Westdeutscher Verlag, 1975.
2. Robert Angell, 'A Critical Review of the Development of the Personal Document Method in Sociology, 1920-1940' in Louis Gottschalk *et al.*, *The Use of Personal Documents in History, Anthropology and Sociology*, New York: United States Social Science Research Council, 1945, pp. 177-8.
3. H.S. Becker, *Sociological Work*, Chicago: Aldine, 1970, ch. 4, 'The Life History and the Scientific Mosaic', pp. 64-72.
4. The main reasons for the failure to complete notes appeared to be forgetfulness and procrastination. Each 'round' of reminders produced a new spurt of returns, but the third round, which was by telephone, had unfortunately to be discontinued on grounds of cost.
5. *Sociological Work*, p. 70.
6. We shall not attempt to elaborate here the case for this approach—to what is in effect the long-standing problem of how a would-be *verstehende* sociology should actually proceed. It is in fact best developed, we believe, in recent writings of Popper and Jarvie (though it also appears in a different philosophical idiom in the work of Schütz). See, in particular, Karl Popper, *Obejctive Knowledge*, Oxford: Clarendon Press, 1972, ch. 4 esp.; and I.C. Jarvie, *Concepts and Society*, London: Routledge, 1972, ch. 1. One point which might, however, be usefully clarified is the following: that seeking to understand a belief as *practically* rational—that is, in the situation in which it is held—does not entail accepting the belief as *epistemically* rational—that is, in the light of philosophically defensible standards of truth. For several useful discussions of the distinction between practical and epistemic rationality, see S.I. Benn and G.W. Mortimore (eds.), *Rationality and the Social Sciences*, London: Routledge, 1976.
7. Here and subsequently the extracts quoted from respondents' life-history notes are intended to illustrate the description or interpretation contained in the preceding paragraph of text. As will be seen, extracts have been taken from a relatively large number of the sets of notes submitted but some respondents have been quoted from

several times over, in part in order to give some idea of the continuity of their accounts. In presenting extracts, we have corrected minor errors in spelling and grammar, and have occasionally changed circumstantial details in order to prevent any possibility of respondents being identified. The details given after each extract have the following format: (respondent's reference number: occupation of father or other head of household at respondent's age 14; respondent's first full-time occupation–respondent's 1974 occupation).

8. It may be taken that those themes characterized as dominant were recognized in at least two-thirds of the life-history notes of the men in question.

9. C. Wright Mills, *The Sociological Imagination*: New York: Oxford University Press, 1959, ch. 1.

10. See above, pp. 128–9.

11. See above, pp. 140–1.

12. In this respect, it is of interest to note that more sophisticated defenders of the free-market economy have in fact rejected the idea of any meritocratic legitimation for the social inequalities that it generates, and largely because of the role that is played by sheer luck in the way in which the operation of markets distributes advantages and rewards. See, e.g., F.A. Hayek, *The Constitution of Liberty*, London: Routledge, 1960, ch. 6 esp.

13. See above, pp. 16–17.

14. For this notion, see Robert Dubin, 'Industrial Workers' Worlds: a Study of the "Central Life Interests" of Industrial Workers', *Social Problems*, vol. 3, 1956.

15. For further discussion of this constraint, see John H. Goldthorpe, David Lockwood, Frank Bechhofer, and Jennifer Platt, *The Affluent Worker: Industrial Attitudes and Behaviour*, Cambridge University Press, 1968, ch. 2; and *The Affluent Worker in the Class Structure*, Cambridge University Press, 1969, ch. 3.

16. The only occasional indications we have of tensions of the kind in question are in regard to overtime and shiftworking. But the latter was also sometimes seen as beneficial to family life in permitting more day-time leisure.

17. In work-life perspective, as we have earlier noted, inter- and intra-occupational mobility tended not to be distinguished; but claims to success on the part of our upwardly mobile respondents in fact typically referred to the former. In the terminology of Tausky and Dubin, one could say that these men usually displayed a 'downward career anchorage'–evaluating their achievement in terms of distance moved from some starting point. In contrast, intergenerationally stable members of Class I more often had an 'upward career anchorage', implying judgement of their success in terms of how close they could get to some occupational peak. Cf. Curt Tausky and Robert Dubin, 'Career Anchorage: Managerial Mobility Motivations', *American Sociological Review*, vol. 30, 1965.

Part Two
Class Mobility in Britain:
Issues of the Present Day

CHAPTER 9

Trends in Class Mobility 1972–1983

(*with* CLIVE PAYNE)

In Part One a recurrent theme was the changing pattern of intergenerational class mobility in Britain over the middle decades of the present century. Chapter 3 was in fact devoted to an examination of mobility trends during this period on the basis of birth-cohort analysis. Respondents to the 1972 inquiry were divided up according to their date of birth (using ten-year intervals), and the mobility experience of individuals was compared across the successive cohorts that were thus formed. As was noted (pp. 69-70), this method has undoubted imperfections and disadvantages. To begin with, one is not operating with true birth cohorts, but only with the survivors of such cohorts after the erosions of mortality and migration; and further, a reliable interpretation of results is always threatened by the confounding of the period effects which are of chief concern to the analyst of trends with the effects of age (or life-cycle) or of cohort membership *per se*. However, while we certainly could not claim to have circumvented such difficulties entirely, we were still able to offer an account of class mobility trends over the period covered by our data which, we felt, was unlikely to be misleading in at least its major conclusions. These could be summarized as follows.

(i) From at least the inter-war years through to the time of the 1972 inquiry, men of *all* class origins had become progressively more likely to move into professional, administrative, and managerial positions—or, we would say, into the service class of modern British society; and, at the same time, they had become less likely to be found in the manual wage-earning positions of the working class.

(ii) These trends could be attributed, more or less entirely, to changes in the shape of the class structure—that is, to the growth of the service class and the contraction of the working class; they were, in other words, the result of changes in objective mobility opportunities, and did not reflect any changes in relative mobility rates or changes in the direction of greater equality of opportunity or 'openness'.

(iii) Thus, while upward mobility into the service class from other class origins steadily increased across successive birth cohorts, downward mobility from service-class origins to other class positions steadily decreased; and correspondingly, while the working class became somewhat less stable intergenerationally, the stability of the service class was enhanced.

The central concern of the present chapter is, then, to investigate whether these elements of change and constancy in the pattern of intergenerational class mobility have persisted for a further decade since 1972. That year has in fact a good claim to be regarded as the last of the post-war period—the period of the 'long boom' during which, it seemed, the sustained and relatively balanced growth of capitalist economies had become successfully institutionalized. In

October 1973, war broke out in the Middle East, and the winter of 1973–4 saw the first major oil price increases. In the following summer came the most severe international economic crisis since 1929 and, from the vantage point of the present, this would appear to have signalled the start of a new phase in the economic history of the western world: one characterized by more intractable macro-economic relationships between inflation and unemployment and by generally reduced rates of growth. In this new context, moreover, Britain has fared worse than most other western nations, and especially in regard to 'de-industrialization' and job losses. Not only has the proportion of the work-force unemployed at any one time been unusually high (reaching an official figure of over 12 per cent by 1983); but further, from around 1975 onwards, a steady build-up has occurred in the numbers of the *long-term* unemployed. In 1983 a million persons had been registered as unemployed for a year or more. The structural change which was the key dynamic element in mobility patterns in the years up to 1972 has usually been understood as a feature of general economic expansion. Thus, one issue which becomes of evident interest is that of whether, in the economic conditions that have more recently prevailed, the creation of favourable mobility opportunities via structural change has been maintained, or whether such opportunities have become increasingly restricted and the risks of unfavourable mobility outcomes have grown.

METHODS AND DATA

In order to address the above issue, and others related to it, we use here a method of investigating mobility trends which is, in principle at least, clearly preferable to that of birth-cohort analysis: namely, the comparison of data from two separate inquiries. We seek to establish trends—or their absence—in inter-generational class mobility by setting the relevant data of the 1972 survey against further data on mobility which we have derived from another nationally based inquiry, the British General Election Study (BGES) of 1983, in which interviews were carried out with a sample designed to be representative of the total British electorate.[1]

The main advantage in examining trends on the basis of inquiries carried out at two different dates is, of course, that period effects can then be isolated. One can compare the mobility experience of individuals at two different points in time while holding age or birth cohort constant. However, the main disadvantage is that in drawing on inquiries undertaken at different times, and usually by different research groups and for different purposes, one can scarcely avoid practical problems of the non-comparability of data-sets. Thus, one major limitation of the BGES, from our point of view, was that no information was sought on a respondent's occupation or employment status on first entry into the labour market, or at any other time than at the date of the inquiry. In using this study, therefore, we can look at intergenerational mobility in the perspective of only one transition—that from a respondent's class of origin (as indexed by the class position of the respondent's father or other head of household at respondent's age 14) to the respondent's 'present' class position.

Moreover, another quite general problem of comparability arose in that all occupational information collected in the 1983 inquiry was coded according to the new system of occupational classification introduced by the Office of Population Censuses and Surveys (OPCS) in 1980,[2] while the corresponding data in the 1972 inquiry had been coded according to the 1970 OPCS system. Clearly, then, before mobility data taken from the BGES could be used in conjunction with those collected in 1972, a large-scale recoding exercise was necessary.

In collaboration with Social and Community Planning Research (SCPR) who were responsible for the BGES fieldwork and data preparation, we designed this exercise as a twofold one, which was carried out by SCPR staff on the following lines.

(i) For all respondents to the BGES, the information collected on their present, and on their father's occupation—and also on the occupation of their spouse—was recoded to the 1970 OPCS system.

(ii) For a sample of approximately 1 in 6 (N = 1,522) of respondents to the 1972 inquiry for whom information on both their present and their father's occupation was available, this information was recoded to the 1980 OPCS system.

Since no significant change was made in 1980 in the OPCS employment status codes, it was then possible, following occupational recoding as in (i) above, to allocate BGES respondents and their fathers to class positions according to the class schema devised for the analysis of the 1972 data, and hence to construct a 1983 intergenerational class mobility table comparable to that available for 1972. However, in order to extend the possibilities for comparison, a new version of the class schema was developed specifically for use with occupational data coded to the 1980 system. The objective of this new version was exactly the same as that of the old (see p. 40 above): to bring together, within the classes distinguished, combinations of occupations and employment statuses whose incumbents would typically share in broadly similar market and work situations; but it was hoped that the more refined occupational classification introduced in 1980 would allow this objective to be achieved somewhat more satisfactorily than before.[3] This new version of the class schema could then be utilized in drawing up two further intergenerational class mobility tables permitting a 1972–83 comparison: one based on the BGES data as originally coded, and the other on the 1972 data recoded, as in (ii) above, to the 1980 system.

In Table 9.1 we present an analysis which draws on our 1972 data to show how the two versions of the class schema relate to each other. It can be seen that non-negligible changes occur in the composition of all classes except Class IV, but it should at the same time be added that over 80 per cent of all cases still fall into the same class of the schema in both its versions.

Our twofold recoding exercise provides us therefore with what we might call a 'double splice' of mobility data for our two points in time. We are able to work with two different pairs of comparable mobility tables, based on two different versions of the class schema and, ultimately, on two different systems of occupational classification, as summarized in Table 9.2.

In this way, then, we gain an advantage in being able to check on the robustness of our results: most obviously, we can give main weight to those results which appear the same on both bases of comparison. But there remains, of course, the question of the reliability achieved in the recoding exercise itself;

Table 9.1

Relationship between old and new versions of the class schema, shown by cross-classification of a sub-sample of respondents to the 1972 inquiry for whom codings to both 1970 and 1980 systems were made (N = 1,522): upper-left figures show % allocation by row of 'old' classes to 'new'; lower-right figures show % composition by column of 'new' classes from 'old'[a]

Old Schema	I	II	III	IV	V	VI	VII	% of total
				New Schema				
1. Higher professional, administrative and managerial	77.3 / 89.9	20.3 / 18.8	0.5 / 1.0	0.5 / 0.7	*1.4* / *2.0*	0	0	13.6
II. Lower professional, administrative and managerial	8.1 / 7.9	85.0 / 65.9	3.5 / 5.9	0	*2.9* / *3.4*	0	*0.6* / *0.2*	11.5
III. Routine non-manual	2.1 / 1.7	13.5 / 8.5	63.8 / 88.2	0	9.9 / 9.5	0	10.6 / 3.6	9.2
IV. Small employers proprietors and self-employed	0	2.1 / 1.3	0	97.9 / 99.3	0	0	0	9.4
V. Lower technical and manual supervisory	0	5.3 / 4.0	0	0	63.9 / 73.5	27.2 / 14.3	*3.6* / *1.5*	11.6
VI. Skilled manual	*0.3* / *0.6*	0	*0.3* / *1.0*	0	3.7 / 8.2	76.8 / 78.3	18.9 / 15.0	21.2
VII. Semi- and unskilled manual	0	*0.8* / *1.3*	1.1 / 4.0	0	1.4 / 3.4	6.6 / 7.5	90.0 / 79.6	23.5
% of total	11.7	14.7	6.7	9.0	9.7	21.1	27.1	

Note: (a) Italicized figures arise from cases of coding disagreement. There were in all 15 such cases. or just under 1% of total.

Table 9.2
Bases of comparative mobility tables, 1972-83

	1972	1983
Old version of class schema (1970 OPCS system)	Nuffield sample original coding (N = 9,434)	BGES sample recoded (N = 1,173)[a]
New version of class schema (1980 OPCS system)	Nuffield sub-sample recoded (N = 1,522)	BGES sample original coding (N = 1,173)[a]

Note: (a) Men aged 20-64 and resident in England and Wales, in order to maintain comparability with the coverage of the 1972 inquiry.

and before we go on to present our substantive findings, we report on two different tests that we carried out in this respect.

First, before starting on the recoding of BGES occupational data to the 1970 system, SCPR staff made trial codings of 300 occupational items from randomly selected 1972 interview schedules, and these were compared with the original codings made in the 1972 study. Of the SCPR codings, 277, or 92 per cent, agreed with the original codings at the level of the 3-digit occupation groups of the OPCS system, and only 9, or 3 per cent, disagreed in such a way that a different allocation to the class schema would have resulted. We can therefore feel reasonably confident that in the case of comparisons based on the 1970 system, where we use occupational data produced by two different teams of coders, no serious differences arose in the interpretation of the OPCS coding rules.

Secondly, once both recoding tasks had been completed, we compared the resulting class distributions of the *fathers* (as at respondent's age 14) of men aged 20-64 from the 1972 inquiry and of men aged 31-75 (and resident in England and Wales) from the 1983 inquiry. Net of the (unknown) effects of differential mortality and migration, one would then expect these two distributions to be the same within the limits of sampling error. The differences between them were in fact found to be clearly non-significant on the 1980 version of the class schema and also fell just short of significance at the 5 per cent level on the 1970 version, where a much larger N was involved (10,472 as against 2,560).[4] Moreover, as is shown in Table 9.3, the main difference apparent was that more Class I but fewer Class VII fathers were found in the 1983 distribution than in the 1972 one; and this, rather than reflecting a lack of consistency in coding practice, could more plausibly be seen as the result of differential mortality and also, perhaps, of an increase in class-differential non-response to social surveys. In sum, our recoding exercise would appear to have achieved a satisfactory standard of reliability, and we have some assurance, in this respect at least, that any differences revealed between our 1972 and 1983 mobility tables will not be seriously artefactual.[5]

Table 9.3
*Class distribution of fathers of men aged 20–64 from 1972 inquiry
and of fathers of men aged 31–75 (and resident in England and
Wales) from 1983 inquiry*

Class	1972 fathers (men aged 20–64)	1983 fathers (men aged 31–75)
	percentage by column	
	Old schema	
I	7.3	9.7
II	5.9	6.9
III	7.4	6.8
IV	14.1	14.9
V	11.5	11.3
VI	27.5	26.6
VII	26.4	23.7
	New schema	
I	7.0	9.7
II	7.5	7.6
III	4.4	5.0
IV	13.7	14.4
V	10.3	11.5
VI	26.6	25.3
VII	30.5	26.5

RELATIVE RATES, 1972–83

In chapter 3, we began with a discussion of trends in absolute (that is, percentage inflow and outflow) rates of class mobility, and then went on to consider how far these reflected changes in relative mobility rates or were rather—as proved in fact to be the case—the outcome essentially of changes in class structure, as mediated through the marginal distributions of the mobility table. Here, it will be more convenient to reverse this procedure. We shall begin by considering relative rates and, specifically, by posing the question of whether the basic stability that we found in the pattern of these rates—or in what we alternatively referred to as the pattern of social fluidity—over the middle decades of the century has extended into the 1980s.

When we previously examined possible changes in relative rates via birth-cohort analysis, we took as an appropriate measure of these rates the set of odds ratios defining the association within the mobility table between class of origin and class of destination. We then tested the hypothesis that relative rates had remained unaltered over time by fitting to the mobility tables for successive birth cohorts a statistical model which postulated the following: (i) that associations exist between cohort and the distributions of both class origins and class destinations; (ii) that an association also exists between class of origin and class of destination; *but* (iii) that this latter association *does not itself vary with cohort*. In other words, the model allowed for structural change and for the fact that mobility would not be perfect—i.e. that relative mobility chances would be unequal; but it required that the pattern of these unequal chances as expressed in odds ratios should be the same from one cohort to another.

In our present analysis, based on the comparison of relative rates from mobility tables of different date, we can then apply this same 'constant social fluidity' model (which is specified formally in the Annex to chapter 3), and merely substitute 'inquiry' for 'cohort' in the labelling of its terms. Thus, the hypothesis that the model now embodies is that the pattern of social fluidity is unchanged as between the mobility tables derived from our 1972 and 1983 inquiries, and the test is that all corresponding odds ratios implicit in these tables should be identical.

In Table 9.4 we show the results obtained when the model is fitted to our data. In our earlier birth-cohort analyses it was necessary, in order to avoid unreliably small cell frequencies, to work with the collapsed threefold version of our class schema. We have used this same collapsed version here also, in addition to the schema in its full sevenfold form, since in the BGES the number of respondents falling within the same population as that studied in 1972 —i.e. males aged 20-64 and resident in England and Wales—is not all that large (N = 1,173), nor indeed is the sample of 1972 respondents (N = 1,522) for whom data were recoded. In all, therefore, we make four tests of the model which proposes constant social fluidity between 1972 and 1983: that is, we fit the model to our data organized on the basis of the old, 1970, and the new, 1980, versions of the class schema in both their collapsed and uncollapsed forms.

Table 9.4
Results of testing the 'constant social fluidity' model against intergenerational class mobility data from the 1972 and 1983 inquiries

		x^2	df	p
Old schema	3 classes	0.08	4	0.99
(N = 10,607)	7 classes	41.57	36	0.24
New schema	3 classes	2.52	4	0.64
(N = 2,693)	7 classes	31.12	36	0.70

As can be seen from Table 9.4, the hypothesis of constant social fluidity, or constant relative rates, is strongly supported. If any deviation from the model that represents this hypothesis is present, it can only be very slight; and moreover, from inspection of residuals, it would appear to follow no pattern of sociological significance. We cannot, for example, find any indication in any of our four tests of one trend which was, arguably, present in our birth cohort analyses: namely, that towards a *worsening* of the chances of men of working-class origins being found in service-class rather than working-class positions, relative to the corresponding chances of men of both service-class and inter-mediate-class origins (pp. 83–5) above.[6]

In Table 9.5 we show, for our three-class analyses, the complete set of odds ratios under the model that we have fitted. These represent our sample estimates of what actually is the pattern of social fluidity that remained constant between

Table 9.5

*Relative intergenerational mobility chances, 1972–83, estimated in
terms of odds ratios: upper figure calculated on old class schema,
lower figure calculated on new class schema*

Pairs of origin classes 'in competition'	I and II/ III–V	I and II/ VI and VII	III–V/ VI and VII
		Pairs of destination classes 'competed for'	
I and II *vs.* III–V	3.00 2.64	5.00 3.61	1.67 1.37
I and II *vs.* VI and VII	3.96 3.15	14.27 10.19	3.61 3.23
III–V *vs.* VI and VII	1.32 1.19	2.85 2.82	2.16 2.37

1972 and 1983. As one might expect, this pattern compares very closely with
that shown by the odds ratios derived from our birth cohort analyses as presented
in Table 3.5.[7] In particular, it may be noted that by far the greatest inequalities
in mobility chances are again shown up in the competition between men of
service-class and working-class origins for service-class rather than working-class
positions—the odds favouring the former by more than ten to one.

It might of course be argued that if mobility data are compared from two
inquiries only a decade apart no large differences of any kind should be expected,
since there will be some considerable overlap between the two populations
studied in the periods in which the crucial mobility experiences of their members occurred. With this point chiefly in mind, we further fitted the 'constant
social fluidity' model to separate 1972 and 1983 mobility tables (in collapsed
form) for men in three different age-groups: 20–34, 35–49 and 50–64. As
Table 9.6 shows, for each age-group alike, and using both versions of the class
schema, the model again performs extremely well. In other words, we may be
reasonably confident that its satisfactory fit to the mobility data for all men
aged 20–64 in 1972 and 1983 does not conceal shifts in relative mobility chances

Table 9.6

*Results of testing the 'constant social fluidity' model against intergenerational
class mobility data from the 1972 and 1983 inquiries, by age-group*

	Age-group	χ^2	df	p
Old schema (3 classes)	50–64	1.46	4	0.83
	35–49	0.68	4	0.95
	20–34	1.98	4	0.74
New schema (3 classes)	50–64	2.64	4	0.62
	35–49	2.41	4	0.66
	20–34	1.83	4	0.77

within particular age-ranges. The fact that the model is as acceptable for the 20–34 age-group as it is for the two older ones is particularly reassuring.

In sum, then, we can give a fairly unequivocal answer to the question from which in this section we began. The stability of relative rates or chances of intergenerational class mobility, which our analyses of the 1972 data suggested went back at least to the 1920s, has *not* been disturbed to any appreciable degree in the first decade after the ending of the post-war era.

ABSOLUTE RATES, 1972–1983

Since in treating relative mobility rates for this period we have accepted the 'constant social fluidity' model, we must regard any changes in absolute rates that are apparent between 1972 and 1983 as the outcome of structural shifts mediated through the marginal distributions of our mobility tables for these years. We can therefore usefully begin here by considering these distributions, as set out in Table 9.7. The upper panel of the table shows the class origins and destinations of the men who figure in our comparative tables according to the collapsed schema (old and new versions), and a very clear picture emerges. If one examines the distributions of 1972 and 1983 class destinations—i.e. of the

Table 9.7

Distribution of respondents and of respondents' fathers (at respondent's age 14), 1972 and 1983 inquiries, according to old and new versions of the class schema

	Old schema				New schema			
	Father		Resp.		Father		Resp.	
Class	percentage by column				percentage by column			
	72	83	72	83	72	83	72	83
I and II	13.2	17.3	25.1	33.1	14.5	17.9	26.4	33.6
III–V	32.9	31.7	30.2	32.3	28.5	29.6	25.4	26.6
VI and VII	53.9	51.0	44.7	34.6	57.0	52.5	48.2	39.8
I	7.3	9.8	13.6	16.9	7.0	9.7	11.7	16.0
II	5.9	7.6	11.5	16.2	7.5	8.2	14.7	17.6
III	7.4	6.6	9.2	9.3	4.4	5.1	6.7	6.7
IV	14.1	14.6	9.4	12.0	13.7	14.0	9.0	11.6
V	11.5	10.5	11.6	11.0	10.3	10.5	9.7	8.4
VI	27.5	25.9	21.2	18.0	26.6	25.0	21.1	19.6
VII	26.4	25.1	23.5	16.6	30.5	27.5	27.1	20.1

Δs for father's and respondent's distributions[a]

	Old schema		New schema	
	1972	1983	1972	1983
3 classes	11.9	16.4	11.9	15.7
7 classes	13.8	18.9	14.2	17.3

Note: (a) Δ is the dissimilarity index showing what percentage of cases in one distribution would have to be reallocated to other categories in order to make the two distributions identical.

'present' class positions of respondents to the two national inquiries—it is evident that the long-term changes in class structure that were emphasized in Part One have continued. The service class has further expanded, and the working class has further contracted. As represented in Table 9.7 these changes may be exaggerated to some extent by the possible increase in class-differential non-response earlier referred to, but there should still be no doubting their reality. They are in fact highly consonant with estimates made in 1981 Census reports.[8] In the lower panel of Table 9.7 the same distributions can be seen over seven classes. Apart from the indication that Class VII, that of semi- and unskilled workers, has declined more than Class VI, that of skilled workers (which may again in part reflect differential non-response), the main interest here lies with the intermediate classes. While Class III has changed little in size and Class V has contracted somewhat, Class IV, that of small proprietors and self-employed workers, has clearly grown—and further analysis suggests that this growth has been greatest among self-employed workers *with* employees.[9]

There is one further point that should be noted from Table 9.7. On whatever basis they are considered, the differences between origin and destination distributions, as indicated by the dissimilarity index, have increased over time. In other words, in 1983 the class distribution of respondents in a sample of the male work-force was more different from the distribution of their fathers than was the case in 1972. This would then imply that, other things being equal, the total intergenerational mobility rate—the proportion of all men found in a different class to that of their father—will have risen somewhat.

Indeed, given constancy in relative rates *and* that class structural shifts have continued on a steady course, then changes in the pattern of absolute mobility rates become in general quite predictable: it must follow that they too will be on the same lines as were revealed in 1972. That this is actually so can be seen from Table 9.8. Again the main feature of the trends displayed—apart from the anticipated slight increase in total mobility—is that men of all class origins have become more likely to be found in service-class positions and less likely to be found in working-class ones. Moreover, this remains still largely the case when in Table 9.9 we once more exploit the possibility open to us of examining differences between 1972 and 1983 mobility rates while holding age-group constant. Of particular interest here are our findings for the youngest age-group. It might have been supposed that, in view of the deterioration in the economic climate, the experience of intergenerational class mobility of men aged 20–34 in 1983 would be less favourable than that of men of similar age in 1972. However, on the evidence of Table 9.9, no such falling off can be claimed. It is true that, at least when the new version of the class schema is used, the chances of young men of service- and intermediate-class origins being themselves found in service-class positions show virtually no *improvement*. But both versions of the schema reveal a continuing increase in the rate of mobility into the service class on the part of young men of working-class origins, and at the same time a continuing decrease in the likelihood of their remaining within the working class.

We could of course also examine the same data as are analysed in Tables 9.8 and 9.9 when organized on the seven-class basis. However, the relevant tables are not here presented (they are available on request) since their cell frequencies,

Table 9.8

*Class distribution of respondents by class of father, 1972 and 1983
inquiries, according to old and new versions of the class schema*

Father's class	Schema	Inquiry	I & II	III–V	VI & VII	N
				Respondent's class		
				percentage by row		
I and II	old	1972	58.8	26.0	15.2	1,242
		1983	65.1	24.7	10.2	204[a]
	new	1972	57.7	23.2	19.1	220
		1983	62.0	22.2	15.8	210
III–V	old	1972	27.6	36.7	35.7	3,105
		1983	34.4	38.3	27.4	372
	new	1972	31.2	31.9	37.0	433
		1983	34.2	34.3	31.5	347
VI and VII	old	1972	15.5	27.2	57.3	5,087
		1983	21.5	31.2	47.3	598
	new	1972	16.0	22.7	61.2	867
		1983	23.6	23.8	52.6	616

Total Mobility Rates (% in cells off main diagonal of mobility table)

	1972	1983
Old schema	49.3	52.5
New schema	47.6	51.1

Note: (a) All Ns given for BGES data, here and subsequently, are weighted values (see n.1
to this chapter) rounded to the nearest whole number.

at least where age divisions are introduced, are often too small to be reliable. We
simply note four refinements to the findings already reported which are suggested
by the seven-class tables for all ages, and which are in fact generally consistent
with the operation of unaltered relative mobility rates within a class structure
that is changing as indicated in Table 9.7.

(i) The increase in immobility within the service class is a feature more of its
lower than of its higher echelons—that is, more of Class II than of Class I.

(ii) The decrease in movement into the working class from all classes of origin
is more marked in the case of movement into Class VII, that of semi- and unskilled workers, than into Class VI, that of skilled workers.

(iii) The slight increase in immobility within the intermediate classes, shown in
Table 9.8, is in fact a feature especially of Class IV, that of the petty bourgeoisie,
and is not at all evident in Class V, that of the blue-collar élite.

(iv) Within the slight increase that is shown in Table 9.8 in mobility from
working-class origins into intermediate-class positions, the clearest tendency is
for more mobility to occur from both Class VI and Class VII origins into self-
employment in Class IV; on both versions of the class schema this outflow rate
rises from around 6 per cent in 1972 to around 9 per cent in 1983.

There is one further way in which we can usefully elaborate on the absolute
rates reported in Table 9.8. To do so we must in fact revert to relative rates, but

Table 9.9

*Class distribution of respondents by class of father, and by
age-groups, 1972 and 1983 inquiries, according to old and
new versions of the class schema*

Age-group	Father's class	Schema	Inquiry	Respondent's class			N
				I & II	III–V	VI & VII	
50–64		old	1972	58.3	26.1	15.6	314
	I and II		1983	70.7	21.6	7.7	52
		new	1972	54.2	25.4	20.3	59
			1983	64.5	24.7	10.8	57
		old	1972	25.3	38.2	36.5	970
	III–V		1983	31.7	37.2	31.1	95
		new	1972	28.5	35.4	36.2	130
			1983	31.6	32.1	36.3	101
		old	1972	14.4	28.6	57.0	1,661
	VI–VII		1983	19.3	33.8	46.9	187
		new	1972	14.0	24.1	61.9	286
			1983	18.9	30.2	50.9	179
35–49		old	1972	64.0	22.5	13.5	378
	I and II		1983	70.7	22.9	6.4	61
		new	1972	62.9	22.9	14.3	70
			1983	67.0	20.5	12.5	63
		old	1972	29.9	37.2	32.9	1,056
	III–V		1983	35.6	37.9	26.5	136
		new	1972	31.2	34.8	34.0	141
			1983	37.2	34.3	28.6	117
		old	1972	16.3	28.9	54.8	1,705
	VI–VII		1983	21.6	32.8	45.5	203
		new	1972	14.9	27.0	58.1	289
			1983	26.3	23.5	50.1	220
20–34		old	1972	55.5	28.4	16.2	550
	I and II		1983	58.0	27.7	14.3	90
		new	1972	56.0	22.0	22.0	91
			1083	56.9	21.7	21.3	90
		old	1972	27.3	34.8	37.8	1,079
	III–V		1983	35.0	39.3	25.7	141
		new	1972	33.3	26.5	40.1	162
			1983	33.5	36.0	30.5	129
		old	1972	15.6	24.2	60.2	1,721
	VI–VII		1983	23.4	27.2	49.4	208
		new	1972	19.2	17.1	63.7	292
			1983	24.6	18.9	56.5	220

as measured by disparity ratios of the kind which were introduced in chapters 2 and 3 rather than by odds ratios. Disparity ratios differ from odds ratios in being sensitive to marginal distributions; but, for this very reason, they are sometimes useful in illuminating the way in which structural changes influence observed mobility patterns.

In analysing our 1972 mobility data, we used disparity ratios to show the chances (or risks) of individuals of different origin being found in a particular destination. Thus, working with the collapsed three-class schema, we observed that the ratio of the chances of access to service-class positions of men of service-class, intermediate-class and working-class origins respectively approximated 4 : 2 : 1, while the corresponding ratio of chances of being found in working-class positions was roughly the reverse—1 : 2 : 4 (the lowest chance being set at 1 in each case). These ratios can be readily recalculated from the outflow percentages for 1972, on the old version of the class schema, that are presented in Table 9.8. The percentages entering the service class of men of service-class, intermediate-class and working-class origins respectively can be seen to be 58.8, 27.6 and 15.5, while the percentages entering the working class are 15.2, 35.7 and 57.3. What is then of interest is to examine these same ratios in 1983. In Table 9.7 the corresponding percentages for 1983 to those given above (i.e. again on the old schema), are 65.1, 34.4 and 21.5, and 10.2, 27.4 and 47.3. Simple arithmetic will then show that a change has occurred, and that what has happened is that inequalities in chances of being found in the service class have diminished somewhat, while those of being found in the working class have widened. In the former case, the disparity ratio has moved from the approximate 4 : 2 : 1 of 1972 to something closer to 3 : 1.5 : 1, while in the latter case, the shift has been from close to 1 : 2 : 4 to almost 1 : 3 : 5. And, it may be added, if one works with the same rates but based on the new version of the class schema, one obtains a comparable result, although the ratios generally are somewhat lower.

It should be clearly understood that there is no inconsistency in finding that relative rates as measured by disparity ratios change, while relative rates as measured by odds ratios do not. As was earlier shown (n. 17, p. 88 above), an odds ratio is in fact the *product* of two complementary disparity ratios. So what we are here discovering is that, underlying the constancy in odds ratios in intergenerational class mobility—or what we can interpret as an unchanging degree of inequality of opportunity over all—there are in fact different, *though essentially offsetting*, trends of change in certain more specific class differentials in mobility chances. To repeat, the relative chances of access to service-class positions have become somewhat more equal, but the relative chances—or risks— of being found in working-class positions have become less equal. Indeed, far from being inconsistent, results of this kind are *necessarily* found where unchanging odds ratios coexist with a sustained transformation of the class structure which significantly affects the relative sizes of classes.

So far in this section we have been concerned entirely with mobility trends viewed in an outflow perspective. Finally, though, we may take advantage of having data from inquiries made at two different points in time in order to adopt also an inflow perspective. In this perspective, interest centres not on changes in the mobility chances of individuals, but rather on changes in the patterns of recruitment of classes, taken as the units of analysis. Since we have comparable data from inquiries made in 1972 and 1983, we can simply set inflow rates for these two dates alongside each other, as is done in Table 9.10.[10]

Table 9.10
Class composition by class of father, 1972 and 1983 inquiries, according to old and new versions of the class schema

Father's class	Respondent's class					
	I and II		III–V		VI and VII	
	1972	1983	1972	1983	1972	1983
			percentage by column			
			Old schema			
I and II	30.8	34.1	11.3	13.3	4.5	5.1
III–V	36.1	32.8	40.0	37.5	26.3	25.1
VI and VII	33.1	33.1	48.6	49.2	69.2	69.7
N	2,372	389	2,848	379	4,214	406
			New schema			
I and II	31.7	33.0	13.2	14.9	5.7	7.1
III–V	33.7	30.1	35.8	38.2	21.8	23.5
VI and VII	34.7	36.9	51.0	46.9	72.4	69.4
N	401	394	386	312	733	467

In examining our 1972 mobility data in inflow terms (pp. 43–7 above), we gave particular emphasis to two features: first, the very wide range of recruitment to the service class, and its consequent heterogeneity as regards the social origins and backgrounds of its members; and second, the large measure of self-recruitment of the working class, which meant that it was overwhelmingly 'second-generation', at least, in its composition. From Table 9.10 it can be seen that both these features are still in evidence in 1983. Indeed, the general impression created by the table is one of little change at all (and the same impression, it may be added, is also given by seven-class tables). However, there is one tendency which, though slight, is apparent with both the old and new versions of the class schema and seems worthy of note: namely, for men of service-class origins to become more important in the composition of *all three* classes—as would indeed be expected, other things being equal, from the steady expansion of this class. One implication of this is of course that self-recruitment to the service class is now on the increase. While still very mixed in its composition and in no sense displaying 'closure', the service class—as was actually anticipated in the light of the 1972 data—is slowly consolidating; and it must in fact continue to do so while ever its growth continues and the pattern of social fluidity remains unaltered.

THE EFFECTS OF UNEMPLOYMENT

In the foregoing analyses we have taken no account of unemployment. In the 1972 inquiry, respondents who were unemployed when interviewed were given a 'present' class position on the basis of their last employment; and we have so far dealt similarly with the unemployed respondents to the 1983 inquiry. However, this is clearly one of those instances where preserving comparability in one respect may well introduce serious non-comparability in another. In 1972, the official rate of unemployment was still under 4 per cent, and of respondents to the 1972 inquiry only 5 per cent reported that they were currently out of work—this including men who had a job arranged and were waiting to take it up.[11] Moreover, there were at this time good grounds for supposing that many of those out of work would be 'between jobs' rather than long-term unemployed; and, further, that the work to which they would eventually return would be of a similar kind to that in which they had previously been engaged. Thus, the practice of giving the unemployed a class allocation based on their last employment would not, in these circumstances, seem likely to be very misleading.[12] But in 1983 a quite different situation prevailed. As already noted, unemployment had reached over 12 per cent and long-term unemployment was now recognized as a major problem. In the BGES sample, almost 9 per cent of men who were aged 20–64 and resident in England and Wales reported that they were unemployed—*excluding* those waiting to take up jobs; and 5 per cent had been unemployed for a year or more.[13] In addition, there is evidence to suggest that, in the present economic context, men who do return to work after a period of unemployment often experience downward mobility in terms of occupational level.[14] Clearly, then, it would be unwise for us in analysing our 1983 mobility data to treat the unemployed in the same way as in 1972 without at least considering whether this might not seriously distort our results; and, more specifically, it would seem important to examine what effect it would have on the 1983 mobility table if unemployment, or at all events long-term unemployment, were itself regarded as a mobility 'status' or outcome.

In this connection, we may ask, to begin with, what class were the unemployed men in the 1983 sample—if we determine their class according to their last employment; and further, what proportion of all in their class did the unemployed constitute. Table 9.11 supplies the answers to these questions, and contains no surprises. The unemployed come predominantly from the working class, and unemployment is clearly more widespread within the working class than within the intermediate classes or the service class. Furthermore, it can be seen that this class bias in the incidence of unemployment is generally accentuated in the case of long-term unemployment.

How far, then, are the patterns of mobility in 1983 altered if the unemployed are treated as having, so to speak, a distinctive class position of their own? Here Table 9.12 provides the relevant information. Again, the results presented might appear rather routine. But, for our present purposes, there is in fact an important conclusion to be drawn which is not immediately apparent, and which becomes so only when the outflow percentages given in Table 9.12 are compared with those of Table 9.8. What then emerges is something that might not have been

Table 9.11

Unemployment by class of last employment, 1983 inquiry

Class	% of all unemployed		% unemployed in class	
	old schema	new schema	old schema	new schema
	(figures for long-term unemployed in brackets)			
I and II	15.9 (10.4)	16.9 (12.1)	4.1 (1.5)	4.3 (1.8)
III–V	20.0 (15.4)	10.0 (5.0)	5.3 (2.3)	3.2 (1.0)
VI and VII	64.1 (74.3)	73.1 (82.9)	16.0 (10.6)	15.8 (10.3)
I	7.1	5.1	3.6	2.8
II	8.8	11.8	4.7	5.8
III	7.1	1.2	6.6	1.5
IV	5.2	4.1	3.7	3.1
V	7.7	4.7	6.1	4.8
VI	31.4	30.8	15.0	13.5
VII	32.7	42.1	17.0	18.1

Table 9.12

Class distribution of respondents by class of father, 1983 inquiry,
according to old and new versions of the class schema and with
the unemployed treated separately

Father's class		Respondent's class					
	Schema	I and II	III–V	VI and VII	U[a]	UL[a]	N
		percentage by row					
I and II	old	63.1	23.2	9.3	4.4	(2.5)	204
	new	60.1	21.2	14.3	4.3	(2.4)	210
III–V	old	32.7	36.2	22.8	8.2	(5.2)	373
	new	31.9	32.9	26.2	9.0	(6.0)	350
VI and VII	old	20.5	29.5	39.5	10.5	(5.9)	599
	new	22.6	23.1	44.0	10.2	(5.5)	616

Note: (a)   U = all unemployed at time of inquiry.
          UL = unemployed at time of inquiry for more than one year.

anticipated: namely, that the principal findings that were derived from Table 9.8 concerning trends in class mobility since 1972 can stand unchanged *even when* in the 1983 table unemployment is regarded as a separate mobility status. That is to say, it still remains the case that men of all class origins have become more likely to be found in service-class positions and less likely to be found in working-class ones. The former trend, it is true, is somewhat muted, but there can be no doubt that it is still present. Moreover, if the data of Table 9.12 are disaggregated by age-group, so that they may be compared with those of Table 9.9 (the relevant tables are available on request), we can in this case likewise say that taking account of unemployment does not require us to modify at all significantly our previous remarks on changes in age-specific mobility patterns.

Although these results are not perhaps ones that would have been widely expected, a moment's reflection will make it apparent that there is no mystery whatever about them. Since it is the case that unemployment is heavily concentrated among men who were previously in working-class positions, treating the unemployed separately will, all other things being equal, reduce outflows to the working class proportionately more than others; and correspondingly, since the incidence of unemployment is lowest within the service class, outflows to service-class positions will be least affected. Thus, the general decline in movement into working-class positions is actually accentuated, while the general increase in movement into the service class becomes less marked but is not eliminated. This outcome could be different only if other things were not equal: for example, if class origins exerted a powerful effect on the chances of becoming unemployed *independently of* the nature of an individual's previous employment. But this is not in fact the case. Further analysis reveals that the association that shows up in Table 9.12 between class origins and unemployment is the product of the associations that exist between class of origin and 'present' class *and* between the latter and unemployment. This apart, class of origin is *not* associated with the likelihood of a man becoming unemployed—a rather unusual instance of the absence of any 'carry-over' effect.[15]

To illustrate the point, we may consider the rate of mobility of men of working-class origins into service-class positions. In Table 9.8 this is shown to be 23.6 per cent for the 1983 sample—using the new version of class schema—as against 16.0 per cent for the 1972 sample; and the rate falls only slightly to 22.6 per cent in Table 9.12 when the 1983 data are reanalysed with the unemployed treated separately. This fall can then be taken as reflecting little more than the slight reduction in the size of the service class that results from the transfer to the 'unemployed' category of those few men who had become unemployed directly from a service-class position. There is no significant tendency apparent in our data for men who have been intergenerationally mobile into the service class from working-class origins to be more likely to become unemployed than men who have been thus mobile from intermediate-class origins or who have remained intergenerationally stable within the service class.

One could, then, easily form an exaggerated idea of the impact of the current level of unemployment on the development of intergenerational mobility patterns. However, this is not to say that unemployment has no implications for mobility at all. The key observation here is in fact the most commonplace one: that unemployment, even when at a high level, remains predominantly a working-class fate. Thus, although the chances of upward mobility into service-class positions have not fallen since 1972, but have in fact continued to improve, what is also evident from our data is that the return of mass unemployment has created a serious new risk of what can only be regarded as downward mobility—*and that this risk is much greater for men in working-class positions, by whatever route they came into them, than it is for any others.*[16]

What can therefore be claimed as regards mobility chances for men of working-class origin is that these have tended not actually to worsen between 1972 and 1983 but, rather, to *polarize*. As can be seen from Table 9.12, more have experienced upward mobility into the service class in 1983 than in 1972;

but more too, we know, have experienced downward mobility into unemployment. To illustrate in more detail, we may consider men of working-class origin aged 20–34—though the point holds good for all age-groups. In 1972, at which time we suppose that we can reasonably neglect unemployment as a mobility outcome, less than 16 per cent of these men (on the basis of the old schema) were found to have been upwardly mobile into the service class, as against 60 per cent who were still in working-class positions. In contrast, when we consider men of working-class origin who were aged 20–34 in 1983, and treat the unemployed as a separate category, we find that while now 22 per cent are upwardly mobile, and only 40 per cent remain in working-class positions, there is a further 11 per cent who have no employment at all, and over half of this group have been without work for more than a year.

A similar kind of polarization can also be traced in the mobility chances of men of intermediate-class origin. Again their chances of upward mobility into the service class have improved somewhat between 1972 and 1983, and the chances of their entering the working class have diminished. *But* their risks of becoming unemployed are not much less than those of men of working-class origin; and further analysis reveals that this largely results from the fact that those men who *have* moved from intermediate-class origins into working-class positions are every bit as likely to become unemployed as men who were born and have remained within the working class.[17]

In sum, one might therefore say that the return of mass unemployment, in the British context at least, has had the general effect of 'raising the stakes' in the mobility 'game'. In particular, the chances of becoming mobile out of the working class or of avoiding mobility into it have taken on a still greater importance than before for the standard and style of life that an individual may anticipate. This is so because to occupy a working-class position so greatly increases the risk of experiencing the rather decisive form of downward social mobility that becoming—and perhaps for long remaining—unemployed must be taken to represent.

MOBILITY AND THE CHANGING CLASS STRUCTURE

The main outcome of our comparison of intergenerational class mobility tables for 1972 and 1983 is then that, despite the transition from one economic era to another which occurred between these dates, a very large measure of continuity can be observed. Relative mobility rates have remained essentially constant on the same pattern that they would appear to have displayed for most of the century; and since the evolution of the class structure has proceeded in much the same direction as throughout the post-war years, it must follow that the same trends in absolute mobility rates as were observed in 1972 will also have extended to 1983. However, we have also shown that the return of large-scale and long-term unemployment does have certain implications for mobility chances. New risks are created of downward mobility into a condition of serious social deprivation, although exposure to them is greatest by far among men who are found in, or who have a high probability of entering, manual wage-earning jobs.

It would thus seem essential both to the description and the interpretation of our findings on mobility trends for the period 1972–83 to recognize that the changing structural context is of prime importance, and that this is one in which a heightening of both opportunities *and* risks occurs. What may then further be remarked is that such a conjunction is something quite unprovided for in—and hence must be a source of doubt about—two current and well-rehearsed theories of apparent relevance: the Marxist 'labour process' theory of class structural change which claims a necessary 'degrading' of work and a progressive prole-tarianization of the work-force under capitalism; and the liberal theory of 'post-industrial' society which claims a general 'upgrading' of the occupational structure, generated by technological advance and the development of a 'service economy'.[18]

The thesis of the degrading of work would in fact appear to be rather flatly contradicted by trends that are consistently revealed in the census statistics of capitalist nations, whatever allowances may be made for the crudity or inaccuracy of these data. It is professional, administrative, and managerial occupations that are in expansion, while the greatest decline is found in manual wage-labour—above all in unskilled grades—and with an incipient decline being in some cases also apparent among more routine nonmanual occupations. Britain is certainly no exception to these trends and, as we have shown, they have continued to be the major source of change in mobility rates and patterns over the last decade, just as they were throughout the post-war years.

This discrepancy between the degrading thesis and the evidence of census data might, however, in some part be attributed to the fact that changes in occupational and class distributions at the societal level can come about quite independently of changes in the organization of production within particular enterprises: that is, through shifts in the division of total employment *among* different industries and sectors, which themselves possess different occupational structures. Thus, in Britain—as, it would appear, in other western societies—the growth of numbers in professional, managerial, and administrative occupations during the post-war period did to a substantial extent result from the increasing importance of the services sector of the economy, within which these occu-pational groupings have always been more prominent than within manufacturing. And in so far as in more recent years of economic difficulty the decline of British manufacturing has been accelerated, it would seem that the expansion of higher-level class positions via such 'shift' effects can only have been enhanced.

More sophisticated adherents of 'labour-process' theories have therefore been able to suggest that, for a time, the consequences of the systematic degrading of work for the shape of the class structure are likely to be masked by an offsetting industrial redistribution of employment. But, they then contend, as the service economy nears its full development, such shift effects must weaken and the reality of widespread proletarianization, together with its very negative impli-cations for mobility opportunities, will at this point become apparent.[19] How-ever, this argument has of late been seriously undermined—as some of its former exponents have in fact come to acknowledge. Analyses of the American, and likewise of the British, experience in the course of the 1970s reveal that in this period professional, administrative, and managerial occupations were still in overall expansion, and manual ones in contraction, *even when* all inter-industry shifts were allowed for. That is to say, in quite direct oppostion to what the thesis of the degrading of work would predict, the major trends apparent in census data were generated not only by industrial and sectoral changes in employment but further by the (net) effects of technological, organizational and other changes determining the occupational 'mix' within production units.[20]

As a last line of defence for the 'degrading' thesis, it may be maintained that some sizeable part of the expansion of administrative and managerial positions in particular should be recognized as more apparent than real. This is so because many of these positions either have been themselves degraded into essentially subordinate ones, involving only routine tasks, or have been created by an upgrading of such subordinate positions of no more than nominal or cosmetic kind. And it has in turn been contended that when such processes are taken into account, the increased upward mobility that is typically displayed in survey-based inquiries must be regarded as in some part spurious.[21] But what has to be pointed out here is, first of all, that no systematic empirical support for such arguments has so far been brought forward, while contrary evidence is growing;[22] and further, that the case made out is one on which our findings can in fact throw serious doubt. If degrading or 'dilution' of the kind claimed *had* gone on over recent decades within the service class of our analyses, one would then expect this to show up in some deterioration of the mobility chances of men originating in this class, relative to those of men of other origins. But, as we have seen, there is no indication of this whatever. Rather, we find still further confirmation of what has elsewhere been referred to as the 'undiminished capacity of the service class to "reproduce" itself, even as its numbers have increased'.[23]

The foregoing might then be taken to imply not only that the degrading thesis is seriously mistaken but, further, that the upgrading thesis is vindicated. However, if this thesis is not, in the same way as the degrading thesis, empirically unsustainable, it is still one which, at least in the economic conditions of present-day Britain, must appear to reflect an unduly partial view. It was a product, one must remember, of the period of the long boom in which employment levels were typically high; and the liberal account of the development of industrial economies and societies of which it forms part was not one that seriously entertained the possibility that unemployment might return and persist on a mass scale.[24]

Thus, it is difficult to accommodate to the upgrading thesis the existence of 'double-digit' unemployment and of a growing pool of men who have been out of work for many months. And in so far as the expansion of professional, administrative and managerial occupations is being promoted by the sectoral shifts involved in the de-industrialization of the British economy, it must appear that the counterpart of this process is not simply that the proportion of the work-force in manual jobs declines, but further that the number of those who have no work at all is enlarged. Furthermore, present economic conditions bring out sharply the continuing differentiation between men in service-class positions and those engaged in manual wage-labour in the degree to which they are threatened by loss of work and, hence, in the nature of the employment relationships in which they are involved.

What then is unacceptable, in the British case at least, is the idea of upgrading as a generalized process at work throughout all levels of the occupational structure and leading towards what has been envisaged as 'the professionalization of everyone'. Even while the expansion of the service class remains a major feature of the structural context of mobility in present-day British society, as it was throughout the post-war period, unemployment is now, as we have seen, another feature of this context which cannot be neglected. For men of working- and intermediate-class origins in particular, the pattern of their possible mobility experience has been significantly reshaped over recent years as unemployment, rather than occupational immobility or decline, has come to represent the alternative pole to gaining entry to a higher-level class position.

We may then conclude that if the upgrading thesis is taken to refer simply to the growth of professional, administrative, and managerial occupations, it captures an important aspect of the changing class structure of advanced industrial societies; but that, on its own, it suggests an over-optimistic perspective on recent economic history, or at all events on the British case. However, the important counter-tendency to be recognized, so far at least as the understanding of current rates and patterns of class mobility is concerned, is not one towards the degrading of work within the capitalist organization of production, as 'labour process' theorists would insist. It is, rather, the elimination of work opportunities of any kind for large numbers of the active population, heavily concentrated among those who had previously been within the ranks of manual wage-earners.[25]

NOTES

1. The British General Election Study of 1983 was directed by Anthony Heath, Roger Jowell, and John Curtice. Fieldwork was undertaken by Social and Community Planning Research between July and October 1983. A total of 3,955 interviews were successfully completed, giving a response rate of 72 per cent. Further details, including information on the weighting of the data here used, are contained in reports by D. Lievesley, available from SCPR; and see also the main report on the study, Anthony Heath, Roger Jowell, and John Curtice, *How Britain Votes*, Oxford: Pergamon, 1985.

2. See OPCS, *Classification of Occupations 1980*, London: HMSO, 1980.

3. The new version of the class schema was devised in collaboration with Anthony Heath. It should be noted that while in constructing the original schema it was convenient to take as basic units the categories of the (collapsed) Hope–Goldthorpe scale of the 'general desirability' of occupations (though without regard to their scale values—see p. 40 above), in constructing the new version the basic units allocated were much finer ones: namely, all permissible combinations of occupation groups and employment statuses under the 1980 OPCS system as shown in *Classification of Occupations 1980*, Table Appendix B.1. A look-up table for allocating individuals to the new schema on the basis of their 1980 occupation and employment status and also a computer program for applying this table are available on request. See further Clive Payne, 'Lookup Tables', *PSTAT UK Newsletter*, no. 1, 1984.

4. Using the old version of the class schema, the test of the null hypothesis that no difference exists between the two distributions returned a χ^2 (likelihood ratio test statistic) of 12.3 which, with 6 degrees of freedom, gives a p-value of 0.06; while using the new version, the χ^2 was 4.6, giving a p-value of 0.60. Dividing the χ^2s by the Ns involved, for purposes of comparison, gives 1.2 in the former case and 1.8 in the latter.

5. A fuller account of this comparison of the fathers' distributions—and of certain problems in the coding of employment status that it revealed—is given in the final report on our research project 'Trends in Occupational and Class Mobility in England and Wales, 1972–1983', submitted to the Economic and Social Research Council in February, 1985.

6. It might therefore seem that one should become increasingly sceptical about this trend—which, if it does exist, is doubtless very slight; but, on the other hand, see the results reported by Macdonald and Ridge on the basis of analyses of data from the British General Election Studies of 1964, 1974 and 1983, which also suggest some slight decline in fluidity. Kenneth Macdonald and John Ridge, 'Social Mobility' in A.H. Halsey (ed.), *British Social Trends since 1900*, London: Macmillan, 2nd ed., 1987.

7. It should be noted that while the odds ratios given in Table 9.5 are based on expected cell values under the 'constant social fluidity' model, those of Table 3.5 are based on actually observed values. Odds ratios derived from expected values in both cases alike would show even greater similarity.

   A more detailed test of the hypothesis that the underlying pattern of social fluidity is the same for our 1972 and 1983 tables could in principle be provided by fitting to the 1983 data the structural model that was developed for the 1972 data in chapter 4. Unfortunately, results obtained in this way cannot be regarded as very reliable in view of the number of small cell values that occur when the 1983 data are organized on the basis of the full sevenfold class schema. The 'eight-level' model finally accepted for the 1972 table (pp. 104–7 above) does in fact also fit the 1983 table fairly well, returning a p-value of 0.12. But it has at the same time to be noted that the 'seven-level' model that we initially proposed in chapter 4 fits the 1983 data even better, with a p-value of 0.57; and further that with both these models the density level for the IV–IV cell, indicating, that is, the propensity for immobility within the petty bourgeoisie, becomes *higher* than that for the I–I cell, indicating the propensity for immobility within the higher echelon of the service class. We would not be inclined to take any of these latter results too seriously. The important point, which would seem beyond question, is that if between 1972 and 1983 the pattern of social fluidity did change at all, then this could only have been in ways that are of quite minor substantive significance.

8. See OPCS, *Census 1981: Economic Activity Great Britain*, London: HMSO, 1984, Table A. The changes made in 1980 in the OPCS system of classifying occupations were so extensive and complex that it did not appear to us worth while to try to extend the time-series established for 1911 to 1971 in Table 2.3 above.

9. Dale has recently argued that 'it is likely that a significant proportion of those moving into self-employment are not acquiring ownership of the means of production and the autonomy over the labour process associated with membership of the petty bourgeoisie, but are, in fact, doing little more than moving into a casualised form of employment.' Angela Dale, 'Social Class and the Self-Employed', *Sociology*, vol. 20, 1986 p. 433. However, while this comment may well have considerable force in the case of women workers, our finding would indicate that, in the case of men, a genuine increase in the size of the petty bourgeoisie has occurred in the recent past. Contrary to what Dale suggests, we believe that most survey researchers *are* aware of the diversity of types of self-employment; and further that this awareness extends to knowing that, again so far as men are concerned, labour-only subcontractors, while obviously important in industries such as construction, amount to only a quite small proportion of those returned as self-employed in nationally based samples.

10. Using birth cohort analysis, one could of course only produce tables showing the pattern of recruitment of men to age-ranges within particular classes, which would not yield any very clear indications as to changes in the total pattern of class recruitment over time.

11. Of those unemployed at time of interview in 1972, 10 per cent had been unemployed for not more than one month and a further 24 per cent for between one and six months.

12. See further R.L. Miller, 'Unemployment as a Mobility Status', Queen's University Belfast, Department of Social Studies, 1984.

13. We shall follow the convention of regarding a continuous period of unemployment of one year or more as constituting 'long-term' unemployment.
14. See in particular Michael White, *Long-Term Unemployment and Labour Markets*, London: Policy Studies Institute, 1983.
15. Thus, a model which embodies the hypothesis that the odds of a man being unemployed rather than employed are dependent on the class of his last employment but not on his class of origin (though allowing for the association between this and his class of last employment) gives an entirely acceptable fit to the 1983 data, whether the old or the new class schema is used (the p-values being 0.95 and 0.83 respectively). The parameter estimates under this model indicate that men whose last employment was a working-class one were approximately four times more likely to be unemployed than others. In multiplicative form the model fitted is

$$F_{ijk} = \eta \;\; t_i^P \;\; t_j^S \;\; t_k^U \;\; t_{ij}^{PS} \;\; t_{jk}^{US}$$

where F_{ijk} is the expected value in cell ijk of a three-way table of class of origin (P) with I categories, class of destination (or of last employment) (S) with J categories and present employment or unemployment (U) with K (=2) categories.

16. It might be thought possible that if unemployment is introduced as a mobility status, our previous finding of essential stability in relative mobility rates between 1972 and 1983 would be undermined. But this is not in fact the case. If we construct for 1972 and 1983 asymmetric mobility tables with three classes of origin but four classes of destination (i.e. the three classes of the schema in its collapsed form plus 'unemployed'), the constant social fluidity model still fits the data very well.
17. In fact, using both versions of the class schema, it turns out that the proportion of men unemployed among those who had been mobile from intermediate-class origins to working-class positions and among those stable within the working class is virtually identical at just over 16 per cent.
18. For major statements of these opposing views, see, on the one hand, H. Braverman, *Labor and Monopoly Capital*, New York: Monthly Review Press, 1974; and, on the other, Daniel Bell, *The Coming of Post-Industrial Society*, New York: Basic Books, 1973. An excellent comparative exposition is provided in Erik Olin Wright and Joachim Singelmann, 'Proletarianisation in the Changing American Class Structure', *American Journal of Sociology*, vol. 88, supplement, 1982.
19. Cf. Joachim Singelmann and Harley L. Browning, 'Industrial Transformation and Occupational Change in the U.S., 1960–70', *Social Forces*, vol. 59, 1980; and Wright and Singelmann, 'Proletarianisation and the Changing American Class Structure'.
20. For Britain and other European countries, see Jay Gershuny, *Social Innovation and the Division of Labour*, Oxford: Oxford University Press, 1983; and for the USA, Joachim Singelmann and Marta Tienda, 'The Process of Occupational Change in a Service Economy: The Case of the United States' in Bryan Roberts, Ruth Finnegan, and Duncan Gallie (eds.), *New Approaches to Economic Life*, Manchester: Manchester University Press, 1985. The—explicit—shift in Singelmann's position, as compared with that adopted in his earlier papers, is notable.
21. Sée, for example, Rosemary Crompton, 'Class Mobility in Modern Britain', *Sociology*, vol. 14, 1980. Cf. Crompton and Gareth Jones, *White-Collar Proletariat: Deskilling and Gender in Clerical Work*, London: Macmillan, 1984.
22. See in particular Rune Åberg, 'Teoriarna om arbets degradering och arbetsmarknadens dualisering—ett försök till empirisik provning', *Sociologisk Forskning*, vol. 2, 1984, and 'Arbetsförhållenden', in Robert Erikson and Åberg (eds.), *Välfärd i Förändring*, Stockholm: Prisma, 1984. Åberg's work is of importance in breaking with the case-study approach which has so far been almost exclusively followed in research in this area. In this connection it must be emphasized that even quite indisputable evidence of degrading derived from particular case studies can be of little value in defending the degrading thesis against the upgrading thesis *in so far as the argument is about class structures*. Supporters of the latter thesis do not seek to deny that deskilling or other forms of degrading occur (although they might wish to see these as integral to the development of industrial, rather than of specifically capitalist societies); but they would still

maintain that the *net* result of technological and organizational change *over the economy as a whole* is an increase in skill levels *and in the proportion of the work-force in salaried or 'bureaucratic' conditions of employment.* In other words, macro-sociological arguments can only be adequately discussed on the basis of macro-sociological data. Moreover, if proponents of the degrading thesis wish to construe this *entirely* in terms of skill and job content, and thus to disregard employment relations, this should be made clear; and, in turn, the implications for their theory of class structure spelled out.

23. John H. Goldthorpe, 'On the Service Class: Its Formation and Future' in Anthony Giddens and Gavin Mackenzie (eds.), *Social Class and the Division of Labour*, Cambridge: Cambridge University Press, 1982, p. 170; cf. also Goldthorpe, 'Reply to Crompton', *Sociology*, vol. 14, 1980.

24. For example, in Bell's *The Coming of Post-Industrial Society*—subtitled 'A Venture in Social Forecasting'—the index contains only three references to unemployment, and these direct one to only passing comments.

25. This is essentially the same position as that reached by Singelmann and Tienda, 'The Process of Occupational Change in a Service Economy'. In fact, however, it would appear to be even more appropriate to the British case than to the American, and especially in view of the form of political economy that has prevailed in Britain since the return of the Conservatives to power in 1979. In opposition to both Marxist and liberal theories of change in class structures of the kind referred to, there would now appear to be a growing awareness of the impact on class structures of *cross-national variation in political economies* within the western world. Cf. the papers collected in John H. Goldthorpe (ed.), *Order and Conflict in Contemporary Capitalism*, Oxford: Clarendon Press, 1984.

CHAPTER 10

The Class Mobility of Women

(*with* CLIVE PAYNE)

The analyses so far presented in this book have been ones based on the mobility experience of men. As earlier described, the sample studied in the course of the 1972 national mobility inquiry was one of the male population of England and Wales, aged 20 to 64; and thus in turn it was men who were studied in the 1974 follow-up inquiry, which entailed the re-interviewing of subsamples of 1972 respondents. In the last chapter, current trends in class mobility were investigated by means of comparisons made between the experience of the men studied in 1972 and that of male respondents to the British General Election Study of 1983.

In recent years mobility research has been repeatedly criticized, in particular by exponents of 'feminist' sociology, for such a concentration on men and the consequent neglect of women; and this 'bias' has then been typically attributed to 'sexism' or 'entrenched androcentrism' on the part of those working in the field.[1] At first sight such criticism may appear cogent, and it has certainly been assured of a sympathetic reception by prevailing sentiment within the socio-logical community. However, a closer examination reveals that the critics' case does not in fact rest on any very close familiarity with the relevant literature, and that their arguments are in various respects lacking in both accuracy and perceptiveness.

To begin with, one may note that while it is true that mobility studies have quite often been designed—like that of 1972—so as to concentrate on men, the impression given by critics that this has been a universal practice is misleading, and the claim that information on the social mobility of women has been more or less unavailable is simply wrong. In the course of the post-war period relevant data have been produced in most of the major industrial nations of the western world. For example, in Britain the pioneering study of social mobility under-taken by Glass and his colleagues in 1949 collected information from a national sample of both men and women; and in the early 1970s data on the mobility of women became obtainable from the General Household Survey. Again, in the USA it has been possible to derive such data from National Opinion Research Centre (NORC) surveys from as early as 1955, and subsequently from a variety of other sources. In France, data have been available from successive national inquiries starting in 1953, and in Sweden from a series of studies initiated in 1968.[2]

Critics would have made a more accurate and a more pertinent point if, instead of alleging a general dearth of information on the social mobility of women, they had rather observed that the data that *have* been produced have not been analysed as intensively, nor for the most part as successfully, as those relating to men. And they might then have gone on to consider why this should be so, and why in particular, if it is indeed the case that the neglect of women imposes 'an enormous limit on our understanding' of mobility,[3] more effort should not have been devoted—and above all by sociologists with feminist commitments—to working on the data in question. Thus, to revert to the British case, it is remarkable that the information on women's mobility collected by Glass should have remained almost entirely unexploited for over thirty years, although accessible in coded form.[4]

If such questions *had* been considered, then, we would suggest, it would not have been found satisfactory to account for the emphasis in the literature of social mobility on the experience of men simply by facile references to 'sexism', and the need for some more serious explanations would have been apparent. Having regard to the availability, but evident under-utilization of material relating to women, we would ourselves advance the following argument: that, despite all assertions of the disastrous consequences for mobility research of the neglect of women, a deep, and inhibiting, uncertainty prevails about just what are the problems to which the study of the social mobility of women should be addressed and, in turn, about what would be the appropriate conceptual approaches and analytical procedures to pursue.

As was shown in chapter 1, an understanding of the historical development of mobility research calls·for recognition of the very different conceptual contexts within which the study of mobility may be carried out; and the importance of conceptual context for the conduct of research is only underlined where the mobility of women is concerned. Thus, for example, if the focus of attention is on women's occupational mobility (or occupational attainment) *per se*, it may well be profitable to take up much the same issues, and via much the same methods, as would be pursued in the case of men, with, then, the possibility of making straightforward comparisons between the sexes.[5] However, if the aim is rather to study the social mobility of women within the context of a class structure (or, for that matter, a status order *stricto sensu*), the situation becomes far more problematic. For in this case undoubtedly complex and disputed issues arise: notably, that of whether for such purposes the individual should still be taken as the unit of analysis or whether this should become the family or household; and, if the latter, that of how the class (or status) position of families or households should be determined. It is the fact that such issues are the subject of continuing debate—and from a diversity of viewpoints—that most clearly testifies to the uncertainty to which we have referred. And the debate does, it should be stressed, have real sociological content: it is not the case, as feminist writers would seem to imply, that all difficulties would be resolved if only the distorted vision of sexist researchers could be corrected.[6]

We do not suppose that in this chapter we shall ourselves bring the debate to any kind of conclusion. We have, rather, two more modest objectives. First, we seek to advance the debate by considering the so far largely neglected question of what difference does it make to the empirical findings that are produced and to the problems that can be addressed when one rather than another of the possible conceptual approaches to the study of women's mobility is adopted. Conceptual choices are obviously not open to empirical refutation in the same way as are substantive propositions. But, as applied to particular cases, they do entail empirical results, and these then have at all events a potential for embarrassment in that they need not be as much in accord with the investigator's theoretical—or ideological—predilections as was the conceptual choice itself. Secondly, we wish to assess, in the light of the empirical results that we are able to report, to just what extent a focus on the mobility experience of men *is* likely to be misleading in so far as the study of specifically *class* mobility is concerned: that is—in the sense that has informed our work throughout—mobility between different locations within the class structure which is consequential for the formation or decomposition of classes understood as collectivities with distinctive life-chances and life-styles, patterns of association, and socio-political orientations and modes of action.

In the following section, we briefly describe the data with which we will work. We then go on to explore, with the above objectives in mind, three different ways in which the location of women within the class structure may be conceptualized and rendered operational. Each of these has been explicitly argued for in the debate to which we have referred, and we label them, following the usage of this debate, the 'conventional', 'individual', and 'dominance' approaches.

DATA

We here again resort to data available from the 1983 British General Election Study, which, as we noted in the previous chapter, was based on interviews undertaken with a sample designed to be representative of the entire national electorate. Specifically, we utilize information, for men and women aged 20 to 64 and resident in England and Wales, on (i) their present (or last) occupation and employment status; (ii) the present (or last) occupation and employment status of their spouses (where cohabiting); and (iii) the occupation and employment status of their fathers (or other 'head of household') at respondent's age 14.

We draw on the information of items (i) and (ii) in order to determine the present class position, or class destination, of respondents—following, in the case of women, the three different approaches that we have referred to; and we take the information of item (iii) as the basis for determining respondent's class origins. We recognize that it might, for our present purposes at least, be contentious not to regard mother's as well as father's employment as an indicator of class origins. However, the relevant information is not available from the BGES, and it should in any event be kept in mind that in the case of older respondents at least, rather few of their mothers would, at the time of the respondents' adolescence, have been found in the labour force. For example, as late as 1951 still only around 20 per cent of married women in England and Wales were engaged in paid employment.

Again as noted in chapter 9, data on occupation and employment status were coded in the BGES according to the 1980 OPCS system—in response to which we then devised a new version of our class schema specifically for use with data in this form. Furthermore, in so doing we made provision for some elaboration of the categories of the schema, and in one respect which is here of particular relevance. That is, in order to make the schema more suited to the class allocation of women—where it is found desirable to do this by reference to their own employment—we provided for Class III, that of routine nonmanual employees, to be split into two sub-classes, labelled IIIa and IIIb. Our aim here was as far as possible to isolate in IIIb occupations which are very largely filled by women and which, moreover, in terms of their characteristic employment relations and conditions, would seem to entail straightforward wage-labour rather than displaying any of the quasi-bureaucratic features associated with other positions covered by Class III. The main occupational groupings in fact allocated to Class IIIb are those of shop assistants, shop cashiers, check-out and wrap operators and various lower-level attendants and receptionists.[7] Thus, where the revised class schema is applied to women in virtue of their own employment and with the aim of making comparisons with men, it would seem an appropriate procedure to combine Class IIIb with Class VII, that of semi- and unskilled manual workers.

In Table 10.1 we show how women and men in the subsample of respondents that we have taken from the BGES are distributed across the classes of our schema in respect of their origins and their present positions. The origins distributions are of course very similar since for both women and men they refer to father's class. But the destination distributions are widely different. The dissimilarity index shows that in this case almost 45 per cent of women, or of men, would have to change positions in order to make the distributions identical. Men are far more likely than women to be found in Class I, and taking Classes I and II together as comprising the more advantaged and desirable service-class positions within modern society, we find that men are still almost twice as likely to occupy them than are women. Much higher proportions of men than of women are also found in Class IV, that of the petty bourgeoisie, and in Classes V and VI, those of the blue-collar élite and skilled manual workers respectively; while women are far more concentrated than men in both of the divisions of Class III and in Class VII, that of non-skilled manual workers.

Table 10.1

Distributions of class origins (father's class at respondent's age 14) and of class destinations (based on present or last employment) of women and men, aged 20–64

| Class | Women | | Men | |
	Origins	Destinations	Origins	Destinations
I	9.8	2.3	9.7	16.0
II	10.4	15.4	8.2	17.6
IIIa	5.2	32.8	4.8	6.1
IIIb	0.2	10.5	0.4	0.6
IV	13.4	3.2	14.0	11.6
V	9.6	2.0	10.5	8.4
VI	25.1	5.2	25.0	19.6
VII	26.5	28.4	27.5	20.1
N	1,204		1,173	

△ for women's destinations/men's destinations = 44.9
△ for women's origins/men's origins = 2.6

THE 'CONVENTIONAL' APPROACH

The 'conventional' approach to the location of women within the class structure starts from the claim that it is the family rather than the individual that forms the basic unit of social stratification. In the context of class analysis, it is then the location of the family member who has the fullest commitment to participation in the labour market that is seen as the most reliable indicator of the location of the family as a whole. For research purposes, the family 'head' in the above sense is usually taken to be an adult male (if one is present in the family) and hence, in application, the conventional approach results in the large majority of married women being accorded the same class position as their husbands.[8]

Exponents of the conventional approach would argue that, to date at least, it is unlikely that studies of class mobility that concentrate on men will have produced any very misleading conclusions. For despite the general tendency in modern societies for the participation of married women in the labour market to increase, their employment still tends to be more intermittent than that of men, is less often full-time, and is only rarely such as to place them in what could be regarded as dominant class positions relative to those held by their husbands. It was in fact considerations of this kind—taken together with ones of cost-effectiveness—that chiefly influenced the decision to restrict the 1972 mobility inquiry to men. As we previously wrote:

> We would wish to maintain the view that—whatever current trends of change in women's work and family life may portend—during the decades preceding our inquiry, and to which our data relate, it has been through the role of their male members within the social division of labour that families have been crucially articulated with the class structure and their class 'fates' crucially determined. Or conversely, one could say, the way in which women have been located in the class structure has reflected their general situation of dependence.[9]

From such a standpoint, one deficiency in class-mobility research that is restricted to men must clearly be acknowledged: that is, the omission of those cases where women live unattached or are themselves family 'heads' in the sense that has been indicated. But this, it may be maintained, is not a sufficiently large problem to create any serious distortion in the general pattern of results obtained.[10] There is, however, another, and more substantial, objection to the neglect of women that can be made without departing from the conventional approach, and indeed by simply following through its logic. This calls here for further examination, and not least because in our earlier work it did not receive the attention that a systematic adherence to the conventional approach would have required.

If women do mostly derive their class positions from those of the male heads of the families to which they belong, then, it may be argued, a full account of class mobility must take in the mobility that occurs as a result of women *marrying*: that is to say, as a result of their moving from their family of origin (or perhaps from an unattached state) to enter into a conjugal family. Moreover, the importance of considering such 'marital' mobility is underlined by suggestions rather frequently encountered in sociological—and also in various kinds of lay—literature to the effect that in modern society marriage does afford particularly wide opportunities for mobility.[11] The main argument that under-lies these suggestions, in so far as one can be detected, would seem to be the following: that the attributes that tend to make women more or less attractive to men as marriage partners—that is, physical and personality attributes—*are less closely associated with social origins* than are those attributes that chiefly influ-ence men's ultimate socio-economic positions—that is, education, qualifications, and of course inherited wealth. Thus, women may be expected to experience greater intergenerational mobility through marriage than do men through employment and their work careers. A supplementary argument which may also appear derives from the claim that unmarried women come disproportionately from more advantaged social origins and unmarried men disproportionately from less advantaged ones. Thus, it can be held, the marital mobility of women will tend to show a net *upward* bias, over and above any which may result from long-term changes in the shape of the class structure and from which they stand to benefit via their husbands.

In sum, then, these arguments would point to the possibility that a study of class mobility which excluded marital mobility from its concerns could well present a misleading picture, and especially in underestimating the degree of openness of the class structure and the range of possibilities for social advance-ment that were offered. However, the question does of course remain of just how valid the foregoing arguments are.

To bring our data into play, we present first, in Table 10.2, a straightforward comparison of the marital mobility rates of women by class and the inter-generational class mobility rates of married men—these being given in both cases in outflow terms. The general impression created by the table is that these rates display some non-negligible differences but within a broad similarity. Some support might be claimed for the idea that women are more mobile via marriage than are men via employment in that the total mobility rate (i.e. the proportion of all cases falling in cells off the main diagonal) works out at 78.2 per cent for the women's matrix in Table 10.2 as compared with 73.0 per cent for the men's. And it can also be calculated that women experience more mobility than men both upwardly into Classes I and II from other class origins (31.0 per cent as against 27.9 per cent) *and* downwardly from Class I and II origins to other class destinations (42.0 per cent as against 33.6 per cent). However, against this, it may be noted from the detail of Table 10.2 that as well as being not all that large, these differences are also not as consistent as might be expected if social processes of the kind that have been suggested did in fact operate to heighten mobility and to create specially favourable opportunities for social ascent via a 'good match'. Thus, for example, the daughters of Class I, and also of Class V, fathers appear more likely to *remain* within their class of origin via marriage than do the sons of such fathers via employment; and so far as Class V and likewise Class VII daughters are concerned, their chances of marrying up into Classes I and II do *not* seem better than the chances that their 'brothers' have of 'working' their way into these more advantaged classes.

The mobility rates shown in Table 10.2 are absolute, percentage ones, which

Table 10.2

Marital mobility of women by class and intergenerational class mobility of married men, outflow rates

Father's class	Daughter's husband's class (upper figures); son's class (lower figures)							Δ	N
	percentage by row								
	I	II	III	IV	V	VI	VII		
I	38.2	29.8	6.6	8.3	5.3	6.4	5.4	4.1	75
	36.2	28.4	9.2	9.1	4.6	6.8	5.6		87
II	27.3	23.3	8.4	18.3	5.5	6.1	11.0	20.2	93
	33.6	34.8	7.4	5.7	7.4	6.7	4.5		71
III	14.7	25.3	6.2	8.8	4.7	34.2	6.1	32.1	48
	24.7	24.2	17.6	5.1	7.6	6.9	13.8		42
IV	19.5	20.7	11.6	17.4	3.9	13.3	13.6	21.1	136
	9.9	18.9	3.3	33.2	7.2	11.9	15.6		130
V	10.2	19.6	2.1	8.8	14.4	20.5	24.4	23.2	93
	22.7	10.9	5.1	14.4	5.8	22.6	18.5		100
VI	15.7	16.8	8.1	6.3	8.6	22.4	22.1	11.1	247
	11.6	13.7	5.6	8.1	12.0	28.3	20.7		231
VII	8.8	14.7	5.5	12.0	9.5	25.7	23.7	11.6	262
	11.7	12.3	4.5	8.2	13.2	21.4	28.7		239
All	16.7	19.2	7.1	11.2	8.0	19.6	18.4	3.7	954
	17.3	17.3	6.0	12.2	9.7	18.7	18.8		900

are thus influenced by marginal distributions. Given the way in which our marital mobility and intergenerational mobility matrices are constructed, differences between their marginal distributions cannot of course be very great: from one point of view, we are simply comparing father-to-son with father-to-son-in-law mobility. None the less, such differences do exist, if only as a result of sampling error and imperfections; and we may find ourselves better able to interpret the data of Table 10.2 if we move on to compare women's marital and men's intergenerational mobility in terms of relative rates—or, in other words, in terms of the patterns of association that exist between class origins and destinations when these are considered net of all marginal effects.

We can do this by the same methods of multiplicative modelling that we have used in earlier chapters. We can in fact apply to the two mobility matrices that are compared in Table 10.2 a model which is formally identical to the 'constant social fluidity' model that we introduced in chapters 3 and 9 but which we can now interpret in a different way. That is to say, instead of using this model to embody the hypothesis that relative mobility or, in other words, a pattern of social fluidity, is constant across cohorts or between inquiries, we can use it to postulate that *common* relative rates, or a common pattern of fluidity, underlies the two different kinds of mobility, one relating to women and one to men, that Table 10.2 displays.[12]

The results of so doing are given in Table 10.3 and, as can be seen, the model does not fit well. It leaves some 20 per cent of the association between class of origin and class of destination unaccounted for,[13] and misclassifies almost 7 per cent of all cases comprised by Table 10.2. Clearly, then, we must accept that the pattern of fluidity that underlies women's marital mobility is *not* the same as that underlying men's intergenerational class mobility.

Table 10.3

Results of testing the common social fluidity model against data on the marital mobility of women by class and the intergenerational class mobility of married men

x^2	df	p	Percentage of association accounted for	Percentage of cases misclassified
68.9	36	0.00	79.8	6.8

However, it does not of course necessarily follow from this that in the former case fluidity is *greater*—that there is a stronger propensity towards mobility rather than immobility. In fact, we may calculate that the women's observed total mobility rate of 78.2 per cent is just 1.6 percentage points higher (and the men's correspondingly lower) than that which would be expected under the 'common social fluidity' model—that is, than the rate which would prevail *if* fluidity were at exactly the same level for both types of mobility considered. And furthermore, if we focus on mobility out of and into Classes I and II of our schema, we discover that while the women's observed rate of marrying down from service-class origins of 42.0 per cent is 4 percentage points higher than would be expected under our model, their observed rate of marrying up into the service class of 31.0 per cent is only 1 percentage point higher than would be expected.

The lack of fit of the model would not therefore seem to result primarily from women's marital mobility offering a generally freer movement between classes—or between Classes I and II and the rest—than men's intergenerational mobility via employment. This being so, what may then be asked is whether the differences shown up between the two types of mobility are in any other way of sociological interest. Inspection of residuals under the model indicates that these differences are rather heterogeneous. There is in fact only one tendency suggested that would appear to merit further comment—chiefly because a similar finding has been reported by other investigators on the basis of results from analyses comparable to those presented here but relating to French, Swedish, and German data: that is, a tendency for the 'exchange' of daughters between the petty bourgeoisie and the service class to be greater than the 'exchange' of sons.[14]

Class IV, the class of the petty bourgeoisie, is that within which the propensity for mobility of daughters most exceeds that of sons. We saw in chapter 4 (and the finding has been confirmed in various other studies[15]) that the propensity for the sons of the petty bourgeoisie to 'succeed' their fathers is distinctively high—in consequence, it would seem, of direct class inheritance via the inter-generational transmission of capital, and often in the form of a 'going concern'. But although Class IV daughters tend more often to move away from their class origins via marriage than do Class IV sons via employment, daughters also, it appears, benefit from Class IV parental resources—that is, by being able to 'marry well'; and another sizeable deviation from the common social fluidity model thus comes about in that their propensity to marry into the service class is greater than that of Class IV sons to enter service-class positions. Turning, on the other hand, to the daughters of the service class, we then find that while those with Class I fathers tend to be mobile or immobile on much the same pattern as their 'brothers', Class II daughters have a lower propensity to remain within the service class via marriage than do Class II sons via employment—perhaps on account of a greater parental concern with sons' education. And in this case, the main compensating deviation from our model that arises is for Class II daughters to show a stronger propensity to enter Class IV by marriage than do Class II sons in the course of their working lives.[16]

From an earlier examination of women's marital mobility (based in fact on data from our 1972 inquiry), Heath reached the conclusion that 'the British class structure would appear to be rather more fluid than consideration of father-to-son mobility alone would have us believe'. Heath did at the same time recognize that differences in pattern between the two types of mobility were 'not all that great' and indeed 'much less remarkable than the similarities', and he also discounted the idea of any significant upward bias in marital mobility.[17] However, the results of our own analyses would incline us to yet greater caution. Specifically, we would not follow Heath in making the general claim that 'a woman's "class fate" is more loosely linked to her social origins than is a man's'.[18] We would rather say, on the basis of the findings we have reported above, that class origins need not always influence to exactly the same degree the class fate of the men and the women who share them. If it then appears that, overall, women are slightly more mobile through marriage than are men through employment, this should, in our view, be understood not as reflecting some general tendency but rather as the net outcome of various different processes of class reproduction and exchange that are of a limited and perhaps contradictory kind.

THE 'INDIVIDUAL' APPROACH

The individual approach to the class location of women could be said to stand in direct opposition to the conventional one, and indeed largely derives from feminist critiques of the latter which allege a 'sexist' bias.[19] Advocates of the individual approach challenge the argument that the family rather than the individual is the unit of class stratification. This is, they claim, in principle dubious and in any event inappropriate once it is the case that the large majority of women participate in the labour market, to some extent or other, after as well as before marriage. In such circumstances, it is misguided to 'derive' the class location of women from the positions occupied by male family 'heads'; rather, women should be seen as holding positions within the class structure that are directly determined by the nature of the employment relations in which they themselves are—or previously have been—engaged. In other words, women should in this respect be treated in exactly the same way as men, and moreover no difference should arise in the treatment of married and unmarried women.

For those who accept this approach, it must then clearly follow that if in the study of class mobility women are excluded—or if attention extends, as an elaboration of the conventional approach, only to their marital mobility—the results produced will be seriously incomplete and defective. When women are assigned class positions on the basis of their own employment, it can be expected that their distribution within the class structure will be very different to, and less favourable than, that of men; and it has indeed been contended that what is in this way brought to light is the remarkable extent to which women are concentrated in 'proletarian' work.[20] Thus, if their fathers' positions are still taken as the indicator of women's class origins, women will display far more *downward* mobility than do men; and consequently, studies of mobility that are restricted to men will give an unduly favourable impression of the prevailing structure of opportunity. In particular, they will entirely overlook the degree to which, because of discrimination against them in employment, women of *all* origins—and whatever their marital mobility—are in fact likely to share in a *common* class fate.

In Table 10.4 we show the results obtained when the class mobility of women is determined following the individual approach and is compared with that of men. It can be seen that there are very wide differences in the rates reported— every dissimilarity index is over 40 per cent—and that the expectation that women will show far more downward mobility is borne out. Thus, the rate of mobility from Class I and II origins to other class destinations may be calculated as 66.2 per cent for women as against 28.3 per cent for men (while their respect- ive rates of mobility into Classes I and II from other class origins are 11.1 and 27.4 per cent). What might be thought of particular note in the detail of Table 10.4 is the large outflow of daughters of Class I fathers to the routine nonmanual positions of Class IIIa and of the daughters of Class II fathers both to IIIa *and* to the still lower-grade types of employment comprised by the combined classes VII and IIIb.

However, before we can know exactly what is the significance to be attached to these findings, we must again ask how far differences in the absolute percent- age rates that are presented simply follow from differences in the marginal distributions of the two matrices in question—their destination marginals being, as one would expect, very divergent; or, on the other hand, how far variation in relative rates, or patterns of fluidity, is also involved. To answer this question, we may revert to the 'common social fluidity' model and apply it to the basic data of Table 10.4, just as we did previously to those of Table 10.2. The main difference is of course that the class destinations of women and men are now determined in a similar way and that in turn we have no need to restrict our analysis to married persons.

As can be seen from Table 10.5, the model does, this time, fit fairly closely, and inspection of residuals reveals no features of evident sociological interest. We can therefore say that the differences in absolute rates shown up in Table 10.4

Table 10.4

Intergenerational class mobility of women (upper figures) and men (lower figures), outflow rates, women's class determined by reference to own present or last employment

Father's class	Respondent's class percentage by row							Δ	N
	I	II	IIIa	IV	V	VI	VII and IIIb		
I	6.1	33.4	46.4	1.6	1.7	1.8	8.9	43.7	118
	32.9	29.1	9.7	7.8	5.2	8.9	6.3		114
II	3.5	24.8	37.0	6.8	0.8	2.4	24.6	44.1	125
	29.2	32.9	9.6	6.4	5.4	8.2	8.3		96
IIIa	4.5	13.1	45.2	1.9	1.5	1.5	32.2	43.6	63
	18.4	23.6	19.9	7.8	7.5	8.8	14.0		56
IV	3.2	17.7	30.8	5.0	0.7	4.4	38.1	51.1	161
	10.8	19.8	3.8	30.7	6.9	13.8	14.2		164
V	2.7	17.5	32.6	4.4	0.8	5.3	36.8	50.1	115
	23.4	10.6	3.2	11.7	6.4	21.7	23.0		123
VI	1.7	11.1	30.6	0.6	3.7	7.8	44.4	46.7	301
	11.9	13.2	5.5	7.4	9.8	29.3	22.9		294
VII and IIIb	0.0	7.7	27.0	3.9	2.2	6.3	53.0	45.0	321
	9.5	13.4	4.0	9.2	10.6	22.1	31.2		327
All	2.3	15.4	32.8	3.2	2.0	5.2	39.0	45.1	1,204
	16.0	17.6	6.1	11.6	8.4	19.6	20.8		1,173

Table 10.5

Results of testing the 'common social fluidity' model against data on women's and men's intergenerational class mobility, women's class determined by reference to own present or last employment

x^2	df	p	Percentage of association accounted for	Percentage of cases misclassified
48.0	36	0.09	88.4	3.9

are almost entirely attributable to differences in marginal distributions; for the pattern of relative rates, or social fluidity, that underlies women's intergenerational class mobility as defined in this table *is virtually the same as that underlying men's mobility*.[21]

This finding stemming from the individual approach (and largely consonant with what has emerged from similar analyses of other national data sets[22]) is then one of undoubted interest. But, we would argue, it is at the same time one which must itself prompt some questioning of the approach, or at all events of arguments closely associated with it. To begin with, one might observe that since the relative rates of class mobility of women, when determined according to their 'own' class positions, turn out to be much the same as those of men, this does of course mean that so far at least as the pattern of fluidity within the class structure is concerned—and assuming the validity of the individual approach—studies restricted to the experience of men will *not* in fact prove misleading. Rather, one could use them as a basis for predicting the experience of women with a high degree of confidence.

But a still more serious point to be made is the following. In view of the good fit of the common social fluidity model to the data of Table 10.4, and of the similarity of the origins distributions involved, the relatively high rates of downward mobility displayed by women must be seen as resulting overwhelmingly from the distinctive pattern of their class *destinations*; or, one could say, from the degree to which sex segregation persists in employment to the general disadvantage of women—a state of affairs which of course can be, and has been, established quite independently of mobility research.[23] What therefore is *not* shown by analyses based on the individual approach is any tendency for women to be 'united in adversity' in the sense that relative mobility chances *are more equal* among them than they are among men. It is not, for example, the case that daughters of Class I and II fathers are less likely as compared with other women to remain in their class of origin than are Class I or II sons as compared to other men. Or, to give another illustration, even if the argument were to be accepted that the majority of employed women are engaged in 'proletarian' work, it would still be important to note that women of all class origins are *not* equally likely to share in this fate. Although women overall confront at any one time a less favourable set of employment opportunities than do men, the forces making for class inequalities in relative mobility chances are not annulled among women. On the contrary, they appear to operate in a way that is quite blind to gender: and hence, women are divided by these inequalities to much the same degree and on much the same pattern as are men.[24]

Finally, then, since women's class positions as 'directly' determined do show a well-defined association with the class positions of their fathers, one is rather naturally led to inquire further, so far as married women are concerned, (i) into the association between their class positions and those of their husbands and (ii) into whether, if these other associations are controlled for, that previously discussed between their fathers' and their husbands' positions still persists. Those who have wished to reject the idea of the family as the unit of stratification have not spelled out at all fully just what they would see as being further entailed by this rejection. But it is, presumably, of importance to their case that any association between wife's class and husband's class or between husband's class and wife's father's class should be rather weak. Exponents of the individual approach have frequently urged that what must now be recognized is not only the extent of married women's labour-market participation but, in addition, the frequency with which women's employment relations are such as to give them clearly different class locations from those of their husbands.[25] And likewise, the argument against the significance of the family and in favour of the 'direct' determination of women's class positions will obviously be strengthened, the more tenuous the connection between father's class and husband's class appears to be.

As a basis for further examining these issues, we present in Table 10.6 a three-way analysis in which we show how women with different experience of class mobility, or immobility, as established via the individual approach, are distributed by class of husband. To simplify matters, the small number of women (5.6 per cent of all married) who were found in Classes IV and V are left out of consideration.

Table 10.6

Distribution of married women with differing experience of class mobility (present class determined by reference to own present or last employment) by class of husband

		Husband's class			
		I and II	IIIa, IV and V	VI, VII and IIIb	N
Father's class	Daughter's class a				
	I and II	85.9	7.9	6.2	63
I and II	IIIa	48.2	32.3	19.5	61
	VI, VII and IIIb	31.3	34.7	33.0	33
	I and II	54.8	25.1	20.1	45
IIIa, IV and V	IIIa	46.2	26.4	27.4	89
	VI, VII and IIIb	22.5	25.3	52.2	118
	I and II	57.6	19.6	22.8	49
VI, VII and IIIb	IIIa	43.7	26.4	29.9	151
	VI, VII and IIIb	16.2	23.1	60.7	276

Note: (a) Women in Classes IV and V omitted.

For present purposes, there are three main points to be noted from Table 10.6. First, many women do indeed appear as having husbands with a different class location to their own. And perhaps the most important instance of this is that a sizeable proportion of women, of all class origins, who might be regarded as 'proletarianized' in being themselves in working-class positions, here defined as those of Classes VI, VII and IIIb have husbands who are *not* in such positions —in fact, 43.7 per cent overall; or, if the definition of proletarianized women is widened to include also those in Class IIIa, then the proportion with non-proletarian husbands is increased to 55.8 per cent. Secondly, however, it is also apparent—as the last-mentioned point serves well to illustrate—that although wives' and husbands' class locations are often different, this still does not prevent there being a marked association between them. And thirdly, it is indicated that father's class *is* still of importance in relation to husband's class. In particular, it may be observed that *even when women's own class is held constant,* daughters of service-class fathers are still clearly less likely to have working-class husbands than are daughters of intermediate- or working-class fathers.[26]

Again, then, empirical findings from an application of the individual approach prove not all that congenial to claims associated with it. Attempts to undermine the unitary conception of the family within class analysis do not receive great support; and, in turn, one has grounds for calling into question the validity of results derived from the individual approach so far as the study of specifically *class* mobility is concerned. The data of Table 10.4 could certainly be read as showing that women have less favourable opportunities for, and hence (across all class origins) less favourable experience of *occupational attainment* than do men—although it would at the same time have to be acknowledged that this is scarcely a novel finding.[27] But what may be disputed is whether the foregoing can be properly translated into an argument concerning class mobility: for example, to the effect that, when the individual approach to the class location of women is adopted, a strong and hitherto neglected tendency for downward class mobility is revealed—with the accompanying subcultural, associational, and socio-political shifts that might be expected. Little or no evidence in support of such an argument has so far been advanced; and, if it is to be maintained, then, we would suggest, its exponents might begin by showing, in the case of those women who appear in Table 10.4 as having moved down from service-class origins, why the 42.2 per cent who (as may be calculted from the data of Table 10.6) are married to service-class men should be regarded as having undergone the same process of *déclassement* as, say, the 24.4 per cent who have working-class husbands.

THE 'DOMINANCE' APPROACH

The dominance approach is one that has been recently proposed by Erikson.[28] Where the focus of interest is on occupational distributions—or, presumably, occupational mobility—Erikson accepts that men and women alike will be appropriately classified according to their individual *work positions*. However, he would still see what we have termed the conventional approach as being valid in associating *class positions* with families: 'the nuclear family is the basic element of the class structure of modern industrial societies, because of the dependence of family members upon each other and the largely shared conditions within the family'.[29] In order to take account of the rapid expansion of the labour-market participation of married women, what is then necessary is not to abandon the conventional conceptualization but rather to implement it differently. It is no longer a satisfactory research practice, Erikson argues, to treat the class position of families as being automatically determined by the type of employment of their *male* 'head'—so that married women's positions become invariably 'derived' ones; some alternative procedure must be found through which women's employment can, in principle at least, influence their families' location.

Erikson considers the idea of 'joint classification'—that is, of allowing the employment of husbands *and* wives (and, perhaps of other family members) to determine the family's class position simultaneously. But, on theoretical and ultimately on empirical grounds also, he rejects methods directed to this end, and comes down in favour of an approach which would still retain the notion of a single family 'head'.[30] What in fact he proposes is that the class position of a nuclear family should be equated with the position of that member of its 'primary generation', *whether male or female*, whose labour-market participation may be regarded as dominant. And as a means of establishing in this respect a 'dominance order', Erikson advances two criteria which may be expressed as follows:[31]

(i) work time—employment dominates non-employment, and full-time employment dominates part-time;

(ii) work position—other things being equal, higher-qualified positions dominate lower-qualified, nonmanual positions dominate manual, and self-employed positions dominate employee ones.

It is evident that an application of the dominance approach would ideally be based on a sample of families—or of households—rather than of individuals. However, for our present purposes, it is still of interest to apply the approach to the female respondents in our data set, and to examine the pattern of their intergenerational mobility as it appears on this basis. To this end, we have determined the (present) class positions of the women in question according to the three rules set out below.

(i) A woman who is unmarried (including widowed or divorced) or who is married but separated from her husband is allocated to a class position by reference to her own (present or last) employment—that is, exactly as she would be following the individual approach.

(ii) A woman who is married and living with her husband is allocated to a class position by reference to her own employment if she stands superior to her husband in the following work-time dominance order, but by reference to her husband's employment if she stand inferior—

1. Employed full-time
2. Employed part-time
3. Not gainfully employed

(iii) A woman who is married and living with her husband and who stands *equal* with him in the above work-time order is allocated by reference to her own employment if it is higher than, or at the same level as, that of her husband in the following work-position dominance order (given in terms of the classes of our schema) or otherwise by reference to her husband's employment.

1. Class I
2. Class II
3. Class IV
4. Class V
5. Class IIIa
6. Class VI
7. Classes IIIb and VII

This order does, we recognize, leave some room for argument, most obviously perhaps about the placing of Class IIIa above Class VI and especially when it is remembered that women and men will be differently distributed among occupational groupings falling *within* these classes. It should, however, be noted that the effect of deciding in favour of the order given will clearly be to raise the probability of a married woman's class position being 'directly' determined rather than derived from that of her husband.

In Table 10.7 we show how women's intergenerational class mobility appears following the dominance approach. Again, we make a comparison with men's mobility, but instead of repeating for this purpose the data for men already included in Table 10.4 it is more convenient to give simply the percentage-point deviations of men's from women's rates. It can be seen that while some

Table 10.7

Intergenerational class mobiliy of women, outflow rates (upper figures) and· deviation of men's rates (lower figures), women's class determined by 'dominance'

Father's class	Daughter's class percentage by row							Δ	N
	I	II	IIIa	IV	V	VI	VII and IIIb		
I	26.3	27.6	25.8	5.3	3.4	4.2	7.4	17.2	117
	6.6	*1.5*	*-16.1*	*2.5*	*1.8*	*4.7*	*-1.1*		
II	22.6	24.9	14.6	17.3	3.3	4.7	12.6	20.2	123
	6.6	*8.0*	*-5.0*	*-10.9*	*2.1*	*3.5*	*-4.3*		
IIIa	14.5	19.6	22.8	6.8	5.2	19.8	11.4	13.9	62
	3.9	*4.0*	*-2.9*	*1.0*	*2.3*	*-11.0*	*2.6*		
IV	17.4	24.5	16.0	13.8	2.7	9.3	16.3	25.6	164
	-6.6	*-4.7*	*-12.2*	*16.9*	*4.2*	*4.5*	*-2.1*		
V	10.1	25.5	9.7	8.0	10.1	14.1	22.5	25.1	114
	13.3	*-14.9*	*-6.5*	*3.7*	*-3.7*	*7.6*	*0.5*		
VI	14.0	18.2	12.1	4.4	8.2	18.9	24.1	15.0	304
	-2.1	*-5.0*	*-6.6*	*3.0*	*1.6*	*10.4*	*-1.2*		
VII and IIIb	7.2	17.3	9.9	10.8	7.2	19.6	28.0	11.4	321
	2.3	*-3.9*	*-5.9*	*-1.6*	*3.4*	*2.5*	*3.2*		
All	14.4	21.2	14.2	9.0	6.2	14.5	20.5	11.7	1,205
	1.6	*-3.6*	*-8.1*	*2.6*	*2.2*	*5.1*	*0.3*		

noteworthy differences between the sexes are thus revealed, they are not of the dramatic kind shown up in Table 10.4, where women's mobility was assessed following the individual approach, and in their magnitude and pattern are more comparable to those of Table 10.2, where we considered women's marital mobility.[32] It is further apparent (despite the slight variation in the categories used) that the women's destination distribution in Table 10.7 is likewise much closer to that of Table 10.2 than to that of Table 10.4

When the contents of Table 10.7 are examined in more detail, it proves to be the case that most of the more sizeable differences between women's and men's mobility can in fact be covered by the following three observations. First, women are less likely than men to be intergenerationally immobile, and especially within Classes I, II, IV, and VI. The total mobility rate for women works out at 78.7 per cent as against 72.2 for men. Secondly, from *all* class origins alike, women are more likely than men to be mobile into Class IIIa. This means of course, *inter alia*, that downward mobility to Class IIIa from service-class origins is more common on the part of women. However, it should further be noted that in so far as this latter difference reflects the experience of the younger, unmarried women in our sample, then the evidence of Table 10.6 would suggest that, following the dominance approach, their downward movement will often prove to be only temporary, since it will be succeeded by 'counter-mobility' back to Classes I and II via marriage, which will in turn increase levels of immobility within these classes. Thirdly, women are more likely than men to be upwardly mobile into Classes I and II from Class IV, petty-bourgeois, origins; and into Class II from 'blue-collar' origins in Classes V, VI, and VII.

Since it is only in this last respect that the differences described are not ones obviously favoured by differences between the two destination distributions of Table 10.7, it is once more of interest to apply the common social fluidity model to the data in order to establish how far variations in relative mobility rates underlie those that show up in absolute, percentage terms. The results of so doing are given in Table 10.8. It can be seen that while the fit of the model is not entirely acceptable, it is still a rather close one; and inspection of the residuals reveals little patterning except, as might be expected, for an echo of the unequal exchange of sons and daughters between the service class and petty bourgeoisie which emerged from the further analysis of the data of Table 10.2. No consistent tendency occurs for the model to over-estimate women's immobility, and as against the observed total mobility rate for women reported above of 78.7 per cent, that expected under the model is only slightly less, at 76.4. In other words, we once more find little support for the claim that if women's mobility is taken into account, the British class structure appears clearly more 'open' than when attention is concentrated on men alone.

Table 10.8

Results of testing the common social fluidity model against
data on women's and men's intergenerational class mobility,
women's class determined by 'dominance'

x^2	df	p	Percentage of association accounted for	Percentage of cases misclassified
54.2	36	0.03	86.2	5.2

Indeed, it must be said that, in general, the adoption of the dominance approach to women's class location is scarcely revelatory so far as questions of mobility are concerned. And an examination of how the approach actually works out in practice indicates why this is so. When applied to the women in our sample, the dominance approach (as we have operationalized it) results in 43 per cent being assigned a class position on the basis of their own employment, and 57 per cent on the basis of their husband's employment. However, more than half of the 43 per cent are unmarried or separated women; and in the case of married women who are living with their husbands, the corresponding proportions to those given above become 26 per cent and 74 per cent. Further still, the large majority—four out of five—of those in the 26 per cent qualify for a 'direct' class assignment because they are equal with their husbands in regard to work-time and have employment at a higher *or at the same* level.

It is, therefore, fairly clear that when the dominance approach to the study of women's class mobility is followed, what is chiefly added to the picture that we gain from studies which are restricted to men is information on the mobility of women who are unattached or themselves family 'heads'. And while this information is of obvious interest in itself, it remains the case (as adherents of the conventional approach have noted) that the numbers involved are scarcely sufficient to call for any major modification of our overall understanding of mobility patterns—and especially when the earlier-mentioned tendency for counter-mobility via marriage on the part of younger women is taken into account.

In our view, the best argument for utilizing the dominance approach is not in fact one which turns on what it can uniquely disclose about mobility rates and patterns within present-day society. It is, rather, the argument that when the dominance approach is applied to contemporary data, as in Table 10.7, a valuable benchmark is thereby provided against which an assessment of future trends may be made. Specifically, the possibility is in this way created of being able to monitor how far the development of women's labour-market participation is such that they more often become 'dominant' in this respect, and the significance of their mobility patterns, within the context of class analysis, is thus enhanced. In other words, the process could in this way be traced—if it were indeed to happen—through which women, by coming to participate in the labour market on more equal terms with men as regards *both* worktime and work-positions, did in fact—to take up Giddens' phraseology—achieve their 'liberation from the family' and *cease to be* 'largely peripheral to the class system'.[33]

We began by arguing that the most serious difficulty that has attened the study of the social mobility of women has not been a general lack of information but rather a persisting uncertainty about what were the central issues to be addressed and what would be the appropriate conceptual approaches and analytical procedures to follow. In the specific case of women's *class* mobility, we noted that rather basic doubts and disagreements have been apparent, centring on the question of how in contemporary society women's class positions should be determined. Our aim in the present chapter has then been to take the debate on this matter further by examining what follows *substantively* from different conceptual choices that may be made, and further to ask, on this basis, how far it is the case that a misleading account of class mobility is obtained if attention is concentrated on the experience of men. We have considered three possible approaches to the class allocation of women which can be taken up in studying their mobility, and our principal conclusions in regard to each may be summarized as follows.

First, if the conventional approach is pursued in what has hitherto been the standard way, so that the class positions of families are seen as following from those of their male 'heads', it can then be convincingly argued that, by the very logic of this approach, mobility research focused on the employment experience of men should be complemented with analyses of women's marital mobility. However, contrary to what might have been supposed from such previous discussion, it does *not* emerge from such analyses that either mobility opportunities or mobility risks for women via marriage are at a generally higher level than are those for men via employment. While a number of specific differences can be detected between the two types of mobility in question—some of which are of evident sociological interest in themselves—they are not ones on a scale that would require any serious revision of our overall understanding of the pattern of either absolute or relative rates of class mobility in modern British society as this understanding has been formed on the basis of studies confined to men.

Secondly, if the individual approach is taken, differences in absolute mobility rates between women and men do clearly appear, and on lines that exponents of this approach would anticipate: in particular, women more often than men display downward mobility from their class origins. However, when women are thus allocated to class positions by reference to their own employment, in the same way as men, it further turns out that the pattern of their relative mobility chances is more or less indistinguishable from that of men. And the implication of this is, then, that the differences shown up in absolute rates must be seen as the result not of endogenous mobility processes *per se*, which would appear essentially invariant to gender, but rather of differing marginal distributions in the mobility table reflecting, most obviously, the degree of sex segregation in the occupational division of labour. Thus, the results of applying the individual approach themselves serve to undermine the notion seemingly favoured by some of its supporters that the general disadvantage of women in the labour market must be associated with a levelling-out of class inequalities among them so far as their chances in regard to prevailing employment opportunities are concerned.[34]

Thirdly, when the dominance approach is followed, we find that while this method of including women in the analysis of class mobility produces some deviations of note from the pattern of absolute rates that is obtained from studies focusing on men, again little or no change is suggested to our picture of the underlying pattern of relative rates. What is chiefly gained by this approach is systematic information on the mobility experience of women who are un-attached or themselves family heads. However, the overall significance of this information, in the present-day context at least, is easily exaggerated, and the major attraction of the dominance approach may be seen in the possibility that it offers for tracing the implications for mobility patterns *if* a future tendency were to develop for the key articulation of family units with the class structure to be increasingly made via women's rather than men's employment.

The upshot is, therefore, that it is only results obtained via the individual approach to women's class location which could lend support to the view that our understanding of mobility within the British class structure is grossly impaired by studies that have concentrated on the experience of men. While findings from the analysis of marital mobility can add valuable refinements to conclusions reached via the conventional approach, as also can those from the dominance approach, it is only when the individual approach is followed that a radically different account of absolute—though not of relative—class mobility rates and patterns is implied. However, the crucial issue which must then be confronted, and which we earlier raised, is that of the *validity* of the results that this approach generates. To repeat, there can be no doubt that findings such as those presented in Table 10.4 above reflect substantial differences in the structure of occupational opportunity for men and for women—to the evident disadvantage of the latter; and attempts to provide a general characterization of rates and patterns of *occupational* mobility which disregard the working lives of women would indeed be highly misleading. But, for present purposes, the question is whether one can take data of this kind at the value which exponents of the individual approach would wish to set upon them: that is, as being indicative of women's experience of intergenerational *class* mobility, or immobility, in the sense that has been earlier spelled out.

This question is not one that can be conclusively determined on the basis of data such as those utilized in this chapter. We have, however, extended our analyses of mobility based on the individual approach to bring out certain results, notably on the relationship between wives' fathers' and husbands' class, which create evident problems for this approach and tend to confirm the idea of the family rather than the individual as being, still, the basic unit of class structure. Moreover, what must be further emphasized is that the onus of proof must here fall on those who would advocate the individual approach, and that they have so far failed to bring forward any systematic evidence in support of their crucial assumption that married women's own employment *can* be reliably taken as the major determinant of their class identity or, say, of their participation in class-linked life-styles, patterns of association, or modes of collective action. Such evidence is all the more needful from their point of view in that the attempts of which we are aware to test this assumption directly have produced clearly negative results—indicating in fact that wives themselves, and not just 'sexist' sociologists, 'derive' their class positions from their husbands' employment rather than from their own.[35] At very least, then, it may be claimed that the validity of the individual approach to the class location of women remains to be demonstrated and that, until it is, the alternative account of class mobility in modern British society that follows from it can scarcely be regarded as compelling.

Finally, to avoid any misunderstanding, we should say that it has not in any way been our intention here to imply that the investigation of issues bearing on the class mobility of women is in itself sociologically unimportant or marginal. Clearly, the results we have presented could only have been arrived at through such investigation, and we believe that they are in various ways of interest. What may, however, be suggested on the basis of these results is, first, that the design of studies of class mobility to focus on men, though obviously incomplete, cannot be automatically dismissed as 'sexist' and may well represent an optimal strategy in this field for the use of inevitably limited research resources;[36] and, secondly, that claims widely made to the effect that studies so designed seriously limit or distort our understanding of class mobility not only prejudged but, as it turns out, largely misjudged the issue.

NOTES

1. See, for example, Joan Acker, 'Women and Social Stratification: A Case of Intellectual Sexism', *American Journal of Sociology*, vol. 78, 1973; Christine Delphy, 'Women in Stratification Studies' in Helen Roberts (ed.), *Doing Feminist Research*, London: Routledge, 1981; Helen Roberts and Diana Woodward, 'Changing Patterns of Women's Employment in Sociology, 1950–80', *British Journal of Sociology*, vol. 32, 1981.

2. For use of the NORC data, see, for example, P.Y. Dejong, M.J. Brawer and S.S. Robin, 'Patterns of Female Intergenerational Occupational Mobility: A Comparison with Male Patterns of Intergenerational Occupational Mobility', *American Sociological Review*, vol. 36, 1971. The French inquiries were conducted by the Institut National de la Statistique et des Études Économiques, and the Swedish ones were successive 'rounds' of the Level of Living Survey undertaken by the Swedish Institute for Social Research. For uses of data from both these sources, see Lucienne Portocarero, 'Social Mobility in Industrial Nations: Women in France and Sweden', *Sociological Review*, n.s. vol. 31, 1983.

3. Roberts and Woodward, 'Changing Patterns of Women's Employment in Sociology: 1950–80', p. 542.

4. Most of the serious work that *has* so far been undertaken on problems of women's social mobility is either American or Scandinavian in provenance (as will emerge from subsequent citations) and has been largely neglected in Britain.

5. See for example the papers by Dejong *et al.* and Portocarero cited in n. 3 above, and further, Andrea Tyree and Judith Treas, 'The Occupational and Marital Mobility of Women', *American Sociological Review*, vol. 39, 1974; Donald J. Treiman and Kermit Terrell, 'Sex and the Process of Status Attainment: A Comparison of Working Women and Men', *American Sociological Review*, vol. 40, 1975; Christine Greenhalgh and Mark B. Stewart, 'Occupational Status and Mobility of Men and Women', Warwick Economic Papers, no. 211, University of Warwick, 1982; and Geoff Payne, Judy Payne and Tony Chapman, 'Trends in Female Social Mobility' in Eva Gamarnikow *et al.* (eds.), *Gender, Class and Work*, London: Heinemann, 1983.

6. See, for example, the exchanges contained in the following: Nicky Britten and Anthony Heath, 'Women, Men and Social Class' in Gamarnikow *et al.* (eds.), *Gender, Class and Work*; John H. Goldthorpe, 'Women and Class Analysis: In Defence of the Conventional View'; Michelle Stanworth, 'Women and Class Analysis: A Reply to John Goldthorpe', *Sociology*, vol. 18, 1984; Anthony Heath and Nicky Britten, 'Women's Jobs do Make a Difference: A Reply to Goldthorpe', ibid.; Goldthorpe, 'Women and Class Analysis: A Reply to the Replies', ibid.; and Robert Erikson, 'Social Class of Men, Women and Families', ibid. Issues arising from the debate are also taken up by several contributors to Rosemary Crompton and Michael Mann (eds.), *Gender and Stratification*, Cambridge: Polity Press, 1986–notably, Walby and Delphy and Leonard–but in a way which seems regressive: that is, by returning to large, vague, and tendentious claims (often referred to as 'theory') rather than attempting to resolve issues by putting them in a form in which research findings might be brought to bear upon them.

7. Ideally, we would have wished also to include in IIIb copy- and audio-typists and some kinds of office machine operators. But unfortunately it is not possible, even with the revised OPCS classification of 1980, to separate these groupings from others which are more appropriately allocated to IIIa.

8. See further, Goldthorpe, 'Women and Class Analysis'.

9. *Social Mobility and Class Structure*, 1st ed., p. 288.

10. Cf. ibid.; also below, p. 294.

11. For reviews and discussion of American findings, see Norval D. Glenn, Adreain A. Ross, and Judy Corder Tully, 'Patterns of Intergenerational Mobility of Females through Marriage', *American Sociological Review*, vol. 39, 1974; and Ivan D. Chase, 'A Comparison of Men's and Women's Intergenerational Mobility in the United States', *American Sociological Review*, vol. 40, 1975.

12. The model may in this case be written as

$$F_{ijk} = \eta \; t_i^P \; t_j^D \; t_k^M \; t_{ij}^{PD} \; t_{ik}^{PM} \; t_{jk}^{DM}$$

where F_{ijk} is the expected frequency in cell ijk of the three-way table which comprises origin, or father's class (P), class of destination (D)—which will be either daughter's husband's class or son's class—*and* type of moblity (M).

13. For the calculation of this statistic, see n. 17, p. 117 above.

14. For France and Sweden see Lucienne Portocarero, 'Social Mobility in France and Sweden: Women, Marriage and Work', *Acta Sociologica*, vol. 28, 1985; and for Germany see Johann Handl, 'Heiratsmobilität und berufliche Mobilität von Frauen', VASMA Working Paper no. 8. Institut für Sozialwissenschaften, University of Mannheim, n.d.

15. Cf. John H. Goldthorpe, 'Soziale Mobilität und Klassenbildung: Zur Erneuerung einer Tradition soziologischer Forschung', in Hermann Strasser and Goldthorpe (eds.), *Die Analyse sozialer Ungleichheit*, Opladen: Westdeutscher Verlag, 1985.

16. If we reapply our common social fluidity model to our data but having first 'blocked' the six cells in the mobility matrices that are involved in the account given in the text (i.e. cells IV-IV, IV-I, IV-II, II-I, II-II, and II-IV), we find that while the fit of the model is still not entirely satisfactory (p = .02), the *improvement* in fit over the original version is clearly significant—a reduction in the χ^2 value of 21.4 being achieved for the loss of the 6 degrees of freedom. Even so, it could still be argued that the best reason for taking this deviation from the model seriously is the corroborative evidence provided by Portocarero and Handl.

17. Anthony Heath, *Social Mobility*, London: Fontana, 1981, pp. 113-14.

18. Ibid., p. 114. As regards the differences between our conclusions and those reached by Heath, it should further be noted, first, that Heath makes comparisons between women's mobility via marriage and men's mobility via employment *only at the level of absolute rates*, and does not consider questions of similarities or differences in underlying patterns of fluidity; and secondly, that while our data come from a sample of women and men, Heath's data, being taken from the 1972 inquiry, are entirely derived from male respondents. Thus, as he recognizes, he is in effect examining women's marital mobility by relating the class of married men to the class of their fathers-in-law. While the difference in sampling units here is probably of no very great importance, we might expect to have the better quality data.

We have in fact fitted our common social fluidity model to the 1972 data utilized by Heath and again find deviation in the form of an unequal exchange of sons and daughters between the petty bourgeoisie and the service class, although this represents a less important part of the total deviation than with our own, 1983, data. When analysed in this way, however, Heath's tables do not differ greatly from ours as regards deviation from the model on the main diagonal. Thus, while we found that the total mobility rate for women via marriage was 1.6 percentage points higher than that expected under the model fitted, the corresponding figure calculated from Heath's tables is 2.1.

19. See, for example, Delphy, 'Women in Stratification Studies'; Stanworth, 'Women and Class Analysis'.

20. See in particular Stanworth, op. cit.

21. If we compare with men only those women whose class allocation in Table 10.4 was based on a full-time job, we find that the fit of our model is entirely acceptable (p = .40), while if the comparison is made with only those women whose class allocation was based on a part-time job, the fit is clearly less satisfactory (p = .01). But in this case again there is no evident pattern in the residuals, although, as would be expected, the women in question are yet more heavily concentrated in relatively disadvantaged positions—the taking of part-time work being often associated with a downward movement in occupational level.

22. See, for example, for the USA, Robert M. Hauser and David L. Featherman, *The Process of Stratification: Trends and Analysis*, New York: Academic Press, 1977, and Nancy Dunton and Featherman, 'Social Mobility through Marriage and Careers: Achievement over the Life Course' in Janet T. Spence (ed.), *Achievement and Achievement Motives*, San Francisco: W.H. Freeman, 1985; for Scandinavia, Seppo Pöntinen,

Social Mobility and Social Structure: A Comparison of Scandinavian Countries, Helsinki: Societas Scientiarum Fennica, 1983, and Robert Erikson and Pöntinen, 'Social Mobility in Finland and Sweden: A Comparison of Men and Women' in Risto Alapuro *et al.*, (eds.), *Small States in Comparative Perspective*, Oslo: Norwegian University Press, 1985; and for Sweden and France, Portocarero, 'Social Mobility in France and Sweden'. All of these studies show either no, or only slight, differences between women's and men's relative class mobility rates; and such differences as would indicate a lower propensity for immobility among women tend to be concentrated within the petty bourgeoisie or farm classes. In the British case, the comparatively small size of the latter classes may well help account for the particularly close fit of the 'common social fluidity' model.

23. See in particular Catherine Hakim, *Occupational Segregation*, London: Department of Employment, Research Paper 9, 1979. One might add that evidence on sex segregation of the kind presented by Hakim has often been taken as warranting claims to the effect that 'the social mobility of men cannot be understood without reference to that of women'. Such claims are, however, unduly imprecise and likely to mislead. To imply that the *relative* mobility rates of men cannot be understood without reference to those of women is simply wrong, as is shown in the text. To argue that the structure of women's employment conditions (favourably) men's objective mobility opportunities, and hence their *absolute* mobility rates, is, on the other hand, valid (and we believe that we were ourselves among the first to document it—see pp. 59–60 above and also in the first edition pp. 294–5). But finally, to suggest that women's employment is the only, or even the primary, such structural influence on men's mobility is again mistaken. Let us suppose a situation in which present patterns of social fluidity remain unaltered, but economically active men and women are distributed in identical ways within the existing structure of employment. It can then be shown—analyses are available on request—that men's outflow mobility rates would change on average, across different classes of origin, by about 17 per cent. (And if allowance were made in the analysis for women working part-time, this figure would be clearly lower). As might be expected, men of all class origins would be less likely to enter Classes I and VI and more likely to enter Classes IIIa and IIIb+VII, while little difference would occur in outflows to Classes II, IV, and V. In cross-national perspective, it is evident that structural effects on men's mobility of at least comparable magnitude could, and do, derive from various other sources—for example, the rate and phasing of the decline of agriculture or of the expansion of higher nonmanual occupations, trends in self-employment etc.

24. Here again the conclusions we reach differ from those of Heath who, on the basis of analysing General Household Survey (GHS) data, argues that 'the relative chances for women from different class backgrounds are more equal than those for men', *Social Mobility*, p. 125. Heath arrives at this view from a consideration of disparity ratios. However, as we have noted above (n. 17, p. 88, and p. 265, disparity ratios, except when taken in strictly complementary pairs so that they become in fact equivalent to odds ratios, are *not* 'margin insensitive' measures. When we apply our common social fluidity model to the GHS data (which Anthony Heath kindly made available to us) we obtain a fit of a very comparable degree of closeness to that reported for our own data in Table 10.5. The χ^2 returned is 43.4 which, with 30 degrees of freedom (from two 6 × 7 tables), gives a p-value of 0.05. Furthermore, 98.6 per cent of the χ^2 from the independence model is accounted for, and only 2 per cent of all classes are misclassified. We would therefore regard the GHS data as in fact providing powerful confirmation of our own results, and especially in view of the much larger sample size involved.

25. See, for example, Stanworth, 'Women and Class Analysis'.

26. After inspection of Table 10.6, it is in fact in no way surprising to discover that its data can only be satisfactorily reproduced by a multiplicative model which postulates *each* of the three possible two-way associations: that is, between a woman's class and her father's class, her own class and her husband's class, *and* her father's class and her husband's class. Moreover, under this model, none of these associations could be

regarded as particularly weak. Thus, although the association between a woman's father's class and her husband's class is the least powerful of the three, we may note, to give some indication of its effect, that *women of service-class origins appear as over three times more likely to have a service-class rather than a working-class husband than are women of working-class origin—these relative chances applying equally across all classes of women as determined by their own employment.* Results closely comparable to our own in this respect are reported for Sweden and for France by Portocarero, 'Social Mobility in France and Sweden'.

27. It might also be observed that *if* the aim is in fact to study women's occupational attainment *rather than* class mobility, it would then be clearly preferable to represent 'destinations' by some specifically occupational classification. Much confusion would appear presently to arise (see e.g. Angela Dale, G. Nigel Gilbert, and Sara Arber, 'Integrating Women into Class Theory', *Sociology*, vol. 19, 1985) between the nature and potential uses of, on the one hand, occupational classifications *per se* and, on the other, categorizations aimed at representing class positions, social status levels, etc. which take occupation as an *indicator*, perhaps along with one or more others, in the way, for instance, that our class schema is based on a combination of occupation *and* employment status. The importance of the distinction in question was already pointed out by Glass in his 'Introduction' to *Social Mobility in Britain*, pp. 5–7.

28. Robert Erikson, 'Om Socio-ekonomiska Indelningar av Hushåll: Övervägenden och ett Förslag', *Statistisk Tidskrift*, vol. 19, 1981; and 'Social Class of Men, Women and Families'.

29. Ibid., p. 502.

30. Two important criteria applied by Erikson here are, first, that a class schema should not result in units showing a high degree of short-term instability; and secondly, that the allocation of units to it should not be 'contaminated' by variation in household composition. The latter may well be an important factor in determining family income, living standards, housing tenure, etc.; but this is no reason for confusing it, analytically or operationally, with class. See also the criticism of 'joint classifications' and arguments for distinguishing between household composition and class effects in Goldthorpe, 'Women and Class Analysis' and 'Women and Class Analysis: A Reply to the Replies'.

31. The exposition in Erikson's paper is somewhat different, but Erikson confirms (personal communication) that we do not here change the substance of his argument.

32. It should moreover be kept in mind that in comparing the mobility rates of men with those of a sample of women who have been allocated to class positions via the dominance approach, we will display greater differences than if we were to compare the mobility rates of men with those that would be obtained if the dominance approach were utilized, as it logically should be, with a sample of families or households. To illustrate the point, we may apply the dominance approach also to the men in our sample, and then compare our 'conventional' mobility table for men only with that produced by summing the tables obtained via the dominance approach for both women and men. When this is done, the differences shown up are clearly lower than those indicated in Table 7, with dissimilarity indices ranging only from 7 to 15.

33. What is intended by this observation appears to have been persistently misunderstood by feminist critics. The essential point being made is that because women still do not participate on equal terms with men in the labour market, women's employment (despite its expansion) continues to play only a relatively minor role as against men's in articulating family units with the class structure. It should be obvious that to maintain this is *not* to claim that women's employment—because of its irregular, part-time or otherwise 'secondary' or 'marginal' character— is unimportant either to the household or the national economy; nor is it to imply that women's employment has no effect on the shape of the class structure or the pattern of mobility opportunities within it. Giddens in fact, like other class analysts (see, for example, above, pp. 59–63) is concerned to stress the importance of precisely such effects in the recent past. And why this should then be supposed to reveal 'inconsistency' (cf. Shirley Dex, *The Sexual Division of Work*, Brighton: Wheatsheaf, 1985, pp. 164–5) is difficult to comprehend.

34. The finding that women's and men's relative mobility rates are essentially the same is in fact one that should be welcomed by feminists. For, as Dunton and Featherman point out, the implication is that 'men and women would achieve equally were it not for sociological features of the economy (e.g. discrimination)' and in turn that 'it is not the ways that females are reared—their values, attitudes, aspirations, or motivations in connection with career and marriage—or their biology that governs their mobility chances and socioeconomic achievements vis-à-vis their brothers and husbands', 'Social Mobility through Marriage and Careers', p. 317.

35. See Mary R. Jackman and Robert W. Jackman, *Class Awareness in the United States*, Berkeley: University of California Press, 1983; and Gudmund Hernes and Knud Knudsen, 'Gender and Class Identification in Norway', paper presented to the ISA Research Committee on Social Stratification and Mobility, Harvard University, September, 1985. In assessing the relation between husbands' and wives' 'objective' class positions and their class identification, the authors of both these studies are careful to control for education, and show that this has important consequences. Cf. also, Pamela Abbott and Roger Sapsford, 'Class Identification of Married Working Women', *British Journal of Sociology*, vol. xxxvii, 1986, and John L. Hammond, 'Wife's Status and Family Social Standing', *Sociological Perspectives*, vol. 30, 1987. The methods used in these studies for determining class identification are not unproblematic as regards either reliability or validity, but they remain to be improved upon. It should moreover be noted that where the attempt has been made to cite evidence in support of the view that wives' class orientations *are* more likely to reflect their own employment experience than their husbands' (see, for example, Stanworth, 'Women and Class Analysis', p. 162), the reference is to very small-scale and highly impressionistic studies, carried out in milieux whose representativeness is unknown and unexamined, and which have produced no publicly available data-sets. And labelling such studies 'qualitative' or 'ethnographic' does not of course mean that they can avoid exactly the same problems of the reliability and validity of data as arise in survey-based research.

36. So far as we can ascertain, none of those who have criticized the 1972 mobility inquiry for its concentration on men has ever shown willing to suggest and defend an alternative design for the study, which—with the fixed resources available—would have allowed women to be included. Attempts to obtain a response from critics on this point, whether through seminars or publications, have failed. The editor of *Sociology* explicitly censored the first sentence of this note in the earlier version of this chapter which appeared as a paper in that journal.

CHAPTER 11

Class Mobility in Britain in Comparative Perspective

In the last chapter, we sought to extend the scope of our analyses of class mobility by considering the implications of the mobility experience of women rather than focusing our attention, as previously, on that of men. In this chapter, we aim to widen the context of our investigations in another way. We view rates and patterns of class mobility in modern Britain in a comparative, cross-national perspective. In commenting on results earlier reported, we have expressed or implied judgements on whether mobility or fluidity within the British class structure might in certain respects be regarded as 'high' or 'low'; but such judgements were for the most part made either in relation to what sociologists would seem generally to have believed about mobility in advanced societies (as in chapter 2) or in relation to formal statistical standards, such as that of 'perfect mobility' (as in chapter 4). If, however, British society is to be characterized as being particularly mobile or immobile, open or closed—or as in any other way displaying patterns of special interest—then there can be little doubt that the most meaningful basis for such assessments is that of comparisons made between Britain and other nations.

It may be remarked that in so far as the topic of comparative social mobility has attracted the attention of social scientists apart from sociologists, or indeed has entered into more popular discussion, interest has centred on the possibility that variation in mobility rates *is* appreciable, and may therefore help in understanding other cross-national differences. Thus, to take two examples relating to the British case, it has become almost conventional among economic historians to suggest that part of the explanation of why this country was the home of the first industrial revolution lies in the relative openness of the form of pre-industrial society in Britain, in comparison, say, with that found in France or Germany; while, in turn, economists who have sought to account for Britain's latter-day decline have invoked the damaging effects on her economic performance of the persistence of 'traditional' and highly impermeable class divisions—which, it is presumed, Britain's competitors have in some way overcome.[1]

However, among sociologists, arguments of this kind have generally met with a good deal of scepticism, not least because of the weakness of their empirical basis. The tendency has rather been to favour, if only as conservative 'null hypotheses', arguments which would in fact go in the contrary direction: that is, ones proposing no significant differences, or at all events a large common element, in mobility rates and patterns among all national societies at a broadly similar developmental stage.

Thus, Lipset and Zetterberg, after analysing results produced by the 'first wave' of national mobility inquiries in the years following the second world war, were led to the conclusion that 'the overall pattern of social mobility appears to be much the same in the industrial societies of various Western countries'—

which, they noted, implied agreement with the impressions formed by virtually all previous investigators from Sorokin onwards.[2] Lipset and Zetterberg's work was of necessity based on crude categorizations and often unreliable data, and utilized only very limited statistical techniques. The cross-national analyses on which they chiefly relied amounted in fact to no more than comparisons of percentage rates of intergenerational outflow mobility as between just two broad occupational groupings, 'manual' and 'nonmanual'. Not surprisingly, therefore, as further and more sophisticated research has been undertaken, their findings have had to be very substantially qualified. What would now be widely accepted is that while overall mobility patterns within advanced societies might still be said to possess some 'family resemblance', far from negligible cross-national differences do arise, and indeed most obviously so in the case of absolute, percentage rates, whether these are viewed in outflow or inflow terms.[3] None the less, what has then further to be noted is that although for a time after the undermining of Lipset and Zetterberg's position the focus of research attention did shift to cross-national differences in mobility and their possible sources, the hypothesis which for the last decade or so has clearly been most influential in the field is again one which places the emphasis on cross-national similarity rather than variation: that is, the hypothesis advanced in 1975 by Featherman, Jones, and Hauser—explicitly as a reformulation of that of Lipset and Zetterberg.[4]

The central claim made by Featherman, Jones, and Hauser is that a basic cross-national similarity will be found, in all societies with market economies and nuclear family systems, *not* in absolute mobility rates, as Lipset and Zetterber sought to show, but rather in *relative* rates or, as we would wish to say, *in patterns of social fluidity*. Absolute rates, it is argued, display mobility at the 'phenotypical' level, at which it will be influenced by a range of structural and other 'exogenous' effects which can indeed be expected to vary in consequence of particular features of the economic, demographic, and political histories of individual nations. But relative rates, referring as they do to mobility considered *net of* such effects, can be taken as displaying mobility at the 'genotypical' level, at which factors 'endogenous' to the prevailing form of stratification will dominate and at which therefore a generic pattern of mobility may be expected to reveal itself.

It is not the purpose of this chapter to add further to the already extensive literature which is concerned with the evaluation of the 'FJH hypothesis'.[5] In this respect, the two points which it is most relevant to make are the following: first, that if taken in its strictest form, as claiming a complete uniformity in cross-national patterns of social fluidity, the hypothesis is not sustainable; but secondly, that it can find far more support if understood in a sense which, though less strict, is still informative. That is, as claiming that fluidity patterns display a very large commonality, across a wide range of industrial and industrializing societies —rather than, say, falling into a series of distinctive *types* which might be differentiated by reference to levels of economic development, political systems, etc.[6] Taken in this latter form, the FJH hypothesis can therefore provide us with a valuable starting point as we attempt to situate what we have already learnt about class mobility in modern Britain within a comparative context.

DATA

Until quite recently, comparative analyses of social mobility were based upon compilations of the already published results of national inquiries. In proceeding thus, major difficulties were encountered in that such inquiries differed, and sometimes quite widely so, not only in their general objectives, design, and quality but, more specifically, in the class or other categories by reference to which their authors sought to define and measure mobility. The data at the analysts' disposal were therefore usually not of an immediately comparable kind, and moreover only quite limited possibilities existed of making any improvement in this respect. Thus, as regards the differing social categorizations used in national inquiries, little could be done other than to 'collapse' these until some cross-nationally common set emerged—which usually turned out to be the simple manual/nonmanual occupational division adopted by Lipset and Zetterberg or, at best, a threefold categorization of manual/nonmanual/farm. Furthermore, the comparability that was in this way achieved was still no more than nominal; and since it can be shown that the manual/nonmanual division is itself one that has been interpreted in substantially different ways from inquiry to inquiry, it would seem clear that much real non-comparability persisted. Indeed, one could say that cross-national mobility data constituted in the way in question are likely to display variation *resulting simply from non-comparability* that is of a similar magnitude to any genuine differences that one might reasonably expect to discover. It is thus difficult to see how the results of studies based on such data can be given any great credence, and it is in no way surprising to find that they are in fact of a confused and often contradictory nature.[7]

However, a major advance in comparative mobility research may be claimed with the development, from the later 1970s, of new methods of assembling cross-national data-sets; that is, through the secondary analysis of the data of the original inquiries taken in their unit-record form. Following such procedures, investigators have far better possibilities of being able to standardize national results in terms of their population coverage etc., and can moreover obtain far greater comparability—and flexibility—in categorization. It is open to them, within limits set only by the basic coding of the original data, first to devise categories that appear appropriate to their own research interests and then to recode to these categories the data of the national studies which they wish to bring together.

The comparative data on which we draw in this chapter derive from an extensive recoding exercise of the kind indicated, which has been carried out under the auspices of the CASMIN (Comparative Analysis of Social Mobility in Industrial Nations) project at the University of Mannheim.[8] As a result of this exercise, data from a number of national mobility inquiries undertaken in the early and middle 1970s have been brought into a comparable form, with the basic categorization being a version of the class schema used in the present study. As can be seen from Table 11.1, the schema is again a sevenfold one, but differs from the original in the following respects. On the one hand, Classes I and II, and V and VI are combined, because of difficulties in making the divisions between them in a cross-nationally consistent way; but, on the other hand, it is

Table 11.1

Version of the class schema as used for cross-national mobility analyses within the CASMIN project

Classes I and II	'service class'–all professionals, administrators and managers (including large proprietors), higher-grade technicians and supervisors of nonmanual workers
Class III	'routine nonmanual'–routine nonmanual employees in administration and commerce, sales personnel and other rank-and-file service workers
Class IVab	'petty bourgeoisie'–small proprietors, self-employed artisans and other 'own account' workers with and without employees (other than in primary production)[a]
Class IVc	'farmers'–farmers, smallholders and other self-employed workers in primary production
Classes V and VI	'skilled workers'–lower-grade technicians, supervisors of manual workers and skilled manual workers
Class VIIa	'non-skilled workers'–semi- and unskilled workers (other than in primary production
Class VIIb	'farm workers'–agricultural and other workers in primary production

Note: (a) Where possible, those with and without employees are differentiated as IVa and IVb respectively.

possible, and for comparative purposes highly desirable, to separate out within Classes IV and VII their agricultural components–that is, to distinguish a class of farmers, Class IVc and a class of agricultural workers, Class VIIb.

So far within the CASMIN project, mobility data have been recoded to what would appear to be a generally acceptable standard of comparability for nine nations: England and Wales (data from the 1972 inquiry), France, the Federal Republic of Germany, Hungary, the Republic of Ireland, Northern Ireland, Poland, Scotland, and Sweden. In addition, data have been recoded with somewhat less satisfactory results for Australia and the USA. In what follows, we shall for the most part confine our attention to the above-mentioned nine nations. In each case, the data utilized will refer to the intergenerational class mobility of men, aged 20–64, with class of origin being indicated by the class of the respondent's father (or other 'head of household') at the time of the respondent's early adolescence.

RELATIVE RATES OR THE PATTERN OF SOCIAL FLUIDITY

We begin by asking how Britain compares with other nations in its relative rates of class mobility or, in other words, in its pattern of social fluidity. This entails the more specific issue of how 'open' is British society–in the sense of how equal are chances of access to different class destinations for individuals of differing class origins. Such questions are of course ones to which the FJH hypothesis is directly relevant, and to the extent that this hypothesis holds good, then, as we have already implied, the answers that we would expect to obtain would have a clearly different emphasis from those suggested in much previous speculation; that is to say, they would point far more to the similarities that prevail between Britain and other nations than to any kind of British distinctiveness.

It is a virtue of the FJH hypothesis that, in its strict form at least, it is capable of being modelled in a rather precise manner. This may in fact be done through the same multiplicative model of constant or common social fluidity which we have previously used in testing hypotheses about the similarity of fluidity patterns over time (that is, as between birth cohorts or successive inquiries) in chapters 3 and 9 or as between the sexes in chapter 10. In order to represent the FJH hypothesis, the model is simply taken as proposing that fluidity patterns will be the same *across nations* or, in other words, that all corresponding odds ratios implicit in comparable national mobility tables will have the same value.[9]

For our present purposes, then, it is of interest first of all to see how well the model fits when we apply it to the mobility table resulting from our 1972 inquiry *taken in turn* with each of the tables for the other eight nations for which we have data of a good standard of comparability. The results obtained from this exercise are shown in Table 11.2.

As a preliminary point, we may note the satisfactory fit that is given by the model of common social fluidity when our 1972 table for England and Wales is compared with that resulting from the Scottish inquiry. This means that for us to take our own data as a basis for talking about Britain as a whole—as we have in fact tended generally to do—is unlikely to be misleading so far at least as patterns of fluidity are concerned. Moreover, the good fit that is also achieved when our 1972 table is compared with that for Northern Ireland would suggest that essentially the same pattern of social fluidity does in fact prevail throughout the United Kingdom.

When we turn to the comparisons made with other nations, we find that our model does not fit in an entirely acceptable way, in that the p-values returned point to real differences between what we may regard as the British pattern and social fluidity elsewhere. And while the standardized χ^2s confirm that it is Scotland and Northern Ireland—together with France—that have relative mobility rates most similar to those found in England and Wales, they also indicate that the poorer fits of the 'common social fluidity' model when other nations are involved are not simply the result of larger sample sizes. However, we must at the same time take account of the further indications given in the last two columns of Table 11.2 that the differences in question here, although real, are in all instances rather small. In each comparison, the 'common social fluidity' model accounts for more than 96 per cent of the association between class of origin and class of destination, and misclassifies less than 3 per cent of all individual cases. In this way, then, the significance of the FJH hypothesis is brought out, even if, taken in its strict sense, the evidence presented would not uphold it. It is difficult to avoid the conclusion that the degree of similarity in patterns of fluidity suggested by the data of Table 11.2 is far more impressive than the extent of any differences that are revealed.[10]

Table 11.2
Results of testing the 'common social fluidity' model against data in inter-generational class mobility for men in England and Wales (N = 9,434) and for men in eight other nations (pairwise comparisons)

Nation compared (N)	χ^2	p^a	standardized $\chi^{2\,b}$	% of association accounted for	% of association misclassified
FRA (18,671)	84.3	0.00	75.1	99.2	1.5
FRG (3,890)	120.9	0.00	224.6	96.5	2.6
HUN (12,005)	160.6	0.00	151.7	96.9	2.6
IRL (1,991)	59.3	0.01	171.2	98.2	1.6
NIR (2,068)	36.2	0.46	99.5	98.9	1.4
POL (32,109)	327.5	0.00	217.0	97.5	2.0
SCO (4,583)	42.7	0.20	70.9	98.8	1.7
SWE (2,097)	74.3	0.00	202.5	97.2	1.8

Notes: (a) df = 36.
(b) i.e. χ^2 returned when each national sample is scaled up or down to an N of 10,000.

What might still be argued is that, even if it is accepted that the range of cross-national variation in social fluidity is not very large, it remains unclear where, within such variation as does occur, British society is located. It is still possible, in other words, that Britain is in some sense an 'outlier'. That this is not in fact the case can, however, be demonstrated with some assurance. In preliminary work within the CASMIN project, the following analysis was undertaken. Working with national sample sizes scaled in each case up or down to 10,000, we fitted the 'common social fluidity' model *to each possible pair* of our nine tables rather than, as described above, to just the eight pairs involving England and Wales. The 36 (= 9 X 8/2) χ^2s that resulted from these fits could thus be treated as indicating the degree of difference between each pair of nations in their social fluidity patterns or, one might say, the 'distance' separating them within the total 'space' into which cross-national variation in fluidity extends. And, in turn, the set of 36 χ^2s could from this point of view be treated as input to a multi-dimensional scaling exercise aimed at 'recovering' the space in question. Such an exercise produced the solution—a three-dimensional one—that is shown in Figure 11.1

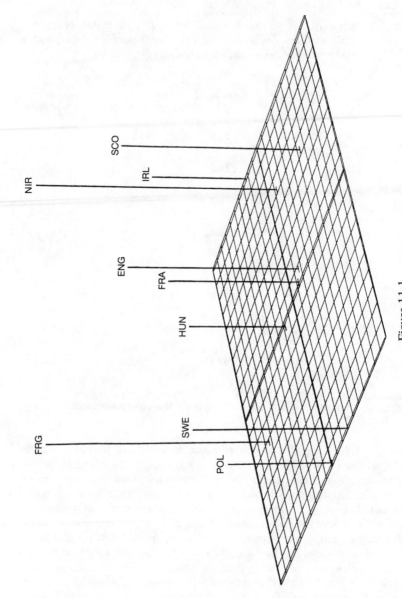

Figure 11.1

*Three-dimensional (ALSCAL) solution for distances between national patterns of social fluidity:
nine nations. Kruskal's stress formula 1 = 0.66*

As can be seen, England and Wales, together with France, turn out to be the most central nations within the configuration that emerges. Scotland and Northern Ireland, along with Hungary, fall into an intermediate band, and it is Poland, Sweden, the FRG, and the Irish Republic which, in that order, represent the most outlying cases. It is not necessary to try to interpret the dimensions of the plot of Figure 11.1—indeed, it may well be that no useful interpretation is possible. But this does not affect the finding that it is England and Wales and France which tend over all to be 'closer' in their patterns of social fluidity to the other nations represented than are the latter to each other.[11] In order to give some test of the robustness of this result, the entire analysis was repeated but with the inclusion of Australia and the USA, despite the problems of comparability that arise with the data for these countries. As shown in Figure 11.2, little change is in fact produced and, if anything, the centrality of England and Wales and France becomes still more apparent as Hungary moves further from the centre of the plot, while the USA falls into the intermediate band and Australia joins the ring of outliers.[12]

The main conclusion to be drawn would seem, then, clear enough. Not only is there a large cross-nationally common element in patterns of social fluidity among the nations for which we have comparative data—as the FJH hypothesis would lead us to expect; but further, in so far as cross-national variation does occur, it is clearly *not* the British case that can best illustrate it. On the contrary, if British social fluidity has any claim to distinctiveness at all, it would seem to be in the degree to which it reproduces the common pattern with only very minor deviation.

ABSOLUTE RATES

Since relative rates of class mobility in modern Britain prove to be so unexceptional, it must follow that if any distinctive features are to be found in absolute rates, they will be the result primarily of distinctive structural effects: that is to say, of effects stemming from the shape of the British class structure and from its pattern of change as these are mediated through the marginal distributions of the mobility table. It would therefore seem an appropriate first step here to consider how the distributions of class origins and destinations in our table for England and Wales—and also in that for Scotland—compare with these distributions in other national tables. This can be done by reference to Table 11.3.

From this table, certain rather well-defined 'British' features can in fact be discerned, and ones which it is not difficult to relate to the particular course followed by British economic history—most obviously to early industrialization and, one might add, to the early abandonment of agricultural protectionism. Thus, from the first panel of the table, in which origin distributions are presented, it can be seen that while men in the two British samples are clearly less likely than those in other national samples to have fathers in Class IVc—that is, to be of farm origins—they are far more likely to have fathers in Classes V+VI or VIIa or, that is, to be of 'blue-collar' origins. In the destination distributions given in the second panel of the table, the small size of the class of farmers in Britain and the relatively large size of the blue-collar classes again show up— although other nations, such as the FRG and Sweden, have achieved contemporary class

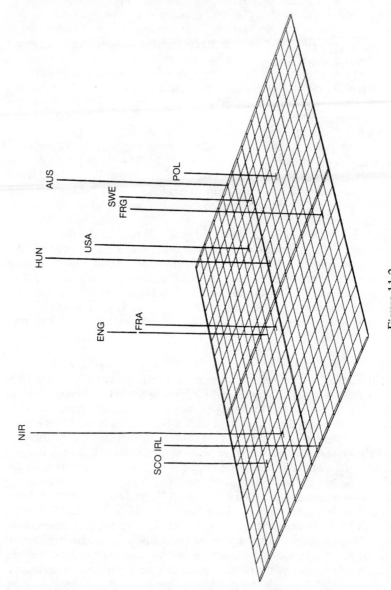

Figure 11.2

Three-dimensional (ALSCAL) solution for distances between national patterns of social fluidity: eleven nations. Kruskal's stress formula 1 = 0.074

Table 11.3
Distribution of class origins and class destinations of men, aged 20-64, in England and Wales and Scotland and in seven other nations (surveys conducted early and mid-1970s)

Class	ENG	SCO	FRA	FRG	HUN	IRL	NIR	POL	SWE
			Class of origin, percent by column[a]						
1+II	13	10	11	14	6	6	9	8	11
III	7	7	9	6	7	5	7	2	3
IVab	10	7	14	11	7	10	9	3	11
IVc	5	5	26	13	27	39	23	53	26
V+VI	39	39	19	37	14	14	21	18	24
VIIa	23	26	15	15	19	20	26	12	20
VIIb	4	5	7	3	22	7	6	4	5
			Class of destination, percent by column						
I+II	26	21	20	28	15	14	18	18	24
III	9	9	10	5	7	9	9	2	8
IVab	8	6	9	7	2	8	10	2	8
IVc	2	3	11	4	1	22	10	25	5
V+VI	33	33	24	37	31	20	26	31	30
VIIa	22	25	21	18	30	21	24	19	22
VIIb	2	3	3	1	14	7	3	3	2
Δ orig./ dest.	13	13	23	17	37	18	17	30	27

Note: (a) So as not to exaggerate the degree of precision involved, in this and all other presentations of comparative data, percentages are rounded to the nearest whole number.

structures of a not very dissimilar kind. Where, however, England and Wales and Scotland are further distinctive is in being the only nations in which, by the early 1970s, fewer men were found in Classes V+VII and VIIa than had fathers in these classes. That is to say, having been the first industrial nations, they would seem also to be among the first in which the structural decline of the working class, as a characteristic of advanced industrialism, comes to play a part in the forming of class mobility patterns. Finally, it should be noted from Table 11.3 that England and Wales and Scotland are also the nations in which, over all, origin and destination distributions differ least. This can again be attributed largely to the early decline of agriculture in Britain—clearly antedating the period to which our data refer—since the greater differences in the other nations can be seen to derive for the most part from the exodus out of farming between the generations of fathers and sons.

How, then, do these distinctive features apparent in the development of the British class structure affect class mobility patterns? In Table 11.4 we show total mobility rates for our nine nations—that is, the percentage of cases found in each national mobility table in cells off the main diagonal, indicating that respondents held a different class position to that of their fathers. Since we have found no marked cross-national variations in social fluidity, it might have been expected that the small differences between origin and destination distributions in the tables for England and Wales and for Scotland would imply that in these nations total mobility rates would be low—for class structural change can have only a rather weak effect in promoting mobility. But, as can be seen, the rates for England and Wales and Scotland fall in fact in the middle of the range that is represented. The further factor that is at work here is that of differences between nations in the sizes of classes with differing propensities to generate mobility or immobility.

Table 11.4
Total mobility rates for England and Wales and Scotland and for seven other nations

Nation	Total mobility rate percent
HUN	76
SWE	73
FRA	65
ENG	64
SCO	64
NIR	63
FRG	62
POL	60
IRL	58

From the analyses reported in chapter 4, we saw that the propensity to generate immobility is notably strong within Class IV, and a series of further studies may be cited which confirm this finding and which moreover show that this propensity is still higher among the agricultural component of Class IV, that is, the class of farmers, than it is among the urban petty bourgeoisie.[13] Since, then, as we noted above, the small differences between origin and destination distributions within our two British samples is associated with the small numbers found in farming and—already in the father's generation—two essentially opposing effects can be said to operate on the total mobility rates that these samples reveal. On the one hand, the lack of any strong 'shift', or 'discrepancy', effect between generations tends to depress mobility; but, on the other hand, the 'compositional' effect of a small class of farmers tends to increase it. Hence, it is not in the end all that surprising that in the rank-order of Table 11.4 the positions held by England and Wales and Scotland should prove to be intermediate ones. Hungary and Sweden, for example, can be seen as ranking above them at the head of the table largely because of the strength of intergenerational shift effects, while Poland and Ireland rank below them at the foot of the table largely because of the compositional effect of a still sizeable class of farmers.

Turning next to inflow rates, we obtain results of a more straightforward kind. In this case, the distinctiveness of the origins distributions of the men in our two British samples is rather directly reflected in mobility patterns. Inspection of the nine national inflow tables that we can draw up reveals that those for England and Wales and Scotland are clearly differentiated from the rest in tending to show, for all classes alike, a higher recruitment of men of blue-collar origins and a lower recruitment of men of farm origins. Rather than reproducing all nine tables in full, we show here in Table 11.5 selected features of inflow patterns where British distinctiveness is most marked and also, one could argue, of greatest sociological significance.

In the first panel of the table we seek to bring out differences in recruitment to the service classes of our nine nations. We have earlier noted, in chapter 2 and again in chapter 9, the extent to which in modern Britain members of the expanding service class have been drawn from among men of working-class, or at all events of blue-collar origins. Table 11.5 would now suggest that in this respect the British pattern should be regarded as standing towards one extreme of the range of cross-national variation. It is not the case that the service class in

Table 11.5

Comparative inflow rates: percentage in selected classes from different class origins

percentage in Classes I+II originating in Classes

V+VI and VIIa		IVc and VIIb	
SCO	49	POL	34
ENG	45	HUN	25
FRG	41	IRL	23
SWE	40	SWE	17
NIR	36	NIR	14
POL	35	FRA	10
HUN	32	FRG	8
FRA	28	ENG	4
IRL	28	SCO	4

percentage in Classes V+VI and VIIa originating in Classes

V+VI and VIIa		IVc and VIIb	
SCO	78	HUN	46
ENG	74	POL	46
FRG	65	SWE	32
NIR	64	FRA	29
IRL	57	IRL	27
SWE	51	NIR	20
FRA	47	FRG	16
POL	42	ENG	7
HUN	39	SCO	7

Britain is characterized by unusually low self-recruitment, nor indeed that it is unusually open to 'recruitment from below': rather, British distinctiveness lies in *where such recruitment comes from*. Within the British pattern, as can be seen, the counterpart of the fact that almost half of all service-class members are the sons of blue-collar workers is that less than one in twenty is the son of a farmer or farm worker. And it is thus that Britain is brought into sharp contrast not only with nations such as Hungary, the Republic of Ireland, or Poland, where recruitment from these two sources is far more equally matched, but also with Sweden, where in the early 1970s more than one in six of all service class members came from off the land, or with France where still well under one in three was of blue-collar origins.

In Britain, several decades elapsed between the period of rapid decline of the agricultural sector and the start of the great expansion of white-collar employment and hence of the service class; and these decades—say from the 1890s through to the 1930s—saw the consolidation of the industrial working class. In nations that industrialized later, the rhythm of structural change was clearly different: the period of expansion of the service class followed much harder upon, or indeed often largely overlapped with, that of rapid agricultural decline. In this way, then, substantial differences between the British pattern of intergenerational recruitment to the service class and that of other nations were assured, independently of whether or not any variation might occur at the level of relative mobility chances.

In the second panel of Table 11.5, we show differences in the intergenerational composition of our blue-collar classes. In this case, the nature of the origins distribution of men in the two British samples is, as would be expected, most significantly reflected in an unusually high level of *self*-recruitment. As well as earlier commenting on the degree to which the service class in modern Britain has been recruited from the working class, we have further emphasized the predominant extent to which the working class itself is 'second generation'—at least—in its composition. The cross-national distinctiveness of this feature also is now made apparent. By the early 1970s, and still, as was seen in chapter 9, in the early 1980s, around three-quarters of all men in blue-collar positions in British society had fathers who had themselves been in similar work—a clearly higher proportion than that found in any of the other nations for which we have comparable data. The main offsetting tendency, as Table 11.5 also shows, is for a sizeable component of the blue-collar work-force in other nations—approaching a third even in such advanced societies as France and Sweden—to be still 'first-generation' or 'green' labour, drawn in from the agricultural sector.

As this latter source of labour supply steadily diminishes, one would of course expect blue-collar recruitment elsewhere to move generally closer to the British pattern. But in societies where the growth of the service class has been largely coincident with the decline of agriculture, it is unlikely that working classes will ever attain *both* the relative size *and* the degree of self-recruitment that have characterized the British working class over the middle decades of the present century. That is to say, the working classes of later industrializing nations will tend to have a large first-generation component still at the time when their growth reaches its limit; and although self-recruitment may from then on increase, it will be within a class that is slowly declining in size as white-collar employment expands and is also recruiting more—unless relative rates change—from among men of white-collar origins. In short, it may well be that the pattern of blue-collar recruitment that we have found in England and Wales and in Scotland is, and will remain, uniquely that of the first industrial nations.

Finally in this section we must consider outflow rates of class mobility. We earlier noted that our mobility tables for England and Wales and for Scotland were less distinctive in their destination than in their origin distributions; and taking this observation together with our finding of a quite unexceptional British pattern of social fluidity, we have little reason to anticipate anything very unusual in the outflow patterns displayed by our two British samples. Inspection of mobility tables expressed in outflow terms does indeed confirm that among the nine nations for which we have comparable data, the rates observed for England and Wales and Scotland are rarely conspicuous. To illustrate the point, we again present, in Table 11.6, a selection of rates of particular interest.

From this table, it can be seen, first of all, that the cross-national differences shown up are much less marked than those revealed by the inflow rates presented in Table 11.5; and secondly, that within this more limited range of variation, England and Wales and Scotland occupy generally intermediate positions. The

Table 11.6

Comparative outflow rates: percentage of those of selected class origins found in different classes

percentage of those of Class I+II origins in Classes

I+II		V+VI and VIIa	
POL	67	HUN	34
FRG	61	FRG	26
FRA	60	POL	25
ENG	59	SWE	25
SCO	59	NIR	24
NIR	57	ENG	22
SWE	56	SCO	22
IRL	55	FRA	21
HUN	52	IRL	21

percentage of those of class V+VI and VIIa categories in Classes

I+II		V+VI and VIIa	
FRG	22	HUN	73
SWE	22	POL	71
POL	21	FRG	69
ENG	18	SCO	69
FRA	17	IRL	68
HUN	16	NIR	68
SCO	16	ENG	66
NIR	14	FRA	63
IRL	11	SWE	61

structural features that are of chief relevance to such variation as does occur in the rates reported are the relative sizes, and intergenerational shifts in the sizes, of service classes and blue-collar classes; and, as may be ascertained by reference back to Table 11.3, in neither of these respects does the British case seem likely to show particularly strong effects. It might be thought that the presence of relatively large blue-collar classes would favour a high rate of intergenerational stability within these classes. But against this must be set the fact earlier noted that our samples for England and Wales and for Scotland comprise more blue-collar fathers than sons; and, as can be seen from Table 11.6, the highest levels of blue-collar stability are in fact to be found in Hungary and Poland, where the intergenerational *increase* in blue-collar workers is greatest.

Over all, then, we must conclude that the distinctive features that can be identified in the historical development of the British class structure are reflected in absolute rates of class mobility only in a number of rather specific ways. They do not result in the total mobility rate in Britain being exceptionally high or low, at least in the light of the cross-national comparisons that we are able to make, nor do they appear to produce any very unusual pattern of outflow rates. Their effects tend rather to be concentrated on the pattern of inflow rates or, in other words, on processes of intergenerational class recruitment. Britain's early industrialization and the unique path that it followed can be rather clearly associated, first, with a service class recruited to an unusual degree from among the sons of blue-collar workers and, secondly, with a broadly defined industrial working class which is to an unusual degree self-recruited or which, one could alternatively say, is highly homogeneous in its composition in terms of its members' social origins. If, therefore, any attempt is to be made to take distinctive patterns of class mobility as explanatory variables in relation to other aspects of modern British society, it is on these particular processes of class recruitment that attention must centre, and not on supposed 'peculiarities' of the British case which refer to rates and patterns of mobility in any more general terms.

'COUNTERFACTUAL' COMPARISONS

In the preceding sections of this chapter the significance of the comparative analyses that we have reported has tended for the most part to be of a negative kind: we have been able to show that much speculation that has gone on concerning supposedly distinctive features of class mobility or immobility in modern Britain is without secure foundation. However, it should be recognized that comparative analyses can also be of value in *stimulating* speculation—while at the same time providing a context within which it may be undertaken with some degree of discipline. Results such as those we have reported on the range of variation in relative and in absolute mobility rates within modern societies serve, on the one hand, to suggest the limits of 'historical possibility' but, on the other, to prompt questions about how mobility in Britain might conceivably be different to what it is. Thus, in the light of these results, we might be led to ask questions such as the following: What would British mobility rates look like if the British class structure had developed on different lines so that it was similar to, say, the French? Or again, what would these rates be like if the British pattern of social fluidity were to change so as to become the same as, say, the Swedish?

Posing, and attempting to answer, questions which depend in this way upon the statement of 'counterfactual' conditions is a procedure notorious for its dangers and difficulties. Most serious, perhaps, is what has become known as the problem of the *ceteris paribus* assumption. If, in the kind of 'thought experiment' that counterfactual analysis implies, one introduces some change in X, so as to be able to consider the effect of this change on Y, one will usually wish further to suppose that 'all other things are equal' or, in other words, are 'held constant'. However, it is not always apparent that it is reasonable to make such a supposition. For if X is taken to be different to what it is, then other things—apart from Y— that are in some way causally connected to X should perhaps be regarded as different also; and it may well be that not all the connections that are involved are known or even knowable. Hence, counterfactual analysis often appears as an impossible 'bootstrap' operation—calling for precisely the kind of theoretical insight that it aims to provide. In the face of this problem, the position that we would here adopt is a pragmatic one. While recognizing that arguments which start from counterfactual conditions must always *be* speculative ones in some degree, we would regard them as still worth taking up to the extent that the feature of social reality in which change is envisaged meets certain criteria; namely, that it is relatively well-defined and delimited and that it appears *not* to be of a highly 'context-dependent' kind. For in so far as these criteria can be met, the making of a *ceteris paribus* assumption would seem still possible without an undue loss of realism being thereby entailed.[14]

If, from this point of view, one considers the two 'counterfactual' questions that were earlier suggested by way of illustration, it is then clearly the *second* that emerges as the more promising type to pursue. To ask what class mobility in Britain would be like if the British class structure had developed in the same way as that of some other nation would require in effect the rethinking of some two centuries of economic and social history, and the problem of what should or should not be seen as changing along with the class structure would be quite unmanageable. However, to ask what class mobility in Britain would be like if the development of the class structure is taken as given, but we suppose that Britain displays the pattern of social fluidity of some other nation, appears rather more meaningful. For although we cannot know for certain that the pattern of fluidity of one nation could coexist with the class structure of another without some mutual modification, we do know that very similar patterns can and widely *do* occur in conjunction with very different structures, and moreover that fluidity patterns typically persist over time as class structures change. Thus, we would feel that in this case we are able to introduce a *ceteris paribus* clause into our analysis without placing too great a strain on either our imagination or our credulity.

In what follows, we show the results that are obtained if we take the marginal distributions of our mobility table for England and Wales for 1972 and, so to speak, 'build into' these distributions the patterns of social fluidity—defined, as always, by odds ratios—of three other western nations. These are the FRG, the Republic of Ireland, and Sweden, each of which, it may be recalled, emerged from our multidimensional scaling analysis as a relative outlier within the 'space' into which cross-national variation in fluidity extends. The method by which we produce our counterfactual mobility tables is well known and straightforward: namely, that of 'simultaneous proportional adjustments', as described, for example, by Mosteller.[15] To produce, say, the table which would embody the German pattern of social fluidity within the distributions of class origins and destinations for England and Wales, we begin with the German mobility table and then, through our method of adjustment, we transform it to one which has identical marginals to that for England and Wales *but which preserves all the odds ratios of the German original.* In Table 11.7 we draw on counterfactual tables thus generated in order to provide comparisons of outflow mobility rates. For each class of origin, we show, first, the actually observed rates for England and Wales, and then these rates as they would have appeared if—and all other things being equal—the German, the Irish, and the Swedish patterns of fluidity respectively had been in operation.

From Table 11.7 we may note to begin with that the differences revealed within each cell, whether between the actual rate and the counterfactual ones or among the latter, tend not to be all that large, and that the actual rate usually holds an intermediate position. Here then we are rediscovering our earlier findings that patterns of social fluidity show a large measure of cross-national similarity and that within the range of variation that is apparent the British pattern is rather central. What our counterfactual analyses can now further provide is some better indication of the orders of magnitude involved. We can, for example, say that if we envisage fluidity patterns in British society being reshaped so as to correspond to those of some of the more 'deviant' western nations, this would not often produce differences in outflow distributions of more than 10 per cent. As the dissimilarity indices show, such shifts occur in only five out of the total of 21 comparisons presented in the table, with four of the five, it may be noted, relating to outflows from agricultural classes where comparability could most easily be questioned. Again, we may observe that the changes brought about in particular outflow rates are rarely greater than five percentage points. There are only four changes of this magnitude produced by the German fluidity pattern, eight by the Irish, and five by the Swedish. What then is clearly suggested is that modifications to British fluidity patterns, made within the range of currently observable possibilities, would scarcely revolutionize absolute class mobility rates.

However, to say this is not to claim that the differences shown up in Table 11.7 are in all respects of negligible significance. Each of the three counter-factual comparisons presented does display some features that are worthy of further attention. For example, it is when we envisage the German fluidity pattern at work that we find three of the five shifts in outflow distributions of 10 per cent or more, yet we may at the same time note that these shifts are not associated with any great change in the level of mobility over all. As recorded in Table 11.4, the actual total mobility rate for England and Wales is 64 per cent, and when the German fluidity pattern is introduced, this rate can be recalculated at 63 per cent. In other words, we are here reminded that differences in fluidity are not necessarily ones simply of 'more' or 'less'; patterns can and do vary in other ways.

Thus, perhaps the most interesting and quantitatively the most important of

Table 11.7

Class distribution of respondents by class of father, observed rates for England and Wales compared with rates which would have resulted under the fluidity patterns prevailing in the FRG, Ireland, and Sweden

Father's class	Fluidity pattern	Respondent's class							
		I+II	III	IVab	IVc	V+VI	VIIa	VIIb	Δ
		percentage by row							
	Observed	59	12	6	1	15	7	0	
I+II	FRG	55	12	9	–	16	8	1	5
(N=1,242)	IRL	65	10	6	1	11	7	0	6
	SWE	51	14	6	0	18	9	1	9
	Observed	34	13	7	0	28	16	1	
III	FRG	37	12	9	0	28	13	1	5
(N=694)	IRL	32	19	7	1	26	15	–	7
	SWE	35	15	9	0	23	16	2	6
	Observed	28	9	21	1	25	16	1	
IVab	FRG	23	15	26	1	20	15	0	11
(N=902)	IRL	29	10	27	1	16	17	1	8
	SWE	27	6	17	2	28	19	1	7
	Observed	16	6	7	23	20	19	9	
IVc	FRG	12	7	6	27	19	27	1	14
(N=427)	IRL	18	6	11	22	13	20	8	9
	SWE	11	9	7	15	25	28	5	17
	Observed	20	9	7	0	41	23	1	
V+VI	FRG	24	9	6	–	41	19	1	4
(N=3,676)	IRL	19	8	4	–	48	21	–	7
	SWE	22	9	6	1	39	22	1	3
	Observed	15	9	6	0	37	32	1	
VIIa	FRG	12	5	3	–	38	39	2	10
(N=2,150)	IRL	12	9	6	1	35	34	3	5
	SWE	17	7	8	1	38	27	1	7
	Observed	8	5	7	3	28	33	16	
VIIb	FRG	9	8	4	1	29	35	14	7
(N=343)	IRL	6	7	13	3	19	39	12	15
	SWE	12	3	5	3	30	40	8	12

the shifts that would be implied under German fluidity would be a greater inequality of mobility chances as between the two blue-collar classes that we distinguish. As can be seen from Table 11.7, while an increase would occur in upward mobility into Classes I+II from Classes V+VI, mobility from Class VIIa into Classes I+II—and likewise into Classes III and IVab—would decrease, and this would be largely offset by greater intergenerational immobility. What is here reflected is in fact a distinctive, and by now quite widely discussed, feature of German social stratification: that is, the division created among the ranks of industrial workers by the national system of vocational education and training—which, one may observe, has of late attracted a number of British admirers. In the FRG chances of access to skilled manual work, and also chances of promotion from manual work to supervisory or managerial positions, have been shown to have an especially close connection with the possession of a formal apprenticeship, secured directly after the completion of full-time education. And, in turn, differences in qualifications and skill level would then appear to map more closely than elsewhere onto lines of sociocultural differentiation within the working class and, in particular, to set nonskilled workers and their families more sharply apart from other classes in their life-styles and life-chances alike.[16]

If, however, we envisage either the Irish or the Swedish fluidity pattern as operating in a British context, the changes implied in outflow distributions, while somewhat slighter than those produced by the German pattern, do appear as ones more readily interpreted in terms of greater or less mobility over all. Under Irish fluidity, four of the eight instances of shifts of more than five percentage points occur in cells on the main diagonal, and in each case *less* intergenerational mobility is indicated—that is, for men of Class I+II, III, IVab, and V+VI origins; while under Swedish fluidity, three of the five instances of shifts of this magnitude are found on the diagonal, and in each case *more* mobility is indicated—that is, for men of Class I+II, IVc, and VIIb origins. It is therefore not surprising to find that the actual total mobility rate for England and Wales of 64 per cent would fall under the Irish pattern to 60 per cent but would rise under the Swedish pattern to 68 per cent.

The main significance of the contrast here revealed is, we would suggest, that it offers some indication of the extent to which, within western societies, the level of social fluidity may be influenced via *political intervention*. We can, on the one hand, take the Swedish case as representing that in which social-democratic 'hegemony' has been most successfully established within a capitalist society, and in which greater equality of condition and greater equality of opportunity have been most strongly pursued as complementary goals; while, on the other hand, we can take the Irish case as being distinctive as one in which social-democratic politics have never been of more than marginal significance, and indeed in which the pursuit of equality has rarely been a serious concern of public policy. From various available comparative indicators, it is apparent that class-linked inequalities in living standards are generally less marked in Sweden than in Ireland,[17] and from our own data it can further be seen that Sweden has a clearly more open class structure. Thus, while other factors may well be involved, the comparison of these two nations would appear to give good *prima facie* grounds at least for supposing that in so far as cross-national variation in social fluidity does occur, politics can play a part in the form that this variation takes.[18] However, even if this is accepted, there is one further question that may still be raised: namely, that of whether what can apparently be achieved by political intervention in creating greater fluidity testifies to the efficacy of social-democratic politics or, rather, to the resistive power of capitalist class structures.

On first consideration, it might not indeed sound all that impressive to say that if the British pattern of fluidity were modified so that it came to correspond with the more open Swedish one, then—all other things being equal—four per cent more men would appear as intergenerationally mobile within the context of our class schema; or, conversely, that if the Irish pattern were to prevail, four per cent more would appear as immobile. The substantive significance of such differences, whatever their statistical interest, could be thought rather slight. However, there are two further points that must here be made. The first is fairly obvious: that within the context of a national population even quite small percentage movements of the kind in question translate into tens of thousands of individual lives. And thus, for those at least who are committed to the idea of creating a more open society—in the sense of steadily diminishing the association between class origins and class destinations—shifts in the level of fluidity which have such an impact can hardly be a matter of indifference. Secondly, it is in any event important not to underestimate the magnitude of such shifts by judging them against an inappropriate standard. It needs be recognized that even if one were to suppose the limiting case of 'perfect mobility', where class of origin and class of destination are entirely independent of each other, it would not of course follow from this that the total mobility rate would be 100 per cent—only that this rate would be determined *solely* by the distribution of class origins and destinations. Taking these distributions for our 1972 mobility table for England and Wales, the total mobility rate under perfect fluidity works out in fact at 77 per cent. And if *this* figure is then regarded as the maximum possible rate (short of providing in some way for a *negative* association between origins and destinations), one could say that a shift from the actually prevailing pattern of fluidity to the Swedish pattern would mean moving almost a third of the way towards the ultimate goal—while a shift to the Irish pattern would mean moving as far in the opposite direction. If, then, it is valid to give a political interpretation of the differences in fluidity between Sweden and Ireland, the potential for generating greater openness through egalitarian economic and social policies appears substantially larger in the perspective suggested than it might on a more superficial assessment; and in turn it becomes less easy to talk—as Marxists in particular have been wont to do—of the 'myths' of social-democratic achievement.

In the introductory section to this chapter, we remarked that the FJH hypothesis could provide a valuable starting point for our attempt to assess class mobility in modern Britain within a comparative perspective. It may likewise prove helpful if, in bringing our assessment to a conclusion, we revert to this hypothesis. As we earlier argued, its authors can best be understood as claiming that a large commonality prevails in patterns of social fluidity across a wide range of modern societies—all those in fact with market economies (broadly defined) and nuclear family systems. Interpreted in this way, the hypothesis can lay claim to a large measure of empirical support. Although comparative research has been able to detect cross-national variations in fluidity that are of undoubted sociological interest, the extent of the cross-national similarity which has at the same time been revealed can only be described as impressive. It is, at all events, by now evident enough that to think of the fluidity patterns of modern societies as falling into some set of more or less distinctive types is far less appropriate than to envisage the large commonality that the FJH hypothesis would propose.

In the foregoing, we have shown that when the British case is viewed in comparative terms, the force of the FJH hypothesis is well brought out. Within the range of such variation in fluidity as is displayed, the British pattern proves to occupy a rather central place; or, one could say, it appears remarkably unexceptional other than perhaps in its *lack* of distinctive features and in the degree to which it does itself instantiate the common pattern. This being so, there are then certain implications of the FJH hypothesis which can be taken as having a quite direct and unqualified relevance for the British case, and which are of particular significance if one comes to consider possible future developments.

First of all, to the extent that the FJH hypothesis holds good, it must of course follow that cross-national variation in absolute mobility rates is largely the result of structural differences—analogously to our finding in chapters 3 and 9 above that variation in these rates over time within the same society is largely the result of structural change. What is here implied is, then, that the question of whether absolute rates of class mobility in Britain will in future tend to become more or less like those found in other nations is essentially a question of how the British and other national class structures will evolve.

One answer obviously available to this question is that of 'convergence' theorists. In their expectation, all major structural features of advanced societies will come to show increasing similarity as variations deriving from distinctive national histories and cultures are ironed out by an inexorable 'logic of industrialism'—or, in other words, by the unremitting functional exigencies of technical and economic rationality.[19] However, this view can no longer be regarded as compelling. That *particular* convergent tendencies are traceable in class structural change is undeniable: for instance, those associated with the decline of agricultural classes or with the expansion of the service class. But these particular tendencies need not and, on the evidence available, do not lead to a general convergence in the shapes of class structures—chiefly because, from society to society, they proceed with such varying pace and rhythm.[20] Thus, as we have indicated, many of the larger differences in absolute rates of class mobility that are to be found among present-day industrial societies in fact derive from differences in the rate at which the decline of agricultural sectors has occurred and in the phasing of this decline relative to other structural changes. And there would seem no reason why future long-run tendencies—such as the now incipient decline in industrial working classes—should not likewise proceed in cross-nationally very differentiated ways and in turn with very differentiated effects on mobility patterns. Moreover, it is not difficult to envisage actually *divergent* tendencies in class structural change. For example, there are already clear indications that, in obvious contradiction with the claims of convergence theory, the urban petty bourgeoisie is in some advanced societies now an expanding rather than a contracting class;[21] and a further major source of structural diversity could well be that of persisting cross-national differences in the level and form of women's work-force participation.

Two things may then be said. On the one hand, there can be little doubt that the distinctive features of British class mobility rates which are currently observable—notably in terms of class recruitment—and which result from Britain's unique route to industrial maturity, will tend to become steadily less prominent. But, on the other hand, there would appear no good grounds for ruling out the possibility that other distinctive structural features and associated mobility patterns will in turn emerge, even though we can have little basis for predicting what these might be.

It may be taken as a second implication of the FJH hypothesis that in so far as deviations from the common patterns of social fluidity do occur, they must stem from influences which are external to the basic form of stratification associated with this pattern (that deriving from a market economy and a nuclear family system) and which in some way modify its operation. Such influences, it may be suggested, are of two main kinds: those exerted by historically formed institutional features specific to different national societies—an example earlier referred to would be the German system of vocational education and training; and those which reflect the political context within which the process of stratification operates, including of course attempts to intervene purposively in this process—as, say, under the social-democratic hegemony established in the Swedish case.

So far as Britain is concerned, the findings that we have reported must obviously make it difficult to claim that historically specific institutional features have any great impact on social fluidity. For, on our evidence, relative rates of class mobility in Britain would in fact appear to represent the common pattern in a rather 'pure' form, and hence there is little need for institutional 'peculiarities' to be invoked. The suggestion which would then follow is that if, within the more immediate future at least, Britain should become somewhat more 'deviant' in its fluidity, this will most likely be as the result of political action—whether this is directed towards mitigating, or to allowing a fuller expression of, the inequalities that the market generates and the family sustains. In other words, and contrary to what has been often supposed, Britain does not appear to possess any kind of 'historical legacy' of established institutions that in itself either distinctively impedes or favours social fluidity. Rather, the important observation to be made is that within the existing range of societal 'openness', Britain holds —and in all probability has held for many decades—an intermediate position. This means, therefore, that the possibility exists of changes being brought about in social fluidity which, without the extent of existing variation being exceeded, could still entail a widening *or* a narrowing of class inequalities in mobility chances of a kind that, as our counterfactual analyses served to show, would be of much more than negligible human and social significance. Whether or not such changes in fluidity are in fact likely to occur in the years ahead and, if so, in what direction, are then questions of evident interest, and are among those that we must seek to address in our final chapter.

NOTES

1. As perhaps the best illustrations, see David Landes, *The Unbound Prometheus*, Cambridge: Cambridge University Press, 1972, chs. 2 and 3 esp.; and Mancur Olson, *The Rise and Decline of Nations*, New Haven: Yale University Press, 1982, ch. 4 esp.

2. S.M. Lipset and Hans L. Zetterberg, 'Social Mobility in Industrial Societies; in Lipset and Bendix, *Social Mobility in Industrial Society*, p. 13. See also Lipset and Zetterberg, 'A Theory of Social Mobility'.
3. See, for example, Miller, 'Comparative Social Mobility'; F. Lancaster Jones, 'Social Mobility and Industrial Society: A Thesis Re-examined', *Sociological Quarterly*, vol. 10, 1969; Robert Erikson, John H. Goldthorpe, and Lucienne Portocarero. 'Intergenerational Mobility in Three Western European Societies', *British Journal of Sociology*, vol. 30, 1979; David B. Grusky and Robert M. Hauser, 'Comparative Social Mobility Revisited', *American Sociological Review*, vol. 49, 1984.
4. David L. Featherman, F. Lancaster Jones, and Robert M. Hauser, 'Assumptions of Mobility Research in the US: The Case of Occupational Status', *Social Science Research*, vol. 4, 1975.
5. See, for illustration and further references, Robert Erikson, John H. Goldthorpe, and Lucienne Portocarero, 'Social Fluidity in Industrial Nations: England, France and Sweden', *British Journal of Sociology*, vol. 33, 1982, and 'Intergenerational Social Mobility and the Convergence Thesis', *British Journal of Sociology*, vol. 34, 1983; and Grusky and Hauser, 'Comparative Social Mobility Revisted'.
6. Thus, for example, if understood in its less strict sense, the FJH hypothesis can claim to apply not only to capitalist societies but further to the state socialist societies of Eastern Europe–despite the degree of political and administrative control that is exerted over market forces within their economies.
7. On all the points raised in this paragraph, see further John H. Goldthorpe 'On Economic Development and Social Mobility', *British Journal of Sociology*, vol. 36, 1985.
8. The CASMIN project is directed by Walter Müller and John H. Goldthorpe from the Institut für Sozialwissenschaften of the University of Mannheim and is funded by the Stiftung Volkswagenwerk. The investigation of intergenerational class mobility, results from which are subsequently used in this chapter, has been jointly undertaken with Robert Erikson of the University of Stockholm.
9. The model may in this case be written as

$$F_{ijk} = \eta \; t_i^P \; t_j^S \; t_k^N \; t_{ij}^{PS} \; t_{ik}^{PN} \; t_{jk}^{SN}$$

where F_{ijk} is the expected frequency in cell ijk of a three-way table which comprises origin, or father's class (P), destination, or son's class (S) and nation (N).
10. It is of further interest to note in this connection that if the common social fluidity model is applied to all nine national mobility tables *simultaneously*, a significant lack of fit is–not surprisingly–indicated, but still 94 per cent of the association between class origin and class of destination is accounted for and less than 5 per cent of all cases are misclassified. See further Robert Erikson and John H. Goldthorpe 'Commonality and Variation in Social Fluidity in Industrial Nations. Part I: a Model for Evaluating the "FJH Hypothesis"; Part II: the Model of Core Social Fluidity Applied', *European Sociological Review*, vol. 3, 1987.
11. On the significance of configurations in multidimensional scaling plots, independently of any interpretation of their axes, see Roger N. Shepard, 'Introduction' in Shepard, A. Kimball Romney, and Sara Beth Nerlove (eds.), *Multidimensional Scaling: Theory and Applications in the Behavioral Sciences*, New York: Seminar Press, 1972. This work also provides a good general introduction to multidimensional scaling for those unfamiliar with the technique. Further details of the analysis referred to in the text are to be found in Erikson and Goldthorpe, 'Commonality and Variation in Social Fluidity in Industrial Nations'.
12. The text commentary on the positioning of nations relative to the centroids of the plots can be confirmed by the calculation of euclidean distances.

In view of the suggestion that has often arisen, both in the sociological literature and more widely, that the USA is characterized by an exceptional degree of openness, it may be worth adding here that if more strictly comparable data had been available, then the USA might well have joined England and France as a 'central' nation. For a detailed treatment of the American case, which reveals little basis for claims of 'exceptionalism', see Robert Erikson and John H. Goldthorpe 'Are American Rates of Social Mobility Exceptionally High? New Evidence on an Old Issue', *European Sociological Review*, vol. 1, 1985.

13. See, for example, McKee J. McClendon, 'Structural and Exchange Components of Occupational Mobility: A Cross-National Analysis', *Sociological Quarterly*, vol. 21, 1980; Erikson, Goldthorpe, and Portocarero, 'Social Fluidity in Industrial Nations'; Grusky and Hauser, 'Comparative Social Mobility Revisited'; and Robert V. Robinson, 'Reproducing Class Relations in Industrial Capitalism', *American Sociological Review*, vol. 49, 1984.

14. This understanding of, and approach to handling, the problems of counterfactual analysis is derived chiefly from contributions to the debate that has arisen over the extensive use of such analysis by 'new' economic historians. See in particular Alexander Gerschenkron, 'Some Methodological Problems in Economic History (with a Postscript)' in *Continuity in History and Other Essays*, Cambridge, Mass.: Harvard University Press, 1968; J.D. Gould, 'Hypothetical History', *Economic History Review*, vol. 22, 1969; and, especially, Peter D. McClelland, *Causal Explanation and Model Building in History, Economics, and the New Economic History*, Ithaca: Cornell University Press, 1975.

15. Frederick Mosteller, 'Association and Estimation in Contingency Tables', *Journal of the American Statistical Association*, vol. 63, 1968; see also W. Edwards Deming, *Statistical Adjustment of Data*, New York: Wiley, 1943.

16. See further M. Maurice, F. Sellier, and J.-J. Silvestre, *Politique d'éducation et organisation industrielle en France et en Allemagne*, Paris: Presses Universitaires de France, 1982; Walter Müller, 'Soziale Mobilität: Die Bundersrepublik im Internationalen Vergleich' in Max Kaase (ed.), *Theorie und Praxis in demokratischer Regierungsweise*, Opladen: Westdeutscher Verlag, 1985; and Wolfgang König and Müller, 'Educational Systems and Labour Markets as Determinants of Worklife Mobility in France and West Germany', *European Sociological Review*, vol. 2, 1986. Such wider social consequences of the German system of vocational education and training seem not to have been fully appreciated by its advocates in this country, who have concentrated their attention on its likely effects on productivity. See, e.g., S.J. Prais, 'Vocational Qualifications and the Labour Force in Britain and Germany', *National Institute Economic Review*, November, 1981.

17. Cf., for example, David B. Rottman, Damian F. Hannan, Niamh Hardiman, and Miriam M. Wiley, *The Distribution of Income in the Republic of Ireland: A Study in Social Class and Family-Cycle Inequalities*, Dublin: The Economic and Social Research Institute, 1982.

18. Two alternative hypotheses that might be suggested regarding Swedish–Irish differences in fluidity are (i) that while Sweden is perhaps the most secularized society in Europe, Ireland is one of the least, and that the higher fluidity in the former case thus reflects the greater prevalence of individualistic over familial values; (ii) that Sweden has been historically a far more egalitarian society than Ireland, on account of its quite different form of agrarian organization, and thus its greater fluidity will extend back for long before the establishment of social-democratic hegemony. Against these hypotheses, it may however be noted (i) that Norway, a clearly less secularized social democracy than Sweden, has been shown to have a similarly high level of fluidity—in contrast with other Nordic nations such as Denmark and Finland, where social-democratic parties have been less successful (see Pöntinen, *Social Mobility and Social Structure*, ch. 8); and (ii) there is clear evidence of a significant *increase* in fluidity in Sweden in the recent past—i.e. among men born in the 1940s and 1950s—and it would appear that previously the Swedish pattern was not all that exceptional (see Robert Erikson, 'Changes in Social Mobility in Industrial Nations: The Case of Sweden' in *Research in Social Stratification and Mobility*, vol. 2, 1983; and Erikson, Goldthorpe, and Portocarero, 'Intergenerational Social Mobility and the Convergence Thesis'.

19. See in particular Clark Kerr, John T. Dunlop, Frederick H. Harbison, and Charles A. Myers, *Industrialism and Industrial Man*, Cambridge, Mass.: Harvard University Press,

1960, and Clark Kerr, *The Future of Industrial Societies*, Cambridge, Mass.: Harvard University Press, 1983.

20. Cf. Joachim Singelman, *From Agriculture to Services: The Transformation of Industrial Employment*, Beverly Hills: Sage, 1978, and Giorgio Gagliani, 'Long-Term Changes in the Occupational Structure', *European Sociological Review*, vol. 1, 1985.

21. See, for example, Suzanne Berger and Michael Piore, *Dualism and Discontinuity in Industrial Societies*, Cambridge: Cambridge University Press, 1980, and Walter Müller, 'Was Bleibt von den Klassenstrukturen?' Institut für Sozialwissenschaften, University of Mannheim, 1986.

CHAPTER 12

Conclusions and Prospects

We stated in our introductory chapter than in this book we view mobility under two different auspices. We regard a particular pattern of mobility as defining a goal to which we have a value-commitment: namely, that of a genuinely open society. But, at the same time, we believe that the likelihood of this goal being achieved, or more closely approximated, will importantly depend on the pattern of mobility that actually prevails: specifically, on how far this pattern, in deviating from openness, is conducive to class formation and action, and in turn to forms of class conflict, through which the class-linked inequalities of life-chances that are the denial of openness may be reduced. In this final chapter we will work towards an assessment of the prospects for openness, made from the position that we have adopted. To this end, we will review the main empirical results of our research and attempt to assess their significance from the standpoint of our two guiding interests in turn.

From what we have learnt about the prevailing degree of openness in British society, one conclusion is clear enough: the goal to which we would aspire is still far off and, moreover, there is little, if any, evidence of progress having been made towards it. Although, as we have seen in the previous chapter, Britain is not characterized by an unduly low level of social fluidity when compared with other industrial nations, it can still be regarded as one in which the barriers to greater mobility have shown a notable persistence from decade to decade.[1] As is revealed by the results reported in chapters 3 and 9, the net association between the class position of individuals in the present-day population and their class origins remains essentially the same in its extent and pattern as that which existed in the inter-war period and even, it seems likely, as that which would have been found at the start of the century.

Over the years to which the data of our 1972 mobility inquiry chiefly relate, Britain enjoyed almost continuous economic growth and often—to judge by national standards at least—at relatively high rates. Concomitantly with this growth, the occupational division of labour was transformed, and rather rapidly so from the 1940s onwards. Also in these post-war years large-scale educational reforms were carried through which greatly increased educational provision, which established a formal equality of educational opportunity, and which were intended, in conjunction with other aspects of social policy, to minimize class influences on processes of social selection. In other words, the project of creating a more open society was undertaken, and in circumstances which might be regarded as highly favourable to it. For it has been a recurrent theme of liberal and (in the British sense) social-democratic theorists that economic expansion is an important desideratum as the context for egalitarian policies, in that it softens any attendant social conflicts and prevents them from taking on a starkly zero-sum form. Thus, the increasing 'room at the top' created by the growth of professional, higher technical, administrative, and managerial positions could provide the occasion, in an analogous way to increasing national wealth, for inequalities in class life-chances to be reduced, but without the members of any class having to become less advantaged than before in absolute terms.

However, the results of our inquiry, as presented in chapter 3, lead clearly to the conclusion that, despite these supposedly propitious circumstances, no significant reduction in class inequalities was in fact achieved. Systematic shifts were evident in the pattern of absolute mobility rates, of a kind that would be expected from the nature of the changes occurring in the occupational structure. But relative mobility rates, which we take as our indicator of the degree of openness, remained generally unaltered; and the only trends that could arguably be discerned (apart from over the early stages of the life-cycle) were indeed ones that would point to a widening of differences in class chances.

Furthermore, in chapter 4 we show that the pattern of relative mobility chances—or, in other words, of social fluidity—associated with the British class structure over the decades in question embodies inequalities that are of a quite striking kind: in particular, those that emerge if one compares the chances of men whose fathers held higher-level service-class positions being themselves found in such positions rather than in working-class ones with the corresponding chances of men of working-class origins. Where inequalities in class chances of this magnitude are displayed—of the order, it may be recalled, of over 30 : 1— then, we believe, the presumption must be that to a substantial extent they do reflect inequalities of opportunity that are rooted in the class structure, and are not simply the outcome of the differential 'take-up' of opportunities by individuals with differing genetic, moral, or other endowments that are unrelated to their class position. At all events, this is the interpretation that must stand until latter-day Social Darwinists or Smilesians are able to offer some alternative account of an empirically credible kind.[2]

The implications of the findings of chapters 3 and 4 have therefore to count as rather grave ones for the general strategy of egalitarian reform that was pursued during the post-war period: in effect, that of seeking to attack social inequalities via legislative and administrative measures which could be carried through without venturing too far beyond the limits of 'consensus' politics. What our results would suggest—and the same point could indeed be made by reference to research on various other topics, such as education or health[3]—is that this strategy grossly misjudges the resistance that the class structure can offer to attempts to change it; or, to speak less figuratively, the flexibility and effectiveness with which the more powerful and advantaged groupings in society can use the resources at their disposal to preserve their privileged positions. There is a serious underestimation of the forces maintaining the situation in which change is sought, relative to the force of the measures through which, it is supposed, change can be implemented.

Consequently, we would add, the main significance of post-war economic growth was not that it facilitated egalitarian reform but rather that it obscured its failure.[4] The fact that the chances of men of all social origins gaining entry into the expanding higher levels of the occupational and class structures steadily increased served effectively to distract attention away from the issue of whether at the same time any equalization of relative mobility chances was being achieved: that is, away from the issue of whether any progress was being made in the direction of a more open, as distinct from simply a more economically developed society. In the more recent period, after the ending of the long boom, the persistence of marked inequalities of condition and opportunity alike is less easily overlooked. The expansion of the service class has, so far at least, continued, with the result that, as was seen in chapter 9, rates of upward mobility are still rising. But the return of large-scale and long-term unemployment has also increased the risks of an unusually damaging form of downward mobility, and especially so, we have shown, for men in working-class positions.

The pattern of relative rates that we have found to obtain in British society through our investigations focused on the class mobility of men is one which, as was revealed in chapter 10, in large degree also underlies the mobility chances of women—whether assessed via marriage or employment, and, moreover, it is one which, in the light of chapter 11, we can regard as highly characteristic of that apparently operating, with only a rather limited range of variation, across a wide range of modern societies. These further results we would then take as reinforcing our argument that if this pattern of fluidity is to be significantly modified, this will not come about in any spontaneous way but only as a political achievement which will be of a highly contested kind and involve conflict between classes in some guise or other. For what is clearly suggested is that the inequalities in mobility chances that the pattern represents are a more or less direct reflection of the distribution of social power and advantage within a rather widely prevailing form of class stratification (that associated, according to the FJH hypothesis, with a market economy and a nuclear family system), and will therefore change only as this distribution itself changes—which can scarcely be expected to occur in a conflict-free way. That is to say, attempts to bring about changes in an egalitarian direction will be met by resistance on the part of those whose power and advantage are placed under threat.[5]

In democratic societies, such conflict has in fact been typically initiated via labour movement, which may be seen as attempts on the part of those most disadvantaged by market-generated inequalities to compensate for their lack of social power as individuals by acting collectively and by using their resources of numbers, organization, and solidarity in order to mount a challenge to the prevailing order. From society to society, this challenge has taken a variety of forms in terms of its historical development, its strategy, and its institutional— or extra-institutional—expression in both the political and industrial arenas. But crucial to its degree of success, one may argue, has always been the cohesion and forcefulness of the class-based action mobilized in its support, as against the class-based opposition with which it has inevitably met. Since, then, we take this view—that it is the dynamics of class relations that will chiefly determine whether or not any change in social fluidity will occur—our assessment of the results of our mobility research from the standpoint of the prevailing lack of openness is not that of ultimate importance. It must yield place to one made from the standpoint of the implications of these results for class formation and action, and it is to this, far more demanding, task that we now turn.

In showing in our introductory chapter the historical diversity of the 'social motives' that have prompted the study of mobility, we outlined a range of different arguments bearing on the relationship between mobility and class formation and, in turn, on the implications of mobility for socio-political change and stability. Here it may be useful, before embarking on a review of our relevant findings, to note among such arguments three major types which are distinct even though sometimes complementary.

First, we may pick out arguments that are concerned with the relationship between mobility and class formation from what may be thought of as an essentially demographic point of view. Specifically, these arguments represent mobility as being inversely related to class formation in the basic sense of the formation of aggregates of individuals or families that are identifiable through the continuity of their class locations over time. Thus, for example, Marx explained the lack of a 'developed formation of classes' in mid-nineteenth century America—and hence the weakness of the labour movement there—in terms of the 'constant flux' of individuals between different class positions and, in particular, the 'continuous conversion of wage labourers into independent, self-sustaining peasants'. Sorokin saw both the theory and the fact of class struggle as being undermined in modern societies through high rates of mobility which produced a decline in the 'stable and permanent' elements of classes and a corresponding increase in the number of individuals whose class positions had to be regarded as provisional and temporary. And, more recently, Giddens has advanced in effect the converse proposition that, under capitalism, classes come into existence as social phenomena primarily through the restriction of mobility within the social division of labour, so that collectivities are created whose members have largely shared market and work situations and common lifetime and intergenerational experience.

Secondly, we may recognize a further set of arguments that also treat mobility and class formation as being opposing social processes, but in terms of their implications for sociopolitical orientations and patterns of action. Such arguments tend to presuppose both some degree of class formation in the basic demographic sense and some amount of mobility between classes, and are then chiefly concerned with the extent to which the latter may serve to prevent the development of class awareness and class consciousness. Thus, Sombart and Michels alike came to the view that the existence of reasonable mobility opportunities for rank-and-file wage-workers encourages within the working class as a whole the growth of individualistic aspirations and ideologies which are inimical to collectivist values and to 'class' interpretations of the social structure and of the fate of individual within it. Blau and Duncan echo this view and add the point that to the extent that mobility does in fact occur, the less evident will classes (or status groups) be as socio-cultural entities, and the greater will be the freedom of the individual from the influence of such collectivities. Finally in this respect, we note the argument also advanced by Blau and Duncan (among others), that as well as encouraging individualistic rather than collectivist orientations, mobility also furthers the acceptance of the *status quo* by giving greater legitimacy to the prevailing structure of social inequality: in a mobile society, inequalities can be more readily regarded as fair and justifiable in that they appear to reflect individual achievement and merit rather than being ones of an evidently ascribed character that are perpetuated from generation to generation.

Thirdly, then, there are arguments which, like the foregoing, are concerned with the effects of mobility at the level of orientations and action, but which see these effects as more likely to *disturb* than to help maintain socio-political stability. These arguments relate basically to the way in which mobility may disrupt established forms of social stratification and to the psychological consequences of this disruption. Most notably, Lipset has contended, as we have seen, that high rates of mobility give rise to a variety of social situations in which individuals will experience serious stress and insecurity, in consequence of which they may abandon their allegiance to the existing order and thus become available for recruitment by extremist political movements whether of the Left or the Right.

So far as class formation in the basic demographic sense is concerned, it is our findings on patterns and trends of absolute mobility rates that are of greatest relevance. Before turning our attention to these findings, though, we should perhaps first recall one point previously made in chapter 2: namely, that the data of our national mobility inquiry are not very informative about the composition of élite groupings in modern British society, if these are strictly defined so as to refer to the small fraction of the population who occupy 'peak' positions *within* professional, administrative, or managerial hierarchies. To the extent that we are able to draw conclusions that relate to élites in this sense, they are ones that appear to be in line with those of more specialized studies in indicating that these groupings are characterized by a high degree of both intergenerational self-recruitment and stability; or, in other words, that they are, or at least have been in the recent past, very well defined and readily indentifiable groupings in terms of their continuity over time.[6] However, the main significance of our findings is in regard to 'mass' rather than 'élite' mobility; and here, we believe, they enable us to give both a more reliable and a more detailed account of the degree of formation of classes via mobility flows than has previously been offered.

In the case, first of all, of the service class, the fact of leading importance for present purposes is that of its continued expansion, which may be seen as the central and indisputable feature of the long-term upgrading of employment within advanced societies that has been emphasized by liberal theorists. Because of this expansion, there is in fact no possibility of service-class positions in present-day British society being largely confined to men of service-class origins: rather, some substantial degree of 'recruitment from below' has been inevitable. Moreover, although very wide inequalities exist in chances of access to the service class, in particular as between men of service-class and working-class origins, this still does not prevent the latter from forming a large component of all service-class entrants—and indeed, as was seen in chapter 12, a distinctively large one on a comparative view. In the light of the data presented in Tables 2.1 and 9.10, the British service class can only be described as highly heterogeneous so far as the social origins of its members are concerned. From the first two columns of the former, more detailed table, it can be seen that each of the seven classes of our schema, considered as a class of origin, contributes at least

10 per cent of the membership of both Class I and II; and this, it may be noted, produces a *greater* degree of heterogeneity than would ensue if men were recruited to these classes according to perfect mobility expectations.[7]

From this point of view, then, the service class would appear as having only a rather low degree of demographic identity. However, against this, it must be recognized first, that, as shown in chapter 9, self-recruitment to the service class is beginning to increase; and secondly, that while the growth of service-class positions has necessarily broadened the basis of recruitment to them, it has at the same time given rise to progressively more favourable conditions for inter-generational stability within the service class. And, as is evident from Table 3.1 and again from Tables 9.8 and 9.9, this stability is also steadily increasing. Thus, in the case of the youngest birth cohort within our 1983 sample to have achieved 'occupational maturity', that of men born 1934-48, *over 70 per cent* of those of Class I and II origins were themselves found in Class I and II positions—as compared with a corresponding figure for the 1908-17 birth cohort in our 1972 sample of 55 per cent. Also comparing these two cohorts, we may further note that the proportion of men who were found in manual, Class VI and VII posi-tions—that is, who could be regarded as having experienced the more decisive kind of *déclassement*—falls from 17 per cent in the older cohort to only 6 per cent in the younger. Thus, we may conclude, while there can be little doubt that over recent decades the service class has been recruited from quite diverse social origins, there is no sign of any falling off in the capacity of its members to transmit social advantage to their offspring. On the contrary, even while expanding, the service class has tended, so to speak, to 'solidify' in the sense that families have become less likely to be detached from it from one generation to the next.

Furthermore, there is one other tendency that we have documented which may also be seen as contributing importantly to the demographic identity of the service class: that is, the tendency for men, once having gained access to this class in the course of their working lives, to remain within it thereafter. For example, indirect but still rather compelling evidence of this tendency is given in Table 5.1, from which it can be seen that the large majority—in fact over 80 per cent—of respondents to our 1972 inquiry whose first full-time occupation was in a Class I or II position were also found in such a position at time of interview.[8] And so far at least as men found in Class I are concerned, we know directly from our 1974 work-history data that from whatever origins and by whatever routes they had first entered the service class, these men had but rarely moved from it subsequently, and even then usually for only brief periods of time. In other words, not only does one observe low, and declining, rates of downward mobility from the service class intergenerationally, but further there would appear to be a very low probability of downward movement from service-class positions intra-generationally in the form of work-life 'demotion'.

Finally in this connection, it is also relevant to again recall that while our data fail to support the thesis of 'counterbalance' between inter- and intragenerational movement into the service class, they do indicate, as is shown in Figure 2.2, that during the post-war period direct routes of access to Classes I and II became *proportionately* more important than indirect ones from all class origins alike;

and there is little reason to suppose any weakening in this tendency in more recent years. Since, therefore, direct routes lead men more quickly into service-class positions than do indirect ones (see above, pp. 127, 137), one may conclude that men are entering into the typically more or less continuous tenure of such positions from a steadily earlier average age.

As we have said, the major factor in understanding the patterns and trends of absolute mobility rates associated with the service class is its expansion. But the continuity with which service-class positions are held and the growing relative importance of direct entry on completion of full-time education serve to high-light another point: namely, that the basis of the expanding service class is an essentially *bureaucratic* one. Bureaucracies, through their very form, tend to establish 'career lines' for those who are employed within them, and success or failure for the latter is then largely defined in terms of how far along these lines they are able to progress. Thus, failure does not usually mean that the individual is actually relegated from the bureaucracy and forced to take up employment of a quite different class character, but only that he achieves relatively little advancement within the bureaucracy. A contrast may be drawn here with the consequences of failure in an entrepreneurial role, which would seem far more likely to lead to a decisive change in class position.[9]

Again—and relatedly—it is a typical feature of bureaucracies that they seek to recruit their personnel on the basis of formal qualifications or at least educational background. In part, no doubt, this is a matter of administrative convenience; but the practice of such 'credentialism' on entry can also be seen as reflecting the subsequent security of tenure that bureaucratic employment offers—in guard-ing, supposedly, against the worst errors of selection. The rate of expansion of the service class in modern Britain, outstripping that of the institutions of higher education at least until the later 1960s, has meant that indirect routes into service-class positions have remained of considerable importance up to the present day. But the influence of bureaucratic selection procedures is, we would argue, now apparent in the growing relative importance of direct routes, and can only be expected to intensify this trend.

In sum, then, we would wish to claim that the last half-century or so has witnessed in Britain not only a significant expansion of professional, higher technical, administrative, and managerial occupations or, in other words, of service-class positions; but further, the emergence of the service class as a new social formation: that is, as a collectivity of individuals and families that main-tains its identity as a class—its location within the structure of class positions—over time. One may say of the service class, as the expanding class of the mid-twentieth century, what Marx said of the industrial proletariat of the mid-nineteenth: that is has been 'recruited from all classes of the population'. But, again like the proletariat of the last century, the service class gains its identity in that its members, despite their diverse origins, display a high degree of both intergenerational stability and work-life continuity. The difference between the two situations is, of course, that while the immobility of the proletariat was the result essentially of constraint—of a lack of opportunity and resources for escape—that of the service class derives rather from the capacity of its members to preserve their positions of relative advantage.[10]

We may turn next to the question of the extent to which the formation of

classes as demographic entities may be observed within the range of the intermediate-class positions of our schema. From the data we have presented, it is
apparent that while Classes III, IV, and V are generally not so heterogeneous in
terms of the social origins of their members as are Classes I and II, they none the
less still have a rather broad basis of recruitment (Tables 2.2 and 9.10); and
further, that men who are of intermediate-class origins are found rather widely
dispersed among other class positions (Tables 2.1, 3.1, 9.8, and 9.9). However,
of much greater significance here is the evidence of chapter 5. This indicates that
men who appear in our basic tables as intergenerationally stable in Classes III,
IV, or V are in fact likely to have experienced a good deal of work-life mobility,
or to be poised for such mobility, both within and beyond the range of intermediate-class positions; and further, that a rather large proportion of men
found at any one time in other class positions will have held intermediate-class
ones at some earlier stage in their lives. In other words, it is clear that it would in
this case be difficult to claim that any very sizeable collectivity or collectivities
can be identified in virtue of the continuity of association of their members with
a given set of class locations. Rather, the positions comprised by the intermediate classes of our schema must be regarded as ones which quite frequently
do not represent final destinations in men's working lives. They are, on the
contrary, ones from which men show a relatively high propensity to be mobile,
whether as the result of choice—as in the pursuit of work-life advancement—or
of constraint.

The one qualification which should perhaps be made to this conclusion relates
to Class IV. It may well be that the degree of work-life continuity that occurs
within the minor proprietorial and entrepreneurial positions comprised by this
class is no greater than that found within our other two intermediate classes, but
several additional points are to be noted. To begin with, Tables 2.1 and 2.2 show
clearly higher values on the main diagonal for Class IV than for Class III or for
Class V; and we have seen in chapter 4, from our analysis of patterns of intergenerational fluidity, that a stronger tendency towards immobility exists within
Class IV than within any other class except Class I. Further, it should be recalled
that our 1974 subsample of men intergenerationally stable in Class IV excluded
those in H–G categories 11 and 13—that is, farmers and small proprietors with
employees—and greater work-life continuity could well be found among the
latter than among the other categories making up Class IV. Finally, our 1983
data show a tendency for Class IV (unlike Classes III and V) to expand in size
somewhat and at the same time to display increasing intergenerational stability.
In terms therefore of both absolute and relative mobility rates, it must be
reckoned that there is a comparatively high probability of men who are at any
one time found in Class IV positions being the sons of men who at some previous
time also held such positions. And what this suggests to us is that a collectivity
of individuals and families does exist in modern British society which is identifiable over time, if not always by the continuity with which its members occupy
the self-employed positions of Class IV, then by what could be regarded as their
'tradition' of self-employment; that is to say, by their propensity to move into
self-employment when opportunity arises and to do so, perhaps, in spite of
previous disappointments or failures in self-employed ventures. It is in this sense,

that the petty bourgeoisie can best be thought of as presently existing as a social formation within the British class structure.

As regards, on the other hand, the unquestionably low degree of both inter-generational stability and work-life continuity that is revealed within Class III and Class V positions, two further observations would seem worth making, albeit ones of a rather negative kind. First, it would seem, in the light of this finding, that the considerable attention devoted by certain Marxist theorists to the ques-tion of the 'true' class affiliations of routine nonmanual employees, lower-grade technicians, and manual supervisory grades is of very doubtful consequence.[11] Whether these groupings are to be regarded as being 'structurally' part of the working class or of a 'new' petty bourgeoisie, or as having 'contradictory' class locations, must in fact be an issue of much diminished significance once the groupings in question are known to be ones with highly fluctuating member-ships even over a relatively short-run period: or, at all events, this must be so if the ultimate interest of the analysis lies in the potentialities for class-based socio-political action rather than in the elaboration and defence of sectarian versions of Marxist theory as an end in itself.[12]

Secondly, and as in part an extension of the foregoing argument, our results must further call into question the more empirical attempts of Marxist authors to revive the thesis of the 'proletarianization' of routine nonmanual employees in positions of the kind covered by our Class III—which are seen to be multiply-ing as a consequence of the systematic deskilling and degrading of all types of labour. Even if one were to accept the degrading thesis—which, as argued in chapter 9, does not accord well with the empirical evidence—its connection with 'proletarianization' is still not all that apparent if, as shown in chapter 5, there is a high frequency of work-life mobility from routine nonmanual positions to both manual *and* higher-level white-collar ones.[13] Moreover, it is difficult to reconcile with any notion of proletarianization our findings that men whose fathers held routine nonmanual positions retain clearly better *de facto* chances of upward mobility into service-class positions than do men of working-class origins (see Table 2.2); and again that, as emerges from the analyses of chapter 4, the general pattern of relative mobility chances associated with Class III positions has a much closer affinity with those of the other two white-collar classes, that is Classes I and II, than with those of Classes VI and VII.

In apparent recognition of these difficulties, exponents of the proletariani-zation thesis have of late tended to shift the focus of their attention to women, emphasizing that it is they who make up the bulk of employees in lower-grade nonmanual positions.[14] However, the thesis remains unconvincing in that, on the one hand, women no less than men appear to hold such employment with only a rather low degree of continuity[15] and, on the other, many of those found in such employment at any one time will, as shown in chapter 10, be married to men in higher-level nonmanual positions, thus obtaining an alternative and, it seems, preferable basis for their class identities.

Finally, then, in the present connection we must consider the question of the degree of demographic identity of the working class. To a certain extent, one may regard the circumstances that prevail here as being the converse of those that exist in the case of the service class. For while the latter has been in expansion, the working class, in the sense of the body of manual wage-workers, has been in decline—rather slowly in the 1950s and 1960s but more rapidly thereafter. Being thus in contraction, the British working class of the mid-twentieth century has not been 'required' to recruit from outside its own ranks, and it is not therefore surprising that the data of Table 2.1 should indicate that Classes VI and VII are clearly more homogeneous than are any others in our schema so far as the social origins of their members are concerned.[16] Indeed, if considered together, these classes form in fact a largely self-recruiting bloc. Of those of our respondents in 1972 who were allocated to Class VI or Class VII, almost 70 per cent had fathers in either Class VI or Class VII, and this figure is virtually unchanged in our 1983 results (Table 9.10). In addition, 10 per cent of men in Class VI and Class VII reported fathers in the third of our blue-collar classes, Class V. In sum, we may regard the present-day working class as being overwhelmingly second-generation blue-collar, at least, in its composition.

It is furthermore evident from Table 2.1 that the picture would not be greatly changed if we were to leave out of account the category of agricultural workers (H–G category 31). In other words, it would also be true to say that the great majority of manual wage-workers *in industry* are at least second-generation. It is in fact the case that 65 per cent of these men in our 1972 sample—that is, of men in Class VI or in Class VII discounting H–G category 31—had fathers who were likewise members of the industrial working class, and that again a further 10 per cent were men whose fathers were allocated to Class V. In this respect, as we have shown in chapter 11, the British working class would appear to have been highly distinctive in its historical development. In the industrial labour forces of other nations, there has far longer remained, and often through to the present day, a sizeable minority of workers who could still in some degree be reckoned as 'green' labour—that is, men who were the sons of, and who had often themselves for some time been, farmers, smallholders or peasants, or agricultural workers.

In terms of the social origins of its members, therefore, the demographic identity of the British working class is well defined. But we must further note that the results we have reported at the same time show a decline in its inter-generational stability. A major factor in this is clearly the growth of the service class and the consequent increase in upward mobility from working-class origins. Thus, from the data of Table 3.1 it can be seen that across the first three of the ten-year birth cohorts within our 1972 sample, the proportion of men of Class VI and VII origins who were found in Class I or II positions steadily rises, while the proportion in Class VI or VII positions steadily falls. And from Table 9.9 it is then apparent that this trend has extended through into the 1980s and has, if anything, strengthened. In the 1983 sample over a fifth of those men with fathers in Classes VI and VII had moved up into service-class positions, and only around a half could themselves be categorized as working-class. Moreover if unemploy-ment is taken as itself a mobility status, then a still more striking result emerges: in 1983 the proportion of all men of working-class origins who were themselves actually employed in manual wage-earning jobs falls to as low as two-fifths (Table 9.12). In other words, one could say that the intergenerational stability of the working class has of late been sharply reduced, concomitantly with what we earlier described as the polarization of working-class mobility chances.

To complete the picture, though, it is again necessary to consider patterns of work-life movement. In several respects, these are clearly favourable to class formation. First of all, the analyses of chapter 5 strongly suggest that men who appear as intergenerationally stable in Class VI or Class VII will tend for the most part to have experienced only very restricted work-life mobility and, in fact, a high degree of continuity in manual wage-earning employment: if they have ever left such employment, they will have moved into other (overwhelmingly intermediate-class) occupations only for quite short periods of time. In general, it would seem that the work-life mobility that occurs away from Class VI and VII positions is of a doubtfully permanent kind. While an upward-mobility route of some importance can be discerned leading from initial employment in a manual occupation, via intermediate-class positions (especially within Class III), to a secure place within the service class, the bulk of the movement that is observed from manual to lower-level nonmanual positions (as of that in the opposite direction) must be accorded a rather high probability of being subsequently reversed.

Secondly, one may suppose that those men whose mobility from the working class *is* most likely to be permanent will tend to leave manual work at a quite early age. For example, although we have shown that those of our 1974 respondents who followed indirect mobility routes to Class I arrived there at an appreciably later age than did those who gained direct entry to the service class, the average at which the former first attained a Class I position was still under 30. Thus, it would seem possible to identify at any one time a very large section of the working class—that, say, of men who have passed their mid-twenties—for whom the chances of any decisive movement from their present class position must be reckoned as rather slight.[17]

Thirdly, it may be noted that while our 1974 work-history data showed that the work experience of men intergenerationally stable in Classes VI and VII was largely confined to manual employment, movement *between* Class VI and Class VII—that is, skilled and nonskilled—occupations was quite frequent. Taken together with the high level of intergenerational mobility and fluidity between these classes that our 1972 and 1983 inquiries reveal, this would suggest that no very powerful or extensive social barriers exist *within* the range of working-class positions as defined by our schema. There are no doubt a number of highly skilled manual occupations, comprised by Class VI, that *are* characterized by a relatively high degree of both 'closure' and work-life continuity on the part of those who gain admittance to them;[18] but our findings would in general lend support to the argument advanced by Westergaard and Resler that the significance of the division between the skilled and nonskilled sections of the working class has over recent decades been much diminished, and that the extent of the mobility that is evident 'within the world of manual work' may be seen both as indicating this increased homogeneity of the working class and as contributing to its greater integration.[19]

The main countervailing tendency in this respect which must now be recognized is clearly that created by the return of mass unemployment, and especially by unemployment of a long-term kind. Our findings reported in chapter 9 brought out the full extent to which unemployment is a working-class 'fate', in the sense of one to which those in manual wage-earning jobs are far more exposed than any other section of the active population. But the possibility evidently exists— and indeed would seem already to be in some degree realized—of a major division opening up within the working class as the long-term unemployed are increasingly set apart from those in work in their standards and styles of living and in their perceived needs and interests. The ultimate result of such a process would be the formation of an 'underclass', concentrated—and in turn isolated and fragmented —within the inner cities and the areas of most rapid industrial decay.

We earlier noted Sorokin's claim that in the economically advanced societies of the West, the long-run tendency is for the 'permanent' core of the working class to decline in importance relative to an expanding 'fluid' element.[20] How- ever, an argument on these lines does not fit well with the British experience. Over the last half century or so, it is evident that the working class has become increasingly self-recruiting and hence more homogenous as regards the social origins of its members. And although the amount of upward mobility into service-class positions has steadily grown, such decisive movement away from working-class origins has been largely restricted to men at an early stage of their careers. Thus, the bulk of the working class, as it exists at any one point in time, is made up of men whose mobility opportunities are in fact relatively few and limited. In short, there is little reason to suppose that any diminution has occurred within the working class in the proportion of those who are, to use Sorokin's own terms, both 'hereditary' *and* 'lifetime proletarians'. In the light of the tendencies that have been reviewed, it may indeed be held that, during the post-war years, economic growth did not so much further the decomposition of the working class as help to bring about its 'maturation', so far at least as its demographic identity is concerned.[21] And in so far as qualifications to this argument would now seem needed, they are ones that reflect not continuing economic success, but rather the conditions that have prevailed in Britain after the ending of the long boom. The former very gradual decline in the size of the working class has given way to a far more dramatic contraction as a consequence of de-industrialization and 'jobless growth'; and a new source of differentiation and potential cleavage within the working class has emerged with the return of unemployment at persistingly high levels.

In the foregoing we have then claimed that, from examination of patterns and trends in mobility within the structure of class positions, it is possible to discern in modern Britain at least two instances of class formation at what we would term the demographic level: instances, that is, of classes existing as collectivities of individuals and families that are identifiable through the degree of continuity of their class locations over time. Such identification is possible, we have concluded, in the case of the service class and the working class; whereas, in con- trast, within the range of intermediate-class positions that we have distinguished— with the possible exception of those of the petty bourgeoisie—the extent and nature of mobility is such that the existence of classes as collectivities that retain their identity through time is highly problematic. Thus, as we turn next to the further implications for class formation that mobility may have at the socio- cultural level and at that of political orientations and action, it is in fact on the service class and the working class that we shall concentrate our attention. We noted earlier in this chapter that arguments had been advanced to suggest that mobility, through its effects at the levels in question, could exert both a support- ive and a destabilizing influence in regard to the existing socio-political order. In what follows we will seek to keep both these possibilities in mind.

As regards the service class, we may perhaps most usefully begin by recalling that we found no evidence to suggest that men who had been upwardly mobile into the higher echelons of this class were at all likely to have experienced their mobility as an unduly stressful or ultimately unrewarding process. The analyses that we reported in chapters 6 and 7 led us to reject the idea that mobility is an inherently dissociative phenomenon which characteristically leads to the disrup- tion of the primary social relations of the mobile individual and in turn to his social isolation or marginality. While relatively long-range mobility of the kind that concerned us could certainly be associated with changes in the social lives of the men who achieved it, these effects, or concomitants, of mobility were clearly more complex and diverse than has been often supposed; and indeed in the case of upward mobility into the higher service class, from working-class origins at least, our findings would suggest that a *widening* in the individual's range of sociable relationships and activities is the most probable outcome.

Furthermore, as we have seen in chapter 8, the material that we obtained from our 1974 respondents in the form of life-history notes points rather consistently to the fact that mobility into the service class was viewed in a highly positive way—typically, that is, as representing an advancement in terms both of income and material living standards and of the possibilities for gaining intrinsic satisfactions from working life. At the same time it is, we believe, sig- nificant that conceptions of mobility as implying movement through a hierarchy of status groups or levels were almost entirely absent from our respondents' accounts. For it is an understanding of mobility of this kind that would appear to lie behind most theories of its disruptive psychological and social consequences. In this connection, we have stressed the importance of recognizing, first, that in modern Britain the upwardly mobile man within the service class can in no way be seen as a conspicuous outsider, but is in fact as likely as not to find that those around him have been upwardly mobile too; and secondly, that as a result, among other things, of the amount of upward mobility, the status order of British society would in any event appear to have considerably decayed in the course of the post-war years.

Rather, then, than mobility having meant that the service class has become permeated by men whose psychological difficulties make them potential dissi- dents against the *status quo*, it would seem from the findings that we have presented that the contrary effect is by far the more probable. That is, that the extent of upward mobility over recent decades, occasioned by the expansion of the service class, has been a major stabilizing influence in British society in creating a sizeable grouping of men within this class who are aware of having 'made their way' and done well for themselves (while not typically being burdened by excessive ambition), and whose attitudes towards the existing order of society would thus seem likely to be ones of acceptance if not indeed of approval and gratitude.

We can therefore offer little support for theories which became fashionable during the 1970s of the emergence of a 'new class' from among the swelling ranks of higher-level white-collar employees which would respresent—according to taste—a major source of socio-cultural dissidence or of moral and political radicalism within 'post-industrial' or 'late-capitalist' society.[22] We would see much greater force in an earlier and far more down-to-earth observation by Wilensky: namely, that 'careers ... are a major source of stability for modern society', in that, while developed to meet the needs of bureaucratic organization, 'they give continuity to the personal experience of the most able and skilled segments of the population'—not to mention obvious material advantages.[23] Furthermore, in the case of our upwardly mobile respondents, the life-history data that we collected would suggest that while an objective widening in mobility opportunities was frequently recognized in intergenerational perspective, work-life mobility, on the other hand, which for many had in fact been the basis of the success, was usually seen—and for quite understandable reasons—as essentially a matter of personal achievement. In other words, the dominant mobility ideology of these men provided neatly for approval and justification *both* of their society *and* of themselves and the positions of advantage that they had attained.

Are we then to conclude that the implications of the extensive 'recruitment from below' into the service class are ones that predominantly favour integration and stability rather than discontent and an impetus to change? This, we believe, must by now represent the most realistic judgement. The service class of present-day British society would appear to stand, like the growing middle class already envisaged by Marx, as a collectivity with a major interest in, and commitment to, the *status quo*, and hence as a barrier to radical change that serves to 'increase the social security and power of the upper ten thousand'. It is true that in consequence of its rapid growth, the service class remains highly heterogeneous in the social origins of its members, and the question thus arises of how far the demographic identity created by the intergenerational and work-life stability of its membership goes together with a corresponding socio-cultural identity and potential for collective action. We have indeed seen from the results of our 1974 inquiry that the life-styles of upwardly mobile men represent, in many respects, some kind of normative compromise between those typical of their class of origin and those typical of the Class I core; and further that these mobile men tend not only to retain ties with their closer kin at least, but also to have associates and friends who are more mixed in their class composition than are those of intergenerationally stable service-class members. It could therefore be that for some time yet political orientations within this class will likewise be substantially influenced by the trajectories that its members have followed in achieving service-class positions as well as by the interests these positions now give them in common. At the same time, though, we have found little to suggest that upwardly mobile men are in any serious way deprived of opportunities for assimilation into their class of destination, and it is notable that in 1974 only a small minority reported *no* ties of sociability with other service-class members: in fact, only 10 per cent among those whose mobility has followed a direct route and 20 per cent among those whose mobility had been indirect. And, looking to the future, the significance is then once more underlined of the steadily increasing importance that direct mobility routes are assuming.

Another consequence of the growth of the service class has been that structural divisions within it—in terms, say, of *situs* or sector or occupational groupings—have become more apparent, and this, it should be noted, has also prompted speculation on possible socio-cultural, and political diversity.[24] That such divisions can be traced within the service class—as within any other—is scarcely to be doubted; but what is not clear is that they are unusually marked. Certainly, so far as mobility between these divisions is concerned, more detailed analyses of our 1972 data would suggest that it is at a rather high level both intra- and intergenerationally. In the former case, the most notable tendency is for professionals eventually to move into administrative and managerial positions; while in the latter, it is, conversely, for the sons of administrators and managers to be, if anything, *more* likely to be found in professional occupations than in ones similar to their fathers'.[25] In addition, further analyses of our 1972 data have also shown that men in different types of employment within the service class have very similar patterns of choice of leisure-time associates, and moreover ones which comprise relatively high levels of inter-association.[26]

In sum, while the service class can still be regarded as one *in statu nascendi*, the indications consistently are that its demographic consolidation is likely to be matched by a steady strengthening of its socio-cultural identity. It may be expected, like other classes, to contain within it segments that have the potential to be mobilized across a range of political ideology and action and, distinctively, to be a source of leaders and activists of all political colorations. But, we would believe, as the service class emerges as an increasingly important basis of collective action, it will be seen to constitute a primarily conservative force within modern society, so far at least as the prevailing structure of class inequality is concerned. In this case, it is then arguments emphasizing the integrative force of high rates of mobility—or, more precisely, of upward mobility—that would appear to be most strongly supported.

Turning now to the working class, we may begin by noting the counterpart of the claim that upward mobility tends to give rise to psychological stress that can alienate the individual from the society within which he has achieved 'success': namely, the claim that downward mobility—or failure to match the achievements of others—will lead to resentment and discontent that can likewise constitute a threat to socio-political stability. However, just as we were unable to find evidence to support the former argument in the case of men who had been upwardly mobile into the higher levels of the service class, so too are we unable to support the latter in the case of those men who had been downwardly mobile from service-class origins to working-class (or for that matter intermediate-class) positions, or in the case of those who had remained intergenerationally stable within the working class.

First, as regards men downwardly mobile from service-class origins, they represent, as our national inquiries show, a small and declining mobility flow, and as a component of the working class they are indeed almost negligible. Moreover, both our 1972 and our 1974 data provide clear indications that their mobility cannot in any event be taken as decisive in that their chances of counter-mobility back to the service class must be reckoned as rather high. In turn, then, it is scarcely surprising to find in the life-history notes of men whom we have categorized as downwardly mobile not only a reluctance to see themselves as failures or even as having been downwardly mobile, but further, in many instances, fairly plausible justifications for their own definition of the situation.[27]

Secondly, as regards men who have remained intergenerationally stable within the working class, what is perhaps most significant—to judge again from our life-history material—is how little resentment they display on account of their immobility. This might be thought surprising, especially in the light of our findings that during the last half-century or so inequalities in class mobility chances have remained essentially unaltered, and have moreover been extreme so far as the relative chances of men of service-class and working-class origins are concerned. But what must be recognized is that trends and patterns in relative mobility rates represent aspects of inequality that are of extremely low social visibility. One is dealing here with 'social facts' that members of a society can have little or no possibility of perceiving in their everyday lives—even though they have a significant bearing on their life-fates—and that we as sociologists have indeed only been able to determine through large-scale and rather elaborate processes of inquiry. There is thus really very little basis for expecting that inequalities of the kind in question should be at all widely reflected in the social conscious-ness of members of the working class, or of any other collectivity.

On the other hand, the actual extent of *upward* mobility, as it has occurred over recent decades, may be regarded as having relatively high social visibility. For if, as is the case, some 20 per cent of men of working-class origins make their way into professional, administrative, and managerial positions, it would seem reasonable to suppose that the large majority of those who remain within the working class will have first-hand knowledge of at least one person—say, a close relative, a former school-friend or an ex-workmate—who has achieved mobility of this kind. And what might then be more plausibly supposed is that in these cir-cumstances a recognition of apparent 'openness' might coexist with some degree of discontent or frustration among those who, so to speak, were left behind. We can, however, suggest a reason why, at least over the post-war years, such a re-sponse should not have been at all widespread. That is, that even those members of the working class whom we would count as immobile were in fact generally aware of having experienced social advancement in an intergenerational perspec-tive. As the life-history notes of our stable working-class respondents revealed, these men predominantly recognized that, relative to their fathers, they enjoyed greatly improved pay and conditions of employment and in general a much higher standard of living, despite the fact that they were still engaged in broadly the same kind of employment. Thus, even if one assumes that men upwardly mobile from the working class do constitute an important reference group for those who remain within it, the comparisons that the latter draw must be thought less likely to give rise to discontent if they are able to feel that they also are involved in a process of social advancement, albeit one of a different character. As Wilensky has argued in suggesting a 'consolation-prize theory of social mobility', in a modern society which is in course of a sustained economic expansion, as was Britain in the 1950s and 1960s, the possibilities for advancement are in fact quite diverse, so that for those who fail to achieve upward mobility in its more decisive and comprehensive forms, there still remain many alternatives that can serve to prevent any widespread sense of deprivation.[28]

At the same time, though, the fact that men who had followed their fathers as manual wage-workers did not on this account tend to feel resentment does not imply that these men were generally well satisfied with their lot. On the contrary, we may draw further on the life-history material supplied by our stable working-class respondents to suggest that while they might show no strong sense of grievance over the extent of inequalities of opportunity, they were none the less well aware of their actual *lack* of opportunity, so far at least as their own working-class lives were concerned. They recognized work as being crucially important to their own and their families' economic and social well-being; but the goals that it appeared possible for them to pursue within work were narrowly restricted: in effect, to ones of a largely instrumental kind which centred on the wage-bargain and which implied a very limited scope for personal achievement or fulfilment. Moreover, in the light of our research findings, such an outlook cannot be regarded as other than a largely realistic one. While the chances for upward mobility of men of working-class origins who themselves began work in manual wage-earning employment did not decline over the post-war years, they became ones which to an increasing degree were confined to men in their early working lives and which, if not then taken up, rather rapidly dwindled. In other words, for the majority of the members of the working class as it existed at any one time, the essential meaning of work—even in the years when work was readily available—was constrained to that of simply a 'job' rather than a career.

What is now of course also of obvious relevance is the likely effect on working-class perceptions of, and responses to, inequalities of opportunity of the return of mass unemployment which, as we saw in chapter 9, has sharply polarized working-class mobility chances. This is not an issue that we can address directly on the basis of our own research but, in the light of various other inquiries, two conclusions of some importance may be reached. On the one hand, it is evident that the experience of unemployment appears, over all, more likely to produce fatalism and apathy than active dissent and protest; but, on the other hand, it would also seem clear that working-class responses may still vary significantly with cross-national differences in political culture and organization. Most importantly perhaps for present purposes, it has been shown that in the British case, in contrast with the American, the unemployed, even if politically quiescent, are far less ready to interpret their situation in individualistic terms and more inclined to see it as a collective and indeed a 'class' fate. And underlying this contrast, it has been suggested, is the lack of any British equivalent to the ideology of the 'American Dream' and a correspondingly greater scepticism over the extent to which individual achievement can override social disadvantage.[29]

In sum, then, one may say that while the patterns and trends of mobility that have prevailed in modern Britain, even after the ending of the long boom, have not served to generate disaffection within the working class, neither does it seem that they have produced any very powerful 'demonstration effect' in favour of an individualistic orientation towards the pursuit of social betterment which has been capable of undermining traditional working-class collectivism. The crucial fact here is, we would argue, that for those who fail to achieve mobility out of the working class, individual initiative can be of only rather limited importance in the achievement of the goals that remain for them or in the avoidance of the risks that threaten them. Their economic fortunes will be determined essentially on a collective basis: that is, through the extent to which they are caught up in, or excluded from, such general economic advance as may occur, and through the extent to which they are able to defend and pursue their interests via collective action.

Finally, then, we must turn to the implications of mobility for the capacity of the working class to engage in action of this kind. We have already stressed the way in which mobility trends have created a present-day working class that is demographically well defined, chiefly in that it is to a large degree intergenerationally self-recruiting. We may now ask, as we did with the service class, how far a demographic identity is matched by a socio-cultural one. In the latter case, we concluded that the main threat to the socio-cultural cohesiveness of the service class came from its diverse sources of recruitment in that mobile men to some extent carry the normative and relational patterns of their class origins into their class of destination. The case of the working class is, however, a clearly different one, since it is *from* its recruitment pattern—that is, from the homogeneity of the social origins of its members—that its demographic identity primarily derives; and in turn, one may then suppose, its socio-cultural homogeneity is in this way also favoured.

The findings that we have earlier presented, in chapter 7 especially, would suggest that although the life-styles and associational patterns displayed by respondents whom we take to represent the working-class core are often not very sharply differentiated from those of men stable in intermediate-class positions (which in view of our data on work-life mobility is not surprising[30]), they are in most respects distinct enough from those of the service-class core. And what then is of chief importance is that within the working-class—in contrast with the service-class—the intergenerationally stable core comprises not a small minority but rather the majority of the membership as a whole. To be sure, the intergenerational stability of the working class is in decline, largely on account of the steady increase in upward mobility from working-class origins; and this no doubt results in more social ties—of kinship, friendship, etc.—linking members of the working class to those in higher-level class positions. But against these developments may be set three further factors promoting the socio-cultural homogeneity of the working class, to each of which we have in fact already referred: first, as a consequence of declining downward mobility, the very small *déclassé* element within the body of manual wage-workers—which several authors have seen as a potentially important source of alternative values to those of collectivism and solidarity;[31] secondly, the similarly small representation of men of farm origins who, to judge from studies made in other industrial societies, tend to differ significantly from more 'established' industrial-urban workers in their characteristic orientations and conduct both in the work-place and more generally;[32] and thirdly, the relatively high rates of both inter- and intragenerational mobility that occur between skilled and nonskilled groupings, thus blurring what may—as in the German case—be a major line of socio-cultural division. In this last connection, it is noteworthy that in the analyses of chapters 6 and 7 we could combine together in our working-class core the two sub-samples of men intergenerationally stable in Class VI and Class VII since no systematic differences were apparent between them across our data relating to life-styles and patterns of association.

Throughout the post-war period it was fashionable for commentators on British society to point to influences—for example, those of rising living standards, the mass media, greater residential mobility, etc.—that were, supposedly, bringing about the decomposition of the working class as a social and cultural entity and its absorption into a predominantly 'middle-class', or 'middle-mass', society. However, the foregoing discussion would suggest that the influence exerted by patterns and trends in class mobility is of a generally opposing kind. Although the British working class has declined in size, and at an increasing rate in the recent past, its 'social metabolism' has been such as to sustain its internal cohesiveness. And in so far as a threat to this cohesiveness now exists, it lies, as we have noted, in the formation of an underclass of the long-term or the recurrently unemployed and their families. In other words, it is one that derives not from the consequences of continuing economic growth and spreading affluence but rather from deteriorating economic performance and widening inequalities of condition and opportunity alike.

We have now attempted to map out, so to speak, the main contours of class formation within present-day British society as these are shaped by mobility flows and their more immediate consequences or concomitants. It thus remains for us in this chapter to consider the implications of the account that we have given for the likelihood of future change in the pattern of relative mobility chances and, in particular, for the possibility of movement away from the essential stability of the last half-century or more in the direction of greater openness.

Writing a decade ago, it was possible, if not to be optimistic about the achievement of a more open society, then at all events to envisage a fairly specific and not entirely implausible course of political development which might lead towards this goal. A working class, increasingly well organized and apparently growing in self-confidence in its own collective strength, could be seen as posing a challenge to the prevailing social order, not in the form of any revolutionary rejection, but rather through its *de facto* unwillingness to limit the pursuit of its interests to ways that could be readily accommodated within this order. This recalcitrance found its most evident and disruptive expression in what were experienced as persisting industrial or economic 'problems'—the strike problem, the productivity problem, the inflation problem. One way of attempting a resolution of these difficulties appeared then to lie, at least under a Labour administration, in processes which, as they had evolved in other western societies, were variously described as those of 'societal bargaining', 'political exchange' or '(neo-)corporatism'. Essential to such forms of political economy was an agreement by organized labour to collaborate with government and with employers in devising and implementing economic strategies which centred on some version of wage regulation, and which thus required that trade unions should hold in check their bargaining power within labour markets and work-places. In return for such restraint, unions would then seek, and expect to obtain, compensating benefits for their members through tax concessions, extensions of workers' legal rights, expansionist employment policies, and, above all, social policies which would be directed towards essentially egalitarian goals. In Britain such an approach had not developed to the same degree as, say, in the Scandinavian nations so as to become in effect the main vehicle of social-democratic politics. But the 'social contract' that operated between the Labour government and the unions during the years 1974–6 could be seen as a serious attempt to start on this route, and one which might be followed by further agreements negotiated on a more ambitious basis.[33]

At the present time, however, such a scenario for radical egalitarian reform must appear very far removed from political realities. With hindsight, the 'social contract' would now seem more likely to have marked the end of a road rather than a new beginning. For not only did successor agreements fail to materialize— underlining major organizational and ideological deficits within the British labour movement—but further this failure was an important factor in Labour's defeat at the General Election of 1979 and the return of a Conservative government committed to a policial economy of a radically different kind: that is, one explicitly aimed at restoring the 'disciplines' of the capitalist market economy and business enterprise and at reducing union power at all levels. Moreover, despite unemployment figures significantly worsened by government policies, and which would have earlier been regarded as 'politically unacceptable', the Conservatives were confirmed in office in 1983, while Labour's share of the popular vote fell by a quarter to 27.6 per cent—lower than it had ever been since 1918. Subsequently, Labour's attempts to rehabilitate itself as a party capable of regaining and effectively using power have been less than convincing, and not least because of its continuing difficulties in presenting its economic and its social policies as being coherently related.

That the issue of social inequality has, over the last decade, been effectively removed from the political agenda—and that its restoration in the foreseeable future is highly uncertain—cannot then be denied. However, what is still open to serious dispute is the account that is to be given of how this situation came about. In particular, it is important in the present context that one interpretation, which has been widely favoured among political commentators, academic and otherwise, should be called into question—on the grounds of its method, content, and implications alike.

In this interpretation, the key factor underlying the recent course of political change in Britain is 'class dealignment'—a weakening of the association between class membership and political allegiance, which is seen as reflecting a general process of class decomposition and, in turn, a decline in the differentiating and mobilizing influence of class.[34] This argument, it should be noted, has not been developed on the basis of any systematic evidence relating to class structure, class mobility, or class values and life-styles in contemporary Britain, but proceeds rather by way of what might be called 'reverse sociologism'. The starting point is with the analysis of political events and tendencies and then, from such analysis, inferences are made back to supposed changes at the level of social structure and process which, it is believed, the events and tendencies must betoken. Thus, when the thesis of class dealignment was first advanced, after Labour's electoral successes of 1974, the main emphasis was on 'middle-class' fragmentation and the declining socio-political solidarity of white-collar groupings. But with the elections of 1979 and 1983, the emphasis correspondingly shifted to the supposed decomposition of the working class and to arguments on this theme which were in fact little more than a restatement of those which, as we have noted above, recurred throughout the post-war years. Labour was failing at the polls because it continued to be a 'class' party—one whose *raison d'être* and appeal presupposed a class-divided society—in a period in which class was of steadily waning significance as a determinant of socio-political orientations, and in particular among the manual workers who had traditionally provided the bulk of Labour's electoral support.[35] In effect, then, the implication of the 'class dealignment' thesis is that the political eclipse of Labour and the consequent fading of the prospects for any radical attack on class inequalities stem ultimately from social changes which at the same time serve to undermine the very relevance of an egalitarian programme: in modern society, in other words, class divisions are of declining significance for political action both as a mainspring *and* as a concern.

If such an interpretation were valid, it would then run counter to much of what has been argued in the foregoing. Claims of class dealignment which focused on an expanding service class might be thought consistent with the diverse bases of recruitment to this class that we have documented; but, as we have also shown, the resulting heterogeneity of social origins and backgrounds has certainly not increased over the last decade. And so far as the working class is concerned, one would have to say that for a politically significant process of decomposition to have occurred, powerful countervailing influences to those of mobility patterns and trends would need to have been at work.

In fact, however, when the class dealignment thesis is tested on the basis of an adequate data-set and through appropriate analytical techniques, it does *not* find confirmation. Using standardized data from the British General Election Surveys of 1964 to 1983, Heath, Jowell, and Curtice have shown that the net association between class (as determined by a version of our own schema) and vote has remained remarkably constant, and that such variation as is revealed is of a trendless kind.[36] To be sure, the proportion of working-class voters supporting Labour declined in 1979 and again, and more sharply, in 1983. But, as Heath and his associates point out, such a shift is one which could be—and in fact *was*—produced by effects other than a weakening in the relative propensity of workers to vote for Labour rather than for other parties. Indeed, what can further be seen in the light of the analyses in question is that claims of empirical support for the class dealignment thesis made in other studies are vitiated precisely because their authors do not employ techniques capable of identifying and separating out the several different effects that a series of class-by-vote tables logically entails.

Specifically, the major sources of Labour's electoral failure that Heath and his associates reveal are two. The first is in fact an essentially political one: the poor performance of Labour as a party, accentuated in 1983 by the emergence of the Alliance, which resulted in a loss of allegiance not only, or distinctively, among the working class but in fact to a similar relative degree across all sections of the electorate. The second source is sociological, but straightforward: not a decline in working-class political cohesiveness but simply the decline in the size of the working class, within which, of course, Labour support has always been heavily concentrated. That these two factors alone can effectively account for the decline in the Labour vote among the working class—and indeed for all other shifts in class voting—is shown by the data of Table 12.1. In this table, the observed distributions of vote by class at the elections of 1979 and 1983 are set against the distributions that would be expected under a model (as applied to data from all elections from 1964 to 1983) which allows for changes in the parties' share of the total vote and in the sizes of classes but *not* in the association between class and vote: that is to say, which requires this association to be constant over the whole period covered. As can be seen, observed and expected values throughout the table are remarkably close, and it is therefore apparent that there is no need—and no warrant—for the introduction of any notion of class decomposition. Or conversely, one could say, *if* such a process were in train, then evidence of a steady weakening in the association of class and vote, net of other effects, *should* have been shown up.[37]

The fact that 'class dealignment' can be rejected as the basis of an account of how a political situation inimical to egalitarian reform came about does not of course alter that situation, but it does set a rather different complexion upon it. For those who share in our own commitment to the idea of a more genuinely open society, it means, first of all, that this commitment cannot be simply dismissed as one that is being outmoded by some apparently spontaneous process of class abatement; and it further implies that, rather than class interests having to be seen as of diminishing significance as the bases of political action, one may still maintain the view that such interests remain inherent in the prevailing structure of class inequalities and will in turn continue to shape political action directed towards either preserving or changing this structure.[38]

Further still, the alternative account to that of 'class dealignment' which emerges from the work of Heath, Jowell, and Curtice, while in no way one calculated to generate great optimism over Labour's electoral future, does at all events lead to a fairly clear definition of the difficulties that have to be overcome if a situation is to be created in which issues of social equality could conceivably return to the political agenda. What is indicated is that the Labour Party must not simply regain the general political efficacy that it displayed in, say, the 1960s—most obviously, by overcoming its internal divisions and organizational and policy weaknesses; it must improve upon this level of performance in order to counter the adverse electoral consequences that it faces from the contraction of the working class. Moreover, since class dealignment in voting has not in fact occurred, it must be reckoned of doubtful value for Labour to attempt to widen its electoral appeal by becoming a 'catch-all' party of the centre. Rather, it must seek to remain a 'class' party but at the same time to create for itself a wider class constituency: that is, to ensure its full potential support from among the body of manual wage-workers while attracting

Table 12.1
*Observed distributions of vote by class at General Elections of 1979
and 1983 (upper rows) compared with distributions expected under
model of constant association between class and vote (lower rows)*[a]

Class[b]	Con.	Lab.	Other	% of total electorate
		percent by row		
1979 (N = 1,436)				
I+II	59 60	22 20	19 20	28
III	48 50	36 33	16 18	19
IV	76 73	13 14	11 13	9
V	40 43	44 42	16 16	11
VI+VII	30 28	55 59	14 12	33
All	47	37	16	100
1983 (N = 3,072)				
I+II	54 55	14 14	32 31	29
III	46 47	25 24	29 28	24
IV	71 70	12 10	17 20	8
V	48 42	26 32	26 26	7
VI+VII	30 30	49 48	21 22	32
All	45	29	26	100

Notes: (a) Estimated from class-by-vote tables for all General Elections, 1964 to 1983.
  (b) Men and women economically active (or retired) categorized according to their
  own present or last occupation and employment status; according to spouse's
  occupation and employment status if not active but married and living with an
  economically active (or retired) spouse.

Source: Standardized data-sets from British General Election Surveys, 1964–83, prepared
  and made available by Anthony Heath.

additional support from among members of other groupings in not radically dissimilar class situations.

In the light of our own findings, the most promising targets here would appear to be the routine clerical, sales, and other service workers of Class III and the lower-level technical and supervisory workers of Class V. We have emphasized— as against Marxist authors—that these groupings cannot be regarded as constituting a ready-made 'new proletariat' that might be taken over *en bloc*; and indeed it is apparent from Table 12.1 that their present levels of Labour voting are quite low. But what may be argued is that since workers of the kind in question occupy class locations which are in our terms 'intermediate'—that is to say, of a mixed or ambiguous character—and, in addition, do so only rather impermanently, in the course of very varied work-life trajectories, one can identify here a quite sizeable pool of voters *within* which favourable possibilities should exist for Labour to mobilize wider electoral support.[39] Moreover, as to the basis on which this mobilization might be attempted, our findings would in turn lead us to underwrite Westergaard's recent suggestion that the line that Labour should seek to emphasize in redefining and enlarging its 'natural' constituency is that separating the 'jobs class' from the 'careers class';[40] for it is indeed the distinction between jobs and careers that is in some way involved in many of the more striking class differences in mobility chances and experience that we have shown up.

It is notable that in several recent studies of social democracy, informed chiefly by the experience of northern and central European nations, different lines of argument have converged on one conclusion. This is that the defining strategy of social democracy is the use of parliamentary institutions, public policy, and ultimately the power of the state in order to redress inequalities in social power and advantage generated by the working of a capitalist economy; *but* that the successful pursuit of this strategy of 'politics against markets', in the interests primarily of the working class, has *always* required social-democratic parties to transcend class structural developments in order to achieve adequate popular support. In other words, it has from the first been necessary for these parties to act politically on the 'raw material' of the class structure so as to create and sustain collective class identities and to form class alliances advantageous to them.[41] In the northern European context especially, this lesson was learnt early, since parties representing the emerging working class could for several decades hope to come to power only if they gained significant backing also from farmers, smallholders, artisans, etc.; and in turn then the need at a later stage of development to win support from among the ranks of new 'intermediate' strata was readily seen. In the British case, in contrast—in which, as we saw in chapter 11, the working class was numerically dominant over an unusually long period—the lesson seems scarcely to have been learnt at all. Within the Labour Party left-wing and also 'labouristic' elements have for long failed to come to grips with the problem of a declining working class,[42] while on the right, where power has chiefly rested, the favoured solution has been the self-defeating one, from a social-democratic point of view, of abandoning class politics altogether. Consequently, opportunities have been repeatedly missed to define and politicize issues in class terms, but in such a way as to associate other groupings with the body of manual wage-workers—for example, over education, pensions, housing, employee rights, etc.[43]

Whether Labour will prove capable of meeting the challenge that lies before it cannot be predicted. But what may be said is that, if it does not, then no movement towards a more open society can be anticipated. For to return to what has been a central theme of this book, there are no grounds for supposing that any tendencies in this direction will be generated 'endogenously'—as, say, part of the inherent 'logic of development' of modern capitalist societies. Prevailing patterns of class-linked inequalities in mobility chances appear to be ones of great durability, and, as we have shown, those presently to be observed in British society are of remarkably long standing. There would then seem little reason to expect any significant reduction in these inequalities other than as a result of 'exogenous' political intervention designed to modify the basic form of class stratification that they express. In the absence of such intervention, any change which might occur would seem far more likely to be towards less rather than greater openness. The general deterioration in the economic climate over the last decade or so has not itself produced such a shift, or at least not one which is so far visible. But in consequence of this deterioration and, since 1979, of the economic and social policies of a government which has explicitly rejected greater social equality as a goal, widening differences are now beginning to appear in standards and styles of living—especially, but not only, through the emergence of a highly disadvantaged underclass. If these tendencies towards greater inequality of condition continue, then, one may suppose, they will at some point be reflected in a widening also in the already marked inequalities of opportunity that we have documented, and that so needlessly limit human development and waste the store of talent in our society.

NOTES

1. While patterns of social fluidity appear generally to show considerable stability over time, evidence of episodes of change or of differences as between studies conducted several decades apart has been produced for several modern societies. See, for example, Erikson, 'Changes in Social Mobility in Industrial Nations: The Case of Sweden'; John H. Goldthorpe and Lucienne Portocarero, 'La Mobilité sociale en France, 1953–1970: Nouvel examen', *Revue française de sociologie*, vol. 22, 1981; and Albert A. Simkus, 'Changes in Occupational Inheritance under Socialism: Hungary 1930–1973', *Research in Social Stratification and Mobility*, vol. 1, 1981.
2. The most recent attempt in this direction, H. Himsworth, 'Epidemiology, Genetics and Sociology', *Journal of Biosocial Science*, vol. 16, 1984, is in no way convincing and reveals a lack of awareness of the results of much recent mobility research. See John H. Goldthorpe, 'Epidemiology, Genetics and Sociology: A Comment', *Journal of Biosocial Science*. vol. 17, 1985.
3. On education, see A.H. Halsey, Anthony Heath, and J.M. Ridge, *Origins and Destinations*, Oxford: Clarendon Press, 1980; and Halsey, 'Schools' and 'Post-Secondary Education' in Halsey (ed.), *British Social Trends since 1900*; and on health, Peter Townsend and Nick Davidson (eds.), *Inequalities in Health*, Harmondsworth: Penguin Books, 1982.

4. In saying that egalitarian policies failed—i.e. did not in fact produce appreciably greater equality in class life-chances—we do not, it should be noted, imply that they have been entirely without egalitarian influence. In their absence, inequalities might have worsened.

5. As Grusky and Hauser have observed ('Comparative Social Mobility Revisited'), the FJH hypothesis must stand in opposition to the argument advanced by Blau and Duncan and others (see pp. 14–15 above) that a steady increase in fluidity may be expected in modern industrial societies as an aspect of their progressive universalism. Cf. Goldthorpe, 'On Economic Development and Social Mobility'.

6. See above, pp. 46–7. An interesting question, which can only be decided by future 'élite' studies, is whether the degree of exclusiveness displayed by élite groupings will be diminished as the effects of more broadly based recruitment to professional, administrative, and managerial occupations begin to show through at élite level, or whether exclusiveness will be maintained through the operation of intra-occupational selection procedures that embody a class bias.

7. To obtain an index of the homogeneity/heterogeneity of the origins of the members of a class, one could regard the inflow percentage distribution as the set of probabilities of a man in this class being from each of the possible classes of origin, and then sum the squares of these probabilities. The maximum value (complete homogeneity) that could thus be achieved would be 1, where the total membership of a class came from the same class of origin; and the minimum value would occur where the men in a class were equally distributed among all classes of origin—this being in fact the reciprocal of the number of such classes, or in our case, $1/7 = .143$. For a given mobility table, it would seem best to express the index for each class as a percentage of this minimum value. If this is done with the inflow data of Table 2.1, the indices for Classes I and II are 112 (110) and 106 (106) respectively, the bracketed figures being those obtained if agricultural categories are included in the analysis. If men were recruited to these two classes on the basis of perfect mobility, so that their inflow distributions were the same as the row marginal distribution of Table 2.1, the index would in each case be 141 (135).

8. And see n. 7, p. 144 above, for evidence on the characteristics of those downwardly mobile from first occupations in Classes I and II, which suggests that such mobility is likely to be often of a temporary kind.

9. While we would doubt if the phenomenon of 'clogs to clogs in three generations' was at all as frequent in the heroic days of modern capitalism as apologists have suggested, we also think it significant that no corresponding folk expression has developed to refer to mobility into and out of what we have termed the service class, considered as in effect the successor to the classic bourgeoisie.

10. See further Goldthorpe, 'On the Service Class: Its Formation and Future'. Note also the significance in this respect of the shifting disparity ratios discussed in chapter 9, p. 265 above.

11. See, e.g., Poulantzas, *Les Classes sociales dans le capitalisme aujourdhui*; G. Carchedi, 'On the Economic Identification of the New Middle Class', *Economy and Society*, vol. 4, 1975; Erik Olin Wright, *Class, Crisis and the State*, London: New Left Books, 1978, and *Classes*, London: Verso, 1986; Rosemary Crompton and John Gubbay, *Economy and Class Structure*, London: Macmillan, 1977.

12. Cf. David Lockwood, 'The Weakest Link in the Chain: Some Comments on the Marxist Theory of Action', *Research in the Sociology of Work*, vol. 1, 1981; Goldthorpe, 'Soziale Mobilität und Klassenbildung'.

13. In the latter respect, one may note further from Figure 2.1 (pp. 52–3 above) the very superior chances of upward work-life mobility that are offered by a first occupation in an intermediate-class—i.e. overwhelmingly Class III or Class V—position, as compared with a first occupation in Class VI or VII. Substantial evidence confirming the favourable mobility chances of male clerical workers is also presented in Stewart, Prandy, and Blackburn, *Social Stratification and Occupations*, although they may well over-generalize from the results of a sample limited to areas of south-eastern England in the 1960s.

14. See in particular Crompton and Jones, *White-Collar Proletariat*.

15. See Goldthorpe, 'Women and Class Analysis' and the further items cited in chapter 10, n. 6.
16. The indices of homogeneity of origins for members of Class VI and Class VII, calculated as previously for Classes I and II, are 195 (187) and 195 (189) respectively. (Those for Classes III, IV, and V are 121 (120), 133 (155), and 150 (148) respectively.)
17. Cf. the discussion in Westergaard and Resler, *Class in a Capitalist Society*, pp. 309–312.
18. Cf. above, pp. 130–1.
19. *Class in a Capitalist Society*, p. 312. In this case, it may be noted, we go directly contrary to the generally received view in suggesting that mobility, rather than militating against class formation, actually contributes to it.
20. And cf. the very similar views advanced by more recent liberal authors: e.g. Lipset, as cited in chapter 1, n. 61 above; Aron, *Progress and Disillusion*, pp. 10–11.
21. Cf. Goldthorpe, 'The Current Inflation: Towards a Sociological Account'.
22. See, e.g., J. Ehrenreich and B. Ehrenreich, 'The Professional-Managerial Class', *Radical America*, vol. 11, 1977; P. Walker (ed.), *Between Capital and Labor*, New York: Monthly Review Press, 1979; B. Bruce Briggs (ed.), *The New Class?* New Brunswick: Transaction Books, 1979; Alvin W. Gouldner, *The Future of the Intellectuals and the Rise of the New Class*, London: Macmillan, 1979. For further critical examination of 'new class' theories, see Goldthorpe, 'On the Service Class: Its Formation and Future'.
23. 'Work, Careers and Social Integration', p. 555.
24. See, e.g., Heath *et al.*, *How Britain Votes*, ch. 5; also Patrick Dunleavy and Christopher T. Husbands, *British Democracy at the Crossroads*, London: Allen and Unwin, 1985, Part III.
25. See further Goldthorpe, 'On the Service Class: Its Formation and Future'.
26. See J. Clyde Mitchell and Frank Critchley, 'Configurational Similarity in Three Class Contexts in British Society', *Sociology*, vol. 19, 1985.
27. For example, to the effect that their downward mobility was of a voluntary (and perhaps short-term) kind, or that they were still only in the early stages of their envisaged careers.
28. H.L. Wilensky, 'Measures and Effects of Social Mobility', in Smelser and Lipset (eds.), *Social Structure and Mobility in Economic Development*.
29. See, e.g., Colin Fraser, Catherine Marsh, and Ray Jobling, 'Political Responses to Unemployment' in Roberts *et al.* (eds.), *New Approaches to Economic Life*; and Gordon Marshall, David Rose, Howard Newby, and Carolyn Vogler, 'Political Quiescence among the Unemployed in Modern Britain' in Rose (ed.), *Economic Decline and Social Change in Britain*, London: Hutchinson, 1987.
30. The greatest similarity, it will be recalled, was with men whose first occupation had been a manual one.
31. See, e.g., Lipset and Gordon, 'Mobility and Trade Union Membership', and H.L. Wilensky and Hugh Edwards, 'The Skidder: Ideological Adjustments of Downwardly Mobile Workers', *American Sociological Review*, vol. 24, 1959.
32. See, e.g., the now extensive literature on the French case including Alain Touraine and Orietta Ragazzi, *Ouvriers d'origine agricole*. Paris: Seuil, 1961; Claude Thélot, *Tel père, tel fils?* Paris: Dunod, 1982, ch. 3 esp.; Duncan Gallie, *Social Inequality and Class Radicalism in France and Britain*, Cambridge: Cambridge University Press.
33. See further on these themes the papers collected in Goldthorpe (ed.), *Order and Conflict in Contemporary Capitalism*.
34. See in particular David Butler and Donald Stokes, *Political Change in Britain: The Evolution of Electoral Choice*, London: Macmillan, 2nd ed., 1974, pp. 206–8 esp.; Ivor Crewe, Bo Särlvik and James Alt, 'Partisan Dealignment in Britain, 1964–74', *British Journal of Political Science*, vol. 7, 1977; Ivor Crewe, 'The Electorate: Partisan Dealignment Ten Years On' in H. Berrington (ed.), *Change in British Politics*, London: Cass, 1984; and Richard Rose and Ian McAllister, *Voters Begin to Choose*, London: Sage, 1986. Note that the thesis of 'class dealignment' supported by these authors is a more specific one than that of 'partisan dealignment'—referring to the electorate's generally declining attachment to the Conservative and Labour Parties—which in some cases they also advance and which is far better founded.

35. Indeed, the same people can be found making more or less the same arguments a quarter of a century apart. Thus, an early instance of 'reverse sociologism' is the claim made by Butler and Rose that the swing to the Conservatives at the 1959 election 'cannot be dismissed as an ephemeral veering of the electoral breeze. Long-term factors were also involved. Traditional working-class attitudes had been eroded by a steady growth of prosperity'. David Butler and Richard Rose, *The British General Election of 1959*, London: Macmillan, 1960, p. 15. No evidence of the 'long-term factors' was adduced. Again then in discussing the result of the 1983 election, Butler and Kavanagh refer to a 'loosening of the class structure'—again without any supporting evidence—which is seen as having been particularly damaging to Labour. David Butler and Dennis Kavanagh, *The British General Election of 1983*, London: Macmillan, 1984, p. 8.

36. *How Britain Votes*, ch. 3 esp. There is no reason to suppose that the result obtained is one that is highly dependent upon the class schema in question; thus, Heath *et al.* show that again no secular decline in the association between class and vote is apparent between 1964 and 1983 if the 'class' variable is a crude manual/nonmanual dichotomy. In this case, a weakening does show up for the 1979 and 1983 elections but, as is pointed out, this would be expected as a result simply of compositional changes within the manual category: in particular, the decline in the proportion of manual wage-earners and the rise in the proportion of those in self-employment—who have very different voting propensities. A failure to see this, and other, weaknesses of the manual/nonmanual division as a basis for investigating the class-vote association is apparent in most of the studies cited in n. 34 above.

37. The model, which is applied by Heath *et al.*, is in fact formally identical to that of constant or common social fluidity to which we have repeatedly resorted in our own analyses above. Instead of representing the hypothesis that, once marginal effects are controlled for, the association between class of origin and class of destination remains unchanged over time, between the sexes, across nations, etc., the model is in this case used to propose that the association between class and vote is unchanged over successive elections. Heath *et al.* specify their model and give the results of various applications in *How Britain Votes*, ch. 3, ns. 13 and 14, pp. 41-2.

     A further noteworthy parallel with mobility analyses is provided by the various ways of measuring the class-vote association adopted by proponents of the class dealignment thesis—for example, the 'Alford index' or the 'index of determination' devised by Rose and McAllister (see *Voters Begin to Choose*, ch. 3). These may be seen as comparable to the similarly *ad hoc* indices used in attempts to measure social fluidity before present techniques of multiplicative modelling had been developed and, in just the same way as such fluidity indices, they are flawed in being 'margin sensitive'. That is to say, they give measures of the class-vote association that are inevitably influenced by the marginal effects of class size and party share of the total vote, which must then make them particularly unsuitable for any attempt at establishing trends in this association. It would be unfair to censure exponents of the class dealignment thesis for using indices of the kind in question before the superiority of other techniques had been shown; and indeed in the first edition of this book (pp. 269-70) we did ourselves draw on some of the earlier class dealignment literature without fully realizing its inadequacies. But what is not creditable is to seek to maintain the class dealignment thesis on the basis of arguments which either ignore, or show a fundamental lack of understanding of, results achieved via the new techniques. See, e.g., Rose and McAllister, *Voters Begin to Choose*; Ivor Crewe, 'On the Death and Resurrection of Class Voting: Some Comments on *How Britain Votes*', *Political Studies*, vol. 35, 1987.

38. For further extensive survey evidence supporting this view, see Gordon Marshall, David Rose, Howard Newby, and Carolyn Vogler, *Social Class in Modern Britian*, London: Hutchinson, forthcoming. Heath *et al.* have themselves produced evidence to indicate that between 1964 and 1983 no decline occurred in subjective class awareness—and they pertinently ask why any such decline should be expected or supposed in view of abundant evidence of persisting, or even widening, class inequalities in many different aspects of social life. See *How Britain Votes* and also 'Trendless Fluctuation: Relative Class Voting 1964-83', *Political Studies*, vol. 35, 1987.

One might add here that a particular danger of the method of 'reverse sociologism' is that it encourages very partial views of current social change. Thus, proponents of the 'class dealignment' thesis have been led by their (faulty) electoral analyses to seek for and emphasize changes within the working class likely to make for greater socio-cultural heterogeneity—for example, increased home-ownership; but they have entirely neglected changes likely to have the opposite effect—for example, the declining visibility and social significance of the distinction between skilled and non-skilled grades. It is notable, and highly consistent with the results of our own analyses, that Heath *et al.* find no difference in the level of Labour support as between Class VI and Class VII voters.

39. Just how large this pool is reckoned to be depends on how one resolves issues raised in chapter 10 concerning the appropriate unit of class analysis. Following the conventional approach, in which the class position of the family is taken to be determined by that of its 'head', Classes III and V together account for about a quarter of the total electorate. For present purposes, at least, this is the approach we would regard as most realistic. But if the individual approach is followed, then Classes III and V account for almost a third of the electorate.

40. John Westergaard, 'The Once and Future Class', in James Curran (ed.), *The Future of the Left*, Cambridge: Polity Press, 1984. This would be close to the strategy followed by the Scandinavian social-democratic parties, and reflected in their tendency increasingly to present themselves as the parties of 'wage-earners' rather of simply the working class.

41. See, e.g., Walter Korpi, *The Democratic Class Struggle*, London: Routledge, 1983; Gösta Esping Andersen, *Politics Against Markets*, Princeton University Press, 1985; and Adam Przeworski, *Capitalism and Social Democracy*, Cambridge: Cambridge University Press, 1985.

42. A belated attempt may be found in some of the papers in M. Jacques and F. Mulhearn (eds.), *The Forward March of Labour Halted*, London: New Left Books, 1981, but the standard of analysis is not impressive. The title essay by Hobsbawm embodies an argument which is in effect little more than the thesis of class dealignment in a *marxisant* idiom.

43. Cf. the insightful comparative comments of Göran Therborn, 'Britain Left Out' in Curran (ed.), *The Future of the Left*.

Bibliography

ABBOTT, PAMELA, and SAPSFORD, ROGER, 'Class Identification of Married Working Women', *British Journal of Sociology*, vol. 37, 1986.

ÅBERG, RUNE, 'Teoriarna om arbets degradiering och arbetsmarknadens dualisering—ett försök till empirisk provning', *Sociologisk Forskning*, vol.2, 1984.

—, 'Arbetsförhållenden', in Robert Erikson and Åberg (eds.), *Välfärd in Förändring*, Stockholm: Prisma, 1984.

ACKER, JOAN, 'Women and Social Stratification: A Case of Intellectual Sexism', *American Journal of Sociology*, vol. 78, 1973.

Acton Society Trust, *Management Succession*, London: Acton Society Trust, 1956.

ADAMS, B.N., *Kinship in an Urban Setting*, Chicago: Markham, 1968.

AIKEN, MICHAEL, and GOLDBERG, DAVID, 'Social Mobility and Kinship: A Re-examination of the Hypothesis', *American Anthropologist*, vol. 71, 1969.

ALLAN, GRAHAM, 'Class Variations in Friendship Patterns', *British Journal of Sociology*, vol. xxviii, 1977.

ANGELL, ROBERT, 'A Critical Review of the Development of the Personal Document Method in Sociology, 1920–1940' in L. Gottschalk *et al., The Use of Personal Documents in History, Anthropology and Sociology*, New York: United States Social Science Research Council, 1945.

ARON, RAYMOND, *Progress and Disillusion: The Dialectics of Modern Society*, London: Pall Mall Press, 1968.

BAIN, G.S., *The Growth of White-Collar Trade Unionism*, Oxford: Clarendon Press, 1970.

—, BACON, ROBERT, and PIMLOTT, JOHN, 'The Labour Force', in Halsey (ed.), *Trends in British Society since 1900*, 1st edn., 1972.

BALÁN, JORGE, BROWNING, HARLEY L., and JELIN, ELIZABETH, *Men in a Developing Society: Geographic and Social Mobility in Monterrey, Mexico*, Austin: University of Texas Press, 1973.

BECHHOFER, FRANK, and ELLIOTT, BRIAN, 'Persistence and Change: the Petite Bourgeoisie in Industrial Society', *Archives européennes de sociologie*, vol. xvii, 1976.

— — and RUSHWORTH, MONICA, 'The Market Situation of Small Shop-keepers', *Scottish Journal of Political Economy*, vol. xviii, 1971.

— — — and BLAND, RICHARD, 'The Petits Bourgeois in the Class Structure', in F. Parkin (ed.), *The Social Analysis of Class Structure*, London: Tavistock, 1974.

BECKER, H.S., *Sociological Work*, Chicago: Aldine, 1970.

BELL, DANIEL, *The Coming of Post-Industrial Society*, New York: Basic Books, 1973.

BENN, S.I., and MORTIMORE, G.W. (eds.), *Rationality and the Social Sciences*, London: Routledge, 1976.

BERGER, SUZANNE, and PIORE, MICHAEL, *Dualism and Discontinuity in Industrial Societies*, Cambridge: Cambridge University Press, 1980.

BERNARD, PAUL, and RENAUD, JEAN, 'Contre-mobilité et effets différés', *Sociologie et sociétés*, vol. 8, 1976.

BERNSTEIN, EDUARD, *Die Voraussetzungen des Sozialismus und die Aufgaben der Sozialdemokratie*, Stuttgart: Dietz, 1899.

BERTAUX, DANIEL, 'Sur l'analyse des tables de mobilité sociale', *Revue française de sociologie*, vol. x, 1969.

—, 'Questions de stratification et de mobilité sociale', *Sociologie du travail*, vol. 13, 1971.

—, 'Mobilité sociale biographique: Une critique de l'approche transversale', *Revue française de sociologie*, vol. xv, 1974.

BETTELHEIM, BRUNO, and JANOWITZ, MORRIS, *The Dynamics of Prejudice*, New York: Harper, 1950.

BILLEWICZ, W.Z., 'Some Remarks on the Measurement of Social Mobility', *Population Studies*, vol. 9, 1955-6.

BLAU, P.M., 'Social Mobility and Interpersonal Relations', *American Sociological Review*, vol. 21, 1956.

— and DUNCAN, O.D., *The American Occupational Structure*, New York: Wiley, 1967.

BOTTOMORE, T.B., *Élites and Society*, London: Watts, 1964.

—, *Classes in Modern Society*, London: Allen and Unwin, 1965.

—, 'The Class Structure in Western Europe, in Margaret S. Archer and Salvador Giner (eds.), *Contemporary Europe: Class, Status and Power*, London: Weidenfeld & Nicolson, 1971.

BOUDON, RAYMOND, *Mathematical Structures of Social Mobility*, Amsterdam: Elsevier, 1973.

—, *L'Inégalité des chances: La Mobilité sociale dans les sociétés industrielles*, Paris: Colin, 1973.

BOURDIEU, PIERRE, 'Cultural Reproduction and Social Reproduction', in R. Brown (ed.), *Knowledge, Education and Cultural Change*, London: Tavistock, 1973.

— and PASSERSON, JEAN-CLAUDE, *La Reproduction: Éléments pour une théorie du système d'enseignement*, Paris: Les Éditions de Minuit, 1970.

BRAVERMAN, H., *Labor and Monopoly Capital*, New York: Monthly Review Press, 1974.

BRIGGS, B. BRUCE (ed.), *The New Class?*, New Brunswick: Transaction Books, 1979.

BRITTEN, NICKY, and HEATH, ANTHONY, 'Women, Men and Social Class', in Gamarnikow *et al.* (eds.), *Gender, Class and Work*.

BUTLER, DAVID, and ROSE, RICHARD, *The British General Election of 1959*, London: Macmillan, 1960.

— and STOKES, DONALD, *Political Change in Britain: The Evolution of Electoral Choice*, London: Macmillan, 2nd edn., 1974.

— and KAVANAGH, DENNIS, *The British General Election of 1983*, London: Macmillan, 1984.

CAIRNES, J.E., *Some Leading Principles of Political Economy Newly Expounded*, London: Macmillan, 1874.

CAPLOW, THEODORE, *The Sociology of Work*, University of Minnesota Press, 1954.

CARCHEDI, G., 'Reproduction of Social Classes at the Level of Production Relations', *Economy and Society*, vol. 4, 1975.

—, 'On the Economic Identification of the New Middle Class', *Economy and Society*, vol. 4, 1975.

CARLSSON, GÖSTA, *Social Mobility and Class Structure*, Lund: CWK Gleerup, 1958.

CHASE, IVAN D., 'A Comparison of Men's and Women's Intergenerational Mobility in the United States', *American Sociological Review*, vol. 40, 1975.

CHILD, JOHN, 'The Industrial Supervisor' in Geoff Esland *et al.* (eds.), *People and Work*, Edinburgh: Holmes McDougall, 1976.

CHINOY, ELY, 'Social Mobility Trends in the United States', *American Sociological Review*, vol. 20, 1955.

CLARK, D., *The Industrial Manager*, London: Business Publications, 1966.

COOLEY, C.M., *Social Process*, New York: Scribners, 1918.

CRAIG, CHRISTINE, *Men in Manufacturing Industry*, Cambridge University, Department of Applied Economics (cyclostyled), 1969.

CREWE, IVOR (ed.), *Élites in Western Democracy: British Political Sociology Yearbook 1*, London: Croom Helm, 1974.

—, 'The Electorate: Partisan Dealignment Ten Years On', in H. Berrington (ed.), *Change in British Politics*, London: Cass, 1984.

—, 'On the Death and Resurrection of Class Voting: Some Comments on *How Britain Votes*', *Political Studies*, vol. 35, 1987.

—, SÄRLVIK, BO, and ALT, JAMES, 'Partisan Dealignment in Britain 1964–1974', *British Journal of Political Science*, vol. 7, 1977.

CROMPTON, ROSEMARY, 'Class Mobility in Modern Britain', *Sociology*, vol. 14, 1980.

— and GUBBAY, JON, *Economy and Class Structure*, London: Macmillan, 1977.

— and JONES, GARETH, *White-Collar Proletariat: Deskilling and Gender in Clerical Work*, London: Macmillan, 1984.

— and MANN, MICHAEL (eds.), *Gender and Stratification*, Cambridge: Polity Press, 1986.

CROSLAND, C.A.R., *The Future of Socialism*, London: Cape, 1956.

CROWDER, N. DAVID, 'A Critique of Duncan's Stratification Research', *Sociology*, vol. 8, 1974.

CURRAN, J. (ed.), *The Future of the Left*, Cambridge: Polity Press, 1984.

CURTIS, RICHARD F., 'Differential Association and the Stratification of the Urban Community', *Social Forces*, vol. 42, 1963.

DAHRENDORF, RALF, *Class and Class Conflict in Industrial Society*, London: Routledge, 1959.

—, 'Recent Changes in the Class Structure of European Societies', *Dædalus*, Winter, 1964.

DALE, ANGELA, 'Social Class and the Self-Employed', *Sociology*, vol. 20, 1986.

—, GILBERT, G. NIGEL and ARBER, SARA, 'Integrating Women into Class Theory', *Sociology*, vol. 19, 1985.

DALE, J.R., *The Clerk in Industry*, Liverpool University Press, 1962.

DANIEL, W.W., *A National Survey of the Unemployed*, London: Political and Economic Planning, 1974.

DAVIS, JAMES, 'Hierarchical Models for Significance Tests in Multivariate Contingency Tables', in Herbert L. Costner (ed.), *Sociological Methodology, 1973-1974*, San Francisco: Jossey-Bass, 1974.

DEJONG, P.Y., BRAWER, M.J., and ROBIN, S.S., 'Patterns of Female Intergenerational Occupational Mobility: A Comparison with Male Patterns of Intergenerational Occupational Mobility', *American Sociological Review*, vol. 36, 1971.

DELPHY, CHRISTINE, 'Women in Stratification Studies', in Helen Roberts (ed.), *Doing Feminist Research*, London: Routledge, 1981.

DEMING, W. EDWARDS, *Statistical Adjustment of Data*, New York: Wiley, 1943.

Department of Employment, *New Earnings Survey 1970*, London: HMSO, 1971.

DEX, SHIRLEY, *The Sexual Division of Work*, Brighton: Wheatsheaf, 1985.

DUBIN, ROBERT, 'Industrial Workers' Worlds: A Study of the "Central Life Interests" of Industrial Workers', *Social Problems*, vol. 3, 1956.

DUNCAN, O.D., 'Occupation Trends and Patterns of Net Mobility in the United States', *Demography*, vol. 3, 1966.

—, 'Social Stratification and Mobility', in Eleanor B. Sheldon and Wilbert E. Moore (eds.), *Indicators of Social Change*, New York: Russell Sage Foundation, 1968.

—, 'Methodological Issues in the Analysis of Social Mobility', in Smelser and Lipset (eds.), *Social Structure and Mobility in Economic Development*.

—, 'Inheritance of Poverty or Inheritance of Race?', in Daniel P. Moynihan (ed.), *On Understanding Poverty*, New York: Basic Books, 1968.

DUNLEAVY, PATRICK, and HUSBANDS, CHRISTOPHER T., *British Democracy at the Crossroads*, London: Allen and Unwin, 1985.

DUNTON, NANCY, and FEATHERMAN, DAVID L., 'Social Mobility through Marriage and Careers: Achievement over the Life Course', in Janet T. Spence (ed.), *Achievement and Achievement Motives*, San Francisco: W.H. Freeman, 1985.

DURBIN, E.F.M., *The Politics of Democratic Socialism*, London: Routledge, 1940.

EHRENREICH, J., and EHRENREICH, B., 'The Professional-Managerial Class', *Radical America*, vol. 11, 1977.

ERIKSON, ROBERT, 'Om Socio-economiska Indelningar av Hushåll: överväganden och ett Förslag', *Statistisk Tidskrift*, vol. 19, 1981.

—, 'Changes in Social Mobility in Industrial Nations: The Case of Sweden', in *Research in Social Stratification and Mobility*, vol. 2, 1983.

—, 'Social Class of Men, Women and Families', *Sociology*, vol. 18, 1984.

— and GOLDTHORPE, JOHN H., 'Are American Rates of Social Mobility Exceptionally High? New Evidence on an Old Issue', *European Sociological Review*, vol. 1, 1985.

— —, 'Commonality and Variation in Social Fluidity in Industrial Nations. Part I: a Model for Evaluating the "FJH hypothesis"; Part II: the Model of Core Social Fluidity Applied', *European Sociological Review*, vol. 3, 1987.

— and PONTINEN, SEPPO, 'Social Mobility in Finland and Sweden: A Comparison of Men and Women', in Risto Alapuro *et al.* (eds.), *Small States in Comparative Perspective*, Oslo: Norwegian University Press, 1985.

—, GOLDTHORPE, JOHN H., and PORTOCARERO, LUCIENNE, 'Intergenerational Mobility in Three Western European Societies', *British Journal of Sociology*, vol. 30, 1979.

— — —, 'Social Fluidity in Industrial Nations: England, France and Sweden', *British Journal of Sociology*, vol. 33, 1982.

— — —, 'Intergenerational Social Mobility and the Convergence Thesis', *British Journal of Sociology*, vol. 34, 1983.

ESPING ANDERSEN, GÖSTA, *Politics Against Markets*, Princeton: Princeton University Press, 1985.

EYSENCK, H. J., *The Inequality of Man*, London: Temple Smith, 1973.

FEATHERMAN, DAVID L., and HAUSER, ROBERT M., *Opportunity and Change*, New York: Academic Press, 1978.

—, JONES, F. LANCASTER, and HAUSER, ROBERT M., 'Assumptions of Mobility Research in the US: The Case of Occupational Status', *Social Science Research*, vol. 4, 1975.

FELLIN, PHILLIP, and LITWAK, EUGENE, 'Neighbourhood Cohesion under Conditions of Mobility', *American Sociological Review*, vol. 28, 1963.

FEUER, LEWIS S. (ed.), *Karl Marx and Friedrich Engels: Basic Writings on Politics and Philosophy*, London: Fontana, 1969.

FRANKEL, H., *Capitalist Society and Modern Sociology*, London: Lawrence & Wishart, 1970.

FRASER, COLIN, MARSH, CATHERINE, and JOBLING, RAY, 'Political Responses to Unemployment', in Roberts *et al.* (eds.), *New Approaches to Economic Life*.

GAGLIANI, GIORGIO, 'Long-Term Changes in the Occupational Structure', *European Sociological Review*, vol. 1, 1985.

GALLIE, DUNCAN, *Social Inequality and Class Radicalism in France*, Cambridge: Cambridge University Press, 1983.

GAMARNIKOW, EVA *et al.* (eds.), *Gender, Class and Work*, London: Heinemann, 1983.

GAY, PETER, *The Dilemma of Democratic Socialism*, New York: Columbia University Press, 1952.

GEIGER, THEODOR, *Soziale Umschichtungen in einer dänischen Mittelstadt*, Aarhus University Press, 1951.

GERMANI, GINO, 'Social and Political Consequences of Mobility', in Smelser and Lipset (eds.), *Social Structure and Mobility in Economic Development*.

GERSCHENKRON, ALEXANDER, *Continuity in History and Other Essays*, Cambridge, Mass.: Harvard University Press, 1968.

GERSHUNY, JAY, *Social Innovation and the Division of Labour*, Oxford: Oxford University Press, 1983.

GERSTL, J.E. and HUTTON, S.P., *Engineers: The Anatomy of a Profession*, London: Tavistock, 1966.

GIBSON, J.B., and YOUNG, MICHAEL, 'Social Mobility and Fertility', in J.E. Meade and A.S. Parkes (eds.), *Biological Aspects of Social Problems*, Edinburgh: Oliver & Boyd, 1965.

GIDDENS, ANTHONY, *The Class Structure of the Advanced Societies*, London: Hutchinson, 1973.

GIROD, ROGER, *Mobilité sociale: Faits établis et problèmes ouverts*, Geneva, Droz, 1971.

—, 'Inégalité des chances: Perspectives nouvelles, *Archives européennes de sociologie*, vol. xvi, 1975.

GLASS, D.V., and HALL, J.R., 'Social Mobility in Britain: A Study of Intergeneration Changes in Status', in Glass (ed.), *Social Mobility in Britain*, London: Routledge, 1954.

GLENN, NORVAL D., ROSS, ADREAIN E., and TULLY, JUDY CORDER, 'Patterns of Intergenerational Mobility of Females through Marriage', *American Sociological Review*, vol. 39, 1974.

GOLDHAMER, H., 'The Analysis of Occupational Mobility', Society for Social Research, Chicago, May, 1948.

GOLDTHORPE, JOHN H., 'Social Stratification in Industrial Society', in Halmos (ed.), *The Development of Industrial Societies*.

—, 'The Current Inflation: Towards a Sociological Account', in Fred Hirsch and

Goldthorpe (eds.), *The Political Economy of Inflation*, London: Martin Robertson, 1978.

——, 'Reply to Crompton', *Sociology*, vol. 14, 1980.

——, 'On the Service Class: Its Formation and Future', in Anthony Giddens and Gavin Mackenzie (eds.), *Social Class and the Division of Labour*, Cambridge: Cambridge University Press, 1982.

——, 'Women and Class Analysis: In Defence of the Conventional View', *Sociology*, vol. 17, 1983.

——, 'Women and Class Analysis: A Reply to the Replies', *Sociology*, vol. 18, 1984.

——, (ed.)., *Order and Conflict in Contemporary Capitalism*, Oxford: Clarendon Press, 1984.

——, 'Epidemiology, Genetics and Sociology: A Comment', *Journal of Biosocial Science*, vol. 17, 1985.

——, 'On Economic Development and Social Mobility', *British Journal of Sociology*, vol. 36, 1985.

——, 'Soziale Mobilität und Klassenbildung: Zur Erneuerung einer Tradition soziologischer Forschung', in Hermann Strasser and Goldthorpe (eds.), *Die Analyse sozialer Ungleichheit*, Opladen: Westdeutscher Verlag, 1985.

—— and HOPE, KEITH, *The Social Grading of Occupations: A New Approach and Scale*, Oxford: Clarendon Press, 1974.

—— and LOCKWOOD, DAVID, 'Affluence and the British Class Structure', *Sociological Review*, n.s. vol. 11, 1963.

—— and PORTOCARERO, LUCIENNE, 'La Mobilité sociale en France, 1953–1970: Nouvel Examen', *Revue française de sociologie*, vol. 22, 1981.

——, LOCKWOOD, DAVID, BECHHOFER, FRANK, and PLATT, JENNIFER, *The Affluent Worker: Industrial Attitudes and Behaviour*, Cambridge: Cambridge University Press, 1968.

—— —— —— ——, *The Affluent Worker in the Class Structure*, Cambridge: Cambridge University Press, 1969.

GOODMAN, L.A., 'A Modified Multiple Regression Approach to the Analysis of Dichotomous Variables', *American Sociological Review*, vol. 37, 1972.

——, 'Some Multiplicative Models for the Analysis of Cross-Classified Variables', *Proceedings of the 6th Berkeley Symposium on Mathematical Statistics and Probability*, Berkeley: University of California Press, 1972.

GOULD, J.D., 'Hypothetical History', *Economic History Review*, vol. 22, 1969.

GOULDNER, ALVIN W., *The Future of the Intellectuals and the Rise of the New Class*, London: Macmillan, 1979.

GRANOVETTER, MARK S., *Getting a Job: A Study of Contacts and Careers*, Cambridge, Mass.: Harvard University Press, 1974.

GREENHALGH, CHRISTINE and STEWART, MARK B., 'Occupational Status and Mobility of Men and Women', *Warwick Economic Papers*, no. 211, University of Warwick, 1982.

GRUSKY, DAVID B., and HAUSER, ROBERT M., 'Comparative Social Mobility Revisited', *American Sociological Review*, vol. 49, 1984.

HAKIM, CATHERINE, *Occupational Segregation*, London: Department of Employment, Research Paper 9, 1979.

HALMOS, P. (ed.), *The Development of Industrial Societies*, Keele: Sociological Review Monographs, No. 8, 1964.

HALSEY, A.H. (ed.), *Trends in British Society since 1900*, London: Macmillan, 1972; *British Social Trends since 1900*, 2nd edn., 1987.

—— and CREWE, IVOR, *Social Survey of the Civil Service*, London: HMSO, 1969.

—, HEATH, ANTHONY and RIDGE, J.M., *Origins and Destinations*, Oxford: Clarendon Press, 1980.

HAMMOND, JOHN L., 'Wife's Status and Family Social Standing', *Sociological Perspectives*, vol. 30, 1987.

HANDL, JOHANN, 'Heiratsmobilität und berufliche Mobilität von Frauen', VASMA Working Paper no. 8, Institut für Sozialwissenschaften, University of Mannheim n.d.

HARRIS, ABRAM LINCOLN, 'Pure Capitalism and the Disappearance of the Middle Class', *Journal of Political Economy*, vol. xlvii, 1939.

HARRIS, AMELIA I., and CLAUSEN, ROSEMARY, *Labour Mobility in Great Britain 1953-63*, London: HMSO, 1967.

HAUSER, ROBERT M., 'A Structural Model of the Mobility Table', *Social Forces*, vol. 56, 1978.

— and FEATHERMAN, DAVID L., *The Process of Stratification: Trends and Analysis*, New York: Academic Press, 1977.

—, KOFFEL, JOHN N., TRAVIS, HARRY P., and DICKINSON, PETER J., 'Temporal Change in Occupational Mobility: Evidence for Men in the United States', *American Sociological Review*, vol. 40, 1975.

HAYEK, F.A., *The Constitution of Liberty*, London: Routledge, 1960.

HEATH, ANTHONY, *Social Mobility*, London: Fontana, 1981.

— and BRITTEN, NICKY, 'Women's Jobs do Make a Difference: A Reply to Goldthorpe', *Sociology*, vol. 18, 1984.

—, JOWELL, ROGER and CURTICE, JOHN, *How Britain Votes*, Oxford: Pergamon, 1985.

— — —, 'Trendless Fluctuation: Relative Class Voting 1964-83', *Political Studies*, vol. 35, 1987.

van HEEK, F., 'Some Introductory Remarks on Social Mobility and Class Structure', *Transactions of the Third World Congress of Sociology*, London: International Sociological Association, 1956.

HERNES, GUDMUND, and KNUDSEN, KNUD, 'Gender and Class Identification in Norway', paper presented to the ISA Research Committee on Social Stratification and Mobility, Harvard University, September, 1985.

HERTZLER, J.O., 'Some Tendencies Towards a Closed Class System in the United States', *Social Forces*, vol. 30, 1952.

HIMSWORTH, H., 'Epidemiology, Genetics and Sociology', *Journal of Biosocial Science*, vol. 16, 1984.

HOLLINGSHEAD, AUGUST B., 'Trends in Social Stratification: A Case Study', *American Sociological Review*, vol. 17, 1952.

HOPE, KEITH, 'Quantifying Constraints on Social Mobility: The Latent Hierarchies of a Contingency Table', in Hope (ed.), *The Analysis of Social Mobility: Methods and Approaches*, Oxford: Clarendon Press, 1972.

—, 'Trends in British Occupational Mobility: A Replication to Test Inferences from Cohort Analysis', in proceedings of Internationale Arbeitstagung, *Anwendung mathematischer Verfahren zur Analyse sozialer Ungleichheit und sozialer Mobilität*, Bad Homburg, March 1974.

—, 'Models of Status Inconsistency and Social Mobility Effects', *American Sociological Review*, vol. 40, 1975.

—, 'Trends in the Openness of British Society in the Present Century', *Research in Social Stratification and Mobility*, vol. 1, 1981.

HOPPER, EARL, 'Educational Systems and Selected Consequences of Patterns of Mobility and Non-Mobility in Industrial Societies: A Theoretical Discussion', in Hopper (ed.), *Readings in the Theory of Educational Systems*, London: Hutchinson, 1971.

JACKMAN, MARY R., and JACKMAN, ROBERT W., *Class Awareness in the United States*, Berkeley: University of California Press, 1983.

JACQUES, M., and MULHEARN, F. (eds.), *The Forward March of Labour Halted*, London: New Left Books, 1981.

JANOWITZ, MORRIS, 'Some Consequences of Social Mobility in the United States', *Transactions of the Third World Congress of Sociology*, London: International Sociological Association, 1956.

JARVIE, I.C., *Concepts and Society*, London: Routledge, 1972.

JONES, F. LANCASTER, 'Social Mobility and Industrial Society: A Thesis Re-Examined', *Sociological Quarterly*, vol. 10, 1969.

KERR, CLARK, *The Future of Industrial Societies*, Cambridge, Mass.: Harvard University Press, 1983.

—, DUNLOP, JOHN T., HARBISON, FREDERICK H., and MYERS, CHARLES A., *Industrialism and Industrial Man*, Cambridge, Mass.: Harvard University Press, 1960.

KLEIN, JOSEPHINE, *Samples from English Cultures*, London: Routledge, 1965.

KÖNIG, WOLFGANG and MÜLLER, WALTER, 'Educational Systems and Labour Markets as Determinants of Worklife Mobility in France and West Germany', *European Sociological Review*, vol. 2, 1986.

KORPI, WALTER, *The Democratic Class Struggle*, London: Routledge, 1983.

KRECKEL, REINHARD, 'Toward a Theoretical Re-orientation of the Sociological Analysis of Vertical Mobility', in Walter Müller and Karl Ulrich Mayer (eds.), *Social Stratification and Career Mobility*, Paris and The Hague: Mouton, 1973.

LANDES, DAVID, *The Unbound Prometheus*, Cambridge: Cambridge University Press, 1972.

LAUMANN, EDWARD O., *Prestige and Association in an Urban Community*, Indianapolis: Bobbs-Merrill, 1966.

—, *Bonds of Pluralism*, New York: Wiley, 1973.

LEE, D.J., 'Class Differentials in Educational Opportunity and Promotion from the Ranks', *Sociology*, vol. 2, 1968.

LENSKI, GERHARD E., 'Trends in Inter-Generational Occupational Mobility in the United States', *American Sociological Review*, vol. 23. 1958.

LEWIS, ROY, and MAUDE, ANGUS, *The English Middle Classes*, London: Phoenix House, 1949.

— —, *Professional People*, London: Phoenix House, 1952.

LIPSET, S.M., *Political Man*, London: Heinemann, 1960.

—, 'The Sources of the "Radical Right"' and 'Three Decades of the Radical Right: Coughlinites, McCarthyites, and Birchers' in Daniel Bell (ed.), *The New American Right*, New York: Doubleday, 2nd edn., 1963.

—, 'The Changing Class Structure of Contemporary European Politics', *Dædalus*, vol. 63, 1964.

—, *Revolution and Counter Revolution*, London: Heinemann, 1969.

—, 'La mobilité sociale et les objectifs socialistes', *Sociologie et sociétés*, November, 1972.

— and BENDIX, REINHARD (eds.), *Class, Status and Power*, London: Routledge, 1st edn. 1954.

— —, *Social Mobility in Industrial Society*, London: Heinemann, 1959.

— and GORDON, JOAN, 'Mobility and Trade Union Membership', in Lipset and Bendix (eds.), *Class, Status and Power*.

— and RAAB, EARL, *The Politics of Unreason*, London: Heinemann, 1970.
— and ZETTERBERG, H.L. 'A Theory of Social Mobility', *Transactions of the Third World Congress of Sociology*, London: International Sociological Association, 1956.
LITWAK, EUGENE, 'Occupational Mobility and Extended Family Cohesion', *American Sociological Review*, vol. 25, 1960.
—, 'Reference Group Theory, Bureaucratic Career, and Neighbourhood Primary Group Cohesion', *Sociometry*, vol. 23, 1960.
— and SZELENYI, IVAN, 'Primary Group Structures and their Functions: Kin, Neighbours and Friends', *American Sociological Review*, vol. 34, 1969.
LOCKWOOD, DAVID, *The Blackcoated Worker*, London: Allen & Unwin, 1958.
—, 'The Weakest Link in the Chain: Some Comments on the Marxist Theory of Action', *Research in the Sociology of Work*, vol. 1, 1981.
LOPREATO, JOSEPH, and HAZELRIGG, LAWRENCE, *Class, Conflict and Mobility*, San Francisco: Chandler, 1972.
MACDONALD, KENNETH, 'The Hall–Jones Scale: A Note on the Interpretation of the Main British Prestige Coding,' in J.M. Ridge (ed.), *Mobility in Britain Reconsidered*, Oxford: Clarendon Press, 1974.
— and RIDGE, JOHN, 'Social Mobility', in Halsey (ed.), *Trends in British Society since 1900*, 2nd edn.
MCCLELLAND, PETER D., *Causal Explanation and Model Building in History, Economics and the New Economic History*, Ithaca: Cornell University Press, 1975.
MCCLENDON, McKEE J., 'Structural and Exchange Components of Occupational Mobility: A Cross-National Analysis', *Sociological Quarterly*, vol. 21, 1980.
MARSHALL, ALFRED, *Principles of Economics*, London: Macmillan, 1890.
MARSHALL, GORDON, ROSE, DAVID, NEWBY, HOWARD, and VOGLER, CAROLYN, 'Political Quiescence among the Unemployed in Modern Britain', in Rose (ed.), *Economic Decline and Social Change in Britain*, London: Hutchinson, 1987.
— — —, *Social Class in Modern Britain*, London: Hutchinson, forthcoming.
MARSHALL, T.H. (ed.), *Class Conflict and Social Stratification*, London: Le Play House Press, 1938.
MARX, KARL, *Theories of Surplus Value*, London: Lawrence & Wishart, 1969.
—, *Capital*, Moscow: Foreign Languages Publishing House, 1959.
— and ENGELS, FRIEDRICH, *Selected Works*, Moscow: Foreign Languages Publishing House, 1958.
MAURICE, M., SELLIER, F., and SILVESTRE, J.-J., *Politique d'éducation et organisation industrielle en France et en Allemagne*, Paris: Presses Universitaires de France, 1982.
MAYER, KARL ULRICH, 'Soziale Mobilität und die Wahrnehmung gesellschaftlicher Ungleichheit', *Zeitschrift für Soziologie*, vol. 1, 1972.
—, *Ungleichheit und Mobilität im sozialen Bewusstsein*, Dusseldorf: Westdeutscher Verlag, 1975.
— and MÜLLER, WALTER, 'Progress in Social Mobility Research?', *Quality and Quantity*, vol. v, 1971.
MERCER, D.E., and WEIR, D.T.H., Attitudes to Work and Trade Unionism among White-Collar Workers', *Industrial Relations*, vol. 3, 1972.
MERTON, R.K., *Social Theory and Social Structure*, Glencoe: Free Press, 1957.
MICHELS, ROBERT, *Umschichtungen in der herrschenden Klassen nach dem Kriege*, Stuttgart and Berlin: Kohlhammer, 1934.
—, *Political Parties*, (trans. Eden and Cedar Paul), New York: Dover, 1959.

—, *First Lectures in Political Sociology* (trans. Alfred de Grazia), New York: Harper & Row, 1965.

MILIBAND, RALPH, *The State in Capitalist Society*, London: Weidenfeld & Nicolson, 1969.

MILL, JOHN StUART, *Principles of Political Economy*, London: John W. Parker, 1848.

MILLER, DELBERT C., and FORM, WILLIAM H., *Industrial Sociology*, New York: Harper, 1951.

MILLER, R.L., 'Unemployment as a Mobility Status', Queen's University Belfast, Department of Social Studies, 1984.

MILLER, S.M., 'Comparative Social Mobility', *Current Sociology*, vol. ix, 1961.

—, 'The Future of Social Mobility Studies', *American Journal of Sociology*, vol. 77, 1971.

—, 'Social Mobility and Equality' in OECD, *Education, Inequality and Life Chances*, Paris: OECD, 1975.

MILLS, C. WRIGHT, *The Sociological Imagination*, New York: Oxford University Press, 1959.

MIRANDE, A.M., 'The Isolated Nuclear Family Hypothesis: A Reanalysis', in J. Edwards (ed.), *The Family and Change*, New York: Knopf, 1969.

MITCHELL, J. CLYDE, 'The Concept and Use of Social Networks', in Mitchell (ed.), *Social Networks in Urban Situations*, Manchester University Press, 1969.

— and CRITCHLEY, FRANK, 'Configurational Similarity in Three Class Contexts in British Society', *Sociology*, vol. 19, 1985.

MITZMAN, ARTHUR, *Sociology and Estrangement*, New York: Knopf, 1973.

MORRISON, DENTON E., and HENKEL, RAMON E. (eds.), *The Significance Test Controversy*, London: Butterworth, 1970.

MOSTELLER, FREDERICK, 'Association and Estimation in Contingency Tables', *Journal of the American Statistical Association*, vol. 63, 1968.

MUKHERJEE, RAMKRISHNA, 'A Further Note on the Analysis of Data on Social Mobility', in Glass (ed.), *Social Mobility in Britain*.

MÜLLER, WALTER, 'Soziale Mobilität: die Bundesrepublik im Internationalen Vergleich', in Max Kaase (ed.), *Theorie und Praxis in demokratischer Regierungsweise*, Opladen: Westdeutscher Verlag, 1985.

—, 'Was Bleibt von den Klassenstrukturen?', Institut für Sozialwissenschaften, University of Mannheim, 1986.

MUSGROVE, F., *The Migratory Élite*, London: Heinemann, 1963.

NAMBOODIRI, N.K., CARTER, L.F., and BLALOCK, H.M. (eds.), *Applied Multivariate Analysis and Experimental Designs*, New York: McGraw Hill, 1975.

NELDER, J.A., 'Log-Linear Models for Contingency Tables', *Applied Statistics*, vol. 23, 1974.

NICOLAUS, MARTIN, 'Proletariat and Middle Class in Marx: Hegelian Choreography and Capitalist Dialectic', *Studies on the Left*, January 1967.

NOBLE, TREVOR, 'Intragenerational Mobility in Britain: A Criticism of the Counter-balance Theory', *Sociology*, vol. 8, 1974.

Office of Population Censuses and Surveys, *Classification of Occupations 1970*, London: HMSO, 1971.

—, *Classification of Occupations 1980*, London: HMSO.

—, *Census 1981: Economic Activity Great Britain*, London: HMSO, 1984.

OLSON, MANCUR, *The Rise and Decline of Nations*, New Haven: Yale University Press, 1982.

OSIPOV, G.B. 'The Class Character of the Theory of Social Mobility', in P. Hollander, (ed.), *American and Soviet Society*, Englewood Cliffs: Prentice Hall, 1969.
PARKIN, FRANK, *Class Inequality and Political Order*, London: McGibbon & Kee, 1971.
— (ed.), *The Social Analysis of Class Structure*, London: Tavistock, 1974.
PARSONS, TALCOTT, 'The Social Structure of the Family', in Ruth Anshen (ed.), *The Family: Its Function and Destiny*, New York: Harper, 1949.
—, 'A Revised Analytical Approach to the Theory of Social Stratification' in Bendix and Lipset (eds.), *Class, Status and Power*.
—, 'The Normal American Family', in S.M. Farber (ed.), *Man and Civilisation: the Family's Search for Survival*, New York: McGraw Hill, 1965.
PAWSON, RAY, 'Empiricist Explanatory Strategies: The Case of Causal Modelling', *Sociological Review*, n.s. vol. 26, 1978.
PAYNE, CLIVE, 'The Log-Linear Model for Contingency Tables', in Payne and Colm O'Muircheartaigh (eds.), *The Analysis of Survey Data*, New York: Wiley, 1977.
—, 'Lookup Tables', *PSTAT UK Newsletter*, no. 1, 1984.
PAYNE, GEOFF, PAYNE, JUDY, and CHAPMAN, TONY, 'Trends in Female Social Mobility', in Gamarnikow *et al.* (eds.), *Gender, Class and Work*.
PETERSON, WILLIAM, 'Is America still the Land of Opportunity?', *Commentary*, vol. 16, 1953.
PICKVANCE, C.G., 'Voluntary Associations', in E. Gittus (ed.), *Key Variables in Social Research*, vol. 2, London: Heinemann, 1974.
PÖNTINEN, SEPPO, *Social Mobility and Social Structure: A Comparison of Scandinavian Countries*, Helsinki: Societas Scientiarum Fennica, 1983.
POPPER, KARL, *Objective Knowledge*, Oxford: Clarendon Press, 1972.
PORTOCARERO, LUCIENNE, 'Social Mobility in Industrial Nations: Women in France and Sweden', *Sociological Review*, ns vol. 31, 1983.
—, 'Social Mobility in France and Sweden: Women, Marriage and Work', *Acta Sociologica*, vol. 28, 1985.
POULANTZAS, NICOS, *Les Classes sociales dans le capitalisme aujourd'hui*, Paris: Seuil, 1974.
PRAIS, S.J., 'Vocational Qualifications of the Labour Force in Britain and Germany', *National Institute Economic Review*, November, 1981.
PRZEWORSKI, ADAM, *Capitalism and Social Democracy*, Cambridge: Cambridge University Press, 1985.
RENNER, KARL, *Wandlungen der Modernen Gesellschaft: Zwei Abhandlungen über die Probleme der Nachkriegszeit*, Vienna: Wiener Volksbuchhandlung, 1953.
RICHARDSON, C.J. *Contemporary Social Mobility*, London: Francis Pinter, 1977.
ROBERTS, B.C., LOVERIDGE, RAY, and GENNARD, JOHN, *The Reluctant Militants*, London: Heinemann, 1972.
ROBERTS, BRYAN, FINNEGAN, RUTH, and GALLIE, DUNCAN (eds.), *New Approaches to Economic Life*, Manchester: Manchester University Press, 1985.
ROBERTS, HELEN, and WOODWARD, DIANA, 'Changing Patterns of Women's Employment in Sociology, 1950–80', *British Journal of Sociology*, vol. 32, 1981.
ROBINSON, ROBERT V., 'Reproducing Class Relations in Industrial Capitalism', *American Sociological Review*, vol. 49, 1984.

ROGIN, MICHAEL P., *The Intellectuals and McCarthy: The Radical Specter*, Cambridge, Mass.: M.I.T. Press, 1967.

ROGOFF, NATALIE, *Recent Trends in Occupational Mobility*, Glencoe: Free Press. 1953.

ROSE, ARNOLD, 'Social Mobility and Social Values', *Archives européennes de sociologie*, vol. 5, 1964.

ROSE, RICHARD, and McALLISTER, IAN, *Voters Begin to Choose*, London: Sage, 1986.

ROSSER, COLIN, and HARRIS, CHRISTOPHER, *The Family and Social Change*, London: Routledge, 1965.

ROTTMAN, DAVID B., HANNAN, DAMIAN F., HARDIMAN, NIAMH, and WILEY, MIRIAM M., *The Distribution of Income in the Republic of Ireland: A Study in Social Class and Family-Cycle Inequalities*, Dublin: The Economic and Social Research Institute, 1982.

ROUTH, GUY, *Occupation and Pay in Great Britain, 1906-60*, Cambridge: Cambridge University Press, 1965.

Royal Commission on the Distribution of Income and Wealth, Report No. 3., *Higher Incomes from Employment*, Cmnd. 6838, London: HMSO, 1976.

SCHNEIDER, DAVID M., and HOMANS, GEORGE, C., 'Kinship Terminology and The American Kinship System', *American Anthropologist*, vol. 57, 1955.

SCOTT, W., 'Reply' [to Billewicz, 'Some Remarks on the Measurement of Social Mobility'], *Population Studies*, vol. 9, 1955-6.

SHEPARD, ROGER N., 'Introduction', in Shepard, A. Kimball Romney, and Sara Beth Nerlove (eds.), *Multidimensional Scaling: Theory and Applications in the Behavioral Sciences*, New York: Seminar Press, 1972.

SIBLEY, ELBRIDGE, 'Some Demographic Clues to Stratification', *American Sociological Review*, vol. 7, 1942.

SIMKUS, ALBERT A., 'Changes in Occupational Inheritance under Socialism: Hungary 1930-1973', *Research in Social Stratification and Mobility*, vol. 1, 1981.

SINGELMANN, JOACHIM, *From Agriculture to Services: The Transformation of Industrial Employment*, Beverly Hills: Sage, 1978.

— and BROWNING, HARLEY L., 'Industrial Transformation and Occupational Change in the U.S., 1960–70', *Social Forces*, vol. 59, 1980.

— and TIENDA, MARTA, 'The Process of Occupational Change in a Service Economy: The Case of the United States', in Roberts *et al.* (eds.), *New Approaches to Economic Life*.

SJOBERG, GIDEON, 'Are Social Classes in America Becoming More Rigid?', *American Sociological Review*, vol. 16, 1951.

SMELSER, N.J., and LIPSET, S.M. (eds.), *Social Structure and Mobility in Economic Development*, London: Routledge' 1968.

SMILES, SAMUEL, *Self Help*, London: John Murray, 1859, and (ed.) Royden Harrison, London: Sphere, 1968.

—, *Lives of the Engineers*, London: John Murray, 1861-2.

SOMBART, WERNER, *Warum gibt es in den Vereinigten Staaten keinen Sozialismus?*, Tubingen: J.C.B. Mohr, 1906.

SØRENSON, AAGE, 'Models of Social Mobility', *Social Science Research*, vol. 4, 1975.

SOROKIN, PITIRIM A., *Social Mobility*, New York: Harper, 1927; enlarged edition, *Social and Cultural Mobility*, Glencoe: Free Press, 1959.

STACEY, BARRIE, 'Some Psychological Consequences of Inter-generation Mobility', *Human Relations*, vol. 20, 1967.

STANWORTH, MICHELLE, 'Women and Class Analysis: A Reply to John Goldthorpe', *Sociology*, vol. 18, 1984.

STANWORTH, PHILIP, and GIDDENS, ANTHONY (eds.), *Élites and Power in British Society*, Cambridge University Press, 1974.

STEINER, H., Grundzüge und Entwicklungstendenzen der westdeutschen Soziologie', in H. Meissner (ed.), *Bürgerliche Ökonomie in modernen Kapitalismus*, Berlin: Dietz, 1967.

STEWART, A., PRANDY, K., and BLACKBURN, R.M., 'Measuring in Class Structure', *Nature*, no. 245, 1973.

— — —, *Social Stratification and Occupations*, London: Macmillan, 1980.

STUCKERT, ROBERT P., 'Occupational Mobility and Family Relationships', *Social Forces*, vol. 41, 1963.

SVALASTOGA, KAARE, *Prestige, Class and Mobility*, Copenhagen: Gyldendal, 1959.

SWEEZY, PAUL, *Modern Capitalism and Other Essays*, New York: Monthly Review Press, 1972.

TAUSKY, CURT, and DUBIN, ROBERT, 'Career Anchorage: Managerial Mobility Motivations', *American Sociological Review*, vol. 30, 1965.

TAVUCHIS, NICHOLAS, 'Mobility and Family: Problems and Prospects', unpublished paper, n.d.

TAWNEY, R.H., *Equality*, London: Allen & Unwin, 3rd edn. 1938.

THÉLOT, CLAUDE, *Tel père, tel fils?*, Paris: Dunod, 1982.

THERBORN, GORAN, 'Britain Left Out', in Curran (ed.), *The Future of the Left*.

THOMAS, G., *Labour Mobility in Great Britain 1945–49*, London: The Social Survey, n.d.

THURLEY, KEITH, and WIRDENIUS, HANS, *Supervision: A Reappraisal*, London: Heinemann, 1973.

TOURAINE, ALAIN, and RAGAZZI, ORIETTA, *Ouvriers d'origine agricole*, Paris: Seuil, 1961.

TOWNSEND, PETER, and DAVIDSON, NICK (eds.), *Inequalities in Health*, Harmondsworth: Penguin Books, 1982.

TREIMAN, DONALD J., 'Industrialization and Social Stratification', in Edward O. Laumann (ed.), *Social Stratification: Research and Theory for the 1970s*, Indianapolis: Bobbs-Merrill, 1970.

— and TERRELL, KERMIT, 'Sex and the Process of Status Attainment: A Comparison of Working Women and Men', *American Sociological Review*, vol. 40, 1975.

TUMIN, MELVIN M., 'Some Unapplauded Consequences of Social Mobility in Mass Society', *Social Forces*, vol. 36, 1957.

TYREE, ANDREA, 'Mobility Ratios and Association in Mobility Tables', *Population Studies*, vol. 27, 1973.

— and TREAS, JUDITH, 'The Occupational and Marital Mobility of Women', *American Sociological Review*, vol. 39, 1974.

WALKER, P. (ed.), *Between Capital and Labor*, New York: Monthly Review Press, 1979.

WEDDERBURN, DOROTHY, and CRAIG, CHRISTINE, 'Relative Deprivation in Work', in Wedderburn (ed.), *Poverty, Inequality and Class Structure*, Cambridge: Cambridge University Press, 1974.

WESOŁOWSKI, W., and SŁOMCZYŃSKI, K., 'Reduction of Social Inequalities and Status Inconsistency', in Polish Sociological Association, *Social Structure: Polish Sociology 1977*, Wrocław: Ossolineum, 1977.

WESTERGAARD, JOHN, 'The Myth of Classlessness', in Robin Blackburn (ed.), *Ideology in Social Science*, London: Fontana, 1972.

——, 'The Once and Future Class', in Curran (ed.), *The Future of the Left*.

—— and LITTLE, ALAN, 'Educational Opportunity and Social Selection in England and Wales: Trends and Policy Implications', in OECD, *Social Objectives in Educational Planning*, Paris: OECD, 1967.

—— and RESLER, HENRIETTA, *Class in a Capitalist Society: A Study of Contemporary Britain*, London: Heinemann, 1975.

WHITE, HARRISON C., 'Cause and Effect in Social Mobility Tables', *Behavioural Science*, vol. 8, 1963.

WHITE, MICHAEL, *Long-term Unemployment and Labour Markets*, London: Policy Studies Institute, 1983.

WILENSKY, H.L., 'Work, Careers and Social Integration', *International Social Science Journal*, vol. 12, 1960.

——, 'Orderly Careers and Social Participation', *American Sociological Review*, vol. 26, 1961.

——, 'Measures and Effects of Social Mobility', in Smelser and Lipset (eds.), *Social Structure and Mobility in Economic Development*.

—— and EDWARDS, HUGH, 'The Skidder: Ideological Adjustments of Downwardly Mobile Workers', *American Sociological Review*, vol. 24, 1959.

WILLMOTT, PETER, and YOUNG, MICHAEL, *Family and Class in a London Suburb*, London: Routledge, 1960.

WRIGHT, ERIK OLIN, *Class, Crisis and the State*, London: New Left Books, 1978.

——, *Classes*, London: Verso, 1986.

—— and SINGELMANN, JOACHIM, 'Proletarianisation in the Changing American Class Structure', *American Journal of Sociology*, vol. 88, supplement, 1982.

YASUDA, SABURO, 'A Methodological Inquiry into Social Mobility', *American Sociological Review*, vol. 29, 1964.

YOUNG, MICHAEL, *The Rise of the Meritocracy*, London: Thames & Hudson, 1958.

—— and WILLMOTT, P., *The Symmetrical Family*, London: Routledge, 1973.

Index